FIRST PEOPLES

A Documentary Survey of American Indian History

Second Edition

COLIN G. CALLOWAY

Dartmouth College

BEDFORD/ST.MARTIN'S   Boston   ◆   New York

For Marcia, Graeme, and Megan, again

For Bedford/St. Martin's

Publisher for History: Patricia A. Rossi
Director of Development for History: Jane Knetzger
Developmental Editor: Sarah Barrash Wilson
Project Manager: Tina Samaha
Senior Production Supervisor: Dennis Conroy
Marketing Manager: Jenna Bookin Barry
Production Assistant: Kristen Merrill
Copyeditor: Lisa Wehrle
Text Design: Wanda Kossak
Cartography: Mapping Specialists Ltd.
Indexer: Steve Csipke
Cover Design: Donna Lee Dennison
Cover Art: Karl Bodmer, *Mandeh-Pachu, Mandan Man.* Joslyn Art Museum, Omaha, Nebraska.
   Gift of Enron Art Foundation.
Composition: Pine Tree Composition
Printing and Binding: R.R. Donnelley & Sons Company, Crawfordsville

President: Joan E. Feinberg
Editorial Director: Denise Wydra
Director of Marketing: Karen R. Melton
Director of Editing, Design, and Production: Marcia Cohen
Managing Editor: Elizabeth M. Schaaf

Library of Congress Card Catalog Number: 2003101689

Manufactured in the United States of America.

8   7   6
h   g

For information, write: Bedford/St. Martin's, 75 Arlington Street, Boston, MA 02116 (617-399-4000)

ISBN-10: 0–312–39889–1
ISBN-13: 978–0–312–39889–7

PREFACE

Colleagues and students from across the country have been generous in their responses to the first edition of *First Peoples*. In countering the often fleeting reference to, and marginalization of, Native Americans in history books, *First Peoples* clearly met a need. It provided an overview of Native American history and offered students a more complete and more richly textured narrative of Indian peoples and their place in United States history. In addition, it provided an opportunity to tackle historical evidence firsthand: I wanted to invite students to try to reconstruct the past through the words of people — Indians and non-Indians — who lived in a different time, saw the world in different ways, and had their own reasons for acting as they did.

The second edition of *First Peoples* follows the same approach and pursues the same goals, with a richer and more varied selection of resources and more information on modern developments. As in the first edition, each chapter includes a narrative section, followed by primary documents and then a picture essay. By combining historical background with textual and visual evidence, the book provides students with enough context to begin asking questions of the documents and pictures. The structure of the book enables instructors to go beyond giving an outline of events, laws, leaders, and battles, and provides them with materials for exploring other issues and examining how Indian history has been written and remembered.

The text has been completely reviewed and, where necessary, revised or expanded to take into account the new books and articles on American history that continue to be published at a tremendous rate, the Indian affairs that continue to make news, and the Indian people who continue to make history. Colleagues, reviewers, and I agree that developments in the twentieth century — and now the twenty-first century — merit more attention than they received in the first edition. In addition, students are often most interested in the most recent events. As a result, I substantially revised and expanded the final chapter. Retitled "Nations Within a Nation: Indian Country Today," it gives students a sense of the continuing struggles waged by America's first peoples as they endeavor to preserve their cultures, promote their economic independence, and protect their sovereignty. The chapter includes information on court cases, the controversy over Indian gaming, and issues of stereotyping that continue to affect Indian people.

In addition to bringing the story up to the beginning of the twenty-first century, this edition provides more information on Alaskan Natives and

Canada's first peoples and expanded coverage of the militancy and activism that developed in Indian Country after World War II. To better articulate and present the nature of the ongoing and evolving history of American Indians, I have strengthened themes and headings throughout.

New documents increase the presence of Native voices in the book. Of the eight documents new to the second edition, five are by Natives: an account of the Pueblo Revolt, a letter by John Ross, the Twenty Points presented to the government during the Trail of Broken Treaties march on Washington, the Proclamation to the Great White Father and to All *His* People issued by the protesters at Alcatraz, and an editorial from *Lakota Times* about mascots. A few of the retained documents have been shortened to increase student accessibility and to create room for the additional selections. In addition, the captivity narrative of Mary Jemison has replaced the captivity narrative of Susanna Johnson that appeared in the first edition. Both women were captured by Indians in the 1750s, but whereas Susanna was a grown woman with children and returned home as soon as she could, Mary was captured as a teenager and lived the rest of her life with the Senecas.

The illustration and map programs received significant attention during the development of the second edition. A greatly enhanced map program features thirteen new maps, including maps that show the approximate tribal locations at first sustained contact with Europeans, the Ohio Country during the Seven Years' War, boundary lines of 1763 and 1783, treaties and land cessions to 1810, and the movement of tribes onto the Plains. To reinforce the expanded final chapter, new maps feature state and federally recognized reservations, Alaska's Native Regional Corporations, Oneida and Maine land claims, proposed and actual nuclear waste sites in Indian Country, and James Bay. Most of the retained maps have been revised to show topography, and reproductions of contemporary maps have been added to help students understand how outsiders perceived the "New World" and the Natives' place in it. In addition, new charts document 2000 census findings, and over thirty new illustrations provide many views of Natives, among them a creation legend, ways of life old and new, historic events, and important women and men in the shared history of the United States and American Indians. The picture essays in Chapters 1 and 7 now include additional examples of early Native American towns and depictions of twentieth-century life by Native American artists, respectively.

Additional pedagogical revisions include calling out the discussion-provoking Questions for Consideration at the end of each document headnote and picture essay and the addition of a Video Resources appendix offering annotated entries for many useful documentaries. The chapter-ending bibliographies have been updated, as has the General Reference Works appendix, and the Web sites found in a separate Internet Resources appendix. In addition, students are encouraged at the end of every chapter's narrative section to look for a more extensive listing of relevant Web sites at www.bedfordstmartins.com/historylinks.

Acknowledgments

I am indebted to the following readers who reviewed the first edition with an eye to preparation of the second edition: S. Carol Berg, College of St. Benedict; José Brandão, Western Michigan University; James Drake, Metropolitan State College of Denver; Emily Greenwald, University of Nebraska–Lincoln; Brian Hosmer, formerly of the University of Wyoming and now Director of the Center for the History of the American Indian at the Newberry Library, Chicago; Barry Joyce, University of Delaware; Margaret Newell, Ohio State University; Greg O'Brien, University of Southern Mississippi; Jeff Pilz, North Iowa Area Community College; Willard Rollings, University of Nevada, Las Vegas; Margaret Connell Szasz, University of New Mexico; and a twelfth, anonymous, reviewer. Their constructive criticisms were invariably helpful, even if their suggestions did not all make their way into the text, and even in cases where different reviewers expressed contrary opinions!

At Dartmouth, I have as always benefited from daily interactions with fine colleagues in both Native American Studies and History. N. Bruce Duthu read my final two chapters with a close eye on issues of Indian law, and Deborah Nichols again fielded my questions about pre-Columbian America. I am grateful to Professor Charles C. Alexander of Ohio University for correcting my understanding of the origins of the Cleveland Indians' team name.

The people at Bedford/St. Martin's again set exemplary standards for the care and attention they give to their books. Chuck Christensen recruited me for my first Bedford project more than a decade ago, and he and Joan Feinberg have been enthusiastic supporters ever since. Tisha Rossi took over the planning for the second edition with a light but efficient hand that made for a smooth transition. Editor Sarah Barrash Wilson approached the project with a fresh perspective and new questions, wrestled with reorganizing as well as editing text, and, it seemed to me, performed wonders in juggling all the different pieces. Her thoroughness, enthusiasm, and skill made this truly a new edition. As in the first edition, the guiding hand of Tina Samaha steered *First Peoples* through production. Tina's professionalism, her patience with getting the details right, and her good humor make her a pleasure to work with and a terrific asset to the project.

Thanks to all of the above for helping to make the second edition of *First Peoples* a better book. Love and thanks to Marcia, Graeme, and Meg for everything else.

BRIEF CONTENTS

CONTENTS

CHAPTER 3   INDIANS IN COLONIAL AND REVOLUTIONARY AMERICA, 1680–1786   137

MAPS AND
CHARTS

INTRODUCTION: AMERICAN INDIANS IN AMERICAN HISTORY

PERSPECTIVES ON THE PAST

In 1870 Charles Windolph emigrated from Prussia to the United States to avoid being drafted into the Franco-Prussian War. But for Windolph America did not live up to its promise as a land of opportunity. Unable to find work in New York, Windolph joined the army—the very fate he had left home to avoid. Six years later, on the night of June 25, 1876, he found himself pinned down with other survivors of Major Marcus Reno's battalion of the 7th Cavalry, on a hill overlooking the Little Big Horn River. That day, Windolph and his comrades had attacked the south end of the great Lakota and Cheyenne village that had assembled in the valley of the Little Big Horn under the leadership of Sitting Bull. Rallying to defend their homes and families, Indian warriors had swept out of the village, routed Reno's command, and sent the survivors scrambling back up the ridge where they dug in for a siege. Only the assault by George Armstrong Custer at the other end of the village saved Windolph and his comrades from being overwhelmed; most of the Indian warriors had hurried off to the north to attack Custer.

That night, as Charles Windolph looked down into the valley, his mind plagued with terrible scenes from the day's disaster and agonizing questions about what had happened to Custer's men, he heard the Indians drumming and singing in what he imagined were "wild victory dances." "We felt terribly alone on that dangerous hilltop," Windolph recalled later. "We were a million miles from nowhere. And death was all around us." He expected to be killed come morning.

But Windolph's peril was more imagined than real. The "wild victory dances" he thought he was hearing were in fact the mourning songs of Lakota and Cheyenne women who had lost husbands, brothers, and sons in the fighting. A Cheyenne warrior named Wooden Leg also recalled that night in his later years. "There was no dancing or celebrating in any of the camps," he said. "Too many people were in mourning. Too many Cheyenne and Sioux women had gashed their arms and legs to show their grief."

Late the next day, the Indians struck their lodges and moved off toward the Big Horn Mountains. On the morning of the 27th, an army relief column arrived. Charles Windolph did not die on Reno Hill. He died in 1950, at the age of ninety-eight, the last American soldier to survive the Battle of the Little Big Horn.[1]

Windolph's experience vividly illustrates some important points about living through and reconstructing historical events, and about the need to use a variety of sources in retelling the past. Windolph's understanding of what was going on down in the Indian village was dead wrong, and any historian who repeated it without question would be equally wrong. Only the Indian people in the village knew what was really happening there and only by hearing from them can we know whether Windolph was really in any danger. But Windolph's terror was also real, and we need his testimony to help us appreciate the depth of his feelings and to remind us that fear, prejudice, and ignorance often shape one group's perceptions of another. Windolph and Wooden Leg remember the same night, and the same events, very differently. Each one gives a vivid account of his own experience, but we need them both to get the full story. In short, Indian sources are vital to understanding Indian history but they can also foster a fuller understanding of non-Indians' history; non-Indian sources, used carefully, can be important for understanding Native American relations with non-Indians and throw light on Indian experiences.

AMERICA'S MASTER NARRATIVE

History is not, as someone once said, "just one damn thing after another." Unless it is badly taught or written, it is not a dry record of events; it is about how people experience, study, and interpret the past. Each generation reviews and rewrites history in the light of its own experiences and understandings, aspirations, and anxieties. Different societies, different groups within society, and even different individuals will often disagree about the meaning of events, the ways in which events happened, and even, sometimes, whether events happened at all. There is no single history that tells the whole story; there can be many different *histories,* telling many different stories, and many different ways of remembering, recording, and recounting the past.[2]

American history, however, was for a long time written and taught as a single story, a narrative of nation building and unending progress that united the diverse participants in the country's past in a single American "experience." It was a national success story, celebrating the human triumphs made possible in a society based on the principles of liberty and equality. American historians tended to ignore or dismiss people whose experiences and interpretations of the past did not conform to the master narrative. The experiences of American Indians during the years of nation building told a story of decline and suffering rather than of "progress" and "the pursuit of happiness." As a result, notes historian Frederick E. Hoxie, the authors of United States history textbooks had "great difficulty shaping the Native American experience to fit the upbeat format of their books."[3] The Indians' story was not the American story; best to leave them out.

When it was told at all, the Indians' story was usually portrayed as one of futile resistance to the march of civilization. As in the movies, "Indian history" was little more than a chronicle of hostility to Euro-American settlers. The image of savage warriors attacking hardy pioneers became firmly fixed in popular conceptions of the past: Writing in the *New York Times Magazine* as recently as 1996, novelist Melissa Bloch said that when she learned she was about to lose a breast to cancer, "The first thing I thought of was ambushed wagon trains, debreasted pioneer women lying in their dying campfires."[4] When Indians were not killing settlers, their "history" was usually a narrative of the federal government's efforts to solve the "Indian problem." In many classrooms and in most history books, Indian people were either conspicuous by their absence or treated in such stereotypical and distorted terms as to rob them of their humanity.

Times change and history—how we understand the past—changes too. Forty years ago, few colleges or universities offered courses in American Indian history or Native American studies. But in the late 1960s and early 1970s, unrest at home and anxiety about America's war in Vietnam caused many people to question long-accepted views about American society and its relation to native peoples. Political pressure from students and community activists produced new college courses, and scholars began to reexamine the Native American past. These *ethnohistorians* endeavored to combine historical research with an understanding of anthropological principles, asking new questions of their sources, and incorporating oral history into their research to gain a better sense of how Indian people perceived, experienced, and shaped their own histories. In doing so, they began to change how historians looked at American history.

History books, films, and television today are likely to portray Indians in a much more positive and romantic light: Indian people lived in harmony with nature and with each other before Europeans arrived, and then fought courageously to defend their lands and way of life against racist and aggressive invaders. No longer savage foes of civilization, Indians are often portrayed as tragic victims of Euro-American expansion. Unfortunately, their basic role in American history has changed little. They continue to be depicted in one-dimensional terms and enter the mainstream narrative of American history only to fight and be defeated.

INDIAN HISTORY: A SHARED PAST

Renditions of United States history that portray Indian people only as warriors or victims may serve to justify past actions or present agendas, but they do not tell a story that includes all participants as real people with human qualities and failings. They assign blame for or excuse the past, allowing us to feel good or guilty about what happened, but do little to help us understand *how* it happened. Understanding the past involves looking at history from the viewpoints of the many people who made it over several centuries rather than from a single modern stance seeking to celebrate or condemn the actions of people who lived in very different times. Indians must be included as a central strand in the history of the United States — after all, the nation was built on Indian land — and their historical experiences require looking beyond stereotypes, old and new, and rethinking some basic assumptions.

The history of the millions of Indian people who have inhabited North America, and of the few million who still do, is important in itself, but it also provides alternative perspectives on the history of the United States. It reminds us that one people's triumph often means another's tragedy; that building a new nation often entails conquest of other, older nations; and that the expansion of one civilization often brings chaos and suffering to another. It demands that we recognize invasion, racism, and acts of genocide, along with pioneering, liberty, and equality, as part of America's history, and that Native struggles to protect their resources and rights continue today. It is a story of conquest and colonization, but it is also a story of resilience, innovation, and survival.

Native American history is more than a mirror image of United States history; it is also part of a shared past. Including Indian people as participants in that history requires us to acknowledge that American history began long *before* 1492 and that Indian history did not end when Indians stopped fighting. Instead of viewing American history as the story of a westward-moving frontier — a line with Indians on one side, Europeans or Americans on the other — it might be more appropriate to think of it as a kaleidoscope, in which numerous Europeans, Africans, and Indians were continually shifting positions. European invasions changed forever the world Indian peoples inhabited. The biological disasters that befell Indian America after 1492 had tremendous repercussions in Indian communities, as well as creating the notion that America was vacant land awaiting European settlement. The policies of European powers and the United States affected Indian lives and limited Indian options. But Indian people also made their own histories and helped shape the story of this country. They responded to invasion in a variety of ways and coexisted with the newcomers as often as they fought against them. They fought to survive as Indians long after the so-called Indian wars were over, and continue to exert influence on the legal, political, economic, cultural, and spiritual climate of the United States. They also, from first contacts to the present, married Europeans, producing families and population of mixed ancestry and multiple heritages.

MAP I.I Approximate Tribal Locations at First Sustained Contact with Europeans
*Many maps which purport to show America in 1492 place Indian tribes in their modern
locations, conveying the impression that these communities remained unchanged in
composition and place. In reality, groups formed, separated, amalgamated, and moved
throughout history. Many so-called "tribes" did not exist in 1492; others were evolving,
and many communities that did exist subsequently disappeared as their members died or
joined other groups. By the time they came into contact with Europeans, many tribes had
incorporated other peoples, and Indian villages commonly included visitors, traders,
spouses, refugees, and others from different tribes. European contact produced additional
disruption, dislocation, and social reorganization.* Colin G. Calloway, *adapted from* New
Worlds for All: Indians, Europeans, and the Remaking of Early America *(Baltimore: Johns Hopkins
University Press, 1997).*

WORKING WITH SOURCES

The shared past is a complicated place. Whether we study American history, Native American history, or any other area and era, we need to draw on multiple perspectives and listen to many voices to get a well-rounded and richly textured picture. I grew up hearing about the Second World War. My parents met while serving in the British Royal Air Force, aunts and uncles served in various capacities across the globe, and everyone remembered the impact of the war on their lives. There were many stories, and I learned things I never could have read in books. But only when I began to read written accounts and histories of the war did I get a sense of the conflict as a whole, and its different meanings for the different countries involved, even as I read things that were contradicted by what I had heard as a child. My understanding of that enormous event was enriched by both sets of sources; it would have been incomplete without either of them. Students of Indian history must consider sources other than the written word, sources they are not accustomed to "reading," and which they are often ill-equipped to understand. Native American pictographs, winter counts or calendars recorded on buffalo robes, events depicted on pages torn from account books and known as ledger art, and oral traditions that rely on stories recounted to an audience may strike us as strange, lacking in "hard evidence," and "inaccessible." As with any other historical source, we need to learn how to "read" these texts, to understand their purposes and conventions, and to interpret them. We must become "literate" in reading these sources so that we can better appreciate them as repositories of knowledge and history and begin to incorporate them into a more fully grounded reconstruction of the past.

Most historians are trained to trust the printed word and many distrust oral sources of history as "unreliable." Samuel Purchas, writing in the early seventeenth century, said that literacy made history possible. "By speech we utter our minds once, at the present, to the present, as present occasions move . . . us: but by writing Man seems immortall." Indians in colonial America soon recognized the power of printed words as employed by Europeans, especially in treaties, but they continued to attribute great power to spoken words, and, living in an oral tradition, stood in what Kiowa writer N. Scott Momaday describes as "a different relation to language." Momaday, himself a master of the written as well as the spoken word, suspects that writing, because it allows us to store vast quantities of words indefinitely, "encourages us to take words for granted." Too many words may actually obscure meaning. But in an oral tradition, words "are rare and therefore dear. They are jealously preserved in the ear and in the mind. . . . They matter, and they must not be taken for granted; they must be taken seriously and they must be remembered." Ritually uttered words possessed magical powers. "By means of words can one quiet the raging weather, bring forth the harvest, ward off evil, rid the body of sickness and pain, subdue an enemy, capture the heart of a lover, live in the proper way, and venture beyond death." For Momaday there is "nothing more powerful" than words, but he has "come to know that much of the power and magic and beauty of words consist not in meaning but in sound."[5]

Other Indian writers echo his sentiments. "Where I come from," says Laguna writer Leslie Marmon Silko, "the words most highly valued are those spoken from the heart, unpremeditated and unrehearsed. Among the Pueblo people, a written speech or statement is highly suspect because the true feelings of the speaker remain hidden as she reads words that are detached from the occasion and the audience."[6]

Written documents are valuable but they are not always to be trusted. They do not convey the "truth" of what happened; they only convey what their authors thought, wanted to think, or wanted others to think happened. Like the oral traditions of native peoples, they were created by individuals and influenced by the times and culture that produced them. The documents that historians use may be simply the ones that survived by chance: how many hundreds more, telling perhaps a different story, have been destroyed by fire, flood, malice, or mice?

Daniel Richter, who has spent years working in colonial records to reconstruct a history of the Iroquois, acknowledges and explains the limitations and frustrations of trying to recapture the lives of people long since dead:

> As a Euro-American of the late twentieth century, I do not pretend to have plumbed the mind of seventeenth-century native Americans, for most of the mental world of the men and women who populate these pages is irrevocably lost. Neither historians who study documents produced by the colonizers, nor anthropologists who make inferences from their knowledge of later culture patterns, nor contemporary Iroquois who are heirs to a rich oral tradition but who live in profoundly changed material circumstances can do more than partially recover it. . . . In more ways than one, we must all remain outsiders to a long-gone Iroquois world because of the inadequacies of the source material available.[7]

As Richter recognizes, the views of a seventeenth-century Jesuit priest about Iroquoian people were shaped by his own experiences, values, and prejudices as a Frenchman in a world that was alien to him. The views of a twentieth-century Iroquois about seventeenth-century missionaries and Indians must surely be shaped by his or her sense of history, views of native and non-native society, and experiences in the modern world. But the views of both, seventeenth-century priest and contemporary Iroquois, are valuable, even essential, in attempting to reconstruct as complete a picture as possible of the Native American past.

Contrary to commonly held opinion, Indian people are not mute in the written records of the past. They spoke often and at length in meetings with Europeans, and Europeans recorded their words. But the fact that Indian words made it into print should not give them instant authority or authenticity, any more than the writings of European people should enjoy such status without question. The Iroquois were master diplomats in colonial America, and the treaty councils in which they spoke are rich and essential sources for understanding Iroquois history and colonial Indian relations. Those speeches also have serious limitations: "all were recorded by Europeans rather than Iroquois," notes Richter; "all were translated by amateur linguists who lost volumes of meaning conveyed in the original, a few were deliberately altered to further colonizers' designs, and none preserves the body language and social context that were central to the native orators' messages."[8]

Just as some historians insist that native oral traditions are unreliable, so some Native Americans insist that only Indian people grounded in their tribal culture and oral traditions can understand or attempt to tell Indian history. They argue that historical records are inevitably biased and inaccurate and that Western concepts of history and time are irrelevant to understanding Native American experiences and worldviews. Certainly many non-Indian observers, like Charles Windolph, totally misunderstood what they saw, and non-Indian writers have often misrepresented Native American life. But although the documents written by observers and the histories written by Euro-American academics may be flawed, they are not always worthless. As Canadian historians Jennifer S. H. Brown and Elizabeth Vibert note in their anthology, *Reading Beyond Words,* "the encounter between Native and non-Native people has been a long and complex engagement of mutual dialogue, communication, and miscommunication. Given the intensity of the engagement, even the most confidently Eurocentric of texts cannot help but provide glimpses of Native actions, traces of Native voices."[9] A Jesuit priest may not have understood, or even liked, the people among whom he lived, but he was there, sometimes for most of his life. He was able to recount things that happened that affected people's lives even if he was unable to understand how they thought or felt about those events.

Documents are invaluable to historians, but they must be used carefully, scrutinized, examined for bias, and checked against other sources. The fact that they are in print does not guarantee their reliability. After all, most documents were produced for particular purposes, not to add to the historical record; if they were produced specifically to inform historians they are probably even more suspect. "There is no such thing as an objective, innocent, primary document," wrote the French historiographer Jacques le Goff. "In the end, there is no documentary truth. Every document is a lie. It is up to historians not to feign innocence."[10] But as anthropologist Marshall Sahlins warns, neither can they adopt cynicism and assume "that an author who may be suspected of lying on the grounds of interest or ideology therefore *is* lying—not even a Christian missionary."[11] Scholars may dream of a "historian's heaven," in which, wrote the late Michael Dorris, "if we have been good little historians," we will finally learn what really happened. In reality, the biases, gaps, and *possible* distortions in the sources, combined with the historian's own subjectivity, sympathies, and biases, mean that anyone attempting to write Indian history had better "admit in advance to fallibility."[12] The sources historians use "present us with complex subjectivities, multiple ways of knowing the world." The different voices in the sources "can be listened for, articulated, balanced with one another; but only through silencing or suppression can they be melded into a single voice or unquestioned truth."[13]

Rather than chase the illusory historian's heaven or attempt to provide a single voice, this book offers a historical overview, in this case written from the perspective of a European student of American Indian history living in the United States, and a selection of documents that present multiple perspectives on the past. The documents have been chosen and edited to illustrate key themes, highlight significant events, and provide broad coverage, but they represent only a small sampling of the many different sources available to scholars and students of Indian history. They should not be read just to gather information, find "the facts," or learn "what really happened." They represent different experiences, perspectives, and agendas. Often, one can learn more by reading critically between the lines than by accepting documents at face value.

The book also includes historic images in a series of picture essays and in-text illustrations. Pictures, like written documents, can help us to understand the past, but they too must be used critically and carefully. They illustrate and help bring history to life, but they also interpret the past, often in subtle ways that might escape those not accustomed to reading and analyzing images. What was the artist's purpose in creating the picture? Where was the picture displayed and for what audience? Is the painting based on firsthand observation, accurate information, pure imagination, or a mixture of all three? Are the images most valuable for what they tell us about the subjects and the events they portray, or for what they reveal about the assumptions, aspirations, and agenda of the artist who created them and his intended audience? What do the images suggest about the power of art in shaping history? As with written documents, each picture "must be evaluated on its own merits," with knowledge acquired from other sources. The late John Ewers, a scholar of Plains Indian history and culture and art of the West, warned that it "is dangerous to appraise the individual works on the basis of the general reputation of the artist who created them."[14] What's more, warns another writer, sometimes each element in a picture must be evaluated separately, since pictures often contain "a mixture of observed facts, added fiction, and borrowed material." It is often said that a picture is worth a thousand words but if it is to be used as an historical source "it may require a thousand words of documentary evidence to show that it is based on actual observation by a credible witness, that it is accurately drawn . . . , and that no well-meaning person has tried to 'improve' it."[15] "Works of art are, of course, historical documents," notes Plains art scholar Janet Berlo, "but . . . they are not *merely* historical documents."[16]

The past is a complex story, made up of many interwoven lives and experiences. American history without Indians is mythology—it never happened. The last five hundred years of American Indian history likewise includes increasing numbers of non-Indian participants in a range of roles. As with the different views of the Battle of the Little Big Horn, we need to take into account many stories and sources if we are to have a history that includes all people and if we are to understand the past not as *his*tory but as **their** story.

A NOTE ON NAME USAGE

Neither *Indian* nor *Native American* is entirely satisfactory as a description of the indigenous peoples of North America. The very term *Indian* is a European conception, or rather misconception, about the first Americans. When Columbus landed in the Caribbean he mistakenly believed he had found a westward route around the world to India. He called the people he met "los Indios," and the name stuck. But both *Indian* and *Native American* serve as collective terms in the absence of any more suitable designation that does not require explanation or create confusion. I use the terms interchangeably, giving preference to *Indian* as stylistically less problematic and because most of the Indian people I have met, especially in the West, employ the term. My preference is to use the term *Indian people,* with *Indian* as an adjective for *people,* rather than on its own as a category.

The names that Indian groups applied to themselves usually translate into "the people," "the real people," or something similar. However, many of the names that have been used historically and continue to be used to designate Indian tribes — *Iroquois, Huron, Sioux* — are names that were applied to them by enemies and carry pejorative connotations. Sioux, for example, is a French corruption of an Algonquian word meaning "snakes" or "adders," that is, "enemies." Some Native people find these terms offensive; others continue to use them. I use the tribal names that seem to be most easily recognizable to readers, and do so in recognition, and with apologies, that some of these terms are inappropriate. I use the term *Lakota* when referring only to the western branch of the Sioux people; I use *Sioux* when referring to that nation in general or to several groups of the nation. The names *Chippewa* and *Ojibwa* are used historically to refer to both bands of essentially the same people; this is still often the case. To use both, or to use one and exclude the other, is confusing, however, and I employ the name that most of these people use to refer to themselves: *Anishinaabeg* (noun) and *Anishinaabe* (adjective), meaning "original people." I use *Pueblos* when referring to the Indian groups living along the Rio Grande and *pueblos* (lowercase) when referring to the towns they inhabited.

References

1. The information on Charles Windolph is from James Welch and Paul Stekler, *Killing Custer: The Battle of the Little Big Horn and the Fate of the Plains Indians* (New York: W. W. Norton, 1994).
2. Peter Nabokov, *A Forest of Time: American Indian Ways of History* (Cambridge: Cambridge University Press, 2002), explores these issues more in depth.
3. Frederick E. Hoxie, "The Indians versus the Textbooks: Is There Any Way Out?" *Perspectives* 23 (April 1985), 18.
4. *New York Times Magazine,* October 6, 1996, 6.
5. Purchas quoted in Jill Lepore, *The Name of War: King Philip's War and the Origins of American Identity* (New York: Knopf, 1998), 26; James Axtell, "The Power of Print in the Eastern Woodlands," in his *After Columbus: Essays in the Ethnohistory of Colonial North America* (New York: Oxford University Press, 1988), 86–99; N. Scott Momaday, *The Man Made of Words* (New York: St. Martin's Press, 1997), 15–16.
6. Leslie Marmon Silko, *Yellow Woman and a Beauty of the Spirit: Essays on Native American Life Today* (New York: Simon and Schuster, 1996), 48.

7. Daniel K. Richter, *The Ordeal of the Longhouse: The Peoples of the Iroquois League in the Era of European Colonization* (Chapel Hill: University of North Carolina Press, 1992), 4–5.

8. Richter, *Ordeal of the Longhouse,* 6.

9. Jennifer S. H. Brown and Elizabeth Vibert, eds., *Reading beyond Words: Contexts for Native History* (Peterboro, Ont.: Broadview Press, 1996), xiv.

10. Jacques le Goff, "Documento/Monumento," *Enciclopedia Einaudi* 4 (1978), 44–45. I am grateful to Annabelle Melzer for bringing this quotation to my attention.

11. Marshall Sahlins, *How "Natives" Think: About Captain Cook, for Example* (Chicago: University of Chicago Press, 1995), 42.

12. Michael Dorris, "Indians on the Shelf," in Calvin Martin, ed., *The American Indian and the Problem of History* (New York: Oxford University Press, 1987), 104.

13. Brown and Vibert, eds., *Reading Beyond Words,* x–xi.

14. John C. Ewers, "Fact and Fiction in the Documentary Art in the American West," in John Francis McDermott, ed., *The Frontier Re-Examined* (Urbana: University of Illinois Press, 1967), 94.

15. Ingeborg Marshall quoted in Arthur Einhorn and Thomas S. Abler, "Bonnets, Plumes, and Headbands in West's Painting of Penn's Treaty," *American Indian Art Magazine* 21 (Summer 1996), 46.

16. Janet Catherine Berlo, ed., *Plains Indian Drawings 1865–1935: Pages from a Visual History* (New York: Harry Abrams, 1996), 10.

AMERICAN HISTORY BEFORE COLUMBUS

DETERMINING WHAT CAME BEFORE

As recently as 1987, a widely used United States history textbook, written by a team of eminent historians and first published in 1959, declared that while human beings elsewhere in the world were developing civilizations over thousands of centuries, "the continents we now know as the Americas stood empty of mankind and its works." The story of America, in the minds of these historians was "the story of the creation of a civilization where none existed." The revised ninth edition of the textbook, published in 1995, acknowledged that there was "as much variety among the civilizations of the Americas as among the civilizations of Europe, Asia and Africa." Nevertheless, it devoted only four of its almost one thousand pages to "America before Columbus."[1]

For Indian people, history did not begin when Christopher Columbus landed in San Salvador in October 1492; it began when their ancestors fell from the sky (Iroquois), emerged from under the earth (Pueblo, Navajo, Mandan), were transformed from ash trees into people (New England Algonquian), entered the world through a hollow log (Kiowa) — or entered North America via the Bering Strait from Siberia (archaeologists). (See "The Beginning," a Navajo emergence story, pages 37–42.) Countless generations of Indian people settled the land and developed ways of living on it, built communities, and maintained relationships with their spirit world. What Columbus "discovered" was not a "new world" but another old world, rich in diverse peoples, histories, communities, and cultures.

Precontact Population

Basing their estimates on numbers recorded by explorers, traders, and colonists who often arrived after diseases had hit Indian America, scholars used to believe that the native population of North America numbered no more than 1 million in 1492. In recent years, scholars employing more sophisticated techniques of demographic calculation have dramatically increased their estimates of pre-Columbian populations. Their figures still vary widely, from as low as 2 million to as much as 18 million people for the area north of Mexico. Most estimates fall between these extremes. The total population of North and South America may have constituted as much as one-fifth of the population of the world at that time: one recent calculation suggests a population of between 43 and 65 million. Whatever the actual figures, much of America was well populated by 1492.

Revisions of Native American population sizes explode many stereotypes about the nature of Indian society on the eve of European invasion. They also discredit old theories that rationalized dispossession and conquest on the premise that America was virgin wilderness and that the few Indians living there "wandered" the land but made no good use of it. Heavier concentrations of population suggest more sophisticated social structures, political systems, and economic activities than most Europeans imagined; they also mean that the idea of America as a pristine landscape before 1492 is a European fiction. In different times and places, Indian peoples had modified the extent and composition of forests, created and expanded grasslands, built towns and earthworks, trails and roads, canals and ditches. They sometimes placed pressure on food sources and occasionally degraded the environment. The notion of America as an untouched land may stem from the observations of seventeenth-century Europeans, who saw it when the Indian presence had largely disappeared after epidemics caused massive declines in Native populations and before European immigrant populations increased significantly.[2]

Creation Stories and Migration Theories

Estimates of how long Indians have lived in America also vary. There is firm archaeological evidence of human presence in North America up to 12,000 years ago, but some estimates push habitation back as far as 40,000 years. The creation stories and oral traditions of most Indian tribes tell how their people had always lived in the land that Europeans called America, but that they knew as Ndakinna (Abenaki), Anishinaabewaki (Anishinaabe), and Dinétah (Navajo). European theories have suggested that American Indians were one of the lost tribes of Israel; that they were descendants of a legendary Welsh prince named Madoc and his followers who arrived in the twelfth century; or that they are descended from early voyagers from Polynesia, Phoenicia, the Middle East, or Japan.

Most non-Indian historians and archaeologists believe that Indian peoples migrated to America from Asia via the Bering Strait, and cite genetic, dental, and even linguistic evidence linking Native populations of the Americas to the peoples of Asia. The theory holds that the Ice Age of c. 75,000 B.C.–8000 B.C. lowered ocean levels worldwide and exposed a land bridge of perhaps a thousand miles across what is now the Bering Strait between Siberia and Alaska. Nomadic hunters made their way across this land bridge over hundreds, perhaps thousands, of years, following migrating game. Finding rich hunting territories and more hospitable climates, they edged their way onward along corridors that opened up as the ice shield receded. The newcomers continued to arrive and scatter as some groups pushed on south to the tip of South America. During the Archaic period (c. 8000 B.C.–1000 B.C.), small bands moved into almost every area of the continent. But migration via land from Asia offers only one explanation of the peopling of America: maritime people would have been more likely to make the trip by sea, expanding back the time when migration may have taken place. Native traditions say the ancestors have always been here.

Key archaeological evidence of early settlement has been found at many North American sites. In 1925, at Folsom, New Mexico, archaeologists found worked flint alongside the bones of a bison species that had been extinct for about 8,000 years. Seven years later, at Clovis, New Mexico, archaeologists discovered weapon points that were even older than the Folsom artifacts. Since then, such Clovis points, as this type of stone weapon is known, have been found from Mexico to Nova Scotia. The oldest Clovis spear points—about 11,500 years old—have generally been considered the benchmark for the beginning of human habitation in the Americas. But the Meadowcroft Rock Shelter in Pennsylvania may have been occupied as long as 20,000 years ago, and some archaeologists say humans could have lived in North America much earlier. The evidence is inconclusive, and many scholars remain skeptical. The most widely accepted estimates for the earliest human occupation of America range between 12,000 and 14,000 years ago, although new evidence and clues emerge each year.

After long debate, many archaeologists reached consensus that humans were inhabiting southern Chile 12,500 years ago. Bone and stone tools found at the Monte Verde site in southern Chile have been dated as more than a thousand years earlier than the oldest Clovis points in North America. "Nothing at Monte Verde was more evocative of its former inhabitants than a single footprint beside a hearth," reported the *New York Times*. "A child had stood there by the fire 12,500 years ago and left a lasting impression in the soft clay." If the people living in Chile migrated south via ice-free corridors through the glaciers that engulfed North America between 13,000 and 20,000 years ago, they must have spread with remarkable speed to the southern end of America. If they did not travel south overland, as previously supposed, they must have come by a different route, perhaps by sea along the western coast. Or they must have entered the Americas more than 20,000 years ago; as Native traditions assert, they must have already been there.[3]

Many Native people refute the idea that their ancestors came to America via the Bering Strait and insist that they are truly indigenous people, not just the first immigrants to America. The Miami chief, Little Turtle, offered a different interpretation of the Bering Strait theory. On a visit to the East, Little Turtle is

Caddo Creation Legend

In many tribal legends the people emerged from below ground, often with corn and other plants to sustain them in their new world. This Caddo creation legend depicted by Creek-Pawnee artist Acee Blue Eagle (1907–59) includes squash and a turtle, too. Caroline Dormon Collection, Cammie G. Henry Research Center, Watson Memorial Library, Northwestern State University of Louisiana.

reported to have met Thomas Jefferson and a group of French scientists who were debating the origins of the American Indians. They pointed out the similarities between American Indians and people from Siberia, which they believed proved that Indians came from Asia. Little Turtle considered the evidence but came to a different conclusion: the Asian people must have migrated from *America,* he concluded.[4] The Lakota writer and scholar Vine Deloria, Jr., takes a more militant position. He dismisses the idea that Indians came to America via the Bering Strait as something that "exists and existed only in the minds of scientists," and asserts that "immense political implications" make it difficult for people to let go of this theory. Portraying Indians as "latecomers who had barely unpacked before Columbus came knocking on the door" allowed Europeans to brush aside Indian claims to aboriginal occupancy based on having "always been here." Lakota writer Joseph Marshall III offers another perspective that might help readers reconcile opposing beliefs about the peopling of America, and to understand Native peoples' insistence that they have always been here, in the face of what may seem to be weighty evidence pointing to Asian origins and Bering Straits migration. The original stories among many Native peoples in North America "do not bother with when," Marshall explains.

Instead, many such stories deal with the obvious fact that we are here and have always been here. When a moment or an event happened so long ago that it has ceased to exist in collective memory, it then begins to exist—as my grandfather liked to say—on the other side of memory. In such an instance, *always* becomes a relative factor. And what emerges as a far more important factor is *first.*[5]

Questions of who was where when continue to spark heated debate today. In 1996, the skeleton of an adult male aged between forty and fifty-five years was discovered on the banks of the Columbia River near Kennewick, Washington. The skeleton showed evidence of violence, including a stone projectile point lodged in the left hip, and was dated as between eight and nine thousand years old. When physical archaeologists reported that the skeleton exhibited

Caucasoid features, suggesting that the man was European rather than Native American, "Kennewick Man" became the center of a storm of controversy. Five tribes demanded that the remains be returned to them for reburial, but, in August 2002, a United States District Court found that scientists must be allowed access to the skeletal remains.[6]

GLIMPSES OF PRECONTACT SOCIETIES

It is too easy to dismiss scholars' skepticism and insistence on meeting scientific criteria as stemming from political or racist motivations. And few scholars today would argue that precontact (the time before interaction with Europeans) America was empty when the Europeans arrived. America was "a pre-European cultural landscape, one that represented the trial and error as well as the achievement of countless human generations."[7] Indian peoples in different times and regions pursued varied activities. They built irrigation systems that allowed them to farm in the deserts. They cultivated new strains of crops, and built settled and populous communities based on corn, beans, and squash. They improved hunting and fishing techniques and crafted more efficient weapons and tools. They exchanged commodities and ideas across far-reaching trade networks. They fought wars, established protocols of diplomacy, and learned to communicate with speakers of many different languages. They developed various forms of architecture suited to particular environments, different seasons, and shifting social and economic purposes. While medieval Christians were erecting Gothic cathedrals in Europe, Indians were constructing temple mounds in the Mississippi basin. They built societies held together by kin, clan, and tradition. They created rich forms of art, music, dance and oral literature, and developed ceremonies and religious rituals that helped keep their world in balance.

West Coast Affluence

People were harvesting the rich marine resources of the California coast ten thousand years ago. As the climate stabilized and came to resemble that of today, the coastal regions of California supported large populations of hunter-gatherers who lived in permanent communities. The inhabitants cultivated only one crop—tobacco—but harvested an abundant variety of natural foods. Women gathered acorns and ground them into bread meal; men fished the rivers and ocean shores and hunted deer and smaller mammals. The Chumash Indians of the Santa Barbara region lived well from the ocean and the land, following an annual cycle of subsistence that allowed them to harvest and store marine mammals, fish, shellfish, acorns, pine nuts, and other wild plants. Chumash traders were part of an extensive regional exchange network, and Chumash villages sometimes housed a thousand people. The sophisticated and diversified hunter-gatherer lifestyle in California supported a population of 300,000 people and a great diversity of languages and cultures before Europeans arrived.

MAP 1.1 Native North America before Columbus: Selected Peoples and Key Sites
Indian peoples sometimes shifted location over time, and different societies developed, changed, and disappeared, but environmental conditions determined broad areas of cultural similarity in Native North America. People exchanged foods, materials, influences, and ideas within and across regions.

On the northwest Pacific coast, from northern California to Alaska, seagoing peoples were harvesting rich marine resources five thousand years ago. Men fished with harpoons and nets from canoes, and villages accumulated reserves of dried fish and sea-mammal meat. Large villages of communal rectangular plank houses were built in sheltered coves. In time, these peoples created prosperous and stratified societies. Craftsmen developed specialized woodworking tools and skills, producing seagoing canoes and ceremonial carvings. At Ozette on the Olympic Peninsula of present-day Washington state, Makah Indians occupied an ideal site for sea-mammal hunting. The village was inhabited for at least two thousand years before a massive springtime mudslide engulfed it—probably around 1700—preserving its contents like a North American Pompeii.

Columbia Plateau Fishers

On the Columbia Plateau, between the Cascade Mountains on the west and the Rocky Mountains on the east, salmon were central to Indian life and culture. Huge and fast-flowing rivers like the Fraser, Columbia, and Snake provided a regular harvest for people inhabiting their banks. At The Dalles, a site at the upstream end of the Long Narrows where the Columbia River rushed for miles through a rocky channel, Indian people harvested salmon runs more than seven

Kettle Falls, Fort Colville
Paul Kane's painting from 1847 shows Indians fishing salmon at Kettle Falls on the upper Columbia River, near present-day Spokane, Washington, as they had done for centuries. Men used harpoons, traps, and dipnets to catch the fish; women dried and stored the catch. Fishing sites often became centers of social and ceremonial activity when the salmon were running. Stark Museum of Art, Orange, Texas.

thousand years ago. Men caught the salmon with harpoons, dipnets, weirs, and traps; women butchered, dried, and stored the catch. Fish were dried or smoked on racks and packed in baskets for eating or for trading, and fishing stations became sites of social and ceremonial activity. Described as "the finest salmon fishery in the world" and located where Chinookan-speaking peoples from downriver met Sahaptian-speakers from upstream, The Dalles became one of the largest trade fairs in western North America, linked to trade routes that extended south to California, east to Yellowstone, and, ultimately, all the way across the continent.[8]

Rituals accompanied the start of the spring salmon runs, and only after the ceremonies were completed was the fishing season open. People threw salmon bones back into the water to allow the spirit of the salmon to return to the sea and ensure that the cycle of abundance would continue. Taboos limited women's contact with salmon and water, especially during menstruation when their blood had the power to offend the salmon and jeopardize the run.[9] Earthquakes and landslides occasionally blocked salmon runs on the Columbia River; and changes in water temperature and mineral content could discourage the fish from returning to their spawning grounds — events explained and retold in Native stories handed down across generations.

Great Basin Foragers

The Great Basin, an area of some 400,000 square miles between the Rocky Mountains and the Sierra Nevadas, embraces tremendous environment and topographical diversity. Ancient inhabitants exploited a broad range of food sources to survive in a hard land. Between ten and twelve thousand years ago, lakes in the region shrank, rivers dried up, and the lusher vegetation retreated to higher elevations and to the north. Temperatures rose until about 4000 or 3000 B.C., and hot, arid conditions continued to characterize the region into historic times. The diverse environments of the Great Basin underwent constant change, and populations moved regularly to take advantage of unevenly distributed and often precarious resources. For instance, on the shores of Pyramid Lake and Walker River in Nevada, people lived in sedentary communities for most of the year, supplementing a staple diet of fish with game and plants. In other areas, people harvested wild plants and small game, a subsistence strategy that required intimate knowledge of the land and its animals, regular movement to take advantage of seasonal diversity and changing conditions, and careful exploitation of the environment. Amid these adaptations, however, hunting and gathering endured for ten thousand years.[10] Trade, too, was a part of Great Basin life: shells from the Pacific coast and obsidian — volcanic glass — from southern Idaho, which may have been present in the Great Basin as early as seven thousand years ago, were traded over vast areas along with food, hides, and other perishable items.

Between about A.D. 400 and 1300, horticultural communities appeared in Utah, eastern Nevada, western Colorado, and southern Idaho, growing corn, making poetry, and living relatively sedentary lives. Called "Fremont Culture" by archaeologists and anthropologists, this way of live proved short lived in Great Basin terms—a mere nine hundred years.

First Buffalo Hunters of the Plains

Life in ancient America was varied and changing, but nowhere did Indians wearing feather headdresses hunt buffalo from horseback; the horse-and-buffalo culture of the Plains Indians developed much later, a byproduct of contact with Europeans. The way of life that popular stereotypes depict as typical of all Indians at all times never existed in most of North America and was not even typical of the Great Plains until the eighteenth and nineteenth centuries.

Between about 12,000 and 8000 B.C., Native American peoples hunted on foot on the Great Plains for big game—mammoths, mastodons, and bison. Over time, these people, known as Paleo-Indians, worked increasingly lethal projectiles, such as Clovis points flaked on both sides, to produce stone spear points bound into split wooden shafts. Experiments by archaeologist George Frison demonstrated that hunters using Clovis point spears could inflict mortal wounds on animals as large as African elephants.[11] As Paleo-Indians refined their hunting toolkits, they also developed more effective methods of hunting large game, such as buffalo drives and corrals. These communal hunting techniques required greater degrees of social organization. At Head Smashed In buffalo jump in Alberta—the largest, oldest, and best-preserved buffalo drive site in the western Plains—Indians hunted and slaughtered buffalo for more than seven thousand years. Many species of large animals became extinct—mastodons, mammoths, giant beaver and bear, saber-toothed cats and American lions, camels, and horses—but the demise of the large Ice Age mammals was a worldwide phenomenon, and most likely the result of climatic change rather than relentless and greedy human predators. By 8500 B.C. most Paleo-Indians were hunting bison. Bows and arrows—a major innovation in hunting and warfare—spread south from the Arctic, and were in use throughout the Plains by A.D. 1000.

When the first Spaniards ventured onto the "vast and beautiful" southern Plains in the 1520s, they saw huge herds of buffalo. They noted that the Indians of the region "live upon them and distribute an incredible number of hides into the interior."[12] Nomadic hunters traded with farming groups on the edges of the Great Plains, but they did not yet travel by horseback. In 1541, Spaniards on the southern Plains encountered peoples who traded each winter with the Pueblos° in the Rio Grande valley and who "go about like nomads with their

---

°The name *Pueblo* comes from the Spanish term for a town and was applied by early Spaniards to the people they met living in multistory adobe towns in New Mexico and Arizona. At the time of first contacts with Europeans, the Pueblo Indians lived in many communities and belonged to eight different language groups. Then, as now, most Pueblo communities nestled in the Rio Grande valley—Taos, San Juan, Cochiti, Acoma—but the Zunis of western New Mexico and the Hopis of Arizona are also regarded as Pueblo Indians.

Pecos Pueblo around 1500
One of the easternmost Pueblo communities, Pecos functioned as a trade center and rendezvous between the farming peoples of the Rio Grande valley and the hunting peoples of the Great Plains long before the Spanish arrived. This 1973 painting by Tom Lovell depicts a harvest-time trade fair at Pecos. The inhabitants of the pueblo trade corn, squash, pottery, and other items to visiting Plains Apaches, who transport the products of the buffalo hunt on dogsleds. Later, Spanish seizures of Pueblo food surpluses disrupted these longstanding trade relationships, while access to Spanish horses increased the Apaches' mobility and military power. Courtesy of Abell-Hanger Foundation and of the Permian Basin Petroleum Museum, Library and Hall of Fame of Midland, Texas, where this painting is on display.

tents and with packs of dogs harnessed with little pads, pack-saddles and girths."[13]

First Farmers of the Southwest

For virtually the entire span of human life on earth, people have survived as hunters and gatherers, living on wild plants and animals. Then, beginning about ten thousand years ago, many hunters became farmers at various places around the world. Within the relatively short period of about five thousand years, people began cultivating domesticated plants in Southeast and Southwest Asia, China, South America, Mesoamerica, and the eastern United States. The transition to agriculture involved more than simply developing a new food source; it entailed a changed relationship with the environment. Ultimately it produced new social structures and organizations,° as people cleared lands, cultivated and stored foods, adopted new technologies for farming, and lived in more populous and sedentary communities.[14]

Between about A.D. 700 and 1100, warmer climatic conditions fostered westward expansion of the tall-grass prairie and peoples living on the eastern edges of the Plains began cultivating corn and beans. By the end of the first millennium, eastern Plains peoples were living in earth-lodge villages, growing corn and beans, as well as hunting and gathering. In the twelfth century, other farming peoples moved into the middle Missouri valley, although agriculture on the Plains became more precarious by the mid-thirteenth century as the climate grew colder and drier.

The ancient inhabitants of the southwestern United States developed agriculturally based societies approximately three thousand years ago. About two thousand years ago in the highlands of the Arizona–New Mexico border and in northwest Mexico, Mogollon people grew corn and squash. They first lived in pit house villages, but later built multi-apartment structures above ground. Southwestern peoples began making clay pots by about A.D. 200, and pottery was widespread by A.D. 500, bringing improved methods for preparing and storing food. Mogollon potters were making the distinctive black on white Mimbres style pottery more than a thousand years ago, although their culture went into decline after about 1100.

Between about 800 and 1400, the Hohokam people, ancestors of the Akimel O'odham or Pimas and Tohono O'odham or Papagos, built sophisticated irrigation systems to tap sources of precious water in their Sonoran Desert homeland. They created a network of canals that transported water hundreds of miles. Freed from dependence on the unpredictable Gila River, the Hohokam people were able to store crops and develop larger and more permanent communities. Snaketown, near present-day Phoenix, had three to six hundred inhabitants and was continuously occupied for twelve hundred years. Drought or increased soil salinity may explain the decline of Hohokam culture after about 1300.

In the four-corners region of the Southwest where the present states of Utah, Colorado, Arizona, and New Mexico meet, the Anasazi culture emerged around A.D. 900 and reached its height between 1100 and 1300, about the time of the Crusades in Europe. Anasazi people grew and stored corn, wove and decorated baskets, made pottery, studied the stars, and were master architects. In Chaco Canyon, in New Mexico's San Juan River basin, they constructed a dozen towns and perhaps two hundred outlying villages. At least five thousand and perhaps as many as fifteen thousand people inhabited the area. D-shaped Pueblo Bonito, one of many such structures in the canyon, contained hun-

---

°Contrary to assumptions that a transition from hunting to farming constituted "progress," however, there is evidence that hunting-and-gathering lifestyles in areas of abundant resources provided a more nutritious diet with less work than did agriculture. In rich and temperate areas like California and the Eastern Woodlands, plant, animal, and fish resources were so abundant that people were able to live in sedentary communities before agriculture became important. For many Indian peoples, the transition to agriculture was an option, not a necessity.

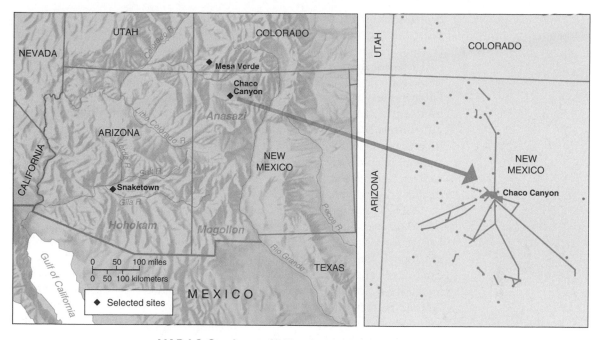

MAP 1.2 Southwest Civilizations and Chaco Canyon as Trade Center, c. 900–1200
*Structures like the cliff-dwellings at Mesa Verde and the town of Pueblo Bonito show that
the ancient Southwest was a region of remarkable activity and lasting achievement.
Pueblo Bonito sat in Chaco Canyon, itself the center of a series of communities in the
San Juan River basin and a focus of trade, in which turquoise was exchanged for goods as
far away as Mexico, California, and the Rocky Mountains. The dots on the detail map
(right) locate some of the outlying settlements. The lines show straight ancient roads,
some of them stretching four hundred miles, that have been documented by either
ground or aerial surveys. Adapted from a drawing by Tracy Wellman. From* Ancient North America
by Brian M. Fagan, copyright © 1995 Thames and Hudson, Ltd.

dreds of rooms and housed hundreds of people, making it "the largest apartment building in North America until New York City surpassed it in the nineteenth century."[15] Most Anasazi villages housed a few families and were located
on mesa tops, but Anasazi people also built impressive cliff dwellings. At Mesa
Verde in southwestern Colorado, people occupied more than two hundred
rooms in a multitiered fortress-like cliff dwelling that provided defense against
enemies. (See Pueblo Bonito and Mesa Verde images, pages 57 and 58.)

With more than four hundred miles of straight roads spoking out from it,
Chaco Canyon was a center of trade. The people of Chaco Canyon exchanged
turquoise to distant peoples, obtaining sea shells from the Gulf of California,
exotic birds and feathers from Central America, and minerals and ores from the
Rocky Mountains.

Natural disaster and climatic change altered the lives and locations of
southwestern peoples. In 1064, near present-day Flagstaff, Arizona, Sunset
Crater volcano erupted, filling the sky with fire and smoke, and causing

dramatic shifts in patterns of settlement. Beginning in the twelfth century, a severe and prolonged cycle of droughts hit the American Southwest. Soil erosion, crop failure, increased competition for farming lands and the ensuing social tensions and warfare seem to have dispersed people into smaller, less stable settlements. Some Anasazi moved south; others joined the Zunis and Hopis in western New Mexico and eastern Arizona. The rest moved east and mingled with Pueblo communities that had developed in the Rio Grande valley, causing a dramatic population upsurge in that area. Some scholars believe that a new religion—what they call the Kachina phenomenon—drew Anasazi people eastward to the Rio Grande; in a period of drought, southwestern farming peoples may well have placed more faith in kachinas, the spirits that brought rain.

According to one account, Pueblo people had a rather different explanation. They said that Anasazi people "kept a great black snake in the kiva,° who had power over their life." They fed him the fruits of the hunt—deer, rabbits, antelope, bison, and birds—and he gave them corn, squash, berries, yucca, cactus, and all they needed to wear. Then one night he left them. They followed his tracks until they disappeared in the water of a big river, the Rio Grande. So they gathered up their things and moved to the river, "where they found another town already living. There they took up their lives again amidst the gods of that place."[16]

Whatever the causes, over the next 150 years, a period known as the Great Migration, Anasazi people abandoned their sophisticated towns and moved away to be amalgamated with other established peoples. No new Chacoan buildings were constructed after 1150, and by 1300 the canyon was abandoned. Great cliff dwellings that had once echoed with human activity became empty and silent. About the same time other movements of peoples altered the populations of the Southwest. Nomadic Athabascan peoples, ancestors of the Apaches and Navajos, began to migrate from far northwestern Canada, probably reaching the Southwest by the 1400s. Long before Europeans arrived in America, Anasazi civilization had emerged in the Southwest, flourished for centuries, and declined. The Pueblo cultures and communities the Spanish invaders encountered in the Southwest in the sixteenth century were descendants of ancient civilizations that stretched back thousands of years. People had migrated, scattered and regrouped, were able to survive and often flourish in a challenging and sometimes harsh environment. When a Spanish expedition reached the Hopi town of Walpi in 1582:

> More than one thousand souls came, laden with very fine earthen jars containing water, and with rabbits, cooked venison, tortillas, atole (corn flour gruel), and beans, cooked calabashes, and quantities of corn and pinole, so that, although our friends were many and we insisted our friends should not bring so much, heaps of food were left over.[17]

°A kiva is an underground ceremonial chamber.

Farmers and Mound Builders of the Eastern Woodlands

Indian women may have begun domesticating indigenous seed plants such as sunflowers, squash, and marsh elder that thrived in the floodplains of the eastern United States as much as four thousand years ago.[18] Some Indians in present-day Illinois were growing squash by 5000 B.C. As long as seven thousand years ago Indian farmers in Mesoamerica crossbred wild grasses and created maize, or corn, which has become a staple food over much of the world; over time, corn cultivation spread north into what is now the United States. It was present in Tennessee about 350 B.C., in the Ohio valley by 300 B.C., and in the Illinois valley by A.D. 650.

Corn does not grow without human care and cultivation; Indian farmers selected the seeds of plants that did best in their environments and developed new strains for particular soils, climates, and growing seasons.

Corn provided people with food they could store. By about A.D. 1000 corn had become the major field crop in the Eastern Woodlands and the core of society and economy. It was a staple of life that also reflected the rhythmic cycle of life. Indian peoples developed a system of agriculture based on corn, beans, and squash—the "sacred three sisters" of the Iroquois—supplemented with a variety of other crops.[19]

"The only reason we have corn today is that for thousands of years humans have selected seeds and planted them," says Jane Mt. Pleasant, an Iroquois agronomist who studies native methods of cultivation and crop yields.[20] "White farmers did not make similar progress in plant breeding until the development of agricultural experiment stations in the late nineteenth century," notes another scholar of Indian agriculture.[21] When Frenchman Jacques Cartier visited the Iroquoian town of Hochelaga (modern Montreal) in 1536, he found it inhabited by several thousand people and surrounded by extensive cornfields. (See Hochelaga image, page 61.) The Hochelagans brought the French fish and loaves of corn bread, "throwing so much of it into our longboats that it seemed to rain bread."[22] Huron Indians north of Lake Ontario tried to grow enough corn each year so that they had a two- or three-year surplus to guard against crop failure and enough left over to trade to other tribes. Huron cornfields were so large that a visiting Frenchman got lost in them.[23]

In the Eastern Woodlands, over a period of about 4,000 years, Indian peoples constructed tens of thousands of large earthen mounds. Archaeologists have discovered a complex of eleven mounds, near the town of Watson Brake in northeast Louisiana, built between 5,000 and 5,400 years ago. It is the earliest mound-building complex yet found in America, predating other known sites by almost 2,000 years.[24] Three thousand years ago at Poverty Point in the Mississippi valley in Louisiana, between two and five thousand people inhabited, or assembled periodically at a town of elaborate earthworks constructed in a semicircle surrounding an open plaza, with a huge ceremonial mound (640 by 710 feet) in the shape of a falcon. The earthworks contained "nearly 1 million cubic yards of dirt and required perhaps 5 million man-hours of sustained, coordinated effort" by people who dug with stone tools and transported

Indian Woman of Florida

John White, who made the voyage to Roanoke in North Carolina in 1585, was the first Englishman to paint Indian people in North America. His watercolors, now in the British Museum, provide a valuable record of the people and plant life of early America. This tattooed Timucuan woman from northeastern Florida offers corn, testifying to the importance of the crop in southeastern Indian culture and to the role of women in producing it. From a sixteenth-century drawing by John White. © British Museum.

the earth in woven baskets. The site received its name in the nineteenth century because it was considered a poor location for a modern plantation, but in its heyday around 1500 B.C. it was "the largest, most prosperous locality in North America," standing at a crossroads of commerce for the whole lower Mississippi valley (see Map 1.1, "Native North America before Columbus: Selected Peoples and Key Sites," page 17).[25] Trade for raw materials for ceremonial use, burial goods, and personal adornment connected peoples as distant as Florida and the Missouri valley. The Poverty Point people seem to have exported stone and clay items and transported heavy, bulky goods by dugout canoe; their imports ranged from copper from the Great Lakes, flint from the Ohio valley, chert (flaked stone) from the Tennessee valley and the Ozarks, to steatite (soapstone) from the Appalachians, and galena (a lead sulphide ore usually ground into a powder and used to make white body paint) from the upper Mississippi valley and southern Missouri.

In the Ohio valley, more than two thousand years ago, people of the Adena culture built mounds that held their honored dead. The Hopewellian culture that emerged from that of the Adena about the first century flourished for some four centuries. Hopewellian people built more elaborate burial mounds and earthen architecture and developed greater ceremonial complexity. Their culture spread through extensive exchange networks, and they obtained valuable raw materials from vast distances: grizzly bears' teeth from the Rockies; obsidian for spear points and blades from Yellowstone; silver from Ontario; copper from the Great Lakes; mica and copper from the southern Appalachians; galena from the upper Mississippi; quartz from Arkansas; pottery, marine shells, turtle shells, shark and alligator teeth from the Gulf of Mexico. Hopewellian craftsmen and artists fashioned the raw materials into tools and intricate ornaments. Many of the items were deposited with the dead in mortuary mounds; others were traded to outside communities.

The Hopewellian culture went into decline

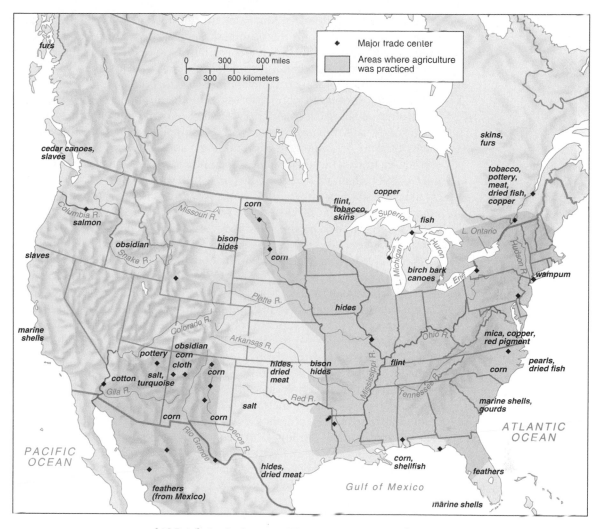

MAP 1.3 Agriculture and Trade in Native America, c. 1450

Europeans often pictured Indians as nomadic hunters living in isolation. In reality, long before European contact, much of Indian America was farming country crisscrossed by well-traveled networks of trade and communication. For centuries, Indian people had been developing and farming corn. Hunting people regularly developed reciprocal economic relations with farming people. Prized items were traded over vast distances, usually along river systems, from community to community or by wide-ranging individual traders. Adapted from The Settling of North America: The Atlas of the Great Migrations into North America from the Ice Age to Ellis Island and Beyond *by Helen Hornbeck Tanner, Janice Reiff, and John H. Long, Editors. Copyright © 1995 by Swanston Publishing Ltd.*

---

around A.D. 300, and seems to have disappeared by about 550. But the spread of corn agriculture throughout eastern North America between 500 and 800 brought population increases and the emergence of more complex societies. Beginning in the lower Mississippi valley around 700 and displaying evidence of Mesoamerican influences, Mississippian cultures spread north to the Great Lakes, east to Florida and the Carolinas, and reached their height between 1100 and 1300. Mississippian societies typically were stable agriculturally based settlements close to floodplains with relatively large populations and complex ceremonial and political structures. Powerful chiefs from elite families collected tribute, mobilized labor, distributed food among their followers, waged war against neighboring chiefdoms, were buried with large quantities of elaborate goods, and appear to have been worshipped as deities. Mississippian towns contained temples, public buildings, and elite residences built atop earthen mounds which surrounded open plazas where ceremonies were conducted and ballgames were played.

The Mississippian town of Cahokia was a thriving urban market center. Founded around A.D. 700 close to the confluence of the Missouri, Mississippi, and Illinois rivers and occupied for about seven hundred years, Cahokia had a population of between 10,000 and 30,000 at its height, about the population of medieval London (see Cahokia Mounds image, page 60). Cahokia was the largest settlement north of the Rio Grande before the end of the eighteenth century, when it was surpassed by New York and Philadelphia. Trade routes linked Cahokia to distant regions of the continent, bringing shells from the Atlantic coast, copper from Lake Superior, obsidian from the Rocky Mountains, and mica from the southern Appalachians. By the fourteenth century, Cahokia was in decline. Most likely, the growing population had exhausted the resources needed to support it in a period of climatic change; archaeological evidence suggests there may have been increasing pressure from enemies. Whatever the causes, the once-thriving metropolis lay abandoned half a century before Columbus. The remains of Cahokia's spectacular mounds can still be seen after five hundred years of erosion—"[t]he great pyramid at Cahokia is greater in extent than that at Gizeh, in Egypt"[26]—and offer impressive testimony to a civilization that developed before Europe entered its middle ages, flourished longer than the United States has existed as a nation, and declined before Europeans set foot in America.

Emerging Tribes and Confederacies

The influences of the Mississippian cultures were still very visible when the Spaniards invaded the Southeast in the sixteenth century. Chiefdoms and temple mound towns were common. Moundville in Alabama, Etowah in Georgia, and Spiro in the Arkansas valley of eastern Oklahoma were mound centers of population, trade, and artistic and ceremonial life. When the Spaniards arrived in northern Florida, the Apalachee and Timucua Indians were living in permanent settlements, planted two crops annually, and rotated their fields to keep the soil fertile; the Spaniards sustained their campaigns by seizing these corn supplies.[27] Political structures—the great chiefdoms that ruled in the South—collapsed in the wake of war and epidemics following contact with the Spaniards in the sixteenth century; out of their ruins emerged the historic peoples of the Southeast: Caddos, Choctaws, Chickasaws, Cherokees, and various tribes of Creeks. The Natchez continued to display significant elements of Mississippian culture until they were effectively destroyed by the French in 1731.

In the North, over the course of several centuries, the Iroquoian-speaking Hurons, Petuns, and Neutrals moved from scattered settlements to fortified villages. Eventually, they formed loose confederacies numbering thousands of peoples. Sometime before direct contact with Europeans, the Iroquoian-speaking peoples of upstate New York ended intertribe conflict and organized a Great League of Peace (see "The Laws of the Confederacy," pages 48–54). The league, composed of Mohawks, Oneidas, Onondagas, Cayugas, and Senecas, met in council and reached decisions by consensus, pursuing common policies on issues of mutual concern. But Iroquois tribes retained autonomy over questions of more local interest, and daily life revolved around the village and the longhouse. Iroquoian villages consisted of elm and bark longhouses, sometimes exceeding a hundred feet, that sheltered families related by clan through the female line. Iroquoian women tended the homes; cultivated and harvested the extensive cornfields that surrounded their villages; gathered berries, fruits, and nuts; made clothing and pottery; and cared for children. Iroquoian men prepared the fields for planting, but the main foci of their activities—war, trade, and diplomacy—lay outside the villages.

The Iroquois fought, traded, and communicated with Algonquian-speaking peoples who surrounded the Iroquoian homeland in New York and Ontario: Ottawas, Algonquins, and Montagnais to the north; Mahicans, Abenakis, and Wampanoags to the east in New England; Delawares and Susquehannocks to the south; and Shawnees, Potawatomis, Anishinaabeg,° Illinois, and Foxes in the west. Algonquians lived in semipermanent villages of wigwams and longhouses and followed a mobile lifestyle, "commuting" from one resource locale to another and practicing varying methods of farming, hunting, and fishing.

SEABORNE STRANGERS

The first Europeans who came to America did not enter a void; they entered a Native American world where alliances, rivalries, commerce, and artistic and cultural exchanges had been going on for centuries, where civilizations had risen and fallen, and where great centers like Chaco Canyon and Cahokia were already ancient history. Europeans, in a sense, entered Indian America "through the back door." They saw only the edges of that world and only hints of its past. Before Europeans, Indian populations and activities had tended to focus on the great river systems in the heart of the continent. After Europeans arrived, Indian peoples "did an about-face toward the new oceanic powers, and were forced to confront seaborne strangers."[28]

°The names *Anishinaabeg* (noun) and *Anishinaabe* (adjective) refer to the peoples variously termed *Ojibwas* or *Chippewas*.

Native traditions from throughout North America tell of ancient prophecies predicting the coming of Europeans. We may suspect these as the products of hindsight or of rumors running along trade networks, but they became an important part of historical memory. Some tribes said that the arrival of Europeans was foretold in dreams; in many East Coast traditions, the strangers arrived on what appeared to be floating islands or giant white seabirds. The prophecies generally carried a sense of foreboding and omens of hard times. Later, other dreams prophesied disaster in the West. "There is a time coming," the Cheyenne prophet Sweet Medicine warned his people, "when many things will change. Strangers called Earth Men will appear among you. Their skins are light-colored and their ways are powerful." Sweet Medicine urged the Cheyennes to keep their own ways but he predicted that "at last you will not remember. . . . You will take after the Earth Men's ways and forget good things by which you have lived and in the end become worse than crazy."[29] Another prophecy, said to have been made by a Spokane Indian just before American missionaries penetrated the Columbia Plateau region of present-day Idaho, Oregon, and Washington, warned the people that, "Soon there will come from the rising sun a different kind of man from any you have yet seen, who will bring with them a book and will teach you everything." After that, said the prophet, "the world will fall to pieces."[30]

The history of Indian peoples in North America stretches back thousands of years, but the last five hundred have been the story of how their world fell to pieces, and of how those who survived tried to rebuild it.

References

1. Richard N. Current, T. Harry Williams, and Alan Brinkley, *American History: A Survey*, quoted in Alvin M. Josephy, ed., *America in 1492: The World of the Indian Peoples before the Arrival of Columbus* (New York: Knopf, 1991), 6, and (from the 1983 edition) Frederick E. Hoxie, "The Indians versus the Textbooks: Is There Any Way Out?" 23 *Perspectives* (April 1985), 19; Alan Brinkley, *American History: A Survey*, 9th ed. (New York: McGraw-Hill, 1995), 1–5.
2. William M. Denevan, "The Pristine Myth: The Landscape of the Americas in 1492," *Annals of the Association of American Geographers* 82 (1992), 369–85 (population figures on page 370).
3. John Noble Wilford, "Human Presence in Americas Is Pushed Back a Millennium," *New York Times,* February 11, 1997.
4. Raymond D. Fogelson, "A Final Look and Glance at the Bearing of Bering Straits on Native American History," D'Arcy McNickle Center for the History of the American Indian, *Occasional Papers in Curriculum Series* 5 (1987), 247.
5. Vine Deloria, Jr., *Red Earth, White Lies: Native Americans and the Myth of Scientific Fact* (New York: Scribner, 1995), chapter 4; Joseph Marshall III, *On Behalf of the Wolf and the First Peoples* (Santa Fe: Red Crane Books, 1995), 207.
6. David Hurst Thomas, *Skull Wars: Kennewick Man, Archaeology, and the Battle for Native American Identity* (New York: Basic Books, 2000); James C. Chatters, *Ancient Encounters: Kennewick Man and the First Americans* (New York: Simon and Schuster, 2001).

7. Karl Butzer, "The Indian Legacy in the American Landscape," in Michael P. Conzen, ed., *The Making of the American Landscape* (Boston: Unwin Hyman, 1990), 27–28.

8. Richard D. Daugherty, "People of the Salmon," in Alvin M. Josephy, Jr., ed., *America in 1492* (New York: Knopf, 1992), 54–55; Brian M. Fagan, *Ancient North America: The Archaeology of a Continent* 3d ed. (London: Thames and Hudson, 2000), 232–34; Kenneth M. Ames and Herbert D. G. Maschner, *Peoples of the Northwest Coast: Their Archaeology and Prehistory* (London: Thames and Hudson, 1999), 23, 83, 115, 127,171.

9. Judith Roche and Meg Hutchinson, eds., *First Fish, First People: Salmon Tales of the North Pacific Rim* (Seattle: University of Washington Press, 1998); Robert Bringhurst, *A Story as Sharp as a Knife: The Classical Haida Mythtellers and Their World* (Vancouver: Douglas and McIntyre, 1999), 65, 120, 155, 288–89.

10. Fagan, *Ancient North America,* chap. 12.

11. George Frison, "Experimental Use of Clovis Weaponry and Tools on African Elephants," *American Antiquity* 54 (1989), 766–84.

12. Cyclone Covey, trans. and ed., *Cabeza de Vaca's Adventures, in the Unknown Interior of America* (Albuquerque: University of New Mexico Press, 1993), 81.

13. Quoted in James P. Ronda, ed., *Revealing America: Image and Imagination in the Exploration of North America* (New York: Simon and Schuster, 1996), 63.

14. T. Douglas Price and Anne Birgette Gebauer, eds., *Last Hunters, First Farmers: New Perspectives on the Prehistoric Transition to Agriculture* (Santa Fe: School of American Research Press, 1995), 3, 6.

15. Francis Jennings, *The Founders of America* (New York: W. W. Norton, 1993), 54.

16. Paul Horgan, *Great River: The Rio Grande in North American History* (Hanover, N.H.: University Press of New England, 1984), 22.

17. Quoted in Stephen Plog, *Ancient Peoples of the American Southwest* (London: Thames and Hudson, 1997), 170–71.

18. Bruce D. Smith, *Rivers of Change: Essays on Early Agriculture in Eastern North America* (Washington, D.C.: Smithsonian Institution Press, 1992); Smith, "Seed Plant Domestication in Eastern North America," in Price and Gebauer, eds., *Last Hunters, First Farmers,* 193–213.

19. R. Douglas Hurt, *Indian Agriculture in America: Prehistory to the Present* (Lawrence: University Press of Kansas, 1987), 11.

20. Quoted in Richard Wolkomir, "Bringing Ancient Ways to Our Farmers' Fields," *Winds of Change* (Summer 1996), 30.

21. Hurt, *Indian Agriculture in America,* 24.

22. Quoted in Ronda, ed., *Revealing America,* 36.

23. Hurt, *Indian Agriculture in America,* 34.

24. "A Mound Complex in Louisiana at 5400–5000 Years before the Present," *Science* 277 (September 1997), 1796–99. I am grateful to my colleague Deborah L. Nichols for providing this source.

25. *Through Indian Eyes* (New York: Reader's Digest, 1995), 31.

26. Roger G. Kennedy, *Hidden Cities: The Discovery and Loss of Ancient North American Civilization* (New York: Penguin, 1994), 12.

27. Hurt, *Indian Agriculture in America,* 27.

28. Lynda Norene Shaffer, *Native Americans before 1492: The Moundbuilding Centers of the Eastern Woodlands* (Armonk, N.Y.: M. E. Sharpe, 1992), 95.

29. John Stands In Timber and Margot Liberty, *Cheyenne Memories* (Lincoln: University of Nebraska Press, 1972), 40.

30. Quoted in Christopher L. Miller, *Prophetic Worlds: Indians and Whites on the Columbia Plateau* (New Brunswick, N.J.: Rutgers University Press, 1985), title page.

Suggested Readings

Ames, Kenneth M., and Herbert D. G. Maschner. *Peoples of the Northwest Coast: Their Archaeology and Prehistory* (London: Thames and Hudson, 1999).

Brose, David S. *Ancient Art of the American Woodland Indians* (New York: Abrams, 1985).

Butzer, Karl W., ed. "The Americas before and after 1492: Current Geographical Research," *Annals of the Association of American Geographers* 82 (1992).

Coe, Michael, et al. *Atlas of Ancient America* (New York: Facts on File, 1986).

Cordell, Linda S. *Ancient Pueblo Peoples* (Washington, D.C.: Smithsonian, 1994).

Dillehay, Thomas D. *The Settlement of the Americas: A New Prehistory* (New York: Basic Books, 2000).

Fagan, Brian M. *Ancient North America: The Archaeology of a Continent,* 3d ed. (London: Thames and Hudson, 2000).

Fagan, Brian M. *The Great Journey: The Peopling of Ancient America* (New York: Thames and Hudson, 1987).

Fiedel, Stuart. *Prehistory of the Americas* (New York: Cambridge University Press, 1987).

Haynes, Gary. *The Early Settlement of North America: The Clovis Era* (Cambridge: Cambridge University Press, 2002).

Jennings, Jesse D. *Prehistory of North America* (Mountain View, Calif.: Mayfield, 1989).

Jennings, Jesse D., ed. *Ancient North Americans* (San Francisco: W. H. Freeman, 1983).

Josephy, Alvin M., Jr., ed. *America in 1492* (New York: Knopf, 1992).

Kennedy, Roger G. *Hidden Cities: The Discovery and Loss of Ancient North American Civilization* (New York: Penguin, 1994).

Kopper, Philip. *The Smithsonian Book of North American Indians: Before the Coming of the Europeans* (Washington, D.C.: Smithsonian, 1986).

Plog, Stephen. *Ancient Peoples of the American Southwest* (London: Thames and Hudson, 1997).

Shaffer, Lynda Norene. *Native Americans before 1492: The Moundbuilding Centers of the Eastern Woodlands* (Armonk, N.Y.: M. E. Sharpe, 1992).

Stuart, David E. *Anasazi America* (Albuquerque: University of New Mexico Press, 2000).

Thomas, David Hurst. *Exploring Native North America* (New York: Oxford University Press, 2000).

Young, Biloine Whiting, and Melvin L. Fowler. *Cahokia: The Great Native American Metropolis* (Urbana: University of Illinois Press, 2000).

D O C U M E N T S

A Navajo Emergence Story

The Navajo Indians, one of the largest Indian tribes in North America today with almost 300,000 people today, emerged into written history in the 1620s when Spaniards began to distinguish from the Apaches a people whom they called "Apaches del Navajo." Long before that—some scholars say as much as five hundred years, others no more than a hundred—the ancestors of the historic Apaches and Navajos migrated from northern Canada and traveled south. The people who became the Navajos, in their own language the Diné, settled in the Colorado Plateau country of what is now northeastern Arizona, northwestern New Mexico, and southeastern Utah. There they raided and traded with Pueblos and Spaniards, and adopted cultural elements from both of them. In time, they evolved from a nomadic hunting people into a more settled farming and herding society.

Sifting through early documents, scholars can piece together increasing "sightings" of the Navajos as they emerge from the distant past into "recorded history," where sources are richer and the light is better. But many Indian peoples have a much clearer sense of their ancient past. Communal stories passed down through the generations link the people to their homelands, explain how they came to be there, and show them how to live in those homelands. "Through the stories we hear who we are," writes Laguna Pueblo author Leslie Marmon Silko:

> . . . the ancient Pueblo people depended upon collective memory through successive generations to maintain and transmit an entire culture, a worldview complete with proven strategies for survival. The oral narrative, or story, became the medium through which the complex of Pueblo knowledge and belief was maintained. Whatever the event or the subject, the ancient people perceived the world and themselves within that world as part of an ancient, continuous story composed of innumerable bundles of other stories.[1]

Like the Navajos who became their neighbors in the Southwest, Pueblo peoples told and continue to tell stories of creation, emergence, and migration that brought the people from lower worlds into the present world.[2] But, explains Silko, the stories "are not to be taken as literally as the anthropologists

MAP 1.4 The Navajo World

Whether they migrated from the far north of Canada or emerged from lower worlds, the Navajos made their home in the Southwest, in an area bordered by sacred mountain ranges representing the four directions, recognized as sources of knowledge, and named for their minerals or the colors they represent: Sisnaajiní (shell white; Blanca Peak); Tsoodził (turquoise; blue; Mount Taylor); Dook'oosłiid (abalone; yellow; San Francisco Peaks), and Dibé nitsaa, (black jet or obsidian; Hesperus Peak). It was also a world surrounded by other peoples with whom, over time, the Navajos experienced both contact and conflict.

might wish." Rather, "the Emergence was an emergence into a precise cultural identity." Linked to prominent features of the landscape, the various narratives tie the people to an ancient world whose lessons they must not forget and to the natural world in which they must survive by maintaining proper relations with other forms of life. "Thus, the journey was an interior process of the imagination," a growing awareness that human beings were different from other forms of life and yet, springing from the same source, never inseparable from them.[3]

Navajo origin stories also tell how people emerged into this world from several lower worlds. There are many versions of these creation and emergence stories, but they share common themes and messages. In some versions, the first world was black, the second blue, the third yellow, and the fourth or present world bright or glittering. First Man and First Woman exist alongside, and talk with, insects and animals—"people" of nonhuman form. But in each of the worlds, they fight, squabble, and behave badly. Each time, the people flee to a higher world, where they meet new people. In one version, the fourth world is covered with water, but eventually the waters recede. Finally, the people emerge into the present world.

Dinétah, the Navajo homeland, takes shape, bounded by four sacred mountains: Abalone Shell Mountain (San Francisco Peak) in the west, Dawn or White Shell Mountain (Blanca Peak) in the east, Blue Bead or Turquoise Mountain (Mount Taylor) in the south, and Obsidian Mountain (Hesperus Peak) to the north. About the time Dinétah was taking form, the sun, moon and stars, night and day, and the four seasons of the year appear. With the four sacred mountains in each of the four directions, the four seasons, men and women living in harmony, and humans living together with the animals and plants, the Navajos have moved from lower worlds of chaos and strife into a higher world of beauty and harmony.

Like the legends of any people, these stories embody communal experience, communal wisdom, and guides for proper conduct, as well as explaining how their world came to be and why things are the way they are. They define the Navajos' place in the world and make as one their history and the landscape of the Southwest. As Keith Basso explains on the basis of his experiences among the Western Apaches:

> For Indian men and women, the past lies embedded in features of the earth—in canyons and lakes, mountains and arroyos, rocks and vacant fields—which together endow their lands with multiple forms of significance that reach into their lives and shape the way they think. Knowledge of places is therefore closely linked to knowledge of the self, to grasping one's position in the larger scheme of things, including one's own community, and to securing a confident sense of who one is as a person.[4]

The stories establish proper relations with other peoples and with other living things. Antisocial behavior and conflict produce misfortune. Aberrant sexual behavior is destructive; good relationships between the sexes, between First Man and First Woman, are crucial to creation and to social harmony. The stories of recurrent movement emphasize the need to restore balance to produce healing; they make clear the Navajos' responsibility for maintaining order and harmony by good living and ritual.

The Navajos "have always progressed intellectually, physically, socially, and spiritually," writes Navajo Rex Lee Jim. "The story of their journey to and settlement in the Southwest is one of wanderers becoming a people. This process lies at the center of the Navajos' sense of their history."[5] The creation story is part of a dynamic Navajo oral tradition. One scholar who studied it in depth found it to be not a single story so much as a "boundless, sprawling narrative with a life of its own." It could change from telling to telling, "depending upon the singer, the audience, the particular storytelling event, and a very complicated set of ceremonial conditions having to do with illness, departure, return, celebration, or any one of a number of social occasions."[6] Any written text can do only partial justice to the poetic and social richness of the storytelling event.

The version of the Navajo creation story reprinted here was told to Aileen O'Bryan in November 1928 at Mesa Verde National Park. The storyteller was a Navajo chief named Sandoval or Hastin Tlo'tsi hee (Old Man Buffalo Grass) whose words were translated by his nephew Sam Ahkeah. "You look at me and you see an ugly old man," Sandoval told O'Bryan, "but within I am filled with great beauty. I sit as on a mountaintop and I look into the future. I see my people and your people living together. In time to come my people will have forgotten their early way of life unless they learn it from white men's books. So you must write down what I tell you; and you must have it made into a book that coming generations may know this truth." O'Bryan recorded the story "without interpolation, and presented it, in so far as is possible, in the old man's words."[7] It is reprinted together with the notes Sandoval provided.

▶ Questions for Consideration

The Navajos' stories of their origins (beginning on page 37) can be read literally or understood metaphorically.

1. What does a specific story convey about the Navajos' view of their place in the world and their relations with animals; of their ideals; of their beliefs about the consequences of wrongdoing?

2. In what ways does the story define Navajo identity? What does it say about what it means to be Navajo?

3. What does it suggest about gender roles in Navajo society?

4. Are the Navajo stories necessarily in conflict with historical explanations of migrations from far north of the continent to the Southwest, with continuous contacts with new people as they move to Dinétah?

5. Sam Ahkeah may have done an excellent job translating his uncle's words into English and O'Bryan may have written them down faithfully. But any translation is inadequate to convey accurately the culturally specific concepts of one people in the language of another people. In such circumstances, can this English version of the Navajo emergence story give us any more than a glimpse of the Navajo worldview?

HASTIN TLO'TSI HEE
The Beginning (1896)

THE FIRST WORLD

These stories were told to Sandoval, Hastin Tlo'tsi hee, by his grandmother, Esdzan Hosh kige. Her ancestor was Esdzan at a', the medicine woman who had the Calendar Stone in her keeping. Here are the stories of the Four Worlds that had no sun, and of the Fifth, the world we live in, which some call the Changeable World.

The First World, Ni'hodilqil,° was black as black wool. It had four corners, and over these appeared four clouds. These four clouds contained within themselves the elements of the First World. They were in color, black, white, blue, and yellow.

The Black Cloud represented the Female Being or Substance. For as a child sleeps when being nursed, so life slept in the darkness of the Female Being. The White Cloud represented the Male Being or Substance. He was the Dawn, the Light-Which-Awakens, of the First World.

In the East, at the place where the Black Cloud and the White Cloud met, First Man, At-se'hastqin, was formed; and with him was formed the white corn, perfect in shape, with kernels covering the whole ear. Dohonot i'ni is the name of this first seed corn,° and it is also the name of the place where the Black Cloud and the White Cloud met.

The First World was small in size, a floating island in mist or water. On it there grew one tree, a pine tree, which was later brought to the present world for firewood.

Man was not, however, in his present form. The conception was of a male and a female being who were to become man and woman. The creatures of the First World are thought of as the Mist People; they had no definite form, but were to change to men, beasts, birds, and reptiles of this world.°

Now on the western side of the First World, in a place that later was to become the Land of Sunset, there appeared the Blue Cloud, and opposite it there appeared the Yellow Cloud. Where they came together First Woman was formed, and with her the yellow corn. This ear of corn was also perfect. With First Woman there came the white shell and the turquoise and the yucca.°

First Man stood on the eastern side of the First World. He represented the Dawn and was the Life Giver. First Woman stood opposite in the West. She represented Darkness and Death.

First Man burned a crystal for a fire. The crystal belonged to the male and was the symbol of the mind and of clear seeing. When First Man burned it, it was the mind's awakening. First Woman burned her turquoise for a fire. They saw each other's lights in the distance. When the Black

---

Source: Aileen O'Bryan, *The Diné: Origin Myths of the Navaho Indians*, Bureau of American Ethnology, Bulletin 163 (Washington, D.C.: U.S. Government Printing Office, 1956), 1–13.

°Five names were given to this First World in its relation to First Man. It was called Dark Earth, Ni'hodilqil; Red Earth, Ni'halchi; One Speech, Sada hat lai; Floating Land, Ni'ta na elth; and One Tree, De east'da eith.

°Where much corn is raised one or two ears are found perfect. These are always kept for seed corn.

°The Navaho people have always believed in evolution.

°Five names were given also the First World in its relation to First Woman: White Bead Standing, Yolgai'na ziha; Turquoise Standing, Dolt i'zhi na ziha; White Bead Floating Place, Yolgai'dana elth gai; Turquoise Floating Place, Dolt 'izhi na elth gai; and Yucca Standing, Tasas y ah gai. Yucca represents cleanliness and things ceremonial.

Cloud and the White Cloud rose higher in the sky First Man set out to find the turquoise light. He went twice without success, and again a third time; then he broke a forked branch from his tree, and, looking through the fork, he marked the place where the light burned. And the fourth time he walked to it and found smoke coming from a home.

"Here is the home I could not find," First Man said.

First Woman answered: "Oh, it is you. I saw you walking around and I wondered why you did not come."

Again the same thing happened when the Blue Cloud and the Yellow Cloud rose higher in the sky. First Woman saw a light and she went out to find it. Three times she was unsuccessful, but the fourth time she saw the smoke and she found the home of First Man.

"I wondered what this thing could be," she said.

"I saw you walking and I wondered why you did not come to me," First Man answered.

First Woman saw that First Man had a crystal for a fire, and she saw that it was stronger than her turquoise fire. And as she was thinking, First Man spoke to her. "Why do you not come with your fire and we will live together." The woman agreed to this. So instead of the man going to the woman, as is the custom now, the woman went to the man.

About this time there came another person, the Great-Coyote-Who-Was-Formed-in-the-Water,° and he was in the form of a male being. He told the two that he had been hatched from an egg. He knew all that was under the water and all that was in the skies. First Man placed this person ahead of himself in all things. The three began to plan what was to come to pass; and while they were thus occupied another being came to them. He

also had the form of a man, but he wore a hairy coat, lined with white fur, that fell to his knees and was belted in at the waist. His name was Atse'hashke', First Angry or Coyote.° He said to the three: "You believe that you were the first persons. You are mistaken. I was living when you were formed."

Then four beings came together. They were yellow in color and were called the tsts'na or wasp people. They knew the secret of shooting evil and could harm others. They were very powerful.

This made eight people.

Four more beings came. They were small in size and wore red shirts and had little black eyes. They were the naazo'zi or spider ants. They knew how to sting, and were a great people.

After these came a whole crowd of beings. Dark colored they were, with thick lips and dark, protruding eyes. They were the wolazhi'ni, the black ants. They also knew the secret of shooting evil and were powerful; but they killed each other steadily.

By this time there were many people. Then came a multitude of little creatures. They were peaceful and harmless, but the odor from them was unpleasant. They were called the wolazhi'ni nlchu nigi, meaning that which emits an odor.°

And after the wasps and the different ant people there came the beetles, dragonflies, bat people, the Spider Man and Woman, and the Salt Man and Woman,° and others that rightfully had no definite form but were among those people who peopled the First World. And this world, being small in size, became crowded, and the

---

°The Great Coyote who was formed in the water, Mai tqo y elth chili.

°Some medicine men claim that witchcraft came with First Man and First Woman, others insist that devil conception or witchcraft originated with the Coyote called First Angry.

°No English name given this insect. Ants cause trouble, as also do wasps and other insects, if their homes are harmed.

°Beetle, ntlsa'go; Dragonfly, tqanil ai'; Bat people, ja aba'ni; Spider Man, nashjei hastqin; Spider Woman, nashjei esdza; Salt Man, ashi hastqin; Salt Woman, ashi esdza.

people quarreled and fought among themselves, and in all ways made living very unhappy.

THE SECOND WORLD

Because of the strife in the First World, First Man, First Woman, the Great-Coyote-Who-Was-Formed-in-the-Water, and the Coyote called First Angry, followed by all the others, climbed up from the world of Darkness and Dampness to the Second or Blue World.°

They found a number of people already living there: blue birds, blue hawks, blue jays, blue herons, and all the blue-feathered beings.° The powerful swallow people° lived there also, and these people made the Second World unpleasant for those who had come from the First World. There was fighting and killing.

The First Four found an opening in the World of Blue Haze; and they climbed through this and led the people up into the Third or Yellow World.

THE THIRD WORLD

The bluebird was the first to reach the Third or Yellow World. After him came the First Four and all the others.

A great river crossed this land from north to south. It was the Female River. There was another river crossing it from east to west, it was the Male River. This Male River flowed through the Female River and on;° and the name of this place is tqo al-na'osdli, the Crossing of the Waters.

There were six mountains in the Third World.° In the East was Sis na' jin, the Standing Black Sash. Its ceremonial name is Yol gai'dzil, the Dawn or White Shell Mountain. In the South stood Tso'dzil, the Great Mountain, also called Mountain Tongue. Its ceremonial name is Yodolt i'zhi dzil, the Blue Bead or Turquoise Mountain. In the West stood Dook'oslid, and the meaning of this name is forgotten. Its ceremonial name is Dichi'li dzil, the Abalone Shell Mountain. In the North stood Debe'ntsa, Many Sheep Mountain. Its ceremonial name is Bash'zhini dzil, Obsidian Mountain. Then there was Dzil na'odili, the Upper Mountain. It was very sacred; and its name means also the Center Place, and the people moved around it. Its ceremonial name is Ntl'is dzil, Precious Stone or Banded Rock Mountain. There was still another mountain called Chol'i'i or Dzil na'odili choli, and it was also a sacred mountain.

There was no sun in this land, only the two rivers and the six mountains. And these rivers and mountains were not in their present form, but rather the substance of mountains and rivers as were First Man, First Woman, and the others. . . .

Within this land there lived the Kisa'ni, the ancients of the Pueblo People. On the six mountains there lived the Cave Dwellers or Great Swallow People.° On the mountains lived also the light

---

°The Second World was the Blue World, Ni'hodotl'ish.

°The names of the blue birds are: bluebird, do'le; blue hawk, gi'ni tso dolt ish; blue jay, jozh ghae'gi; and blue heron, tqualtl a'gaale.

°The swallow is called tqash ji'zhi.

°The introduction of generation.

°Sis na' jin, Mount Baldy near Alamosa, Colo.; Tso'dzil, Mount Taylor, N. Mex.; Dook'oslid, San Francisco Mountain, Ariz.; Debe'ntsa, San Juan Mountains, Colo.; Dzil na'odili, El Huerfano Peak, N. Mex.; and Choli, also given as El Huerfano or El Huerfanito Peak, N. Mex. These mountains of the Third World were not in their true form, but rather the substance of the mountains.

Recorder's note: Although both Matthews and the Franciscan Fathers give Sis na' jin as Pelado Peak, Sam Ahkeah, the interpreter, after checking, identified it as Mount Baldy near Alamosa, Colo. Also, although the Franciscan Fathers give Dzil na odili choli as Herfanito Peak, Sam Ahkeah says that it is the Mother Mountain near Taos.

°The Great Swallow People, Tqashji'zhi ndilk'si, lived in rough houses of mud and sticks. They entered them from holes in the roof.

and dark squirrels, chipmunks, mice, rats, the turkey people, the deer and cat people, the spider people, and the lizards and snakes. The beaver people lived along the rivers, and the frogs and turtles and all the underwater people in the water. So far all the people were similar. They had no definite form, but they had been given different names because of different characteristics.

Now the plan was to plant.

First Man called the people together. He brought forth the white corn which had been formed with him. First Woman brought the yellow corn. They laid the perfect ears side by side; then they asked one person from among the many to come and help them. The Turkey stepped forward. They asked him where he had come from, and he said that he had come from the Gray Mountain.° He danced back and forth four times, then he shook his feather coat and there dropped from his clothing four kernels of corn, one gray, one blue, one black, and one red. Another person was asked to help in the plan of the planting. The Big Snake came forward. He likewise brought forth four seeds, the pumpkin, the watermelon, the cantaloup, and the muskmelon. His plants all crawl on the ground.

They planted the seeds, and their harvest was great. . . .

At this time the Great-Coyote-Who-Was-Formed-in-the-Water came to First Man and told him to cross the river. They made a big raft and crossed at the place where the Male River followed through the Female River. And all the male beings left the female beings on the river bank; and as they rowed across the river they looked back and saw that First Woman and the female beings were laughing. They were also behaving very wickedly.

In the beginning the women did not mind being alone. They cleared and planted a small field.

On the other side of the river First Man and the chiefs hunted and planted their seeds. They had a good harvest. Nadle° ground the corn and cooked the food. Four seasons passed. The men continued to have plenty and were happy; but the women became lazy, and only weeds grew on their land. The women wanted fresh meat. Some of them tried to join the men and were drowned in the river.

First Woman made a plan. As the women had no way to satisfy their passions, some fashioned long narrow rocks, some used the feathers of the turkey, and some used strange plants (cactus). First Woman told them to use these things. One woman brought forth a big stone. This stone-child was later the Great Stone that rolled over the earth killing men. Another woman brought forth the Big Birds of Tsa bida'hi; and others gave birth to the giants and monsters who later destroyed many people.

On the opposite side of the river the same condition existed. The men, wishing to satisfy their passions, killed the females of mountain sheep, lion, and antelope. Lightning struck these men. When First Man learned of this he warned his men that they would all be killed. He told them that they were indulging in a dangerous practice. Then the second chief spoke: he said that life was hard and that it was a pity to see women drowned. He asked why they should not bring the women across the river and all live together again.

"Now we can see for ourselves what comes from our wrong doing," he said. "We will know how to act in the future." The three other chiefs of the animals agreed with him, so First Man told them to go and bring the women.

°The Gray Mountain is the home of the Gray Yei, Hasch el'ba'i, whose other name is Water Sprinkler. The turkey is connected with water and rain.

Interpreter's note: Gray Mountain is San Francisco Mountain, Ariz. Tqo'neinili, the Water Sprinkler, whose color is gray, lives there. He is also called the Gray God, Hasch e'lbai, and the Clown whose call is "do do," and whose name is Hasch e'dodi.

°Nadle means that which changes.

After the women had been brought over the river First Man spoke: "We must be purified," he said. "Everyone must bathe. The men must dry themselves with white corn meal, and the women, with yellow."

This they did, living apart for 4 days. After the fourth day First Woman came and threw her right arm around her husband. She spoke to the others and said that she could see her mistakes, but with her husband's help she would henceforth lead a good life. Then all the male and female beings came and lived with each other again.

The people moved to different parts of the land. Some time passed; then First Woman became troubled by the monotony of life. She made a plan. She went to Atse'hashke, the Coyote called First Angry, and giving him the rainbow she said: "I have suffered greatly in the past. I have suffered from want of meat and corn and clothing. Many of my maidens have died. I have suffered many things. Take the rainbow and go to the place where the rivers cross. Bring me the two pretty children of Tqo holt sodi, the Water Buffalo, a boy and a girl."

The Coyote agreed to do this. He walked over the rainbow. He entered the home of the Water Buffalo and stole the two children; and these he hid in his big skin coat with the white fur lining. And when he returned he refused to take off his coat, but pulled it around himself and looked very wise.

After this happened the people saw white light in the East and in the South and West and North. One of the deer people ran to the East, and returning, said that the white light was a great sheet of water. The sparrow hawk flew to the South, the great hawk to the West, and the kingfisher to the North. They returned and said that a flood was coming. The kingfisher said that the water was greater in the North, and that it was near.

The flood was coming and the Earth was sinking. And all this happened because the Coyote had stolen the two children of the Water Buffalo, and only First Woman and the Coyote knew the truth.

When First Man learned of the coming of the water he sent word to all the people, and he told them to come to the mountain called Sis na'jin. He told them to bring with them all of the seeds of the plants used for food. All living beings were to gather on the top of Sis na'jin. First Man traveled to the six sacred mountains, and, gathering earth from them, he put it in his medicine bag.

The water rose steadily.

When all the people were halfway up Sis na'jin, First Man discovered that he had forgotten his medicine bag. Now this bag contained not only the earth from the six sacred mountains, but his magic, the medicine he used to call the rain down upon the earth and to make things grow. He could not live without his medicine bag, and he wished to jump into the rising water; but the others begged him not to do this. They went to the kingfisher and asked him to dive into the water and recover the bag. This the bird did. When First Man had his medicine bag again in his possession he breathed on it four times and thanked his people. . . .

First Man had with him his spruce tree° which he planted on the top of Sis na'jin. He used his fox medicine° to make it grow; but the spruce tree began to send out branches and to taper at the top, so First Man planted the big Male Reed.° All the people blew on it, and it grew and grew until it reached the canopy of the sky. They tried to blow inside the reed, but it was solid. They asked the woodpecker to drill out the hard heart. Soon they were able to peek through the opening, but they had to blow and blow before it was large enough to climb through. They climbed up inside the big male reed, and after them the water continued to rise.

°Recorder's note: That the tree is here called a spruce and earlier a pine is not explained.

°First Man's name, Aste'hastqin, corresponds to the sacred name of the kit fox.

°The big Male Reed is called luka'tso. It grows near Santo Domingo Pueblo, not far from the home of the Turquoise Boy, the little turquoise mountain south of Santa Fe, N. Mex.

THE FOURTH WORLD

When the people reached the Fourth World they saw that it was not a very large place. Some say that it was called the White World; but not all medicine men agree that this is so. °...

THE FIFTH WORLD

First Man was not satisfied with the Fourth World. It was a small, barren land; and the great water had soaked the earth and made the sowing of seeds impossible. He planted the big Female Reed° and it grew up to the vaulted roof of this Fourth World. First Man sent the newcomer, the badger, up inside the reed, but before he reached the upper world water began to drip, so he returned and said that he was frightened. . . .

Now two dark clouds and two white clouds rose, and this meant that two nights and two days had passed, for there was still no sun. First Man again sent the badger to the upper world, and he returned covered with mud, terrible mud. First Man gathered chips of turquoise which he offered to the five Chiefs of the Winds° who lived in the uppermost world of all. They were pleased with

the gift, and they sent down the winds and dried the Fifth World.

First Man and his people saw four dark clouds and four white clouds pass, and then they sent the badger up the reed. This time when the badger returned he said that he had come out on solid earth. So First Man and First Woman led the people to the Fifth World, which some call the Many Colored Earth and some the Changeable Earth. They emerged through a lake surrounded by four mountains. The water bubbles in this lake when anyone goes near.°

Now after all the people had emerged from the lower worlds First Man and First Woman dressed the Mountain Lion with yellow, black, white, and grayish corn and placed him on one side. They dressed the Wolf with white tail feathers and placed him on the other side. They divided the people into two groups. The first group was told to choose whichever chief they wished. They made their choice, and, although they thought they had chosen the Mountain Lion, they found that they had taken the Wolf for their chief. The Mountain Lion was the chief for the other side. And these people who had the Mountain Lion for their chief turned out to be the people of the Earth. They were to plant seeds and harvest corn. The followers of the Wolf chief became the animals and birds; they turned into all the creatures that fly and crawl and run and swim.

And after all the beings were divided, and each had his own form, they went their ways.

This is the story of the Four Dark Worlds and the Fifth, the World we live in. Some medicine men tell us that there are two worlds above us, the first is the World of the Spirits of Living Things, the second is the Place of Melting into One.

°The Four Worlds were really twelve worlds, or stages of development; but different medicine men divide them differently according to the ceremony held. For the narrative they call them the Four Dark Worlds, and the Fifth World, the one we live in. An old medicine man explained that the Sixth World would be that of the spirit; and that the one above that would be "cosmic," melting into one.

°The big Female Reed is thought to be the joint cane which grows along the Colorado River.

°The First Chief, Nlchi ntla'ie, the Left Course Wind; the Second Chief, Nlchi lichi, the Red Wind; the Third Chief, Nlchi shada ji na'laghali, the Wind Turning from the Sun; the Fourth Chief, Nlchi qa'hashchi, the Wind with Many Points; the Fifth Chief, Nlchi che do et siedee, the Wind with the Fiery Temper.

°The place of emergence is said to be near Pagosa Springs, Colo. The white people have put a wire fence around our Sacred Lake.

References

1. Leslie Marmon Silko, *Yellow Woman and a Beauty of the Spirit: Essays on Native American Life Today* (New York: Simon and Schuster, 1996), 30–31.
2. See, for example, Frank Waters, *Book of the Hopi* (New York: Viking, 1963), p. 1.
3. Silko, *Yellow Woman and a Beauty of the Spirit,* 30–36.
4. Keith H. Basso, *Wisdom Sits in Places: Landscape and Language among the Western Apache* (Albuquerque: University of New Mexico Press, 1996), 34.
5. Rex Lee Jim, "Navajo," in Frederick E. Hoxie, ed., *Encyclopedia of North American Indians: Native American History, Culture, and Life from Paleo-Indians to the Present* (Boston: Houghton Mifflin, 1996), 422.
6. Paul G. Zolbrod, *Diné bahané: The Navajo Creation Story* (Albuquerque: University of New Mexico Press, 1984), 19.
7. Aileen O'Bryan, *The Diné: Origin Myths of the Navaho Indians,* Bureau of American Ethnology, Bulletin 163 (Washington, D.C.: U.S. Government Printing Office, 1956), vii.

Suggested Readings

Between Sacred Mountains: Navajo Stories and Lessons from the Land (Tucson: Sun Tracks and the University of Arizona Press, 1984).

Evers, Larry, ed. *The South Corner of Time: Hopi, Navajo, Papago, Yaqui Tribal Literature* (Tucson: University of Arizona Press, 1980).

Goodman, James M. *The Navajo Atlas: Environments, Resources, People, and History of the Diné Bikeyah* (Norman: University of Oklahoma Press, 1982).

Iverson, Peter. *The Navajos* (New York: Chelsea House, 1990).

Luckert, Karl W., ed. *The Upward Moving and Emergence Way: The Gishin Biyé Version by Father Berard Haile.* (Lincoln: University of Nebraska Press, 1981).

Matthews, Washington, comp. and trans. *Navaho Legends* (1897; reprinted Salt Lake City: University of Utah Press, 1994).

Silko, Leslie Marmon. *Yellow Woman and a Beauty of the Spirit: Essays on Native American Life Today* (New York: Simon and Schuster, 1996).

Yazzie, Ethelou. *Navajo History* (Chinle, Ariz.: Rough Rock Press, 1971).

Zolbrod, Paul G. *Dine bahané: The Navajo Creation Story* (Albuquerque: University of New Mexico Press, 1984).

The Iroquois Great League
of Peace

When the French, Dutch, and English began to penetrate present-day up-state New York in the early seventeenth century, they encountered the remarkable political system of the Hodenosaunee or "People of the Longhouse." Five Iroquoian nations—the Mohawks, Oneidas, Onondagas, Cayugas, and Senecas—occupied the region from the Hudson valley in the east to Lake Erie in the west and cooperated in a league that preserved peace among its members and exerted tremendous influence upon its neighbors. This League of the Iroquois, as the Europeans called it, played a dominant role in the history of northeastern North America before the American Revolution, and Iroquois power and foreign policies shaped colonial, intertribal, and international relations. Despite the devastating impact of the colonial and revolutionary wars, the league continues to function today, and is one of the oldest political bodies in North America.

No one knows exactly when the league was formed. A committee of Six Nations chiefs in 1900 estimated that it "took place about the year 1390," and some Iroquois assert that it was even earlier. One recent article argues that the league was founded on the afternoon of August 31, 1142! Archaeologist and anthropologist Dean Snow, on the other hand, maintains that "Iroquois oral tradition and archaeological evidence for endemic warfare suggest that the League could not have formed prior to around 1450," and suggests that the confederation "was probably complete by around 1525."[1] Whatever the date, Iroquois people already referred to their league as ancient by the time they first met Europeans: "We, the five Iroquois Nations, compose but one cabin," a Mohawk envoy declared in 1654; "we maintain but one fire; and we have, from time immemorial, dwelt under one and the same roof."[2]

The league that united the Iroquois in peace was forged in a time of violence. Before its formation, the traditions say, Iroquois people lived in a state of constant warfare: "Everywhere there was peril and everywhere mourning. . . . Feuds with outer nations, feuds with brother nations, feuds of sister towns and feuds of families and of clans made every warrior a stealthy man who liked to kill. . . . A man's life was valued as nothing."[3] Warriors fought to avenge the deaths of relatives in an endless cycle of killing and retribution.

An Onondaga chieftain, who became known to posterity as Hayenwatha or Hiawatha, lost three daughters. Some traditions attributed their deaths to the evil powers of Atotarho or Tadodaho, an Onondaga shaman twisted in body and mind, with snakes twined in his hair. The "mourning war" culture of the Iroquois demanded that Hiawatha assuage his grief and appease the spirits of his loved ones by taking the life of an enemy; instead, he chose to break the cycle of vengeance and violence and create a new world order for the Iroquois. The stories tell how, wandering the forests in his grief, Hiawatha met a Huron called Deganawidah [sometimes Dekanahwideh] who came from north of Lake Ontario. In some versions of the tradition, Deganawidah was a Huron; in others he was an adopted Mohawk; in others he was a healing spirit who had assumed human form. Whatever his identity, he became known as the Peacemaker. He eased Hiawatha's grief with words of condolence and beads of wampum, symbolically wiping his tears and restoring his reason. The rituals became part of the protocol of the Iroquois league and of their diplomatic dealings with outsiders: healing words, not bloody deeds, assuaged grief and redressed wrongs. Deganawidah and Hiawatha composed the laws of a great peace that would restore order and preserve harmony in Iroquois country. Recording each law on a string of wampum so that future generations would remember and observe them, the two set out to carry their message to the warring tribes.

They traveled from village to village, teaching the laws of peace and persuading people to replace war and weapons with words and wampum. The Mohawks agreed; then the Oneidas, Cayugas, and Senecas. The fierce Tadodaho resisted but Hiawatha is said to have combed the snakes from his hair to ease his torment. Finally Tadodaho accepted the pact. Onondaga became the site of the league's central council fire and Tadodaho the fire's guardian. Deganawidah placed deer antlers on the heads of the chiefs of the Five Nations as symbols of their authority.

The Five Nations agreed to stop fighting among themselves and unite in common defense. The individual tribes retained control of their own affairs at the local level but acted through the Grand Council at Onondaga in matters of common concern. The league reflected the traditional Iroquois longhouse, sheltering many families, each with their own fire but who from time to time gathered around a central fire and functioned as one family. Like a longhouse, the league could be expanded to incorporate new members, as occurred early in the eighteenth century when the Tuscaroras migrated from the South and joined the league as a junior, sixth nation. The Mohawks, who defended the eastern borders of the Iroquois homeland, were designated the Keepers of the Eastern Door; the Senecas were Keepers of the Western Door; the Onondagas were Keepers of the Council Fire. Iroquois people likened their league to a bundle of arrows, symbolizing the strength they achieved in unity: single arrows could be snapped easily but a bundle was difficult to break. The Five Nations saw their league as a great tree providing shelter to other peoples who would follow its roots of peace and take their place in its shade. They adopted so many captives and took in so many refugees that by the seventeenth century French observers estimated there were more non-Iroquois than Iroquois in Iroquois country.

Fifty council chiefs or sachems (called "lords" in the document reprinted here), were chosen by clan mothers from the member tribes. The names of the

Forming the League of the Iroquois (The Council with Tadodaho as the League Was Started)

In this 1936 painting by Seneca artist Ernest Smith (1907–75), Tadodaho, with snakes in his hair, becomes a reformed character as Hiawatha and Deganawidah describe the principles and purposes of their league of peace.

© Rochester Museum and Science Center.

original chiefs passed as titles from generation to generation, as new chiefs succeeded the older ones in the council. (The Mohawks had/have nine sachems, the Oneidas nine, the Onondagas fourteen, Cayugas ten, and Senecas eight.) League sachems had to be thick-skinned—"seven thumbs thick," said Deganawidah—and above criticism and petty jealousies. "Tadodaho represents the mind which promotes peace and the welfare of all people," said Chief Leon Shenandoah, who held the title of Tadodaho from 1967 until his death in 1996. "He must be kind to the people and express love for their welfare, and he must never hurt anybody."[4] The league sachems met, and still meet, at Onondaga, near Syracuse, New York. "They hold every year a general assembly," wrote a Jesuit observer in 1688. "There all the Deputies from the different Nations are present, to make their complaints and receive the necessary satisfaction in mutual gifts,—by means of which they maintain a good understanding with one another."[5] The sachems were divided into two moieties or "sides"—the elder moiety included the Mohawks, Onondagas, and Senecas; the younger, the Oneidas and Cayugas. The two moieties exchanged the ceremonial words of condolence prescribed by Deganawidah to wipe away the grief of those who had lost chiefs and to renew the league. The Mohawks and the Senecas passed matters for discussion back and forth to the Oneidas and Cayugas, with the Onondagas and Tadodaho, the Firekeeper, presiding and mediating, until consensus was reached or the matter was dropped. The sachems possessed no power of coercion: the chiefs had to be "of one mind." People who could not abide by the general consensus were free to go their own way so long as their actions did not threaten the league as a whole.

The league functioned to make and preserve peace, but freed from internal conflict and with new strength in unity, Iroquois warriors were able to turn their attentions to outside enemies. "By 1600," says historian Daniel Richter,

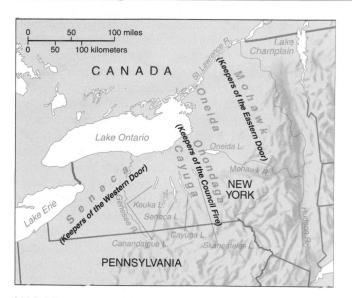

MAP 1.5 The Five Nations of the Iroquois
The Iroquois saw their league as an extended longhouse, stretching from the Mohawk Valley to Lake Erie. Each member tribe occupied a position and performed a role, and the longhouse could be extended to include other people who sought its shelter. The Tuscaroras joined the league as the sixth nation around 1722 after moving north from the Carolinas.

"the cultural ideal of peace and the everyday reality of war had long been intertwined."[6] European invasion unleashed new forces that threw Indian peoples into increasing competition and conflict with rival colonial powers and with other Indian tribes. Formed to end war, the League of Peace found itself participating in wars on a scale unknown earlier to native North America. Iroquois power made the Six Nations key players in the contests for North America. "The firmness of this league, the great extent of land it claims, the number of great warriors it produces, and the undaunted courage and skill which distinguish the members of it," wrote English trader John Long, "all conspire to prove the good policy of an alliance with them."[7] The league was able to negotiate from a position of strength and to pursue a path of formal neutrality in the wars of the eighteenth century. The American Revolution imposed strains the confederacy could not withstand and produced civil war in Iroquois country, but the ideas and ideals of the league survived.

Many Iroquois people and some non-Iroquois scholars believe that the League of the Iroquois served as a model for the Constitution of the United States. In 1987, the United States Senate passed a resolution acknowledging "the historical debt" which the United States owed to the Iroquois "for their demonstration of enlightened, democratic principles of government and their example of a free association of independent Indian nations." The Iroquois model was there for the colonists to emulate—in 1744 the Onondaga orator Canasatego urged them to follow the model of "union and amity" established by "our wise Forefathers," and Benjamin Franklin asked why, if the Six Nations could create "such a Union," could not a dozen or so colonies do likewise?[8] But whether or not the founding fathers looked to the Iroquois league in creating their constitution remains a hotly contested debate.

The Great Law of the League that Deganawidah gave to the Iroquois was preserved for generations through oral tradition before it was written in the nineteenth century, most notably by Lewis Henry Morgan in his *League of the Hodenosaunee,* published in 1851. Several versions now exist. In 1900, the Six Nations Council of Grand River in Ontario appointed a committee of ten chiefs to prepare an "official version" of the code of Deganawidah and the tradition of the formation of the league. The chiefs noted that "books have been written by white men in the past, but these have been found to be too voluminous and inaccurate in some cases." They offered instead a record compiled "by the elder ceremonial chiefs" who perpetuated "that system of government by hereditary succession as it was constituted by Deganawidah." They acknowledged that some of the ancient traditions had been modified or lost. But they noted that the traditions relating to the formation of the league and the procedures for installing chiefs which Deganawidah established had been handed down from father to son for centuries and were "still strictly observed and adhered to by the chiefs of the Six Nations and their people." They produced their history "so that the future generations of the people of the Six Nations may have preserved to them the traditions of their forefathers which otherwise in time would become lost."[9] The laws of the confederacy reprinted here are taken from this "chiefs' version."

▶ **Questions for Consideration**

1. What are the rights and duties of the chiefs as described below in the Laws of the Confederacy?

2. Consider the meaning and purpose of the emblems, metaphors, and rituals.

3. Compare the Constitution of the United States with that of the Iroquois reprinted here. Evaluate the evidence suggesting that the former was modeled on the latter.

CHIEFS OF THE SIX NATIONS
The Laws of the Confederacy (1900)

Then Dekanahwideh again said: "We have completed the Confederation of the Five Nations, now therefore it shall be that hereafter the lords who shall be appointed in the future to fill vacancies caused by death or removals shall be appointed from the same families and clans from which the first lords were created, and from which families the hereditary title of lordships shall descend."

Then Dekanahwideh further said: "I now transfer and set over to the women who have the lordships' title vested in them, that they shall in the future have the power to appoint the successors from time to time to fill vacancies caused by death or removals from whatever cause."

Then Dekanahwideh continued and said: "We shall now build a confederate council fire from which the smoke shall arise and pierce the

Source: Arthur C. Parker, *The Constitution of the Five Nations or the Iroquois Book of the Great Law* (Albany: New York State Museum Bulletin, No. 184, 1916), 97–113.

skies and all nations and people shall see this smoke. And now to you, Thadodahho, your brother and cousin colleagues shall be left the care and protection of the confederate council fire, by the Confederate Nations."

Then Dekanahwideh further said: "The lords have unanimously decided to spread before you on the ground this great white wampum belt Ska-no-dah-ken-rah-ko-wah and Ka-yah-ne-renh-ko-wah, which respectfully signify purity and great peace, and the lords have also laid before you this great wing, Ska-weh-yeh-seh-ko-wah, and whenever any dust or stain of any description falls upon the great belt of white wampum, then you shall take this great wing and sweep it clean." (Dust or stain means evil of any description which might have a tendency to cause trouble in the Confederate Council.)

Then Dekanahwideh said: "The lords of this confederacy have unanimously decided to lay by you this rod (Ska-nah-ka-res) and whenever you see any creeping thing which might have a tendency to harm our grandchildren or see a thing creeping toward the great white wampum belt (meaning the Great Peace), then you shall take this rod and pry it away with it, and if you and your colleagues fail to pry the creeping, evil thing out, you shall then call out loudly that all the Confederate Nations may hear and they will come immediately to your assistance."

Then Dekanahwideh said: "Now you, the lords of the several Confederate Nations, shall divide yourselves and sit on opposite sides of the council fire as follows: You and your brother colleagues shall sit on one side of the council fire (this was said to the Mohawks and the Senecas), and your sons, the Oneidas and Cayugas, shall sit on the opposite side of the council fire. Thus you will begin to work and carry out the principles of the Great Peace (Ka-yah-ne-renh-ko-wah) and you will be guided in this by the great white wampum belt (Ska-no-dah-ke-rah-ko-wah) which signifies Great Peace."

Then Dekanahwideh said: "You, Thadodahho, shall be the fire keeper, and your duty shall be to open the Confederate Council with praise and thanksgiving to the Great Ruler and close the same."

Then Dekanahwideh also said: "When the council is opened, Hahyonhwatha and his colleagues shall be the first to consider and give their opinion upon any subject which may come before the council for consideration, and when they have arrived at a decision, then shall they transfer the matter to their brethren, the Senecas, for their consideration, and when they, the Senecas, shall have arrived at a decision on the matter then they shall refer it back to Hahyonhwatha and his colleagues. Then Hahyonhwatha will announce the decision to the opposite side of the council fire.

"Then Ohdahtshedeh and his colleagues will consider the matter in question and when they have arrived at a decision they will refer the matter to their brethren, the Cayugas, for their consideration and after they have arrived at a decision, they will refer the matter back to Ohdahtshedeh and his colleagues. Then Ohdahtshedeh will announce their decision to the opposite side of the council fire. Then Hahyonhwatha will refer the matter to Thadodahho and his colleagues for their careful consideration and opinion of the matter in question and if Thadodahho and his colleagues find that the matter has not been well considered or decided, then they shall refer the matter back again to the two sides of the council fire, and they shall point out where, in their estimation, the decision was faulty and the question not fully considered, and then the two sides of the council will take up the question again and reconsider the matter, and after the two sides of the council have fully reconsidered the question, then Hahyonhwatha will again refer it to Thadodahho and his colleagues, then they will again consider the matter and if they see that the decision of the two sides of the council is correct, then Thadodahho and his colleagues will confirm the decision."

Then Dekanahwideh further said: "If the brethren of the Mohawks and the Senecas are divided in their opinion and can not agree on any matter which they may have for their consideration, then Hahyonhwatha shall announce the two decisions to the opposite of the council fire. Then Ohdahtshedeh and his brother colleagues, after they have considered the matter, and if they also are divided in their decision, shall so report, but if the divided factions each agree with the decision announced from the opposite side of the council, then Ohdahtshedeh shall also announce their two decisions to the other side of the council fire; then Hahyonhwatha shall refer the matter to Thadodahho and his colleagues who are the fire keepers. They will fully consider the matter and whichever decision they consider correct they will confirm."

Then Dekanahwideh said: "If it should so happen that the lords of the Mohawks and the lords of the Senecas disagree on any matter and also on the opposite side of the council fire, the lords of the Oneidas and the lords of the Cayugas disagree among themselves and do not agree with either of the two decisions of the opposite side of the council fire but of themselves give two decisions which are diverse from each other, then Hahyonhwatha shall refer the four decisions to Thadodahho and his colleagues who shall consider the matter and give their decision and their decision shall be final."

Then Dekanahwideh said: "We have now completed the system for our Confederate Council."

Then Dekanahwideh further said: "We now, each nation, shall adopt all the rules and regulations governing the Confederate Council which we have here made and we shall apply them to all our respective settlements and thereby we shall carry out the principles set forth in the message of Good Tidings of Peace and Power, and in dealing with the affairs of our people of the various dominions, thus we shall secure to them contentment and happiness."

Then he, Dekanahwideh, said: "You, Kanyen-ke-ha-ka (Mohawk), you, Dekarihoken,

Hahyonhwatha and Sadekarihwadeh, you shall sit in the middle between your brother lords of the Mohawks, and your cousin lords of the Mohawks, and all matters under discussion shall be referred to you by your brother lords and your cousin lords for your approval or disapproval.

"You, O-nen-do-wa-ka (Senecas), you, Skanyhadahriyoh and Sadeh-ka-ronh-yes, you shall sit in the middle or between your brother lords and your cousin lords of the Senecas and all matters under discussion shall be referred to you by them for your approval or disapproval.

"You, Ohnenyohdehaka (Oneidas), you, Ohdahtshedeh, Kanonkweyoudoh and Deyouhahkwedeh, you shall sit in the middle between your brother lords and your cousin lords of the Oneidas and all matters under discussion shall be referred to you by them for your approval or disapproval.

"You, the Que-yenh-kwe-ha-ka (Cayugas), you, Dekaehyonh and Jinondahwehonh, you shall sit in the middle between your lords and your cousin lords of the Cayugas and all matters under discussion shall be referred to you by them for your approval or disapproval."

Then Dekanahwideh said: "We have now completed arranging the system of our local councils and we shall hold our annual Confederate Council at the settlement of Thadodahho, the capitol or seat of government of the Five Nations' Confederacy."

Dekanahwideh said: "Now I and you lords of the Confederate Nations shall plant a tree Ska-renj-heh-se-go-wah (meaning a tall and mighty tree) and we shall call it Jo-ne-rak-deh-ke-wah (the tree of the great long leaves).

"Now this tree which we have planted shall shoot forth four great, long, white roots (Jo-doh-ra-ken-rah-ko-wah). These great, long, white roots shall shoot forth one to the north and one to the south and one to the east and one to the west, and we shall place on the top of it Oh-don-yonh (an eagle) which has great power of long vision, and we shall transact all our business beneath the shade of this great tree. The meaning of planting this great tree, Skarehhehsegowah, is to symbolize Ka-yah-ne-renh-ko-wa, which means Great Peace, and Jo-deh-ra-ken-rah-ke-wah, meaning Good Tidings of Peace and Power. The nations of the earth shall see it and shall accept and follow the roots and shall follow them to the tree and when they arrive here you shall receive them and shall seat them in the midst of your confederacy. The object of placing an eagle, Skadjíenä', on the top of the great, tall tree is that it may watch the roots which extend to the north and to the south and to the east and to the west, and whose duty shall be to discover if any evil is approaching your confederacy, and he shall scream loudly and give the alarm and all the nations of the confederacy at once shall heed the alarm and come to the rescue."

Then Dekanahwideh again said: "We shall now combine our individual power into one great power which is this confederacy and we shall therefore symbolize the union of these powers by each nation contributing one arrow, which we shall tie up together in a bundle which, when it is made and completely tied together, no one can bend or break."

Then Dekanahwideh further said: "We have now completed this union by securing one arrow from each nation. It is not good that one should be lacking or taken from the bundle, for it would weaken our power and it would be still worse if two arrows were taken from the bundle. And if three arrows were taken any one could break the remaining arrows in the bundle."

Then Dekanahwideh continued his address and said: "We shall tie this bundle of arrows together with deer sinew which is strong, durable and lasting and then also this institution shall be strong and unchangeable. This bundle of arrows signifies that all the lords and all the warriors and all the women of the Confederacy have become united as one person."

Then Dekanahwideh again said: "We have now completed binding this bundle of arrows and we shall leave it beside the great tree (Skare-

hhehsegowah) and beside the Confederate Council fire of Thadodahho."

Then Dekanahwideh said: "We have now completed our power so that we the Five Nations' Confederacy shall in the future have one body, one head and one heart."

Then he (Dekanahwideh) further said: "If any evil should befall us in the future, we shall stand or fall united as one man."

Then Dekanahwideh said: "You lords shall be symbolized as trees of the Five Confederate Nations. We therefore bind ourselves together by taking hold of each other's hands firmly and forming a circle so strong that if a tree shall fall prostrate upon it, it could neither shake nor break it, and thus our people and our grandchildren shall remain in the circle in security, peace and happiness. And if any lord who is crowned with the emblem of deer's horns shall break through this circle of unity, his horns shall become fastened in the circle, and if he persists after warning from the chief matron, he shall go through it without his horns and the horns shall remain in the circle, and when he has passed through the circle, he shall no longer be lord, but shall be as an ordinary warrior and shall not be further qualified to fill any office."

Then Dekanahwideh further said: "We have now completed everything in connection with the matter of Peace and Power, and it remains only for us to consider and adopt some measure as to what we shall do with reference to the disposal of the weapons of war which we have taken from our people."

Then the lords considered the latter and decided that the best way which they could adopt with reference to the disposal of the weapons would be to uproot the great tall tree which they had planted and in uprooting the tree a chasm would form so deep that it would come or reach the swift current of the waters under it, into which the weapons of war would be thrown, and they would be borne and swept away forever by the current so that their grandchildren would never see them again. And they then uprooted the great tree and they cast into the chasm all manner of weapons of war which their people had been in the custom of using, and they then replaced the tree in its original position.

Then Dekanahwideh further continued and said: "We have completed clearing away all manner of weapons from the paths of our people."

Then Dekanahwideh continued and said: "We have still one matter left to be considered and that is with reference to the hunting grounds of our people from which they derive their living."

They, the lords, said with reference to this matter: "We shall now do this: We shall only have one dish (or bowl) in which will be placed one beaver's tail and we shall all have coequal right to it, and there shall be no knife in it, for if there be a knife in it, there would be danger that it might cut some one and blood would thereby be shed." (This one dish or bowl signifies that they will make their hunting grounds one common tract and all have a coequal right to hunt within it. The knife being prohibited from being placed into the dish or bowl signifies that all would be removed from shedding blood by the people of these different nations of the confederacy caused by differences of the right of the hunting grounds.)

Then Dekanahwideh continued and said: "We have now accomplished and completed forming the great Confederacy of the Five Nations together with adopting rules and regulations in connection therewith."

Then he, Dekanahwideh, continued and said: "I will now leave all matters in the hands of your lords and you are to work and carry out the principles of all that I have just laid before you for the welfare of your people and others, and I now place the power in your hands and to add to the rules and regulations whenever necessary and I now charge each of you lords that you must never seriously disagree among yourselves. You are all of equal standing and of equal power, and if you seriously disagree the consequences will be most serious and this disagreement will cause you to dis-

regard each other, and while you are quarreling with each other, the white panther (the fire dragon of discord) will come and take your rights and privileges away. Then your grandchildren will suffer and be reduced to poverty and disgrace." . . .

Then Dekanahwideh said: "I shall now therefore charge each of your lords, that your skin be of the thickness of seven spreads of the hands (from end of thumb to the end of the great finger) so that no matter how sharp a cutting instrument may be used it will not penetrate the thickness of your skin. (The meaning of the great thickness of your skins is patience and forbearance, so that no matter what nature of question or business may come before you, no matter how sharp or aggravating it may be, it will not penetrate to your skins, but you will forbear with great patience and good will in all your deliberations and never disgrace yourselves by becoming angry.) You lords shall always be guided in all your councils and deliberations by the Good Tidings of Peace and Power."

Then Dekanahwideh said: "Now, you lords of the different nations of the confederacy, I charge you to cultivate the good feeling of friendship, love and honor amongst yourselves. I have now fulfilled my duty in assisting you in the establishment and organization of this great confederacy, and if this confederation is carefully guarded it shall continue and endure from generation to generation and as long as the sun shines. I shall now, therefore, go home, conceal and cover myself with bark and there shall none other be called by my name."

Then Dekanahwideh further continued and said: "If at any time through the negligence and carelessness of the lords, they fail to carry out the principles of the Good Tidings of Peace and Power and the rules and regulations of the confederacy and the people are reduced to poverty and great suffering, I will return."

Then Dekanahwideh said: "And it shall so happen that when you hear my name mentioned disrespectfully without reason or just cause, but spoken in levity, you shall then know that you are on the verge of trouble and sorrow. And it shall be that the only time when it shall be proper for my name to be mentioned is when the condolence ceremonies are being performed or when the Good Tidings of Peace and Power which I have established and organized are being discussed or rehearsed."

Then the lords (Ro-de-ya-ner-shoh) said: "We shall begin to work and carry out the instructions which you, Dekanahwideh, have laid before us."

Then they said: "We shall therefore begin first with the Confederate Council of the Five Nations and other nations who shall accept and come under the Great Law of the confederacy will become as props, supports of the long house.

"The pure white wampum strings shall be the token or emblem of the council fire, and it shall be that when the fire keepers shall open the council, he shall pick up this string of wampum and hold it on his hand while he is offering thanksgiving to the Great Ruler and opening the council." And then they also said: "That while the council is in session the strings of the white wampum should be placed conspicuously in their midst and when they should adjourn then, the fire keepers should pick up these strings of wampum again, offer thanksgiving, close the council and all business in connection with the council should then be adjourned."

Then they said: "We shall now establish as a custom that when our annual Confederate Council shall meet we shall smoke the pipe of peace."

And they, the lords, then said: "We shall now proceed to define the obligations and position of the lords of the Confederacy as follows:

"If a lord is found guilty of wilful murder, he shall be deposed without the warning (as shall be provided for later on) by the lords of the confederacy, and his horns (emblem of power) shall be handed back to the chief matron of his family and clan.

"If a lord is guilty of rape he shall be deposed without the usual warning by the lords of the confederacy, and his horns (the emblem of power) shall be handed back to the chief matron of his family and clan.

"If a lord is found guilty of theft, he shall be deposed without the usual warning by the lords of the confederacy and his horns (the emblem of power) shall be handed back to the chief matron of his family and clan.

"If a lord is guilty of unwarrantably opposing the object of decisions of the council and in that his own erroneous will in these matters be carried out, he shall be approached and admonished by the chief matron of his family and clan to desist from such evil practices and she shall urge him to come back and act in harmony with his brother lords.

"If the lord refuses to comply with the request of the chief matron of his family and clan and still persists in his evil practices of unwarrantably opposing his brother lords, then a warrior of his family and clan will also approach him and admonish him to desist from pursuing his evil course.

"If the lord still refuses to listen and obey, then the chief matron and warrior shall go together to the warrior and they shall inform him that they have admonished their lord and he refused to obey. Then the chief warrior will arise and go there to the lord and will say to him: 'Your nephew and niece have admonished you to desist from your evil course, and you have refused to obey.' Then the chief warrior will say: 'I will now admonish you for the last time and if you continue to resist, refuse to accede and disobey this request, then your duties as lord of our family and clan will cease, and I shall take the deer's horns from off your head, and with a broad edged stone axe I shall cut down the tree' (meaning that he shall be deposed from his position as lord or chief of the confederacy). Then, if the lord merits dismissal, the chief warrior shall hand back the deer's horns (the emblem of power) of the deposed lord to the chief matron of the family or clan."

Whenever it occurs that a lord is thus deposed, then the chief matron shall select and appoint another warrior of her family or clan and crown him with the deer's horns and thus a new lord shall be created in the place of the one deposed.

The lords of each of the confederate nations shall have one assistant and their duty, each of them, shall be to carry messages through the forests between our settlements and also in the absence of the lord through illness or any other impediment he shall be deputed by him (his lord) to act in his place in council.

The lords then said: "We have now completed defining the obligations and positions of a lord (Royaner) and therefore in accordance with the custom which we now have established, it shall be that when a lord is deposed and the deer's horns (emblem of power) are taken from him, he shall no longer be allowed to sit in council or even hold an office again."

Then the lords continued and said: "What shall we do in case some of us lords are removed by sudden death and in whom so much dependence is placed?"

"In such case (this shall be done), the chief matron and the warriors of the family and clan of the deceased lord, shall nominate another lord from the warriors of the family and clan of the dead lord to succeed him, then the matter will be submitted to the brother lords and if they (the brother lords) confirm the nomination, then the matter will be further submitted to their cousin lords and if they also confirm the nomination, then the candidate shall be qualified to be raised by the condolence ceremony (Honda nas)."

Then the lords continued and said: "In case the family and clan in which a lordship title is vested shall become extinct, this shall be done: It shall then be transferred and vested in the hands of the confederate lords and they will consider the matter and nominate and appoint a successor from any family of the brother lords of the deceased lord, and the lords may in their discretion vest the said lordship title in some family, and such title will remain in that family so long as the lords are satisfied.

"If ever it should occur that the chief matron in a family or clan in which a lordship title is vested should be removed by death and leave female infants who, owing to their infancy can not nominate a candidate to bear their lordship title, then the lords (of the same nation) at their pleasure may appoint an adult female of a sister family who shall make a temporary appointment, shall come before the lords and request that the lordship title be restored to them, then the lords must obtain the title and restore it accordingly."

Then the lords continued and said: "We now have completed laying the foundation of our rules and methods (Kayanehrenokowa) and we will now proceed to follow and carry out the working of these rules and methods of the confederacy, and the local affairs of our respective settlements, and whenever we discover a warrior who is wise and trustworthy and who will render his services for the benefit of the people and thus aid the lords of the confederacy, we will claim him into our midst and confer upon him the title of 'He has sprung up as a Pine Tree' (Eh-ka-neh-do-deh) and his title shall only last during his lifetime and shall not be hereditary and at his death it shall die with him. "...

References

1. Arthur C. Parker, *The Constitution of the Five Nations or the Iroquois Book of the Great Law* (Albany: New York State Museum Bulletin, No. 184, 1916), 61; Barbara A. Mann and Jerry L. Fields, "A Sign in the Sky: Dating the League of the Haudenosaunee," *American Indian Culture and Research Journal* 21 (1977), 105–63; Dean R. Snow, *The Iroquois* (Oxford: Blackwell, 1994), 60.
2. Quoted in Matthew Dennis, *Cultivating a Landscape of Peace: Iroquois-European Encounters in Seventeenth-Century America* (Ithaca, N.Y.: Cornell University Press, 1993), 76.

3. Parker, *The Constitution of the Five Nations*, 17.

4. Leon Shenandoah, "Foreword" to Paul Wallace, *The White Roots of Peace: The Iroquois Book of Life* (Santa Fe: Clear Light Publishers, 1994), 13.

5. Quoted in Daniel K. Richter, *The Ordeal of the Longhouse: The Peoples of the Iroquois League in the Era of European Colonization* (Chapel Hill: University of North Carolina Press, 1992), 39.

6. Richter, *The Ordeal of the Longhouse*, 31.

7. Milo M. Quaife, ed., *John Long's Voyages and Travels in the Years 1768–1788* (Chicago: R. R. Donnelley, 1922), 18.

8. Canasatego's speech is reprinted in Colin G. Calloway, ed., *The World Turned Upside Down: Indian Voices from Early America* (Boston: Bedford Books, 1994), 104; Franklin's opinion is quoted in Bruce E. Johansen, *Forgotten Founders: Benjamin Franklin, the Iroquois, and the Rationale for the American Revolution* (Ipswich, Mass.: Gambit Publishers, 1982), 66.

9. Parker, *The Constitution of the Five Nations*, 61–63.

Suggested Readings

Dennis, Matthew. *Cultivating a Landscape of Peace: Iroquois-European Encounters in Seventeenth-Century America* (Ithaca, N.Y.: Cornell University Press, 1993).

Fenton, William N. *The Great Law and the Longhouse: A Political History of the Iroquois Confederacy* (Norman: University of Oklahoma Press, 1998).

Fenton, William N., ed. *Parker on the Iroquois: Iroquois Uses of Maize and Other Food Plants, the Code of Handsome Lake, the Seneca Prophet, The Constitution of the Five Nations, by Arthur C. Parker* (Syracuse: Syracuse University Press, 1968).

"Forum: The 'Iroquois Influence' Thesis—Con and Pro," *William and Mary Quarterly,* 3d series, 53 (1996), 587–636.

Grinde, Donald, Jr., and Bruce E. Johansen, eds. *Exemplar of Liberty: Native America and the Evolution of Democracy* (Los Angeles: UCLA American Indian Studies Center, 1991).

Johansen, Bruce E., and Elisabeth Tooker. "Commentary on the Iroquois and the U.S. Constitution," *Ethnohistory* 37 (1990), 279–301.

Lyons, Oren, et al. *Exiled in the Land of the Free: Democracy, Indian Nations, and the U.S. Constitution* (Santa Fe: Clear Light Publishers, 1992).

Morgan, Lewis Henry. *League of the Hodenosaunee, or Iroquois* (Rochester, N.Y.: Sage and Brother, 1851).

Richter, Daniel K. *The Ordeal of the Longhouse: The Peoples of the Iroquois League in the Era of European Colonization* (Chapel Hill: University of North Carolina Press, 1992).

Snow, Dean R. *The Iroquois* (Oxford: Blackwell, 1994).

Wallace, Paul. *The White Roots of Peace: The Iroquois Book of Life* (Santa Fe: Clear Light Publishers, 1994).

Early American Towns and Cities

—◆—

European colonists often depicted the Indians they encountered in North America as "wandering savages," hunting people who lacked permanent settlements. Americans inherited this view and the United States government incorporated it into its Indian policies which, throughout the nineteenth century, operated on the conviction that Indians must be taught to farm and live in one place if they were ever to become "civilized." The notion that Indians were nomads who lived in small hunting bands with no fixed homes helped justify their dispossession: Euro-Americans needed the land for agriculture and they had every right to take it because the Indians were not using it anyway.

Throughout North America, Indian people lived in small villages *and* hunted. In some areas, Indians were nomadic and followed game in small hunting bands. But most Indians were farmers and some inhabited towns that were as large as those of contemporary Europeans and colonists. Southwestern Indian peoples constructed multistory apartment buildings; Mississippian societies erected towns and temples on earthen mounds; Iroquoian people lived in towns of multifamily longhouses surrounded by palisades and cornfields. Arriving in the wake of Indian losses to epidemic diseases, Europeans often saw only traces of the civilizations that had existed in North America. On the basis of these impressions, history books portrayed Indian people as only hunters and village dwellers, rarely as farmers and city dwellers.

As the illustrations here indicate, there was an "urban America" long before Europeans arrived. The ruins and remains of some of these places provide clues to American Indian worlds and experiences that must have been very different from those described by most European observers and most American historians.

Pueblo Bonito (Beautiful Town) (Figure 1.1) was the largest of the towns built in Chaco Canyon. It was a planned, multistoried community of between 650 and 800 rooms laid out as a giant D-shaped amphitheater around a central plaza covering three acres. The walls were constructed of stones and filled with rubble; thousands of wooden roof beams were made from logs carried from almost fifty miles away. Ring-dated beams indicate that Pueblo Bonito was built between A.D. 919 and 1085.

At Mesa Verde in southeastern Colorado, people were living in many small villages on top of the mesa as early as A.D. 700. As the villages increased in size, the inhabitants developed more sophisticated structures and building tech-

FIGURE 1.1 **Artist's Reconstruction of Pueblo Bonito**

From Lewis Henry Moran, Houses and House-Life of the American Aborgines *(1881).*

niques. By 1150, most of the inhabitants were living in large cliff houses constructed within the huge caves in the canyon walls, which provided security against attack. As many as seven thousand people may have lived in the area. Cliff Palace (Figure 1.2) was the largest cliff dwelling in the area, with two hundred rooms and twenty kivas, but there may have been between five hundred and one thousand cliff houses at Mesa Verde during its peak in the mid-thirteenth century.[1]

As people abandoned some sites, they congregated in others. By the time Spaniards arrived in New Mexico around 1540, Indian populations were concentrated in the Rio Grande valley and they were living in towns (which the Spaniards called pueblos). Taos Pueblo (Figure 1.3), photographed here in the 1870s, had been inhabited for centuries before Europeans arrived. It is still inhabited today.

At its height around A.D. 1050 and 1250, Cahokia (Figure 1.4) covered two thousand acres and was the largest city north of Mexico, with a population of at least 10,000 and perhaps more than 30,000 residents. By contrast, Philadelphia, the largest city in colonial North America, had a population of only 23,000 as late as 1763. Cahokia was a city of ceremonial pyramids, open plazas, extensive cornfields, satellite villages, and suburbs. The rectangular field with two poles in the middle of the plaza was a ball court. The circle of posts at the far left—known as "Woodhenge" to archaeologists—seems to have been a calen-

FIGURE 1.2 **Cliff Palace at Mesa Verde**
Arizona State Museum, University of Arizona. Helga Teiwes, photographer.

dric device that allowed priests to predict the coming of the solstices and equinoxes and to predict the correct timing for planting and ceremonies. The Cahokia site has been eroded over the years by farming, highways, and building developments, but impressive mounds remain at Cahokia State Park as testimony to the metropolis that once thrived there.

Mississippian societies constructed mound-based towns and cities throughout the Mississippi and Ohio valleys and the Southeast. The stockaded town at Aztalan along the Crawfish River, near Lake Mills in southern Wis-

FIGURE 1.3 **Taos Pueblo**
Library of Congress.

consin, depicted in Figure 1.5 as it may have looked in its heyday between A.D. 1100 and 1300, housed some five hundred people and was probably the northernmost outpost of Mississippian culture. The town appears to have been destroyed by burning, but it is not known by whom.

Indian communities were not haphazard towns and villages. They were carefully planned to meet the social, political, economic, and ceremonial needs of the people. The drawing of the fortified town of Hochelaga (Figure 1.6) at the site of present-day Montreal was done shortly after Jacques Cartier visited in 1535. The drawing is a stylized rendition of what was most likely a palisaded town of longhouses, but it conveys that the Europeans saw Hochelaga as an organized and substantial community and a thriving center of Native life.

John White's drawing of the Algonquian village of Secoton in Virginia in 1585 (Figure 1.6) is in the form of a town plan, showing the various purposes and functions of the buildings and spaces and leading the viewer up the "main street" from foreground to background. The multifamily houses are constructed of saplings bent over and covered with bark and woven mats that could be removed to let in air and light. The inhabitants depended on corn and practiced field rotation (note the three fields of corn at different stages of growth at the right of the picture—"rype corne," "greene corn," and "corne newly sprung"), but supplemented their diet with hunting. A fire burns at "the place of solemn prayer" while, across the main street, a ritual is in progress.

FIGURE 1.4 Cahokia Mounds, c. A.D. 1100–1150
Cahokia Mounds State Historic Site. Painting by William R. Iseminger.

FIGURE 1.5 Aztalan, an Artist's Conception
Courtesy Milwaukee Public Museum.

Figure 1.6 John White, *Indian Village of Secoton* **(1585)**
Copyright British Museum.

White's English viewers would have recognized many similarities with English towns and fields. It is possible that White's *Indian Village* was a composite painting, depicting various aspects of Indian life.

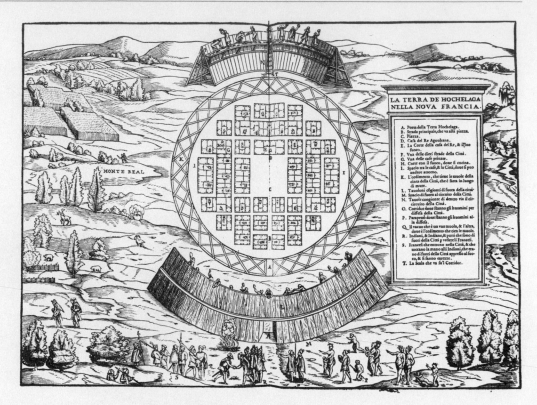

FIGURE 1.7 Hochelaga
Newberry Library.

▶ Questions for Consideration

1. What do these images of Indian towns, villages, and other cities reveal about how these inhabitants lived in relation to their environment? About how they organized their space and their societies? About their religious obligations, economic activities, and needs for defense?

2. What are the differences between a village, a town, and a city?

3. Why, and with what effects, did white Americans tend to refer to all Indian settlements, regardless of their size, as villages?

References

1. Stuart J. Fiedel, *Prehistory of the Americas* (Cambridge: Cambridge University Press, 1987), 219.

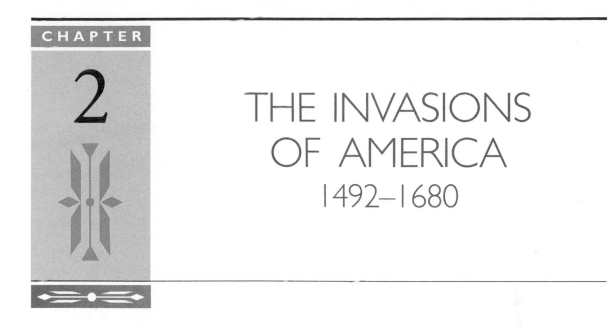

THE INVASIONS OF AMERICA
1492–1680

FIRST CONTACTS AND ENDURING IMAGES

Some people argue that Africans from the Nile Delta, Buddhist monks from Japan, Celtic priests, or even visitors from outer space got to America long before Columbus. Viking sagas and archaeological evidence confirm that Scandinavian seafarers made contact with Indian people—Skraelings, the Vikings called them—in Newfoundland and Labrador around A.D. 1000. Relations with the natives broke down in violence, and the Viking colonies were short-lived.

But at the end of the fifteenth century, Europe broke its bounds and embarked on a program of expansion overseas that reached into America, Asia, Africa, and Australia. The American phase of this expansion entailed the defeat and dispossession of the native inhabitants over almost four centuries of coercion and conflict. It also witnessed widespread and sometimes violent competition between rival European powers. In the seventeenth century, Spanish, French, Dutch, Swedish, and English colonizers all contended for a foothold on the American continent. European immigrants who encroached on Indian country in the seventeenth and eighteenth century included Finns, Germans, Scots, Irish, and many others, and Russian expansion eastward, which began in Siberia in the sixteenth and seventeenth centuries, brought traders and missionaries to Alaska and northern California in the eighteenth and nineteenth centuries. But Spain, France, and Britain came to dominate the struggle for hegemony and had the most enduring effects on Indian America.

European colonists endeavored to create societies that mirrored those they had left behind giving them names that evoked home—New Spain, New

Mexico, New France, New England, Nova Scotia, New Netherlands—but the communities that emerged were quite different from their European counterparts. At the same time, the invasion of European peoples, plants, products, and plagues transformed America, creating what historian James Merrell aptly described as "a new world" for Indian peoples.[1]

The first Europeans to arrive in America brought with them European germs, animals, plants, technologies, and concepts of land use and ownership that would forever change the face of North America. They also brought attitudes and opinions about "primitive" people that would govern their relations with the native peoples they encountered and established images of Indians that endured for centuries.

Because the recent development of the printing press had greatly increased the circulation of news and literature, Europeans soon had access to a variety of descriptions of the "New World" and the people who lived here. Some of these were favorable: Columbus described the first Indians he met as simple children of nature, timid, generous, and guileless. They were "very well formed, with handsome bodies and good faces" and went "as naked as their mothers bore them." They accepted whatever they were offered in trade and "gave of what they had very willingly." With an eye to what he saw in store for these people, the admiral reckoned they would make "good and intelligent servants" and "would become Christians very easily, for it seemed to me that they had no religion." The Indians were "very gentle and do not know what evil is."[2] Other observers spoke of the Indians' agility, health, dignity, and bravery. The image of Indians as "noble savages" and "simple children of nature" took a firm hold in the imagination of Europeans. At the same time, however, Columbus and others reported stories of fierce cannibals, and the idea of Indians as "treacherous savages" and "dirty savages" also became a common image. The very diversity in Native American life that the label "Indian" ignored presented Europeans with contradictions in what they found and thus produced a conflicting set of beliefs about Indians.

Inevitably, Europeans judged Indians by European values. They assessed them in terms of Western views of civilization, noting what they lacked rather than what they had achieved. By "civilization" Europeans usually meant wearing "proper" clothing, speaking a language intelligible to their ears, living in "orderly" social and political structures, practicing a sedentary agricultural economy in which men, not women, did the farming, dwelling in permanent housing, and observing some form of Christianity. They saw that Indians had no sailing ships, printing presses, wheeled vehicles, stone arches, iron tools, steel weapons, or guns. Based on their observations, most Europeans did not think they were displacing existing civilizations when they came to America.

For the most part, Indian people greeted the newcomers with cautious hospitality and goodwill. They seem to have been impressed by the Europeans' technology, particularly their ships, guns, and metal tools, but shocked by their appearance, language, and behavior. Europeans frequently claimed that Indians regarded them with awe, as godlike, but Indians regularly dismissed European pretensions to superiority. "You are always fighting and quarreling among yourselves," Micmac Indians in Nova Scotia told Frenchmen in the early seven-

MAP 2.1 **European Invasions of Indian America**

At different times in the course of the sixteenth, seventeenth, and eighteenth centuries, various major European nations penetrated North America. Other peoples—Finns, Scotch-Irish, Germans, African slaves—also pushed into the continent. Their intrusion set off ripple effects throughout Indian country, often affecting the lives of Indian people who had never laid eyes on a European.

teenth century. "You are envious and are all the time slandering each other; you are thieves and deceivers; you are covetous, and are neither generous nor kind; as for us, if we have a morsel of bread we share it with our neighbor."[3] A Micmac elder reiterated a similar theme in the 1670s, telling missionary Chrestien LeClerq in no uncertain terms that the French had no cause to look down on

Indians: "miserable as we seem in thine eyes, we consider ourselves neverthe-less much happier than thou in this, that we are content with the little that we have; . . . thou deceivest thyself greatly if thou thinkest to persuade us that thy country is better than ours. For if France, as thou sayest, is a little terrestrial par-adise, art thou sensible to leave it?" He concluded, "there is no Indian who does not consider himself infinitely more happy and more powerful than the French."[4]

Even as European numbers increased, Natives and newcomers often found ways of coexisting and cooperating, adapting to each other's presence, and bor-rowing from what the other had to offer. But hospitality turned to hostility when understanding failed to bridge the cultural gulf and Indians began to ex-perience mistreatment at the hands of Europeans. As early as 1524, the Flo-rentine explorer Giovanni Verrazzano found that Indians on the coast of Maine would not allow his crew ashore to trade; they had already had dealings with Europeans, perhaps Basque or Breton sailors and fisherman, or perhaps a Por-tuguese expedition that had passed through the area the year before. It was not long before Indians and Europeans clashed. To Europeans, the Indians' hostil-ity was proof of their savagery. Like later Americans, they invoked that sav-agery to justify their actions and continued assaults on Indian cultures.

But the notion of Indians as "noble savages" endured. From the journals of Columbus in 1492, through the writings of eighteenth-century philosophers like Jean Jacques Rousseau, to movies like *Dances with Wolves* in 1990, many non-Indians portrayed Indians living lives of simplicity and purity as a contrast to their own societies, which they depicted as aggressive and materialistic. The habit of viewing the diverse native inhabitants of North America as a single col-lective category in mirror image of Western society had roots in the first con-tacts between Indian and European people and has persisted for more than five hundred years. Non-Indian images of Indians usually reveal more about how the image makers feel about themselves and their own society than they do about real Indian people.

COLUMBIAN EXCHANGES

In 1493, Columbus made his second voyage to Hispaniola (an island now di-vided between Haiti and the Dominican Republic). This time his purpose was colonization of the lands he had "discovered." He took with him seventeen ships, more than a thousand settlers, and a cargo that included horses, pigs, cat-tle, sheep, goats, chickens, dogs, seeds, and cuttings for fruit trees, wheat, and sugarcane. Columbus's cargo illustrated the many levels on which the European invasion of America occurred as animals, plants, insects, germs, and new tech-nologies accompanied European peoples into Indian country. Even though this invasion was one-way, from Europe to America, an exchange was in fact taking shape: in time, American people, foods, and ideas spread across the Atlantic to permanently change the Old World, and Native American ways of life subtly in-fluenced the European colonists. Contact between Europe and America initiated what historian Alfred Crosby has termed "the Columbian exchange" between two worlds. That exchange also brought America into contact with Africa via slaving and trade routes. Interaction with Indian people also finally contributed to transforming European colonists into Americans.

Changing New World Landscapes

Europeans entered a continent that bore the marks of thousands of years of human habitation and activity. As they moved inland, they continued to encounter settled or recently abandoned agricultural landscapes. Assisted by Indian guides and subsisting on native food, "the pioneers at the head of the Euro-American advance followed the signposts of cleared fields and orchards that recorded the long experience of Native Americans in selecting good soils and managing local ecologies."[5] But Europeans began to alter the landscape in ways Native Americans never had. They brought new plants and crops: rice, wheat, barley, oats; and new grasses and weeds, along with fruits such as peaches and oranges. They introduced domesticated animals such as horses, sheep, goats, and pigs, which trod down grasses unaccustomed to pastoralism, trampled Indian cornfields, and drove away wild game. Their world, quite literally, changed before Indians' eyes as European colonists transformed the forest into farmland: "these English have gotten our land," declared a Narragansett chief only twenty years after the Pilgrims arrived in New England. "They with scythes cut down the grass, and with axes fell the trees; their cows and horses eat the grass, and their hogs spoil our clam banks."[6] In the Southeast, hogs ran wild. Sheep and goats became permanent parts of the economy and culture of Pueblo and Navajo peoples in the Southwest. Horses transformed the lives and cultures of Indian peoples on the Plains. Europeans also brought honeybees, black rats, cats, and cockroaches to America.

Some Indians crossed the Atlantic eastward to Europe, as kidnap victims, slaves, and diplomats—for instance, when "four Indian kings" (in fact, three Mohawks and one Mahican) visited Queen Anne in London in 1710—but most American exports were the foods that Native peoples had developed and cultivated. Potatoes transformed the diets of ordinary people in northern Europe; tomatoes became quickly incorporated into Italian cooking. Corn, which had long been the key component in many Indian diets, quickly became a staple of life for European pioneers in frontier America.

Biological Catastrophes

Europe's deadliest export was invisible. Nothing hit Indian societies harder or did more to shape the subsequent course of American history than European diseases. The inhabitants of both North America and Europe suffered from ailments and injuries and had a life expectancy that most twenty-first-century Westerners would find shocking. But until 1492 Indians were isolated from the massive, deadly epidemics that ravaged Europe and Asia in me-

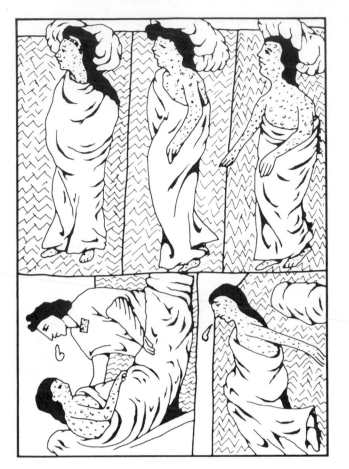

Silent Killer

This sixteenth-century portrayal of smallpox records the effects of a disease that would strike Native peoples repeatedly from first contacts to the twentieth century. From Stolen Continents *by Ronald Wright. Copyright © 1992 by Ronald Wright. Reprinted with permission of Houghton Mifflin Company. All rights reserved.*

dieval times. When Europeans arrived on the continent they carried germs and viruses that exploded into "virgin soil epidemics" among Native American populations who had no acquired immunity to these new diseases.[7]

Epidemics of smallpox, measles, bubonic plague, influenza, cholera, and other killer diseases spread like wildfire through Indian societies. Different diseases struck different regions at different times, and populations varied in their responses. In some cases entire populations perished; 90 percent mortality rates were common. In some areas populations recovered, or even increased, as they incorporated refugees from other areas. But sooner or later imported diseases struck all native populations. Some scholars may have produced inflated estimates of population size and decline, but their work points to one of the greatest demographic disasters in history. The population of Hispaniola was estimated at some 8 million in 1492; by 1535 the original inhabitants were all but extinct; the native population of Mexico dropped from an estimated 25 million in 1519 to perhaps 1.3 million by the end of the century; Peru's population dwindled from as high as 9 million to a half million in 1600.

The pattern of epidemic diseases and depopulation in North America is not fully understood, and estimates of precontact Indian populations in North America must always be tentative since so many people died before Europeans conducted headcounts of survivors. In some areas, populations increased as refugees sought shelter from war and disease elsewhere. Combined with the impacts of increased warfare, famine, and other traumas of colonization, recurrent epidemics and chronic diseases caused continual attrition of Indian numbers from the fifteenth to the twentieth century and steadily eroded Indian capacity for dealing with the invaders. A recent estimate suggests that the Native population of North America fell by 74 percent between 1492 and 1800, while that of the hemisphere as a whole plummeted by 89 percent between 1492 and 1650.[8] The Indians whom European invaders encountered were often the survivors of shattered societies: abandoned villages and pockmarked faces testified to the suffering that had preceded the colonists.

INDIANS CONFRONT THE SPANISH

In the late fall of 1528, Indians in eastern Texas came upon a group of bearded and bedraggled men who had washed up on the Gulf coast. The Indian men, probably Karankawas, were astonished and brought their women and children to look at the strangers. The Indians took pity on them, fed them roots and fish, and gave them shelter in their village. Eventually "half the natives died from a disease of the bowels."[9] The strange men were Spanish soldiers, would-be conquistadors and survivors of an ill-fated expedition that had landed in Florida. Four of them—including the royal treasurer of the expedition, Álvar Núñez Cabeza de Vaca—later lived for years among the Indians. It was the first of many encounters in North America, and not the last in which Spaniards and Indians would live in close contact. But the power dynamics in subsequent years would very often be reversed.

A Mission for Gold and God

Spanish soldiers, priests, and colonizers in the South and Southwest preceded English colonists on the Atlantic coast by almost a century. Christopher Columbus had sailed west in 1492 in the employ of the Spanish monarchs, Ferdinand and Isabella. Recently liberated from Moslem power that had both limited Spain's expansion and influenced its development throughout the Middle Ages, Spaniards looked to the New World as an area for empire building. Seven centuries of warfare to drive the "infidels" out of the Iberian peninsula left an indelible mark on the militant Christian warrior culture of Spain: young noblemen now looked elsewhere for infidels to fight. In the next hundred years or so, Spaniards came into contact with Indian peoples from Florida to California, from Peru to the Great Plains.

The Spanish believed they had a divine and royal mandate to reduce Indian peoples to submission. Spanish law required the conquistadors to read to the Indians they encountered the *Requerimiento*. This document, worked out by theologians in 1513 at the request of the King of Spain, required Indians to "acknowledge the Church as the Ruler and Superior of the whole world," the Pope as high priest, and the king and queen of Spain as lords of their lands. If they did so, the Spaniards would "receive you in all love and charity, . . . leave you, your wives, and your children, and your lands, free without servitude, . . . and . . . not compel you to turn Christians." But, the *Requerimiento* continued,

> if you do not do this, and wickedly and intentionally delay to do so, I certify to you that, with the help of God, we shall forcibly enter into your country and shall make war against you in all ways and manners that we

can, and shall subject you to the yoke and obedience of the Church and of their Highnesses; we shall take you and your wives and your children, and shall make slaves of them, and as such shall sell and dispose of them as their Highnesses may command; and we shall take away your goods, and shall do all the harm and damage that we can, as to vassals who do not obey, and refuse to receive their lord, and resist and contradict him; and we protest that the deaths and losses which shall accrue from this are your fault, and not that of their Highnesses, or ours, nor of these gentlemen who come with us.

Read in Spanish to Indian people who understood neither its language nor its concepts, the *Requerimiento* became little more than a "ceremony of possession," allowing the Spaniards to justify conquest—and any accompanying atrocities.[10]

The Spanish had settlements in the Caribbean, especially on Cuba and Hispaniola, before 1520. Despite mass enslavements of the native populations, these colonies did not produce the wealth the colonizers had hoped for. Legends and reports of great riches on the mainland attracted Spanish attention and ambitions. In the next thirty years, Spanish forces penetrated as far as Mexico and the central plateau of the Andes, destroyed the civilizations they encountered, and took possession of the most densely populated areas of the Americas, thereby establishing the first European land empire overseas.

Conquest of the Aztecs

In 1519, the Aztecs of central Mexico began to hear reports of strange white men, wearing armor and riding animals. The news followed a series of bad omens and portents of disaster. Aztec life revolved around cyclical rituals based on a solar year of eighteen months. The end of a cycle was regarded as a time of great peril. Around 1507, a major cycle of the Aztec calendar had come to an end. Fifteen years later the Aztec empire lay in ruins. The conqueror was Hernán Cortés who landed near Vera Cruz in 1519 with a force of only 508 men, burned his ships to demonstrate there was no turning back, and marched inland.

The Spaniards were entering a complex and highly structured civilization whose impressive cities left the invaders in wonderment. The Aztecs were only the most recent in a *series* of ruling peoples in the area. Invading from the north, they had achieved ascendancy relatively recently, in the fifteenth century, and exacted tribute and labor from subject peoples over a wide area. The Aztec emperor headed a society rigidly divided by castes, attuned to the predictions of priests, and dependent on human sacrifice as the key to ensuring agricultural fertility and the daily return of the sun. Efficiently irrigated fields produced crops of maize, tobacco, potatoes, and tomatoes—all unknown in Europe at that time—and pyramid-shaped temples dominated the large plazas of Aztec towns. The capital, Tenochtitlán, on the site of present-day Mexico City, housed more than 200,000 people, making it several times the size of most European capitals at the time. Then, as now, Mexico City was one of the largest cities in the world.

Boldly marching through jungle to the high plateau of central Mexico, the Spaniards won over the outlying towns as tribes eager to throw off Aztec rule joined them. Communication with the Indians was aided by an Aztec woman who could speak both Mayan and Nahuatl, the language of the Aztecs, and whom the Spaniards called Doña Marina; she served as Cortés's mistress and interpreter — one of the first of many people to serve as a culture broker between Indians and Europeans.° Hearing advance warning of their arrival, the Aztec emperor Montezuma sent gifts to the invaders and allowed them to enter Tenochtitlán; in return, Cortés seized Montezuma and held him hostage in his own palace.

In 1520, after a tenuous peace, Spanish cruelties and desecration of temples finally produced a furious Aztec counterassault. Montezuma was killed by disaffected Aztecs, and Cortés had to fight his way out of the city. The Spaniards lost a third of their men but regrouped for another attack. Meanwhile, a massive smallpox epidemic broke out in Tenochtitlán. It lasted for seventy days, according to a native text, "striking every where in the city and killing a vast number of our people."[11] It killed Montezuma's brother, Cuitláhuac, who had spearheaded the Aztec resistance. Strengthened by allies from the coastal tribes and by Spanish reinforcements from Cuba, in 1521 Cortés's troops looted and destroyed Tenochtitlán. A year later, Cortés was appointed "Captain General of New Spain." Bernal Díaz, a young foot soldier in the invasion, wrote a lengthy account of the conquest in his old age. He recalled the march inland, the awe with which the Spaniards viewed island cities built in the water, the long causeway leading straight for Tenochtitlán, rich orchards, and rose gardens. "Some of our soldiers even asked whether the things that we saw were not a dream," he said. "Seeing things as we did that had never been heard of or seen before, not even dreamed about." But he was imagining a paradise before the fall: "Of all these wonders that I then beheld today all is overthrown and lost, nothing [is] left standing."[12]

Contemporaries and many later historians saw the rapid and total collapse of the Aztec Empire as evidence of European superiority over Native people. The Spaniards fought with courage, discipline, and ruthless brutality, and had the advantage of horses, firearms, and metal armor. The Aztecs were unable to sustain — or even, perhaps, to understand — the kind of prolonged campaign mounted by Spaniards who, driven by a single-minded faith in their mission and a lust for gold, laid siege to cities and starved and killed whole populations. But there were major internal reasons for the collapse of the highly structured

---

°Doña Marina, or Malinche, had apparently been stolen in childhood by traders and sold to the Tabascans. The Tabascans gave her to Cortés. Her native language was Nahuatl, but in Tabasca she had learned the Maya language. She spoke in Mayan to Jeronimo de Aguilar, a shipwrecked Spaniard who lived among Mayan-speaking Indians, who then translated from Mayan to Spanish for Cortés. Patricia de Fuentes, trans. and ed., *The Conquistadors: First-Person Accounts of the Conquest of Mexico* (Norman: University of Oklahoma Press, 1993), 21, 24, 215.

Aztec Empire. Rebellious subject peoples sided with the invaders, and Indian defenders died from disease faster than Spaniards could kill them.

Searching for Other Empires

In the wake of Cortés's stunning conquest, the Spaniards sent expeditions into other areas of America. In 1532, Francisco Pizarro invaded Peru with 168 men and 67 horses. The people of the Inca Empire were learned in mathematics and astronomy, irrigated their fields, built huge temples and palaces, and constructed a network of paved roads linking major towns with the capital city, Cuzco. But smallpox preceded Pizarro to Peru, and the Spaniards caught the Incas in the midst of a civil upheaval with a usurper named Atahualpa on the throne. Pizarro captured Atahualpa by treachery, held him hostage until his people filled a storeroom with a ransom of treasure, and then had him strangled. The Spanish suppressed resistance to them with bloody reprisals, and Incan civilization was soon reduced to ruins, although Indian resistance to Spanish colonial rule continued for generations.

Indian peoples in the area of the present-day United States encountered Spanish soldiers and missionaries as other expeditions pushed north. New Spain's northern frontier ultimately stretched from California to Florida. In 1513, Juan Ponce de León sailed along the coast of Florida. Calusa Indians traded and skirmished with his party. Eight years later Ponce died after a pitched battle with the Indians. Other Spaniards explored the Florida coastline, some of them looking for slaves. Lucas Vásquez de Ayllón attempted to establish a colony in 1526, but disease, hunger, and Indian resistance defeated his efforts.

In 1528, Pánfilo de Narváez landed on the west coast of Florida and divided his force, marching inland with his troops while his ships paralleled their route up the coast carrying supplies. After an arduous trek, the Spaniards reached the Indian town of Apalachee in northern Florida, but the Indians harassed them with guerilla-style tactics and the Spaniards headed for the coast. The ships were nowhere to be seen. In desperation, the Spaniards built makeshift barges and set sail. Narváez and most of his followers were never seen again. Cabeza de Vaca and other survivors made it to an island off the coast of eastern Texas where local Indians took them in. After six years living among the coastal Indians, often as slaves, Cabeza de Vaca and three companions escaped. They spent two more years wandering across the Southwest, "through so many different villages of such diverse tongues that my memory gets confused." They earned a reputation as healers and "the Indians treated us kindly . . . deprived themselves of food to give to us, and presented us skins and other tokens of gratitude." After passing through Pima country in present-day Arizona, they saw signs they were nearing their objective: Spanish slavers had been at work, carrying off women and children. "With heavy hearts we looked out over the lavishly watered, fertile, and beautiful land," wrote Cabeza de Vaca, "now abandoned and burned and the people thin and weak, scattered or hiding in fright." The Indians could not believe that the sun-darkened Cabeza de Vaca and his companions were the same people as the Christians who raided them for slaves: "We had come from the sunrise, they from the sunset; we healed the sick, they killed the sound; we came naked and barefoot, they clothed, horsed, and lanced; we coveted nothing but gave whatever we were given, while they robbed whomever they found and bestowed nothing on anyone."[13]

Cabeza de Vaca and his companions made their way to Mexico City. The stories they brought back of finding emerald arrowheads and of wealthy Indian nations to the north convinced some that Spain was on the brink of locating the famed Seven Cities of Cibola, which, legend had it, had been founded centuries before somewhere in the west by seven fugitive bishops.

In what is now the southeastern United States, between 1539 and 1543 Indian peoples faced a brutal invasion by Hernando de Soto and an army of some six hundred men, with two hundred horses, herds of pigs, and dogs trained for war. De Soto already had a reputation even among fellow conquistadors as an accomplished Indian-killer. His troops occupied Indian towns, commandeered food supplies, women, and guides, and pressed on in a relentless search for gold. Spanish diseases, terror tactics, firearms, and war dogs left a trail of devastation from Florida to Texas. Indian people tried to deal with the strangers by established methods of diplomacy and gift-giving, fled from their approach, harassed them with hit-and-run guerilla tactics, and fought desperate battles. After De Soto died in 1542, his lieutenants brought the straggling survivors back to Spanish settlements in Mexico. Several members of the expedition kept journals and later wrote accounts of the campaign (see "A Narrative of the De Soto Invasion," pages 96–104). Most of the powerful and populous chiefdoms that dotted the Southeast in 1540 finally disappeared in the wake of the De Soto expedition. Their descendants rebuilt smaller communities and regrouped to become the peoples Europeans encountered as Creeks, Choctaws, Chickasaws, and others.

As De Soto's men pushed west toward and beyond the Mississippi, another Spanish expedition approached the great river from the west. From 1540 to 1542, Francisco Vásquez de Coronado led an expedition of Spanish soldiers and Indian allies north from New Spain in search of treasures. A Franciscan friar named Marcos de Niza had reported seeing the cities of Cibola in 1539 when he looked from a distance on the Zuni pueblos in western New Mexico. Coronado found the Zuni towns but the inhabitants of Hawikuh resisted in a desperate battle in 1540. As the Spaniards commandeered food, most Pueblo peoples adopted a strategy of urging the invaders north in the hope they would get lost in the Great Plains. An Indian guide whom the Spaniards acquired at the pueblo of Pecos spoke of his native country to the east as a land of great riches. The Spaniards called this place Quivira and wandered on to the Great Plains looking for it. When they reached the villages they called Quivira, probably those of the Wichitas in Kansas, they realized there were no cities of gold and strangled their guide. Meanwhile, in 1542, Juan Rodríguez Cabrillo sailed up the coast of California.

In 1550, the impact of the Spanish invasions on Indian peoples gave rise to a formal debate about the moral basis of Spanish treatment of those peoples. According to a priest named Bartolomé de Las Casas, "What we committed in the Indies stands out among the most unpardonable offenses committed against God and mankind."[14] Las Casas's opponent, Juan de Sepulveda, declared that Indians were naturally inferior and therefore were meant to be slaves; if the Indians refused to submit, the Spanish were justified in using force against them. Indians were like children and would benefit from subordination to "civilized" Christians. Sepulveda would not be the last person to justify taking Indian lands and destroying Indian culture on the assumption that "it was good for them" or that assimilation was their only alternative to destruction.

North American Attempts to Colonize and Christianize

Spaniards established permanent colonies along with conducting expeditions through Indian country. They established missions among the Florida tribes and founded St. Augustine in 1565. In 1598, Juan de Oñate led a colonizing expedition into New Mexico. As elsewhere, the Spaniards aimed to transform Indian peoples into Christians and laborers. In the wake of their conquests to the south, Spaniards established the *encomienda* system, whereby the authorities assigned Indian workers to mines and plantation owners on the understanding that the recipients would pay taxes and teach the workers Christianity. After 1550, however, that system was largely replaced by the *repartimento,* which required Indian towns to supply a pool of labor. Indians resisted the systems, and Spanish missionaries often played a leading role in extracting labor as well as confessions of faith from Indian people. The Spaniards founded Santa Fe in 1610, though Indian laborers built most of the city.

Indian people who survived the demographic disasters unleashed by the diseases the Spaniards brought responded to invasion and colonization in a variety of ways. Many fled from the invaders, generating a "domino effect" of population pressures and group migrations over thousands of miles. Others resisted violently. Guale Indians in Florida killed missionaries in 1597. A year later and more than two thousand miles to the west, the people of Ácoma Pueblo attacked a party of Spanish soldiers; Juan de Oñate retaliated by despatching troops who climbed to the top of the mesa where Ácoma sat, turned cannons on the inhabitants, and killed as many as eight hundred people. The Spaniards put the survivors on trial and "made an example" of them: males over the age of twenty-five were sentenced to have one foot cut off; women over twelve years of age were sentenced to twenty years of servitude; children under twelve were placed in the care of missionaries to be raised as Christians and as servants.

Franciscan friars among the Pueblos forbade dancing and ceremonies and even raided kivas to confiscate religious objects. They also demanded that Pueblo people change their attitudes toward sex: what Pueblo men and women regarded as a natural, life-affirming, and perhaps even a sacred act that united male and female, missionaries taught were "sins of the flesh." Pueblo women traditionally enjoyed considerable influence as a result of their control of the household, their production of corn, and their fertility. The patriarchal Catholic church sought to undermine female influence and rights in Pueblo communities.[15] Pueblo people resisted in subtle ways. They accommodated the Spanish presence and adopted some of the outward forms of Catholicism but kept Spanish missionaries at arm's length, preserving their religion underground in the kivas. Missionaries were unable to stamp out traditional beliefs and rituals even among Pueblos who participated in Catholic services. Friars did not supplant local religious leaders and medicine men. "Kivas and village plazas, not churches and mission compounds, remained the focus of village life," wrote Pueblo anthropologist Alfonso Ortiz. "The Christian faith was, if accepted to any degree, regarded as a supplement, not an alternative, to a religion that had served the Pueblos and their ancestors well."[16]

The Pueblo War of Independence

In 1680, after years of economic and religious oppression, the Rio Grande Pueblos rose in synchronized revolt against the Spaniards. The Pueblo Revolt was one of the most effective Indian resistance movements in American history, what Pueblo historian Joe S. Sando calls "the first American revolution."[17] For more than eighty years, Pueblo peoples had endured Spanish persecution of their religious practices, Spanish demands for corn and labor, and Spanish abuses of their women. New diseases as well as famines resulting from the disruption of their traditional economies had scythed their numbers, from as many as 100,000 in the late sixteenth century to a mere 17,000 by 1680.[18] Many Pueblos blamed their misfortunes on Spanish assaults on the religious ceremonies that kept their world in balance, and there was a resurgence of the ancient rituals. Spanish officials responded with intensified oppression: in 1675 they hanged three Pueblo religious leaders and whipped many others. Meanwhile, drought produced food scarcities among Plains nomads to the east, and the Apaches stepped up their raids on Pueblo farming communities: "the whole land is at war with the widespread heathen nation of the Apache Indians, who kill all the Christian Indians they can find," wrote a Franciscan friar in 1669.[19] By 1680, the Pueblos were facing crisis. They could no longer save themselves by coexistence and accommodation.

The move to open confrontation came initially from northern Pueblo leaders. The Spaniards credited Popé, a medicine man from San Juan Pueblo who had been publicly flogged and fled, with masterminding the revolt. But Luis Tupàtü, governor of Picuris Pueblo and "an Indian respected among all the nations,"[20] and other leaders also played important roles. They made plans to strike at a time when the Spaniards would be low on supplies—just before the arrival of a Spanish supply caravan from the south. Their goals were to cut off the Spanish capital at Santa Fe and overwhelm Spanish settlements in the outlying areas. As historian David Weber notes, it required careful planning to coordinate "an offensive involving some 17,000 Pueblos living in more than two dozen independent towns spread out over several hundred miles and further separated by at least six different languages and countless dialects, many of them mutually unintelligible."[21] Runners carrying knotted strings that indi-

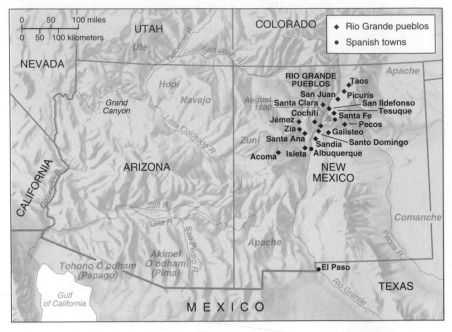

MAP 2.2 The Pueblos and Their Neighbors, c. 1680
The Pueblo War of Independence brought together most of the Pueblo communities of the Rio Grande Valley in unprecedented united action culminating in the siege of the Spaniards at Santa Fe in August 1680 and securing a twelve-year liberation from Spanish rule.

cated the number of days until the revolt went from pueblo to pueblo, "under penalty of death if they revealed the secret."[22]

Word of the planned revolt leaked but Popé advanced the date and, as the viceroy of New Spain reported to the King the following February, the Indians

> fell upon all the pueblos and farms at the same time with such vigor and cruelty that they killed twenty-one missionary religious—nineteen priests and two lay brothers—and more than three hundred and eighty Spaniards, not sparing the defenselessness of the women and children. They set fire to the temples, seizing the images of the saints and profaning the holy vessels with such shocking desecrations and insolences that it is indecent to mention them. They left thirty-four pueblos totally desolated and destroyed, not counting many other farms and haciendas. . . .[23]

Some Indians plunged into rivers to scrub themselves and their clothing, believing that in this way they would be cleansed of "the character of the holy sacraments."[24]

The Indians laid siege to Santa Fe for nine days and cut off the town's water supply. Rather than face the prospect of dying from starvation and thirst, Gov-

Pueblo Revolt at Hopi

In 1680, after years of abuse and amid growing crises, Pueblo Indians turned on their Spanish oppressors and their Franciscan missionaries. In this 1976 painting by artist Fred Kabotie (1900–86), Hopi people at Shongopovi string up and prepare to burn their priest. Other Hopis dismantle the church he had forced them to build and attend. Image 54019/13 Painting by Fred Kabotie, Nakayoma, Hopi (1976). Museum of Indian Arts and Culture/Laboratory of Anthropology, Museum of New Mexico. Photograph by Blair Clark.

ernor Don Antonio de Otermín fought his way through the Pueblo cordon and led about one thousand Spanish soldiers, "their families and servants . . . Mexican natives, and all classes of people" in retreat south to El Paso.[25] Bewildered by the scale and success of the uprising, Spaniards interrogated captured Indians to understand how it happened (see "Declaration of the Indian Juan," pages 106–08).

The coalition that Popé and others had woven together began to unravel soon after the Pueblos had liberated their land. Beginning in 1692, Diego de Vargas reconquered New Mexico for the Spanish. Pueblos revolted again in 1696 but resistance was promptly crushed. Some Pueblos moved beyond the Spaniards' reach, joining Hopis or Navajos in what is now Arizona. Most opted for more subtle forms of resistance, quietly maintaining their cultures and communities, preserving a Pueblo world within a Spanish colony. The Spaniards for their part learned to govern with less of an iron hand. They reduced demands for labor and tribute, and the *encomienda* system was never reestablished after 1680. They assigned land grants to individual Pueblos, giving them clear European title to their own lands. And they adopted a more tolerant approach to the traditional religion of the Pueblos. Spanish New Mexico in the eighteenth century became more concerned with defending its northern borders against Apache, Navajo, Ute, and Comanche attacks than it was with subjugating and converting its Pueblo populations. Change occurred at a slower rate and in both directions as Hispanic and Pueblo people interacted and intermarried. The Spanish colony was restored and survived in New Mexico, but not entirely on Spanish terms. Pueblo people had to make adjustments and accommodations in order to survive, but their resistance and resilience also reshaped Spanish New Mexico.

By the time Mexico surrendered California, Arizona, New Mexico, and parts of Utah and Colorado to the United States in 1848, Indian peoples living in those regions had been in contact with Spanish-speaking peoples for almost three hundred years. Many of them displayed the marks of that contact: they rode horses, tended sheep and goats, carried crucifixes, spoke Spanish, and wore Spanish-style clothing. Indians and Hispanos had intermarried extensively. Despite population collapse and the surface addition of new elements and practices, these people also had long experience of preserving their identity and culture in the face of tremendous pressures. The United States stepped up the pressures, but it was dealing with veterans in a long war for cultural survival.

INDIANS CONFRONT THE FRENCH

While Indian peoples were encountering, accommodating, and resisting Spanish soldiers and priests in the Southeast and Southwest, Indians in the Northeast faced French explorers, traders, and priests. Indians on the Atlantic Coast probably made contact with French fishermen in the fifteenth century. When the Montagnais Indians on the banks of the St. Lawrence River saw their first French ship, they thought it was a floating island; when French sailors then offered them biscuits and wine, the Indians remarked that "the Frenchmen drank blood and ate wood," and threw the biscuits overboard. Micmac people likewise saw an island float close to shore: "there were trees on it, and branches to the trees, on which a number of bears, as they supposed, were crawling about." They soon found that these were not bears, but men with hairy faces. One was a priest "who came towards them making signs of friendship, raising his hands towards heaven, and addressing them in an earnest manner, but in a language which they could not understand."[26] These tribal traditions recall the opening contacts in a relationship in which Frenchmen and Indians met, traded, lived together, and fought over huge areas of North America.

Commerce and Conflict

In 1534, Jacques Cartier sailed up the St. Lawrence River. He visited populous Indian towns at Stadaconna (near present-day Quebec) and Hochelaga and reported extensive crops and orchards covering the banks of the river. Seventy years later, when Samuel de Champlain traveled the same route in 1603, everything had changed. Deadly diseases and intertribal warfare generated by competition for European trade had raged through the valley. The villages were gone and the river banks were overgrown.

Champlain founded Quebec City, explored the lake that bears his name, and helped put France on the path that led to an empire built on the fur trade. But Indians played crucial roles in establishing the patterns and terms of that empire. Champlain began a policy of sending young traders into Indian villages to learn native ways of living and languages. He made alliances with local tribes like the Algonquins and Montagnais to gain access to rich fur territories farther west; the Indians pursued alliances with the French as a means of securing European trade goods.

However, this cooperation threatened the powerful Iroquois of upstate New York. In 1609, a group of Algonquins and Hurons with whom Champlain was traveling encountered an Iroquois war party at the southern end of Lake Champlain. The two groups of Indians engaged in a ritual exchange of insults, paddled their canoes to the shore, and lined up in preparation for battle. Traditionally, such a conflict would have involved firing arrows and hurling spears, with relatively few casualties. Champlain and his French companions, however, introduced a deadly new element into American Indian warfare. Stepping forward with their guns loaded, they opened fire on the Iroquois, killing several of the startled Indians outright and putting the rest to flight.

Indians quickly developed new ways of fighting to adapt to the new equipment. When Indian warriors obtained guns they adopted guerilla tactics that allowed them to employ the new weapons with deadly effect. Indian people traded for a wide range of European manufactured goods, but firearms and metal weapons were among the most sought after. In the hands of skilled archers who could fire arrows accurately and in rapid succession, bows and arrows possessed some notable advantages over seventeenth-century firearms, which were heavy, unreliable, inaccurate, and required constant maintenance. Ethnohistorians now question the degree to which Indian people became immediately dependent on European firearms and are reassessing the long-held belief that Iroquois warfare in this period became driven by the pelts-for-guns trade. The Iroquois continued to wage wars for traditional reasons—to secure honor, revenge, and captives—even as they fought in a world of new economic threats and opportunities.[27] Nevertheless, guns brought supremacy over unarmed neighbors, and a tribe needed guns to survive. Guns could be acquired only by trade with Europeans, and Europeans wanted only one thing: beaver pelts. Indian hunters frequently "trapped out" beaver territories in an effort to supply an endless demand, and competition between Indian bands for trade and furs became intense at the same time that guns made intertribal conflict more lethal. The Iroquois turned to Dutch traders on the Hudson River to supply them with guns. They fought and defeated the local Mahican Indians in the 1620s to secure easier access to the Dutch trade. In the so-called Beaver Wars of the mid-seventeenth century, Iroquois attacked the Huron people and their neighbors who lived in the Great Lakes region, and raided as far afield as

Champlain's Fight with the Iroquois
This engraving from The Voyages of Samuel de Champlain *(1613) is often attributed to Champlain himself, but the inaccuracies in the picture suggest that the artist was not present at the battle. The depiction of this fight in 1609 between Mohawks (right) and Champlain and his Indian allies (left) contains many errors: there are no palm trees on the shores of Lake Champlain, the Indians did not use hammocks, and the boats at the water's edge do not resemble canoes. Nevertheless, the picture does convey the deadly impact of firearms on warriors accustomed to fighting in ranks, using bows and arrows, and protected by wooden or wicker shields.* National Library of Canada.

Quebec, New England, and the Carolinas. The Hurons were still reeling from the impact of a series of epidemic diseases, and the Iroquois assault in 1649 dispersed and destroyed their confederacy. Other tribes in the Ohio valley and Great Lakes area waged recurrent warfare in contests for guns, goods, and furs.

Pelts and Priests

France's empire, based on the fur trade, needed Indian alliances to sustain it. The French offered their religion and metal goods in the hope of winning Indian converts, customers, and allies. Over the course of the seventeenth century,

The French-Indian World, Mid-Seventeenth Century
French knowledge of the geography of North America grew piecemeal as explorers, missionaries, and traders penetrated Indian country and learned about the continent from Native guides and informants. Library of Congress.

French explorers, missionaries, and traders made contact with Indian peoples deep in the heart of the continent. Louis Joliet and Jacques Marquette reached Green Bay and explored the Mississippi River in 1673; Robert de la Salle followed the Mississippi to the Gulf of Mexico in 1682 and claimed the region—Louisiana—for his king, Louis XIV. French traders and explorers pushed out on to the Great Plains in the eighteenth century. French traders lived with Indian tribes, and people of French descent continued to be active in the fur trade long after the collapse of the French empire in North America. Many modern North American cities, including Detroit, St. Louis, and Montreal, began life as early French trading posts, and many families in the Great Lakes region descended from French and Indian marriages.

Black-robed Jesuit priests worked diligently among northern tribes like the Abenaki, Huron, and Algonquin. They learned Indian languages and spent much of their lives in Indian country. Often the missionaries brought their message of salvation at a time when the Indians saw their world falling apart under the impact of new diseases. Father Jean de Brébeuf led the Jesuits to Huron country, north of Lake Ontario, in 1634, but the missionaries en-

Radisson and Groseilliers (1906)

American artist Frederic Remington portrayed the history of the American West in romantic and heroic terms. Here he depicts a typical scene in the French penetration of North America where French explorers, traders, and missionaries relied on Indian paddlers and guides. Pierre Esprit Radisson (1636–1710) was captured by the Iroquois, lived as an adopted Mohawk, and then worked as an interpreter. His brother-in-law, Médard Chouart, Sieur des Groseilliers (c. 1618–c. 1697), worked with Jesuit missionaries in Huronia from 1641 to 1646 (see pages 109–12) and became a coureur de bois *or Indian trader after the Iroquois-Huron wars. Radisson and Groseilliers journeyed west to Lake Superior and Lake Michigan in 1659–60, making contact with Anishinaabeg, Ottawas, Potawatomis, and perhaps Sioux. Buffalo Bill Historical Center, Cody, Wyo. Gift of Mrs. Karl Frank; 14.86.*

countered considerable resistance (see "The Jesuits in New France," pages 109–20). Growing dependence on French trade, increasing assaults from the Iroquois, and devastating smallpox epidemics brought turmoil to Huron villages, however, and hundreds of Hurons turned from the ensuing chaos to the Jesuits.

Throughout New France, many Indians converted to the Catholic faith, settled in French mission villages, attended Mass, and wore crucifixes. Kateri Tekakwitha, a Mohawk girl who lost her family to smallpox when she was a child and was herself disfigured by the disease, converted to Christianity and found meaning and hope in the church. She fled to the Jesuit mission at Kahnawake or Caughnawaga near Montreal, and modeled her life on that of the

Catherine tekakoüita Iroquoise du Saut S. Louis de Montreal en Canada morte en odeur de Sainieté.

Kateri Tekakwitha

Scarred by smallpox and family tragedy in her youth, Kateri Tekakwitha (1656–80) embraced Catholicism and an ascetic way of life at the mission village of Kahnawake. She was beatified in 1980 and may soon be canonized by the Catholic church as the first Native American saint. Newberry Library.

local nuns. She so devoted herself to a life of chastity, prayer, and penitence that when she died at the age of twenty-four in 1680, pilgrims began to visit her shrine, and in the twentieth century the Catholic church began the process of conferring sainthood on her. Others, however, continued to practice their traditional religion or to observe a mixture of the two, and the French did not resort to forced conversions as the Spaniards did.

Recognizing that their empire depended on maintaining a network of Indian alliances, French officials, traders, and officers in Indian country tried to employ diplomacy, tact, and respect for native culture. In the Great Lakes region, French leaders and Indian chiefs worked tirelessly to create order out of the chaos that followed the Beaver Wars. Each group adjusted to the presence and the cultural expectations of the other and shared a common interest in maintaining peace and trade. As historian Richard White observed, French and Indians negotiated "a middle ground" of coexistence that could only be maintained by constant mediation and compromise. Employing the kinship language of forest diplomacy, the French claimed to be "fathers" to the Indians, and Indians often addressed them as such; but fulfilling that role in Indian country meant giving gifts, not giving orders, observing rituals, not expecting obedience, and bestowing protection, not invoking paternal authority.[28] Indian peoples in the Great Lakes and Mississippi valley regions often incorporated Frenchmen into their societies through marriage and the ritual of the calumet, the ceremonial pipe, that brought peace and order to relationships and turned strangers into kinfolk.

Franco-Indian relations were not always smooth. Some Mohawks embraced French Catholicism, but most Iroquois resisted French expansion into their homelands, compelling the French to focus their energies on the West and build a trade empire along the Great Lakes and the area north of the Ohio River. French armies invaded Iroquois country several times in the late seventeenth century. In the 1720s and '30s, the French waged genocidal wars against the Chickasaws and Natchez in the lower Mississippi valley, and against the Fox Indians in Wisconsin. The fur trade that lay at the heart of Franco-Indian relations also produced chaos in Indian country as it facilitated the spread of guns, contagious diseases, and alcohol. Jesuit missionaries who worked to save souls also generated social and political divisions in Indian communities.

Religious and commercial ties bound many tribes to the French, however. Confronted with a powerful rival in the form of English colonies to the south, the French in Canada needed Indian allies to provide assistance in the event of war. The French were relatively few in number, wanted Indian furs rather than land, and carefully cultivated Indian alliances. Confronted with the threat of English settlers encroaching on their lands, many Indians saw the French as their best hope for protection and military support. Thus, the stage was set for Indian involvement in over a half century of bitter conflict between France and England in eighteenth-century North America.

INDIANS CONFRONT THE ENGLISH

The English were relative latecomers in the invasion and colonization of North America. John Cabot explored the coasts of Maine and Nova Scotia in 1497 and 1498, but not until 1607 was the first permanent English settlement founded at Jamestown, Virginia. But the English were not new to colonization: from the Middle Ages, England had extended dominion north into Scotland, west to Wales, and across the Irish Sea. Many of the attitudes and ways of treating "heathen people" that the English developed in Ireland carried over into their dealings with Indians in America. Also, Indian policies that the various English colonies and the British government developed over a century and a half of Indian relations established important precedents for later United States Indian policies. For the Indians, however, relations with the English took place in a context of increasing warfare, as initially amicable relations broke down under intensifying pressure for Indian lands and gave way to open conflict.

Securing a Beachhead in Virginia

One of the first settlements in North America—at Roanoke Island off Virginia in 1585–88—seems to have been destroyed after the English alienated the local Indians. Anglo-Indian relations in Virginia followed a similar course after the establishment of Jamestown. Many of the settlers at Jamestown were soldiers of fortune expecting to win great riches in their enterprise, not farmers who knew how to extract a modest living from the land. Half the settlers died in the first year. Recent findings from analyses of cypress tree growth rings indicate that English attempts to establish colonies at Roanoke and Jamestown occurred during one of the worst droughts ever to affect that area.[29] Few in number, and evidently inept in their new environment, the English cannot have seemed much of a threat to the local Indians, members of the powerful Powhatan chiefdom that embraced some thirty tribes and extended across most of eastern Virginia. The Indians supplied corn to the colonists and the paramount chief, Powhatan, seems to have tried to incorporate the English into his

English View of Virginia

Captain John Smith sought to make the Powhatan Indians of Virginia vassals of the King of England, and the map displays the royal coat of arms. But the map, which Smith made with the help of Indian informants, also reveals the arrogance of English pretension. The English colony at Jamestown is one small settlement in a world full of Indian villages. The detail at top left refers to Smith's capture by Chief Powhatan. Private Collection/The Stapleton Collection/Bridgeman Art Library.

domain. John Smith, the leader of the colonists, recalled several years later how he was captured by the Indians in December 1607 and saved from execution by Powhatan's daughter, Pocahontas, "a childe of twelve or thirteene years of age." Pocahontas threw her body across his "at the minute of my execution." Smith's account has become legendary, perpetuated in history books and Disney movies for its romantic impact rather than its accuracy. In fact, if the events occurred as Smith described them, Pocahontas was most likely performing a prescribed role in a standard ritual by which Powhatan could adopt Smith and make him a *werowance,* or subordinate chieftain.[30]

But Smith was not interested in becoming a secondary leader. Rather, he looked to Spanish experiences in Mexico as his guide to dealing with Indians. The English began to demand and seize corn. "What will it availe you to take that by force you may quickly have by love, or destroy them that provide you food?" asked Powhatan in bewilderment.[31] Tensions increased as the English expanded up the James River. After Smith left the colony in 1609, fighting broke out between

Pocahontas

Pocahontas has been the subject of paintings, movies, and legends. The real Pocahontas was daughter of chief Powhatan, married English colonist John Rolfe, and acted as an intermediary in relations between the English and the Powhatan Indians. She posed for this portrait in 1616 during her visit to England. Dressed in the costume of a lady at court, she looked the part of an "Indian princess" for her English audience. She was about twenty-one and never saw Virginia again; she died not long after the portrait was painted. National Portrait Gallery, Smithsonian Institution/Art Resource.

Indians and English. Pocahontas seems to have played an intermediary role between Indians and colonists, and her marriage to John Rolfe, one of the colonists, in 1614 helped restore peace. She traveled to England with him, only to die there in 1617 as her ship was about to leave for America. In 1622, Powhatan's brother Opechancanough led Indians in what the English called "the Virginia massacre"; four hundred colonists died. But the Indians were unable to drive the English away. The colonists retaliated and kept up pressure on Indian lands. War broke out again in 1644, and the English captured and killed the aged and now blind Opechancanough.

In 1676, without permission from the governor of Virginia, Nathaniel Bacon, an English aristocrat who had come to America three years earlier, led a series of attacks on Indians in the colony. Bacon coerced the Virginia House of Burgesses into appointing him commander-in-chief in the Indian war, but the governor of Virginia declared Bacon a rebel and "Bacon's Rebellion" collapsed when he died soon after in October 1676. As a result of the rebellion, several small reservations—the first in the present United States—were established for the survivors of the tribes that had once comprised the powerful Powhatan chiefdom.

Making a New England

In New England, the English adventurer Sir Humphrey Gilbert dreamed of establishing a colony in the region of Maine, which he called Norumbega, in the 1580s, but died at sea before any of his ambitions could be realized. Several English expeditions skirted the coast of Maine in the first decade of the seventeenth century, trading with the Indians and, on occasion, kidnapping and fighting with them. In 1607, the English established a short-lived colony at Sagadahoc at the mouth of the Kennebec River in Maine. In 1614, John Smith voyaged to the region, produced a detailed map of the area, and renamed it: from Norumbega, or North Virginia, it became New England.

Permanent English settlement in New England began when the Pilgrims settled north of Cape Cod in 1620 and established Plymouth Colony. They found the coast of Massachusetts depopulated by an epidemic that had ravaged the area between 1616 and 1619. God, so the Pilgrims believed, had prepared the way for their coming by sending a plague among the Indians. Fewer than half the Pilgrims survived their first winter in America, but God seemed to offer help again when, early in the spring, "a certaine Indian came bouldly amongst them and spoke to them in broken English, which they could well understand, but marvelled at it."[32] The Indian was Samoset, an Abenaki from Maine who had been brought to Cape Cod on an English ship and learned the language from the sailors. Samoset introduced the Pilgrims to Squanto, a local Patuxet Indian who had been captured, taken to Spain, traveled to England and then back home, only to find his people wiped out by disease. Squanto helped the Pilgrims adjust to their new world; he showed them how to plant corn and where to fish, and functioned as interpreter and intermediary in their dealings with the local Indians. He was, said Governor William Bradford of Plymouth, "a spetiall instrument sent of God."[33] In 1621, Massasoit, chief of the Wampanoags of southern Massachusetts and Rhode Island, made a treaty of peace and friendship with the Pilgrims. The English presence in New England grew when in 1629, the Crown chartered the Massachusetts Bay Colony and more than 20,000 English colonists arrived over the next fourteen years. Boston was founded in 1630 and was soon ringed by English towns inland.

As English settlers arrived at an increasing rate, Indian people found themselves pushed off their lands, deprived of game, and cheated in trade. Smallpox struck the Indians of New England in 1633–34. On the Connecticut River, wrote William Bradford, "it pleased God to visite these Indeans with a great sickness, and such a mortalitie that of a 1000. above 900. and a halfe of them dyed, and many of them did rott above ground for want of buriall."[34] The Pequot Indians of southern Connecticut suffered appalling losses in the epidemic. Two years later, the English went to war against them. The Pequots were a once-powerful people whose location at the mouth of the Connecticut River allowed them to control the region's trade in wampum — strings of shells used in intertribal trade and diplomacy.

The Pequot war has been a source of controversy among historians: some blame the Pequots; others see it as an act of genocide on the part of the English. A recent scholar of the conflict concludes that it was "the messy outgrowth of petty squabbles over trade, tribute, and land" among various Indian tribes, Dutch traders, and English Puritans. The Puritans, however, transformed it into a mythic struggle between savagery and civilization.[35] A Puritan army broke Pequot resistance in a surprise attack on their main village in 1637. Surrounding the palisaded village, the soldiers put the Pequots' lodges to the torch. William Bradford described the ensuing slaughter:

> Those that scaped the fire were slaine with the sword; some hewed to peeces, others rune throw with their rapiers, so as they were quickly dispatchte, and very few escaped. It was conceived they thus destroyed about 400. at this time. It was a fearfull sight to see them thus frying in the fryer, and the streams of blood quenching the same, and horrible was the stinck & sente ther of; but the victory seemed a sweete sacrifice, and they gave the prays thereof to God, who had wrought so wonderfully for them, thus to inclose their enimise in their hands, and give them so speedy a victory over so proud & insulting an enimie."[36]

The English Attack on the Pequots at Their Mystic River Village in 1637
This stylized engraving of the massacre, from John Underhill's Newes from America (1638), shows English soldiers, armed with muskets and backed by a ring of Narragansett Indian allies armed with bows and arrows. They surround the palisaded Pequot village and shoot down the inhabitants as they attempt to escape. Library of Congress.

The English hunted down the survivors, executing some, selling women and children into slavery, and handing over others to the Mohegans and Narragansetts who had assisted the English in the war. At the Treaty of Hartford in 1638, the English terminated Pequot sovereignty and outlawed the use of the tribal name. In the 1640s, the Dutch in New York inflicted similar crushing defeats on the Indians of the lower Hudson valley and Long Island.

In Massachusetts, meanwhile, the Puritan missionary John Eliot worked to convert the Indians to Christianity, gathering converts into "praying towns" where they were expected to give up Indian ways and live like their Christian English neighbors. Working with an Indian interpreter and an Indian printer, Eliot even translated the Bible into the Algonquian language for his Indian congregations. Indian people embraced Christianity in varying degrees and for a variety of reasons. Some found it offered hope and strength in a world that seemed to be unraveling under the impact of disease, alcohol, and escalating violence. For some, Christian services and prayers replaced or supplemented traditional rituals that provided no protection against diseases new to them. Some found in a Christian community, even in Eliot's rigidly regulated praying towns, a refuge from English racism and the turmoil in their own villages. In the pray-ing town of Natick, Massachusetts, for example, individuals and families from several different tribal groups rebuilt a community within their southeastern New England homeland.[37] Algonquian women sometimes found that Christianity honored their traditional roles and gave them an opportunity to learn to read and write. Many Indians blended elements of old and new religions, invested Christian messages and rituals with Native meanings, and made Christianity an Indian religion. Christianity, for some, was a strategy of survival.

King Philip's War

After Massasoit made peace with the English in 1621, he worked to preserve it. Colonists and Indians became, to a degree, economically interdependent. Even the Puritan war against the Pequots of Connecticut in 1636–37 did not spill over into conflict with the Wampanoags. Indians and English managed for a time to share the same world. But Puritans held to the belief that Indians were heathen savages and continued to trespass on Indian lands. Relations rapidly deteriorated after Massasoit's death in 1661. His son, Wamsutta, whom the English called Alexander, continued his father's policy of selling lands to the English, but in 1662, fearing they could not control the young sachem, the Plymouth colonists brought Wamsutta to Plymouth at gunpoint for questioning. Wamsutta was ill, and the colonists released him but kept his two sons as hostages. The ordeal proved too much for the leader, and he died on the way home. Many Wampanoags believed the Puritans had poisoned their sachem.

Wamsutta's younger brother, Metacomet (called King Philip by the English), now became the leader of his people at a critical juncture. The Puritans continued to encroach on Wampanoag land and to assert their judicial authority over Indian actions. Indian hunters found themselves being arrested and jailed for "trespassing" on lands the English now claimed as their own. As the Indians displayed growing resentment, the colonists in 1671 demanded that Metacomet surrender the Wampanoags' weapons. Metacomet was backed into a corner: "I am determined not to live until I have no country," he said.[38] The Plymouth colonists and the Wampanoags squared off for a fight. Rumors of impending war flew through the settlements.

In December 1674, John Sassamon, a Christian Indian, reported to Plymouth governor John Winslow that Metacomet was preparing for war. The next month, Sassamon was found under the ice of a pond with a broken neck. In June, the Puritans seized three Wampanoags and charged them with Sassamon's murder. The evidence was flimsy, but a Plymouth jury found the men guilty and executed them. (Indians sat on the jury but they had no vote.) It was the first time the English had executed an Indian for a crime committed against another Indian.

Metacomet began to forge a multitribal coalition, and Indians and colonists steeled themselves for war. An Indian was shot as he ransacked a colonist's house; a party of Indians retaliated by killing a colonist and his son. Metacomet withdrew from his home in present-day Rhode Island at Montaup, or

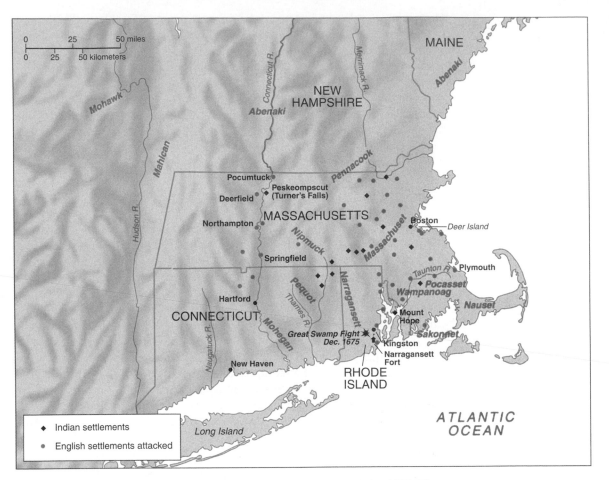

MAP 2.3 New England in King Philip's War, 1675–76

In proportion to population, King Philip's War is reckoned to have been the bloodiest conflict in American history. English towns were attacked and burned. Unknown numbers of Indians died, and many—even the Christian Indians from John Eliot's praying towns west of Boston—were relocated and suffered terrible hardship confined on Deer Island in Boston Harbor.

Mount Hope to the English, and took refuge with Wetamoo, the "squaw sachem" of the Pocassets and widow of Wamsutta. Some Indians faced difficult decisions and divided loyalties as the impending war threatened to sever ties they had built with English neighbors over the previous generation.[39] Wetamoo seems to have been reluctant to commit to war but many of her warriors rallied to Metacomet, as did most Nipmucks in central Massachusetts. Awashunkes, squaw sachem of the Sakonnets of Rhode Island, put her people under the protection of the Plymouth colony. The Mohegan sachem, Uncas, supported the English as he had in the Pequot War as a way of preserving Mohegan autonomy and enhancing his own position.[40] The powerful Narragansetts declared their intention to remain neutral, and many of Metacomet's followers sent their women and children to take refuge with them. Many Christian Indians supported the English but, fearing all Indians, the colonists incarcerated even the Christian Indians from John Eliot's praying towns on Deer Island in Boston Harbor.

Scattered acts of violence escalated into the brutal conflict known as King Philip's War. Metacomet's warriors ambushed English militia companies and burned English towns. In November 1675, the English declared war against the Narragansetts, interpreting their offer of sanctuary to noncombatants from other tribes as an act of hostility. The next month, an English army of more than a thousand men marched through deep snow and attacked the main Narragansett stronghold near Kingston, Rhode Island. Hundreds of Narragansett men, women, and children died in what became known as the Great Swamp Fight. An Englishman, Joshua Tefft, who had an Indian wife and was in the Narragansett stronghold at the time of the attack, was captured, hanged, and quartered by the Puritans (an incident mentioned on page 127 by William Apess in the document "Eulogy on King Philip"[41]). The surviving Narragansetts joined Metacomet's war of resistance.

Both sides suffered terribly that winter from cold and hunger. English homes lay in ruins and fields lay barren. Puritan ministers thundered from pulpits that the war was God's way of punishing his sinful people. Disease broke out in the Indian camps. Metacomet tried to broaden the conflict by bringing in the Mahicans and Abenakis; Governor Edmund Andros of New York prevailed upon the Mohawks to attack Metacomet's army in its winter camps, a devastating blow to the Wampanoag alliance which now found itself fighting on two fronts.

In February 1676, the Indians attacked and burned Lancaster, Massachusetts. They took two dozen prisoners, including Mary Rowlandson, who later produced a narrative of her experience as a captive with Metacomet's army as the war was slipping away from the Indians.[42] The tribal coalition was falling apart and Indian resistance was faltering. In April, the colonists captured the Narragansett sachem Canonchet and handed him over to their Mohegan allies for execution. In May, Captain William Turner attacked an Indian encampment at Peskeompscut, now Turner's Falls, Massachusetts, where families had gathered for springtime fishing on the Connecticut River. Surprising the Indians at dawn, Turner's men killed hundreds of people. Captain Benjamin Church, effectively applying Indian tactics of guerilla warfare, harried Metacomet's remaining followers. That summer, he captured Metacomet's wife, Wootonekanuska, and nine-year-old son and sent them to Plymouth for trial; they were probably sold as slaves in the West Indies. On the night of August 11, Church and his men, including some Indian allies, caught up with Metacomet. Jolted from sleep, Metacomet ran for safety but was shot and killed. Church ordered Metacomet's head cut off and his body cut into quarters. Even after the leader's death, the war continued along the coast of Maine, but Indian power and independence in southern New England were broken. Many Indians fled north, joining Abenakis in Maine, Vermont, and New Hampshire and siding with the French in future conflicts against the English who had driven them from their homelands. The war left a searing impression on New England and a bitter legacy for Anglo-Indian relations (see "Two Views of King Philip, pages 121–30).

Within the five-year period 1675–80, Indian peoples in New England and New Mexico fought wars of independence against Europeans who had invaded and had begun colonizing their homelands. In both instances, the Indians scored impressive victories. The defeat of those movements did not mean the end of Indian resistance, which continued in other ways and other places, but it did mark the end of a phase: on both sides of the continent, Europeans had weathered their most severe test and secured their beachheads. By the end of the seventeenth century, the outposts of New France dotted the shores of the St. Lawrence, the Great Lakes, and the Mississippi. New Spain included Florida and New Mexico. New Netherland had fallen. English colonists had settled from New England to Georgia. African slaves were being shipped to American ports to provide labor for colonial agriculture. Throughout most of North America, Indian peoples followed their ancient cycles of life without disruption, participated in ceremonies to keep crops growing, game plentiful, and the universe in harmony, and lived, fought, and traded with other Indians, not with Europeans. But European people, European animals, and European diseases were infiltrating North America. Europeans were a permanent presence, and colonial America was being established in Indian America.

References

1. James H. Merrell, *The Indians' New World: Catawbas and Their Neighbors from European Contact through the Era of Removal* (Chapel Hill: University of North Carolina Press, 1989).
2. Oliver Dunn and James E. Kelley, Jr., trans. and eds., *The Diario of Christopher Columbus's First Voyage to America, 1492–1493* (Norman: University of Oklahoma Press, 1989), 65–69, 143.
3. Reuben G. Thwaites, ed., *The Jesuit Relations and Allied Documents: Travels and Explorations of the Jesuit Missionaries in New France, 1610–1791,* 71 vols. (Cleveland: Burrows Brothers, 1896–1901), 1:175.
4. Quoted in Colin G. Calloway, ed., *The World Turned Upside Down: Indian Voices from Early America* (Boston: Bedford Books, 1994), 50–52.
5. Karl W. Butzer, ed., "The Americas before and after 1492: Current Geographical Research," *Annals of the Association of American Geographers* 82 (1992), 359.
6. Calloway, ed., *The World Turned Upside Down,* 80.
7. Alfred W. Crosby, Jr., "Virgin Soil Epidemics as a Factor in the Aboriginal Depopulation in America," *William and Mary Quarterly,* 3d series, 33 (1976), 289–99.
8. Russell Thornton, *American Indian Holocaust and Survival: A Population History since 1492* (Norman: University of Oklahoma Press, 1987); Thornton, "Aboriginal North American Population and Rates of Decline, ca. A.D. 1500–1900," *Current Anthropology* 38 (1997), 310–15; Noble David Cook, *Born to Die: Disease and New World Conquest, 1492–1650* (Cambridge: Cambridge University Press, 1998). The depopulation estimates are by William M. Denevan, ed., *The Native Population of the Americas in 1492,* 2d ed. (Madison: University of Wisconsin Press, 1992),

xvii–xxix. David Henige, *Numbers from Nowhere: The American Indian Contact Population Debate* (Norman: University of Oklahoma Press, 1998), critiques the premises, methodology, and conclusions of scholars he calls "the High Counters."

9. Cyclone Covey, trans. and ed., *Cabeza de Vaca's Adventures in the Unknown Interior of America* (Albuquerque: University of New Mexico Press, 1993), 56–60.

10. The *Requerimiento* is quoted in Albert L. Hurtado and Peter Iverson, eds., *Major Problems in American Indian History: Documents and Essays* (Lexington, Mass.: D. C. Heath, 1994), 83–84. Patricia Seed examines Spanish protocols of conquest in *Ceremonies of Possession in Europe's Conquest of the New World, 1492–1640* (Cambridge: Cambridge University Press, 1995), chap. 3.

11. Quoted in W. George Lovell, "'Heavy Shadows and Black Night': Disease and Depopulation in Colonial Spanish America," in Butzer, ed., "The Americas before and after 1492," 429.

12. Bernal Díaz del Castillo, *The Discovery and Conquest of Mexico* (New York: Farrar, Straus, 1956), 190–91. See also Stuart B. Schwartz, ed., *Victors and Vanquished: Spanish and Nahua Views of the Conquest of Mexico* (Boston: Bedford/St. Martin's, 2000).

13. Covey, trans. and ed., *Cabeza de Vaca's Adventures in the Unknown Interior of America,* 56, 65, 106, 123, 128.

14. Bartolomé de Las Casas, *History of the Indies* (New York: Harper and Row, 1971), 289.

15. Ramón A. Gutiérrez, *When Jesus Came, the Corn Mothers Went Away: Marriage, Sexuality, and Power in New Mexico, 1500–1846* (Stanford: Stanford University Press, 1991).

16. Alfonso Ortiz, *The Pueblo* (New York: Chelsea House, 1994), 50.

17. Joe S. Sando, *Pueblo Nations: Eight Centuries of Pueblo Indian History* (Santa Fe: Clear Light Publishers, 1992), 63.

18. Daniel T. Reff, *Disease, Depopulation, and Culture Change in Northwestern New Spain, 1518–1764* (Salt Lake City: University of Utah Press, 1991), 229.

19. Quoted in Andrew L. Knaut, *The Pueblo Revolt of 1680: Conquest and Resistance in Seventeenth-Century New Mexico* (Norman: University of Oklahoma Press, 1995), 162.

20. Charles Wilson Hackett, ed., and Charmon Clair Shelby, trans., *The Revolt of the Pueblo Indians of New Mexico and Otermín's Attempted Reconquest, 1680–1682,* 2 vols. (Albuquerque: University of New Mexico Press, 1942), 2:237.

21. David J. Weber, *The Spanish Frontier in North America* (New Haven: Yale University Press, 1992), 134.

22. Hackett, ed., *The Revolt of the Pueblo Indians,* 2:246. Pueblo people still commemorate this event each year with foot races along the routes taken by the runners. Peter Nabokov, *Indian Running* (Santa Barbara: Capra Press, 1981).

23. Hackett, ed., *The Revolt of the Pueblo Indians,* 2:3.

24. Hackett, ed., *The Revolt of the Pueblo Indians,* 2:247.

25. Hackett, ed., *The Revolt of the Pueblo Indians,* 1:19.

26. Calloway, ed., *The World Turned Upside Down,* 33–34.

27. Brian J. Given, *A Most Pernicious Thing: Gun Trading and Native Warfare in the Early Contact Period* (Ottawa: Carleton University Press, 1994). Jose Antonio Brandao, *"Your Fyre Shall Burn No More": Iroquois Policy toward New France and Its Native Allies to 1701* (Lincoln: University of Nebraska Press, 1997), provides a thorough reassessment of the "Beaver Wars" thesis.

28. Richard White, *The Middle Ground: Indians, Empires, and Republics in the Upper Great Lakes, 1650–1815* (Cambridge: Cambridge University Press, 1991).

29. "Drought May Have Doomed Lost Colony" (*New York Times*, April 24, 1998, A1, A14).

30. Smith's account of his rescue, embellished in a letter to the Queen of England at the time Pocahontas visited London, is reprinted in Karen Ordahl Kupperman, ed., *Captain John Smith: A Select Edition of His Writings* (Chapel Hill: University of North Carolina Press, 1988), 69. In Smith's writings of his life and his adventures, beautiful women save him from dire peril "not once but three times." Helen C. Rountree, *Pocahontas's People: The Powhatan Indians of Virginia through Four Centuries* (Norman: University of Oklahoma Press, 1990), 38. For a discussion of the rescue as ritual adoption see Frederic W. Gleach, *Powhatan's World and Colonial Virginia: A Conflict of Cultures* (Lincoln: University of Nebraska Press, 1997), chap. 4.

31. Quoted in Calloway, ed., *The World Turned Upside Down*, 39.

32. Harvey Wish, ed., *William Bradford: Of Plymouth Plantation* (New York: Capricorn Books, 1962), 72.

33. Wish, ed., *William Bradford: Of Plymouth Plantation*, 73.

34. Wish, ed., *William Bradford: Of Plymouth Plantation*, 176.

35. Alden T. Vaughan, *New England Frontier: Puritans and Indians, 1620–1675* (New York: W. W. Norton, 1979), and Francis Jennings, *The Invasion of America: Indians, Colonialism, and the Cant of Conquest* (New York: W. W. Norton, 1976), represent the polar positions in the debate. Alfred A. Cave, *The Pequot War* (Amherst: University of Massachusetts Press, 1996), 178.

36. Wish, ed., *William Bradford: Of Plymouth Plantation*, 184.

37. Jean M. O'Brien, *Dispossession by Degrees: Indian Land and Identity in Natick, Massachusetts, 1650–1790* (Cambridge: Cambridge University Press, 1997), 11.

38. Quoted in Russell Bourne, *The Red King's Rebellion: Racial Politics in New England, 1675–1678* (New York: Oxford University Press, 1990), 107.

39. James D. Drake, *King Philip's War: Civil War in New England* (Amherst: University of Massachusetts Press, 1999).

40. On Uncas and Awashunkes, see Eric S. Johnson, "Uncas and the Politics of Contact," and Ann Marie Plane, "Putting a Face on Colonization: Factionalism and Gender Politics in the Life History of Awashunkes, the 'Squaw Sachem' of Saconet," in Robert S. Grumet, ed., *Northeastern Indian Lives, 1636–1816* (Amherst: University of Massachusetts Press, 1996), 39–47, 140–65.

41. Colin G. Calloway, "Rhode Island Renegade: The Enigma of Joshua Tefft," *Rhode Island History* 19 (1984), 136–45.

42. Neal Salisbury, ed., *The Sovereignty and Goodness of God by Mary Rowlandson* (Boston: Bedford Books, 1997).

Suggested Readings

Bourne, Russell. *The Red King's Rebellion: Racial Politics in New England, 1675–1678* (New York: Oxford University Press, 1990).

Cave, Alfred. *The Pequot War* (Amherst: University of Massachusetts Press, 1996).

Cronon, William. *Changes in the Land: Indians, Colonists, and the Ecology of New England* (New York: Hill and Wang, 1983).

Crosby, Alfred. *The Columbian Exchange: Biological and Cultural Consequences of 1492* (Westport, Conn.: Greenwood Press, 1972).

Delâge, Denys. *Bitter Feast: Amerindians and Europeans in Northeastern North America* (Vancouver: University of British Columbia Press, 1993).

Drake, James D. *King Philip's War: Civil War in New England* (Amherst: University of Massachusetts Press, 1999).

Gallay, Alan. *The Indian Slave Trade: The Rise of the English Empire in the American South, 1677–1717* (New Haven: Yale University Press, 2002).

Gleach, Frederic W. Powhatan's *World and Colonial Virginia: A Conflict of Cultures* (Lincoln: University of Nebraska Press, 1997).

Henige, David. *Numbers from Nowhere: The American Indian Contact Population Debate* (Norman: University of Oklahoma Press, 1998).

Hudson, Charles. *Knights of Spain, Warriors of the Sun: Hernando de Soto and the South's Ancient Chiefdoms* (Athens: University of Georgia Press, 1997).

Jennings, Francis. *The Invasion of America: Indians, Colonialism, and the Cant of Conquest* (New York: W. W. Norton, 1976).

Knaut, Andrew. *The Pueblo Revolt: Conquest and Resistance in Seventeenth-Century New Mexico* (Norman: University of Oklahoma Press, 1995).

Kupperman, Karen Ordahl. *Indians and English: Facing Off in Early America* (Ithaca: Cornell University Press, 2000).

Lepore, Jill. *The Name of War: King Philip's War and the Origins of American Identity* (New York: Knopf, 1998).

Mancall, Peter C., and James H. Merrell, eds. *American Encounters: European Contact to Indian Removal, 1500–1850* (New York: Routledge, 2000).

Milanich, Jerald T. *Florida Indians and the Invasion from Europe* (Gainesville: University Press of Florida, 1995).

Richter, Daniel K. *Facing East from Indian Country: A Native History of Early America* (Cambridge, Mass.: Harvard University Press, 2000).

Rountree, Helen C. *Pocahontas's People: The Powhatan Indians of Virginia through Four Centuries* (Norman: University of Oklahoma Press, 1990).

Salisbury, Neal. *Manitou and Providence: Indians, Europeans, and the Making of New England, 1500–1643* (New York: Oxford University Press, 1982).

Steele, Ian K. *Warpaths: Invasions of North America* (New York: Oxford University Press, 1994).

Thornton, Russell. *American Indian Holocaust and Survival: A Population History since 1492* (Norman: University of Oklahoma Press, 1987).

Trigger, Bruce G. *Natives and Newcomers: Canada's "Heroic Age" Reconsidered* (Montreal: McGill-Queen's University Press, 1986).

Weber, David J. *The Spanish Frontier in North America* (New Haven: Yale University Press, 1992).

White, Richard. *The Middle Ground: Indians, Empires, and Republics in the Upper Great Lakes, 1650–1815* (Cambridge: Cambridge University Press, 1991).

D O C U M E N T S

A Narrative of the De Soto Invasion

The invasion of what is now the southeastern United States by Hernando de Soto in 1539 produced the first major encounter between Indian peoples and Europeans east of the Mississippi. For four years, De Soto and his army of more than six hundred men blundered and plundered their way through present-day Florida, Georgia, Alabama, North and South Carolina, Tennessee, Mississippi, Louisiana, Arkansas, and Texas, searching for riches to match those won by Cortés in Mexico and Pizarro in Peru. De Soto's men encountered thousands of Indian people and generated immeasurable chaos in Indian country. They killed, kidnapped, raped, and enslaved hundreds of people. Disease and famine killed thousands more in the wake of the expedition.

Hernando de Soto was born in poverty in southeastern Spain a few years after Columbus's first voyage to America. He came to the New Spain as a teenager and won his spurs in the bloody Spanish conquest of Panama between 1517 and 1523. He participated in the invasion of Nicaragua in 1523–27, and was one of Pizarro's captains in the conquest of Peru in 1531–35. He earned a reputation for ruthlessness and courage and returned to Spain in 1536 a wealthy man. Appointed governor of Cuba, he secured official approval to undertake the conquest of La Florida, the Spanish designation for the entire region we now know as the southeastern United States.

Leaving Spain in 1538, De Soto organized his expedition in Cuba, and landed at Tampa Bay on the west coast of Florida in May 1539. On a foray inland, the Spaniards came upon one of their countrymen, Juan Ortiz, who had been with an expedition of Pánfilo de Narváez in 1528 and for ten years had been held captive by the Indians. Ortiz served as an interpreter for the expedition until his death in the winter of 1541–42. Pushing north, the Spaniards passed the following winter in Apalachee country near present-day Tallahassee. In 1540, they headed through Georgia, the Carolinas, and Tennessee. Moving south into Alabama, the conquistadors encountered the tall cacique or chief, Tascaluça, who lured them into ambush and a bloody day-long battle at the town of Mabila in October. The Spaniards passed a hard winter in Mississippi. Crossing the great river in 1541, they moved from village to village through Arkansas during the winter of 1541–42, and then swung back into Louisiana. There, De Soto died of fever in May 1542. His followers tied his body to a log and sank it in the Mississippi to prevent the Indians from finding it.

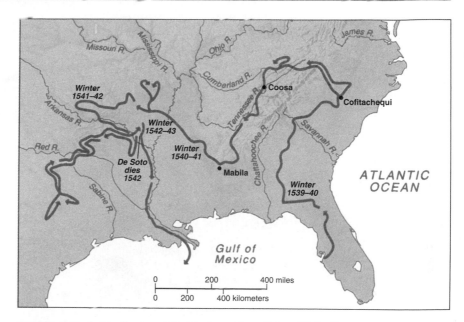

MAP 2.4 Probable Route of the De Soto Expedition, 1539–42
The conquistadors' hopes of finding great wealth and emulating the successes of Cortés and Pizarro drew them across vast expanses of the American South, disrupting Indian lives and destabilizing relations between chiefdoms.
Based on Charles Hudson and Carmen C. Tesser, eds., The Forgotten Centuries (Athens: University of Georgia Press, 1994).

    With Luis de Moscoso de Alvarado as leader, the bedraggled remnants of De Soto's once-formidable army tried to reach Mexico via Texas. Failing to do so, they returned again to the Mississippi, built barges, and sailed into the Gulf of Mexico. The survivors reached the Spanish settlement at Vera Cruz in September 1543. After four years and four months and crossing almost four thousand miles of Indian country, the conquistadors had found no great riches. Almost half of them had died in the attempt.[1]

    If the expedition was a failure from the Spanish point of view, it was a disaster for the Indians. De Soto's men entered a world full of Indians, passed through some densely settled regions, and dealt with powerful chiefs. When Europeans returned to the interior of the Southeast in the next century, the great chiefdoms were gone, many of the towns had disappeared, and the people they met were fewer in number, poorer, and more scattered. De Soto's army spent one hundred days plundering and terrorizing the wealthy chiefdom of Coosa in Georgia in 1540; just twenty years later, another Spanish expedition led by Tristan de Luna found the region overgrown and depopulated. Luna's men almost starved in places where De Soto's men had found thriving and well-fed

Spaniards Meet with a Mississippian Chief
Standing at the head of structured and ranked social systems, Mississippian chiefs com-
manded reverence from their followers and expected respect from visitors. As this twenti-
eth-century painting by John Berkey shows, De Soto and his conquistadors sometimes
tried to secure what they wanted—food, information, women, and wealth—by diplo-
macy as well as by force, and in such instances they relied heavily on the linguistic skills of
former Indian captive Juan Ortiz. More often, however, the Spaniards employed the
threat or reality of force and often kidnapped chiefs as a way of securing safe and sure
passage from one chiefdom to the next. John Berkey/National Geographic Society.

Indian communities. In southern Alabama, where the slaughter at Mabila had
occurred, Indians "told the Spaniards their country had once been great and
powerful, until strangers looking like them had come and destroyed their crops
and cities, and killed their people."[2] The human landscape of the South changed
forever after De Soto's men cut their bloody trail across it, although we'll never
know how much of the massive depopulation and collapse of previously flour-
ishing Mississippian societies was directly attributable to the *entrada*.[3]

Like the soldiers who followed Cortés and Pizarro, De Soto's men believed they were engaged in a great adventure, making history. Several participants produced chronicles of the expedition. These accounts provide glimpses of the Indian civilizations encountered and offer scholars a source that, combined with archaeological and ethnohistorical evidence, is crucial in reconstructing a picture of southeastern Mississippian societies at the time of first contacts with Europeans. Nevertheless, the chronicles have serious limitations as historical sources. For the most part they focus on the epic qualities of the invasion rather than on detailed and accurate portrayals of native peoples. Most were written long after the event and drew on each other; many exaggerated the scale of the battles and the heroism of the Spaniards in overcoming adversity.

The most detailed eyewitness account was written by an anonymous Portuguese officer in De Soto's army who called himself the Gentleman of Elvas. First published in Portuguese in 1557, fourteen years after the expedition, and later translated into Spanish, Dutch, French, and English, Elvas's account is generally considered dependable, but he probably wrote it from memory several years after the expedition, made some errors, and inserted long, flowery speeches to bolster the romantic quality of the narrative.[4] Long after the event and based on other sources as well as stories he had heard and interviews with survivors of the expedition, Garçilaso de la Vega wrote a lengthy and literary account entitled *The Florida of the Inca.* The son of a Spanish captain and an Inca noblewoman, Garçilaso was "a true son of the colonial society that was built on the wreckage of the Inca empire," and gives a *mestizo*° perspective on the invasion. His account is rich in detail and imagery, but mingles fact and fiction in an attempt to dramatize the glories of the bloody conquest. A modern ethnohistorian describes it as "a fancifully embellished compendium of participants' memoirs, folklore, and literary allusions."[5]

The account whose extract is reprinted here is attributed to Rodrigo Rangel, De Soto's private secretary, who evidently kept a diary on the expedition, although this has never been found. This account is generally considered accurate, but was written a few years after the expedition by Gonzalo Fernandez de Oviedo, the royal historian, who added passages of his own to the text and used it to depict De Soto, whom he had known, as a liar and a butcher.°[6]

Accounts of conquest written by the invaders can give at best only a one-sided view of events. However, the work produced by Rangel and/or Oviedo is useful on a number of levels. It dispels the notion that the Spaniards were a monolithic force driven by single-minded purpose, and reveals disunity within the Spanish ranks. The account begins as the Spaniards approach the town of Tascaluça or Tuscaloosa, just prior to the battle at Mabila in October 1540.

°A *mestizo* is a person of mixed Indian and European ancestry or parentage.

°Although Oviedo is believed to have gathered his information from Rangel by 1546, the manuscript was not published in Spanish until 1851. The first English translation appeared in 1904.

▶ **Questions for Consideration**

1. What purposes and biases are evident in the Rangel document? What evidence is there that it might have been the work of two authors? Which parts may have been added at a later date by Oviedo?

2. Other accounts of the expedition often emphasize the courage and nobility of the Spaniards as explorers and conquistadors, but this one portrays the men of the expedition as "lost" in more ways than one. What does the document reveal about Spanish strategies for sustaining their expedition and maintaining power?

3. What particular aspects of Spanish behavior most infuriated the Indians? Were they necessarily the ones the chronicler found most reprehensible?

4. What does the document reveal about the nature of the societies the Spaniards encountered and about the Indians' strategies for dealing with the invaders?

RODRIGO RANGEL
Account of the Northern Conquest and Discovery of Hernando de Soto (c. 1546)

The historian [Oviedo] asked a well-informed gentleman who found himself present with this Governor and who went with him all through that northern land, why, in each place that this Governor and his army arrived, they asked for those tamemes or burden-bearing Indians, and why they took so many women, and these not old nor the most ugly; and after giving them what they had, why they detained the caciques° and

Source: *Account of the Northern Conquest and Discovery of Hernando de Soto* by Rodrigo Rangel, in Lawrence A. Clayton, Vernon James Knight, Jr., and Edward C. Moore, eds., *The De Soto Chronicles: The Expedition of Hernando de Soto to North America in 1539–1543*, 2 vols. (Tuscaloosa: University of Alabama Press, 1993), 1:288–94. Copyright © 1993 by The University of Alabama Press. Reprinted with the permission of the publisher.
    °Village chiefs.

principal Indians, and why, where they went, they never halted or settled anywhere; saying that was neither to populate nor to conquer, but rather to disturb and devastate the land and take away the liberty of all the natives, and not to convert or make one Indian a Christian or a friend. He responded and said: that they took those burden-bearing Indians or tamemes in order to have more slaves and servants, and to carry their supplies, and whatever they stole or what they gave them; and that some died and others fled or weakened, and thus they had need to renew and take more; and that they wanted the women also in order to make use of them and for their lewdness and lust, and that they baptized them more for their carnal intercourse than to instruct them in the faith; and that if they detained the caciques and principal Indians, this was advisable so that the others, their subjects, would be quiet and not obstruct their thefts and prevent what they might wish to do in their land. As to where they were going, neither the Governor nor they knew, except that his intent was to find some land so rich that it might sate his greed, and to find out about the great secrets that the Governor said that he had heard about those places, according to many reports that had been given to him. And that as regards disturbing the land and not settling it, nothing else could be done until they came upon a site that would satisfy them. Oh, lost people; oh, diabolical greed; oh, bad conscience; oh, unfortunate soldiers; how you did not understand in how much danger you walked, and how wasted your lives and without tranquility your souls! Why did you not remember that truth that the glorious St. Augustine, deploring of the present misery of this life, says: "This life is a life of misery, decrepit and uncertain, a toilsome and unclean life, a life, my Lord, of evils, queen of the proud, filled with miseries and with dread; this is not life, nor can it be called that, but rather death, since in a moment it is finished by various mutations and diverse kinds of death"? Listen well, Catholic reader, and do not lament any less the conquered Indians than their Christian conquerors, or killers of themselves and of those others, and attend to the incidents of this ill-governed Governor, instructed in the school of Pedrarias de Avila, in the dissipation and devastation of the Indians of Castilla de Oro, graduate in the killing of the natives of Nicaragua and canonized in Peru, according to the Order of the Pizarros. And freed from all those hellish passages, and having gone to Spain loaded with gold, neither as a bachelor nor a married man could he rest, nor did he know how to, without returning to the Indies to spill human blood, not content with that already spilled, and to depart this life in the manner that farther on will be related; and giving cause for so many sinners, deceived by his vain words, to be lost with him. See how much more he wanted than what that queen or cacica of Cofitachequi, lady of Talimeco, offered him, where she told him that in that place of hers he

would find so many pearls that all the horses of his army would not be able to carry them; and receiving him with such humanity, see how he treated her. Let us go on, and do not forget this truth that you have read, how in proof of how many pearls she offered him, this Governor and his people now carried eight or nine arrobas of pearls, and you will see what enjoyment they got of them in what follows. . . .

On Sunday, the tenth of October [1540], the Governor entered in the town of Tascaluça, which was called Athahachi, a new town; and the cacique was on a balcony that was made on a mound to one side of the plaza, about his head a certain headdress like an *almaizar*° worn like a Moor, which gave him an appearance of authority, and a *pelote* or blanket of feathers down to his feet, very authoritative, seated upon some high cushions, and many principals of his Indians with him. He was of as tall a stature as that Antonico of the guard of the Emperor our lord, and of very good proportions, a very well built and noble man; he had a young son as tall as he, but he was more slender. Always in front of this cacique was a very graceful Indian on foot, with a sunshade, on a pole, which was like a round and very large fly-flap, with a white cross similar to that which the knights of the Order of St. John of Rhodes wear, in the middle of a black field. And although the Governor entered in the plaza and dismounted and went up to him, he did not rise but rather was quiet and composed, as if he were a king, and with much gravity. The Governor sat with him a bit, and after a little while he rose and said that they should go to eat and took him with him, and Indians came to dance; and they danced very well in the way of the peasants of Spain, in such a manner that it was a pleasure to see.

At night he wished to go, but the adelantado° [De Soto] told him that he had to sleep there; and

---

°A type of turban.
°An honorific title for a commander.

he understood it and showed that he scoffed at such a decision, being lord, to give him so suddenly a restraint or impediment to his liberty; and concealing his intentions in the matter, he then dispatched his principal Indians, each one by himself, and he slept there to his sorrow. The next day the Governor asked for tamemes and one hundred Indian women, and the cacique gave them four hundred tamemes and said that he would give them the rest of the tamemes and the women in Mabila, the province of a principal vassal of his, and the Governor was content that the rest of that his unjust demand would be satisfied in Mabila. And he commanded that he be given a horse and some buskins and a cloak of scarlet cloth to keep him content. But as the cacique had already given him four hundred tamemes, or more accurately slaves, and was to give him one hundred women in Mabila, and those which they most desired, see what contentment could be given him by those buskins and mantle and the chance to ride on horseback, since he thought that he was riding on a tiger or on a ferocious lion, because horses were held in great dread among those people.

Finally, Tuesday, the twelfth of October, they left from that town of Atahachi, taking the cacique, as has been said, and with him many principals and always the Indian with the sunshade in front of his lord, and another with a cushion; and that day they spent the night in the open. And the next day, Wednesday, they arrived at Piachi, which is a high town, upon the bluff of a rocky river, and its cacique was malicious, and he took a position to resist the crossing; but in fact they crossed the river with difficulty, and two Christians were killed, and the principals who accompanied the cacique went away. In that town Piachi it was found out that they had killed Don Teodoro, and a black man, who came forth from the boats of Pánfilo de Narváez.

On Saturday, the sixteenth of October, they departed from there and went to a forest, where one of the two Christians that the Governor had sent to Mabila came; and he said that there was a great gathering of armed people in Mabila. The next day they went to a palisaded town, and messengers from Mabila came who brought to the cacique much chestnut bread, for there are many and good chestnuts in his land. On Monday, the eighteenth of October, the day of St. Luke, the Governor arrived at Mabila, having passed that day through some towns. But these towns detained the soldiers, pillaging and scattering themselves, for the land seemed populous; thus only forty on horseback arrived in advance guard with the Governor, and since they were a little detained, in order for the Governor not to show weakness, he entered in the town with the cacique, and all entered with him. The Indians then did an *areito*, which is their kind of ball with dancing and singing.

While watching this, some soldiers saw them placing bundles of bows and arrows secretively in some palm leaves, and other Christians saw that the huts were filled high and low with concealed people. The Governor was warned, and he placed his helmet on his head and commanded that all should mount their horses and warn all the soldiers who had arrived; and scarcely had they left, when the Indians took command of the gates of the wall of the town. And Luis de Moscoso and Baltasar de Gallegos and Espíndola, Captain of the guard, and seven or eight soldiers remained with the Governor. And the cacique plunged into a hut and refused to come out from it; and then they began to shoot arrows at the Governor. Baltasar de Gallegos entered for the cacique, and he not wanting to leave, he [Gallegos] cut off the arm of a principal Indian with a slash. Luis de Moscoso, awaiting him at the door in order not to leave him alone, was fighting like a knight, and he did everything possible, until he could suffer no more, and said: "Señor Baltasar de Gallegos, come forth, or I will have to leave you, for I cannot wait for you any longer."

During this time Solís, a resident of Triana of Seville, and Rodrigo Rangel, had mounted. They were the first, and for his sins Solís was then shot down dead. Rodrigo Rangel arrived near the gate of the town at the time that the Governor and two soldiers of his guard with him were leaving, and about him [the Governor] were more than seventy Indians, who halted out of fear of the horse of Rodrigo Rangel, and he [the Governor] wishing him to give it to him, a black man arrived with his own [horse]; and he commanded Rodrigo Rangel to aid the Captain of the guard who remained behind, who came out very fatigued, and with him a soldier of the guard, and he on horseback faced his enemies until he got out of danger. And Rodrigo Rangel returned to the Governor, and he drew out more than twenty arrows that he carried hanging from his armor, which was a quilted tunic of thick cotton; and he commanded Rangel to guard [the body of] Solís until he could bring him out from among their enemies, so that they might not carry him within, and so that the Governor might go to collect the soldiers. There was so much virtue and shame this day in all those who found themselves in this first attack and the beginning of this bad day. They fought admirably, and each Christian did his duty as a most valiant soldier. Luis de Moscoso and Baltasar de Gallegos left with the remaining soldiers through another gate.

In effect, the Indians ended up with the town and all the property of the Christians and with the horses that they left tied within, which they then killed. The Governor gathered all the forty on horseback who were there, and they arrived at a large plaza in front of the principal gate of Mabila, and there the Indians came forth, without daring to venture far from the palisade; and in order to draw them out, they pretended that those on horseback were fleeing at a gallop, withdrawing far from the ramparts, and the Indians, believing it, ventured from the town and from the palisade in their pursuit, desirous of employing their arrows, and when it was time, those on horseback turned around on their enemies, and before they could take shelter, they lanced many.

Don Carlos wished to go with his horse up to the gate, and they gave his horse an arrow wound in the breast, and not being able to turn [his horse], he dismounted to draw out the arrow, and another came which struck him in the neck, above his shoulder, from which, asking for confession, he fell dead. The Indians did not dare to venture again from the palisade. Then, the adelantado encircled them on many sides until all the army arrived, and they entered it through three sides setting fire, first cutting through the palisade with axes; and the fire traveled so that the nine arrobas of pearls that they brought were burned, and all the clothes and ornaments and chalices and moulds for wafers, and the wine for saying mass, and they were left like Arabs, empty-handed and with great hardship.

The Christian women, who were slaves of the Governor, had remained in a hut, and some pages, a friar, a cleric, and a cook and some soldiers; they defended themselves very well from the Indians, who could not enter until the Christians arrived with the fire and brought them out. And all the Spaniards fought like men of great spirit, and twenty-two of them died, and they wounded another one hundred and forty-eight with six hundred and eighty-eight arrow wounds, and they killed seven horses and wounded twenty-nine others. The women and even boys of four years struggled against the Christians, and many Indians hanged themselves in order not to fall into their hands, and others plunged into the fire willingly. See what spirit those tamemes had. There were many great arrow shots sent with such fine will and force, that the lance of a gentleman, named Nuño de Tovar, which was of two pieces of ash and very good, was pierced by an arrow through the middle from side to side, like a drill, without splintering anything, and the arrow made a cross on the lance.

Don Carlos died this day, and also Francisco de Soto, nephew of the Governor, and Juan de Gamez de Jaen, and Men Rodríguez, a good Portuguese gentleman, and Espinosa, a good gentleman, and another called Velez, and one Blasco de Barcarrota and other very honored soldiers; and the wounded were most of the people of worth and of honor. They killed three thousand Indians, in addition to which there were many others wounded, which they found afterward dead in the huts and by the roads. Nothing was ever learned of the cacique [Tascaluça], either dead or alive; the son was found lanced.°

The battle having taken place in the manner stated above, they rested there until Sunday, the fourteenth of November, treating the wounded and the horses, and they burned a great part of the land. From the time that this Governor and his armies entered in the land of Florida up to the time that they left from there, all the dead were one hundred and two Christians, and not all, to my way of thinking, in true penitence. . . .

°According to Charles Hudson, Rangel provides probably the most accurate estimate of casualaties. Armor kept Spanish casualties low, although the Spaniards sustained a total of 668 wounds. See Charles Hudson, *Knights of Spain, Warriors of the Sun* (Athens: University of Georgia Press, 1997), 244.

References

1. Charles Hudson, a leading scholar of the De Soto expedition, provides a concise itinerary in Hudson and Carmen Chaves Tesser, eds., *The Forgotten Centuries: Indians and Europeans in the American South, 1521–1704* (Athens: University of Georgia Press, 1994), 74–103; and in his *Knights of Spain, Warriors of the Sun: Hernando de Soto and the South's Ancient Chiefdoms* (Athens: University of Georgia Press, 1997).
2. David Ewing Duncan, *Hernando de Soto: A Savage Quest in the Americas* (New York: Crown Publishers, 1995), 388.
3. See, for example, Russell Thornton, Jonathan Warren, and Tim Miller, "Depopulation in the Southeast after 1492," in John W. Verano and Douglas H. Ubelaker, eds., *Disease and Demography in the Americas* (Washington, D.C.: Smithsonian Institution Press, 1992), 187–95. Ann F. Ramenofsky and Patricia Galloway in "Disease and the Soto Entrada," in Patricia Galloway, ed., *The Hernando de Soto Expedition: History, Historiography and "Discovery" in the Southeast* (Lincoln: University of Nebraska Press, 1997), 259–79, list nineteen diseases possibly brought by the Spanish and, despite slim evidence, identify ten diseases that were likely to have been transmitted to the Indians.
4. Duncan, *Hernando de Soto: A Savage Quest in the Americas*, xxiv–xxv.
5. Hudson, *Knights of Spain, Warriors of the Sun*, 448; Patricia Galloway, *Choctaw Genesis, 1500–1700* (Lincoln: University of Nebraska Press, 1995), 20. See Frances G. Crowley, "Garçilaso de la Vega, the Inca," in Lawrence A. Clayton, Vernon James Knight, Jr., and Edward C. Moore, eds., *The De Soto Chronicles: The Expedition of Hernando de Soto to North America in 1539–1543*, 2 vols. (Tuscaloosa: University of Alabama Press, 1993), 2:1–24.
6. Clayton, Knight, and Moore, eds., *The De Soto Chronicles* 1:249. On Oviedo, see Juan Bautista de Avalle-Arce, "Gonzalo Fernández de Oviedo y Valdés: Chronicler of the Indies," and José Rabasa, "The Representation of Violence in the Soto

Narratives," in Galloway, ed., *The Hernando de Soto Expedition,* 369–79, 380–409. Galloway contains valuable discussions of the various source materials of the expedition.

Suggested Readings

Clayton, Lawrence A., Vernon James Knight, Jr., and Edward C. Moore, eds. *The De Soto Chronicles: The Expedition of Hernando de Soto to North America in 1539–1543,* 2 vols. (Tuscaloosa: University of Alabama Press, 1993).

Duncan, David Ewing. *Hernando de Soto: A Savage Quest in the Americas* (New York: Crown Publishers, 1995).

Galloway, Patricia, ed. *The Hernando de Soto Expedition: History, Historiography, and "Discovery" in the Southeast* (Lincoln: University of Nebraska Press, 1997).

Hudson, Charles. *Knights of Spain, Warriors of the Sun: Hernando de Soto and the South's Ancient Chiefdoms* (Athens: University of Georgia Press, 1997).

Hudson, Charles, and Jerald T. Milanich. *Hernando de Soto and the Indians of Florida* (Gainesville: University Press of Florida, 1993).

Hudson, Charles, and Carmen Chaves Tesser, eds. *The Forgotten Centuries: Indians and Europeans in the American South, 1521–1704* (Athens: University of Georgia Press, 1994).

An Indian Explanation
of the Pueblo Revolt

In 1681, Governor Otermín attempted to retake New Mexico. Divisions had surfaced among the Pueblos, and the town of Isleta welcomed the returning Spaniards. But elsewhere, Pueblo resistance remained strong, and Otermín was able to do little more than interrogate captured Indians as to their reasons "for rebelling, forsaking the law of God and obedience to his Majesty, and committing such grave and atrocious crimes." The Indians said "that the uprising had been deliberated upon for a long time." Some placed blame on Popé or the devil. Others cited continued Spanish oppression and said "they were tired of the work they had to do for the Spaniards . . . and, that being weary, they rebelled." One eighty-year-old man, whose life spanned the era of Spanish colonial rule, declared "that the resentment which all the Indians have in their hearts has been so strong, from the time this kingdom was discovered, because the religious and the Spaniards took away their idols and forbade their sorceries and idolatries." He had "heard this resentment spoken of since he was of an age to understand."[1]

A twenty-eight-year old Indian named Juan, from the pueblo of Tesuque, provided the following information after Spanish priests absolved him and had him swear an oath to tell the truth.

▶ Questions for Consideration

1. What do the interrogation of Juan and his answers indicate about the Spaniards' understanding of the revolt?

2. What do they reveal about the respondent's understanding of Spaniards?

3. What information do they convey about the causes of the revolt and the situation in Pueblo country?

Declaration of the Indian Juan (1681)

Having been questioned according to the tenor of the case, and asked for what reasons and causes all the Indians of the kingdom in general rebelled, returning to idolatry, forsaking the law of God and obedience to his Majesty, burning images and temples, and committing the other crimes which they did, he said that what he knows concerning this question is that not all of them joined the said rebellion willingly; that the chief mover of it is an Indian who is a native of the pueblo of San Juan, named El Popé, and that from fear of this Indian all of them joined in the plot that he made. Thus he replied.

Asked why they held the said Popé in such fear and obeyed him, and whether he was the chief man of the pueblo, or a good Christian, or a sorcerer, he said that the common report that circulated and still is current among all the natives is that the said Indian Popé talks with the devil, and for this reason all held him in terror, obeying his commands although they were contrary to the orders of the señores governors, the prelate and the religious, and the Spaniards, he giving them to understand that the word which he spoke was better than that of all the rest; and he states that it was a matter of common knowledge that the Indian Popé, talking with the devil, killed in his own house a son-in-law of his named Nicolás Bua, the governor of the pueblo of San Juan. On being asked why he killed him, he said that it was so that he might not warn the Spaniards of the rebellion, as he intended to do. And he said that after the rebellion was over, and the señor governor and cap-

tain-general had left, defeated, the said Indian Popé went in company with another native of the pueblo of Taos named Saca through all the pueblos of the kingdom, being very well pleased, saying and giving the people to understand that he had carried out the said uprising, and that because of his wish and desire the things that had happened had been done, the religious and the people who died had been killed, and those who remained alive had been driven out. He [the deponent] said that the time when he learned of the rebellion was three days before it was carried out.

Asked how the said Indian, Popé, convoked all the people of the kingdom so that they obeyed him in the treason, he said that he took a cord made of maguey fiber and tied some knots in it which indicated the number of days until the perpetration of the treason. He sent it through all the pueblos as far as that of La Isleta, there remaining in the whole kingdom only the nation of the Piros who did not receive it; and the order which the said Popé gave when he sent the said cord was under strict charge of secrecy, commanding that the war captains take it from pueblo to pueblo. He [the deponent] learned of this circumstance after the kingdom was depopulated.

Asked to state and declare what things occurred after they found themselves without religious or Spaniards, he said that what he, the declarant, knows concerning this question is that following the departure of the señor governor and captain-general, the religious, and the Spaniards who were left alive, the said Indian, Popé, came down in person with all the war captains and many other Indians, proclaiming through the pueblos that the devil was very strong and much better than God, and that they should burn all the images and temples, rosaries and crosses, and that all the people should discard the names given

Source: Declaration of the Indian Juan, December 18, 1681, in Charles Wilson Hackett, ed., *Revolt of the Pueblo Indians of New Mexico and Otermín's Attempted Reconquest, 1680–1682*, 2 vols. (Albuquerque: University of New Mexico Press, 1942), vol. 2, 233–35.

them in holy baptism and call themselves whatever they liked. They should leave the wives whom they had taken in holy matrimony and take any one whom they might wish, and they were not to mention in any manner the name of God, of the most holy Virgin, or of the Saints, on pain of severe punishment, particularly that of lashing, saying that the commands of the devil were better than that which they taught them of the law of God. They were ordered likewise not to teach the Castilian language in any pueblo and to burn the seeds which the Spaniards sowed and to plant only maize and beans, which were the crops of their ancestors. And he said that all the nations obeyed in everything except in the command concerning Spanish seeds, which some of them sowed because of their fondness for the Spaniards. Thus he replied.

Asked whether they thought that perhaps the Spaniards would never return to this kingdom at any time, or that they would have to return as their ancestors did, and in this case what plans or dispositions they would make, and what else he knew about this matter, he said that they were of different minds regarding it, because some said that if the Spaniards should come they would have to fight to the death, and others said that in the end they must come and gain the kingdom because they were sons of the land and had grown up with the natives.

References

1. Charles Wilson Hackett, ed., *The Revolt of the Pueblo Indians of New Mexico and Otermín's Attempted Reconquest, 1680–1682,* 2 vols. (Albuquerque: University of New Mexico Press, 1942), 1:24–25, 61; 2:232–49.

Suggested Readings

Gutiérrez, Ramón. *When Jesus Came the Corn Mothers Went Away: Marriage, Sexuality, and Power in New Mexico, 1500–1846* (Stanford: Stanford University Press, 1991).

Hackett, Charles Wilson, ed., *The Revolt of the Pueblo Indians of New Mexico and Otermín's Attempted Reconquest, 1680–1682,* 2 vols. (Albuquerque: University of New Mexico Press, 1942).

Knaut, Andrew L. *The Pueblo Revolt of 1680: Conquest and Resistance in Seventeenth-Century New Mexico* (Norman: University of Oklahoma Press, 1995).

Riley, Carroll L. *The Kachina and the Cross: Indians and Spaniards in the Early Southwest* (Salt Lake City: University of Utah Press, 1999).

Sando, Joe S. *Pueblo Nations: Eight Centuries of Pueblo Indian History* (Santa Fe: Clear Light Publishers, 1992).

Weber, David J., ed. *What Caused the Pueblo Revolt of 1680?* (Boston: Bedford/St. Martin's, 1999).

Jesuits in New France

The Huron or Wendat Indians were early and important allies of the French. Huronia, their homeland, was relatively small, no more than twenty miles north to south and thirty-five miles across, between Lake Simcoe and Georgian Bay in present-day Ontario. The area was densely settled, with between twenty and thirty thousand people living in villages. Lying at the northern limit of southern Ontario's rich farmland, it was also an important center of trade between hunters and farmers in the upper Great Lakes region. From the villages of the Hurons, French traders and missionaries could set forth north, west, and south into distant Indian regions.

In 1609, Huron and Algonquin warriors arrived at Quebec to ask Samuel de Champlain for support in a raid against their Iroquois enemies. Champlain was anxious to establish commercial relations with the Hurons and Algonquins and agreed. He accompanied the Indians to Lake Champlain and participated in a skirmish with the Mohawks. Three years later, Champlain despatched a young man named Étienne Brulé to live among the Hurons and strengthen Franco-Huron trade connections. (Brulé "went Indian" and spent the rest of his life in Indian country.) In 1615, Champlain journeyed to Huronia himself and was compelled to join the Hurons in another battle against the Iroquois. The Iroquois became increasingly disturbed at the threat posed by this alliance between their old enemies and the French. Meanwhile, the French looked to Huronia as the potential center of a new Catholic and commercial empire. Father Gabriel Sagard, a Recollect missionary who traveled to Huronia and lived there in the winter of 1623–24, found much in Huron life that was distasteful, and reported many things he did not understand, but he acknowledged the love Hurons showed one another: "If they were Christians these would be families among whom God would take pleasure to dwell," he wrote.[1]

An English expedition captured Quebec in 1629 and Champlain returned to France. But this loss was reversed by a peace settlement in Europe and Champlain was back in 1633. Accompanying him was Father Jean de Brébeuf. Born to a noble family in Normandy in 1593, Brébeuf entered the Society of Jesus in 1617 and was sent to Canada in 1625 as one of the first Jesuit missionaries. After a year among the Montagnais on the north shore of the St. Lawrence, he went to Huronia in 1626, where he lived for three years in the village of Toanché, and learned the Huron's language. In 1634, he set out again for Huronia. With the exception of three years in Quebec, Brébeuf spent the rest of his life in Indian country.

The Jesuit order had a long record of missionary work, and their North American venture was launched with characteristic zeal. They learned native languages, committed their lives to their work, and risked (some would say sought) martyrdom in their efforts to save people they regarded as heathen. At first, the Jesuits, like earlier Recollect missionaries in New France and Puritan ministers in New England, tried to coerce their Indian converts to abandon traditional ways. In time, they tempered their approach, realizing that Indian people were more likely to accept a new religion if they did not have to give up being Indians in order to become Christians. Jesuits adopted Indian words and ways to get their message across: Brébeuf himself presented the Huron council with a wampum belt of 1200 beads to "smooth their road to Paradise."[2]

Even so, Brébeuf's mission struggled in its early years. The Hurons tolerated the black-gowned Jesuits because they wanted to maintain trade relations with the French, but they resented the missionaries' intrusion in their rituals and ceremonies. The Jesuits criticized Huron sexual practices, gender relations, child-rearing, and festivals. They won few converts in these early years.

Then disease began to take its toll. The location and participation of the Hurons in trade networks reaching to the Atlantic guaranteed that European germs as well as European goods would enter their villages. Smallpox struck in the mid-1630s. Influenza hit in 1636. Smallpox returned in 1639. At first, many Hurons blamed the Jesuits for the disaster and some sought vengeance, but soon Huron people began to ask for baptism.

By 1640, smallpox had killed as many as half the Hurons. The disease devastated Huron society, killing children and elders. With their loved ones dying before their eyes, many Hurons began to listen to the words of Jesuit missionaries who, unaffected by the disease, were clearly men of great power. The Huron shamans had failed to forewarn or protect their people from the catastrophe; perhaps the Jesuit shamans had some answers, perhaps they were right that the Hurons were being punished for living in sin. At the same time, escalating raids by Iroquois war parties threatened the Hurons. By the mid-1640s, hundreds of Hurons were accepting baptism from the Jesuit fathers, although they may well have seen it as a curative ritual rather than a path to heaven.

Whether or not the Jesuits saved the Hurons from damnation, they were unable to save them from the Iroquois. In the spring of 1649, the Iroquois launched a massive assault on Huronia. They destroyed the mission villages at St. Ignace and St. Louis, captured Fathers Brébeuf and Gabriel Lalemant, and tortured them to death. Huronia was destroyed, its people killed, starved, and scattered; many of the survivors were adopted into Iroquois communities as was the tradition with captives. The missions lay in ruins and the Jesuits abandoned Huronia. Some Hurons eventually resettled at the mission village of Lorette near Quebec.

The Jesuits blamed the Iroquois for the destruction of Huronia and historians have generally followed their lead, but as the Huron scholar Georges Sioui reminds us, European microbes had already done their deadly work, leaving relatively little for the Iroquois to destroy. In Sioui's view, Hurons and Iroquois were both engaged in a desperate war for cultural survival in the wake of Eu-

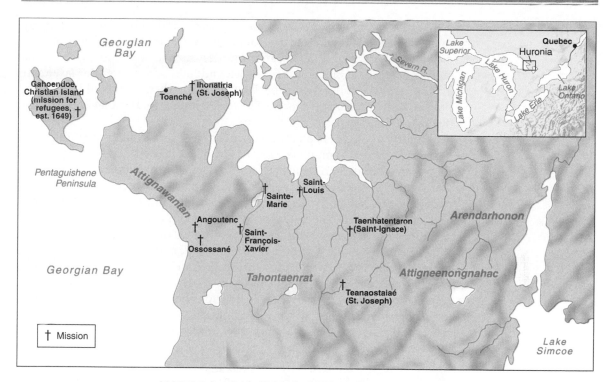

MAP 2.5 Jesuits in Huronia, 1615–1650

In the early seventeenth century, the Hurons—four major tribes living in between eighteen and twenty-five villages—represented a rich field for Jesuit missionaries. This map shows the location of the major tribal groups, key Jesuit missions, and the village of Toanché, with which Brébeuf was associated. From Bitter Feast: Amerindians and Europeans in Northeastern North America, 1600–1664, *by Denys Delâge, translated by Jane Brierly.*
© *The University of British Columbia Press, 1993. Reprinted with permission of the publisher. All rights reserved by the publisher.*

ropean invasion, and the Iroquois were less interested in destroying an economic rival than in adopting captives to offset their own losses.[3] The Jesuits themselves contributed to the collapse of Huronia by undermining stabilizing traditions, advocating social revolution, and promoting factionalism.

Brébeuf's account of his journey to Huronia and his work there in 1635 gives a graphic portrayal of the hardships Jesuit missionaries faced as they trekked deep into Indian country and of the challenges they then faced in Huron villages. Brébeuf also wrote an instruction manual for subsequent missionaries to the Hurons, telling them what to expect and how to behave. These instructions convey Jesuit strategy in dealing with the Indians and suggest some of the reasons why they fared better than their English rivals in winning Indian converts. Jesuit missionaries went into Indian country and adapted to the way of life there. They did not die of smallpox, they did not seek Indian land, they did not molest Indian women. Instead, they traveled with Indians by canoe and snowshoe, they shared Indian lodges and Indian food, they displayed impressive shamanistic powers, and they dedicated their lives to their calling. Brébeuf himself paid with his life and shared in the disaster that befell Huronia in 1649.

Brébeuf wrote based on his experience of daily life among the Hurons, but his relation allows us only a glimpse of Huronia filtered through the eyes of a seventeenth-century missionary. From 1611 to 1768, Jesuit missionaries in North America followed the practice of sending lengthy reports to their superior in Quebec, who compiled them into *Relations* and sent them on to Paris. The Jesuit order published the reports from 1632 to 1673 to publicize its missionary work. The *Jesuit Relations* was edited and translated by American historian Reuben Gold Thwaites in 71 volumes and published at the turn of the twentieth century; it is one of the most comprehensive sources of Indian-European encounters in seventeenth-century North America. These reports contain information on everyday life, religious beliefs, and customs, but their main purpose was to record the progress of the missions rather than to document the life of the Indians. Jesuits went into Indian country to change the culture they saw, not to study it.

▶ **Questions for Consideration**

In Jesuit eyes, Indians were humans, but they were heathen savages who needed to be saved from eternal damnation. In the following document, Brébeuf sees only part of the Huron universe.

1. What does he see and not see?

2. What does he not understand?

3. What could he never understand?

JEAN DE BRÉBEUF
The Mission to the Hurons (1635–37)

RELATION OF WHAT OCCURRED AMONG THE HURONS IN THE YEAR 1635

. . . I arrived among the Hurons on the fifth of August, after being thirty days on the road in continual work, except one day of rest, which we took in the country of the Bissiriniens.° I landed at the port of the village of Toanché or of *Teandeouiata*, where we had formerly lived; but it was with a little misfortune. My Savages, — forgetting the kindness I had lavished upon them and the help I had afforded them in their sickness, and notwithstanding all the fair words and promises they had given me, — after having landed me with some Church ornaments and some other little outfit, left me there quite alone, and resumed their route toward their villages, some seven leagues distant.° My trouble was that the village of Toanché had changed since my departure, and that I did not know precisely in what place it was situated. The shore being no longer frequented, I could not easily ascertain my way; and, if I had known it, I could not from weakness have carried all my little baggage at once; nor could I risk, in that place, doing this in two trips. That is why I entreated my Savages to accompany me as far as the village, or at least to sleep on the shore for the night, to watch my clothes while I went to make inquiries.

But their ears were deaf to my remonstrances. The only consolation they gave me was to tell me that some one would find me there. Having considered that this shore was deserted, and that I might remain there a long time before any one in the village would come to find me, I hid my packages in the woods; and, taking what was most precious, I set out to find the village, which fortunately I came upon at about three-quarters of a league — having seen with tenderness and emotion, as I passed along, the place where we had lived, and had celebrated the Holy sacrifice of the Mass during three years, now turned into a fine field; and also the sight of the old village, where, except one cabin, nothing remained but the ruins of the others. . . .

I was occupied some two weeks in visiting the villages, and bringing together, at much expense and trouble, all our party, who landed here and there, and who, not knowing the language, could only have found us out after much toil. It is true that one of our men was able to come without any other address than these two words, *Echom, Ihonatiria*,° which are my name and that of our village. Among all the French I do not find anyone who has had more trouble than Father Davost and Baron; the Father from the wicked treatment of his Savages, Baron from the length of the journey. He occupied forty days on the road; often he was alone with a Savage, paddling in a canoe very large and very heavily laden. He had to carry all his packages himself; he had narrow escapes three or four times in the torrents; and, to crown his

---

Source: Reuben G. Thwaites, ed., *The Jesuit Relations and Allied Documents: Travels and Explorations of the Jesuit Missionaries in New France, 1610–1791*, 71 vols. (Cleveland: Burrows Brothers, 1896–1901), 8:89–153; 12:117–24.

°The Bissiriniens were the Nipissing Indians who lived north of the Hurons.

°The village of Toanché was located northeast of Thunder Bay on the Penetanguishene peninsula.

°Ihonatiria was the most northerly Huron village, on the Penetanguishene peninsula.

difficulty, much of his property was stolen. Truly, to come here, much strength and patience are needed; and he who thinks of coming here for any other than God, will have made a sad mistake. . . .

Although it is a desirable thing to gather more fruit, and to have more listeners in our assemblies, which would make us choose the larger villages, rather than the small, nevertheless, for a beginning, we have thought it more suitable to keep in the shadow, as it were, near a little village where the inhabitants are already disposed to associate with the French, than to put ourselves suddenly in a great one, where the people are not accustomed to our mode of doing things. To do otherwise would have been to expose new men, ignorant of the language, to a numerous youth, who by their annoyances and mockery, would have brought about some disturbance. . . .

I cannot better express the fashion of the Huron dwellings than to compare them to bowers or garden arbors,— some of which, in place of branches and vegetation, are covered with cedar bark, some others with large pieces of ash, elm, fir, or spruce bark; and, although the cedar bark is best, according to common opinion and usage, there is, nevertheless, this inconvenience, that they are almost as susceptible to fire as matches. Hence arise many of the conflagrations of entire villages. There are cabins or arbors of various sizes, some two brasses° in length, others of twenty, of thirty, of forty; the usual width is about four brasses, their height is about the same. There are no different stories; there is no cellar, no chamber, no garret. It has neither window nor chimney, only a miserable hole in the top of the cabin, left to permit the smoke to escape. This is the way they built our cabin for us.

The people of Oënrio° and of our village were employed at this by means of presents given them. It has cost us much exertion to secure its comple-

tion, we were almost into October before we were under cover. As to the interior, we have suited ourselves; so that, even if it does not amount to much, the Savages never weary of coming to see it, and seeing it, to admire it. We have divided it into three parts. The first compartment, nearest the door, serves as an ante-chamber, as a storm door, and as a storeroom for our provisions, in the fashion of the Savages. The second is that in which we live, and is our kitchen, our carpenter shop, our mill, or place for grinding wheat, our Refectory, our parlor and our bedroom. On both sides, in the fashion of the Hurons, are two benches which they call *Endicha,* on which are boxes to hold our clothes and other little conveniences; but below, in the place where the Hurons keep their wood, we have contrived some little bunks to sleep in, and to store away some of our clothing from the thieving hands of the Hurons. They sleep beside the fire, but still they and we have only the earth for bedstead; for mattress and pillows, some bark or boughs covered with a rush mat; for sheets and coverings, our clothes and some skins do duty.

The third part of our cabin is also divided into two parts by means of a bit of carpentry which gives it a fairly good appearance, and which is admired here for its novelty. In the one is our little Chapel, in which we celebrate every day holy Mass, and we retire there daily to pray to God. It is true that the almost continual noise they make usually hinders us, and compels us to go outside to say our prayers. In the other part we put our utensils. The whole cabin is only six brasses long, and about three and a half wide. That is how we are lodged, doubtless not so well that we may not have in this abode a good share of rain, snow and cold. However, they never cease coming to visit us from admiration, especially since we have put on two doors, made by a carpenter, and since our mill and our clock have been set to work. It would be impossible to describe the astonishment of these good people, and how much they admire the intelligence of the French. No one has come who has not wished to turn the mill; nevertheless

---

°A linear measure; one brass equals about five feet.
°A village due south of Toanché.

we have not used it much, inasmuch as we have learned that our Sagamités° are better pounded in a wooden mortar, in the fashion of the Savages, than ground within the mill. I believe it is because the mill makes the flour too fine. As to the clock, a thousand things are said of it. They all think it is some living thing, for they cannot imagine how it sounds of itself; and when it is going to strike, they look to see if we are all there, and if some one has not hidden, in order to shake it.

They think it hears, especially when, for a joke, one of our Frenchmen calls out at the last stroke of the hammer, "That's enough," and then it immediately becomes silent. They call it the Captain of the day. When it strikes they say it is speaking; and they ask when they come to see us how many times the Captain has already spoken. They ask us about its food; they remain for a whole hour, and sometimes several, in order to be able to hear it speak. They used to ask at first what it said. We told them two things that they have remembered very well; one, that when it sounded four o'clock of the afternoon, during winter, it was saying, "Go out, go away that we may close the door," for immediately they arose, and went out. The other, that at midday it said, *yo eiouahuoua,* that is, "Come, put on the kettle;" and this speech is better remembered than the other, for some of these spongers never fail to come at that hour, to get a share of our Sagamité. They eat at all hours, when they have the wherewithal, but usually they have only two meals a day, in the morning and in the evening; consequently they are very glad during the day to take a share with us.

Speaking of their expressions of admiration, I might here set down several on the subject of the loadstone, into which they looked to see if there was some paste; and of a glass with eleven facets, which represented a single object many

times, of a little phial in which a flea appears as large as a beetle; of the prism, of the joiner's tools; but above all, of the writing; for they could not conceive how, what one of us, being in the village, had said to them, and put down at the same time in writing, another, who meantime was in a house far away, could say readily on seeing the writing. I believe they have made a hundred trials of it. All this serves to gain their affections, and to render them more docile when we introduce the admirable and incomprehensible mysteries of our Faith; for the belief they have in our intelligence and capacity causes them to accept without reply what we say to them.

It remains now to say something of the country, of the manners and customs of the Hurons, of the inclination they have to the Faith, and of our insignificant labors.

As to the first, the little paper and leisure we have compels me to say in a few words what might justly fill a volume. The Huron country is not large, its greatest extent can be traversed in three or four days. Its situation is fine, the greater part of it consisting of plains. It is surrounded and intersected by a number of very beautiful lakes or rather seas, whence it comes that the one to the North and to the Northwest is called "fresh-water sea."° We pass through it in coming from the Bissiriniens. There are twenty Towns, which indicate about 30,000 souls speaking the same tongue, which is not difficult to one who has a master. It has distinctions of genders, number, tense, person, moods; and, in short, it is very complete and very regular, contrary to the opinion of many. . . .

It is so evident that there is a Divinity who has made Heaven and earth that our Hurons cannot entirely ignore it. But they misapprehend him grossly. For they have neither Temples, nor Priests, nor Feasts, nor any ceremonies.

°Corn pounded into meal and boiled in water, sometimes with meat, fish, or vegetables added; called "samp" or "hominy" by the English.

°Lake Huron.

They say that a certain woman called *Eataensic* is the one who made earth and man. They give her an assistant, one named *Jouskeha,* whom they declare to be her little son, with whom she governs the world. This *Jouskeha* has care of the living, and of the things that concern life, and consequently they say that he is good. *Eataensic* has care of souls; and, because they believe that she makes men die, they say that she is wicked. And there are among them mysteries so hidden that only the old men, who can speak with authority about them, are believed.

This God and Goddess live like themselves, but without famine; make feasts as they do, are lustful as they are; in short, they imagine them exactly like themselves. And still, though they make them human and corporeal, they seem nevertheless to attribute to them a certain immensity in all places.

They say that this *Eataensic* fell from the Sky, where there are inhabitants as on earth, and when she fell, she was with child. If you ask them who made the sky and its inhabitants, they have no other reply than that they know nothing about it. And when we preach to them of one God, Creator of Heaven and earth, and of all things, and even when we talk to them of Hell and Paradise and of our other mysteries, the headstrong reply that this is good for our Country and not for theirs; that every Country has its own fashions. But having pointed out to them, by means of a little globe that we had brought, that there is only one world, they remain without reply.

I find in their marriage customs two things that greatly please me; the first, that they have only one wife; the second, that they do not marry their relatives in a direct or collateral line, however distant they may be. There is, on the other hand, sufficient to censure, were it only the frequent changes the men make of their wives, and the women of their husbands.

They believe in the immortality of the soul, which they believe to be corporeal. The greatest part of their Religion consists of this point. We have seen several stripped, or almost so, of all their goods, because several of their friends were dead, to whose souls they had made presents. Moreover, dogs, fish, deer, and other animals have, in their opinion, immortal and reasonable souls. In proof of this, the old men relate certain fables, which they represent as true; they make no mention either of punishment or reward, in the place to which souls go after death. And so they do not make any distinction between the good and the bad, the virtuous and the vicious; and they honor equally the interment of both, even as we have seen in the case of a young man who poisoned himself from the grief he felt because his wife had been taken away from him. Their superstitions are infinite, their feast, their medicines, their fishing, their hunting, their wars, — in short almost their whole life turns upon this pivot; dreams, above all have here great credit.

As regards morals, the Hurons are lascivious, although in two leading points less so than many Christians, who will blush some day in their presence. You will see no kissing nor immodest caressing; and in marriage a man will remain two or three years apart from his wife, while she is nursing. They are gluttons, even to disgorging; it is true, that does not happen often, but only in some superstitious feasts,° — these, however, they do not attend willingly. Besides they endure hunger much better than we, — so well that after having fasted two or three entire days you will see them still paddling, carrying loads, singing, laughing, bantering, as if they had dined well. They are very lazy, are liars, thieves, pertinacious beggars. Some consider them vindictive; but, in my opinion, this vice is more noticeable elsewhere than here.

We see shining among them some rather noble moral virtues. You note, in the first place, a

---

°"Eat all feasts," where guests were expected to consume everything, even if they had to empty their stomachs by vomiting in order to do so, usually had a ritual purpose. Bruce G. Trigger, *The Huron: Farmers of the North* (New York: Holt, Rinehart and Winston, 1969), 96.

great love and union, which they are careful to cultivate by means of their marriages, of their presents, of their feasts, and of their frequent visits. On returning from their fishing, their hunting, and their trading, they exchange many gifts; if they have thus obtained something unusually good, even if they have bought it, or if it has been given to them, they make a feast to the whole village with it. Their hospitality towards all sorts of strangers is remarkable; they present to them, in their feasts, the best of what they have prepared, and, as I have already said, I do not know if anything similar, in this regard, is to be found anywhere. They never close the door upon a Stranger, and, once having received him into their houses, they share with him the best they have; they never send him away, and when he goes away of his own accord, he repays them by a simple "thank you."

What shall I say of their strange patience in poverty, famine, and sickness? We have seen this year whole villages prostrated, their food a little insipid sagamité; and yet not a word of complaint, not a movement of impatience. They receive indeed the news of death with more constancy than those Christian Gentlemen and Ladies to whom one would not dare to mention it. Our Savages hear of it not only without despair, but without troubling themselves, without the slightest pallor or change of countenance. We have especially admired the constancy of our new Christians. The next to the last one who died, named Joseph *Oatij*, lay on the bare ground during four or five months, not only before but after his Baptism,—so thin that he was nothing but bones; in a lodge so wretched that the winds blew in on all sides; covered during the cold of winter with a very light skin of some black animals, perhaps black squirrels, and very poorly nourished. He was never heard to make a complaint. . . .

About the month of December, the snow began to lie on the ground, and the savages settled down into the village. For, during the whole Summer and Autumn, they are for the most part either in their rural cabins, taking care of their crops, or on the lake fishing, or trading; which makes it not a little inconvenient to instruct them. Seeing them, therefore, thus gathered together at the beginning of this year, we resolved to preach publicly to all, and to acquaint them with the reason of our coming into their Country, which is not for their furs, but to declare to them the true God and his son, Jesus Christ, the universal Saviour of our souls.

The usual method that we follow is this: We call together the people by the help of the Captain of the village, who assembles them all in our house as in Council, or perhaps by the sound of the bell. I use the surplice and the square cap, to give more majesty to my appearance. At the beginning we chant on our knees the *Pater noster,* translated into Huron verse. Father Daniel, as its author, chants a couplet alone, and then we all together chant it again; and those among the Hurons, principally the little ones, who already know it, take pleasure in chanting it with us. That done, when every one is seated, I rise and make the sign of the Cross for all; then, having recapitulated what I said last time, I explain something new. After that we question the young children and the girls, giving a little bead of glass or porcelain to those who deserve it. The parents are very glad to see their children answer well and carry off some little prize, of which they render themselves worthy by the care they take to come privately to get instruction. On our part, to arouse their emulation, we have each lesson retraced by our two little French boys, who question each other,—which transports the Savages with admiration. Finally the whole is concluded by the talk of the Old Men, who propound their difficulties, and sometimes make me listen in my turn to the statement of their belief.

Two things among others have aided us very much in the little we have been able to do here, by the grace of our Lord; the first is, as I have already said, the good health that God has granted us in the midst of sickness so general and so widespread. The second is the temporal assistance we have rendered to the sick. Having brought for ourselves some few delicacies, we shared them with them, giving to one a few prunes, and to another a few raisins, to others something else. The poor people came from great distances to get their share.

Our French servants having succeeded very well in hunting, during the Autumn, we carried portions of game to all the sick. That chiefly won their hearts, as they were dying, having neither flesh nor fish to season their sagamité. . . .

YOUR REVERENCE'S:
From our little House of St. Joseph, in the village of Ihonatiria in the Huron country, this 27th of May, 1635, the day on which the Holy Spirit descended visibly upon the Apostles.
Very humble and obedient
servant in our Lord,
JEAN DE BRÉBEUF.

INSTRUCTIONS FOR THE FATHERS OF OUR SOCIETY WHO SHALL BE SENT TO THE HURONS, 1637

The Fathers and Brethren whom God shall call to the holy Mission of the Hurons ought to exercise careful foresight in regard to all the hardships, annoyances, and perils that must be encountered in making this journey, in order to be prepared betimes for all emergencies that may arise.

You must have sincere affection for the Savages,— looking upon them as ransomed by the blood of the son of God, and as our Brethren with whom we are to pass the rest of our lives.

To conciliate the Savages, you must be careful never to make them wait for you in embarking.

You must provide yourself with a tinder box or with a burning mirror, or with both, to furnish them fire in the daytime to light their pipes, and in the evening when they have to encamp; these little services win their hearts.

You should try to eat their sagamité or salmagundi in the way they prepare it, although it may be dirty, half-cooked, and very tasteless. As to the other numerous things which may be unpleasant, they must be endured for the love of God, without saying anything or appearing to notice them.

It is well at first to take everything they offer, although you may not be able to eat it all; for, when one becomes somewhat accustomed to it, there is not too much.

You must try and eat at daybreak unless you can take your meal with you in the canoe; for the day is very long, if you have to pass it without eating. The Barbarians eat only at Sunrise and Sunset, when they are on their journeys.

You must be prompt in embarking and disembarking; and tuck up your gowns so that they will not get wet, and so that you will not carry either water or sand into the canoe. To be properly dressed, you must have your feet and legs bare; while crossing the rapids, you can wear your shoes, and, in the long portages, even your leggings.

You must so conduct yourself as not to be at all troublesome to even one of these Barbarians.

It is not well to ask many questions, nor should you yield to your desire to learn the language and to make observations on the way; this may be carried too far. You must relieve those in your canoe of this annoyance, especially as you cannot profit much by it during the work. Silence is a good equipment at such a time.

You must bear their imperfections without saying a word, yes, even without seeming to notice them. Even if it be necessary to criticise anything, it must be done modestly, and with words and signs which evince love and not aversion. In short, you must try to be, and to appear, always cheerful.

Each one should be provided with half a gross of awls, two or three dozen little knives called jam-bettes (pocket-knives), a hundred fish-hooks, with some beads of plain and colored glass, with which to buy fish or other articles when the tribes meet each other, so as to feast the Savages; and it would be well to say to them in the beginning, "Here is something with which to buy fish." Each one will try, at the portages, to carry some little thing, according to his strength; however little one carries, it greatly pleases the savages, if it be only a kettle.

You must not be ceremonious with the Savages, but accept the comforts they offer you, such as a good place in the cabin. The greatest conveniences are attended with very great inconvenience, and these ceremonies offend them.

Be careful not to annoy anyone in the canoe with your hat; it would be better to take your nightcap. There is no impropriety among the Savages.

Do not undertake anything unless you desire to continue it; for example, do not begin to paddle unless you are inclined to continue paddling. Take from the start the place in the canoe that you wish to keep; do not lend them your garments, unless you are willing to surrender them during the whole journey. It is easier to refuse at first than to ask them back, to change, or to desist afterwards.

Finally, understand that the Savages will retain the same opinion of you in their own country that they will have formed on the way; and one who has passed for an irritable and troublesome person will have considerable difficulty afterwards in removing this opinion. You have to do not only with those of your own canoe, but also (if it must be so stated) with all those of the country; you meet some today and others tomorrow, who do not fail to inquire, from those who brought you, what sort of man you are. It is almost incredible, how they observe and remember even the slightest fault. When you meet Savages on the way, as you cannot yet greet them with kind words, at least show them a cheerful face, and thus prove that you endure gayly the fatigues of the voyage. You will thus have put to good use the hardships on the way, and have already advanced considerably in gaining the affection of the Savages.

This is a lesson which is easy enough to learn, but very difficult to put into practice; for, leaving a highly civilized community, you fall into the hands of barbarous people who care but little for your Philosophy or your Theology. All the fine qualities which might make you loved and respected in France are like pearls trampled under the feet of swine, or rather mules, which utterly despise you when they see that you are not as good pack animals as they are. If you could go naked, and carry the load of a horse upon your back, as they do, then you would be wise according to their doctrine, and would be recognized as a great man, otherwise not. Jesus Christ is our true greatness; it is He alone and His cross that should be sought in running after these people, for, if you strive for anything else, you will find naught but bodily and spiritual affliction. But having found Jesus Christ in His cross, you have found the roses in the thorns, sweetness in bitterness, all in nothing.

References

1. George M. Wrong, ed., *The Long Journey to the Country of the Hurons by Father Gabriel Sagard* (Toronto: The Champlain Society, 1939), 102.
2. Reuben G. Thwaites, ed., *The Jesuit Relations and Allied Documents: Travels and Explorations of the Jesuit Missionaries in New France, 1610–1791*, 71 vols. (Cleveland: Burrows Brothers, 1896–1901), 10:27–29.
3. Georges E. Sioui, *For an Amerindian Autohistory* (Montreal: McGill-Queen's University Press, 1992), chap. 4.

Suggested Readings

Axtell, James. *The Invasion Within: The Contest of Cultures in Colonial North America* (New York: Oxford University Press, 1985).

Bowden, Henry Warner. *American Indians and Christian Missions: Studies in Cultural Conflict* (Chicago: University of Chicago Press, 1981).

Grant, John Webster. The Moon of Wintertime: *Missionaries and the Indians of Canada in Encounter since 1534* (Toronto: University of Toronto Press, 1984).

Harris, R. Cole, ed. *Historical Atlas of Canada,* Vol. 1. (Toronto: University of Toronto Press, 1987). Includes maps of trade networks around Huronia.

Parkman, Francis. *The Jesuits in North America in the Seventeenth Century* (Lincoln: University of Nebraska Press; Bison Books, 1997). Originally published in 1867, and heavily ethnocentric, Parkman's work focuses on the Jesuit mission to the Hurons.

Sioui, Georges E. *For an Amerindian Autohistory* (Montreal: McGill-Queen's University Press, 1992).

Sioui, Georges, E. *Huron-Wendat: The Heritage of the Circle* (Vancouver: University of British Columbia Press; East Lansing: Michigan State University Press, 1999).

Tooker, Elisabeth. *An Ethnography of the Huron Indians, 1615–1649.* Reprint ed. (Syracuse: Syracuse University Press, 1991).

Trigger, Bruce G. *The Children of Aetaentsic: A History of the Huron People to 1660.* 2 vols. (Montreal: McGill-Queen's University Press, 1976).

Trigger, Bruce G. *The Huron, Farmers of the North* (New York: Holt, Rinehart and Winston, 1969).

Two Views of King Philip

King Philip's War was one of the bloodiest conflicts in American history. In terms of proportionate populations it was *the* bloodiest. It shattered two generations of coexistence between Indians and English in Massachusetts. Fifty-two English towns were attacked, a dozen were destroyed, and many Indian villages were burned. More than 2,500 colonists died, perhaps 30 percent of the English population of New England. At least twice as many Indians died in the fighting and some estimates suggest that the combined effects of war, disease, and starvation killed half the Indian population of New England. The war left an enduring legacy in its imprint on subsequent attitudes and policies towards Indian peoples in America.

Not surprisingly, interpretation of the war has generated extreme views, as participants and historians recount the catastrophe and evaluate its meaning. The English at the time saw the conflict as a civil rebellion[1] and laid the blame squarely on the shoulders of Metacomet, whom they called King Philip. Even as the English preached the war as divine punishment for their own erring ways, they regarded Metacomet as a fiend and traitor who deserved the traitor's death and dismemberment he received. Generations of American historians, accepting the Puritans' accounts of the conflict as fact, portrayed the war as a vital victory in securing the Anglo-Saxon beachhead in North America, and saw it as forging a new American identity that forever excluded Indians. Indian people and most modern ethnohistorians blame Puritan land hunger, arrogance, and aggression for triggering the bloodshed. Historian Francis Jennings in 1975 renamed King Philip's War "The Second Puritan Conquest" (the first being the Pequot War) and denounced vicious and hypocritical colonists for fomenting war in a campaign to seize Indian lands.[2] More than three hundred years later, historians are still trying to achieve a balanced understanding of a racial war that shattered patterns of coexistence.[3]

Sometimes, how wars are remembered and written about can be as important as how they were fought, and a "contest of words" ensues over the memory and meaning of the conflict.[4] In this war, perhaps more than any other, the winners wrote the history books. The Puritans, not the Wampanoags, recorded assessments of Metacomet, and their views were the primary ones available to later historians. Reverend Increase Mather wrote a typically scathing indictment. Mather, one of the leading scholars and theologians in Puritan New England, wrote two books about King Philip's War, one of them while the war was still in progress. For Mather, as for most Puritans, the war was both divine punishment and an ordeal that tested the colonists' virtue, courage, and devotion to God. In Mather's account, the Puritans brought the war on them-

MR. WILLIAM APES,

A NATIVE MISSIONARY OF THE PEQUOT TRIBE

OF INDIANS.

William Apess

Pequot William Apess (1798–1839) was, at one time or another, a soldier, a Methodist preacher, a writer, and a leading figure in an Indian "rebellion" in Massachusetts. This undated portrait was imprinted on a card with a ticket for the lecture "Eulogy on King Philip" which he delivered in Boston in 1836. Courtesy American Antiquarian Society.

selves by their sinful ways amongst each other, not by their treatment of the Indians. Despite this placement of blame, he named the Indians as the instigators of the conflict: "The Heathen people amongst whom we live, and whose Land the Lord God of our Fathers hath given us for a rightfull Possession, have at sundry times been plotting mischievous devices," he wrote.[5] Metacomet was the villain and had to be destroyed. The extracts from Mather's "Brief History" of the war that follow trace Metacomet's final days as Captain Benjamin Church and the English with their Indian allies first capture his family, then kill Metacomet himself.

Although no Indian voices could challenge Mather in the wake of the bloody war, Puritan views of the conflict did not go unchallenged before the twentieth century. In 1836, 160 years after Metacomet's death, a Pequot Indian, William Apess, delivered a remarkable speech in Boston, eulogizing Metacomet and giving a very different view of the war. Most New Englanders supposed that the Pequots had been exterminated in 1637 and that Indians had, to all intents and purposes, disappeared from the region after King Philip's War. William Apess (1798–1839) exposed both notions as fallacies. Born into poverty and a broken home, beaten as a child by his drunken grandmother, William Apess also experienced firsthand the effects of racism in New England. As a young man he served in the American army in the War of 1812. He later became a Methodist preacher and one of the first Native American writers.

The 1830s were not good times to be an Indian. United States policy mandated the removal of all Indians from east of the Mississippi, and thousands were forced out of their ancestral homelands in the Southeast. In New England, where Indians had been dispossessed long before, many people criticized the government's policies and opposed the actions of the southern states. Rather than keep his head down in such times, William Apess stood up as an Indian;

rather than curry favor with New Englanders by expressing gratitude for their antiremoval stance, he confronted them with their own history and hypocrisy. He related in detail the aggression and oppression of their ancestors in dealing with the Indians and portrayed Metacomet as a patriot, like George Washington, who, after having made every possible compromise, fought to defend his people's rights and freedom.

► Questions for Consideration

1. What value does Apess's account (page 124), written long after the event, have as a historical record?

2. Is it more or less useful to historians than that written by Increase Mather at the time of the war? How does the language employed by Apess differ from Mather's?

3. Does Apess's account tell us more about Indian New England in Metacomet's time or in Apess's time, about Metacomet or about Apess?

INCREASE MATHER

From *A Brief History of the Warr with the Indians in New England* (1676)

August 1. Captain *Church* with thirty *English-men,* and twenty *Indians* following *Philip* and those with him, by their track, took twenty and three Indians. The next morning they came upon *Philips* head quarters, killed and took about an hundred and thirty Indians, with the loss of but one English-man. In probability many of the English-Souldiers had been cut off at this time, but that an Indian called *Matthias,* who fought for the English, when they were come very near the Enemy, called to them in their own Language with much vehemency, telling them they were all dead men if they did but fire a Gun, which did so amuse and amaze the Indians that they lost a great advantage against the English. *Philip* hardly es-caped with his life this day also. He fled and left his *Peag°* behind him, also his *Squaw and his Son were taken Captives,* and are now Prisoners in *Plimouth.* Thus hath God brought that grand Enemy into great misery before he quite destroy him. It must needs be bitter as death to him, to loose his Wife and only Son (for the Indians are

Source: Increase Mather, *A Brief History of the Warr with the Indians in New England* (Boston, 1676), reprinted in Richard Slotkin and James K. Folsom, eds., *So Dreadfull a Judgment: Puritan Responses to King Philip's War,* 1676–1677 (Middletown, Conn.: Wesleyan University Press, 1978), 136, 138–39. Reprinted with the permission of Wesleyan University Press.
°Wampum, from the Algonquian wampompeag.

marvellous fond and affectionate towards their Children) besides other Relations, and almost all his Subjects and Country too. . . .

August 12. This is the memorable day wherein *Philip,* the perfidious and bloudy Author of the War and wofull miseryes that have thence ensued, was taken and slain. And God brought it to pass, chiefly by Indians themselves. For one of *Philips* men (being disgusted at him, for killing an Indian who had propounded an expedient for peace with the English) ran away from him and coming to Road-Island, informed that *Philip* was now returned again to *Mount-Hope,* and undertook to bring them to the Swamp where he hid himself. Divine Providence so disposed, as that Capt. *Church* of *Plymouth* was then in Road-Island, in order to recruiting his Souldiers, who had been wearied with a tedious march that week. But immediately upon this Intelligence, he set forth again, with a small company of English and Indians. It seemeth that night *Philip* (like the man in the Host of *Midian*) dreamed that he was fallen into the hands of the English, and just as he was saying to those that were with him, that they must fly for their lives that day, lest the Indian that was gone from him should discover where he was, Our Souldiers came upon him, and surrounded the *Swamp* (where he with seven of his men ab-sconded)[.] Thereupon he betook himself to flight, but as he was coming out of the Swamp, an English-man and an Indian endeavoured to fire at him, the English-man missed of his aime, but the Indian shot him through the heart, so as that he fell down dead. The Indian who thus killed *Philip,* did formerly belong to Squaw-Sachim of *Pocasset,* being known by the name of *Alderman.* In the beginning of the war, he came to the Governour of *Plymouth,* manifesting his desire to be at peace with the English, and immediately withdrew to an Island not having ingaged against the English nor for them, before this time. Thus when *Philip* had made an end to deal treacherously, his own Subjects dealt treacherously with him. This Wo was brought upon him that spoyled when he was not spoyled.° And in that very place where he first contrived and began his mischief, was he taken and destroyed, and there was he (Like as Agag was hewed in pieces before the Lord)° cut into four quarters, and is now hanged up as a monument of revenging Justice, his head being cut off and carried away to Plymouth, his Hands were brought to *Boston. So let all thine Enemies perish, O Lord!*

°Meaning that Metacomet attacked the colonists but the English had not attacked him.

°1 Samuel 15:33.

WILLIAM APESS
From "Eulogy on King Philip" (1836)

Until the execution of these three Indians,° supposed to be the murderers of Sassamon, no hos-tility was committed by Philip or his warriors. About the time of their trial, he was said to be marching his men up and down the country in arms; but when it was known, he could no longer restrain his young men, who, upon the 24th of June [1675], provoked the people of Swansea by killing their cattle and other injuries, which was a signal to commence the war, and what they had

Source: William Apess, from "Eulogy on King Philip," 1836, reprinted in Barry O'Connell, ed., *On Our Own Ground: The Complete Writings of William Apess, a Pequot* (Amherst: University of Massachusetts Press, 1992), 119–28.

See page 89.

desired, as a superstitious notion prevailed among the Indians that whoever fired the first gun of either party would be conquered, doubtless a notion they had received from the Pilgrims. It was upon a fast day, too, when the first gun was fired; and as the people were returning from church, they were fired upon by the Indians, when several of them were killed. It is not supposed that Philip directed this attack but was opposed to it. Though it is not doubted that he meant to be revenged upon his enemies; for during some time he had been cementing his countrymen together, as it appears that he had sent to all the disaffected tribes, who also had watched the movements of the comers from the New World° and were as dissatisfied as Philip himself was with their proceedings. . . .

At this council it appears that Philip made the following speech to his chiefs, counselors, and warriors:

> Brothers, you see this vast country before us, which the Great Spirit gave to our fathers and us; you see the buffalo° and deer that now are our support. Brothers, you see these little ones, our wives and children, who are looking to us for food and raiment; and you now see the foe before you, that they have grown insolent and bold; that all our ancient customs are disregarded; the treaties made by our fathers and us are broken, and all of us insulted; our council fires disregarded, and all the ancient customs of our fathers; our brothers murdered before our eyes, and their spirits cry to us for revenge. Brothers, these people from the unknown world will cut down our groves, spoil our hunting and planting grounds, and drive us and our children from

the graves of our fathers, and our council fires, and enslave our women and children.

This famous speech of Philip was calculated to arouse them to arms, to do the best they could in protecting and defending their rights. The blow had now been struck, the die was cast, and nothing but blood and carnage was before them. And we find Philip as active as the wind, as dexterous as a giant, firm as the pillows of heaven, and fierce as a lion, a powerful foe to contend with indeed, and as swift as an eagle, gathering together his forces to prepare them for the battle. And as it would swell our address too full to mention all the tribes in Philip's train of warriors, suffice it to say that from six to seven were with him at different times. When he begins the war, he goes forward and musters about five hundred of his men and arms them complete, and about nine hundred of the other, making in all about fourteen hundred warriors when he commenced. It must be recollected that this war was legally declared by Philip, so that the colonies had a fair warning. It was no savage war of surprise, as some suppose, but one sorely provoked by the Pilgrims themselves. But when Philip and his men fought as they were accustomed to do and according to their mode of war, it was more than what could be expected. But we hear no particular acts of cruelty committed by Philip during the siege. But we find more manly nobility in him than we do in all the head Pilgrims put together, as we shall see exploits and to lead captive their haughty lords. It does appear that every Indian heart had been lighted up at the council fires, at Philip's speech, and that the forest was literally alive with this injured race. And now town after town fell before them. The Pilgrims with their forces were marching ever in one direction, while Philip and his forces were marching in another, burning all before them, until Middleborough, Taunton, and Dartmouth were laid in ruins and forsaken by its inhabitants.

At the great fight at Pocasset, Philip commanded in person, where he also was discovered with his host in a dismal swamp. He had retired

---

°This may be a slip of the pen or deliberate irony on the part of Apess, reminding his listeners that Europe was a new world to Indian people. Barry O'Connell, ed., *On Our Own Ground: The Complete Writings of William Apess, a Pequot* (Amherst: University of Massachusetts Press, 1992), 294.

°A species of buffalo had once lived in New England.

here with his army to secure a safe retreat from the Pilgrims, who were in close pursuit of him, and their numbers were so powerful they thought the fate of Philip was sealed. They surrounded the swamp, in hopes to destroy him and his army. At the edge of the swamp Philip had secreted a few of his men to draw them into ambush, upon which the Pilgrims showed fight, Philip's men retreating and the whites pursuing them till they were surrounded by Philip and nearly all cut off. This was a sorry time to them; the Pilgrims, however, reinforced but ordered a retreat, supposing it impossible for Philip to escape; and knowing his forces to be great, it was conjectured by some to build a fort to starve him out, as he had lost but few men in the fight. The situation of Philip was rather peculiar, as there was but one outlet to the swamp and a river before him nearly seven miles to descend. The Pilgrims placed a guard around the swamp for thirteen days, which gave Philip and his men time to prepare canoes to make good his retreat, in which he did, to the Connecticut River, and in his retreat lost but fourteen men. We may look upon this move of Philip's to be equal, if not superior, to that of Washington crossing the Delaware. For while Washington was assisted by all the knowledge that art and science could give, together with all the instruments of defense and edged tools to prepare rafts and the like helps for safety across the river, Philip was naked as to any of these things, possessing only what nature, his mother, had bestowed upon him; and yet makes his escape with equal praise. But he would not even [have] lost a man had it not been for Indians who were hired to fight against Indians, with promise of their enjoying equal rights with their white brethren; but not one of those promises have as yet been fulfilled by the Pilgrims or their children, though they must acknowledge that without the aid of Indians and their guides they must inevitably been swept off. It was only, then, by deception that the Pilgrims gained the country, ⸱ their word has never been fulfilled in regard to ⸱ian rights.

Philip having now taken possession of the back settlements of Massachusetts, one town after another was swept off. . . .

The Pilgrims determined to break down Philip's power, if possible, with the Narragansetts: Thus they raised an army of fifteen hundred strong, to go against them and destroy them if possible. In this, Massachusetts, Plymouth, and Connecticut all join in severally, to crush Philip. Accordingly, in December, in 1675, the Pilgrims set forward to destroy them. Preceding their march, Philip had made all arrangements for the winter and had fortified himself beyond what was common for his countrymen to do, upon a small island near South Kingston, R.I. Here he intended to pass the winter with his warriors and their wives and children. About five hundred Indian houses was erected of a superior kind, in which was deposited all their stores, tubs of corn, and other things, piled up to a great height, which rendered it bulletproof. It was supposed that three thousand persons had taken up their residence in it. (I would remark that Indians took better care of themselves in those days than they have been able to since.) Accordingly, on the 19th day of December, after the Pilgrims had been out in the extreme cold for nearly one month, lodging in tents, and their provision being short, and the air full of snow, they had no other alternative than to attack Philip in the fort. Treachery, however, hastened his ruin; one of his men, by hope of reward from the deceptive Pilgrims, betrayed his country into their hands. The traitor's name was Peter. No white man was acquainted with the way, and it would have been almost impossible for them to have found it, much less to have captured it. There was but one point where it could have been entered or assailed with any success, and this was fortified much like a blockhouse, directly in front of the entrance, and also flankers to cover a crossfire—besides high palisades, an immense hedge of fallen trees of nearly a rod in thickness. Thus surrounded by trees and water, there was but one place that the Pilgrims could pass. Nevertheless, they made the attempt Philip now had directed his men to fire, and every platoon of the Indians swept every white man from the path one after another, until six captains, with a great many of the men, had fallen. In the meantime, one Captain Moseley with some of his men had somehow or other gotten into the fort in another way and surprised them, by which the Pilgrims were enabled to capture the fort, at the same time setting fire to it and hewing down men, women, and children indiscriminately. Philip, however, was enabled to escape with many of his warriors. It is said at this battle eighty whites were killed and one hundred and fifty wounded, many of whom died of their wounds afterward, not being able to dress them till they had marched eighteen miles, also leaving many of their dead in the fort. It is said that seven hundred of the Narragansetts perished, the greater part of them being women and children.

It appears that God did not prosper them much, after all. It is believed that the sufferings of the Pilgrims were without a parallel in history; and it is supposed that the horrors and burning elements of Moscow will bear but a faint resemblance of that scene.° The thousands and ten thousands assembled there with their well-disciplined forces bear but little comparison to that of modern Europe, when the inhabitants, science, manners, and customs are taken into consideration. We might as well admit the above fact and say the like was never known among any heathen nation in the world; for none but those worse than heathens would have suffered so much, for the sake of being revenged upon those of their enemies. Philip had repaired to his quarters to take care of his people and not to have them exposed. We should not have wondered quite so much if Philip had gone forward and acted thus. But when a people calling themselves Christians conduct in

this manner, we think they are censurable, and no pity at all ought to be had for them.

It appears that one of the whites [Joshua Tefft] had married one of Philip's countrymen; and they, the Pilgrims, said he was a traitor, and therefore they said he must die. So they quartered him; and as history informs us, they said, he being a heathen, but a few tears were shed at his funeral. Here, then, because a man would not turn and fight against his own wife and family, or leave them, he was condemned as a heathen. We presume that no honest men will commend those ancient fathers for such absurd conduct. Soon after this, Philip and his men left that part of the country and retired farther back, near the Mohawks, where, in July 1676, some of his men were slain by the Mohawks. Notwithstanding this, he strove to get them to join him; and here it is said that Philip did not do that which was right, that he killed some of the Mohawks and laid it to the whites in order that he might get them to join him. If so, we cannot consistently believe he did right. But he was so exasperated that nothing but revenge would satisfy him. All this act was no worse than our political men do in our days, of their strife to wrong each other, who profess to be enlightened; and all for the sake of carrying their points. Heathenlike, either by the sword, calumny, or deception of every kind; and the late duels among the [so-] called high men of honor is sufficient to warrant my statements. But while we pursue our history in regard to Philip, we find that he made many successful attempts against the Pilgrims, in surprising and driving them from their posts, during the year 1676, in February and through till August, in which time many of the Christian Indians joined him. It is thought by many that all would have joined him, if they had been left to their choice, as it appears they did not like their white brethren very well. It appears that Philip treated his prisoners with a great deal more Christian-like spirit than the Pilgrims did; even Mrs. Rowlandson, although speaking with bitterness sometimes of the Indians, yet in her journal

°A reference to Napoleon Bonaparte's burning of Moscow in 1812 and the disastrous French retreat through the Russian winter.

she speaks not a word against him. Philip even hires her to work for him, and pays her for her work, and then invites her to dine with him and to smoke with him. And we have many testimonies that he was kind to his prisoners; and when the English wanted to redeem Philip's prisoners, they had the privilege.

Now, did Governor Winthrop or any of those ancient divines use any of his men so? No. Was it known that they received any of their female captives into their houses and fed them? No, it cannot be found upon history. Were not the females completely safe, and none of them were violated, as they acknowledge themselves? But was it so when the Indian women fell into the hands of the Pilgrims? No. Did the Indians get a chance to redeem their prisoners? No. But when they were taken they were either compelled to turn traitors and join their enemies or be butchered upon the spot. And this is the dishonest method that the famous Captain Church used in doing his great exploits; and in no other way could he ever gained one battle. So, after all, Church only owes his exploits to the honesty of the Indians, who told the truth, and to his own deceptive heart in duping them. Here it is to be understood that the whites have always imposed upon the credulity of the Indians. It is with shame, I acknowledge, that I have to notice so much corruption of a people calling themselves Christians. If they were like my people, professing no purity at all, then their crimes would not appear to have such magnitude. But while they appear to be by profession more virtuous, their crimes still blacken. It makes them truly to appear to be like mountains filled with smoke, and thick darkness covering them all around.

But we have another dark and corrupt deed for the sons of Pilgrims to look at, and that is the fight and capture of Philip's son and wife and many of his warriors, in which Philip lost about 130 men killed and wounded; this was in August 1676. But the most horrid act was in taking 'lip's son, about ten years of age, and selling be a slave away from his father and mother.

While I am writing, I can hardly restrain my feelings, to think a people calling themselves Christians should conduct so scandalous, so outrageous, making themselves appear so despicable in the eyes of the Indians; and even now, in this audience, I doubt but there is men honorable enough to despise the conduct of those pretended Christians. And surely none but such as believe they did right will ever go and undertake to celebrate that day of their landing, the 22nd of December. Only look at it; then stop and pause: My fathers came here for liberty themselves, and then they must go and chain that mind, that image they professed to serve, not content to rob and cheat the poor ignorant Indians but must take one of the king's sons and make a slave of him. Gentlemen and ladies, I blush at these tales, if you do not, especially when they professed to be a free and humane people. Yes, they did; they took a part of my tribe and sold them to the Spaniards in Bermuda, and many others, and then on the Sabbath day, these people would gather themselves together and say that God is no respecter of persons; while the divines would pour forth, "He says that he loves God and hates his brother is a liar, and the truth is not in him"—and at the same time they [are] hating and selling their fellow men in bondage. And there is no manner of doubt but that all my countrymen would have been enslaved if they had tamely submitted. But no sooner would they butcher every white man that come in their way, and even put an end to their own wives and children, and that was all that prevented them from being slaves; yes, *all*. It was not the good will of those holy Pilgrims that prevented. No. But I would speak, and I could wish it might be like the voice of thunder, that it might be heard afar off, even to the ends of the earth. He that will advocate slavery is worse than a beast, is a being devoid of shame, and has gathered around him the most corrupt and debasing principles in the world; and I care not whether he be a minister or member of any church in the world—no, not excepting the head men of the nation. And he that will not set his face against its corrupt principles is a coward and not worthy of being numbered among men and Christians—and conduct, too, that libels the laws of the country, and the word of God, that men profess to believe in.

After Philip had his wife and son taken, sorrow filled his heart, but notwithstanding, as determined as ever to be revenged, though [he] was pursued by the duped Indians and Church into a swamp, one of the men proposing to Philip that he had better make peace with the enemy, upon which he slew him upon the spot. . . .

Philip's forces had now become very small, so many having been duped away by the whites and killed that it was now easy surrounding him. Therefore, upon the 12th of August, Captain Church surrounded the swamp where Philip and his men had encamped, early in the morning, before they had risen, doubtless led on by an Indian who was either compelled or hired to turn traitor. Church had now placed his guard so that it was impossible for Philip to escape without being shot. It is doubtful, however, whether they would have taken him if he had not been surprised. Suffice it to say, however, this was the case. A sorrowful morning to the poor Indians, to lose such a valuable man. When coming out of the swamp, he was fired upon by an Indian and killed dead upon the spot.

I rejoice that it was even so, that the Pilgrims did not have the pleasure of tormenting him. The white man's gun, missing fire, lost the honor of killing the truly great man, Philip. The place where Philip fell was very muddy. Upon this news, the Pilgrims gave three cheers; then Church ordering his body to be pulled out of the mud, while one of those tender-hearted Christians exclaims, "What a dirty creature he looks like." And we have also Church's speech upon that subject, as follows: "For as much as he has caused many a Pilgrim to lie above ground unburied, to rot, not one of his bones shall be buried." With him fell five of his best and most trusty men, one the son of a chief, who fired the first gun in the war.

Captain Church now orders him to be cut up. Accordingly, he was quartered and hung up upon four trees, his head and one hand given to the Indian who shot him, to carry about to show, at which sight it so overjoyed the Pilgrims that they would give him money for it, and in this way obtained a considerable sum. After which his head was sent to Plymouth and exposed upon a gibbet for twenty years; and his hand to Boston, where it was exhibited in savage triumph. . . .

Now, while we sum up this subject, does it not appear that the cause of all wars from beginning to end was and is for the want of good usage? That the whites have always been the aggressors, and the wars, cruelties, and bloodshed is a job of their own seeking, and not the Indians? Did you ever know of Indians hurting those who was kind to them? No. We have a thousand witnesses to the contrary. Yea, every male and female declare it to be the fact. We often hear of the wars breaking out upon the frontiers, and it is because the same spirit reigns there that reigned here in New England; and wherever there are any Indians, that spirit still reigns; and at present, there is no law to stop it. What, then, is to be done? Let every friend of the Indians now seize the mantle of Liberty and throw it over those burning elements that has spread with such fearful rapidity, and at once extinguish them forever. It is true that now and then a feeble voice has been raised in our favor. Yes, we might speak of distinguished men, but they fall so far short in the minority that it is heard but at a small distance. We want trumpets that sound like thunder, and men to act as though they were going at war with those corrupt and degrading principles that robs one of all rights, merely because he is ignorant and of a little different color. Let us have principles that will give everyone his due; and then shall wars cease, and the weary find rest. Give the Indian his rights, and you may be assured war will cease.

But by this time you have been enabled to see that Philip's prophecy has come to pass; therefore, as a man of natural abilities, I shall pronounce him the greatest man that was ever in America; and so it will stand, until he is proved to the contrary, to the everlasting disgrace of the Pilgrims' fathers.

References

1. James D. Drake, *King Philip's War: Civil War in New England* (Amherst: University of Massachusetts Press, 1999).
2. Francis Jennings, *The Invasion of America: Indians, Colonialism, and the Cant of Conquest* (New York: W. W. Norton, 1976), 298.
3. For example, Russell Bourne, *The Red King's Rebellion: Racial Politics in New England, 1675–1678* (New York: Oxford University Press, 1990).
4. Jill Lepore, *The Name of War: King Philip's War and the Origins of American Identity* (New York: Knopf, 1998).
5. Mather's "Brief History" of the war, first published in 1676, is reprinted in Richard Slotkin and James K. Folsom, eds., *So Dreadfull a Judgment: Puritan Responses to King Philip's War, 1676–1677* (Middletown, Conn.: Wesleyan University Press, 1978), quote on p. 86.

Suggested Readings

Bourne, Russell. *The Red King's Rebellion: Racial Politics in New England, 1675–1678* (New York: Oxford University Press, 1990).

Drake, James D. *King Philip's War: Civil War in New England* (Amherst: University of Massachusetts Press, 1999).

Jennings, Francis. *The Invasion of America: Indians, Colonialism, and the Cant of Conquest* (New York: W. W. Norton, 1976).

Leach, Douglas Edward. *Flintlock and Tomahawk: New England in King Philip's War* (New York: W. W. Norton, 1966).

Lepore, Jill. *The Name of War: King Philip's War and the Origins of American Identity* (New York: Knopf, 1998).

O'Connell, Barry, ed. *On Our Own Ground: The Complete Writings of William Apess, a Pequot* (Amherst: University of Massachusetts Press, 1992).

Peyer, Bernd C. "William Apess, Pequot-Mashpee Insurrectionist of the Removal Era," in Peyer, *The Tutor'd Mind: Indian Missionary-Writers in Antebellum America* (Amherst: University of Massachusetts Press, 1997), 117–65.

Salisbury, Neal, ed. *The Sovereignty and Goodness of God by Mary Rowlandson, with related documents* (Boston: Bedford Books, 1997).

Slotkin, Richard, and James K. Folsom, eds. *So Dreadfull a Judgment: Puritan Responses to King Philip's War, 1676–1677* (Middletown, Conn.: Wesleyan University Press, 1978).

Images of Invasion

The idea that America was ever invaded strikes many people as odd. The arrival of Europeans usually has been portrayed in terms of exploration, settlement, and building a new society and nation. But viewed from Indian country that same story was one of invasion, conquest, and assault on the societies they had previously constructed. The pictograph of mounted Spaniards bearing lances etched by native hands into the wall of Cañon del Muerto in Arizona gives some sense of the impression the arrival of militant strangers made on the Indian inhabitants (Figure 2.1).

Euro-American artists created powerful images that celebrated the arrival of European civilization in the Americas, though their pictures are often heavy on symbolism but lighter on historical or ethnographic accuracy. In 1836, Congress commissioned a series of four murals portraying scenes from early

FIGURE 2.1 Spaniards on Horseback
Arizona State Museum, University of Arizona. Helga Teiwes, photographer.

FIGURE 2.2 **William Powell, *The Discovery of the Mississippi by De Soto in 1541* (1853)**
Architect of the Capitol.

American history for the rotunda of the United States Capitol. Such art in public places reduced complex historical developments to specific memorable events and interpreted events of the past as progress. The first scene, painted by John Vanderlyn in 1846, shows the landing of Christopher Columbus in the West Indies in October 1492. Columbus holds his banner aloft and looks into the distance (i.e., the future), while Indians flee in terror in the background. "His right to conquer, as an agent bringing civilization to the New World, is taken for granted."[1] In the second painting, William Powell presents Hernando de Soto "discovering" the Mississippi in 1541 (Figure 2.2). The Indians are awed and submissive in the face of Spanish power and the coming of "civilization." The Indians of the area (about thirty miles south of modern Memphis) would in fact have inhabited Mississippian-style towns, not Plains-style tepees. The half-naked Indian women at the feet of De Soto's charger also satisfy nineteenth-century convention: like the land, the women are suggested to be vulnerable and available to European conquest—they are both submissive and alluring. In reality, the Indians would have been more likely to hide their women, knowing in advance that De Soto's expedition had been "a nightmare of rape and abuse" for hundreds of Indian women farther east. By the time De Soto's bedraggled and half-starved army reached the Mississippi, they were more interested in seizing corn from the Indians than in

FIGURE 2.3 **John Gadsby Chapman,** *The Baptism of Pocahontas at Jamestown, Virginia, 1613* **(1840)**
Architect of the Capitol.

impressing them with displays of European pageantry. "The real Hernando de Soto," in the words of a recent biographer, "was probably feeling somewhat less than triumphant. . . . Dressed like his men in a motley blend of animal skins, furs, and armor, his face emaciated by hunger and creased by the strain of command, he undoubtedly saw this mile-wide strip of roiling water not as the highway for settlement and commerce it later became, but as a monumental nuisance—for the very practical reason that he had to cross it."[2]

The third of the four scenes in the Capitol shows the Pilgrims embarking for their New World. The fourth, John Gadsby Chapman's *The Baptism of Pocahontas* (Figure 2.3), was supposed to represent the first conversion in 1613 of an American Indian, at Jamestown, Virginia. In Chapman's view, "Christianity was the ordained religion of progress and . . . as the nation expanded and prospered only those who shared the faith would benefit." Chapman, apparently, had never seen an Indian firsthand and turned for models to the works of his former teacher, Charles Bird King. Behind the kneeling Pocahontas stand her brother, Nantequaus, who turns his head away, and John Rolfe. Again, Indians sit on the ground in a subordinate position: Pocahontas's sister with her baby and "her plotting uncle," seated in the foreground with his arms folded.[3] There

FIGURE 2.4 Jean L. G. Ferris, *The First Thanksgiving*
© *Bettmann/CORBIS.*

is a long history of artistic representations of Pocahontas, saving John Smith's life, marrying John Rolfe, dressed as a lady at the English court (see image on page 86 also), and so on. In fact, for a long time, Pocahontas and Sacagawea were the only two Indian women accorded a significant role in American history—they both assisted whites and therefore were identified with progress and the future. In fact, Pocahontas's future was short: she died of an unidentified disease in England at the age of twenty-two.

Indian societies regularly gave—and give—thanks for the earth's bounty, but the historical evidence for the first Euro-American Thanksgiving, reputedly in November 1621, is rather slim—a few sources mention a meal shared with Indians. But with the designation in the nineteenth century of the last Thursday in November as a national holiday, the meal became a defining moment in American history. Numerous artists portrayed it as they imagined it had happened, usually with Indians resplendent in Plains-style buckskins and feathers (Figure 2.4). Such romanticized paintings recall the extent to which early English colonists depended on Indian food for their very survival. Few works of art conveyed the historical reality that Indians in coastal New England had little to

FIGURE 2.5 Emanuel Leutze, *The Founding of Maryland* (1860)
The Maryland Historical Society.

be thankful for: most of the local population had already been wiped out by European disease.

In Emanuel Leutze's *The Founding of Maryland* (Figure 2.5) Sir George Calvert, first Lord Baltimore, meets with a local Indian chief, while soldiers, colonists, and their livestock mingle. The soldiers lend a military character to the colony, but the elegant couple in the foreground and the house under construction in the background signify that "civilization" has arrived. A priest says Mass or confers blessing on the meeting in the shadow of a huge cross, while a shaman sits dejected at bottom left. Indian women bring corn, game, and oysters. "One is reminded of Thanksgiving and the Fourth of July, all rolled into a single high-spirited festival," writes one critic. "The standard of Lord Baltimore is raised above the crowd, a patriotic vignette in which one could substitute the Stars and Stripes."[4]

Jonathan Warm Day's twentieth-century work, *The Last Supper* (Figure 2.6) presents a much more restrained and ominous view of encounter. Ironically invoking the image of Christ's final meal with his disciples, the Pueblo artist shows a Pueblo family disturbed by the arrival of dark Spanish soldiers and priests. The viewer looks at the Spaniards through the home and the life of the Indian family, but also with the knowledge of what lies in store for them.

FIGURE 2.6 Jonathan Warm Day, *The Last Supper* (1991)

"The Last Supper," Jonathan Warm Day, Taos Pueblo, MRM 1991–46. Courtesy of Millicent Rogers Museum of Northern New Mexico.

▶ Questions for Consideration

1. What do these different images suggest about how Native and non-Native peoples experienced and remembered their earliest encounters?

2. Several of the pictures were painted in the mid-nineteenth century. What meanings do the painters seem to have attached to the events they depict? Why?

3. Which pictures might be viewed as creating or contributing to a national mythology? In what ways?

References

1. William H. Truettner, ed., *The West as America: Reinterpreting Images of the Frontier, 1820–1920* (Washington, D.C.: Smithsonian Institution, 1991), 70.
2. David Ewing Duncan, *Hernando de Soto: A Savage Quest in the Americas* (New York: Crown Publishers, 1995), xxxiii, 295, 401–02.
3. Truettner, ed., *The West as America,* 71; Patricia Trenton and Patrick T. Houlihan, *Native Americans: Five Centuries of Changing Images* (New York: Abrams, 1989), 24–25.
4. Truettner, ed., *The West as America,* 89.

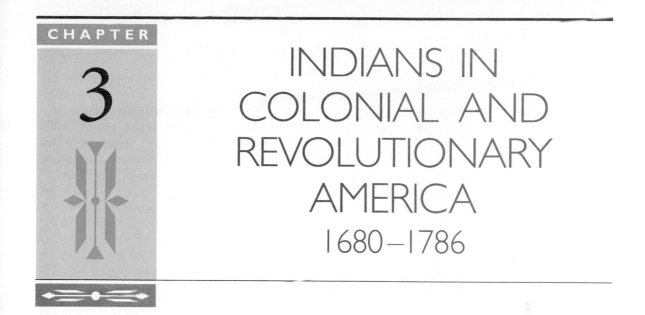

INDIANS IN COLONIAL AND REVOLUTIONARY AMERICA
1680–1786

ECONOMIC AND CULTURAL EXCHANGES

Despite the cartographic claims of rival European powers and the ravages of war and disease inflicted on Indian populations, at the beginning of the eighteenth century the European presence existed only on the edges and along the arteries of the continent. Indian people still held sway over the interior. Indians used their power to resist and limit European intrusion, but also sought out Europeans as sources of new commercial opportunities and political alliance. Indian people came to colonial settlements and cities to trade and otherwise participate in the economic life of the new communities. Indians lived near, and sometimes in, colonial societies. Indians and Europeans coexisted and adjusted to each other's presence. They also engaged in what historian James Axtell describes as a "contest of cultures:"[1] colonial governments, teachers, and missionaries endeavored to change Indians into "civilized Christians," but Indian ways also exerted subtle influence on many Europeans who experienced them firsthand. Indian captors often tried to convert their captives to Indian ways, with some successes. Indians and Europeans also killed each other in a world of escalating violence. While Indians participated in colonial wars, the outcome of those wars was the creation of a new nation committed to expansion onto Indian lands and the exclusion of everything Indian from society.

Indians in Colonial Society

Indian people played important roles in helping Europeans establish their initial settlements in North America. They served as guides, sometimes willingly, sometimes under coercion; they acted as interpreters and intermediaries with more distant tribes; they provided food supplies and taught Europeans how to grow, hunt, and fish for their own food in an unfamiliar environment.

Indians often constituted an integral part of the colonial societies and economies. In New Spain, Indians were subjected to labor drafts, worked in Spanish mines, plantations, and households, and built Spanish missions and towns. The trade in Indian slaves reached far beyond the arena of Spanish control, involving Ute Indians from the Rockies, Plains Apaches, and many other peoples. Indian slaves in colonial New Mexico came to comprise a separate class, known as *genizaros*, looked down upon by Pueblo Indians and Hispanic settlers alike. Indian women cooked in Spanish kitchens, sold pottery and foodstuffs in markets at St. Augustine, New Orleans, and Santa Fe, and wove textiles in Santa Fe. Indian men worked on Spanish ranches and herded Spanish cattle.

Franciscan priests established missions in Florida, New Mexico, and, after 1769, in California. They assaulted the Indians' traditional religions, insisted on baptism, and tried to transform them into communities of Christian peasants living within sound of the mission bells. Concentrating Indian populations into mission communities at a time when new epidemic diseases stalked the land often proved fatal. As it had among the Pueblos in 1680, Franciscan oppression, backed by the Spanish military and combined with the disruption of traditional lifeways and economies, produced suffering and resentment that occasionally burst out into open violence, as when Indians attacked the mission at San Diego in 1775. Nevertheless, thousands of Indians became at least nominal Catholics. Accepting certain tenets and symbols of Christianity to which they attached their own meanings, without abandoning their traditional beliefs and rituals, Indians created their own versions of Christianity. Indians and Spaniards intermarried and borrowed each other's foods, clothing, technologies, and words. The centuries-long influence of Spanish people and culture on Indians, and of Indian culture and peoples on Hispanos, is evident in areas of the Southwest today.

On the Atlantic seaboard, Indians mingled with Dutch, Swedes, Finns, Scots, Irish, Englishmen, Germans, and African slaves, although British population and power predominated by the eighteenth century. Despite intense pressures on their lands and periodic eruptions of hostilities, Indians lived in and around colonial settlements and took advantage of the new economic opportunities they afforded even as those same settlements curtailed their traditional mobile economy. They worked for wages in colonial towns, labored on colonial plantations alongside African slaves, served on colonial ships, and enlisted in colonial armies. Sometimes, Indians lived with the colonial families who employed them. Indian healers, many of them women, drew on their extensive knowledge of plant-derived medicines to cure European as well as Indian patients. Indian men traded the products of their hunting; Indian women traded the corn they grew and the baskets they made. In South Carolina, many Catawbas "took to the road as peddlers, their packs bulging with moccasins,

26

Mission Indians of California

Indian converts at the Spanish mission at Carmel, California, line up to receive visiting Frenchmen in 1786. Spanish priests worked to produce dutiful congregations of "mission Indians." However, beneath the appearance of order and contentment depicted on occasions such as this, Indians in Spanish missions often suffered hunger, disease, and abuse. One of the French visitors compared the mission to a slave plantation. Indians frequently ran away from the missions and sometimes, as at San Diego in 1775, resorted to violent resistance. Courtesy of the Bancroft Library, University of California, Berkeley.

baskets, table mats, and . . . pottery." Like basketmaking, pottery was an ancient skill, and Indians "simply put old skills to new uses" and began manufacturing baskets and pots for sale.[2]

Some Indians worshipped, married, and were buried in colonial churches. Sometimes, they established and maintained their own Christian churches, with their own deacons and ministers. Others attended colonial schools, where they were taught to read and write, to study the Bible, and to dress and behave in English ways. Some colonial colleges, like Harvard, William and Mary, and Dartmouth, had "Indian schools." Many Indian people recognized the power of literacy and saw the new education as a useful tool. Some used their education to work as interpreters or to assume a larger role as culture brokers: Mohegan minister Samson Occom, for example, worked to extend Christianity to Indian peoples and also traveled to Britain to raise money for the Indian school at Dartmouth College.

Other Indians were more guarded in their responses. At the Treaty of Lancaster, Pennsylvania, in 1744, commissioners from Virginia invited the Iroquois delegates to send their children to William and Mary, where they would receive the benefits of an English education. The Onondaga orator, Canasatego, thanked them for their kind offer, "but our Customs differing from yours, you will be so good as to excuse us." In the expanded version of his reply recorded by Benjamin Franklin (who printed many colonial Indian treaties), Canasatego went further. Young Indians who had gone to school in the colonies, he said, came home "good for nothing," unable to hunt a deer, paddle a canoe, or find their way in the woods. Tongue in cheek, he returned the compliment: if the Virginians would like to send some of their young men to the Iroquois, the Indians would teach them their ways and make real men of them![3]

Colonists in Indian Societies

At the same time, colonists mingled with Indians. France's North American empire constituted a veneer of French population and culture spread thinly over an Indian world. Indian converts and customers were attracted to French missions and trading posts, and French traders, priests, soldiers, and agents ventured into Indian country to bolster Indian allegiance, but the French population remained relatively small and scattered in settlements from the mouth of the St. Lawrence to the mouth of the Mississippi. Nevertheless, in regions like Louisiana, French settlers and Indians interacted and intermarried, exchanged foods, commodities, and knowledge, and, along with African slaves, "forged a network of cross-cultural interaction that routinely brought individuals into small-scale, face-to-face episodes of exchange."[4]

Many Europeans who pushed into Indian country adopted Indian ways. They hunted using Indian techniques, dressed in Indian hunting shirts, leggings, and moccasins, wore their hair Indian style, bore body paint and tattoos, spoke Indian languages, and smoked Indian pipes. Colonial authorities sometimes became alarmed by the numbers of their citizens who "went Indian." Some individuals chose to live with Indians and even fought beside them against Europeans. Indians also took hundreds of captives from European settlements during the colonial wars, adopting them into their societies and turning them from strangers into relatives. Some of these captives became so accustomed to life in Indian country and Indian communities that they stayed permanently, even refusing opportunities to return home.

THE IMPACT OF THE FUR TRADE

Trade in animal hides was a major component of the economy of early America. The exchange of beaver pelts for European goods was already established when Micmac Indians in Chaleur Bay on the coast of present-day New

Brunswick saw Jacques Cartier in 1534 and held aloft furs, indicating their desire to trade. Beaver pelts trapped in Canada and the northern British colonies were extremely valuable in Europe, where wearing fur provided warmth and social prestige. Farther south, deerskins, originating in the interior and shipped out of Charleston to European tanners, were equally sought after. Metal tools, weapons, and utensils, woven cloth, and other European goods exchanged for furs were equally valuable to Indians.

Swedes, Dutch, French, British, Spaniards, Russians, and Americans all participated in the pelt trade. In Alaska, Russian traders, *promyshleniki,* began to hunt for sea otter pelts after Vitus Bering, a Dane in the czar's service who gave his name to the straits, reached the Aleutian Islands in 1741. In 1775, the English sea captain James Cook led an expedition to the northwest coast, and by the end of the eighteenth century, ships from several European nations and from New England plied the coastline from Oregon to Alaska, trading for sea otter pelts that they then transported across the Pacific and sold at great profits in China.

Many cities — Albany, New York, Montreal, St. Louis, Detroit, and Charleston — began as fur or deerskin trade markets, and many individual and family fortunes were built on the production and marketing of beaver and deerskins. Trading posts became focus points of cultural as well as economic interaction. The search for new sources of furs and new customers fueled continued European exploration and penetration of Indian country. The fur trade was part of everyday life in early America; and it continued for centuries: the British Hudson Bay Company, established by royal charter in 1670, joked that its initials stood for "Here Before Christ."

Europeans provided capital, organization, manufactured goods, and equipment for the trade. Indians provided much of the labor force: they hunted the animals, guided the fur traders, and paddled the canoes that carried pelts to market. Indian women prepared the skins. Various Indian groups acted as middlemen, securing a lucrative role by conveying pelts and manufactured goods between Europeans and more distant Indian tribes. Indian women played a valuable role as cultural mediators[5] and frequently married European traders, who thereby attained a place in the kinship networks of Indian societies. The children of these unions often grew to become influential leaders in Indian communities and skilled negotiators with colonial society. In areas of Canada and around the Great Lakes, Indian women and French traders produced a new population, known as Métis.[6] In tribes where descent followed the father's line, children of European traders who lacked clan membership might lack a place in their Indian mother's society. But in matrilineal societies, children of mixed ancestry inherited their mother's clan and community: by the eighteenth century, it was not uncommon to find Creek and Cherokee Indians in the Southeast bearing the names of the Scottish traders who fathered them — McIntosh, McGillivray, Ross, and McDonald.

In return for the pelts they supplied and the services they provided, Indians obtained steel knives and axes, firearms, metal cooking vessels, woolen blankets and clothing, glass beads, mirrors, scissors, awls, spoons, linen shirts, hats, buckles, and a host of other goods. The new items sometimes replaced tra-

Fur Trading

This detail from William Fadden, "A Map of the Inhabited Part of Canada . . . With the Frontiers of New York and New England," engraved in London in 1777, shows the commerce that became crucial to the economy of Indian and colonial America. Indian hunters traded beaver pelts and other skins for European merchandise. This scene was part of a centuries-long exchange between Indian America and industrializing Europe, although the participants often attached very different values and meanings to the items being exchanged. National Archives of Canada C-7300.

ditional ones: metal axes were better than stone ones. Sometimes they simply supplemented existing items: birchbark containers continued to be used for maple sugaring long after copper kettles were introduced. Sometimes Indians refashioned the new items in traditional ways: metal pots might be cut up for jewelry. Few Europeans understood why some items cheaply produced in European factories and traded as trinkets and tools took on a social and spiritual significance once they entered Indian hands. For northeastern Algonquian peoples, glass beads and metal objects were often identified with native crystal and copper which possessed special healthful properties.[7]

The Cost of the Fur Trade

But the costs of the fur trade to Indians were enormous. Contagious diseases spread from tribe to tribe as Indians traded with Europeans and then with other Indians. Overhunting depleted animal populations to the point of extinction in some regions and undermined traditional hunting rituals and reciprocal relationships in which hunters treated animal spirits with respect and animals allowed themselves to be hunted. New tools made life easier but traditional craft skills sometimes declined. Competition for new weapons made warfare more common and new weapons made warfare more lethal. Balanced and diversified patterns of subsistence were disrupted as communities focused their energies on hunting and trapping to meet the insatiable demands of European fur markets. Indian people in some areas traded for European goods but resisted being pulled into a dependent relationship on traders; others became heavily dependent on European goods: "Every necessary of life we must have from the white people," a Cherokee chief lamented in the 1750s. "We have been used so long to wrap up our Children as soon as they are born in Goods procured of the white People," said a Creek in the 1770s, "that we cannot do without it."[8] As Native environments became degraded, subsistence patterns changed and Indian people became increasingly dependent on Europeans for goods, clothing, and food. Europeans in turn sought to bring Native resources, land, and labor into the market.[9] Indians were becoming tied to developing European capitalism as both producers and consumers, and being incorporated into a world market. They fell into debt to European traders who offered credit, then sometimes demanded land in payment for accumulated debts. And traders brought alcohol into Indian country.

Alcohol was a crucial commodity for European traders. It could be transported easily in concentrated form and diluted for sale at huge profits, and it was quickly consumed. Traders soon found that liquor was a good way of attracting Indians to trade and then getting them to make that trade on favorable terms. Not all Indians drank and not all who did suffered from it, but alcohol had disastrous effects in many Indian societies. Indian hunters who sold their catch for a bottle of rum often left their families in poverty. Drunken brawls disrupted social relations in communities that traditionally stressed harmony and help between individuals and families. "You Rot Your grain in Tubs, out of which you take and make Strong Spirits You sell it to our young men," said the Catawba chief, Hagler, to his English neighbors in South Carolina in the 1750s; "it Rots their guts and Causes our men to get very sick and many of our people has Lately Died by the Effects of that Strong Drink."[10]

Scholars and clinicians still do not fully understand the exact causes and nature of alcoholism. Like other people, Indians who drank to excess did so for a variety of social, cultural, genetic, and behavioral reasons. Some drank because they enjoyed the sensations alcohol produced; some sought solace in alcohol as they were forced "to reorient their daily lives" in times of wrenching change. Indian leaders throughout colonial America complained about the rum trade and asked that it be halted, but colonial governments could not or would not stem the tide of alcohol into Indian villages.[11]

WAR AND DIPLOMACY IN COLONIAL AMERICA

History books have often portrayed a colonial America in which European settlers built new homes in a new world, wresting the land from Indians who emerged from the forests to burn cabins and lift scalps. In reality, the lines of conflict and competition were more complicated, and colonial America was often a more dangerous place for Indians than for Europeans. The invasion of America by European powers created a bewildering and volatile situation, involving many

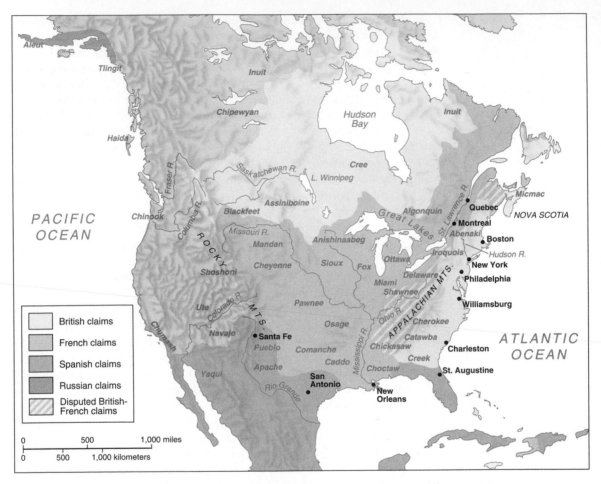

MAP 3.1 Indian Nations and European Territorial Claims, c. 1750
Eighteenth-century maps showed North America as a vast zone of competing and some-times overlapping European claims. In most regions, the actual European presence was slight or nonexistent and Indian people and power predominated. Yet European ambi-tions generated repercussions that reached far into Indian country.

players in changing roles. European settlers competed with Indians for prime lands. European powers competed for North American resources and domi-nance, as well as for Indian allies to help them secure that dominance. Indians re-sisted European intrusions and pretensions yet often forged alliances with the newcomers. Europeans competed for Indian trade; Indians competed with other Indians for European trade. Relations between different tribes sometimes altered dramatically; friends became enemies and vice versa. Indian nations developed their own foreign policies for dealing with the representatives of various European powers, colonial governments, and other tribes. Europeans sought Indian allies and learned the customs of doing business in Indian country.

Relations often broke down in bloody conflict. As they had in King Philip's War and the Pueblo War of Independence, Indian warriors fought for tribal lands and independence in recurrent conflicts against colonial expansion. Increasingly, wars between Indians and Europeans occurred in a larger context of wars between Europeans. The so-called French and Indian wars (which included King William's War, Queen Anne's War, and King George's War, as well as the Seven Years' War or French and Indian War proper—see Table 3.1, page 149) involved Indian warriors fighting on both sides *beside* European armies, as well as fighting *against* European armies invading Indian country. But through it all, Europeans and Indians also reached across cultural divides and engaged in negotiation to achieve what they wanted—peace, trade, land—through diplomacy rather than war.

The Language and Lessons of Diplomacy

France's North American empire, huge in extent but sparsely populated, depended on maintaining the goodwill of an array of Indian peoples. Lacking the advantages in population and in the price and quality of trade goods enjoyed by their British rivals, the French developed diplomacy into a fine art. French officers and agents lived in Indian country, learned Indian ways, and became adept at speaking Indian languages. They followed appropriate protocol, smoking the long-stemmed calumet or "peace pipe," presenting and receiving wampum belts, giving gifts, and making lengthy orations. Failure to do so risked courting disaster: when Antoine de la Mothe Cadillac, founder of Detroit and governor of Louisiana, refused to stop and smoke the calumet with the Natchez Indians on a trip down the Mississippi in 1715, the Natchez interpreted the refusal as an act of war and killed four French traders in retaliation.[12] Preserving Indian alliances was expensive and time-consuming but unavoidable: "one is a slave to Indians in this country," sighed one French officer.[13]

In the Southwest, after the Pueblo War of Independence of 1680, Spaniards learned to temper force with diplomacy in their dealings with Indian peoples. In the eighteenth century, mounted Ute, Comanche, and Apache nomads proved more than a match for heavily equipped European soldiers in thinly spread garrisons. Spaniards came to rely on Pueblo and Pima allies and on diplomacy to defend their provinces. In the eighteenth century, Governor and Captain General of New Mexico Don Tomás Vélez Cachupín recognized that Spain had been too quick to respond with the sword and had alienated Indians whose friendship might have been secured by trade and diplomacy. Vélez made peace with the Utes; he then defeated the Comanches in 1751, and then cultivated peace with them, sitting down and smoking with the Comanche chiefs who visited trade fairs at the Pueblo towns. In Vélez's view, the Spaniards had no choice but to try and preserve peace with the Comanches, Utes, and Apaches because if these tribes joined forces they would crush the small Spanish garrisons in the province.[14] Spanish-Comanche relations continued to be marred by hostilities, however, until Governor Don Juan Bautista de Anza defeated and killed the Comanche chief Cuerno Verde (Green Horn) in 1779 and then

Wyandot Chief with Wampum Belt

Indicative of the interplay of influences that characterized frontier diplomacy, this Wyandot chief wears a European coat and medals but speaks on a wampum belt in traditional manner. In the forest diplomacy of eighteenth-century northeastern North America, wampum belts—pieces of polished shell or beads roped together into strands—conveyed messages, initiated proceedings, recorded agreements, and guaranteed promises. Iroquois orators opened councils by offering wampum to produce a state of mind conducive to calm discussion. Speakers punctuated their talks by handing wampum belts to their listeners; refusing a wampum belt (see page 191) meant the listener rejected what was said. When talks were finished, the wampum belts became part of the tribal record and the collective memory. Canadian Museum of Civilization, image number 80-6675.

made peace between New Mexico and the Comanches in 1786. After meeting with the chiefs of the Comanches, Anza realized "that if the nation had been managed with gentleness and justice since we had known it, the arms of the king perhaps would not have had to spend a grain of powder among them."[15]

Despite a reputation for unrelenting land hunger that prevented anything but hostile and exploitive relations with Indians, the British, like the Spanish, also became skilled in the art of diplomacy and recognized the importance of Indians to their imperial ambitions. "The Importance of Indians is now generally known and understood," wrote South Carolina merchant and Superintendent of Indian Affairs Edmond Atkin in his report to the Board of Trade in England in 1755. "[A] Doubt remains not, that the prosperity of our Colonies on the Continent, will stand or fall with our Interest and favour among them. While they are our Friends, they are the Cheapest and strongest Barrier for the Protection of our Settlements; when Enemies, they are capable by ravaging in their method of War, in spite of all we can do, to render those Possessions almost useless."[16] Englishmen regarded treaties and property deeds as legitimate ways to acquire Indian lands, even though they sometimes practiced fraud and deception in securing these documents. They also used treaties as a forum in which to assert that Indians were subjects of the king, that they were subject to English laws, that they must provide assistance against the French and hostile Indian tribes, and that Indians bore responsibility for past conflicts. Indians regarded treaties and councils as an opportunity to make and cement alliances, air their grievances, secure goods and guarantees in return for land, and exercise a small measure of control over the diminution of their homelands. Indians also, on occasion, rejected English claims to sovereignty and jurisdiction and pointed out English breaches of former agreements. Indians who read the texts of treaties, or who had them read to them, sometimes complained that "these writings appear to contain things that are not," and cited English misinterpretations and misrepresentations of their words point by point.[17] Nevertheless, the English established the system of treaty-making as the principal means by which to acquire and legitimize the acquisition of Indian land; inherited and continued by the United States government, this system was the vehicle through which much of America passed from Indian to non-Indian hands.

Anglo-Indian relations varied from colony to colony. Indian leaders often dealt with representatives of several colonies; they sometimes exploited the situation to their advantage and to preserve their independence. In Pennsylvania, William Penn and the Quakers earned a reputation in the late seventeenth century for fair dealings with the Indians by obtaining their lands through negotiated treaties and deeds. But the Quakers lost control of the colonial legislature, and unfair trade practices, demands for Indian land, and the influx of land-hungry Scotch-Irish settlers turned Pennsylvania into a bloody battleground in the eighteenth century. The Delawares lost the last of their lands in the upper Delaware and Lehigh valleys in the infamous "Walking Purchase" of 1737, when Pennsylvanians produced a team of runners to measure out an old deed that supposedly granted William Penn and his heirs land "as far as a man can go in a day and a half." William Penn's "peaceable kingdom" became a zone of racial hatred and frontier conflict with no place for cultural mediators, a decline into violence that revealed "the final incompatibility of colonial and native dreams about the continent they shared."[18] The Delawares continued to retreat westward before the advancing edge of the colonial frontier.

In New York, the Iroquois dealt with the Dutch until 1664. After the English takeover, they shifted their diplomatic attentions to the British crown and its representatives, building an alliance they likened to the links of a "Covenant Chain," and entering King William's War against the French in the 1680s and '90s. But the war took a heavy toll. French campaigns struck Iroquois villages and starvation stalked the longhouses. By 1700, Iroquois population had been cut in half. Iroquois diplomats traveled to Montreal, Albany, and to the Great Lakes region to make peace with France, Britain, and their Indian allies. They charted a new course of neutrality between competing powers that allowed them to halt their losses and restore some power. The Iroquois combined statesmanship with a reputation for military prowess and held the balance of power in northeastern North America well into the eighteenth century. They compelled the British, like the French, to deal with them and to do so on Iroquois terms, paying constant attention to keeping strong the Covenant Chain that symbolically linked the Iroquois and their allies. The British Superintendent of Indian Affairs in the north during the mid-eighteenth century, Sir William Johnson, set the tone of the British Indian Department for more than a generation. A former trader, Irishman Johnson took a Mohawk wife, immersed himself in Mohawk culture, spoke Mohawk, and became an expert practitioner in the intricate world of Iroquois politics. Known to Mohawks as Warraghiyagey, "he who does much business," or "a man who undertakes great things," he cultivated good relations with important chiefs, gave generous gifts, and mastered the protocol of council-fire diplomacy. Other agents of the British Indian Department married into Indian societies and functioned as intermediaries between crown and tribe.

European Indian agents learned to speak Indian languages, to understand the metaphors of Indian speeches, to smoke the calumet pipe, and to provide a steady flow of gifts that indicated they were men of their word and representatives of a powerful and generous king. In turn, Indians had to adjust and hone their diplomatic skills to survive and succeed in a dangerous new world. Powerful strategically located tribes like the Iroquois in New York and the Choctaws in the lower Mississippi valley were able to play one European power off another to secure trade while maintaining independence. "To preserve the Ballance between us and the French," wrote one British colonial official, "is the great ruling Principle of the Modern Indian Politics."[19] Smaller tribes surrounded by European populations sometimes pursued similar strategies at a local level. The Catawbas of South Carolina, reduced to fewer than five hundred people by 1760 and dependent on Europeans for trade goods, admitted "we cannot live without the assistance of the English." But, as historian James Merrell observes, "they were not willing to become English themselves." In the mid-eighteenth century the Catawba chief, Hagler, practiced a skillful diplomatic balancing act that secured the support of colonial authorities without sacrificing Catawba autonomy.[20] Indian leaders soon realized that Europeans who invited them to the treaty table generally wanted their land, resources, or young men as soldiers. They juggled competing demands, weighing what they gave against what they got, walking a fine line to preserve their independence in an environment of increasing dependency.

Wars for America

Indians and Europeans alike spent tremendous amounts of time and energy talking in an effort to maintain peace, establish and restore friendships, settle disputes, and transfer land. But, as international, intercolonial, interethnic, and intertribal rivalries escalated in North America, diplomacy often unraveled followed by a bloodbath.

King William's War, Queen Anne's War, King George's War, and the Seven Years' (or French and Indian) War all had origins in the old world rivalry of England and France but also produced fighting in North America that involved Indian warriors as well as French and English soldiers and militia. Algonquian tribes like the Abenakis, Ottawas, Shawnees, Delawares, and Potawatomis tended to support their French allies in these wars. Mohegans and Mahicans (sometimes spelled Mohicans) often supplied scouts to the English; when the Iroquois abandoned their neutrality, the Mohawks tended to side with the British, although Senecas occasionally fought with the French.

The Abenakis of northern New England found themselves occupying a borderland between the two competing European powers. French and English agents, missionaries, and traders competed for Abenaki allegiance, and Abenakis sometimes kept their options open, praying with the French yet traveling south to get better prices and goods at English trading posts. As English pressure on Abenaki lands increased, however, most Abenakis made common cause with the French. For almost eighty years, Abenaki warriors launched

TABLE 3.1 A Century of Conflict, 1689–1783

Dates	American Conflict	European Conflict
1689–97	King William's War	War of the League of Augsburg
1702–13	Queen Anne's War	War of the Spanish Succession
1712	Tuscarora War in North Carolina	
1715	Yamassee War in South Carolina	
1723–27	Abenaki wars in Maine and Vermont	
1744–48	King George's War	War of the Austrian Succession
1756–63	French and Indian War	Seven Years' War
1759–61	Cherokee War	
1763–65	"Pontiac's War"	
1774	Lord Dunmore's War	
1775–83	American Revolution	

lightning raids, stalling the northward advance of the English frontier. Abenakis earned a reputation as stalwart allies of the French and implacable enemies of New England. The nineteenth-century historian Francis Parkman, describing the Abenakis at the time of the Seven Years' War, wrote:

> They were nominal Christians, and had been under the control of their missionaries for three generations; but though zealous and sometimes fanatical to the forms of Romanism,° they remained thorough savages in dress, habits, and character. They were the scourge of the New England borders, where they surprised and burned farmhouses and small hamlets, killed men, women, and children without distinction, carried prisoners to their village, subjected them to the torture of "running the gauntlet," and compelled them to witness dances of triumph around the scalps of parents, children, and friends.[21]

Phineas Stevens, a trader and militia captain on the upper Connecticut River, had been captured by Abenakis as a boy, traded with them, and fought them during King George's War. He blamed Abenaki hostility to the English on the French: "were it not for ye French," he said in the early 1750s, "it would be Easy to Live at peace with ye Indians."[22] But the Abenakis did not agree. At a conference in Montreal in 1752, which Stevens attended as an emissary from the governor of Massachusetts, an Abenaki named Ateawanto made clear that Abenakis believed the causes of conflict lay elsewhere: "We hear on all sides that this Governor and the Bostonians [the Abenaki term for the English] say that the Abenakis are bad people," he said. But he insisted "It is you, brother, that always attack us; your mouth is of sugar but your heart of gall. In truth, the moment you begin we are on our guard." The Abenakis were determined to keep

---

°Catholicism.

Watercolor of an Abenaki Man and Woman from the Mission Village at Bécancouer, Quebec

By the eighteenth century, many Abenaki people from Maine, Vermont, and New Hampshire had moved north and built new communities at French mission villages like St. Francis (Odanak) and Bécancouer on the St. Lawrence River. With assistance from their French allies, they raided English colonists on their former homelands during the French and Indian Wars. The conical peaked caps worn by these people were also common among the Penobscots, Passamaquoddies, and Micmacs; they may have been modeled and adapted from Basque caps worn by early French sailors in Canada. Courtesy of the City of Montreal, Records Management and Archives.

their lands but did not seek war: "we ask nothing better than to be quiet, and it depends, brothers, only on you English, to have peace with us."[23] Like other Indians who turned out during the French and Indian Wars, the Abenakis fought for their own reasons.

At the same time, Indians often sought European allies in their struggles against other Indian tribes. As war became endemic in eighteenth-century North America, Indian villages and countryside bore the brunt of the fighting. War had always played an important but limited role in Indian societies; now it began to dominate Indian life. Communities found that they had to survive on a war footing. Traditional nonmilitary activities were often disrupted as husbands, sons, and fathers—producers and protectors—spent more time at war away from the villages, placing greater burdens on the women. Ceremonial and social calendars were interrupted, and cycles of planting, harvesting, hunting, and fishing were subordinated to the demands of campaigns. Indians became more dependent on European allies for goods and provisions. Destruction of crops by enemy forces resulted in hunger and rendered people more susceptible to disease.

Indians fled from regions that had been transformed into battlegrounds between French and English, European and Indian, Indian and Indian. Algonquian people driven from southern and central New England after King Philip's War took refuge to the north in Abenaki country; as English pressure increased along the southern edges of Abenaki territory, many Abenakis in turn withdrew further north. Tuscarora war refugees migrated north from North Carolina to the country of the Iroquois in 1722 where they were adopted as the sixth tribe of the Iroquois confederacy. (Thereafter, the English referred to the Iroquois as the Six Nations.) Coocoochee, a Mohawk woman born near Montreal around 1740, was forced to move five times during a quarter century of war and upheaval in the Northeast, and finally took up residence among the Shawnees in the Ohio country. The Shawnees had mi-

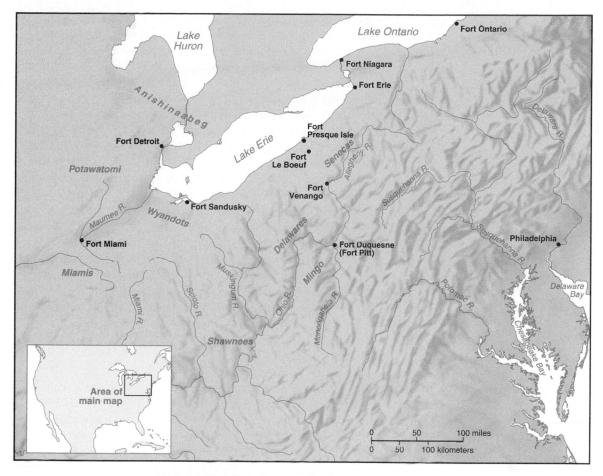

MAP 3.2 The Ohio Country During the Seven Years' War
By the mid-eighteenth century, the Ohio country was home to many Indian peoples, some of them pushed there by the pressure of European settlement in the east. The forks of the Ohio (where the French built Fort Duquesne and the British later built Fort Pitt) were regarded as the key to the West and became the focus of Anglo-French rivalry. When war broke out, the Ohio country became an international and intertribal battleground.

grated from their Ohio homelands in the late seventeenth century in the wake of the Iroquois wars. Many of them relocated to the Southeast, where they developed close contacts with the Creeks and encountered the English. By the mid-eighteenth century most of them were back in Ohio, where they were joined by Mingoes (Iroquois people who had moved west), Delawares, and other displaced peoples in a zone of escalating imperial friction.[24]

Escalating conflict between Britain and France came to a head in the Ohio valley and erupted into what became known as the Seven Years' War (the French and Indian War). When the French began to construct a line of forts there in 1753, the British attempted to drive them out. France's Indian allies routed

General Edward Braddock's army in 1755 as it marched to attack Fort Duquesne at the forks of the Ohio. But the British recovered from early defeats and won stunning victories all around the globe. In 1758 they sent peace overtures to the Ohio Indians. "Why don't you & the French fight in the old country and on the sea?" Delawares asked. "Why do you come to fight on our land? This makes everybody believe you want only to take & settle the Land."[25] Why would the English "wonder at our joining with the French in this present war?" they asked; "were we but sure that you will not take our Lands on the Ohio, or the West side of Allegeny Hills from us; we [could] drive away the French when we please."[26] The British assured them they would protect their homelands and the Ohio Indians made peace, clearing the way for the British to advance on Fort Duquesne. Unable to hold the fort without Indian support, the French blew it up and retreated. In 1759 the British also took Fort Niagara, captured Quebec, and won command of the seas. France could no longer supply the West. The Franco-Indian alliance came apart so rapidly that some Indians became alarmed: they did not want French troops and forts on their land, but the French collapse left no counterweight to British power. The Indians' goal throughout the war had been to keep their lands independent of foreign domination. They watched with apprehension as the British built Fort Pitt on the ruins of Fort Duquesne.[27]

Division within Tribal Communities

Some tribes split into factions over issues of peace, war, and alliance with competing European powers. Militants from different tribes joined forces in intertribal alliances, while divisions grew at home with those who advocated a less militant stance.[28] New communities formed as refugees from different tribes fled to safer areas or congregated in armed camps to continue the fight.

Recurrent warfare produced repercussions on social and political structures. Most Indian societies in the Eastern Woodlands had two classes of chiefs. Older civil or village chiefs, often called sachems, guided the community in daily affairs and in reaching consensus on issues of importance. Younger chiefs with impressive military records led warriors on campaign but relinquished authority when they returned to the village. Violent deeds had no place in kin-based Indian communities where, with no courts, police, or jails, social harmony was a common and necessary condition, not just an ideal. Now, as war became a normal state of affairs and war parties came and went with increasing regularity, war chiefs exerted more influence in tribal councils. European allies bolstered their position with supplies of guns and gifts of medals and uniforms, and the number of contenders for such support increased. Civil or peace chiefs saw their influence decline. A group of Seneca warriors in 1762 told Sir William Johnson that they, not the sachems, had "the power & Ability to settle Matters"; the sachems, they said, were "a parcell of Old People who say Much, but who Mean or Act very little." Civil chiefs lost their ability to restrain headstrong young warriors, which had provided an important generational balance in many Indian societies. "Formerly the Warriors were governed by the wisdom of their uncles the Sachems," said an Onondaga chief during the Revolution, "but now they take their own way & dispose of themselves without consulting their uncles the Sachems."[29] Consequently, the voices for war in Indian communities grew louder and less restrained. Generations of recurrent warfare left an indelible mark on Indian societies and cultures, and helped create the stereotype of warlike Indians that Europeans and later Americans invoked to justify treating them as "savages."

European involvement also sometimes undercut the influence of Indian women in councils and decision-making. Iroquois men did the hunting, fighting, trading, and diplomacy, which took them away from the villages and into the forest, but an Iroquois town "was largely a female world," perhaps increasingly so as men went away to war more often. Men cleared the fields but women did the planting, cultivating, and harvesting, and women possessed the power attributed to fertility that was necessary in performing rituals that ensured successful crops. Men built them, but women controlled the longhouses that sheltered Iroquois clans and families. Women's economic power gave them considerable political power. Clan mothers could decide the fate of captives, elect and remove council chiefs, and influence decisions for war or peace: "the Elders decide no important affair without their advice," noted one French missionary.[30]

However, Europeans were primarily interested in Indians as allies (or enemies) in war and as customers in the fur and deerskin trades and expected to deal with men—the warriors and hunters—not women. Even Sir William Johnson, who married Mohawk Molly Brant and who understood the role of women in Iroquois politics, tried to ignore them. At a council meeting in the spring of 1762, Johnson barred women or children and invited "none but those who were Qualified for, and Authorized to proceed on business." When the Iroquois men reminded him that it was customary for their women to be present on such occasions "being of Much Estimation Amongst Us, in that we proceed from them," Johnson replied that he appreciated the women's "Zeal & Desire to promote a good work," but insisted that "No more persons would Attend any meeting than were necessary for the Discharge of the business on Which they were Summoned." In the eyes of the British superintendent, Indian women were politically unnecessary.[31] But European males failed to eradicate the influence of Iroquois clan mothers; Molly Brant's influence actually increased as a result of her connection to Sir William Johnson. After his death in 1774, she remained a considerable presence in British Iroquois diplomacy: an officer during the Revolution rated "Miss Molly Brants Influence" over her people as "far superior to that of all their Chiefs put together."[32] In some ways, the changes bombarding Indian society affected women's lives less than men's. Many women "continued to hoe their corn, raise their children, and exercise traditional kinds of power as they always had."[33]

Captives Taken, Captives Returned

Another result of ongoing warfare was the increase in the number of captives, Indian and European. Indians carried off prisoners as slaves or adopted them to bolster populations in place of relatives killed in battle. French movement

The Indians Delivering up the English Captives to Colonel Bouquet

"Liberating" the young captives in 1764 in compliance with the terms of the peace treaty proved to be a heartbreaking experience for the captives and for their adoptive Shawnee and Delaware families. This engraving by Benjamin West accompanied William Smith's An Historical Account of the Expedition against the Ohio Indians in the Year 1764, *published in 1766. Dartmouth College Library.*

down the Mississippi and westward penetration of English traders from Charleston, South Carolina, brought guns and slave raiding to the lower Mississippi valley by the end of the seventeenth century. Newly armed bands of Indians raided villages on both sides of the Mississippi for slaves whom they sold to English traders. The slaves were then marched east to Charleston, to be used in colonial households and plantations or to be shipped as slaves to the Caribbean.

Europeans who fell into Indian hands as war captives sometimes experienced a different fate. In February 1704, a war party of Abenakis, Mohawks from Kahnawake or Caughnawaga, and Hurons from Lorette (both on the St. Lawrence in Quebec), together with their French allies, sacked the town of Deerfield, Massachusetts, and carried off more than a hundred people, including the town's minister, the Rev. John Williams, and his family. As the Indians fled north along the frozen Connecticut River, they tomahawked Williams's wife who had recently given birth and could not keep up the pace. But they carried, or pulled along on toboggans, the captive children, including Williams's seven-year-old daughter, Eunice. When John Williams was liberated after two and a half years in captivity, he wrote an account of his experiences, *The Redeemed Captive Returning to Zion.* In it, he expounded the Puritan view of captivity as a testing of good Protestants, an ordeal which, with God's help, they survived by resisting the torments of Indian savages and the inducements of evil Jesuit priests who tried to turn them into Catholics. But Eunice's fate said something different about the experiences of some captives in Indian society. She stayed with the Indians, converted to Catholicism, and married a Mohawk of Kahnawake. Despite repeated entreaties from her father and brother, she refused to return home. One emissary reported that Eunice was "thoroughly naturalized" to the Indian way of life and "obstinately resolved to live and dye here." Another reported that the Indians "would as soon part with their hearts" as let Eunice return home. To her family's dismay and her countrymen's consternation, Eunice Williams—although she later visited her New England relatives—lived with the Indians for more than eighty years and died among the people with whom she had made her life, her home, and her own family.[34]

Other captives at other times and places followed Eunice's example. Mary Jemison, who was captured and adopted by the Senecas as a teenager in 1758, married an Indian husband and raised a family. In time, she came to share fully in the lives of Seneca women (see Mary Jemison's account, pages 167–70).

Captives who did return to colonial society did not always come home happily. After Colonel Henry Bouquet defeated the Indians of the Ohio valley at Bushy Run in 1763, he dictated peace terms that required the Indians to hand over all captives they had taken during the French and Indian War. The Shawnees and Delawares complied, but they reminded Bouquet that the captives "have been all tied to us by Adoption. . . . we have taken as much care of these Prisoners, as if they were [our] own Flesh, and blood." Many of the Shawnees' captives resisted their "liberation." An observer who was present when the Indians delivered their captives to Bouquet said that the children had become "accustomed to look upon the Indians as the only connexions they had, having been tenderly treated by them, and speaking their language," and "they considered their new state in the light of a captivity, and parted from the savages with tears." Some of the adult captives were equally reluctant to return, and the Shawnees "were obliged to bind several of their prisoners and force them along to the camp; and some women, who had been delivered up, afterwards found means to escape and run back to the Indian towns. Some, who could not make their escape, clung to their savage acquaintances at parting, and continued many days in bitter lamentations, even refusing sustenance."[35]

Women and children were more likely to remain with the Indians than were men, but Eunice Williams and Mary Jemison were not typical. Many women, clung to hopes of returning home and gathering back their children.

INDIANS AND THE AMERICAN REVOLUTION

By 1763, after more than half a century of conflict with France, Britain emerged as the victorious colonial power in North America. Indian tribes which had traded and allied with the French now found that they had to deal with the representatives of King George. Many British officials regarded the Indians as a defeated people and, with the war won, saw little reason to drain a depleted treasury by giving them gifts. The Iroquois could no longer play off the English and the French, and with peace a flood of English settlers invaded Indian lands. Inevitably, conflict ensued. In one of the most famous Indian wars for independence, named after the Ottawa chief Pontiac, tribes in the Great Lakes and the Ohio valley regions rallied against the British. Pontiac's warriors drove the redcoats back on almost every front until the combination of European military superiority and disease turned the tide. In a calculated strategic move, Jefferey Amherst, the commander of the British army in North America at the end of the French and Indian War, may have ordered that blankets infected with smallpox be distributed to the Indians.

Attempting to Draw a Line

In 1763, the British attempted to regulate the frontier and avoid further Indian wars of resistance by prohibiting settlement on Indian lands west of the Appalachian Mountains. Many colonials felt cheated and land speculators like George Washington, who had investments in the West, began to protest against the empire they had formerly served. Like Indian sachems who were unable to control their young men, the British government was unable to prevent its subjects from encroaching on Indian lands. The Royal Proclamation that attempted to contain westward expansion became one of the first steps on the road to the American Revolution.

The British themselves did not intend the proclamation line to be a permanent barrier. The king's agents, meeting with Indian tribes in formal and open council, could negotiate cessions of land to the crown that would push the

The Proclamation Line of 1763
The British Proclamation of 1763 was a major development in British Indian policy, triggered events that contributed to the American Revolution, and remains fundamental to many First Nations land claims today in Canada. It also received plenty of attention at the time; this map depicting the line was published in The Gentleman's Magazine, *an eighteenth-century news journal. Courtesy of the John Carter Brown Library at Brown University.*

Joseph Brant (c. 1797) by Charles Wilson Peale

The Mohawk Joseph Brant (1743–1807) was probably the most famous Indian of his day. He sat for portraits by such noted artists as George Romney and Gilbert Stuart, as well as by Peale. Educated at Eleazar Wheelock's Indian Charity School in Connecticut, Brant was bilingual and literate, and assisted in translating the gospel into Mohawk. He visited England twice, was received at court, and befriended the Prince of Wales. He was the protégé of Sir William Johnson, who married Brant's sister. Brant became a war leader on the British side during the Revolution. Though bitterly disappointed by Britain's abandonment of its Indian allies in 1783, he continued to play a pivotal role in relations between the northeastern Indians, the British, and the new United States. Courtesy of Independence National Historical Park Collection.

line westward. However, when Sir William Johnson met with the Iroquois at Fort Stanwix in 1768, he exceeded his authority and purchased a huge tract of land from the assembled Indian delegates. Most of the land the Iroquois sold was south of the Ohio River—hunting territory claimed by the Shawnees and Cherokees, who were not at the treaty negotiations. The Iroquois delegates deftly diverted colonial expansion south of their own land, but lost prestige among western tribes who regarded the Fort Stanwix treaty as an act of betrayal. (See page 160 and page 202 [Map 4.1, United States Treaty and Land Cessions in 1810].) The treaty thrust a wedge into the heart of Indian country. Colonists swarmed into Kentucky, confident that these lands had been duly ceded, and came into open conflict with Shawnee and Cherokee warriors determined to defend their hunting grounds against trespassers.

Continued encroachment on Shawnee land produced open conflict with the Virginians in 1774 in a war named after Lord Dunmore, the colonial governor of Virginia. The Shawnee chief Cornstalk argued against war but led his warriors at the Battle of Point Pleasant at the junction of the Ohio and Kanawha rivers in present-day West Virginia. The Shawnees were defeated and made peace, reaffirming the Ohio River as their boundary, but hostilities had hardly ceased before the American Revolution broke out. The Shawnees and their neighbors would once again fight for their lands.

Taking Sides

The American Revolution was a source of considerable confusion to Indian peoples: the British appeared to have fallen to fighting among themselves. Both the Americans and the British tried to enlist Indian allies. At first most Indians chose to remain neutral in what they regarded as a family quarrel. But diplomatic and economic pressures rendered neutrality difficult and dangerous. For the most part, Indians who fought in the Revolution sided with the British. They recognized that the war was a contest for Indian land as well as for American independence, and their experiences of the land hunger of American settlers convinced them that their best hopes of survival lay in supporting the crown. Different motives prompted different groups, but by and large the Indians were fighting for their freedom just as much as American patriots were.

The Revolution brought both suffering and civil war to Indian country. Cherokee warriors ignored the warnings of their elders and went to war in the hope that they could drive out American trespassers (see "The Revolution Comes to the Cherokees" pages 172–80). Instead, American expeditions during the war burned Cherokee towns and American peacemakers exacted even more land. The Iroquois Confederacy split as the Oneidas and Tuscaroras joined the Americans, while the Mohawks, Onondagas, Cayugas, and Senecas supported the British. Iroquois warriors killed each other in battle. In the fall of 1779, responding to raids on the frontiers of New York and Pennsylvania, George Washington dispatched an American expedition to burn out the Iroquois. General John Sullivan's army marched through the heart of Iroquois country, burned some forty towns, cut down orchards, destroyed crops, "and left nothing but the bare soil and timber." The Indians pulled back as Sullivan advanced but returned to find their homes laid waste. The winter that followed was bitter. Mary Jemison, who was living with the Senecas at the time, remembered in her old age "our feelings when we found that there was not a mouthful of any kind of sustenance left, not even enough to keep a child one day from perishing with hunger." The snow fell to a depth of five feet and the weather became so bitterly cold "that almost all the game upon which the Indians depended for subsistence, perished, and reduced them almost to a state of starvation through that and three or four succeeding years."[36] Deprived of food and shelter, Iroquois refugees crowded around the British garrison at Fort Niagara, which their warriors used as a base to resume the war in the spring. American soldiers who had accompanied Sullivan told of the fertile lands they had marched through, and American settlers and land speculators eagerly awaited the end of the war.

In the Ohio valley, Delawares and Shawnees found themselves pressured by British agents from Detroit and American agents from Fort Pitt to join their side as allies. Efforts to remain neutral proved futile. Led by the pro-American chief White Eyes, the Delawares signed a treaty with the United States in 1778, but the Americans were unable to deliver the promised supplies and protection. American militia killed White Eyes that same year and in 1781 at Gnadenhütten, a Moravian mission, slaughtered a village of pacifist Delawares who had converted to the Moravian religion. The Shawnee chief, Cornstalk, also worked to keep his people out of the war, but American soldiers killed him under a flag of truce in 1777. By the end of the war, Delaware and Shawnee warriors were fighting alongside the British and inflicting defeats on American forces in the West. In 1782, the Indians lured Daniel Boone and the Kentucky militia into an ambush and routed them at the Battle of Blue Licks.

In New England, most Indians supported their American neighbors. Warriors from the mission town of Stockbridge in western Massachusetts were among the first Indians to fight in the conflict, joining Washington's army at the siege of Boston in 1775. They suffered heavy casualties throughout the war, only to find that their American neighbors had taken over their lands and town while they were away fighting. Other Indian towns in New England also sustained heavy casualties but secured few rewards for their services.

Peace Treaties

In 1783, at the Treaty of Paris, Britain recognized the independence of the United States and acknowledged American sovereignty over all territory south of the Great Lakes, east of the Mississippi, and north of Florida. In doing so, Britain abandoned its Indian allies to the mercy of the Americans. Many Indians had fought for the king throughout the war, but they were neither represented nor included in the peace treaty. Now they faced a new power which regarded them as defeated enemies who had forfeited both lands and rights. The Peace of Paris brought little peace in Indian country. The Iroquois were "thunderstruck" when they heard of the peace terms, and the Mohawk chief Joseph

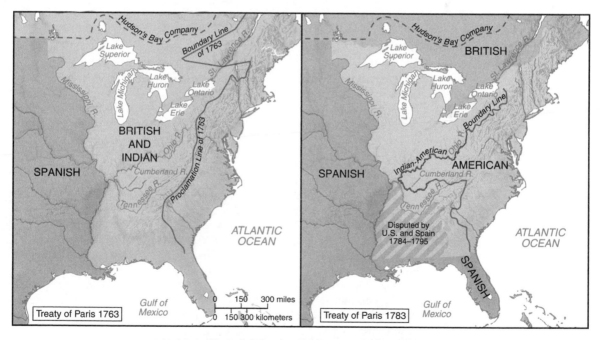

MAP 3.3 Changing Territorial Claims, 1763–1783

At the Treaty of Paris in 1763, which ended the Seven Years' War, France ceded its North American territorial claims to Britain (France had ceded its lands west of the Mississippi to Spain to keep them out of British hands). Twenty years later another Treaty of Paris ended the War of American Independence, and Britain ceded territory east of the Mississippi, south of the Great Lakes, and north of Florida to the new United States. In all of these agreements, the bulk of the territories transferred were Indian homelands, and Indian power stood between paper claims and actual possession of the lands.

Brant, who had fought for the British throughout the war, was enraged and "cast down" to be betrayed by "Our Allies for whom we have so often freely Bled."[37]

In the summer of 1784, more than two hundred Indians—Iroquois, Shawnees, Cherokees, Creeks, and others—who were visiting St. Louis told the Spanish governor they were already feeling the effects of the American victory: "The Americans, a great deal more ambitious and numerous than the English, put us out of our lands, forming therein great settlements, extending themselves like a plague of locusts in the territories of the Ohio River which we inhabit." For them, the American victory meant continued warfare and hunger; it was, they said, "the greatest blow that could have been dealt us."[38] Indian delegates met with American treaty commissioners at Fort Stanwix (1784) in New York, Fort McIntosh (1785) in western Pennsylvania, and Fort Finney (1786) in southwestern Ohio (see "The Treaty of Fort Finney with the Shawnees," pages 181–92). They recognized American sovereignty and handed over enormous tracts of land as the price of peace. American veterans who had seen fertile lands while campaigning in Indian country were eager to return and occupy them.

References

1. James Axtell, *The Invasion Within: The Contest of Cultures in Colonial North America* (New York: Oxford University Press, 1985).
2. James H. Merrell, *The Indians' New World: Catawbas and Their Neighbors from European Contact through the Era of Removal* (Chapel Hill: University of North Carolina Press, 1989), 210.
3. Colin G. Calloway, ed., *The World Turned Upside Down*, 101–4; Franklin's version is in Leonard W. Labaree, ed., *Papers of Benjamin Franklin,* 36 vols to date. (New Haven: Yale University Press, 1959–61), 4:483. For broader coverage of Indian education, see Margaret Connell Szasz, *Indian Education in the American Colonies, 1607–1783* (Albuquerque: University of New Mexico Press, 1988), and Axtell, *The Invasion Within.*
4. Daniel H. Usner, Jr., *Indians, Settlers, and Slaves in a Frontier Exchange Economy: The Lower Mississippi Valley before 1783* (Chapel Hill: University of North Carolina Press, 1992), quote at 277.
5. Clara Sue Kidwell, "Indian Women as Cultural Mediators," *Ethnohistory* 39 (1992), 97–107. On cultural mediators more generally, see Margaret Connell Szasz, ed., *Between Indians and White Worlds: The Cultural Broker* (Norman: University of Oklahoma Press, 1994).
6. Jacqueline Peterson and Jennifer S. H. Brown, eds., *The New Peoples: Being and Becoming Métis in North America* (Lincoln: University of Nebraska Press, 1985); Susan Sleeper-Smith, *Indian Women and French Men: Retinking Cultural Encounter in the Western Great Lakes* (Amherst: University of Massachusetts Press, 2001).
7. Christopher L. Miller and George R. Hamell explore the spiritual associations of glass beads and other trade items in "New Perspectives on Indian-White Contact: Cultural Symbols and Colonial Trade," *Journal of American History* 73 (1988), 311–28.

8. Quoted in Colin G. Calloway, *The American Revolution in Indian Country: Crisis and Diversity in Native American Communities* (New York: Cambridge University Press, 1995), 11.

9. Richard White, *The Roots of Dependency: Subsistence, Environment, and Social Change among the Choctaws, Pawnees, and Navajos* (Lincoln: University of Nebraska Press, 1983).

10. Quoted in Colin G. Calloway, ed., *The World Turned Upside Down: Indian Voices from Early America* (Boston: Bedford Books, 1994), 108.

11. Peter C. Mancall, *Deadly Medicine: Indians and Alcohol in Early America* (Ithaca: Cornell University Press, 1995), esp. 5–8.

12. Usner, *Indians, Settlers, and Slaves in a Frontier Exchange Economy,* 29.

13. Edward P. Hamilton, ed., *Adventure in the Wilderness: The American Journals of Louis Antoine de Bougainville, 1756–1760* (Norman: University of Oklahoma Press, 1964), 170.

14. Alfred Barnaby Thomas, ed., *The Plains Indians and New Mexico: A Collection of Documents Illustrative of the History of the Eastern Frontier of New Mexico* (Albuquerque: University of New Mexico Press, 1940), 137.

15. Alfred Barnaby Thomas, trans. and ed., *Forgotten Frontiers: A Study of the Spanish Indian Policy of Don Juan Bautista de Anza, Governor of New Mexico 1777–1787* (Norman: University of Oklahoma Press, 1932), 317.

16. Wilbur R. Jacobs, ed., *The Appalachian Indian Frontier: The Edmond Atkin Report and Plan of 1755* (Lincoln: University of Nebraska Press, 1967), 3–4.

17. Quoted in Calloway, ed., *The World Turned Upside Down,* 92.

18. James H. Merrell, *Into the American Woods: Negotiators on the Pennsylvania Frontier* (New York: W. W. Norton, 1999).

19. Quoted in Daniel K. Richter, *The Ordeal of the Longhouse: The Peoples of the Iroquois League in the Era of European Colonization* (Chapel Hill: University of North Carolina Press, 1992), 206.

20. James H. Merrell, "'Minding the Business of the Nation': Hagler as Catawba Leader," *Ethnohistory* 33 (1986), 55–70; quote from Merrell, *The Indians' New World,* 166.

21. Francis Parkman, *Montcalm and Wolfe: The French and Indian War* (New York: Da Capo Press, 1995), 452–53.

22. Quoted in Colin G. Calloway, *The Western Abenakis of Vermont 1600–1800: War, Migration, and the Survival of an Indian People* (Norman: University of Oklahoma Press, 1990), 162.

23. Colin G. Calloway, ed., *Dawnland Encounters: Indians and Europeans in Northern New England* (Hanover, N.H.: University Press of New England, 1991), 121.

24. Michael N. McConnell, *A Country Between: The Upper Ohio Valley and Its Peoples, 1724–1774* (Lincoln: University of Nebraska Press, 1992).

25. Calloway, ed., *The World Turned Upside Down,* 133–34.

26. *Pennsylvania Archives,* 1st series, 3 (1853), 548–49.

27. Fred Anderson, *The Crucible of War: The Seven Years' War and the Fate of Empire in British North America* (New York: Knopf, 1999).

28. Gregory Evans Dowd, *A Spirited Resistance: The North American Indian Struggle for Unity, 1745–1815* (Baltimore: Johns Hopkins University Press, 1992).

29. Seneca and Onondaga quotes from Calloway, *The American Revolution in Indian Country,* 7, 59.

30. Richter, *The Ordeal of the Longhouse,* 22, 43.

31. James Axtell, ed., *The Indian Peoples of Eastern America: A Documentary History of the Sexes* (New York: Oxford University Press, 1981), 156–57.

32. Quoted in Lois M. Feister and Bonnie Pulis, "Molly Brant: Her Domestic and Political Roles," in Robert S. Grumet, ed., *Northeastern Indian Lives, 1632–1816* (Amherst: University of Massachusetts Press, 1996), 313.

33. Theda Perdue, *Cherokee Women: Gender and Culture Change, 1700–1835* (Lincoln: University of Nebraska Press, 1998), 186.

34. John Demos, *The Unredeemed Captive: A Family Story from Early America* (New York: Knopf, 1994); see also Evan Haefeli and Kevin Sweeney, "Revisiting *The Redeemed Captive: New Perspectives on the 1704 Attack on Deerfield*," *William and Mary Quarterly*, 3d series, 52 (1995), 3–46; reprinted in Colin G. Calloway, ed., *After King Philip's War: Presence and Persistence in Indian New England* (Hanover, N.H.: University Press of New England, 1997).

35. William Smith, *Historical Account of the Expedition against the Ohio Indians in the Year 1764* (Cincinnati, 1868), 80–81.

36. Quoted in Calloway, ed., *The World Turned Upside Down*, 159–60.

37. Calloway, ed., *The World Turned Upside Down*, 167–69.

38. Quoted in Calloway, *The American Revolution in Indian Country*, vi, 281.

Suggested Readings

Anderson, Fred. *Crucible of War: The Seven Years' War and the Fate of Empire in British North America* (New York: Knopf, 2000).

Axtell, James. *The Invasion Within: The Contest of Cultures in Colonial North America* (New York: Oxford University Press, 1985).

Axtell, James, ed. *Natives and Newcomers: The Cultural Origins of North America* (New York: Oxford University Press, 2001).

Calloway, Colin G. *The American Revolution in Indian Country: Crisis and Diversity in Native American Communities* (New York: Cambridge University Press, 1995).

Calloway, Colin G. *New Worlds for All: Indians, Europeans, and the Remaking of Early America* (Baltimore: Johns Hopkins University Press, 1997).

Calloway, Colin G., ed. *The World Turned Upside Down: Indian Voices from Early America* (Boston: Bedford Books, 1994).

Clayton, Andrew R. L., and Frederika J. Teute, eds. *Contact Points: American Frontiers from the Mohawk Valley to the Mississippi, 1750–1830* (Chapel Hill: University of North Carolina Press, 1998).

Dowd, Gregory Evans. *A Spirited Resistance: The North American Indian Struggle for Unity, 1745–1815* (Baltimore: Johns Hopkins University Press, 1992).

Dowd, Gregory Evans. *War Under Heaven: Pontiac, the Indian Nations, and the British Empire* (Baltimore: Johns Hopkins University Press, 2002).

Hinderaker, Eric. *Elusive Empires: Constructing Colonialism in the Ohio Valley, 1673–1800* (Cambridge: Cambridge University Press, 1997).

Mancall, Peter C. *Deadly Medicine: Indians and Alcohol in Early America* (Ithaca: Cornell University Press, 1995).

Mancall, Peter C., and James H. Merrell, eds. *American Encounters: Natives and Newcomers from European Contact to Indian Removal, 1500–1850* (New York: Routledge, 2000).

Mandell, Daniel R. *Behind the Frontier: Indians in Eighteenth-Century Eastern Massachusetts* (Lincoln: University of Nebraska Press, 1996).

Merrell, James H. *The Indians' New World: Catawbas and Their Neighbors from European Contact through the Era of Removal* (Chapel Hill: University of North Carolina Press, 1989).

Merrell, James H. *Into the American Woods: Negotiators on the Pennsylvania Frontier* (New York: W. W. Norton, 1999).

Merritt, Jane T. *At the Crossroads: Indians and Empires on a Mid-Atlantic Frontier, 1700–1763* (Chapel Hill: University of North Carolina Press, 2003).

O'Brien, Jean. *Dispossession by Degrees: Indian Land and Identity in Natick, Massachusetts, 1650–1790* (Cambridge: Cambridge University Press, 1997).

Perdue, Theda. *Cherokee Women: Gender and Culture Change, 1700–1835* (Lincoln: University of Nebraska Press, 1998).

Richter, Daniel K. *Facing East from Indian Country: A Native History of Early America* (Cambridge, Mass.: Harvard University Press, 2001).

Richter, Daniel K. *The Ordeal of the Longhouse: The Peoples of the Iroquois League in the Era of European Colonization* (Chapel Hill: University of North Carolina Press, 1992).

Usner, Daniel H., Jr. *Indians, Settlers, and Slaves in a Frontier Exchange Economy: The Lower Mississippi Valley before 1783* (Chapel Hill: University of North Carolina Press, 1992).

White, Richard. *The Middle Ground: Indians, Empires, and Republics in the Great Lakes Region, 1650–1815* (New York: Cambridge University Press, 1991).

Wood, Peter H., Gregory A. Waselkov, and M. Thomas Hatley, eds. *Powhatan's Mantle: Indians in the Colonial Southeast* (Lincoln: University of Nebraska Press, 1989).

A Captive with the Senecas

People who had endured and survived captivity often wrote or related narratives of their experiences in which they, or their editors, portrayed Indians as bloodthirsty savages who scalped and tortured men, tomahawked children indiscriminately, and subjected women to "unspeakable horrors." Some twentieth-century writers and film-makers have perpetuated such images of Indian savagery. Although many captives suffered violent treatment, Indian captors often had another purpose. They frequently took captives with the intention of adopting them into their family and community.

Indians in the northeastern woodlands took captives to assuage the grief of bereaved relatives and appease the spirits of deceased kinsfolk. War parties often made raids for the specific purpose of taking captives, and they sometimes brought extra clothing and moccasins for the prisoners they expected to seize. With escalating losses to war and diseases in the wake of European invasion, captive-taking became a way of maintaining population levels as well as patching holes torn in the social fabric of kin- and clan-based Indian communities: captives were often adopted to fill the specific place of a deceased relative. The imperial wars waged between England and France from 1689 to 1763 introduced an additional incentive for taking captives, as the French bought prisoners to ransom to the English. During the French and Indian Wars, Indians abducted more than 1,600 people from New England alone, carrying them north to Canada. Some of the captives did not survive the ordeal — they succumbed to hardships of travel, hunger and disease, or were killed by their captors. Many of those who survived the grueling journey northwards were sold to the French and later ransomed to the English. Some made new lives for themselves in Canada. Others were adopted into Indian communities.

The captives' fates and experiences varied according to their age, gender, and health, the character and feelings of their captors, and chance. Older people, adult males, and crying infants might be tomahawked and left for dead, but women and children were often treated with consideration once the raiding party escaped pursuit. Indian warriors generally treated kindly those captives who were likely to be adopted. Contrary to popular fears, Indian warriors in the Eastern Woodlands did not rape female captives. Warriors ritually prepared for war and invoked spiritual assistance; preserving the purity of their war medicine demanded sexual abstinence, while intercourse with someone who might be adopted into one's clan constituted incest. "None of the Indians were

Mary Jemison
Captured by Indians in 1758 at age fifteen, Mary Jemison (ca. 1742–1833) was adopted by Senecas and spent the rest of her life as an Iroquois woman. Known locally as "the white woman of the Genesee," she is memorialized in this statue in Letchworth State Park in the Genesee River Valley in New York. Her life story, which she related in her old age, was first published in 1824 and has been reprinted more than thirty times. Rochester Museum and Science Center.

disposed to show insults of any nature," former captive Susanna Johnson recalled.[1] Hard travel in moccasins in harsh weather and over rugged terrain, irregular meals and unfamiliar diet, and separation from family and home all took a toll on captives. But these experiences also initiated them into a new way of life.

Once the trek into Indian country was over, captives faced new ordeals. Arriving at a village, they might be made to run a gauntlet between two ranks of Indians brandishing sticks and clubs. Indians mourning relatives might vent their grief by demanding that a captive be tortured to death. But often they dressed and painted the captives in Indian style and ritually adopted them into a family. Time and the wealth of kinship relations that captives found in Indian society healed many wounds. Some captives preferred not to return home even when the opportunity arose, and most found things they admired in Indian society. Many women appear to have found life in an Indian community more rewarding than the isolation and hard work that was the common lot of a wife on the colonial frontier.

Children proved especially susceptible to adoptive "Indianization." Titus King, captured by Abenakis in Massachusetts, saw many English children held by Indians in Canada. He estimated it took only six months for children to forsake their parents, forget their homes, refuse to speak their own language, and "be holley swollowed up with the Indians" and adopt their ways.[2] Susanna Johnson's son, Sylvanus, whom she described as having become "a perfect Indian" after three years with the Abenakis, apparently never lost his Indian ways. According to the nineteenth-century town history of Charlestown, New Hampshire, "he so much preferred the modes of Indian life to the customs of civilization that he often expressed regret at having been ransomed. He always maintained, and no arguments could convince him to the contrary, that the Indians were a far more moral race than the whites."[3]

Captives who returned home were permanently changed by the experience. For some, it was a nightmare never to be forgotten. Others retained lasting connections to Indian communities and real affection for the families which had adopted them. It was not unusual for former captors to visit former captives in the English settlements, bringing news of Indian friends and relatives.

Some former captives became intermediaries between Indians and whites. Phineas Stevens, the former Abenaki captive and militia captain during King George's War, ran a trading post where his adoptive Abenaki father visited him. Stevens seems to have enjoyed the respect and business of English settlers and Abenakis alike.

Accurate information about and viewpoints from Native American women in colonial times are extremely scarce, and historians usually have tried to reconstruct the experiences of Indian women through words written by European men. One of the few exceptions is the life story of Mary Jemison, a white woman who was captured by Shawnees and adopted by the Senecas at about age fifteen in 1758. The Iroquois traditionally adopted captives into their society to fill the place of deceased relatives. Mary Jemison married an Indian husband and raised a family. In time and in cultural allegiance she became a Seneca, sharing fully the lives of eighteenth-century Seneca women. She lived most of her life in the Genesee country of western New York, the Seneca heartland, and became known as the "white woman of the Genesee." In her old age, she dictated her story. Though the narrative of her life is flawed by the intrusive influence of her nineteenth-century writer, it nevertheless provides us with a rare opportunity to read the words of a woman who was living in Indian country in times of dramatic change.

These extracts from the autobiography of Mary Jemison give insights into the ways in which — by adoption, acceptance, kind treatment, and family ties — one woman came to be a "white Indian." After the American Revolution, Mary Jemison had the chance to return to white society but refused. By the time she died, she had had two husbands (one a Delaware, the other a Seneca), she had borne eight children (only three of whom survived her), and she had thirty-nine grandchildren and fourteen great-grandchildren. Jemison is still a prominent name among the Senecas.

▶ Questions for Consideration

1. European males typically depicted Indian women as living in unremitting hardship, and colonial literature often told of European women being raped and abused when captured by Indians. What indications does Mary Jemison in the following document give that the lives of women — Indian or European — in Seneca society were rather different?

2. What information does Jemison offer about Indian societies and intercultural interaction in early America?

3. What value can the narrative of a captive have as a historical source providing a view of events in Indian country?

MARY JEMISON
A Narrative of Her Life (1824)

At night we arrived at a small Seneca Indian town, at the mouth of a small river, that was called by the Indians, in the Seneca language, She-nan-jee, where the two Squaws to whom I belonged resided. There we landed, and the Indians went on; which was the last I ever saw of them.

Having made fast to the shore, the Squaws left me in the canoe while they went to their wigwam or house in the town, and returned with a suit of Indian clothing, all new, and very clean and nice. My clothes, though whole and good when I was taken, were now torn in pieces, so that I was almost naked. They first undressed me and threw my rags into the river; then washed me clean and dressed me in the new suit they had just brought, in complete Indian style; and then led me home and seated me in the center of their wigwam.

I had been in that situation but a few minutes, before all the Squaws in the town came in to see me. I was soon surrounded by them, and they immediately set up a most dismal howling, crying bitterly, and wringing their hands in all the agonies of grief for a deceased relative.

Their tears flowed freely, and they exhibited all the signs of real mourning. At the commencement of this scene, one of their number began, in a voice somewhat between speaking and singing, to recite some words to the following purport, and continued the recitation till the ceremony was ended; the company at the same time varying the appearance of their countenances, gestures and tone of voice, so as to correspond with the sentiments expressed by their leader:

Source: Colin G. Galloway, *The World Turned Upside Down: Indian Voices in Early America* (Boston: Bedford Books, 1994), 73–77.

"Oh our brother! Alas! He is dead—he has gone; he will never return! Friendless he died on the field of the slain, where his bones are yet lying unburied! Oh, who will not mourn his sad fate? No tears dropped around him; oh, no! No tears of his sisters were there! He fell in his prime, when his arm was most needed to keep us from danger! Alas! he has gone! and left us in sorrow, his loss to bewail: Oh where is his spirit? His spirit went naked, and hungry it wanders, and thirsty and wounded it groans to return! Oh helpless and wretched, our brother has gone! No blanket nor food to nourish and warm him; nor candles to light him, nor weapons of war:—Oh, none of those comforts had he! But well we remember his deeds!—The deer he could take on the chase! The panther shrunk back at the sight of his strength! His enemies fell at his feet! He was brave and courageous in war! As the fawn he was harmless: his friendship was ardent: his temper was gentle: his pity was great! Oh! Our friend, our companion is dead! Our brother, our brother, alas! he is gone! But why do we grieve for his loss? In the strength of a warrior, undaunted he left us, to fight by the side of the Chiefs! His warwhoop was shrill! His rifle well aimed laid his enemies low: his tomahawk drank of their blood: and his knife flayed their scalps while yet covered with gore! And why do we mourn? Though he fell on the field of the slain, with glory he fell, and his spirit went up to the land of his fathers in war! Then why do we mourn? With transports of joy they received him, and fed him, and clothed him, and welcomed him there! Oh friends, he is happy; then dry up your tears! His spirit has seen our distress, and sent us a helper whom with pleasure we greet. Dickewamis has come: then let us receive her with joy! She is handsome and pleasant! Oh! she is our sister, and gladly we welcome her here. In the place of our brother she stands in our tribe. With care we will guard her from trouble; and may she be happy till her spirit shall leave us."

In the courts of that ceremony, from mourning they became serene—joy sparkled in their countenances, and they seemed to rejoice over me as over a long lost child. I was made welcome amongst them as a sister to the two Squaws before mentioned, and was called Dickewamis; which being interpreted, signifies a pretty girl, a handsome girl, or a pleasant, good thing. That is the name by which I have ever since been called by the Indians.

I afterwards learned that the ceremony I at that time passed through, was that of adoption. The two squaws had lost a brother in Washington's war,° sometime in the year before, and in consequence of his death went up to Fort Pitt, on the day on which I arrived there, in order to receive a prisoner or an enemy's scalp, to supply their loss.

It is a custom of the Indians, when one of their number is slain or taken prisoner in battle, to give to the nearest relative to the dead or absent, a prisoner, if they have chanced to take one, and if not, to give him the scalp of an enemy. On the return of the Indians from conquest, which is always announced by peculiar shoutings, demonstrations of joy, and the exhibition of some trophy of victory, the mourners come forward and make their claims. If they receive a prisoner, it is at their option either to satiate their vengeance by taking his life in the most cruel manner they can conceive of; or, to receive and adopt him into the family, in the place of him whom they have lost. All the prisoners that are taken in battle and carried to the encampment or town by the Indians, are given to the bereaved families, till their number is made good. And unless the mourners have but just received the news of their bereavement, and are under the operation of a paroxysm of grief, anger and revenge; or, unless the prisoner is very old, sickly, or homely, they generally save him, and treat him kindly. But if their mental wound is fresh, their loss so great that they deem it irreparable, or if their prisoner or prisoners do not meet their approbation, no torture, let it be ever so cruel, seems sufficient to make them satisfaction. It is family, and not national, sacrifices amongst the Indians, that has given them an indelible stamp as barbarians, and identified their character with the idea which is generally formed of unfeeling ferocity, and the most abandoned cruelty.

It was my happy lot to be accepted for adoption; and at the time of the ceremony I was received by the two squaws, to supply the place of their brother in the family; and I was ever considered and treated by them as a real sister, the same as though I had been born of their mother.

During my adoption, I sat motionless, nearly terrified to death at the appearance and actions of the company, expecting every moment to feel their vengeance, and suffer death on the spot. I was, however, happily disappointed, when at the close of the ceremony the company retired, and my sisters went about employing every means for my consolation and comfort.

Being now settled and provided with a home, I was employed in nursing the children, and doing light work about the house. Occasionally I was sent out with the Indian hunters, when they went but a short distance, to help them carry their game. My situation was easy; I had no particular hardships to endure. But still, the recollection of my parents, my brothers and sisters, my home, and my own captivity, destroyed my happiness, and made me constantly solitary, lonesome and gloomy.

°The Seven Years' War, although in Iroquois memory, Washington is more often associated with the war of the Revolution, during which he earned the name "Town Destroyer."

My sisters would not allow me to speak English in their hearing; but remembering the charge that my dear mother gave me at the time I left her, whenever I chanced to be alone I made a business of repeating my prayer, catechism, or something I had learned in order that I might not forget my own language. By practising in that way I retained it till I came to Genesee flats, where I soon became acquainted with English people with whom I have been almost daily in the habit of conversing.

My sisters were diligent in teaching me their language; and to their great satisfaction I soon learned so that I could understand it readily, and speak it fluently. I was very fortunate in falling into their hands; for they were kind good natured women; peaceable and mild in their dispositions; temperate and decent in their habits, and very tender and gentle towards me. I have great reason to respect them, though they have been dead a great number of years.

The town where they lived was pleasantly situated on the Ohio, at the mouth of the Shenanjee: the land produced good corn; the woods furnished a plenty of game, and the waters abounded with fish. Another river emptied itself into the Ohio, directly opposite the mouth of the Shenanjee. We spent the summer at that place, where we planted, hoed, and harvested a large crop of corn, of an excellent quality.

I had then been with the Indians four summers and four winters, and had become so far accustomed to their mode of living, habits and dispositions, that my anxiety to get away, to be set at liberty, and leave them, had almost subsided. With them was my home; my family was there, and there I had many friends to whom I was warmly attached in consideration of the favors, affection and friendship with which they had uniformly treated me, from the time of my adoption. Our labor was not severe; and that of one year was exactly similar, in almost every respect, to that of the others, without that endless variety that is to be observed in the common labor of the white

people. Notwithstanding the Indian women have all the fuel and bread to procure, and the cooking to perform, their task is probably not harder than that of white women, who have those articles provided for them; and their cares certainly are not half as numerous, nor as great. In the summer season, we planted, tended and harvested our corn, and generally had all our children with us; but had no master to oversee or drive us, so that we could work as leisurely as we pleased. We had no ploughs on the Ohio; but performed the whole process of planting and hoeing with a small tool that resembled, in some respects, a hoe with a very short handle.

Our cooking consisted in pounding our corn into samp or hommany, boiling the hommany, making now and then a cake and baking it in the ashes, and in boiling or roasting our venison. As our cooking and eating utensils consisted of a hommany block and pestle, a small kettle, a knife or two, and a few vessels of bark or wood, it required but little time to keep them in order for use.

Spinning, weaving, sewing, stocking knitting, and the like, are arts which have never been practised in the Indian tribes generally. After the revolutionary war, I learned to sew, so that I could make my own clothing after a poor fashion; but the other domestic arts I have been wholly ignorant of the application of, since my captivity. In the season of hunting, it was our business, in addition to our cooking, to bring home the game that was taken by the Indians, dress it, and carefully preserve the eatable meat, and prepare or dress the skins. Our clothing was fastened together with strings of deer skin, and tied on with the same.

In that manner we lived, without any of those jealousies, quarrels, and revengeful battles between families and individuals, which have been common in the Indian tribes since the introduction of ardent spirits amongst them.

The use of ardent spirits amongst the Indians, and the attempts which have been made to civilize and christianize them by the white people, has constantly made them worse and worse; increased their vices, and robbed them of many of their virtues; and will ultimately produce their extermination. I have seen, in a number of instances, the effects of education upon some of our Indians, who were taken when young, from their families, and placed at school before they had had an opportunity to contract many Indian habits, and there kept till they arrived to manhood; but I have never seen one of those but what was an Indian in every respect after he returned. Indians must and will be Indians, in spite of all the means that can be used for their cultivation in the sciences and arts.

One thing only marred my happiness, while I lived with them on the Ohio; and that was the recollection that I had once had tender parents, and a home that I loved. Aside from that consideration, or, if I had been taken in infancy, I should have been contented in my situation. Notwithstanding all that has been said against the Indians, in consequence of their cruelties to their enemies—cruelties that I have witnessed, and had abundant proof of—it is a fact that they are naturally kind, tender and peaceable towards their friends, and strictly honest; and that those cruelties have been practiced, only upon their enemies, according to their idea of justice.

References

1. "A Narrative of the Captivity of Mrs. Johnson," in Colin G. Calloway, comp., *North Country Captives: Selected Narratives of Indian Captivity from Vermont and New Hampshire* (Hanover, N.H.: University Press of New England, 1992), 62.
2. Colin G. Calloway, ed., *Dawnland Encounters: Indians and Europeans in Northern New England* (Hanover, N.H.: University Press of New England, 1991), 239.
3. Rev. Henry H. Saunderson, *History of Charlestown, New Hampshire* (Claremont, N.H., 1876).

Suggested Readings

Axtell, James. "The White Indians of Colonial America," in *The European and the Indian: Essays in the Ethnohistory of Colonial America* (New York: Oxford University Press, 1981).

Calloway, Colin G., comp. *North Country Captives: Selected Narratives of Indian Captivity from Vermont and New Hampshire* (Hanover, N.H.: University Press of New England, 1992).

Coleman, Emma Lewis. *New England Captives Carried to Canada between 1677 and 1760 during the French and Indian Wars.* 2 vols. (Portland, Maine: The Southworth Press, 1925).

Demos, John. *The Unredeemed Captive: A Family Story from Early America* (New York: Knopf, 1994).

Fleary, Rebecca Bevins. *Cartographies of Desire: Captivity, Race, and Sex in the Shaping of an American Nation* (Norman: University of Oklahoma Press, 1999).

Namias, June. *White Captives: Gender and Ethnicity on American Frontiers* (Chapel Hill: University of North Carolina Press, 1993).

Namias, June, ed. *A Narrative of the Life of Mary Jemison* (Norman: University of Oklahoma Press, 1992).

Vaughan, Alden T., and Edward W. Clark, eds. *Puritans among the Indians: Accounts of Captivity and Redemption 1676–1724* (Cambridge, Mass.: The Belknap Press of Harvard University Press, 1981).

The Revolution Comes
to the Cherokees

In the Southeast, the Cherokee Indians experienced revolutionary changes
long before the American Revolution. Traditional subsistence practices and
settlement patterns changed as Cherokees participated in the deerskin trade and
adopted English styles of farming and domesticating animals. English traders
funneled new goods, new values, and deadly alcohol into Cherokee communities. Some Cherokees began to traffic in and eventually own African slaves.
Cherokee political structure became more unified as English colonial governments insisted that the various Cherokee towns function as a single tribe. Smallpox cut their population in half in 1738 and returned in 1759. British armies
burned Cherokee crops and villages in 1760 and 1761. And Cherokee lands
were steadily whittled away.

The tempo of Cherokee land loss increased dramatically in the decade before the Revolution. In 1768, Iroquois delegates to the Treaty of Fort Stanwix
with Sir William Johnson handed away Cherokee hunting lands north of the
Tennessee River. That same year, the Treaty of Hard Labor in South Carolina
fixed boundaries to Cherokee territory. Cherokee chiefs met with colonial officials from North and South Carolina and drew a border between their respective lands by burning marks on a strip of trees, but constant pressure from
colonial settlers compelled the Cherokees to agree to new limits two years later
at the Treaty of Lochaber. The surveyors lopped off another chunk of Cherokee land when they ran the treaty line. In 1772, Virginia demanded another cession of everything east of the Kentucky River. No matter how much land Cherokees gave up, settlers kept coming: Cherokees complained that they could "see
the smoke of the Virginians from their doors."[1]

In March 1775, a group of North Carolina land speculators led by Richard
Henderson pulled off one of the biggest real estate deals in frontier history at
Sycamore Shoals on the Watauga River in Tennessee. The Cherokee chiefs Attakullakulla (Little Carpenter), Oconostota, and Savunkah (the Raven of Chota)
sold Henderson 27,000 square miles of territory between the Cumberland River
in the south and the Kentucky River in the north in exchange for a cabin full
of trade goods. The deal contravened the Royal Proclamation of 1763 as well as
Cherokee tribal law, and the chiefs later declared that Henderson had deceived
them as to what they were signing. Settlers were soon filling up the ceded lands,
and the Cherokees found themselves cut off from both the Ohio River and
their Kentucky hunting grounds. Even then the invasion of Cherokee lands did
not stop: settlers encroached on the Watauga and upper Holston rivers in

TABLE 3.2 Cherokee Land Cessions in the Colonial and Revolutionary Eras

Date of Treaty	State Where Ceded Lands Are Located	Area in Square Miles	Area in Acres
1721	South Carolina	2,623	1,678,720
November 24, 1755	South Carolina	8,635	5,526,400
October 14, 1768	Virginia	850	544,000
October 18, 1770	Virginia	4,500	2,880,000
	West Virginia	4,300	2,752,000
	Tennessee	150	96,000
	Kentucky	250	160,000
1772	Kentucky	10,135	6,486,400
	West Virginia	437	279,680
	Virginia	345	220,800
June 1, 1773	Georgia	1,050	672,000
March 17, 1775	Kentucky	22,600	14,464,000
	Virginia	1,800	1,152,000
	Tennessee	2,650	1,696,000
May 20, 1777	South Carolina	2,051	1,312,640
July 20, 1777	North Carolina	4,414	2,824,960
	Tennessee	1,760	1,126,400
May 31, 1783	Georgia	1,650	1,056,000
November 28, 1785	North Carolina	550	352,000
	Tennessee	4,914	3,144,960
	Kentucky	917	586,880

Source: Charles C. Royce, *The Cherokee Nation of Indians* (Washington, D.C., U.S. Government Printing Office, 1887).

northeastern Tennessee. (See Map 4.1, "United States Treaties and Indian Land Cessions to 1810," page 202.)

The older chiefs may have been trying to buy time for their people by creating a buffer zone of ceded territory between Cherokees and colonists, but younger Cherokees bitterly resented the recurrent sacrifice of homeland and hunting grounds. Attakullakulla's son, Dragging Canoe (Chincanacina), stormed out of the negotiations at Sycamore Shoals and is reputed to have warned Henderson that he would make the lands "dark and bloody." He told British Deputy Superintendent of Indian Affairs Henry Stuart "that he had no hand in making these Bargains but blamed some of their Old Men who he said were too old to hunt and who by their Poverty had been induced to sell their Land but that for his part he had a great many young fellows that would support him and that were determined to have their Land."[2] The outbreak of the American Revolution seemed to offer the younger warriors the opportunity, with British support, to drive invaders off their homelands, but first they had

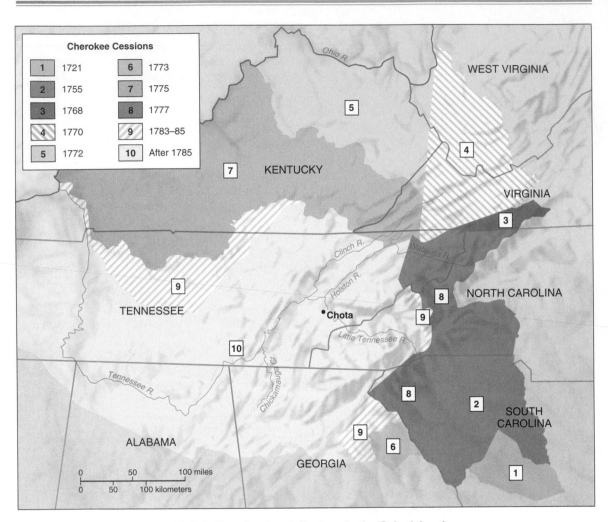

MAP 3.4 Cherokee Land Cessions in the Colonial and Revolutionary Eras, 1721–85

By the outbreak of the American Revolution, when their delegates assembled at Chota, the Cherokees had seen their lands whittled away in a series of treaties. The Treaty of Sycamore Shoals in 1775 that gobbled up most of the remaining Cherokee land in Kentucky (No. 7) was especially devastating. Many younger Cherokee warriors blamed the older chiefs for selling their homelands. The Cherokee decision to go to war, and the restoration of peace, did little to stem the pressures on Cherokee land. Adapted from Charles Royce, The Cherokee Nation of Indians (Washington, D.C.: U.S. Government Printing Office, 1887), 256.

to challenge the authority of the older chiefs and gain the upper hand in the councils of the Cherokee nation.

Their opportunity to make this challenge came in May 1776 when a delegation of Shawnee, Delaware, Mohawk, and other Indians from the north arrived at Chota, the Cherokee capital or "beloved town" on the Little Tennessee River and urged the Cherokees to join them in a war of united resistance against the Americans. Delegates from the various Cherokee towns assembled at the council house to hear the northern Indians' talk. Henry Stuart and Alexander Cameron, the British agent to the Overhill Cherokees, were also there.° John Stuart, British Superintendent for the Southern Indians, who had taken refuge at St. Augustine, had sent his brother Henry to Chota. Henry had a difficult mission: to arm the Cherokees in readiness for war against the colonists, but to restrain them until the British could coordinate their attacks in the southern colonies. Like the older chiefs, the British did not want the Cherokees to go to war—yet.

But recurrent losses of Cherokee territory had undermined the prestige of the older chiefs. When Dragging Canoe and the younger warriors accepted the war belt the northern Indians offered them, they effectively staged a coup, seizing authority from the chiefs and reversing their policies of appeasement. Cherokee warriors attacked American settlements on the Watauga River the following month.

The war was a disaster for the Cherokees. American expeditions from Georgia, Virginia, and the Carolinas marched into Cherokee country, burning towns and destroying cornfields. As Cherokee refugees fled the smoking ruins of their towns, the accommodationist chiefs began to reassert their influence and open negotiations for peace. The Americans granted them peace, but at a price: the Cherokees lost more than five million acres in treaties with Georgia, Virginia, North and South Carolina. Dragging Canoe and his followers refused to be party to the treaties and retreated to the southwestern reaches of Cherokee country, building new towns on the Chickamauga River and fracturing the ancient balance between old and young in Cherokee society. The Chickamauga Cherokees, as they became known, continued their war against the Americans. The Americans retaliated, often without making a distinction between different groups of Cherokees: in 1780, they burned Chota itself.

By the end of the Revolution, the Cherokees' population had dropped to perhaps ten thousand people; they had lost three-quarters of their territory and more than half their towns had been destroyed. Their world was in chaos. The Chickamaugas made common cause with militant factions among the Creeks and Shawnees and continued to resist American expansion. Other Cherokees, closer to the Americans and with bitter memories of the war, pre-

---

°The British divided the Cherokees into four main divisions: the Overhill Towns in the north on the Little Tennessee and Tellico rivers, the Valley and Middle Towns in the Blue Ridge region, and the Lower Towns in South Carolina.

ferred to try to survive by peace. In 1785, the Cherokees signed the Treaty of Hopewell, their first treaty with the United States. Many tried to earn themselves a place in the new nation by following a path of accommodation and controlled change. It worked—for a time.

Henry Stuart's presence at Chota in May 1776 and his report on the momentous council meeting that occurred there affords us a rare glimpse of the change that the American Revolution generated in Cherokee society. Stuart clearly wanted to portray his own efforts in a good light, but his account reminds us that Indian people who fought in the American Revolution did so for their own, not for British, reasons. Cherokees were struggling to survive in a world that was crumbling around them, and they attempted different strategies in their struggle. Continued pressure on their lands had pushed the Cherokees to the brink of disintegration by 1776. The traditional division between young and old, warrior and councillor, that had served for generations to preserve balance in Cherokee society became the fault line around which the nation split and from which a new tribe would emerge.

▶ **Questions for Consideration**

1. What information does Stuart's account below convey about the workings of inter- and intratribal politics and in an era of crisis?

2. Whom does Stuart blame for the premature outbreak of war?

3. Stuart was watching events from the wings but was vitally interested in their outcome: in what ways does this affect the reliability of the report he wrote?

HENRY STUART
Report from Cherokee Country (1776)

The young fellows [Cherokee warriors] began now to be impatient and to be apprehensive that an army was preparing to come against them; while they were in this turn of mind a Deputation of fourteen Indians with a Cherokee fellow as in-

Source: William L. Saunders, ed., *The Colonial Records of North Carolina*, vol. 10 (Raleigh: State Printer, 1890), 773–84.

terpreter arrived from the Northern Nations. They consisted of some from the Confederate Nations and from the Mohawks, Ottowas, Nantucas, Shawnees and Delawares. We were sent for to Chote [Chota] the day that they made their Entrance; they came in all black. They gave an account of their Journey and the news which served sufficiently to intimate their Errand. They said they had been seventy days on their Journey; that when they attempted to pass through that Country from Pittsburgh to their Nation, which but very lately used to be the Shawnees and Delawares hunting grounds (where they used to see nothing but Deer Bear and Buffaloe), they found the Country thickly inhabited and the people all in arms; That at Pittsburgh there were 2000 Men assembled; That at a fort on Cedar River which falls into the Ohio there were 1500 Men assembled; that at a Fort on Louisa River there were 1000; that on Green River beyond Cumberland Mountain there were 1000 men. They laid down several other Forts where they said there were Bodys of Men assembled. Their salt Springs and their Buffaloe grounds they said had numbers of Inhabitants and fortified places round them; That they were obliged to go down a great way on the other side of the Ohio and to take a round of near 300 Miles to avoid being discovered; that between Cumberland Mountain and the Cherokee Nation where the road goes from the Settlements on the Ohio to Holston's River they discovered fresh Tracks of a Great Body of People with Horses and Cattle. The Mohawks said that early in the Spring a Body of the White People inhabiting the Country near them had come into one of their Towns and surprised their people and killed many of them; that they took Sir William Johnson's son prisoner and put him to death in a cruel manner; that there were two attempts made afterwards and that the Indians gave them battle and defeated them with a very great Slaughter.° They said that they had got all the Northern Tribes to assist them to take Satisfaction and that the French have supplied them with a great quantity of Ammunition and Arms and Provisions and have promised to support them; that they told them that the King's Troops would soon fall on their Enemies towards the Sea and if they united and fell on them on this side they would find them nothing; That now all

Nations of Indians were at peace with one another; that they had sent messengers to the Oubacks° to the Tribes there to secure their friendship, and that they would not trouble the Cherokees any more. This they said was all they had to say now, which they might depend was all Truth; they apprehended the 10th day from the day of their arrival for their grand Talk, when they hoped there would be people from the different parts of the Nation. After this day every young Fellow's face in the Overhills Towns appeared Blackened, and nothing was now talked of but War. The people of Tellico and the Island° were busily employed in preparing Spears, Clubs and scalping Knives. We still continued to diswade them from their Intentions of attacking the Settlements by representing to them the dangerous consequences that were likely to follow to their Nation, the danger of making an indiscriminate attack and the impossibility of their being able without a Body of White People to join them to make any distinction; that it would be the means of drawing on them the King's displeasure and of uniting all parties against them. . . .

The grand Talk from the Northern Indians was to have been in two days. The standard of war was erected, the Flag Staff and Posts of the Town House were painted black and red. . . . The Deputies being now assembled from the different parts of the Nation and the day being come for hearing the Grand Talk, we went to Chote where we could easily judge their different inclinations from their appearances; those from the Great Island except Otacite° & two or three men were all black, also all the Chilhowie and Settico [Tellico]° people and some from every Town were blacked. The Northern Deputies being seated they said

---

°The rumors of the murder of Johnson's son were untrue.

°The tribes of the Wabash River: the Weas, Piankeshaws, and others.

°Great Island was one of the Overhill Towns.

°Outacite or Judd's Friend, who also had the title Mankiller.

°Settico and Tellico were different towns.

they would now tell them what they came about and begged that they would listen with attention.

The principal Deputy for the Mohawks and six Nations began. He produced a belt of white and purple Whampum with strings of white beads and purple whampum fixed to it; He said he supposed there was not a man present that could not read his Talk; the back settlers of the Northern Provinces whom he termed the Long Knife had without any provocation come into one of their Towns and murdered their people and the son of their Great Beloved Man; that what was their case one day might be the case of another Nation another day; That his Nation was fighting at this time and that he was sent by them to secure the friendship of all Nations for he considered their interests as one, and that at this time they should forget all their quarrels among themselves and turn their eyes and their thoughts one way. The Belt was delivered to Chincanacina.

The principal Deputy of the Ottowas produced a white Belt with some purple figures; they expressed their desire of confirming a lasting bond of true friendship with all their red Brethren; that they were almost constantly at war one Nation against another, and reduced by degrees, while their common enemies were taking the advantage of their situation; that they were willing & they hoped every Nation would be the same to drop all their former quarrels and to join in one common cause, and that altho' the Trade to their Nation and all the other Northern Nations had been stopped, that their friends, the French in Canada, had found means to supply them and would assist them. Chincanacina received this Belt.

The Talk of the Nations was much to the same effect, he produced a white Belt and it was received by the Raven.

There was only a boy of the Delaware Nation. The Talk was now to be finished by the Shawnees Deputy, formerly (as I am informed) a noted French partizan. He produced a War Belt about 9 feet long and six inches wide of purple Wham-

pum strewed over with vermilion. He began with pathetically enumerating the distresses of his own and other Nations. He complained particularly of the Virginians who after having taken away all their Lands and cruelly and treacherously treated some of their people, had unjustly brought war upon their Nation and destroyed many of their people; that in a very few years their Nation from being a great people were now reduced to a handful; that their Nation possessed Lands almost to the Sea Shore and that the red people who were once Masters of the whole Country hardly possessed ground enough to stand on; that the Lands where but lately they hunted close to their Nations were thickly inhabited and covered with Forts & armed men; that wherever a Fort appeared in their neighbourhood, they might depend there would soon be Towns and Settlements; that it was plain, there was an intention to extirpate them, and that he thought it better to die like men than to diminish away by inches; That their Fathers the French who seemed long dead were now alive again; that they had supplied them plentifully with ammunition, arms and provisions and that they promised to assist them against the Virginians; that their cause was just and that they hoped the Great Being who governs everything would favour their cause; that now is the time to begin; that there is no time to be lost, and if they fought like men they might hope to enlarge their Bounds; that the Cherokees had a Hatchett which was brought in six years ago & desired that they would take it up and use it immediately; That they intended to carry their Talks through every Nation to the Southward and that that Nation which should refuse to be their Friends on this occasion should forever hereafter be considered as their common enemy and that they would all fall on them when affairs with the White People should be settled.

The Belt was received by Chincanacina. It was some minutes before any one got up to give his Assent which was to be done by laying hold of the Belt. At last a Head man of Chilhowie who had lived long in the Mohawk Nation and whose wife had constantly lived in Sir William Johnson's house was the first who rose up to take the Belt from Chincanacina. He sung the war song and all the Northern Indians joined in the chorus. Almost all the young warriors from the different parts of the Nation followed his example, though many of them expressed their uneasiness at being concerned in a war against the white people. But the principal Chiefs, who were averse to the measure and remembered the Calamities brought on their Nation by the last war, instead of opposing the rashness of the young people with spirit, sat down dejected and silent. The Deputies proposed that Mr Cameron and I with all the white People that were present should take up the Belt as the King's friends among them and all the French had done, which we refused. We told them that Indians did not understand our written Talks and we did not understand their Beads, nor what were their intentions; That for my part I was determined not to give any sanction to a war that was likely to bring destruction on their Nation, especially as I had not forgot the use that they made of my telling them that the King should expect their assistance if it should be asked to bring his disobedient and obstinate children to order; That the Virginians when they were not above half the number that they are at present had withstood the French and the combined Force of all the Indian Nations when they were twice as numerous as they are at present and that now they are in Arms ready to go against the King's forces; that if they went to war they had no white People to direct them against their proper Enemy as the Northern Tribes had, and if they should go over the Boundary Line or fall on indiscriminately to kill women and children and to attack the King's friends as well as his enemies, they would draw on themselves all the force that was intended against the King's Troops and the resentment of those that otherwise would have been their friends, and would have assisted them; that their Father was willing to support them and supply

them with ammunition while they paid regard to our Talks, But that we did not yet think it time for them to go out unless they were certain that there was an Army coming against them and therefore could not give our consent, as it was your desire that they should remain quiet until they should hear from you.

Cahetoy delivered this very distinctly. The Raven of Chote told them that they would consider of their Talks before they gave them a full answer and a meeting was appointed next day at Settico [Tellico,] where we were told the young fellows expressed a great deal of dissatisfaction at our not laying hold of their Belt, and from what we were afterwards informed passed there, and from the insinuations of one James Branham a half breed who had been in the settlements and was sent in with a design to injure Mr Cameron, that our lives and the lives of all the white people of the Nation had been in great danger. . . .

It was in vain to talk any more of Peace, all that could now be done was to give them strict charge not to pass the Boundary Line, not to injure any of the King's faithful subjects, not to kill any women and children, and to stop hostilities when you should desire it notwithstanding any promises to the contrary given to the Shawnese. All these instructions they promised strictly to adhere to, and they begged that I would acquaint you of this, and that altho' they had been rash and listened too readily to the Talks of the Northward Indians, that the usage you had received, the threats against Mr Cameron, and the cruelty used to Sir William Johnson's son were the causes that spurred them on and they therefore hoped that you would not be angry with them nor cast them off, but continue your assistance & support. They blamed Chincanacina the Warrior of Chilhowie as the cause of their beginning before they received your Orders.

The Indians seemed very inclinable that any of the King's loyal Subjects that were at Nonatluchky should be invited to come to them or desired to assemble themselves together and put up a white flag. Captain Guest offered to undertake to give them notice if he could get four white men that knew the woods and some Indians. The Tish of Settico [Tellico] a very sensible Indian offered himself with his Nephew who is Interpreter; they sent a message on this subject to the Warrior of Cowie. The very night before they were to have set out the four men that were chosen to go run away, they were all Virginians which was likely to prove fatal to the people who remained. All the white People in the Nation thought that the only security they now could have for their safety, was to go out with the Indians. Some went out with the Indians from the Overhills and Middle Settlements and all the rest offered to accompany Mr Cameron who was to set out in a few days for the Lower Towns. I left the Nation the 12th July, when the Toquah and Chote People which were the last Parties in the Nation set out very much dejected which I am informed was the case with the greatest part of the Nation.

References

1. Quoted in Colin G. Calloway, *The American Revolution in Indian Country: Crisis and Diversity in Native American Communities* (New York: Cambridge University Press, 1995), 189.
2. William L. Sanders, ed., *The Colonial Records of North Carolina,* vol. 10 (Raleigh: State Printer, 1890), 764.

Suggested Readings

Calloway, Colin G. *The American Revolution in Indian Country: Crisis and Diversity in Native American Communities* (New York: Cambridge University Press, 1995).

Dowd, Gregory Evans. *A Spirited Resistance: The North American Indian Struggle for Unity, 1745–1815* (Baltimore: Johns Hopkins University Press, 1992).

Hatley, Tom. *The Dividing Paths: Cherokees and South Carolinians through the Era of the Revolution* (New York: Oxford University Press, 1993).

O'Donnell, James H., III. *The Southern Indians in the American Revolution* (Knoxville: University of Tennessee Press, 1973).

Oliphant, John. *Peace and War on the Anglo-Cherokee Frontier, 1756–63* (Baton Rouge: Louisiana State University Press, 2001).

Snapp, J. Russell. *John Stuart and the Struggle for Empire on the Southern Frontier* (Baton Rouge: Louisiana State University Press, 1996).

The Treaty of Fort Finney with the Shawnees

The Peace of Paris in 1783 between Great Britain and the United States brought a formal end to the American War of Independence. However, it did not bring an end to the struggle of Indian peoples to preserve their independence. In the treaty, Britain recognized its thirteen former colonies as a new nation. It also, without consulting or even mentioning the Indian inhabitants of the area, handed over to the United States all territory east of the Mississippi, south of the Great Lakes, and north of Florida. With an empty treasury to fill to support the new government, the United States set about converting Indian territory into American real estate. It concentrated its efforts north of the Ohio, where individual states relinquished their claims to western lands to the national government.

European colonial powers had learned to deal with Indian peoples by mastering their languages and the protocols of council-fire diplomacy, dealing with the Indians on their own terms, and lubricating negotiations with a steady supply of gifts and alcohol. Like the French before them, the British came to understand that compromise, conciliation, and respectful dealings were generally more effective than force, or the threat of force, in a world where Indian power was significant and where Indian nations usually had a choice of European allies. The British developed a policy whereby transfers of Indian lands were supposed to occur only in open council between tribal delegates and the king's authorized agents, although the crown was unable to enforce this policy on the borders of colonial settlement.

The American colonists fought for independence from Britain, in part for the freedom to acquire Indian lands that had been barred to them by British policies. Like the British before them, the new United States preferred to achieve its goals by treaty rather than by war and to obtain Indian lands by purchase rather than by risky and expensive military action, but it too lacked the ability to enforce its policies on distant and turbulent frontiers. Moreover, with the British defeated, the United States was eager to impress on the Indians that a new era had dawned, and that the Americans were people not be trifled with. Commissioners from "the Thirteen Fires" (the United States) traveled into Indian country and employed the rhetoric and symbols of council-fire diplomacy, but they never deviated from their purpose: to obtain tribal acquiescence to the claim that the United States had acquired all territory east of the Mississippi by right of conquest.

At Fort Stanwix in New York in the fall of 1784, United States commissioners with troops at their backs met with delegates from the Six Nations. The

Iroquois were also being pressured by commissioners from the states of New York and Pennsylvania to cede lands. The Americans said they were masters of all Indian lands "and can dispose of the Lands as we think proper or most convenient to ourselves." They demanded huge cessions of Iroquois country as the price of peace. The Iroquois tried to argue for the Ohio River as a boundary but the Americans would have none of it. "You are a subdued people," they were told. Still divided by the war and now abandoned by their British allies, the Iroquois delegates agreed to cede much of the Seneca land in western New York and Pennsylvania as well as all their territory west of Pennsylvania, giving six hostages to guarantee their compliance.[1] When they returned home they were met with scorn. The Six Nations in council refused to ratify the proposed treaty, but the United States proceeded as if the treaty were valid. Even the Oneidas and Tuscaroras, two of the Iroquois nations which had supported the Americans during the war, found their lands, too, were soon under pressure.

In January 1785 at Fort McIntosh in western Pennsylvania, United States commissioners met with delegates from the Wyandots, Anishinaabeg, Delawares, and Ottawas and demanded large cessions of land. When the Indians objected that the king of England had no right to transfer their lands to the United States, the Americans reminded them they were a defeated people. The delegates attached their marks to a treaty that was dictated to them. Of the Indian tribes north of the Ohio River who had fought against the Americans during the Revolution, only the Shawnees had refused to come in and make peace.

The Shawnees had a long history of fighting for their lands. Originally located in the Ohio valley, they had dispersed under Iroquois pressure in the mid-1600s, and many had migrated to the Southeast, only to encounter English colonists pushing inland. By the middle of the eighteenth century, most Shawnees had regrouped in southern Ohio, where they found themselves in the front lines of the Indian struggle to prevent white settlement beyond the Ohio River. When colonial hunters and settlers flooded into Shawnee hunting grounds in Kentucky after the first Treaty of Fort Stanwix in 1768, tensions and killings escalated. Defeated by a Virginian army in a day-long battle at Point Pleasant in 1774, the Shawnees were forced to cede all lands south of the Ohio as the terms of peace. (See Map 4.1, United States Treaties and Indian Land Cessions to 1810, page 202).

For most Shawnees, the outbreak of the American Revolution in 1775 meant a continuation of the struggle to defend their lands against aggression, although Cornstalk, their principal chief, worked hard to maintain peace, and perhaps as much as half the tribe migrated west beyond the Mississippi rather than continue the endless conflict. The British wooed the Shawnees with promises of support and warnings that the Americans planned to destroy them. British agents like Alexander McKee and Matthew Elliot, both of whom had Shawnee wives, exerted considerable influence in Shawnee councils. But not until the Americans murdered Chief Cornstalk in 1777 did most Shawnees fully commit to the British. For the rest of the war, Shawnee war parties spear-headed the Anglo-Indian war effort in the West. They captured Daniel Boone, laid siege to Boonesboro, and routed the Kentucky militia at Blue Licks. In retaliation, American armies launched raids from Kentucky against Shawnee villages in Ohio, propelling a gradual Shawnee exodus to the northwest.

Then word came that the war was over — or, as the Americans told the Shawnees, "Your Fathers the English have made Peace with us for themselves, but forgot you their Children, who Fought with them, and neglected you like Bastards."[2] The Shawnees knew from past experience that peace for them could only be bought with land and they refused to attend the multitribal meeting at Fort McIntosh in 1785. The Americans realized that no peace in the West would last if it did not include the Shawnees and they dispatched emissaries to Shawnee villages to induce them to make peace. In January 1786, more than two hundred Shawnees finally met the American commissioners at Fort Finney, where the Great Miami River meets the Ohio in southwestern Ohio. Most of them were Maquachakes, the most conciliatory division whose traditional responsibilities included healing and negotiation. The Americans they met, however, were in no mood for conciliation. General Richard Butler had fought with Colonel Henry Bouquet against the Shawnees and Delawares in 1764 and was a veteran of the Revolutionary War. George Rogers Clark, the other American commissioner, had made a name for himself as an Indian fighter during the Revolution and led assaults on Shawnee villages in 1780 and 1782. At the siege of Vincennes in 1779 he had tomahawked Indian prisoners within sight of the British garrison and tossed their still-kicking bodies into the river. "To excel them in barbarity," Clark declared "is the only way to make war upon Indians."[3] Clark had little patience for the protocols of Indian diplomacy as practiced by the British and the French, preferring instead to dictate terms with the threat of force. "I am a man and a Warriour and not a councillor," he told Indians on the Wabash River in 1778; "I carry in my Right hand war and Peace in my left."[4]

The negotiations at Fort Finney graphically illustrate the contrast between the old and new ways of conducting diplomacy in Indian country. The Shawnees approached the treaty grounds in ceremonial fashion, and the proceedings opened with traditional speeches of welcome, smoking peace pipes, and dining. But this was not a meeting between equals. The Americans were determined to negotiate from a position of strength. When a Shawnee chief named Kekewepellethe or Captain Johnny balked at the terms of the treaty, the Americans threw the Shawnees' wampum belt to the table and threatened them with destruction. Moluntha, a Maquachake chief, urged the Shawnees to reconsider, and they grudgingly accepted the American terms.

But there was to be no peace for the Shawnees. Many who did not attend the treaty were outraged by the terms and some refused to give up their captives, the "flesh and blood," required by the treaty. Younger warriors, who had grown up knowing nothing but war, accused Moluntha and the older chiefs of selling out to the Americans. Before the year was over, Kentucky militia raided Shawnee country again. At Moluntha's village, the old chief, carrying a copy of the treaty he had made at Fort Finney, met the militia, while his people hoisted an American flag. The Kentuckians destroyed the town and killed Moluntha in cold blood.

Shawnees then became leaders in forming a multitribal coalition committed to resisting American expansion. The coalition routed General Arthur St. Clair's army in western Ohio in 1791; Richard Butler was killed in the battle. After General Anthony Wayne defeated the Indians at the Battle of Fallen Timbers in northwestern Ohio in 1794, Shawnee leaders who had fought the Americans since before the Revolution signed the Treaty of Greenville in 1795, ceding most of Ohio to the United States. Shawnee resistance then passed to a younger generation and shifted west.

▶ **Questions for Consideration**

1. What does the American record of the treaty negotiations at Fort Finney described below suggest about the participants' different understandings of the nature of those negotiations and the respective positions of power from which they operated?

2. What does the record reveal about the divisions in Indian society at the time and about the strategies Indians employed to adjust to the new situation created by American independence?

3. As the journal of one of the commissioners dictating terms to the Shawnees, does Butler's account have any value other than as a one-sided record of the negotiations?

RICHARD BUTLER

The Journal of General Richard Butler at the Treaty of Fort Finney (1786)

Saturday, Jan. 14th. [1786]

Every thing being ready for the reception of the Shawnese, we waited till 12 o'clock, when Mi-animeeca arrived and told us they were coming on, also that they would fire to salute us; we told them we would return the salute, and that our messengers would go to meet them, and bring them in by the hand, and set them down by the council fire, which seemed very grateful to them.

Source: Neville B. Craig, ed., *The Olden Time*, 2 vols. (Pittsburgh, 1848), 2:510–25.

Mr. Elliott, Mr. Ranken, and Maj. Montgomery went to meet them; and Mr. Boggs waited at the Council house to direct them where to sit.° Shortly after these arrangements they appeared, in number about 150 men and 80 women, in very regular order; the chiefs in front, beating a drum, with young warriors dancing a peculiar dance for such occasions. This is so particular that I shall here describe it; the oldest chief leads, and carries a small drum, on which he beats time and sings; two young warriors, who dance well, carry each the stem of a pipe painted, and decorated with feathers of the bald eagle, and wampum, these are joined in the dance by several other young men, who dance and keep time to the drum; the whole of the party painted and dressed in the most elegant manner, in their way, which is truly fantastic, but elegant, though savage. The chief who headed this party is called Melonthe. These were followed by the chief warrior Aweecanny, and last the warriors armed; then come the head woman called Ca-we-chile, in front of all the women and children. When they came near the Council-house, Aweecanny got on a stump, and ordered the whole to halt. They then sung for some time, when he gave a signal, and the song ceased. He then ordered the armed men to make ready, which they did, then to fire, which was performed in the Indian style, which is a running fire; this was repeated three times, on which our troops returned the salute, with three vollies from a platoon, well performed, the drum beating an American march. We then entered and took our seats; they then arrived, and after dancing a short time at the door, by way of salute, they entered at the west door, the chief on our left, the warriors on our right and round on the east end till they joined the chiefs; the old chief beating the drum,

and the young men dancing and waving the feathers over us, whilst the others were seated; this done, the women entered at the east door, and took their seats on the east end, with great form. This over, the chief enquired who were the Commissioners, which the young warrior, John Harris, told them, and pointed us out. After a short song, the chiefs called on Ke-kewe-pellethe, a Wagatommochie° man, who immediately rose to address us. His speech was short, but pathetic and sensible. He said that in consequence of our invitation, they had come to our council fire—that they had also brought their women and children—that they had shut their ears against all that advised them not to come, and now stood before us; they hoped, on our part, we would also shut our ears against evil stories, and banish from our memory every evil impression, that they cleared our ears, wiped our eyes, and with the string of wampum removed all sorrow from our hearts; they hoped therefore we would be strong, pity their women and children, and go on with the good work of peace, and suffer no evil report to prevent us carrying it into effect.

This done, we addressed them, as per our speech of this date. All being over, we invited the old man and some of their captains to dine with us, and ordered the rest to remain in the council house till cooked provision was brought them; we also ordered a drink of grog, with pipes and tobacco. After these articles came in, we introduced Capt. Finney and the other officers to them; this done, the chiefs and dancers arose and shook hands with the Commissioners and suit; the old Captain, Aweecanny went at the head of the warriors, and shook hands with the officers.

I find at the commencement of a treaty of peace the Chiefs or Kings shake the hands of those who have to treat with them, but the warriors and women not till the business is concluded; the rea-

°Daniel Elliott, Colonel Samuel Montgomery, John Boggs, and a James Rinker traveled into Indian country in the summer of 1785 to persuade the tribes to attend the proposed treaty negotiations with the United States.

°Wagatommochie was Wakatomica, a Shawnee town on the Muskingum River.

son they give is that the heads of the people should be on an easy and familiar footing, but that the warriors and women, who are the strength of the nation, more distant till peace is certain. We then retired to dine, and the provision was taken to the long house, where all were well regaled and pleased on going away. The young fellows wished a little more drink; this the head men disapproved, but thought it better to gratify them for the present, therefore requested two gallons, which was given, and they went away pleased. . . .

Tuesday, Jan. 17th.

It froze very hard last night, which we fear will prevent the arrival of the boats, which we expect are on their way with supplies, the drift of ice being so much increased. Several of the Shawnese remain, and one sick, after their drink. They remained in the long house till after they had dined, and set off then to camp. I find that many of the young fellows which have grown up through the course of the war, and *trained like young hounds to blood,* have a great attachment to the British; but the chiefs of any repute are and have been averse to the war, but their influence is not of sufficient weight to prevent them from committing mischief, which they regret very much.

Wednesday, Jan. 18th.

This morning snow—the ice driving in the Ohio. About 11 o'clock the Pipe° came in, and stayed some time. I had a free conversation with him and explained many things respecting the late treaty, and their situation, which gave him much satisfaction. He thanked me for my advice and candor, observing at the same time that he respected the Commissioners for the punctuality with which all their engagements were fulfilled, and that his heart which had been in pain for many years, now begins to feel ease, and that he hopes to feel great pleasure on the conclusion of the present business.

The Pipe, Half-King and others,° dined with the Commissioners, after which they went home well pleased. I now find that some opinions which I had formed respecting the necessity of having a more general conference and eclaircisement of the treaty held last year with the Wyandots and Delawares were just; for although we had some of the principal chiefs, who, in the name of the Delaware nation, concluded the treaty, these have been very much reflected on by those who did not attend, and by being ignorant of the real state of their situation as to the U.S. right on the country, often charged the chiefs with having broke faith with them, and sold their lands.

This animosity will, in all probability, now be wiped away, and matters so settled that our frontier to the Wabash, will be freed from the distress and horror of an Indian war. Congress have it in their power to survey and sell the lands, and settle some kind of government in this country. . . .

Tuesday, Jan. 24th.

The Chiefs of the Wyandots and Delawares attended in council; explained to them clearly the treaty with Great Britain; showed them the boundary between their subjects, and the U.S. citizens; also, the treaty of Fort McIntosh with the United States and their nation, clearly delineating the boundary line, which they acknowledged gave them great satisfaction. Had an address from one of their chiefs, expressing their full satisfaction with the treaty. We told them our Surveyors would be out in the spring, that some of their sensible men and young men should attend them to see that we do not pass the described bounds, and

---

°Captain Pipe or Hopocan was a Delaware war chief who had supported the British during the Revolution but had signed the Treaty of Fort McIntosh, for which he was criticized as having sold out to the Americans.

°Half-King was a Wyandot chief who had sided with the British. A delegation of Delawares and Wyandots were in attendance at the treaty negotiations.

advised them to collect their nations within their own territory; by doing which they would have their people more compact, and the influence of their head men of course greater. All which seemed to give them pleasure; it also cleared the Pipe of the opinion they had formed of his having sold the land to the U.S.

Wednesday, Jan. 25th.

The Commissioners met and settled the plan, for opening the treaty with the Shawnese Indians, on which I was requested to draw up a speech, which was done.

Thursday, Jan. 26th.

The speech being prepared, was laid before the Board of Commissioners; some few alterations being made, was agreed to.

The Chiefs of the Shawnese were at the council, and the speech read and explained to them.

Friday, Jan. 27th.

The Shawnese chiefs requested a private conference. Having met them, they recapitulated the speech, in order to be fully satisfied that they understood it, which we found they did. On our informing them so, they replied they were fully convinced our observations were just — that they had been led into folly by the British — that they were sensible they had done wrong, but they hoped for pity from the 13 fires, and that they hoped these things would be forgotten.

They then took up the story of the Big Cat, the Delaware chief. This they declare to be totally false, and stated that the Weachtinos and Miamies had sent people to the town, but that they had not turned back.° They say these people were sent by their nation to them to know if a treaty was carrying on, which they informed them fully. These deputies told them that they had no directions to go to it, as they had heard some things in their towns that such an event was to take place, that they would now return and inform their chiefs, and they might act as they thought proper; but that some of the British people had been very busy among them, and advised them to stay at home and not attend the treaty.

Saturday, Jan. 28th.

The chiefs and young people and women of the Shawnese were called to public council, all of the chiefs of the Wyandots and Delawares, with Packanchichiles,° and chiefs of the last mentioned nations. The Commissioners sent for the Shawnese chiefs, and had a private conference on the nature of the speech, and their intention for framing it in this manner. That by putting their young men in mind of the ills they have done, and danger to which they have exposed their nation, it will have a tendency to induce them to listen to the advise of their chiefs, and give weight to that advice. This done, we went into council, which was very full.

Tetapaxica,° a Delaware chief, addressed the Commissioners and the Shawnese, stating the good work which we were upon, and admonished each party to go on with it in temper, and hasten it to a happy conclusion. He then addressed Packanchichiles, and gave a very handsome complimentary account of his conduct on being informed of the terms and principles on which the peace between the U.S. and his nation were founded, and advised the head warriors of the Shawnese to be strong and follow his example. That he had laid down the hatchet, and would never more take it up.

After he had concluded I began the address, and went through it clearly; I also went into an ex-

---

°Big Cat had earlier accused the Shawnees of turning back Miami and other Indians from the Wabash. The Weachtinos were probably Weas.

°Packanchichiles was the Delaware war chief, Buckongahelas.

°Tetapaxica or Tetapachksit was a councilor of the Delaware Turtle clan. He signed the Treaty of Greenville in 1795.

planation, or rather recapitulation of their breach of all the treaties which they had made with the United States; the mischiefs they have done to our citizens; the distress they had involved their nation in by their conduct, and that they were now left to the mercy of the United States, which they may yet experience if their conduct can convince us of their determination to live in peace for the future. We then closed, and required their answer, which was promised when they considered what we had said.

Sunday, Jan. 29th.

The Shawnese informed us they will give us their answer to-day; on which the Wyandot and Delaware chiefs were called, the whole collected, and Kekewepellethe, a Shawnee Captain, spoke in a very clear and masterly manner, recapitulating the substance of our address, acknowledging the truths which we related, and advising his young men to be attentive, that they might remember it—and hoped we would forget all that was passed; he told us we should have our flesh and blood, that three of their principal people (warriors) should go to the towns and collect them every one, and bring them; that they had three here which they would take back to collect the others, and bring them all together; he added that he was a warrior, that the warriors had done the mischief, and they should restore as much as possible the prisoners; that they attended fully to what we had said respecting the conduct of the British to them; that it is all true, and we have taken pains to prove it to them, and they perfectly believe it; that they hoped what we have said would not be from our lips only, but from our hearts—that this is their determination, that God sees our actions, and hears our mutual promises, and they hoped whatever may be now done shall last forever; that they cover our blood and bury the hatchet that there shall be no war.

The council being over, the Commissioners met in council, and concluded on the article of treaty, which they requested Gen. Parsons° to draw up, to which he agreed.

John Harris then spoke.

Grand-fathers: The Delawares, young brothers, the Wyandots are brothers of the 13 fires. Hearken to my words: You have heard what our captains and warriors have said. They have buried our hatchet deep, and covered over your blood. They have promised to collect and bring in your flesh and blood, and to deliver them up to you 13 fires. We now request that you will also lay down the hatchet, bury it deep, let no sharp weapon remain in your hands. You told us that our fathers once lived in friendship; we wish you to recollect that friendship again, and let it be as great between us as it hath been between them of old.

He then produced a large belt and a road belt. These belts I only show you that it may bring the friendship which has been mentioned fresh to your memories. These are belts which our kings have kept by them. They are the belts received from the 13 fires at the beginning of the war; and although some of our young people have been led astray by the evil advice of the British, and have done you much mischief, our kings never gave their consent or advice for the war, but have sat still as they promised; they have also kept the road belt, and although the road has been stopped for some time, we have now wiped it clean, and nothing shall stop it in future, and that they will still hold fast these belts.

Monday, Jan. 30th.

The Commissioners met and examined the articles, which being approved, the chiefs of the Shawnese were sent for, and the whole explained fully to them; also the boundary line which we first proposed. This not pleasing, they complaining that we were putting them to live on ponds, and leaving them no land to live or raise corn on.

°General Samuel Parsons, an Indian commissioner and land speculator.

This being found to be the case, on inquiry, we agreed to enlarge the boundary from a branch to the main of the Miami river, and joining on the southwest corner of the lands of the Wyandots and Delawares. This did not seem fully to satisfy, but we would go no further.

The whole of the chiefs of the Wyandot, Delaware, and Shawnese nations being collected, the Commissioners went to Council. All being seated, the Commissioners spoke as follows:

Chiefs, &c., We have listened attentively to your speech of yesterday, and considered every part thereof. Your professions and declarations to concur with us in completing the work of peace pleases us. We will do every thing which is just, on our part, and the Great Spirit sees our actions; our declarations are from our hearts, and not from our lips only. We are glad to see that your eyes are open to your interest, and that you understand us fully, that you are sensible who led you astray, plunged your nation into error and distress, and left you without a friend, and that you are determined in future to shut your ears against their evil counselors. You tell us that the evils of the war sprung from the warriors, and not from your kings, and that the warriors must make us all the reparation in their power; that you have appointed three of them to collect and bring our people to this place, and give them up. Your proposals, so far, please us. It is a mark of your sincerity, and we advise you to be strong, that the thoughts of past injuries may be forgotten; and that what we conclude at this council fire may last forever, and each become great and happy. Nothing will tend to effect this more than a cheerful compliance, on your part, with the articles of treaty which we shall propose, and speedy return of our people. This will dry the tears of sorrow from the eyes of our women, and appease the anger of our men. We are sorry to find one of your proposals such as we cannot comply with. It is that of your taking back the three of our prisoners which you have here. These must be immediately given to us, and the most speedy and effec-

tual measures taken by you to bring in all the others, white and black, to this place, without fail.

Chiefs, &c., We have shown you the situation in which you stand with the United States. This you say you understand clearly, and that you are sensible of the truth and justice of all we have said. It therefore only remains for us to tell you the terms on which the United States will grant you peace, and receive your nation into friendship and protection. These are the articles of treaty:

1st. Three hostages to remain till all our prisoners, white and black, are delivered, who are in your nation, &c.

2d. The Shawnese acknowledge the United States have the sole and absolute sovereignty of the whole country ceded by the King of Great Britain, &c.

3d. Any Indian who may commit a murder or robbery on a citizen of the U.S. shall be given up to be punished by the laws of the U.S. Any citizen who may commit the like on an Indian, to be punished by the laws of the U.S., &c.

4th. The Shawnese having knowledge of a war being waged by any Indian nation, shall give information thereof, or be considered enemies. The United States the same obligation.

5th. The U.S. grant peace, and receive into protection, &c.

6th. The U.S. grant to the Shawnese lands on the west of the main branch of the Miami, &c., as described.

7th. Any citizen presuming to settle on the lands assigned to the Indians, is out of the protection of the U.S., &c.

The chiefs and people being collected, the Commissioners, Officers, civil and military, the chiefs and warriors of the Shawnese, the chiefs of the Wyandots and Delawares; the business was opened by a head Captain of the Shawnese, Kekewepellethe, he recapitulated the speech and articles of treaty, and explained them to the whole. He then addressed the Commissioners:

Brothers: By what you have said to us yesterday, we expected every thing past would be forgotten; that our proposals for collecting the prisoners were satisfactory, and that we would have been placed on the same footing as before the war. To-day you demand hostages till your prisoners are returned. You next say you will divide the lands. I now tell you it is not the custom of the Shawnese to give hostages, our words are to be believed, when we say a thing we stand to it, we are Shawnese—and as to the lands, God gave us this country, we do not understand measuring out the lands, it is all ours. You say you have goods for our women and children; you may keep your goods, and give them to the other nations, we will have none of them. Brothers, you seem to grow proud, because you have thrown down the King of England; and as we feel sorry for our past faults, you rise in your demands on us. This we think hard. You need not doubt our words; what we have promised we will perform. We told you we had appointed three good men of our nation to go to the towns and collect your flesh and blood; they shall be brought in. We have never given hostages, and we will not comply with this demand. *A black string.*

The Commissioners conferred a short time on this answer, and resolved they would not recede from any of the articles, considering them just and as liberal as the interests of the U.S. would admit of. Whereupon, I addressed them in this short manner:

Shawnese—You have addressed us with great warmth. We think the answer unwise and ungrateful; and in return for just and generous proposals, you have not only given us improper language, but asserted the greatest falsehoods. You say you cannot give hostages for the performances of your promises, as it is contrary to your usages, and that you never break your word. Have you forgotten your breach of treaties in the beginning of the late war with Britain, between the United States and your chiefs, in '75 and '76? Do you think us ignorant of those treaties? Do you think we have forgotten the burning of our towns, the murder and captivity of our people in conse-

quence of your perfidy, or have you forgotten them? Don't you remember when Col. Bouquet came to Tuscarawas, that you there gave hostages?° Do you forget that you gave hostages to Lord Dunmore? Do you forget that when he had agreed to send people to collect the prisoners, that they had like to have been murdered in your towns? Recollect, and you might know that these are truths. You gave to both of these great men hostages for the performance of your promises; and even under that engagement, you paid so little regard to your faith, which you had pledged, that it was with difficulty our people got from amongst you; and although you had promised to do the business yourselves, you did not even attempt to protect these men who went to assist you. We know these things to be truths, with much more we could relate, equally aggravating. You cannot, therefore, expect we will believe you; I tell you we cannot believe you, or rely on your words; and the burning of the houses of our people, and barbarously ravaging our frontier, besides the repeated violations of treaties of the most sacred nature. Are your barbarous murders, and the cruelty shown our prisoners, marks of your fidelity, or proofs of your pacific disposition, or a desire of enjoying the blessings of peace in common with us. I say, they are not. These are the gifts of heaven, and they cannot be enjoyed under such circumstances. You joined the British King against us, and followed his fortunes; we have overcome him, he has cast you off, and given us your country; and Congress, in bounty and mercy, offer you country and peace. We have told you the terms on which you shall have it; these terms we will not alter, they are liberal, they are just, and we will not depart from them; we now tell you, if you have been so unfortunate and unwise as to determine and adhere to what you have said, and to refuse the terms we have offered to give to your nation

---

°A reference to Colonel Henry Bouquet's expedition and dictated peace in 1764.

peace, friendship, and protection, you may depart in peace; you shall have provisions to take you to your towns, and no man shall touch you for eight days after this day; but after that time is expired, be assured that we shall consider ourselves freed from all the ties of protection to you, and you may depend the U.S. will take the most effectual measures to protect their citizens, and to distress your obstinate nation. It rests now with you, the destruction of your women and children, or their future happiness, depends on your present choice. Peace or war is in your power; make your choice like men, and judge for yourselves. We shall only add this: had you judged as it is your interest to do, you would have considered us as your friends, and followed our counsel; but if you choose to follow the opinion which you have expressed, you are guided either by evil counsel or rashness, and are blinded. We plainly tell you that this country belongs to the United States — their blood hath defended it, and will forever protect it. Their proposals are liberal and just; and you instead of acting as you have done, and instead of persisting in your folly, should be thankful for the forgiveness and offers of kindness of the United States, instead of the sentiments which this string imparts, and the manner in which you have delivered it. We shall not receive it or any other from you in any such way. (I then took it up and dashed it on the table.) We therefore leave you to consider of what hath been said, and to determine as you please.

We then left them and threw down a black and white string. In the afternoon, the Shawnese sent a message requesting we would attend in the Council-house; on which we went in. Kekewepellethe then arose and spoke as follows:

Brothers, the 13 Fires — We feel sorry that a mistake has caused you to be displeased at us this morning. You must have misunderstood us. We told you yesterday that three of our men were to go off immediately to collect your flesh and blood; we had also appointed persons to remain with you till this is performed; they are here and shall stay with you. Brethren, our people are sensible of the truths you have told them. You have every thing in your power — you are great, and we see you own all the country; we therefore hope, as you have everything in your power, that you will take pity on our women and children. Brothers, everything shall be as you wish; we came here to do that which is good, and we agree to all you have proposed, and hope, in future, we shall both enjoy peace, and be secure. (A white string.)

The Commissioners then told them they were glad to find they had reconsidered their speech, and rectified the mistake, and that their sensible men had considered the good of their nation, and were likely to act a proper and prudent part, which alone can secure the friendship of the United States, and give their nation peace. (A white string.)

The Half-king of the Wyandots then rose and addressed the Commissioners and Shawnese.

Brothers: I feel pleased and happy that the disagreeable difference which arose between you is now settled. I hope you will now conclude a peace which shall last forever between the United States and the Shawnese, and that you may both be as brothers. (A string.)

The council then broke up. It was worthy of observation to see the different degrees of agitation which appeared in the young Indians, at the delivery of Kekewepellethe's speech; they appeared raised and ready for war; on the speech I spoke they appeared rather distressed and chagrined by the contrast of the speeches, and convinced of the futility of their arguments.

References

1. Colin G. Calloway, ed., "Revolution and Confederation," in Alden T. Vaughan, gen. ed., *Early American Indian Documents: Treaties and Laws, 1607–1789,* vol. 18 (Bethesda, Md.: University Publications of America, 1994), 284, 313–27.
2. Quoted in Colin G. Calloway, *The American Revolution in Indian Country: Crisis and Diversity in Native American Communities* (New York: Cambridge University Press, 1995), 174.
3. Quoted in Calloway, *American Revolution in Indian Country,* 48.
4. Quoted in Calloway, ed., *Revolution and Confederation,* 158.

Suggested Readings

Calloway, Colin G. *The American Revolution in Indian Country: Crisis and Diversity in Native American Communities* (New York: Cambridge University Press, 1995).

Dowd, Gregory Evans. *A Spirited Resistance: The North American Indian Struggle for Unity, 1745–1815* (Baltimore: Johns Hopkins University Press, 1992).

Downes, Randolph C. *Council Fires on the Upper Ohio: A Narrative of Indian Affairs in the Upper Ohio Valley until 1795* (Pittsburgh: University of Pennsylvania Press, 1940).

Hinderaker, Eric. *Elusive Empires: Constructing Colonialism in the Ohio Valley, 1673–1800* (Cambridge: Cambridge University Press, 1997).

Horsman, Reginald. *Expansion and American Indian Policy* (East Lansing: Michigan State University Press, 1967).

Sugden, John. *Blue Jacket, Warrior of the Shawnees* (Lincoln: University of Nebraska Press, 2000).

Sword, Wiley. *President Washington's Indian War* (Norman: University of Oklahoma Press, 1985).

Tanner, Helen Hornbeck, ed. *Atlas of Great Lakes Indian History* (Norman: University of Oklahoma Press, 1987).

White, Richard. *The Middle Ground: Indians, Empires, and Republics in the Great Lakes Region, 1650–1815* (New York: Cambridge University Press, 1991).

Painting the Past:
Indians in the Art of an Emerging Nation

As the colonies secured their independence and Americans embarked on building a new nation, American artists encoded in national art powerful images of Indians that produced lasting legacies. Indians were accorded a limited role: giving way to American colonists, threatening the pioneers who struggled to build civilization, but doomed to disappear before the advance of that civilization. In the art of the new nation, as in the new nation itself, Indians were consigned to the past; there was no place for them to survive, as Indians, in the new society that was emerging. Looking back over the recurrent conflicts that had punctuated the colonial and Revolutionary era — the nation's formative years — Americans tended to regard Indians as inherently warlike. The art of the young nation provided its citizens with compelling imagery of Indians in the past and armed them with powerful justifications for excluding Indians from the future.

Benjamin West's famous painting of William Penn's *Treaty with the Indians When He Founded the Province of Pennsylvania in North America* (1771) shows Penn meeting with the Delawares under an elm tree at Shackamaxon in 1682 (Figure 3.1). The Indians exchange land for bales of cloth and other manufactured goods while "civilization" advances in the background with ships in the harbor and houses under construction edging onto the forested area of Indian lodges. The workmen on the bottom left and the Indian family at bottom right direct the viewer's attention to the central meeting of Indians with English Quakers and merchants. The central Indian figure ponders the sale of Indian land, but otherwise it is the Indians rather than the colonists who seem eager to make the trade. West observed Indian people firsthand and includes some valuable ethnographic documentation in the picture, which is often reproduced as an actual portrayal of a historical event. But the meeting never happened as he depicted it, the Indians wear clothing combining the styles of several tribes, and most scholars see the picture instead as an allegory of colonial America and a representation of a succession of Indian treaties. By the time West painted this picture in 1771, Pennsylvania had experienced bloody conflicts: colonists often killed Indians out of hand and seized their lands by whatever means they could. Thomas Penn, the proprietor of Pennsylvania, commissioned the painting ostensibly as a tribute to his father, but probably to invoke an image of more peaceful times that would reinforce the Penn family claim to proprietorship of the colony during a time of political dissension.

FIGURE 3.1 Benjamin West, *Penn's Treaty with the Indians* (1771)
Courtesy of the Pennsylvania Academy of the Fine Arts, Philadelphia. Gift of Mrs. Sarah Harrison (The Joseph H. Harrison, Jr., Collection).

West's depiction of the Delawares as willing participants in the sale of their land permanently established the image of William Penn as a man of peace, but it also justified more recent and more blatant thefts of Indian land.[1]

The abduction of women into captivity by Indian warriors was a common theme in the literature of colonial America and the art of early national America. It alarmed contemporaries and provided later generations of Americans with powerful allegories of the clash of "civilization"—white, female, defenseless, and vulnerable—and "savagery"—dark-skinned, male, armed, and dangerous. One of the more famous stories of captivity and rescue involved Daniel Boone's daughter Jemima. It was told and retold in stories, writings, sketches, and paintings, including Carl Wimar's (1828–62) 1853 painting of her abduction (Figure 3.2). Wimar was a German-born American artist who settled in St. Louis and specialized in painting scenes from the American frontier. Toward the end of his short life he painted a series of murals in the rotunda of the St. Louis courthouse which included a version of Hernando de Soto discovering the

FIGURE 3.2 **Charles F. Wimar,** *The Abduction of Daniel Boone's Daughter by the Indians* **(1853)**

Oil on Canvas, 46 ¹/₈″ × 56 ¹/₄″. Washington University Gallery of Art, St. Louis, Gift of Mr. John T. Davis, Jr, 1954.

Mississippi. Wimar traveled up the Missouri to see Indians firsthand, but his painting reflected the attitudes of mid-nineteenth-century America: Indians were either "savage foes" or "noble redmen" doomed to extinction. As in many of Wimar's pictures, Indian subjects are portrayed against the background of a symbolically setting sun.[2] Three muscular Shawnee warriors surround the Madonna-like figure of the heroine, but the Indians are wary and have a hunted look about them: Daniel Boone and "civilization" are sure to catch up with them.

In the *The Death of Jane McCrea* (Figure 3.3), painted in 1804, John Vanderlyn likewise took a historical event and depicted it in a way that gave it enduring power. Jane McCrea, it seems, was murdered by Indian allies of General

FIGURE 3.3 John Vanderlyn, *The Death of Jane McCrea* (1804)

The Wadsworth Atheneum Museum of Art, Hartford, Connecticut. Purchased by the Wadsworth Atheneum.

John Burgoyne during the abortive British invasion of New England in 1777. News of the murder helped to rally colonial resistance; Burgoyne surrendered at Saratoga in 1777. The facts of the case are not clear and if McCrea was killed by Indian allies of Burgoyne, the killers were almost certainly Christians from the mission villages on the St. Lawrence River. But Vanderlyn's painting reflected and fueled popular stereotypes and fears: a European woman, her

FIGURE 3.4 **John Mix Stanley,** *The Last of Their Race* **(1857)**
Buffalo Bill Historical Center, Cody, Wyoming; 5.75.

breasts partially exposed, falls victim to the tomahawk blows of Indian warriors. It graphically imprinted on the minds of generations of Americans the notion embodied in the Declaration of Independence that Native Americans were "merciless Indian savages, whose known rule of warfare is an undistinguished destruction of all ages, sexes, and conditions."

Euro-Americans who headed west into Indian country carried with them assumptions that Indians were, at best, noble but tragic figures who would inevitably disappear as civilization advanced, and at worst, vicious savages who should be hunted to extinction. Assuming that extinction was assured, some American artists also indulged in nostalgic mourning for a passing way of life. In 1857, John Mix Stanley's *The Last of Their Race* (Figure 3.4) allegorically depicted a group of Indians driven to the Pacific where they await and contemplate their final extinction against a setting sun.

▶ Questions for Consideration

1. These four pictures tell us much about how Americans viewed Indians during the colonial and Revolutionary period of the nation's history. Do they reveal anything about the Indians themselves?

2. Are they of any value in understanding Native American historical experiences?

3. Why did the way Indians were depicted in art matter to the young nation?

References

1. Ann Uhry Abrams, "Benjamin West's Documentation of Colonial History: *William Penn's Treaty with the Indians*," *Art Bulletin* 64 (1982), 59–75; Arthur Einhorn and Thomas S. Abler, "Bonnets, Plumes, and Headbands in West's Painting of Penn's Treaty," *American Indian Art Magazine* 21 (Summer 1996), 45–53; Patricia Trenton and Patrick T Houlihan, *Native Americans: Five Centuries of Changing Images* (New York: Abrams, 1989), 26–30; Anne Cannon Palumbo, "Averting 'Present Commotions': History as Politics in Penn's Treaty," *American Art*, 9 (Fall 1995), 29–55.
2. See Rick Stewart, Joseph D. Kettner II, and Angela L. Miller, *Carl Wimar: Chronicler of the Missouri River Frontier* (Abrams, 1991), 45–50.

AMERICAN INDIANS AND THE NEW NATION

1783–1838

THE NEW NATION EXPANDS

While competing powers waged wars of empire in the East, large areas of Indian America in the West remained untouched by European contact. There life went on in traditional ways, and Indian people made choices and changes without much thought to Europeans. Once the United States had won its liberty from Britain, it began to build its own domain in the territory that Britain had transferred at the peace treaty of 1783 — lands inhabited by Indian peoples. Inevitably, war and treaty-making came to dominate U.S.–Indian relations, although the federal government developed policies aimed at robbing Indians of their cultures as well as their lands. The United States regarded its expansion as inevitable, even divinely ordained, and recognized that its growth would entail dispossessing the original Indian inhabitants. But Indians challenged the policy that threatened to transform their homelands into national real estate. "Our lands are our life and our breath," declared the Creek chief Hallowing King in 1787. "If we part with them, we part with our blood."[1] Giving up land meant more than shrinking a tribe's territorial base: it reduced the people's mobility and restricted the range of resources available to them; it uprooted them from ancestral places to which they felt bound by communal traditions and stories.

While the American victory in the East brought changing relations between Indian Americans and white Americans, a massive smallpox epidemic in the West also generated far-reaching changes. Breaking out in Mexico City in 1779, the epidemic had spread in all directions, traveling through the Southwest, north across the Great Plains and Rocky Mountains, and into the forests of Canada by 1783. Thousands of Indians died.[2] A generation later, the new United States began to venture beyond the Mississippi. Like the Pilgrims who landed at Plymouth in 1620, they were setting foot in a land already devastated and depopulated by disease.

Developing an Indian Policy

The new United States followed the British example in Indian relations: they set up an Indian department, established rules for the sale and transfer of Indian lands, and tried to regulate the advance of the frontier. The United States Constitution established national authority over the conduct of Indian relations, permitting only the federal government to negotiate and make treaties with Indian nations. The War Department assumed responsibility for Indian affairs, and the first secretary of war, Henry Knox, proved relatively humanitarian in his dealings with Indians. In the 1780s, with dust from the Revolution not quite settled on the frontiers, it made sense for Indian affairs to be under the juris-

The United States in 1783
The Treaty of Paris in 1783 recognized the independence of the United States and established the borders of the new nation at the Great Lakes, the Mississippi, and the northern boundary of Florida. As the map shows, most of this territory was inhabited by Indian nations. The Indians were not mentioned in the Peace of Paris, and American expansion entailed taking possession of their lands by war or treaty. National Archives of Canada.

diction of the War Department. Furthermore, the United States in the 1780s was still an infant power, with hostile European neighbors on its northern and southern borders. Both the British in Canada and the Spanish in Florida continued to encourage and support Indians living within the United States territory in resisting American expansion, while the young nation lacked the military resources and economic strength to establish control over its frontiers. The Indian Office, later known as the Bureau of Indian Affairs, was established in 1824; not until 1849 was it transferred from the War Department to the Department of the Interior.

Indian policy, and the machinery for conducting Indian relations, in the words of historian Francis Paul Prucha, "grew bit by bit."[3] Nevertheless, a clear and basic object of United States Indian policy from the end of the American Revolution to the Indian removals of the 1830s was the acquisition of lands between the Appalachians and the Mississippi. Many government leaders were conscious of their position as the only republic on the world stage and wanted to ensure that national expansion be pursued with honor, but the drive to acquire land was constant. Indians responded to American policies and presumptions in a variety of ways, and Indian power continued to limit American expansion for many years. Nevertheless, by 1815 the United States had effectively destroyed Indian power east of the Mississippi.

Regulating an Indian—and a Land—Policy

In the decade following the Revolution, the United States claimed Indian lands east of the Mississippi by right of conquest. These territories were a vital national resource that would provide land for citizens, fill an empty treasury, and guarantee a future of continuous growth and prosperity. But formulating and implementing national policy was frequently hampered and frustrated.

In an effort to regulate conditions on the frontier and reaffirm that conduct of Indian affairs was reserved to the federal government, not the states, Congress passed the Indian Trade and Intercourse Act in 1790. Only licensed traders were permitted to operate in Indian country, and no transfers of Indian land were valid without congressional approval. The Trade and Intercourse Acts were renewed periodically until 1834. But, like the British after 1763, the fledgling United States government failed to control its own citizens on distant frontiers. Frontier settlers, squatters, and speculators seldom shared their government's concern for expansion with honor—all they wanted was expansion. Individual states, resentful of attempts by the federal government to restrict their rights, frequently made treaties that never received congressional approval.

Further complicating the government's land policy were conflicting colonial charters; because of them, seven of the original states had land claims stretching to the Mississippi valley. The parties agreed that these claims should be ceded to the national government for the common good before the Articles of Confederation went into effect in 1781 and that the lands lying beyond these boundaries should fall into the public domain. By 1786, the states had ceded

MAP 4.1 United States Treaties and Indian Land Cessions to 1810
Although individual states exerted pressure on the southern tribes, the new United States government devoted most energy to acquiring Indian lands beyond the Ohio River and to defeating the multitribal coalitions that resisted American expansion there. Treaties, by which Indian nations sold lands or ceded them in return for peace, became major instruments in the United States' policy of national expansion.

most of the lands north of the Ohio River. Southern states proved less compliant, however. Virginia retained claims to Kentucky, North Carolina did not cede Tennessee until 1789, and Georgia did not relinquish its claims to the territory of Alabama and Mississippi until 1802. In the early years of the republic, national expansion focused north of the Ohio, since the government had no lands to sell in the South.

In 1787, the Northwest Ordinance proclaimed that the United States would observe "the utmost good faith" in its dealings with Indian people and that their lands would not be invaded or taken except in "just and lawful wars authorized by Congress." But the Ordinance also laid out a blueprint for national expansion: the Northwest Territory was to be divided into districts which, after passing through territorial status, would become states. Ohio, Indiana, Illinois, Michigan, and Wisconsin eventually entered the Union as states carved from the Northwest Territory. Indians who resisted American expansion soon found themselves subjected to "just and lawful wars."

INDIANS CONFRONT EXPANSION

While American power was relatively weak after the Revolution, Indian power remained formidable in much of the western territory that the United States claimed. Indian tribes usually acted in the specific interests of family and band rather than as a "race," but in times of crisis, Indian peoples often cooperated in impressive displays of unity. For Indian people, American independence ushered in a new era in which they struggled again to preserve their homelands and freedom. Not only did various tribes come together to negotiate and fight those who pushed them off their land, in some cases they also collectively sought hope in new religious movements.

Building a United Defense

In the 1780s, as Americans dictated treaties to separate tribes, the Mohawk leader Joseph Brant emerged as a leading spokesman in a confederacy of northwestern tribes. The confederacy rejected treaties signed by individual tribes and refused to accept any American settlement west of the Ohio River. Delegates from the Iroquois, Hurons, Delawares, Shawnees, Ottawas, Anishinaabeg, Potawatomis, Miamis, and Wabash River tribes assembled in council at the mouth of the Detroit River in December 1786. They sent a message to Congress, assuring the Americans of their desire for peace, but insisting that "as landed matters are often the subject of our councils with you, a matter of the greatest importance and of general concern to us," any cession of lands "should be made in the most public manner, and by the united voice of the confederacy; holding all partial treaties as void and of no effect."[4] The confederacy prepared to resist American expansion, by armed force if necessary.

Early American efforts at a military solution met with little success. In 1790, General Josiah Harmar invaded Indian country with some 1,500 men, but the warriors of the western tribes, ably led by the Miami war chief Little Turtle and Blue Jacket of the Shawnees, inflicted a decisive defeat. Worse was to come. In 1791, Little Turtle routed an American army under General Arthur St. Clair in the heaviest defeat Indians ever inflicted on the United States. St. Clair suffered over 900 casualties, with some 600 dead, at a time when the young republic had neither the manpower nor the resources to sustain such losses. American claims to Indian land by right of conquest looked empty.

For a time it seemed as if the United States would negotiate a compromise agreement with the Indian tribes of the Old Northwest. However, while the Americans rebuilt their army, deep divisions appeared in Indian ranks. After the defeat of St. Clair, Joseph Brant and the Iroquois recommended reaching a

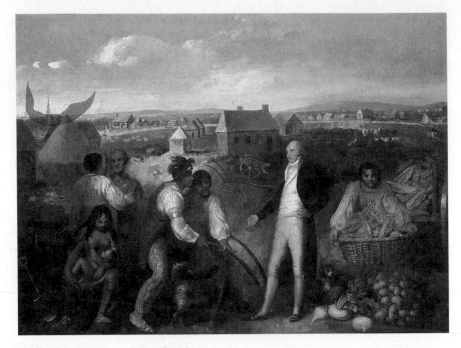

Benjamin Hawkins and the Creeks
United States Indian agent Benjamin Hawkins is shown introducing Creek Indians to plows, steel tools, and Euro-American farming techniques. For Hawkins, promoting agriculture meant transforming Indian men from hunters to farmers; Indian women, who produced the cornucopia portrayed here, were to be allotted more "domestic" chores.
Greenville County Museum of Art, Greenville, South Carolina. Gift of the Museum Association, Inc.

settlement with the United States. Brant and the Iroquois continued to exert influence in Indian country after the Revolution, but many of the western tribes regarded them with increasing suspicion. Western warriors who had already defeated two American armies rejected the idea of compromise. "Money, to us, is of no value," representatives of the united tribes told American commissioners in 1793, and "no consideration whatever can induce us to sell the lands on which we get sustenance for our women and children." They assumed that the settlers who trespassed across the Ohio were poor and proposed that the United States take the money it was offering to purchase Indian land, add to it "the great sums you must expend in raising and paying Armies" and divide the total among the settlers. Thus accommodated, the settlers would happily remove from Indian lands and peace could be restored. All the Indians wanted was "the peaceable possession of a small part of our once great Country." They could not give up the Ohio River as their boundary: "Look back and view the lands from whence we have been driven, we can retreat no further."[5]

Meanwhile, Congress was appropriating $1 million to raise, equip, and train a new army, the Legion of the United States, to be led by General Anthony Wayne against the Indian alliance. By the time Wayne and his army entered Indian country in 1794, the confederacy was no longer united. On the west bank of the Maumee River, south of Lake Erie, a reduced Indian force confronted Wayne's troops in a tangle of trees felled by a tornado. Outnumbered and out-gunned, the Indians were driven from the field by the American cannon, cavalry, and bayonets. "We were driven by the sharp end of the guns of the Long Knives," recalled one Indian leader. "Our moccasins trickled with blood in the sand, and the water was red in the river."[6] They fled to a nearby British fort, where they believed they would receive assistance. But although the British were willing to encourage Indian hostility to the United States, they were not interested in another war in America while faced with trouble in Europe and a revolutionary government in France. The fleeing Indians found the gates of the fort barred against them. The lack of British support dispirited the Indians more than the actual battle at Fallen Timbers, where their losses were relatively light. In 1795, at the signing of the Treaty of Greenville, more than a thousand Indian delegates accepted Wayne's terms and ceded to the United States two-thirds of present-day Ohio and part of Indiana. In return, the Indians were promised a lasting boundary between their lands and American territory.

Accommodating and Resisting Change

Military pressures were not the only ones that Indian peoples experienced in these years. Americans sought to eradicate the Indians' way of life at the same time as they took away their lands. Men like Benjamin Hawkins, United States agent to the Creek (or Muskogee) Indians from 1796–1816, attempted to im-pose a social revolution on Indian country, organize Indian economic life around intensive agriculture, and redefine gender roles in Indian families. The Creeks, Cherokees, and most other Eastern Woodland peoples had farmed for centuries, but in the American program, men, not women, were to do the farm-ing and were to give up hunting for a life behind a plow. Women were to take up spinning, weaving, and other "domestic chores." As Indians spent less time hunting, they would need less land and could sell the "surplus" land to the United States. As men spent more time at home, the nuclear family, with the male at its head, would supplant the matrilineal clans. As families acquired more property, they would adopt Anglo-American principles of ownership and inheritance. "Ultimately," concludes one scholar "the Muskogees would become good yeoman farmers, settlers with a slightly darker skin and some quaint ethnic memories. The men would display 'the manners of a well bred man,' the women the 'neatness and economy of a white woman.' This was Hawkins' dream."[7]

Missionaries and other groups in American society believed it was their duty to "civilize" the Indians by destroying their traditions and culture and transforming them into Christians. Some Indians were quick to point out what they saw as the Americans' hypocrisy. The Seneca chief Red Jacket, for example, asked missionaries to explain why they were so sure that theirs was the one true religion. The Great Spirit had made Indians and white men different in many respects, so why not accept that He had given them different religions to suit

Handsome Lake Preaching
Handsome Lake preaches his new religion in the Seneca longhouse at Tonawanda, New York, in a twentieth-century watercolor by Ernest Smith, who was born at Tonawanda. Handsome Lake's Teachings resulted in the Longhouse Religion, which many Iroquois people still practice. Rochester Museum and Science Center.

their needs? The Indians might be more inclined to accept Christianity, he said, if the Christians they saw around them served as better examples. But since they saw lying, cheating, drunkenness, and theft, the Indians thought they were better off with their own religion.[8]

In a period of intense pressure and crisis, many Indians found solace in new forms of religion. Time and again, Indian people turned to ritual and belief to restore balance and harmony to a world that had gone chaotic. The Delaware prophet Neolin had headed one such movement in the 1760s; his renunciation of European material goods and influences, helped fuel Pontiac's war of resistance against the British.

By 1800, the Iroquois Confederacy was broken. Iroquois people who had once dominated the northeastern United States were now confined to reservations in small areas of their traditional homelands or lived in exile in Canada. The Senecas once held some 4 million acres of western New York and Pennsylvania; now they lived on fewer than 200,000 acres, divided into ten separate tracts. Many sought refuge in alcohol. In 1799, a hard-drinking Seneca named Handsome Lake, who lay ill and apparently close to death, experienced a vision in which the Creator awakened him to a new religion and a new way of life for Iroquois people. Handsome Lake renounced his former life of drunkenness and embarked on a mission to bring his teachings, *Gaiwiio,* or "the Good Message," to his people. The "Longhouse Religion" that developed based on his teachings combined traditional beliefs with some Christian additions, adopted from Quaker missionaries to the Senecas. Handsome Lake preached that Iroquois people should live in peace with the United States and with one another, and based many of his teachings on the Great Law of Peace (see "The Iroquois Great League of Peace," pages 44–55). He denounced alcohol and factionalism and emphasized the importance of education and farming. He espoused the new social gospel in which men now did the farming, and husbands headed the nuclear family, in place of society based on matrilineal, extended families that had traditionally inhabited the clan mothers' longhouses.[9] At the same time, his teachings incorporated thanksgiving festivals and other ceremonies from the old religion and denounced the sale of lands. For many, the new religion meant a new way of living, but it also offered hope in a time of spiritual crisis and a means of coping. The Longhouse Religion and the code of values Handsome Lake preached continue as a way of life for many Iroquois people today.

The Last Phases of United Indian Resistance

Like the Iroquois, the Shawnee Indians had lost lands, suffered defeat in battle, and seen their culture assaulted. In the first decade of the nineteenth century, however, Shawnees emerged as leaders in a pan-Indian religious and political movement. Like Handsome Lake, the Shawnee Prophet, Tenskwatawa, lived an early life of drunkenness and debauchery. Like Handsome Lake, he fell into a trance and experienced a vision in 1805, which caused him to transform his life and bring a message of hope to his people. Tenskwatawa preached that the Master of Life had selected him to spread the new religion among the Indians. Indian people were warned to avoid contact with the Americans, who were "children of the Evil Spirit." They were urged to give up alcohol, refuse intermarriage, reject Christianity, lay down manufactured tools, and throw off white man's clothing. Instead of eating the meat of domesticated animals, they should return to a diet of corn, beans, maple sugar, and other traditional foods. They should avoid intertribal conflict and practice communal ownership of property. Tenskwatawa's teachings promised a revitalization of Shawnee culture but his message also drew adherents from the Delawares, Kickapoos, Ottawas, Potawatomis, Anishinaabeg, and other tribes, especially after he accurately predicted a total eclipse of the sun on June 16, 1806. Many Indians rejected his message, but hundreds of others flocked to the village he established at Prophetstown on the Tippecanoe River in Indiana.

However, it was the Shawnee Prophet's brother, Tecumseh, who gave strongest direction to the developing movement of Indian unity. Tecumseh had fought at the Battle of Fallen Timbers in 1794 but he refused to sign the Treaty of Greenville. Identifying American expansion and piecemeal cessions of land as the major threat to Indian survival, Tecumseh argued that no tribe had the right to sell their lands, because the lands belonged to all Indians. He denounced older chiefs who signed away tribal territory, and his influence soared after pro-American chiefs ceded more than three million acres to the United States at a "whiskey treaty" at Fort Wayne in 1809. Tecumseh traveled from the Great Lakes to Florida, carrying his message of pan-Indian land tenure and preaching a vision of an Indian nation stretching from Canada to the Gulf of Mexico.

Tenskwatawa's teachings and Tecumseh's vision alarmed the United States government. In 1811, an American army under General William Harrison launched a preemptive strike against the Prophet's village at Tippecanoe while Tecumseh was away in the South. The battle was a relatively minor affair— Tecumseh dismissed it as "a scuffle between children"—but the Americans claimed a victory, the Prophet lost prestige, and Tecumseh's confederacy suffered a setback. Tension between Indians and Americans persisted into the War of 1812. In that conflict, Tecumseh sided with the British in a last attempt to stem the tide of American expansion. The British–Indian alliance scored some early victories—in 1812 Tecumseh and General Isaac Brock captured Detroit—but Britain was distracted by its involvement in European resistance to Napoleon. When Tecumseh was killed at the Battle of the Thames in Ontario in 1813, the last hope of Indian unity east of the Mississippi also died.

In the South, Alexander McGillivray (1759–93) of the Creeks headed a confederacy of tribes whose united power represented a considerable force in the decade after the Revolution. McGillivray was the son of a Scottish trader who provided him an education in Charleston, South Carolina, and a French-Creek mother who gave him membership in the influential Wind clan. He tried to protect Creek lands and independence in a region of competing and threatening international, intertribal, and state ambitions. McGillivray refused to recognize any claims of the United States to Creek lands based on the treaty with Britain in 1783 because the Indians took no part in the treaty. In 1784, he signed a treaty with Spain at Pensacola, securing Spanish trade and protection of Creek lands. The United States signed its first treaty with the other major southeastern tribes—the Cherokees, Choctaws, and Chickasaws—at Hopewell in Georgia in 1785–86, reaffirming tribal boundaries in an effort to avoid all-out war on the southern frontier. In 1790, McGillivray led a delegation of Creek chiefs to New York where they signed a treaty in which the United States guaranteed Creek territorial boundaries. But the southern states posed a more immediate threat than Congress, and Georgia continued to encroach on Creek and Cherokee lands.

McGillivray was opposed by some chiefs who favored a policy of appeasement and land cessions in dealing with Georgia. Tension within the Creek confederacy increased after McGillivray's death in 1793, and escalated after Tecumseh traveled the Southeast with his message of united Indian resistance in 1811. Upper Creek towns tended to favor adopting a militant stance in dealing with the United States; Lower Creek towns tended to advocate peace and accommodation. Conflicts within the Creek confederacy spilled over into attacks on American settlers, and the United States responded with swift military action against the militant Creeks, or "Red Sticks." In the Creek War of 1813–14, General Andrew Jackson directed a series of devastating campaigns that culminated in the slaughter of some eight hundred Creek warriors at the Battle of

Tohopeka or Horseshoe Bend on the Tallapoosa River in present-day Alabama in March 1814. About five hundred Cherokees and one hundred Lower Creeks helped Jackson win his victory. But at the Treaty of Fort Jackson the general dictated punitive terms that divested the Creek Nation of 14 million acres, two-thirds of their tribal domain. It was the single largest cession of territory ever made in the Southeast and initiated a boom in land sales and cotton production in the deep South.

As the deerskin trade declined and the Cotton Kingdom expanded into new lands in Mississippi, the Choctaws and Chickasaws adjusted to new economic conditions. They changed their farming and settlement patterns, raised more stock, mingled with African American slaves, and grew cotton for the market.[10] The age of Indian confederacies in the East and of Indian power that delayed American expansion was over by the end of the War of 1812, but Indians did not disappear just because they stopped fighting.

INDIAN REMOVALS

The state of Oklahoma today is home to numerous tribes: Cherokee, Creek, Chickasaw, Choctaw, Seminole, Caddo, Comanche, Southern Cheyenne, Southern Arapaho, Kiowa, Apache, Shawnee, Potawatomi, Wyandot, Quapaw, Osage, Peoria, Ottawa, Seneca, Pawnee, Ponca, Oto, Kansa, Tonkawa, Kickapoo, Modoc, Wichita, Iowa, Sauk and Fox, as well as to members and descendants of many other tribes. Few of these peoples were indigenous to the Oklahoma region; most live there because nineteenth-century United States policies designated the region "Indian Territory" and relocated thousands of Indian people there from other areas of the country.

The policy of removing Indian peoples from their eastern homelands to the West was implemented in the late 1820s and 1830s, but it originated in earlier periods when Americans had considered various solutions to the problem of what to do with Indians in the eastern United States. The government could try to (1) destroy the Indians; (2) assimilate them into American society; (3) protect them on their ancestral lands; (4) remove them to more distant lands. Most Americans favored the last option as the only practical course. Removal became a policy on which almost all sectors of American society could agree. Even some Indians came to believe that removal represented their best strategy for survival.

Roots of Removal Policy

The beginnings of removals went back to the presidency of Thomas Jefferson. In 1802, the state of Georgia ceded its western land claims to the United States, but in return Congress agreed to secure on "reasonable and peaceful" terms title to Cherokee and Creek lands within the state as soon as possible. In 1803, American emissaries in Paris purchased the Louisiana Territory—some

827,000 square miles of territory between the Mississippi and the Rocky Mountains—for a mere $15 million, and the United States doubled its size overnight. Jefferson soon dispatched Meriwether Lewis and William Clark on an epic journey (1804–06) to the Pacific to discover what the United States had bought (see "The Lewis and Clark Expedition," pages 225–39). The Lewis and Clark expedition initiated a new era of American interest in the West and, ultimately, a new era for the Indian peoples living there. The explorers did not enter an isolated and unchanging world. They met Indian people who had had contacts with European cultures—who rode horses, carried guns, wore woolen clothing, sometimes bore pock-marked faces, and, on occasion, swore like sailors. They encountered sedentary agricultural villages where the inhabitants did a brisk business trading corn and tobacco with hunters from the plains; some of these plains hunters had, until relatively recently, been farmers. Direct and indirect contact with the outside world had transformed the Indian West long before Lewis and Clark arrived. But many Americans saw the West as barren and virtually empty. Removal of the eastern Indians to presumably "empty" lands beyond the Mississippi became a practical possibility after 1803.

Jefferson and others easily solved the dilemma of how to take Indian lands with honor by determining that too much land was a disincentive for Indians to become "civilized." Ignoring the role of agriculture in Eastern Woodland societies, they argued that Indians would continue to hunt rather than settle down as farmers unless their options were restricted. Taking their lands forced Indians into a settled, agricultural, and "civilized" way of life and was, therefore, good for them in the long run. As Indians took up farming, Jefferson wrote in 1803 to William Henry Harrison, governor of Indiana Territory, "they will perceive how useless to them are their extensive forests, and will be willing to pare them off from time to time in exchange for necessaries for their farms and families." To promote this process "we shall push our trading houses, and be glad to see the good and influential individuals run into debt, because we observe that when these debts get beyond what the individuals can pay, they become willing to lop them off by a cession of lands." In this way, American settlements would gradually surround the Indians "and they will in time either incorporate with us as citizens of the United States, or remove beyond the Mississippi."[11] The process of dispossession could be comfortably accomplished within Jefferson's philosophy of minimal government. The government could do little to regulate the frontier and protect Indian lands, causing Indians to fight for their land. The government would have no choice but to invade Indian country, suppress the uprising, and dictate treaties in which defeated Indians signed away land. The stage was then set for the process to repeat itself. Jefferson's strategy for acquiring Indian lands resulted in some thirty treaties with a dozen or so tribal groups and the cession of almost 200,000 square miles of Indian territory in nine states. Jefferson regretted that Indians seemed doomed to extinction, but he showed little compunction in taking away their homelands.[12]

Some Indians moved west voluntarily; others determined never to abandon their ancestral lands. But in the early decades of the century the pressure to move west mounted steadily. Americans who hated Indians and desired their lands favored removal as a means of freeing up territory. Although many New

Englanders denounced the removal policies in the South, many other Americans who were sympathetic to the Indians also favored removal as the only way to protect them from their rapacious neighbors. Proremoval forces received a boost when Andrew Jackson, a renowned Indian-fighter and a staunch advocate of removal, was elected president in 1828. Jackson knew the settled and agriculturally based Creeks and Cherokees firsthand, but in his State of the Union Address in 1830 he depicted them as wandering hunters: "What good man would prefer a country covered with forests and ranged by a few thousand savages to our extensive republic studied with cities, towns and prosperous farms, embellished with all the improvements that art can devise or industry execute, occupied by more than 12 million happy people and filled with all the blessings of civilization, liberty and religion?" he asked.[13] The Indians would be better off in the West, where they could live undisturbed, Jackson argued. Other politicians expressed similar views, declaring that a few thousand Indians could not be allowed to stand in the way of human progress. Indians did not put the land to good use, they said, and could not be allowed to deny that land to American farmers. "Civilization" and "progress" demanded that the Indians be removed.

The Cherokee Resistance

The irony in Jackson's argument lay in the fact that the Indians whom Americans seemed most anxious to expel from their lands were people whom, even by their own definition, Americans termed civilized. Many Cherokees, Creeks, Chickasaws, and Choctaws had accommodated to American ways, wore European styles of clothing, plowed fields and fenced lands, cultivated corn and cotton. Some held slaves; some were Christian and literate. In 1827, the Cherokees restructured their tribal government into a constitutional republic modeled after that of the United States, with a written constitution, an independent judiciary, a supreme court, a principal chief, and a two-house legislature. They had a written language based on the syllabary developed by Sequoyah (a.k.a. George Gist, c. 1770–1843), who devoted a dozen years to developing a written version of the Cherokee language. In 1828 they established a newspaper, the *Cherokee Phoenix*. Its editor, Elias Boudinot, had received an education at a Moravian school in North Carolina and at the Cornwall Foreign Mission School in Connecticut. The *Phoenix* was published in both Cherokee and English. Some Cherokees were literate in two languages: they displayed more of the attributes of supposedly "civilized" society than did many of the American frontiersmen who were so eager to occupy their lands. A census taken among the Cherokees in 1825 showed that they owned 33 grist mills, 13 saw mills, one powder mill, 69 blacksmith shops, two tan yards, 762 looms, 2,486 spinning wheels, 172 wagons, 2,923 plows, 7,683 horses, 22,531 cattle, 46,732 pigs, and 2,566 sheep.[14] The Cherokees seemed to have everything the United States required of them to take their place in the new nation as a self-supporting, functioning republic of farmers. "You asked us to throw off the hunter and warrior state," said Cherokee John Ridge in a speech in Philadelphia in 1832. "We did

John Ridge

John Ridge (1803–39) was the son of Major Ridge, speaker of the Cherokee Council who fought as an ally of Andrew Jackson during the Creek War of 1813–14. Along with his cousin Elias Boudinot, John attended the American Board's Foreign Mission School in Cornwall, Connecticut. When the two young men fell in love with women in the town and proposed marriage, the citizens of Cornwall responded with an outburst of racist attacks. The young people married anyway, John taking Sarah Bird Northrup as his wife. Ridge wrote for the Cherokee Phoenix and served as an interpreter and secretary in delegations to Washington. Along with his father and Elias Boudinot, he came to believe that continued opposition to removal was futile. He was one of the so-called Treaty party who signed the Treaty of New Echota in 1835, committing the Cherokees to westward removal by 1838. From the Collection of Gilcrease Museum, Tulsa.

so—you asked us to form a republican government: We did so—adopting your own as a model. You asked us to cultivate the earth, and learn the mechanic arts: We did so. You asked us to learn to read: We did so. You asked us to cast away our idols, and worship your God: We did so."[15]

But it did not save them. Indeed, their very success and prosperity only increased pressure from neighbors eager to get their hands on Cherokee land. Cherokee territory originally extended into five southeastern states, but by the 1820s most of the remaining Cherokees were confined to Georgia. Gold was discovered in Cherokee country in 1827 and prospectors flooded into the area. In December the Georgia legislature passed a resolution asserting its sovereignty over Cherokee lands within the state's borders. Georgia demanded that the United States government begin negotiations to compel the Cherokees to cede their land: "The lands in question *belong* to Georgia," the legislators asserted. "She *must* and *will* have them."[16] Georgia subjected the Cherokees to a systematic campaign of harassment, intimidation, and deception, culminating in a sustained assault on their government. The state applied to the Cherokees not only general laws governing all citizens, but also special laws aimed only at Cherokees with "a direct intent to destroy the political, economic, and social infrastructure of the nation."[17] It prohibited meetings of the tribal council and closed down the tribal courts. In 1830, Georgia created a police force—the Georgia Guard—to patrol Cherokee country. Over the next few years the Guard harassed Cherokee people, arrested Principal Chief John Ross and seized his papers, and confiscated the Cherokee printing press. Elias Boudinot appealed to Washington in words that proved prophetic:

> The State of Georgia has taken a strong stance against us, and the United States must either defend us in our rights, or leave us to our foe. In the former case, the General Government will redeem her pledge solemnly given in treaties. In the latter, she will violate her promise of protection, and we cannot, in future, depend consistently, upon any guarantee made by her to us, either here or beyond the Mississippi.[18]

Implementing Removal

In May 1830, after extensive debate and a close vote in both houses, Congress passed the Indian Removal Act, authorizing the president to negotiate treaties of removal with all Indian tribes living east of the Mississippi. Almost immediately, surveyors and squatters entered Cherokee country and Georgia stepped up its campaign of harassment. The Cherokees decided to fight Georgia in the federal courts. In 1830, John Ross hired William Wirt, the former attorney general, and other lawyers to represent his people's interests. Wirt filed a series of test cases. He first obtained a writ of error from Supreme Court Justice John Marshall to stay the execution of a Cherokee named Corn Tassel. Corn Tassel had been sentenced to death by a Georgia court for killing another Indian in Cherokee country, a crime the Cherokees and their supporters argued should fall under Indian jurisdiction. In a special session, the Georgia legislature voted to defy the writ, and Corn Tassel was hanged. "The conduct of the Georgia Legislature is indeed surprising," wrote Elias Boudinot in another prophetic passage. "[T]hey . . . authorize their governor to hoist the flag of rebellion against the United States! If such proceedings are sanctioned by the majority of the people of the U. States, the Union is but a tottering fabric which will soon fall and crumble into atoms."[19]

In 1831, the Cherokee Nation brought suit against the state of Georgia in the United States Supreme Court (see "Foundations at Federal Indian Law, and

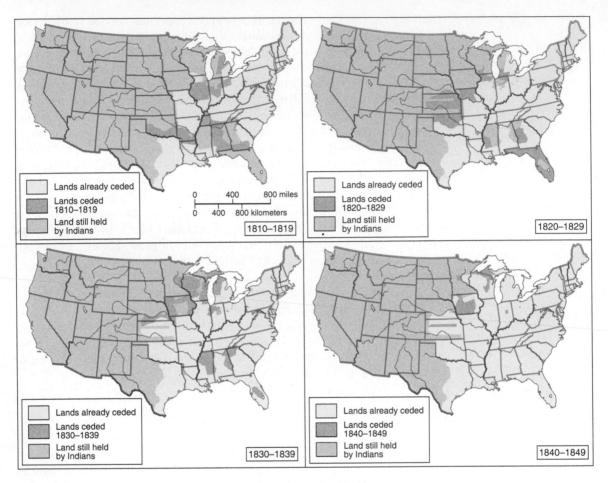

MAP 4.2 Indian Land Cessions, 1810–49
Between 1810 and 1849, the United States quashed the final Indian military resistance east of the Mississippi and implemented the policy of removing eastern Indian peoples to the west of the Mississippi. The result was massive loss of Indian homelands.

a Native Response," pages 240–49). Chief Justice John Marshall declared that the court lacked jurisdiction over the case since the Cherokees were neither U.S. citizens nor an independent nation; they were, he said, "domestic dependent nations." The next year, however, a Vermont missionary brought suit challenging Georgia's right to exert its authority over him in Cherokee country. Because the suit involved a U.S. citizen, it fell within the Supreme Court's jurisdiction. In *Worcester v. Georgia* the court found that the Cherokee Nation was "a distinct community, occupying its own territory" in which "the laws of Georgia can have no force."[20] The court's decision was one of the most important in the history of U.S.–Indian relations, but it was not enough to save the Cherokees.

The Trail of Tears
A decade before American pioneers headed west in search of new opportunities, thousands of southeastern Indians were forced, often at gunpoint, to gather what possessions they could and trek west beyond the Mississippi. The Cherokee ordeal, portrayed in this 1942 painting, became known as "The Path Where They Cried," or "The Trail of Tears." Woolaroc Museum, Bartlesville, Oklahoma.

Georgia would not tolerate a sovereign Cherokee nation within its boundaries; nor would it tolerate federal protection of that sovereignty. Georgia ignored the Supreme Court's ruling.

By the 1830s, the South was producing about half the cotton consumed in the world, and growing rich exporting most of it to the cotton mills of northern England. Southeastern Indian lands were too valuable to be left in Indian hands. Southern Indians faced a choice between destitution and removal. Most bowed to the inevitable. As early as 1820, the Choctaw chief Pushmataha made a treaty with Jackson at Doak's Stand, ceding lands in Mississippi to the United States and accepting new lands in the West in return. Ten years later, the Choctaws signed the Treaty of Dancing Rabbit Creek, ensuring the removal of most of the tribe, although some Choctaws remained in Mississippi. The Creeks tried to resist: a Creek chief named William McIn-

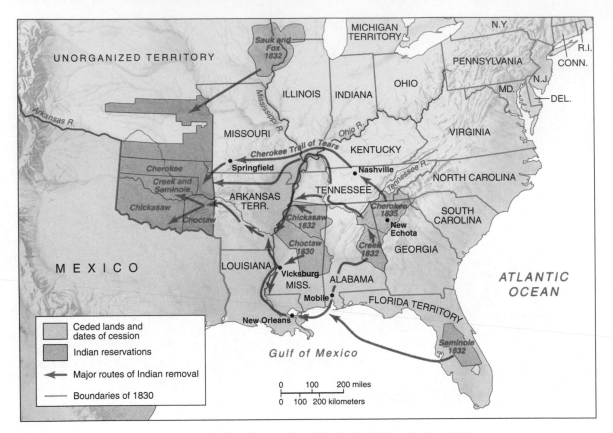

MAP 4.3 Indian Removal and the Trail of Tears in the 1830s
The United States' government policy of removing Indians west of the Mississippi brought tremendous suffering to the uprooted people and disrupted the lives of the people already inhabiting the region to which they moved. As many as a quarter of the Cherokees died on their Trail of Tears in 1838. But not all Indians were removed: groups of Cherokees, Seminoles and Choctaws still live in their traditional homelands.

tosh was executed by fellow tribesmen in 1825 for selling lands in contravention of tribal law. But in 1836, the Creeks embarked on a bitter march west.

In 1835, the United States signed the Treaty of New Echota with a minority of Cherokees who agreed to move west voluntarily. The "Treaty Party" included Elias Boudinot, John Ridge, and others who now felt they had no alternative but to migrate. Principal Chief John Ross and the majority of his people denounced the treaty and refused to abide by it. In 1838, citing the Treaty of New Echota, federal troops moved in and forced out the Cherokees. Thousands of Creeks, Cherokees, and others died on the journeys west, on the aptly named "Trail of Tears." Alexis de Tocqueville, a French visitor to the United States, observed the removal process and concluded that, whereas the Spaniards had earned a reputation for brutality in their dispossession of the Indians, the Americans had attained the same objective under the pretense of legality and philanthropy. It was, he wrote, "impossible to destroy men with more respect to the laws of humanity."[21]

For most of the Cherokees, the march west to Indian Territory was the beginning of a new era in which they would have to adjust to life in a strange land and re-create their societies in the area that became the state of Oklahoma. In 1839, unknown assailants killed Major Ridge, John Ridge, and Elias Boudinot, the leaders of the Treaty Party who had ceded Cherokee land, and civil strife continued to divide the Cherokees in their new homes. Nevertheless, the Cherokees rebuilt their nation in the West. They reestablished their political institutions, centering their government at Tahlequah, in northeastern Oklahoma. They established churches and Protestant seminaries for both men and women and provided free coeducation in their public schools—the first west of the Mississippi. Once again, Cherokees were the vanguard of "civilization."

Some southern Indians managed to stay in the traditional lands. Florida Seminoles refused to remove and, in the Second Seminole War (1835–42), fought the United States to a standstill from their stronghold in the Everglades. The federal government spent millions of dollars, deployed thousands of troops, and lost 1,500 men. Despite the capture by treachery of the chief, Osceola, under a flag of truce and his subsequent death in prison, some Seminoles remained undefeated and defiant in their Florida homelands. Some Cherokees also evaded the American drive west, and survive in North Carolina as the Eastern Band of Cherokees.

In the North, implementing the removal policy meant dealing with a variety of tribes and bands, many of which had migrated from one region to another, and many of which were already living on a fraction of their former lands. Between 1829 and 1851, the United States signed eighty-six treaties with twenty-six northern tribes between New York and the Mississippi. Sometimes several tribes participated in a treaty; sometimes a single tribe signed several treaties.[22] In New York, pressure to remove the remaining Indians mounted steadily. In 1838, the United States negotiated the Treaty of Buffalo Creek, in which the Senecas agreed to give up their four reservations in New York and move to Kansas. But charges of bribery and fraud by the commissioners impeded the treaty's ratification by the Senate and the Senecas were able to negotiate a compromise treaty four years later which allowed most of them to stay in western New York. In the Great Lakes region, the Potawatomis alone participated in nineteen treaties. Most Anishinaabe bands managed to preserve reservations in their Michigan, Wisconsin, and Minnesota homelands. Often they signed treaties that ceded large chunks of territory but guaranteed their rights to continue hunting, fishing, and gathering wild rice on the ceded lands and the rivers and lakes—rights that they had to reassert in confrontations and court cases in the late twentieth century. Some Potawatomis, Anishinaabeg, and Ottawas moved north into Canada rather than go west to Kansas and Oklahoma.

Other tribes joined the general pattern of coerced migration beyond the Mississippi. In 1832, the Sauk chief Black Hawk returned with his people to plant corn in their Illinois homelands after wintering in Iowa. American settlers

Black Hawk

Black Hawk or Makataimeshekiakiak consistently defended his people's homeland against American expansion. He denounced the Treaty of St. Louis of 1804, whereby a small delegation of tribal leaders ceded all Sauk lands east of the Mississippi; he fought with the British against the United States in the War of 1812; and in 1832 he led his band across the Mississippi and into a disastrous defeat.

The Warner Collection of Gulf States Paper Corporation, Tuscaloosa, Alabama.

occupying the area claimed that they were being invaded. The Illinois militia was called out and federal troops were brought in. The so-called "Black Hawk War" culminated in the slaughter of many of Black Hawk's band at the Battle of Bad Axe as they were trying to escape across the Mississippi. Black Hawk was captured and imprisoned, but later was taken on a tour of the East and related his autobiography. Citing the "unprovoked" war as justification, the United States stripped the Sauks of their lands in treaties in 1833, 1836, 1837, and 1842. Most Sauks eventually removed to new homes in Kansas.

Contrary to what some Americans asserted, the country to which the eastern tribes were removed was not empty. The United States carved its "Indian Territory" out of the homelands of Omahas, Otos, Missouris, Kansas, Pawnees, and Osages, who regarded the newcomers as invaders. The Osages, who had dominated the southern prairies in the eighteenth century, clashed repeatedly with Cherokees in the Arkansas country. Relations between Native inhabitants and Native immigrants from the East remained tense for years.[23]

SURVIVING BEHIND THE FRONTIER

Despite the pressures to remove west, many Indian people remained on their traditional homelands throughout the eastern United States. They continued the fight to remain Indian in the midst of an alien society that denied the validity of their culture and in time ignored their very presence. In New England, Indian people remained long after New Englanders believed they had resolved their Indian "problem." Confined to tiny reservations and subjected to increasing regulation by individual states, they saw their lands whittled away. In Vermont and New Hampshire, as Americans occupied their lands, Abenakis pulled back into the farthest reaches of their territory or maintained a low profile on the peripheries of the new towns, villages, and farms. Newcomers assumed that Indians were fast disappearing from the region, or insisted that those they saw were from St. Francis and belonged in Canada, not in Vermont.[24] In Maine, Penobscots and Passamaquoddies, who had supported the American cause during the Revolution, appealed to Congress for justice as their former allies invaded their hunting territories. But, in defiance of the Indian Trade and Intercourse Act of 1790, first Massachusetts and then after 1820 the new state of Maine imposed treaties that gobbled up huge areas of Indian land without obtaining congressional approval. In 1794, the Passamaquoddies ceded more than one million acres to Massachusetts. Two years later, the Penobscots ceded almost 200,000 acres in the Penobscot valley; in 1818, they relinquished all their remaining lands except an island in the Penobscot River and four six-mile square townships. In 1833, Maine bought the four townships for $50,000. By mid-century, the Penobscots were confined to Indian Island at Old Town, near Orono, Maine, and the Passamaquoddies were reduced to two reservations.

Massachusetts reinstituted a guardian system for Indians after the Revolution, placing Indian communities and lands under the supervision of state-appointed overseers who were entrusted with protecting Indian interests but

Cornelius Krieghoff, *The Basket Seller* (c. 1850)

With traditional economies disrupted and their men often away from home, many Indian women in New England and eastern Canada found that making and selling baskets offered a way of both preserving traditional craft skills and making ends meet. Some women peddled their wares from village to village and house to house, often a humiliating experience. William Apess's grandmother barely earned enough to feed her family. A minister in Ledyard, Connecticut, recalled, as a small boy, seeing an Indian woman named Anne Wampy every spring selling baskets she had made during the winter. "When she started from home she carried upon her shoulders a bundle of baskets so large as almost to hide her from view," he wrote. Her fine baskets found customers at almost every house. After two or three days her load would be sold, but "sad to relate," noted the minister, she would spend much of her earnings on strong drink before she reached home. (Quoted in Barry O'Connell, ed., On Our Own Ground: The Complete Writings of William Apess, a Pequot *(Amherst: University of Massachusetts Press, 1992), 153.) Art Gallery of Ontario, Toronto. Gift from the Fund of the T. Eaton Co., Ltd. for Canadian Works of Art, 1951.*

who often exploited their position for their own ends. At places like Natick and Stockbridge, where Indians and Anglo-Americans shared the same town, Indians were edged out of town offices and off the land. Stephen Badger, minister at Natick, reported in 1798 that Indians were "generally considered by white people, and placed, as if by common consent, in an inferiour and degraded situation, and treated accordingly." Covetous neighbors "took every advantage of them that they could, under colour of legal authority . . . to dishearten and depress them."[25]

Indian people who had once moved seasonally for subsistence purposes were now compelled to move about by poverty and the search for either work or dislocated relatives. New England towns added to the numbers of Indian people traveling the roads by "warning out" needy people to avoid paying poor relief. Many Indian men went away to sea, often on lengthy whaling voyages, and their wives had to assume the burden of supporting the family. Many women married non-Indians. Some Mashpee women of Cape Cod married Africans, Portuguese sailors, or German veterans of the Revolutionary War. Indian people who moved to Boston, Providence, Worcester, and other cities often took up residence among the growing African American population. Stephen Badger said in 1798 that the Indians of Natick were "frequently shifting their place of residence, and are intermarried with blacks, and some with whites; and the various shades between those, and those descended from them." Indians in some parts of Massachusetts had become "almost extinct," and seemed to "vanish" among "people of color."[26]

Former president John Adams, writing to Thomas Jefferson in 1812, recalled growing up in Massachusetts seventy years earlier with Indians for neighbors and as visitors to his father's house. "But the Girls

Captain Amos Haskins: Daguerreotype by an Unknown Photographer

Haskins (1816–61), a Wampanoag Indian from New Bedford, Massachusetts, was one of many New England Indians who worked in deep-sea whaling in the nineteenth century. He probably began whaling in the early 1830s. By the time this picture was made, probably in the mid-1850s, he had achieved the rank of ship's captain and made his fortune. Few Indian whalers were so fortunate. New Bedford Whaling Museum.

went out to Service and the Boys to Sea, till not a Soul is left," he wrote. "We scarcely see an Indian in a year."[27] In his *Report on Indian Affairs,* submitted to the secretary of war in 1822, Jedidiah Morse portrayed the Indian communities in New England as a "few feeble remnants" teetering on the brink of extinction.[28] Writing in 1833, after his visit to the United States, Alexis de Tocqueville declared, "All the Indian tribes who once inhabited the territory of New England—the Narragansetts, the Mohicans, the Pequots—now live only in men's memories."[29] The prevailing view among Anglo-Americans was that Indians were a doomed race—an idea embodied in James Fenimore Cooper's *The Last of the Mohicans* (1826).

They were wrong. The same year that Tocqueville pronounced them gone, the Mashpee Indians openly defied the authority of Massachusetts and staged a "revolt" which, though never violent, did win them a measure of self-government and was a limited victory for Indian rights.[30] William Apess, who delivered a eulogy for King Philip (see "Two Views of King Philip," pages 121–30) in 1836, took an active role in the revolt and worked hard to make sure that Americans did not forget that New England had once been, and on one level still was, Indian country. Addressing those New Englanders who protested against Georgia's treatment of the Cherokees, Apess demanded: "How will the white man of Massachusetts ask favor for the red men of the South, while the poor Marshpee [sic] red men, his near neighbors, sigh in bondage?" In "An Indian's Looking Glass for the White Man," he reminded his readers that the new American nation was built on Indian land and with African slave labor: "Can you charge the Indians with robbing a nation almost of their continent, and murdering their women and children, and then depriving the remainder of their lawful rights, that nature and God require them to have? And to cap the climax, rob another nation to till their grounds and welter out their days under the lash with hunger and fatigue under the scorching rays of a burning sun?" If all the races of the world were put together, "and each skin had its national crimes written upon it," he asked, "which skin do you think would have the greatest?"[31] For at least some of Apess's readers in the United States of the 1830s, it was a hard question.

References

1. Quoted in Colin G. Calloway, ed., *Early American Indian Documents: Treaties and Laws, 1607–1789. Vol. 18: Revolution and Confederation* (Bethesda, Md.: University Publications of America, 1994), xxv.

2. Elizabeth E. Fenn, *Pox Americana: The Great Smallpox Epidemic of 1775–1782* (New York: Hill and Wang, 2001).

3. Francis Paul Prucha, *American Indian Policy in the Formative Years: The Indian Trade and Intercourse Acts, 1790–1834* (Lincoln: University of Nebraska Press, 1970), vii, 1–2.

4. Colin G. Calloway, ed., *The World Turned Upside Down: Indian Voices from Early America* (Boston: Bedford Books, 1994), 175–76.

5. Calloway, ed., *The World Turned Upside Down,* 181–83.

6. Dresden W. H. Howard, "The Battle of Fallen Timbers as Told by Chief Kin-Jo-I-No," *Northwest Ohio Quarterly* 20 (1948), 37–49, quotes at 46–47.

7. Joel Martin, *Sacred Revolt: The Muskogees' Struggle for a New World* (Boston: Beacon Press, 1991), 98.

8. Quoted in Peter Nabokov, ed., *Native American Testimony* (New York: Harper and Row, 1978), 69–70.

9. Joy Bilharz, "First Among Equals? The Changing Status of Seneca Women," in Laura F. Klein and Lillian A. Ackerman, eds., *Women and Power in Native North America* (Norman: University of Oklahoma Press, 1995), 108.

10. Daniel H. Usner, Jr., "American Indians on the Cotton Frontier: Changing Economic Relations with Citizens and Slaves in the Mississippi Territory," *Journal of American History* 72 (1985), 297–317.

11. Quoted in Francis Paul Prucha, ed., *Documents of United States Indian Policy* (Lincoln: University of Nebraska Press, 1975), 22–23.

12. Anthony F. C. Wallace, *Jefferson and the Indians: The Tragic Fate of the First Americans* (Cambridge, Mass.: Harvard University Press, 1999).

13. Virgil J. Vogel, ed., *This Country Was Ours: A Documentary History of the American Indian* (New York: Harper and Row, 1972), 289.

14. Quoted in Theda Perdue and Michael D. Green, eds., *The Cherokee Removal: A Brief History with Documents* (Boston: Bedford Books, 1995), 119–20.

15. Quoted in John Ehle, *Trail of Tears: The Rise and Fall of the Cherokee Nation* (New York: Doubleday, 1988), 254.

16. Quoted in William G. McLoughlin, *Cherokee Renascence in the New Republic* (Princeton, N.J.: Princeton University Press, 1986), 412.

17. Sidney L. Harring, *Crow Dog's Case: American Indian Sovereignty, Tribal Law, and United States Law in the Nineteenth Century* (Cambridge: Cambridge University Press, 1994), 32.

18. Theda Perdue, ed., *Cherokee Editor: The Writings of Elias Boudinot* (Knoxville: University of Tennessee Press, 1983), 105–06.

19. Perdue, ed., *Cherokee Editor,* 121.

20. Perdue and Green, eds., *The Cherokee Removal,* 74.

21. J. P. Mayer, ed., *Democracy in America by Alexis de Tocqueville* (New York: Harper and Row, 1966), 339.

22. Francis Paul Prucha, *American Indian Treaties: The History of a Political Anomaly* (Lincoln: University of Nebraska Press, 1994), 184.

23. Willard H. Rollings, *The Osage: An Ethnohistorical Study of Hegemony on the Prairie-Plains* (Columbia: University of Missouri Press, 1992). For an Osage ac-

count of the troubles, see John Joseph Matthews, *The Osages: Children of the Middle Waters* (Norman: University of Oklahoma Press, 1961), chaps. 44–45.

24. Colin G. Calloway, *The Western Abenakis of Vermont, 1600–1800: War, Migration, and the Survival of an Indian People* (Norman: University of Oklahoma Press, 1990).

25. Stephen Badger, "Historical and Characteristic Traits of the American Indians in General, and Those of Natick in Particular," *Collections* of the Massachusetts Historical Society, 1st series, 5 (1798), 38–39.

26. Badger, "Historical and Characteristic Traits," 35, 43.

27. Lester J. Cappon, ed., *The Adams-Jefferson Letters: The Complete Correspondence between Thomas Jefferson and Abigail and John Adams,* 2 vols. (Chapel Hill: University of North Carolina Press, 1959), 2:310–11.

28. Rev. Jedidiah Morse, *A Report to the Secretary of War of the United States, on Indian Affairs* (New Haven: S. Converse, 1822), 64–75.

29. Mayer, ed., *Democracy in America,* 321.

30. Donald M. Nielsen, "The Mashpee Indian Revolt of 1833," *New England Quarterly* 88 (1985), 400–20.

31. Barry O'Connell, ed., *On Our Own Ground: The Complete Writings of William Apess, a Pequot* (Amherst: University of Massachusetts Press, 1992), 157, 205.

Suggested Readings

Calloway, Colin G., ed. *After King Philip's War: Presence and Persistence in Indian New England* (Hanover, N.H.: University Press of New England, 1997).

Dowd, Gregory Evans. *A Spirited Resistance: The North American Indian Struggle for Unity, 1745–1815* (Baltimore: Johns Hopkins University Press, 1992).

Edmunds, R. David. *The Shawnee Prophet* (Lincoln: University of Nebraska Press, 1983).

Horsman, Reginald. *Expansion and American Indian Policy, 1783–1812.* Reprint ed. (Norman: University of Oklahoma Press, 1992).

Hurt, R. Douglas, *The Indian Frontier, 1763–1846* (Albuquerque: University of New Mexico Press, 2002).

Jackson, Donald, ed. *Black Hawk: An Autobiography* (Urbana: University of Illinois Press, 1964).

Martin, Joel. *Sacred Revolt: The Muskogees' Struggle for a New World* (Boston: Beacon Press, 1991).

McLoughlin, William G. *Cherokee Renascence in the New Republic* (Princeton, N.J.: Princeton University Press, 1986).

O'Connell, Barry, ed. *On Our Own Ground: The Complete Writings of William Apess, a Pequot* (Amherst: University of Massachusetts Press, 1992).

Perdue, Theda. *Cherokee Women: Gender and Culture Change, 1700–1835* (Lincoln: University of Nebraska Press, 1998).

Perdue, Theda, and Michael D. Green, eds. *The Cherokee Removal: A Brief History with Documents* (Boston: Bedford Books, 1995).

Prucha, Francis Paul. *The Great Father: The United States Government and the American Indians,* 2 vols. (Lincoln: University of Nebraska Press, 1984).

Ronda, James P. *Lewis and Clark among the Indians* (Lincoln: University of Nebraska Press, 1984).

Sheehan, Bernard W. *Seeds of Extinction: Jeffersonian Philanthropy and the American Indian* (Chapel Hill: University of North Carolina Press, 1973).

Sugden, John. *Blue Jacket: Warrior of the Shawnees* (Lincoln: University of Nebraska Press, 2000).

Sugden, John. *Tecumseh: A Life* (New York: Henry Holt, 1998).

Wallace, Anthony F. C. *The Death and Rebirth of the Seneca* (New York: Knopf, 1969).

Wallace, Anthony F. C. *Jefferson and the Indians: The Tragic Fate of the First Americans* (Cambridge, Mass.: Harvard University Press, 1999).

Wallace, Anthony F. C. *The Long, Bitter Trail: Andrew Jackson and the Indians* (New York: Hill and Wang, 1993).

The Lewis and Clark Expedition

E ven before the United States purchased the Louisiana Territory from France in 1803, President Thomas Jefferson was making plans for an American expedition to explore the Missouri River to its sources and from there to the Pacific. The first European to cross the continent north of Mexico was Alexander Mackenzie, a Scotsman in the employ of the Montreal-based North West Company, who traveled in 1793 from Saskatchewan to the Pacific. In 1801, Mackenzie published *Voyages from Montreal,* which not only described his travels but also spelled out his ideas for British settlement in the West. Jefferson read this book in 1802 and it galvanized him to action. In the words of Lewis and Clark scholar James Ronda, "The Lewis and Clark Expedition—Jefferson's imperial response to Mackenzie's challenge—began the moment the president read the final pages of *Voyages from Montreal.*"[1] By the time the expedition—led by two Virginians, Jefferson's personal secretary Meriwether Lewis and William Clark—left St. Louis in 1804, the Louisiana Territory was "American," and the president was eager to learn what he had acquired.

In reality, of course, the vast territory that lay roughly between the Mississippi and the Rocky Mountains was not American, French, or Spanish, although those nations passed claim to it among themselves. It was Indian country. It was a world in which the presence of British, French, and Spanish traders and the aspirations of competing European nations had been felt for some time, but where Indian people and Indian power were still dominant. The Corps of Discovery, as the Lewis and Clark expedition was known, would have to travel through Indian country, deal with Indian tribes, and develop a working knowledge of Indian politics, as would the American traders, settlers, and agents that Jefferson envisioned following in their wake. Lewis and Clark's purpose, therefore, was to proclaim American sovereignty over the area, prepare the way for American commerce with the tribes, and gather as much information as possible about this "new land" and the many Indian peoples who inhabited it. The success of the expedition depended on cultivating amicable relations: "In all your intercourse with the natives," Jefferson instructed Lewis, "treat them in the most friendly and conciliatory manner which their own conduct will permit."[2]

On the whole, the expedition succeeded in doing so. The explorers carried with them flags and gifts to present to Indian chiefs; they met and smoked with Indians in council after council, proclaiming the new era of peace and pros-

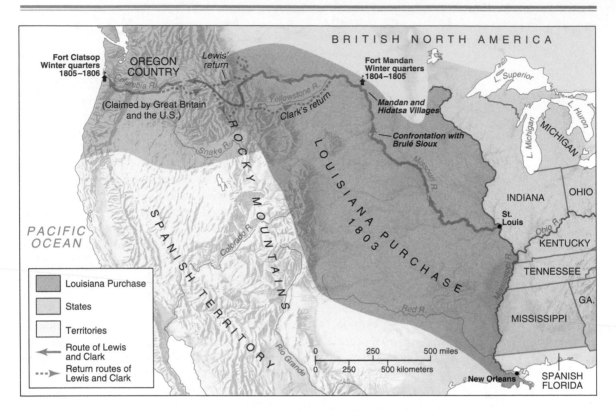

MAP 4.4 The Lewis and Clark Expedition and the Louisiana Purchase
The Louisiana Purchase (1803) added to the United States an enormous amount of land inhabited by a great variety of Indian peoples. In their expedition across and beyond that territory in 1804–06, Lewis and Clark encountered many Indians who had plenty of experience dealing with European traders, but for most of the Indians in the West the expedition marked their first encounter with representatives of the new American nation that now laid claim to their lands.

perity that would surely come to the Indians now that their land "belonged" to the Great Father in Washington. Lewis and Clark painstakingly gathered information on the names, numbers, and customs of the tribes they encountered. They experienced only one openly violent confrontation, with Piegan Blackfeet on the return trip. Indian knowledge, guidance, assistance, transportation, and food helped the expedition to the Pacific and back.

The expedition did not get off to an auspicious start. Leaving St. Louis in June 1804, the explorers headed up the Missouri River — about fifty men,° in-

°That number included St. Louis boatmen and United States soldiers attached to the expedition as far as the Mandan villages, as well as the core party of twenty-nine.

cluding Clark's African American servant, York, who was to cause quite a stir among the Indians—in half a dozen canoes and two pirogues. They tested their skills at Indian diplomacy among the Otos, Omahas, and Missouris, once-powerful tribes already badly reduced by the ravages of disease. In September 1804, they encountered a band of Brulé or Sicangu Sioux. The Sioux were accustomed to levying tribute from St. Louis traders—Clark called them "the pirates of the Missouri"—and were not about to allow the American strangers to pass upriver to other tribes without exacting some share of their cargo. Eager to demonstrate that the United States would not be bullied, the Americans were equally determined not to concede. There was a tense and ugly scene in which each side stood to arms. Only the presence of Indian women and children and the quick-thinking statesmanship of the Brulé chief Black Buffalo averted conflict. The Americans tossed the Indians some tobacco as a token tribute and were allowed to proceed. But it was touch-and-go. Lewis and Clark had failed in the first serious challenge to their Indian diplomacy. They still had a lot to learn if the expedition was to navigate successfully the turbulent waters of inter- and intratribal politics. A winter in the Mandan villages provided an invaluable crash-course.[3]

Passing the Arikaras, who had been cut down by smallpox and Sioux attacks from "eighteen fairly large villages" to "three very mediocre ones," according to French-Canadian trader Pierre-Antoine Tabeau,[4] the Americans reached the Mandans in the late fall. The Mandan Indians, located on the Knife River near the great bend of the Missouri in present-day North Dakota, were especially crucial to the expedition's plans, progress, and ultimate success. The Mandans and their Hidatsa (also known as Gros Ventres or Minnetarees) neighbors had lived for centuries along the Missouri, their ancestors having arrived there perhaps as early as the eleventh century. By the end of the eighteenth century the earth-lodge villages of the Mandans and Hidatsas formed the hub of a huge intertribal trading network in which Plains Indians exchanged horses and the products of buffalo hunting for guns, trade goods, and agricultural produce. The two tribes lived where the Canadian and St. Louis-based spheres of trade overlapped; traders from the Hudson Bay Company and North West Company competed there with independent traders and representatives of the Missouri Company, a coalition of Spanish merchants in St. Louis.

The tribes also lived where the expanding horse frontier from the southwest met the expanding gun frontier from the northeast. The Mandans and Hidatsas were thus able to distribute horses to their northern neighbors and guns to their neighbors on the plains, "often at a 100 percent markup from their original purchase price."[5] Indian traders from deep in the Plains traveled to the upper Missouri villages, then returned to exchange the goods they acquired to other Indian peoples: Crows traded with their Hidatsa relatives and with Shoshonis (also known as Snakes) and Flatheads in the Rocky Mountains; Cheyennes, Arapahos, Kiowas, Kiowa-Apaches, and Comanches traded at the Missouri villages, with each other, and with Spaniards in the Southwest. Spanish, British, and French-Canadian traders operated in and around the Missouri villages. Tabeau, who lived among the Arikaras in 1803–04 and who met Lewis and Clark, believed that if a trading post was established at the Mandan villages, it "would be a gathering-place for more than twenty nations."[6] Unfortunately, the same location and circumstances that made the villages a gathering place of the nations guaranteed that they would be transformed into death-traps when epidemic diseases raced along the trade routes: the smallpox epidemic of 1779–81 hit the villagers hard; there was another outbreak on the Missouri early in the nineteenth century, and the epidemic of 1837 virtually destroyed the Mandans.

Like their neighbors, the Mandans had once inhabited more villages, but in 1804 they lived in just two: Mitutanka (which Lewis and Clark called Matootonha) and, farther upstream: Rooptarhee. The expedition passed abandoned Mandan villages before they reached Mitutanka. The Mandans were a shadow of the powerful tribe they had once been and they were under increasing pressure from the Sioux, who appear to have suffered less devastation from epidemic diseases than had their more sedentary neighbors. The principal chief of Mitutanka was Shahaka, Big White; Posecopsahe, Black Cat, was principal chief of Rooptarhee. Across the Missouri, along the Knife River, lay the three Hidatsa villages. Surrounded by extensive fields of corn, beans, squash, and sunflowers which the women cultivated and which were the basis of their prosperity and trade, the villages straddling the Missouri River highway comprised a great marketplace and crossroads. The residents were accustomed to visitors—French, English, Scots, Spanish, Crees, Assiniboines, Crows, Cheyennes, Arapahoes, Kiowas—and they were accomplished traders.

The Mandan villages were the first major objective in Lewis and Clark's transcontinental odyssey. In Mandan lodges, they found shelter from winter on the northern plains and corn to get them through the season. From Mandan people they learned about tribes they could expect to encounter when they resumed their journey westward in the spring. From the Mandans' Hidatsa neighbors, the expedition was joined by a Shoshoni woman—actually a teenager—whom the Hidatsas had captured in a raid as a child. Sacagawea was married to Toussaint Charbonneau, a French-Canadian trader, who became one of the expedition's interpreters. She would prove invaluable when the Americans made contact with the Shoshonis in the Rocky Mountains.

Lewis and Clark pinned great hopes on the Mandans as a source of information, access to other tribes, and future trade with Americans. They also hoped to promote an alliance of the Mandans, Hidatsas, and Arikaras against the Sioux. Such a coalition seemed natural to them, but it proved to be more difficult to arrange than simply handing out medals, flags, and fine speeches. Tribal politics were still in flux after villages reassembled in the wake of disease, and the presence of British and French-Canadian traders in the area complicated things further.

Bird's Eye View of the Mandan Village, 1,800 Miles above St. Louis
On the edges of the Great Plains, Mandans, Hidatsas, Arikaras, Pawnees, Omahas, and other people inhabited earth-lodge villages for hundreds of years before whites saw them. Lewis and Clark headed for the Mandan villages on the first leg of their trek in 1804, knowing that there they would find the food and shelter to get them through a winter on the northern Plains. By the time George Catlin painted this village in the 1830s, the Mandans, Hidatsas, and Arikaras on the upper Missouri had been ravaged by recurrent epidemics. Smithsonian American Art Museum/Art Resource.

The American captains spent much of that winter gathering information about the tribes of the West. Meanwhile, Mandans and Americans visited back and forth, joined in each other's dances, hunted buffalo together, and together pursued Sioux horse raiders. Members of the expedition slept with Mandan women, and the expedition blacksmith mended Mandan axes and hoes in exchange for corn. During their six months among the Mandans, the members of the expedition produced detailed ethnographic records of the life and culture they observed and got a good introduction to the challenges and pitfalls of trying to apply predetermined American policies in Indian country.

The Lewis and Clark expedition was not a total success. It failed to find a water route to the Pacific—the fabled "Northwest Passage" giving access to the markets of the Far East which had been the dream of empire builders for generations—because none existed. It failed to establish intertribal peace on the Missouri River, and instead cemented Sioux and Blackfoot hostility to the United States. But the winter among the Mandans was one of its high points. They enjoyed good relations with other Indian peoples—the Shoshonis and Nez Percés, in particular—but with no other group did they live so closely, for so long, and on such good terms. The winter spent with the Mandans demonstrated the capacity of one group of humans to coexist harmoniously with another, at least for a time; it was not an experience repeated often in subsequent relations between the United States and the Indians of the West.

▶ Questions for Consideration

1. In the following account, contrast the diplomacy of Meriwether Lewis and William Clark among the Mandans with the diplomacy of Richard Butler and George Rogers Clark (William's older brother) at Fort Finney (see "The Treaty of Fort Finney with the Shawnees" pages 181–91) and consider the different circumstances and agenda governing American conduct.

2. What do the extracts from Lewis and Clark's journal reveal about the nature of intertribal relations on the Upper Missouri?

3. Why were the men of the Lewis and Clark expedition able to maintain good relations with the Mandans during the winter they spent there?

MERIWETHER LEWIS AND WILLIAM CLARK
A Winter with the Mandans (1804–1805)

Mandans

[Clark]   *27th of October Satturday 1804*
we Set out arly   Came too at this Village on the L. S.°   this village is Situated on an eminance of about 50 feet above the Water in a handson Plain   it Containes houses in a kind of Picket work.°   the houses are round and Verry large Containing Several families, as also their horses which is tied on one Side of the enterance, a Discription of those houses will be given hereafter, I walked up & Smoked a pipe with the Cheifs of this Village   they were anxious that I would Stay and eat with them, my indisposition provented my eating which displeased them, untill a full explination took place, I returned to the boat and Sent 2 Carrots of Tobacco for them to Smoke, and proceeded on, passed the 2d Village and Camped opsd. the Village of the *Weter Soon*°   or ah wah har ways which is Situated on an eminance in a plain on the L. S. this Village is Small and Contains but fiew inhabitents.   above this village & also above the Knife river on the Same Side of the Missouri the Big bellies [Gros Ventres] Towns are Situated   a further Discription will be given here after as also of the Town of Mandans on this Side of the river i' e' S. Side—

a fine worm Day   we met with a french man by the name of *Jassamme*° which we imploy as an interpeter   This man has a wife & Children in the Village—   Great numbers on both Sides flocked down to the bank to view us as wce passed.

Capt. Lewis with the Interpetr. walked down to the village below our Camp After delaying one hour he returned and informed me the Indians had returned to their village &c., &c., we Sent three (twists) Carrots of Tobacco by three young men, to the three Villages above inviting them to come Down & Council with us tomorrow. many Indians Came to view us   Some Stayed all night in the Camp of our party—   we procured Some information of Mr. Jessomme of the Chiefs of the Different Nations. . . .

[Clark]   *31st of October Wednesday 1804*
a fine morning, the Chief of the Mandans Sent a 2d Chief to invite us to his Lodge to recive Some Corn & here what he had to Say   I walked

Source: Gary E. Moulton, ed., *The Journals of the Lewis and Clark Expedition,* 13 vols. (Lincoln: University of Nebraska Press, 1986–2001), 3:204, 218, 228, 233–34, 237–39, 242, 244–47, 261, 268–69, 272, 275–76, 289–91, 311–12, 322; 4:7–10. Copyright © 1987 by the University of Nebraska Press. Reprinted with permission of the publishers.

Note: Lewis and Clark recorded their observations in hundreds of pages of leather-bound notebook journals. Over the years, various writers and editors have worked on them: the first was Nicholas Biddle, around 1810, whose additions and corrections are indicated by *NB.* The extracts from the journals reprinted here are taken from the most recent edition, nearing completion after twenty-years' work. The editor of the current edition retained Lewis and Clark's erratic and often ingenious spelling, capitalization, and punctuation. Some words are corrected in square brackets for clarity. Words in italics in square brackets indicate a correction or addition made by Lewis, Clark, Biddle, or an unknown person, shown by *X.* Words in brackets thus < > were scored out by Lewis or Clark but restored by the editor to allow us to follow the writer's thinking.

Volume 13 of *The Journals of the Lewis and Clark Expedition* consists of a comprehensive index. For the story of the entire publication project, see Gary E. Moulton, "The Journals of Lewis and Clark: Almost Home," *Montana, The Magazine of Western History* 48 (Summer 1998), 72–79.

°"L. S." means "larboard side" (i.e., to the left); "S. S." or "starboard side" indicated to the right.

°Patrick Gass, a member of the expedition, said the village contained forty or fifty lodges.

°The Waterson were a division of the Hidatsas.

°René Jassaume was an independent trader who had spent ten years among the Mandans.

down and with great ceremoney was Seeted on a roab by the Side of the Chief, he threw a handsom Roabe over me and after smokeing the pipe with Several old men arround, the Chief Spoke

Said he believed what we had told them, and that peace would be general, which not only gave him Satisfaction but all his people, they now Could hunt without fear, & ther womin Could work in the fields without looking everry moment for the Enemey, and put off their mockersons at night, [*NB: sign of peace undress*]. . . .

[Clark]

4th of Novr. a french man by Name Chabonah,° who Speaks the Big Belley language visit us, he wished to hire & informed us his 2 Squars were Snake Indians, we engau him to go on with us and take one of his wives to interpet the Snake language   The Indians Horses & Dogs live in the Same Lodge with themselves. . . .

[Clark]   12th *November Monday 1804*

a verry Cold night   early this morning the Big White princapal Chief of the lower Village of the Mandans Came Down, he packd about 100 W. of fine meet on his Squar for us, we made Some Small presents <on> to the Squar, & Child   gave a Small ax which She was much pleased—   3 men Sick with the [*blank*]. . . . The interpeter Says that the Mandan nation as they old men Say Came out of a <Small lake> [*NB: Subterraneous village & a lake*] where they had Gardins, maney years ago they lived in Several Villages on the Missourie low down, the Smallpox destroyed the greater part of the nation and reduced them to one large Village and Some Small ones, all <the> nations before this maladey was affrd. [*NB: afraid*] of them   after they were reduced the Sioux and other Indians waged war, and killed a great maney, and they moved up the Missourie, those Indians Still con-

tinued to wage war, and they moved Still higher, untill they got in the Countrey of the Panias, whith this ntn. [nation] they lived in friendship maney years, inhabiting the Same neighbourhood untill that people waged war, They moved up near the *watersoons & winataree* where they now live in peace with those nations, the mandans Specke a language peculial to themselves <verry much>

they can rase about 350 men, the Winatarees [*NB: <or> the <600, 700> Wittassoons or Maharha 80*] about 80 and the Big bellies [*NB: or Minitarres*] about 600 or 650 men. the mandans and Seauex [*X: <Shoe Tribe of Minataras>*] have the Same word for water—   The Big bellies [*NB: or*] Winitarees & ravin [*NB: & Wattassoons, as also the Crow (or Raven)*] Indians Speake nearly the Same language and the presumption is they were originally the Same nation   The Ravin Indians "have 400 Lodges & about 1200 men, & follow the Buffalow, or hunt for their Subsistance in the plains & on the Court noi & Rock Mountains, & are at war with the Sioux [and] Snake Indians["]°

The Big bellies & Watersoons are at war with the Snake Indians & Seauex, and were at war with the *Ricares* until we made peace a fiew days passd.—The Mandans are at War with all who make war on them, at present with the Seauex only, and wish to be at peace with *all* nations, Seldom the agressors—. . . .

[Clark]   18th *Novr. Sunday 1804*

a Cold morning   Some wind   the Black Cat, Chief of the Mandans Came to See us, he made Great inquiries respecting our fashions.   he also Stated the Situation of their nation, he mentioned that a Council had been held the day before and it was thought advisable to put up with the

---

°Toussaint Charbonneau was a trader and the husband of Sacagawea.

°The Hidatsas were also known as Big Bellies (Gros Ventres) and Minnetarees. The Crows were once the same people as the Hidatsas and split off from them, migrating to the Yellowstone valley. They were also known as the People of the Long Beaked Bird, or the Raven. The Snake Indians were the Shoshonis.

resent insults of the Ossiniboins & Christonoes° untill they were Convinced that what had been told thim by us, <untill> Mr. Evins° had deceived them & we might also, he promised to return & furnish them with guns & amunitiion, we advised them to remain at peace & that they might depend upon Getting *Supplies* through the Channel of the Missouri, but it requred time to put the trade in opperation. The Assiniboins &c have the trade of those nations in their power and treat them badly as the Soux does the *Ricarees* and they cannot resent for fear of loseing their trade &.°

[Clark]   20th *November Tuesday 1804*

Capt Lewis & my Self move into our huts, a verry hard wind from the W. all the after part of the day a temperate day Several Indians Came Down to Eat fresh meat, three Chiefs from the 2d Mandan Village Stay all Day, they are verry Curious in examining our works. Those Chiefs informs us that the Souix settled on the Missourie above Dog [*NB: Chayenne*] River, threten to attacked them this winter, and have treated 2 Ricares who Carried the pipe of peace to them Verry roughly. whiped & took their horses from them &c. &c. & is much displeased with Ricares for makeing a peace with the Mandans &. &. through us, &. we gave them a Sattisfactory answer. &c. &c.

[Clark]   28th *Novr. Wednesday 1804*

a cold morning wind from the N. W river full of floating ice, began to Snow at 7 oClock *a' m* and continued all day at 8 oClock the *Poss-cop-so-he* or Black Cat Grand Chief of the Mandans Came to See us, after Showing Those Chiefs many thing which was Curiossities to them, and Giveing

a fiew presents of Curioes Handkerchiefs arm bans & paint with a twist of Tobaco they departed at 1 oClock much pleased, at parting we had Some little talk on the Subject of the British Trader Mr. Le rock Giveing Meadils & Flags, and told those Chiefs to impress it on the minds of their nations that those Simbells were not to be recved by any from them, without they wished incur the displieasure of their Great American Father—a verry disagreeable day—no work done to day river fall 1 Inch to day

[Clark]   29th *November Thursday 1804*

A verry Cold windey day wind from the N. W by W. Some Snow last night the Detpt of the Snow is various in the wood about 13 inches, The river Closed at the Village above and fell last night two feet Mr. *La Rock* and one of his men Came to visit us we informed him what we had herd of his intentions of makeing Chiefs &c. and forbid him to give meadels or flags to the Indians, he Denied haveing any Such intention, we agreed that one of our interpeters Should Speak for him on Conditions he did not Say any thing more than what tended to trade alone— he gave fair promises &.°

[Clark]   30th *of November Friday 1804*

This morning at 8 oClock an Indian Calld from the other Side and informed that he had Something of Consequence to Communicate. we Sent a perogue for him & he informed us as follows. Viz: "five men of the Mandan Nation out hunting in a S. W. derection about Eight Leagues was Suprised by a large party of *Sceoux*

°Assiniboines and Crees.

°Welshman John Evans was employed by the St. Louis-based Missouri Company.

°As James Ronda has pointed out, the Sioux-Arikara relationship was more complex and reciprocal than Lewis and Clark appreciated. Ronda, *Lewis and Clark among the Indians*, 49–50.

°The Mandans were trying to deter the Hidatsas from visiting Fort Mandan until the Mandans could secure the coveted middleman position in trade with the Americans. Charbonneau was the interpreter. In his account of the incident, Larocque noted "As I had neither flags nor medals, I ran no riske of disobeying those orders." Reuben G. Thwaites, ed., *Original Journals of the Lewis and Clark Expedition*, 8 vols. (New York: Dodd, Mead, 1904–05), 1:229n.

& Panies° one man was Killed and two wounded with arrows & 9 Horses taken, 4 of the We ter Soon nation was missing, & they expected to be attacked by the Souix &c. &.["]   we thought it well to Show a Disposition to ade and assist them against their enimies, perticularly those who Came in oppersition to our Councils, and I Deturmined to go to the town with Some men, and if the Sceoux were comeing to attact the nation to Collect the worriers from each Village and meet them, thos Ideas were also those of Capt Lewis, I crossed the river in about an hour after the arrival of the Indian express with 23 men including the interpeters and flankd the Town & came up on the back part—   The Indians not expecting <not> to receive Such Strong aide in So Short a time was much Supprised, and a littled allarmed at the formadable appearance of my party—   The principal Chiefs met me Some Distance from the town (Say 200 yards) and invited me in to town, I ord my pty into dft. lodges &. . . .

I told this nation that we Should be always willing and ready to defend them from the insults of any nation who would dare to Come to doe them injurey dureing the time we would <Stay> remain in their neighbourhood, and requstd. that they would inform us of any party who may at any time be discovered by their Patroles or Scouts;

I was Sorry that the Snow in the Plains had fallen So Deep Sence the Murder of the young Chief by the Scioux as prevented, their horses from traveling I wished to meet those Scioux & all others who will not open their ears, but make war on our dutifull Children, and let you See that the Wariers of your great father will Chastize the enimies of his dutifull Children the Man-

dans, wetersoons & Winitarees, who have opend. their ears to his advice—   you Say that the Panies or Ricares were with the *Sciaux,*   Some bad men may have been with the *Sciaux*   you know there is bad men in all nations, do not get mad with the racarees untill we know if those bad men are Counternoncd. by their nation, and we are Convsd. those people do not intend to follow our Councils—   you know that the Sceaux have great influence over the ricarees and perhaps have led Some of them astray—   you know that the Ricarees, are Dependant on the Sceaux for their guns, powder, & Ball, and it was policy in them to keep on as good terms as possible with the Siaux untill they had Some other means of getting those articles &c. &.   you know your Selves that you are Compelled to put up with little insults from the *Christinoes & Ossinaboins* (or Stone Inds.) because if you go to war with those people, they will provent the traders in the north from bringing you Guns Powder & Ball and by that means distress you verry much, but whin you will have Certain Suppliers from your Great American father of all those articls you will not Suffer any nation to insult you &c.   after about two hours conversation on various Subjects all of which tended towards their Situation &c. I informed them I Should return to the fort, the Chief Said they all thanked me verry much for the fatherly protection which I Showed towards them, that the Village had been Crying all the night and day for the death of the brave young man, who fell but now they would wipe away their tears, and rejoice in their fathers protection—and Cry no more—. . . .

[Clark]   *23rd December Sunday 1804*
a fine Day   great numbers of indians of all discriptions Came to the fort many of them bringing Corn to trade, the *little Crow,* loadd. his wife & Sun with corn for us, Cap. Lewis gave him a few presents as also his wife, She made a Kettle

---

°Pawnees, but here may mean Arikaras, who were related to the Pawnees.

of boild Simnins, beens, Corn & Choke Cherris with the Stones which was paletable

This Dish is Considered, as a treat among those people, The Chiefs of the Mandans are fond of Stayin & Sleeping in the fort. . . .

[Clark]   25th *December Christmass* Tuesday
I was awakened before Day by a discharge of 3 platoons from the Party and the french, the men merrily Disposed, I give them all a little Taffia [a dram] and permited 3 Cannon fired, at raising Our flag, Some men went out to hunt & the Others to Danceing and Continued untill 9 oClock P, M, when the frolick ended &c. . . .

[Clark]   5th of *January Satturday 1805*
a cold day   Some Snow, Several Indians visit us with thier axes to get them mended, I imploy my Self drawing a Connection of the Countery from what information I have recved— a Buffalow Dance (or Medison) [*NB: medecine*] for 3 nights passed in the 1st Village, a curious Custom the old men arrange themselves in a circle & after Smoke a pipe, which is handed them by a young man, Dress up for the purpose, the young men who have their wives back of the circle <Com> go to one of the old men with a whining tone and [*NB?: request*] the old man to take his wife (who presents necked except a robe) and—(or Sleep with him)   the Girl then takes the Old man (who verry often can Scercely walk) and leades him to a Convenient place for the business, after which they return to the lodge, if the Old man (or a white man) returns to the lodge without gratifying the man & his wife, he offers her again and again; it is often the Case that after the 2d time <he> without Kissing the Husband throws a nice robe over the old man & and begs him not to dispise him, & his wife

(we Sent a man to this Medisan <Dance> last night, they gave him 4 Girls)

all this is to cause the buffalow to Come near So that They may kill thim°

                                    Fort Mandan
[Clark]   7th of *January Monday 1805*
a verry Cold clear Day, the Themtr Stood at 22 d below o wind N W., the river fell 1 inch Several indians returned from hunting, one of them the Big White Chef of the Lower Mandan Village, Dined with us, and gave me a Scetch of the Countery as far as the high mountains, & on the South Side of the River Rejone,° he Says that the river rejone recves [*NB: receives*] 6 Small rivers on the S. Side, & that the Countery is verry hilley and the greater part Covered with timber, Great numbers of beaver &c.—. . . . I continue to Draw a connected plote from the information of Traders, Indians & my own observation & idea— from the best information, the Great falls is about [*NB?: 800*] miles nearly west,—

[Clark]   13th of January Sunday (1805)
a Cold Clear Day (great number of Indians move Down the River to hunt) those people Kill a number of Buffalow near their Villages and Save a great perpotion of the meat, their Custom of makeing this article of life General [*NB: see note common*] leaves them more than half of their time without meat° Their Corn & Beans &c they Keep

---

°The Mandans and other northern Plains people believed that spiritual power could be transferred through sexual intercourse. Young men could acquire the wisdom of old men, the skills of hunters, or the spiritual powers of white strangers by having their wives sleep with them. "Nothing in his cultural heritage prepared Clark to comprehend all this," wrote James Ronda, "but he had the good sense to make an accurate record of the event." Ronda, *Lewis and Clark among the Indians*, 131–32. See Alice B. Kehoe, "The Function of Ceremonial Sexual Intercourse among the Northern Plains Indians," *Plains Anthropologist* 15 (1970), 99–103.
°Clark's attempt at the French name "Roche Jaune," i.e., the Yellowstone.
°A reference to the practice of sharing the game among all the families of the tribe.

for the Summer, and as a reserve in Case of an at-tack from the Soues, which they are always in dread, and Sildom go far to hunt except in large parties, about 1/2 the Mandan nation passed this to day to hunt on the river below, they will Stay out Some Days, Mr. Chabonee (our inturpeter) and one man that accompanied him to Some loges of the Minatarees near the Turtle Hill° re-turned, both frosed in their faces.

Chaboneu informs that the Clerk of the Hud-sons Bay Co. with the *Me ne tar res* has been Speak-ing Some fiew expressns. unfavourable towards us, and that it is Said the N W Co. intends building a fort   at the *Mene tar re's*—   he Saw the Grand Chief of the *Big bellies* who Spoke Slightly of the Americans, Saying if we would give our great flag to him he would Come to See us. . . .

[Clark]   16th *January Wednesday 1805*
     about thirty Mandans Came to the fort to day, 6 Chiefs. Those Me ne ta rees told them they were liars, had told them if they came to the fort the whites men would kill them, they had been with them all night, Smoked in the pipe and have been treated well and the whites had danced for them, observing the Mandans were bad and ought to hide themselves—   one of the 1st War Chiefs of the big belles nation Came to See us to day with one man and his Squar [*NB: (his wife handsome)*] to wate on him [*NB: requested that she might be used for the night*]   we Shot the Air gun, and gave two Shots with the Cannon which pleased them verry much, the little Crow 2d Chf of the lower village came & brought us Corn &.   4 men of ours who had been hunting returned one frost'd <but not bad>

This war Chief gave us a Chart in his way of the Missourie, he informed us of his intentions of going to war in the Spring against the Snake Indi-ans   we advised him to look back at the number of nations who had been distroyed by war, and re-flect upon what he was about to do, observing if he

wished the hapiness of his nation, he would be at peace with all, by that by being at peace and have-ing plenty of goods amongst them & a free inter-course with those defenceless nations, they would get on easy terms a great Number of horses, and that nation would increas, if he went to war against those Defenceless people, he would displease his great father, and he would not receive that pertec-tion & Care from him as other nations who lis-tened to his word—   This Chief who is a young man 26 yr. old replied that if his going to war against the Snake indians would be displeasing to us he would not go, he had horses enough.

we observed that what we had Said was the words of his Great father, and what we had Spo-ken to all the nations which we Saw on our pas-sage up, they all promis to open their ears and we do not know as yet if any of them has Shut them (we are doubtfull of the Souxs)   if they do not at-tend to what we have told them their great father will open their ears—   This Cheif Said that he would advise all his nation to Stay at home untill we Saw the Snake Indians & Knew if they would be friendly, he himself would attend to what we had told him—. . . .

[Lewis]   *7th February Thursday 1805.*
     This morning was fair   Thermometer at 18° above naught much warmer than it has been for some days; wind S. E.   continue to be visited by the natives. The Sergt. of the guard reported that the Indian women (wives to our interpreters[)] were in the habit of unbaring the fort gate at any time of night and admitting their Indian visitors, I therefore directed a lock to be put to the gate and ordered that no Indian but those attatched to the garrison should be permitted to remain all night within the fort or admitted during the period which the gate had been previously ordered to be kept shut which was from sunset untill sunrise.—

[Lewis]   *8th February Friday 1805.*
     This morning was fair wind S. E.   the weather still warm and pleasant—   visited by the *black-*

°On the Little Missouri River.

Cat the principal chief of the Roop-tar-he, or upper mandane vilage.   this man possesses more integrety, firmness, inteligence and perspicuety of mind than any indian I have met with in this quarter, and I think with a little management he may be made a usefull agent in furthering the views of our government. The black Cat presented me with a bow and apologized for not having completed the shield he had promised alledging that the weather had been too could to permit his making it, I gave him som small shot 6 fishing-hooks and 2 yards of ribbon   his squaw also presented me with 2 pair of mockersons for which in return I gave a small lookingglass and a couples of nedles.   the chief dined with me and left me in the evening.   he informed me that his people suffered very much for the article of meat, and that he had not himself tasted any for several days. —. . . .

[Lewis]   *11th February Monday 1805.*
. . . about five oclock this evening one of the wives of Charbono was delivered of a fine boy.° it is worthy of remark that this was the first child which this woman had boarn and as is common in such cases her labour was tedious and the pain violent; Mr. Jessome informed me that he had frequently administered a small portion of the rattle of the rattle-snake, which he assured me had never failed to produce the desired effect, that of hastening the birth of the child; having the rattle of a snake by me I gave it to him and he administered two rings of it to the woman broken in small pieces with the fingers and added to a small quantity of water. Whether this medicine was truly the cause or not I shall not undertake to determine, but I was informed that she had not taken it more than ten minutes before she brought forth   perhaps this remedy may be worthy of future experiments, but I must confess that I want faith as to it's efficacy. —. . . .

°This was Sacagawea. The son was named Jean Baptiste and accompanied the expedition.

[Clark]   10th of *March Sunday* 1805.
a Cold winday Day.   we are visited by the Black mockersons, Chief of the 2d Manetarre Village and the Chief of the Shoeman [*NB: Shoe or Mocassin Tr:*] Village or Mah hâ ha V. [*NB: Wattassoans*]   those Chiefs Stayed all day and the latter all night and gave us man[y] Strang accounts of his nation &c   this Little tribe or band of Menitaraies Call themselves Ah-nah-hâ-way or people whose village is on the hill. [*NB: Insert this Ahnahaway is the nation Mahhaha the village*]   nation formerleyed lived about 30 miles below this but beeing oppressed by the Asinniboins & Sous were Compelled to move <near> 5 miles the Minitaries, where, the Assinniboins Killed the most of them those remaining built a village verry near to the Minitarries at the mouth of Knife R where they now live and Can raise about 50 men, they are intermixed with the Mandans & Minatariers—   the Mandans formerly lived in 6 [*NB: nine*] large villages at and above the mouth of *Chischeter* or Heart River   five [*NB: six*] Villages on the West Side [*NB: of the Missouri*] & two [*NB: three*] on the East   one of those Villages on the East Side of the Missouri & the larges was intirely Cut off by the Sioux & the greater part of the others and the Small Pox reduced the others. . . .

[*March 29, 1805*]
[Clark]   *30th of March Sunday 1805*
The obstickle broke away above & the ice came dow in great quantites   the river rose 13 inches the last 24 hours   I observed extrodanary dexterity of the Indians in jumping from one Cake of ice to another, for the purpose of Catching the buffalow as they float down maney of the Cakes of ice which they pass over are not two feet Square. The Plains are on fire in view of the fort on both Sides of the River, it is Said to be common for the Indians to burn the Plains near their villages every Spring for the benifit of ther horse, and to induce the Buffalow to come near to them.

[Clark]   [*March 30, 1805*]

31h of March Monday 1805   Cloudy   Several gangus of Ducks and Gees pass up   not much ice floating. All the party in high Spirits, but fiew nights pass without a Dance   they are helth. except the—vn. [venereal]—which is common with the Indians and have been communicated to many of our party at this place—   those favores bieng easy acquired.   all Tranquille. . . .

[Lewis]   Fort Mandan April 7th 1805.

Having on this day at 4 P.M. completed every arrangement necessary for our departure, we dismissed the barge and crew with orders to return without loss of time to S. Louis, a small canoe with two French hunters accompanyed the barge; these men had assended the missouri with us the last year as engages. . . .

At same moment that the Barge departed from Fort Mandan, Capt. Clark embaked with our party and proceeded up the river. as I had used no exercise for several weeks, I determined to walk on shore as far as our encampment of this evening; accordingly I continued my walk on the N. side of the River about six miles, to the upper Village of the Mandans, and called on the Black Cat or Pose cop'se há, the great chief of the Mandans; he was not at home; I rested myself a minutes, and finding that the party had not arrived I returned about 2 miles and joined them at their encampment on the N. side of the river opposite the lower Mandan village. Our party now consisted of the following Individuals. Sergts. John Ordway, Nathaniel Prior, & Patric Gass; Privates, William Bratton, John Colter, Reubin, and Joseph Fields, John Shields, George Gibson, George Shannon, John Potts, John Collins, Joseph Whitehouse, Richard Windsor, Alexander Willard, Hugh Hall, Silas Goodrich, Robert Frazier, Peter Crouzatt, John Baptiest la Page, Francis Labiech, Hue McNeal, William Werner, Thomas P. Howard, Peter Wiser, and John B. Thompson. —

Interpreters, George Drewyer and Tauasant Charbono also a Black man by the name of York, servant to Capt. Clark, an Indian Woman wife to Charbono with a young child, and a Mandan man who had promised us to accompany us as far as the Snake Indians with a view to bring about a good understanding and friendly intercourse between that nation and his own, the Minetares and Ahwahharways.

Our vessels consisted of six small canoes, and two large perogues. This little fleet altho' not quite so rispectable as those of Columbus or Capt. Cook° were still viewed by us with as much pleasure as those deservedly famed adventurers ever beheld theirs; and I dare say with quite as much anxiety for their safety and preservation.   we were now about to penetrate a country at least two thousand miles in width, on which the foot of civillized man had never trodden; the good or evil it had in store for us was for experiment yet to determine, and these little vessells contained every article by which we were to expect to subsist or defend ourselves.   however as this the state of mind in which we are, generally gives the colouring to events, when the immagination is suffered to wander into futurity, the picture which now presented itself to me was a most pleasing one. entertaing <now> as I do, the most confident hope of succeeding in a voyage which had formed a da[r]ling project of mine for the last ten years <of my life>, I could but esteem this moment of my <our> departure as among the most happy of my life.°

°James Cook (1728–79), British explorer of the Pacific.
°Lewis committed suicide four years later.

References

1. James P. Ronda, ed., *Revealing America: Image and Imagination in the Exploration of North America* (Lexington, Mass.: D. C. Heath, 1996), 140.
2. James P. Ronda, *Lewis and Clark among the Indians* (Lincoln: University of Nebraska Press, 1984), quote at p. 1.
3. Ronda, *Lewis and Clark among the Indians.* Chapter 2 provides an excellent account of the confrontation with the Brulé Sioux.
4. Annie Heloise Abel, ed., *Tabeau's Narrative of Loisel's Expedition to the Upper Missouri River* (Norman: University of Oklahoma Press, 1939), 123–24. Other traders claimed three smallpox epidemics had scythed the Arikaras from thirty-two villages to two before 1795; John C. Ewers, ed., *Five Indian Tribes of the Upper Missouri. By Edwin Thompson Denig* (Norman: University of Oklahoma Press, 1961), 41n.
5. Raymond W. Wood and David D. Thiessen, eds., *Early Fur Trade on the Northern Plains: Canadian Traders among the Mandan and Hidatsa Indians, 1738–1818* (Norman: University of Oklahoma Press, 1985), 3–4; John C. Ewers, "The Indian Trade of the Upper Missouri before Lewis and Clark," in *Indian Life on the Upper Missouri* (Norman: University of Oklahoma Press, 1968), 14–34.
6. Abel, ed., *Tabeau's Narrative*, 165.

Suggested Readings

Ambrose, Stephen E. *Undaunted Courage: Meriwether Lewis, Thomas Jefferson, and the Opening of the American West* (New York: Simon and Schuster, 1996).

Barth, Gunther, ed. *The Lewis and Clark Expedition: Selections from the Journals, Arranged by Topic* (Boston: Bedford Books, 1998).

Calloway, Colin G. *One Vast Winter Count: The Native American West before Lewis and Clark* (Lincoln: University of Nebraska Press, 2003).

Duncan, Dayton, and Ken Burns. *Lewis and Clark: The Journey of the Corps of Discovery* (New York: Knopf, 1997).

Meyer, Roy W. *The Village Indians of the Upper Missouri* (Lincoln: University of Nebraska Press, 1977).

Moulton, Gary E., ed. *The Journals of the Lewis and Clark Expedition*, 13 vols. (Lincoln: University of Nebraska Press, 1986–2001).

Ronda, James P. *Finding the West: Explorations with Lewis and Clark* (Albuquerque: University of New Mexico Press, 2001).

Ronda, James P. *Lewis and Clark among the Indians* (Lincoln: University of Nebraska Press, 1984).

Wood, W. Raymond, and Thomas D. Thiessen, eds. *Early Fur Trade on the Northern Plains: Canadian Traders among the Mandan and Hidatsa Indians, 1738–1818* (Norman: University of Oklahoma Press, 1985).

Foundations of Federal Indian Law and a Native Response

Americans who advocated the removal of the Cherokees and their neighbors from the southeastern United States to new homes west of the Mississippi often justified that removal on the grounds that the Indians were, after all, "savages." Such assertions ignored the realities of Cherokee culture, Cherokee history, and Cherokee success in adapting to the demands of American mores in the early nineteenth century. The Cherokees created and participated in a republican form of government modeled on the United States Constitution, and built a capital at New Echota with impressive public buildings. Testimony to the degree to which Cherokees had adapted and incorporated the "civilized ways" of their non-Indian neighbors was their response to Georgia's assault on their society and government: the Cherokees did not resort to violence, striking the war post as Dragging Canoe and his followers had done more than half a century earlier — they took Georgia to court.

Since colonial times, Indians had used British colonial and United States courts to seek legal protection and redress of grievances. But the Cherokees were the first to bring a case to the United States Supreme Court. They hired as their lawyer former attorney general of the United States William Wirt. Wirt sought an injunction to stop Georgia from executing or enforcing its laws in Cherokee country. The sitting chief justice, John Marshall, had presided over the Supreme Court since 1801, and he consciously used his position to mold the evolving law of the young nation. Despite the precedents of English, colonial, natural, and international law, Marshall believed that "the United States had to have an *American* law developed by American jurists attending to American needs." The Cherokee cases — *Cherokee Nation v. Georgia* (1831) and *Worcester v. Georgia* (1832) — have been called "the central fury of . . . one of the greatest constitutional crises in the history of the nation." Marshall used the Cherokee cases that came before the court "to establish the legal doctrine . . . of an American law of United States–Native American relations."[1]

In an earlier case, *Johnson v. McIntosh* (1823), Marshall had restricted tribal rights to transfer lands only to the United States government and "focused his opinion exclusively on the need for rationalizing the process of land acquisition in a country originally inhabited by a savage people but gradually overtaken by a foreign invader."[2] In *Cherokee Nation v. Georgia,* the Supreme Court found that it lacked original jurisdiction, but Marshall tried to define the exact status of the Cherokees, and by extension all Indian tribes, within the United States.

The Cherokees, he decided, were "a domestic, dependent nation," who had retained some aspects of their sovereignty through treaties. He likened the Indians' relationship to the government to that between a ward and a guardian. However, without a strong show of federal power to enforce United States laws protecting tribal sovereignty, the Cherokees were vulnerable to Georgia's strong antisovereignty position. In the opinion of legal scholar Sidney Harring, "Marshall's opinion was a feeble gesture compared with Georgia's dramatic assertion of state power when it hung Corn Tassel."[3]

In 1832, the Cherokees succeeded in getting into the Supreme Court via a United States citizen. In a test case, Samuel Worcester, a missionary from Vermont, defied a law passed by the Georgia legislature requiring non-Indians living in Cherokee country to take an oath of allegiance to Georgia. Worcester and another missionary, Elihu Butler, were arrested and sentenced to four years hard labor. Worcester and Butler petitioned the Supreme Court, which accepted the case. As in *Cherokee Nation,* Georgia refused to appear. Marshall, seventy-five-years old and in poor health, took just two weeks to write the court's opinion. In March 1832, the Supreme Court rendered its decision. Worcester's arrest, said Marshall, was illegal. Georgia had no authority to execute its laws within an Indian nation protected under the treaty clause of the United States Constitution. The Cherokee Nation was "a distinct community, occupying its own territory . . . in which the law of Georgia can have no right to enter but with the assent of the Cherokees."

The cases clearly asserted the authority of the federal government, but where did they leave the legal status of the Cherokees? Georgia refused to release the missionaries and openly defied the court. President Andrew Jackson had no intention of executing the law in this case, and the two missionaries remained in prison until 1833 when a new governor released them. Georgia continued its campaign to undermine Cherokee government. Many Cherokees and their supporters came to believe that in their Supreme Court victory they had, in fact, lost their last battle.

But John Marshall's opinions established the legal foundation for the existence of Indian tribes within the borders of the United States. Indians were to be considered domestic, dependent nations, but Indian country had distinct legal boundaries within which state law did not apply. As John Wunder notes in his study of Indians and the Bill of Rights, some of the chickens hatched in *Cherokee Nation v. Georgia* came home to roost in modern times: "Whereas nineteenth-century law focused on defining 'domestic' and 'dependent' for nineteenth-century audiences anxious to take Indian lands, twentieth-century courts after World War II expanded the meaning of 'nation.'"[4] Law professor Charles F. Wilkinson maintains that one can interpret aspects of Marshall's decision in various ways but "the thrust of *Worcester* cannot be disputed. Tribes are sovereign nations with broad inherent powers that, almost without exception, exist by dint of inherent right, not by delegation." Regardless of subject matter, it is "one of the Supreme Court's most lasting statements." The prin-

John Ross, Principal Chief of the Cherokees (1790–1866)
Ross was a steadfast opponent of removal, lobbying in Congress and taking the Cherokee case to the United States Supreme Court. On the Trail of Tears, Ross's wife, Quatie, died. In Indian Territory, he set about rebuilding the Cherokee Nation and his own fortune. The divisions occasioned by removal persisted, however, and surfaced again during the Civil War. Ross first advocated neutrality but later supported the Union. Many Cherokees supported the pro-Confederate chief, Stand Watie. A regular visitor to Washington, Ross died there in 1866 while serving in a treaty delegation. From the Collection of Gilcrease Museum, Tulsa.

ciples enunciated in *Worcester* "guide the modern Court's protective stance toward Indian self-government. *Worcester* constitutes the headwaters of modern Indian law—one cannot really understand the field without understanding *Worcester*."[5]

Marshall's opinions in *Cherokee Nation* and *Worcester* thus define the status of Indian tribes in the United States. *Cherokee Nation* defines the tribes' relationship to the federal government, *Worcester* their relationship to the states.

Tribes are under the protection of the federal government but they possess sufficient sovereignty to defend themselves from intrusion by the states.[6] The federal government, of course, has not always carried out its responsibility to protect tribal sovereignty against state encroachment, but legal relationships — and the existence of federal, state, and tribal jurisdictions — laid out in *Cherokee Nation* and *Worcester* are keys to understanding many aspect of U.S.–Indian affairs in the past and many developments in Indian country today.

John Ross, whose reactions to *Worcester v. Georgia* are reprinted here, had fought long and hard against passage of the Indian Removal Act. As he wrote to Davy Crockett, who as Democratic congressman from Tennessee had broken party ranks and voted against the removal bill, he lived in hope that humanity and justice would ultimately prevail over greed, intrigue, and corruption. "Whether this day will come in time to save the suffering Cherokees from violence and fraud, it is for wisdom, magnanimity & justice of the United States to determine."[7] The Supreme Court decision was a victory for justice, but Ross knew all too well the forces and interests arrayed against its implementation, as his letter to fellow Cherokees makes clear.

In 1992, the Georgia State Board of Pardons and Paroles acted "to remove a stain on the history of criminal justice in Georgia": 160 years after *Worcester v. Georgia*, the board issued full and unconditional pardons to Samuel Worcester and Elihu Butler.[8]

▶ **Questions for Consideration**

1. What do the following Marshall and Ross documents reveal about the status of Indian nations in the United States? Identify key passages and consider their bearing on the standing and sovereignty of Indian tribes.

2. How does Marshall define the place of Indian tribes in the federal constitutional system? Which of his statements about Indian rights and sovereignty seem to be most important — and most relevant to the political aspirations of Indian peoples today?

3. What does John Ross identify as the "strong shield" of Cherokee rights, and what does he see as the threat to those rights?

JOHN MARSHALL
Cherokee Nation v. State of Georgia (1831)
and Worcester v. Georgia (1832)

CHEROKEE NATION v. STATE OF GEORGIA

Mr. Chief Justice *Marshall* delivered the opinion of the court:

This bill is brought by the Cherokee Nation, praying an injunction to restrain the State of Georgia from the execution of certain laws of that State, which as it is alleged, go directly to annihilate the Cherokees as a political society, and to seize, for the use of Georgia, the lands of the nation which have been assured to them by the United States in solemn treaties repeatedly made and still in force.

If the courts were permitted to indulge their sympathies, a case better calculated to excite them can scarcely be imagined. A people once numerous, powerful, and truly independent, found by our ancestors in the quiet and uncontrolled possession of an ample domain, gradually sinking beneath our superior policy, our arts and our arms, have yielded their lands by successive treaties, each of which contains a solemn guarantee of the residue, until they retain no more of their formerly extensive territory than is deemed necessary to their comfortable subsistence. To preserve this remnant the present application is made.

Before we can look into the merits of the case, a preliminary inquiry presents itself. Has this court jurisdiction of the cause?

The third article of the Constitution describes the extent of the judicial power. The second section closes an enumeration of the cases to which it is extended, with "controversies" "between the State or the citizens thereof, and foreign states, citizens, or subjects." A subsequent clause of the same section gives the Supreme Court original jurisdiction in all cases in which a state shall be a party. The party defendant may then unquestionably be sued in this court. May the plaintiff sue in it? Is the Cherokee Nation a foreign state in the sense in which that term is used in the Constitution?

The counsel for the plaintiffs have maintained the affirmative of this proposition with great earnestness and ability. So much of the argument as was intended to prove the character of the Cherokees as a State, as a distinct political society separated from others, capable of managing its own affairs and governing itself, has, in the opinion of a majority of the judges, been completely successful. They have been uniformly treated as a State from the settlement of our country. The numerous treaties made with them by the United States recognize them as a people capable of maintaining the relations of peace and war, of being responsible in their political character for any violation of their engagements, or for any aggression committed on the citizens of the United States by any individual of their community. Laws have been enacted in the spirit of these treaties. The acts of our government plainly recognize the Cherokee Nation as a State, and the courts are bound by those acts.

A question of much more difficulty remains. Do the Cherokees constitute a foreign state in the sense of the Constitution?

The counsel have shown conclusively that they are not a State of the Union, and have in-

Source: Supreme Court of the United States, 1831. 30 U.S. (5 Pet.) 1, 8 L.Ed. 25. Supreme Court of the United States, 1832. 31 U.S. (6 Pet.) 515, 8 L.Ed. 583.

sisted that individually they are aliens, not owing allegiance to the United States. An aggregate of aliens composing a State must, they say be a foreign state. Each individual being foreign, the whole must be foreign.

This argument is imposing, but we must examine it more closely before we yield to it. The condition of the Indians in relation to the United States is perhaps unlike that of any other two people in existence. In the general, nations not owing a common allegiance are foreign to each other. The term "foreign nation" is, with strict propriety, applicable by either to the other. But the relation of the Indians to the United States is marked by peculiar and cardinal distinctions which exist nowhere else.

The Indian Territory is admitted to compose part of the United States. In all our maps, geographical treaties, histories and laws, it is so considered. In all our intercourse with foreign nations, in our commercial regulations, in any attempt at intercourse between Indians, and foreign nations, they are considered as within the jurisdictional limits of the United States, subject to many of those restraints which are imposed upon our own citizens. They acknowledge themselves in their treaties to be under the protection of the United States; they admit that the United States shall have the sole and exclusive right of regulating the trade with them, and managing all their affairs as they think proper; and the Cherokees in particular were allowed by the treaty of Hopewell, which preceded the Constitution, "to send a deputy of their choice, whenever they think fit, to Congress." Treaties were made with some tribes by the State of New York under a then unsettled construction of the confederation, by which they ceded all their lands to that State, taking back a limited grant to themselves, in which they admit their dependence.

Though the Indians are acknowledged to have an unquestionable, and, heretofore, unquestioned right to the lands they occupy until that right shall be extinguished by a voluntary cession to our government, yet it may well be doubted whether those tribes which reside within the acknowledged boundaries of the United States can, with strict accuracy, be denominated foreign nations. They may, more correctly, perhaps, be denominated domestic dependent nations. They occupy a territory to which we assert a title independent of their will, which must take effect in point of possession when their right of possession ceases. Meanwhile they are in a state of pupilage. Their relation to the United States resembles that of a ward to his guardian.

They look to our government for protection; rely upon its kindness and its power; appeal to it for relief to their wants; and address the President as their great father. They and their country are considered by foreign nations, as well as by ourselves, as being so completely under the sovereignty and dominion of the United States, that any attempt to acquire their lands, or to form a political connection with them, would be considered by all as an invasion of our territory, and an act of hostility.

These considerations go far to support the opinion that the framers of our Constitution had not the Indian tribes in view when they opened the courts of the Union to controversies between a State or the citizens thereof, and foreign states.

In considering this subject, the habits and usages of the Indians in their intercourse with their white neighbors ought not to be entirely disregarded. At the time the Constitution was framed, the idea of appealing to an American court of justice for an assertion of right or a redress of wrong, had perhaps never entered the mind of an Indian or of his tribe. Their appeal was to the tomahawk, or to the government. This was well understood by the statesmen who framed the Constitution of the United States, and might furnish some reason for omitting to enumerate them among the parties who might sue in the courts of the Union. Be this as it may, the peculiar relations between the United States and the Indians occupying our territory are such that we should feel much difficulty in considering them as designated by the term "foreign State," were there no other part of the Constitution which might shed light on the meaning of these words. But we think that in construing them, considerable aid is furnished by that clause in the eighth section of the third article, which empowers Congress to "regulate commerce with foreign nations, and among the several States, and with the Indian tribes."

In this clause they are as clearly contradistinguished by a name appropriate to themselves from foreign nations as from the several States composing the Union. They are designated by a distinct appellation; and as this appellation can be applied to neither of the others, neither can the appellation distinguishing either of the others be in fair construction applied to them. The objects to which the power of regulating commerce might be directed, are divided into three distinct classes—foreign nations, the several States, and Indian tribes. When forming this article, the convention considered them as entirely distinct. We cannot assume that the distinction was lost in framing a subsequent article, unless there be something in its language to authorize the assumption.

WORCESTER v. GEORGIA

The Indian nations had always been considered as distinct, independent political communities, retaining their original natural rights, as the undisputed possessors of the soil from time immemorial, with the single exception of that imposed by irresistible power, which excluded them from intercourse with any other European potentate than the first discoverer of the coast of the particular region claimed: and this was a restriction which those European potentates imposed on themselves, as well as on the Indians. The very term "nation," so generally applied to them, means "a people distinct from others." The Constitution, by declaring treaties already made, as

well as those to be made, to be the supreme law of the land, has adopted and sanctioned the previous treaties with the Indian nations, and consequently admits their rank among those powers who are capable of making treaties. The words "treaty" and "nation" are words of our own language, selected in our diplomatic and legislative proceedings, by ourselves, having each a definite and well understood meaning. We have applied them to Indians, as we have applied them to the other nations of the earth. They are applied to all in the same sense.

Georgia herself has furnished conclusive evidence that her former opinions on this subject concurred with those entertained by her sister States, and by the government of the United States. Various acts of her Legislature have been cited in the argument, including the contract of cession made in the year 1802,° all tending to prove her acquiescence in the universal conviction that the Indian nations possessed a full right to the lands they occupied, until that right should be extinguished by the United States, with their consent; that their territory was separated from that of any State within whose chartered limits they might reside, by a boundary line, established by treaties; that, within their boundary, they possessed rights with which no State could interfere, and that the whole power of regulating the intercourse with them was vested in the United States. A review of these acts, on the part of Georgia, would occupy too much time, and is the less necessary because they have been accurately detailed in the argument at the bar. Her new series of laws, manifesting her abandonment of these opinions, appears to have commenced in December, 1828.

In opposition to this original right, possessed by the undisputed occupants of every country; to this recognition of that right, which is evidenced by our history, in every change through which we

---

°The Compact of 1802, by which Georgia ceded her western land claims to the federal government. See page 209.

have passed, is placed the charters granted by the monarch of a distant and distinct region, parceling out a territory in possession of others whom he could not remove and did not attempt to remove, and the cession made of his claims by the Treaty of Peace.

The actual state of things at the time, and all history since, explain these charters; and the King of Great Britain, at the Treaty of Peace, could cede only what belonged to his crown. These newly asserted titles can derive no aid from the articles so often repeated in Indian treaties; extending to them, first, the protection of Great Britain, and afterwards that of the United States. These articles are associated with others, recognizing their title to self-government. The very fact of repeated treaties with them recognizes it; and the settled doctrine of the law of nations is that a weaker power does not surrender its independence — its right to self-government, by associating with a stronger and taking its protection. A weak State in order to provide for its safety, may place itself under the protection of one more powerful without stripping itself of the right of government, and ceasing to be a State. Examples of this kind

are not wanting in Europe. "Tributary and feuda-tory states," says Vattel,° "do not thereby cease to be sovereign and independent states so long as self-government and sovereign and independent authority are left in the administration of the state." At the present day, more than one State may be considered as holding its right of self-government under the guaranty and protection of one or more allies.

The Cherokee nation, then, is a distinct community, occupying its own territory, with boundaries accurately described, in which the laws of Georgia can have no force, and which the citizens of Georgia have no right to enter but with the assent of the Cherokees themselves or in conformity with treaties and with the acts of Congress. The whole intercourse between the United States and this nation is, by our Constitution and laws, vested in the government of the United States.

The act of the State of Georgia under which the plaintiff in error was prosecuted is consequently void, and the judgment a nullity.

°Emer de Vattel (1714–67), a Swiss diplomat.

JOHN ROSS

Reactions to *Worcester v. Georgia:* Letter to Richard Taylor, John Baldridge, Sleeping Rabbit, Sicketowee, and Wahachee (April 28, 1832)

My Friends,

. . . The Supreme Court in the case of Worcester & Butler vs. the State of Georgia has determined the question of our national rights as fully as can be.

The decision is final & cannot be revoked: but the course of legal proceedings is necessarily attended with tardiness, consequently should the authorities of Georgia, refuse, as they have done, to release immediately those much injured imprisoned gentlemen, and continue still to arrest & oppress our citizens, we should not be discouraged, because the President, out of his disappointment, may still pursue a political course towards us,

Source: Gary E. Moulton, ed., *The Papers of Chief John Ross*, 2 vols. (Norman: University of Oklahoma Press, 1985) 2: 242–43.

under the hope that by withholding from us the protection of the government, a Treaty may yet be effected previous to the time when it shall become his imperious duty to act for the enforcement of this decision of the Supreme Court [in *Worcester v. Georgia*]. The conflict is now between the United States & Georgia. The final issue ere long will be seen. Should Georgia prevail, the Union of the States is dissolved: but should the United States regard the constitutional liberties guaranteed to their citizens, Georgia must submit to see the Cherokees triumph over their oppressions under her usurped authority; therefore, let the people endure patiently to await the final result. We have gained a great point and they should be watchful over the conduct of such disappointed traitors as may be found amongst them. Thro' the false impressions made by them upon the government, our sufferings have been prolonged, and protections withheld from us. Our country is again full of surveyors who are engaged by the authorities of Georgia, to run out a large portion of our Territory into small lots. This illegal proceeding can have no effect to weaken our national rights, even should they proceed so far as to draw for the lands: the title granted by the drawer of lots will not be valid, unless our national title be first extinguished by a Treaty with the United States, which contingency can never take place, if our people continue to remain firm & be united in the support of our common interests. I cannot believe that the General Govern-

ment would allow Georgia to go so far as to draw for and *occupy our lands by force*. The President has repeatedly said to us, that the Cherokees will be *protected in their territorial possessions;* and he has also boasted of never having told a red brother a lie, nor ever having spoke to them with a forked tongue. We have a right, however, to judge of this bravado for ourselves from his own acts. The decision of the Supreme Court, under the Treaties, Laws & Constitution, is the strong shield by which our rights must be respected & protected; and under any other administration than Gen. Jackson, there would be no trouble or difficulty on the subject. Even under his, the crisis is at hand to induce him to act otherwise than he had done, or else his political career will be prostrated. I beseech the people to continue to be patient, firm & united & to have as little intercourse with the white intruders in our country as possible, & above all things, to discountenance & refrain from the introduction & use of ardent spirits. A tippling shop is the fountain from which every species of evil that befalls our citizens & our country flows; and it should be spurned & shunned as the bosom of desolation, by every true friend to humanity & patriotism.

Your friend

Jno Ross

References

1. David H. Getches, Charles F. Wilkinson, and Robert A. Williams, Jr., eds., *Cases and Materials on Federal Indian Law,* 4th ed. (St. Paul: West Group, 1998), 102.
2. Robert A. Williams, Jr., *The American Indian in Western Legal Thought: The Discourses of Conquest* (New York: Oxford University Press, 1990), 312.
3. Sidney L. Harring, *Crow Dog's Case: American Indian Sovereignty, Tribal Law, and United States Law in the Nineteenth Century* (Cambridge: Cambridge University Press, 1994), 31–32.

4. John R. Wunder, *"Retained by the People": A History of American Indians and the Bill of Rights* (New York: Oxford University Press, 1994), 27.
5. Charles F. Wilkinson, *American Indians, Time, and the Law* (New Haven: Yale University Press, 1987), 30, 95–96.
6. Vine Deloria, Jr., and Clifford M. Lytle, *American Indians, American Justice* (Austin: University of Texas Press, 1983), 33.
7. Gary E. Moulton, ed., *The Papers of Chief John Ross*, 2 vols. (Norman: University of Oklahoma Press, 1985) 1:210.
8. Quoted in Norgren, *The Cherokee Cases: The Confrontation of Law and Politics* (New York: McGraw-Hill, 1996), 1–2.

Suggested Readings

Deloria, Vine, Jr., and Clifford M. Lytle. *American Indians, American Justice* (Austin: University of Texas Press, 1983).

Garrison, Tim Alan. *The Legal Ideology of Removal: The Southern Judiciary of Native American Nations* (Athens: University of Georgia Press, 2002).

Getches, David H., and Charles F. Wilkinson. *Federal Indian Law: Cases and Materials,* 2d ed. (St. Paul: West Publishing Company, 1986).

McLoughlin, William G. *Cherokee Renascence in the New Republic* (Princeton, N.J.: Princeton University Press, 1986).

Moulton, Gary E., ed. *The Papers of Chief John Ross*, 2 vols. (Norman: University of Oklahoma Press, 1985).

Norgren, Jill. *The Cherokee Cases: The Confrontation of Law and Politics* (New York: McGraw-Hill, 1996).

Perdue, Theda, and Michael D. Green, eds. *The Cherokee Removal: A Brief History with Documents* (Boston: Bedford Books, 1995).

Wilkins, David E. *American Indian Sovereignty and the U.S. Supreme Court: The Masking of Justice* (Austin: University of Texas Press, 1997).

Wilkinson, Charles F. *American Indians, Time, and the Law* (New Haven: Yale University Press, 1987).

Indian Life on the Upper Missouri:
A Catlin/Bodmer Portfolio

—=◆=—

Their central importance as the hub of intersecting trade networks ensured that the villages of the Mandans and Hidatsas received a regular stream of visitors. Indians from dozens of other tribes went there to trade and smoke; French, Canadian, and Spanish traders centered their operations there; and Lewis and Clark wintered there in 1804–1805. In the early 1830s, the Swiss artist Karl Bodmer and American artist George Catlin both traveled up the Missouri River, stopped off at the Mandan villages and other locations, and painted portraits of Indian people and scenes of Indian life much as Lewis and Clark would have seen them thirty years earlier.

Catlin, a Pennsylvania lawyer-turned-artist, made several trips to the West including a voyage up the Missouri River in 1832. In 1837–38, he exhibited more than six hundred paintings and his collection of Indian artifacts in eastern cities, and he hoped to sell his "Indian gallery" to Congress for a national museum. Failing to gain congressional support, he tried his luck in Europe, but was finally forced to sell his collection to meet his debts. Many of his sketches and paintings appeared as illustrations to his published accounts of travel among the Indians of the West.[1]

Karl Bodmer traveled up the Missouri in 1833. He had been hired by a German prince, Maximilian of Wied, to accompany him on a scientific tour of the United States. Bodmer's watercolors and sketches illustrated the prince's account of his travels, published in German in 1839 and in English in 1840.[2]

Between them, these two artists left an invaluable visual record of Indian life on the upper Missouri in the years just before the smallpox epidemic of 1837 devastated the tribes and virtually annihilated the Mandans. They depicted the earth-lodge villages of the Mandans and their neighbors and scenes of everyday life inside these lodges, such as Lewis and Clark would have experienced during their winter sojourn.

Bodmer's painting of the interior of a Mandan earth lodge (Figure 4.1(a)) shows the occupants sitting on buffalo robes between the four central posts and under the open skylight. (Figure 4.1(b) is a diagrammatic sketch of the interior of such a lodge, which shows how space was organized and allocated in these communities.) The lodge housed an extended family and contains their valued possessions, including prized horses. The men's weapons lean against a post in the foreground. Mandan women were the producers of

FIGURE 4.1(a) **Karl Bodmer, *The Interior of the Hut of a Mandan Chief***
Joslyn Art Museum, Omaha, Nebraska.

food—a wooden mortar and pestle used for grinding corn and large baskets in the background testify to the food supplies that supported the tribe's prosperity and trade system. Catlin and Bodmer both provide pictures of Mandan women. Shakoha, or Mint, whom Catlin calls "a pretty girl with piercing black eyes" (Figure 4.2), was twelve years old when Catlin painted her in 1832, but he said she was already famous for her conquests. Bodmer's *Ptihn-Tak-Ochata, Dance of the Mandan Women* (Figure 4.3) captures a glimpse of the ceremonial roles of women and shows elderly women of the White Buffalo Cow Society wearing headgear made from the fur of the sacred white buffalo.[3]

In his painting of Pehriska-Ruhpa or Two Ravens, Bodmer shows a Hidatsa warrior of the Dog Society (Figure 4.4). Two Ravens wears a headdress of owl, raven, and magpie feathers, designed to be seen in motion, an eagle bone whistle hangs from his neck, and he carries a rattle made of small hooves in one

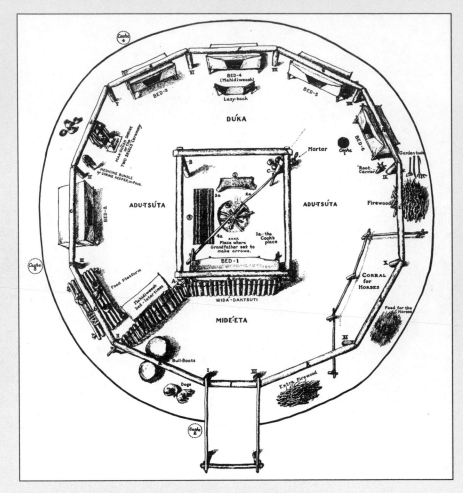

FIGURE 4.1(b) Diagram of the Interior of an Earth Lodge
American Museum of Natural History Library.

hand, bow and arrows in the other. Bodmer did a watercolor of the subject but reworked it for publication as an engraving, adding motion to the figure and meticulous detail to the costume. "I have long considered this the finest full-length portrait of an Indian I have seen," wrote the late scholar of northern Plains art and history, John C. Ewers.[4]

Both artists executed fine portraits of Indian males in warrior regalia, but they also recorded other aspects of Mandan male life. Mandeh-Pahchu or Eagle's Beak (Figure 4.5) holds a flute, not a tomahawk. The young man wears beads, dentalium, and abalone shells in his hair and ears and around his neck. He may have been going courting, since flutes were often used by young men to play songs to girls.

FIGURE 4.2 George Catlin, *Mint, a Pretty Girl*
Smithsonian American Art Museum, Washington, D.C./Art Resource.

The artists also shared and shaped the prejudices and perspectives of their time, however. They regarded Indians as part of a vanishing frontier, doomed as "civilization" engulfed their world. Catlin's paintings of the Assiniboine chief Ah-jon-jon (Figure 4.6), also known as the Light (or, according to Catlin, Pigeon's Egg Head), exemplify this view. Catlin saw Ah-jon-jon in St. Louis in 1832 when the chief was on his way to Washington as part of a

FIGURE 4.3 **Karl Bodmer,** *Ptihn-Tak-Ochata, Dance of the Mandan Women*
Joslyn Art Museum, Omaha, Nebraska.

delegation from the upper Missouri; he saw him again as a fellow-passenger on the steamboat, *Yellow Stone,* heading back up the Missouri on his return home. Struck by the transformation in Ah-jon-jon, Catlin painted a full-length, two-figure oil portrait depicting the contrast. Military coat, top hat, high-heeled boots, and white gloves have replaced buckskins, headdress, and moccasins. In Catlin's portrait, the Indian has lost his dignified bearing and cuts a ridiculous figure as he returns home with umbrella, fan, and rum bottle in his coat pocket. In Catlin's view, Ah-jon-jon was an Indian betrayed by civilization.

Ah-jon-jon came to a tragic end. He acted as the government hoped Indian delegates to the capital would and tried to convince his people of the superiority of American power by describing the wonders he had seen in the East. His people came to regard him as a braggart and the chief was eventually killed by one of his own tribe.[5] It seemed as if Catlin's assessment of the impact of contact with "civilization" was accurate. Ah-jon-jon passed into recorded history as a victim and as something of a fool.

But Ah-jon-jon's present-day descendants remember a different man and

FIGURE 4.4 Karl Bodmer, *Pehriska-Ruhpa, Moennitarri Warrior, in the Costume of the Dog Danse*

Joslyn Art Museum, Omaha, Nebraska.

FIGURE 4.5 Karl Bodmer, *Mandeh-Pachu, Mandan Man*
Joslyn Art Museum, Omaha, Nebraska.

a more complex personality, and Catlin's assumption that outward forms of cultural borrowing represent cultural suicide was too simple. Ah-jon-jon may have alienated people with his stories and his boasting, but he discarded his fancy clothes soon after he returned home. Every year thousands of people from the eastern United States visit the West and stagger home in cowboy hats and boots without abandoning their eastern way of life. It might be more accurate to see Ah-jon-jon as a tourist rather than a symbol of a disappearing way of life.

FIGURE 4.6 George Catlin, *Pigeon's Egg Head (The Light) Going to and Returning from Washington*

Smithsonian American Art Museum, Washington, D.C./Art Resource.

► **Questions for Consideration**

1. What do the pictures and diagram reveal about Mandan and Hidatsa social organization?

2. What do Catlin and Bodmer, two outsiders, manage to convey about Indian life on the upper Missouri?

3. Which aspects of Indian life do the artists seem to have been most interested in?

References

1. George Catlin, *Letters and Notes on the Manners, Customs, and Conditions of North American Indians,* 2 vols. (London: Author, 1844); Brian W. Dippie, *Catlin and His Contemporaries: The Politics of Patronage* (Lincoln: University of Nebraska Press, 1990).
2. "Prince Maximilian of Wied's Travels in the Interior of North America, 1832–1834," in Reuben G. Thwaites, ed., *Early Western Travels, 1748–1846,* vols. 22–25 (Cleveland: The Arthur H. Clark Co., 1906).
3. John C. Ewers, *Views of a Vanishing Frontier* (Lincoln: University of Nebraska Press and Joslyn Art Museum, 1984), 65.
4. Ewers, *Views of a Vanishing Frontier,* 65.
5. John C. Ewers, "When the Light Shone in Washington," in *Indian Life on the Upper Missouri* (Norman: University of Oklahoma Press, 1968), 75–90.

CHAPTER

5

DEFENDING THE WEST
1830–90

THE INDIAN WEST BEFORE 1830

The Indian peoples who lived on the Great Plains in the early nineteenth century can be divided into two broad categories. On the edges of the Plains, along the Missouri River, lived sedentary farming tribes like the Mandan, Hidatsa, Arikara, Pawnee, and Omaha. These peoples had lived in the region for hundreds of years. They inhabited earth-lodge villages, cultivated extensive acreage of crops, practiced elaborate rituals, and observed rank and status within their societies. British, French, Canadian, and Spanish merchants traded in their villages, Lewis and Clark wintered with the Mandans on their way west, and artists George Catlin and Karl Bodmer painted them during their trips up the Missouri River in the early 1830s. (See Picture Essay, "Indian Life on the Upper Missouri: A Catlin/Bodmer Portfolio," pages 250–58.)

By comparison, many of the nomadic buffalo-hunting Indians of the Plains were relatively recent arrivals. The Lakota Sioux, Cheyennes, Arapahos, Crows, Kiowas, Comanches, Shoshonis, and Blackfeet have histories linking them to other areas. Some, like the Blackfeet, Arapahos, and Shoshonis seem to have been on the Plains before the first Europeans ventured onto the area; others, like the Lakotas, arrived in the late eighteenth and early nineteenth century. Although there was great diversity among these tribes in their languages, social structures, and historical experiences, in comparison with the village peoples of the Missouri River they shared some common characteristics. They depended on the buffalo for subsistence. Easily transportable skin tepees and a fluid band structure (living most of the year in relatively small bands and coming together at times in larger gatherings) enabled them to follow the herds at will, and authority and restraints on individual freedom were kept to a minimum. Public opinion and tradition exerted more influence than the words of chiefs, whose position depended on their own prestige and the example they set.

Horses Transform the Plains

The Plains Indians' way of life was the product of interplay between their environment, vast herds of roaming buffalo, and horses introduced by the Spanish invaders to the south. The animals spread by trade and raids and reached virtually every tribe on the Plains in the mid-eighteenth century. Apaches traded horses to Pueblos; Kiowas and Kiowa-Apaches traded them to Caddos; Wichitas and Pawnees traded them to Osages; Comanches and Utes traded them to Shoshonis. Shoshonis then traded them to Crows and to the Flatheads and Nez Percés in the Plateau region, who traded them to the Blackfeet, as did the Arapahos. Blackfeet and Gros Ventres° traded them to Assiniboines. Crows, Kiowas, Arapahos, Cheyennes, and others brought horses to the villages of the Mandans, Hidatsas, and Arikaras. Lakotas° obtained horses at the Arikara villages and traded them to their eastern Yankton, Yanktonai, and Dakota relatives.[1] (See Map 5.2, "The Diffusion of Guns and Horses across the Plains, 1680–1750," page 263.)

Horses transformed Plains Indians into mobile communities, capable of traveling great distances and fully exploiting the rich resources of their environment. In Cheyenne tradition, the prophet Sweet Medicine foretold the coming of the horse and how it would change people's lives: "This animal will carry you on its back and help you in many ways," he said. "Those far hills that seem only a blue vision in the distance take many days to reach now; but with this animal you can get there in a short time, so fear him not." When the first Cheyenne saw horses, sometime in the early eighteenth century, "he thought of the prophecy of Sweet Medicine, that there would be animals with round hoofs and

---

°Also known as Atsinas, the Gros Ventres of Montana were a different people from the Gros Ventres of the Missouri, also known as the Hidatsas.

°The Sioux comprised various divisions, tribes, and bands, roughly as follows:

Lakota (Western, Teton)	Nakota (Middle, Yankton)	Dakota (Eastern, Santee)
Oglala	Yankton	Mdwekanton
Hunkpapa	Yanktonai	Wahpeton
Miniconjou		Wahpekute
Brulé (Sicangu)		Sisseton
Blackfoot (Sihaspa)		
Two Kettle		
Sans Arc		

shaggy manes and tails, and men could ride on their backs into the Blue Vision. He went back to the village and told the old Indians, and they remembered."[2]

The buffalo that Plains Indians began to hunt from horseback provided the tribes with food, shelter, clothing, tools, and weapons; it became the economic and cultural base of the societies that developed on the Plains. This new way of life emphasized the man's role as warrior and hunter and seems to have brought an increase in polygyny in some societies. Successful hunters could afford more wives, and the increasingly successful hunts meant more hides for the women to tan and prepare, especially as trade with Euro-Americans developed. The Crow woman, Pretty Shield, recalled her grandmothers' talk about the hard lives they had lived before horses and decided that horses had changed everything for the better: "there was always fat meat, glad singing, and much dancing in our villages," she remembered nostalgically.[3] The new horse-buffalo complex of the Plains was the source of power and prosperity for Plains societies. It also constituted the vulnerable point of those societies: when American soldiers and hunters destroyed the buffalo herds in the second half of the nineteenth century, they eradicated the foundations of Plains Indian society, reducing mobile hunters to dependence on government rations.[4]

Jostling for Position on the Plains

The rich resources of the Plains were a magnet for Indian peoples at a time when other areas were feeling the effects and pressures generated by Euro-American invasion. Soon the Plains were transformed into a huge arena of competition between rival tribes jostling for position and for rich hunting territories.

When the first Europeans arrived on the northern Plains in the eighteenth century they met many Shoshoni or Snake Indians. Descendants of peoples who once inhabited the Great Basin region of Nevada, the Shoshonis had moved north and east. They acquired horses early in the eighteenth century from Ute and Comanche relatives to the south and pushed onto the northern Plains. But the Shoshonis pulled back into the Rocky Mountains as other groups edged onto the Plains and as the Blackfeet to the north acquired both horses and guns. Some Kiowa and Comanche bands were still on the northern Plains at the end of the century, but they continued their migration southward to the area of present-day Texas and Oklahoma. En route, the Comanches came into conflict with Apache bands, whom they pushed west off the Plains and into areas of Arizona and New Mexico. The Apaches and Navajos had themselves migrated from the north several hundred years before, coming into contact and conflict with the Pueblo Indians of the Southwest and with the northern frontier of Spain's empire.

Other groups entered the Plains from the east. The Crow Indians split off from their Hidatsa relatives sometime before 1700, moved onto the Plains, and eventually took up residence in the rich hunting territory of the Yellowstone region. The Cheyennes, who once lived in sedentary farming villages in Minnesota and then North Dakota, crossed the Missouri River and took up life as

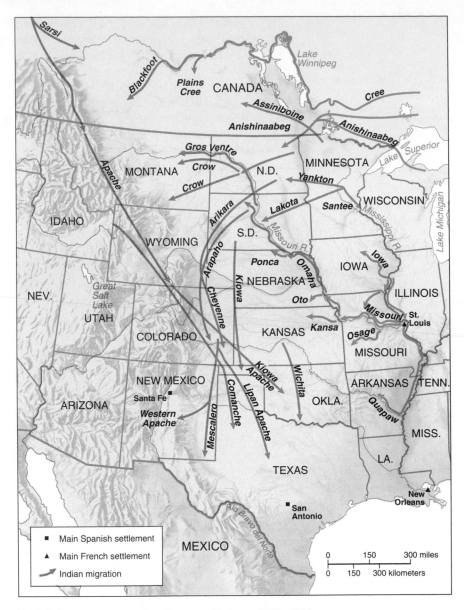

MAP 5.1 Movement of Peoples onto Plains, c.1500–1800

Long before Euro-Americans pushed west onto the Great Plains, Indian peoples had been moving into and across the vast grasslands. Some peoples, like the Quapaws, Osages, Omahas, and Poncas, followed river valleys west before horses reached the plains. Others, like the Cheyennes, Comanches, and Lakotas, migrated deep into the plains to take advantage of new opportunities presented by the spread of horses. Some peoples were still in motion and competing for position on the plains when the Americans arrived. Adapted from The Settling of North America: The Atlas of the Great Migrations into North America from the Ice Age to Ellis Island and Beyond *by Helen Hornbeck Tanner, Janice Reiff, and John H. Long, eds. Copyright © 1995 by Swanston Publishing Ltd.*

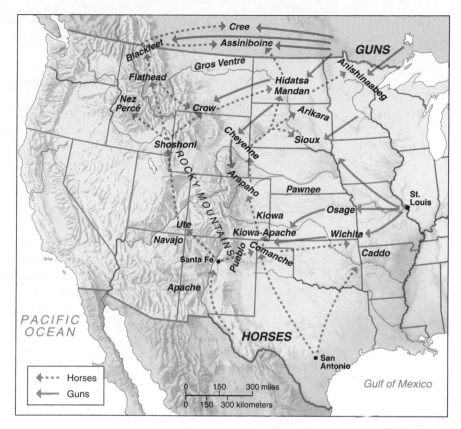

MAP 5.2 The Diffusion of Guns and Horses across the Plains, 1680–1750
In the late seventeenth and eighteenth centuries, Indian peoples on the Great Plains incorporated into their cultures major factors of change brought by Europeans: horses, introduced by Spaniards in the Southwest, and firearms, introduced primarily by French and British traders to the northeast.

mounted hunters on the Plains in the late 1700s and early 1800s. Moving first to the Black Hills, they swung south to the central Plains after 1800. Like American settlers who came later, they were "drawn westward by alluring opportunities"; but in their case the opportunities were the vast buffalo herds and "the chance to become middlemen in a sprawling trade system that reached from New Mexico to Canada."[5]

At the Confluence of Guns and Horses

By the eighteenth century the Great Plains became a battleground. Warriors raided for horses and fought for honor; tribes clashed over hunting grounds and resources. War became an integral part of Plains Indian life. Young men sought visions that would bring them success in battle against their enemies, joined warrior societies that encouraged and sustained their martial spirit, and participated in elaborate rituals in preparation for war. Success in war brought status and prestige. Counting coup (striking or just touching) on an enemy without harming him, or stealing horses from an enemy camp, carried more prestige than killing or conquering. However, as intertribal competition intensified on the Plains, warfare became more deadly. European and American traders introduced a lethal new factor: guns. As had Eastern Woodland peoples in the seventeenth century, Plains Indians found that they had to have guns to survive in an increasingly dangerous world.

By the end of the century, guns were dispersing across the Plains through a series of networks. Like other Indians in North America, Plains Indians were accustomed to trading over long distances. Indian hunters living deep in the Plains traveled to the Missouri River trading centers to exchange meat and leather for the corn, tobacco, and other crops grown by women in the Mandan and Hidatsa villages; now they went there to obtain manufactured goods and guns as well. Bands of Crows and Cheyennes brought horses and meat to the villages, traded for guns and goods, and then headed back to the Plains where they traded those guns and goods to more distant neighbors. Crow traders often traveled to a rendezvous with the Shoshonis in southwestern Wyoming; the Shoshonis in turn traded with the Nez Percés, Flatheads, and other groups in the mountains. Many of those groups were in contact in turn with Native traders at The Dalles on the Columbia River who dealt with European and American maritime traders on the Pacific coast.

The Sioux, living in Minnesota around the headwaters of the Mississippi, had contested hunting territories in the western Great Lakes region against Anishinaabe and Cree enemies armed with guns. But like later Americans, the Sioux in the late eighteenth century looked to the rich resources and opportunities available in the West. The Lakotas or western tribes of the Sioux—the Oglala, Hunkpapa, Brulé or Sicangu, Miniconjou, Sans Arc, Two Kettle, and Sihaspa or Blackfoot Sioux—began to move onto the Plains. As they migrated out onto the northern and central Plains they pushed Omahas, Otos, Missouris, Iowas, and Cheyennes to the south and west, seizing hunting territories to support their large population. By the time Lewis and Clark encountered the Brulés on the Missouri River, the Sioux were dominating the area and threatening the trade network that focused on the upper Missouri villages. The Sioux held their own rendezvous in direct contact with traders from the East. As the Lakotas continued to move west, they formed alliances with the Cheyennes and Arapahos, pushed the Crows west to the Powder River, and attacked the Pawnees in Nebraska. They dominated the northern and central Plains by the mid-nineteenth century.[6]

INVADERS FROM THE EAST

But other new peoples were also advancing on to the Plains in force. In the 1830s, Indians expelled from their eastern homelands by United States removal policies migrated into areas of present-day Oklahoma, Arkansas, Kansas, and

Missouri. There they came into conflict with local tribes like the Osages, pushing them into increased conflict with Comanche enemies to their southwest, and southern Plains Indians resisted the invasion of the homelands by the five tribes from the Southeast.[7] Indian peoples west of the Mississippi first encountered American explorers and traders early in the nineteenth century, and the expanding power of the Lakotas and their Cheyenne and Arapaho allies would soon clash head-on with the expanding power of the United States. The newcomers did not enter a static situation; they added to the far-reaching changes already taking place in Indian society and encountered Indian peoples who had been contesting among themselves for generations. The West was still Indian country. But as American expansion gathered pace, the doctrine of Manifest Destiny proclaimed that Americans had a God-given right to occupy all land west to the Pacific and a duty to extend the blessings of American democracy to the peoples already living there, whether Mexican or Indian. The Indian nations of the western United States came under siege by disease and emigrants looking for land — and gold.

The Ravages of Smallpox

Epidemics of smallpox had hit the Indians of the West hard in the eighteenth and nineteenth century. Perhaps as many as half of Plains Indians died in the smallpox pandemic in 1779–81, which spread along the routes which Indians followed to trade horses at Santa Fe and other towns.[8] Smallpox struck again in 1801–02: Lewis and Clark passed deserted villages on the Missouri River in 1804. Disease struck the sedentary tribes harder than the nomads, further shifting the balance of power in the region from river peoples like the Mandans and Hidatsas to Plains groups like the Lakotas. But nomads also suffered terribly. As many as four thousand Comanches died in a smallpox epidemic in 1816; another epidemic hit the Sioux in 1819.

Half of the Pawnees died in an epidemic on the central Plains in the early 1830s. Then, in June 1837, an American steamboat carrying smallpox docked at the Mandan villages on the upper Missouri River in North Dakota. Within a few weeks, fever appeared. Soon people were dying by the hundreds. "I Keep no a/c of the dead, as they die so fast it is impossible," wrote Francis Chadron, a trader at Fort Clark near the Mandan villages. The Mandans' population, as many as 15,000 when the French first met them in 1738, declined steadily. Their location at the center of a trade network on the Missouri River guaranteed that Mandans received germs as well as goods from Europeans. They suffered heavily during the smallpox pandemic of 1779–81 and probably numbered no more than 2,000 by June 1837. By October only 138 remained. Between 1837 and 1840 the disease spread thousands of miles and killed thousands of people: half of the Assiniboines, two-thirds of the Blackfeet, half of the Arikaras, a third of the Crows, and perhaps a quarter of the Pawnees. At Fort Union, where the Yellowstone River meets the Missouri, a trader reported "such a stench in the fort that it could be smelt at a distance of 300 yards." So many Assiniboines died that bodies were buried in large pits until the ground froze, after which there was no choice but "to throw them into the river."[9] A Kiowa winter count recorded 1839–40 as a year of smallpox on the southern Plains (see "Sixty Years of Kiowa History," pages 290–93).

The discovery of gold in California in 1848 brought increased traffic across the Plains. Immigrants on the overland trails brought more diseases to the Indians. Cholera, measles, and scarlet fever were soon adding to the toll of Indian deaths. "If I could see this thing, if I knew where it came from, I would go there and fight it," cried an anguished Cheyenne warrior as cholera raged through the tribe in 1849.[10] Smallpox hit the Blackfeet again in 1869 and continued to ravage Indian country into the next century. The American military conquest of the West took place in the wake of biological disasters that had reduced Indian power to resist and, for some pock-marked survivors who watched these horrible deaths, the will to live.

The Arrival of Miners and Settlers

Those who did survive had to deal with more and more American intruders as the United States pushed west to realize its "Manifest Destiny" and occupy the continent from the Atlantic to the Pacific. Americans colonized Texas and won its independence from Mexico in 1836. American settlement of Texas entailed the defeat and dispossession of the Indian inhabitants: emigrant Indians from the east were driven north or into Mexico; Kiowas and Comanches and Texans fought a bitter struggle for survival and supremacy. The Texas Rangers, formed in the 1830s, battled the Comanches until the end of the southern Plains wars in 1875. The Americans conquered California, Arizona, New Mexico, and parts of Utah and Colorado during the war with Mexico in 1846–48. Americans soon were encroaching on lands that the Indians of the Southwest regarded as their own, not to be transferred from Mexico to the United States without their consent. Pueblo Indians had seen Spanish, Mexican, and now American invaders claim their land and once again revolted in 1847. Apaches watched with concern as American surveyors ran a boundary line between the United States and Mexico, and wondered where Apache country figured into the picture.[11]

In California, the Indian population was shattered by the massive upheavals that followed the discovery of gold in 1848. As many as 300,000 people lived in the area at the time of first contact with Spaniards. By 1848, the Indian numbers had been cut in half at least. Disease, starvation, enslavement, and murder reduced them to a mere 30,000 by 1861. Miners, settlers, and "volunteer companies" hunted down Indians in systematic campaigns of extermination. When Pomo Indians killed two avaricious miners who had ruthlessly exploited their Indian laborer, American soldiers retaliated in 1850, killing more than one hundred Pomo men, women, and children, "a perfect slaughter pen" according to the officer commanding the troops.[12] Thousands of women and children throughout California were sold into slavery. The U.S. government created a series of reservations in the early 1850s, but in some ways "they functioned more as refugee camps in this period of bloodshed."[13]

California Indians faced an ongoing struggle to remain on their traditional lands. Debris from mining and logging operations choked fishing streams; the newcomers' fences and "property rights" kept Indians from places where they had formerly fished, hunted, and gathered. Cahuilla Indians sent a petition to the Commissioner of Indian Affairs in 1856, complaining that the Americans not only took their best farming and grazing lands but also diverted the water they needed for irrigation. In some instances the water had been "wholly monopolized by the white settlers thereby depriving us of the most essential means for the successful cultivation of our crops," and forcing them "to abandon portions of our improved lands greatly to the detriment and distress of our people."[14] Many of the Indians who survived in California became part of the market economy and the agricultural labor force. Indians, said one California farmer in 1851, were "all *among* us, *around* us, *with* us—hardly a farm house—a kitchen without them."[15]

Indians in Oregon Territory experienced less population loss than those in California, but they too suffered from newly introduced diseases. When a measles epidemic hit the Cayuse Indians in 1847, missionary Marcus Whitman and his wife treated Indian as well as non-Indian children, but the Cayuse children died while others recovered. The Cayuses feared the Whitmans were poisoning their children and murdered them and a dozen other settlers. The ensuing war lasted until 1850. Such "Indian massacres" were used to justify military reprisals and dispossessions, but contrary to Hollywood's obsession with Indian raids on wagon trains, emigrants crossing the plains to Oregon and California experienced relatively little hostility from Indians. Of 250,000 emigrants who crossed the Plains between 1840 and 1860, only 362 died in all the recorded conflicts with Indians. More often, Indians acted as pilots and guides, aided emigrants at river crossings, and traded horses and food for guns and cloth. But tensions were inevitable. The Indians regarded the emigrants as trespassers and expected them to pay tribute. "The Indians say that the whites have no right to be in their country without their consent," reported Thomas H. Harvey, the Superintendent of Indian Affairs at St. Louis in 1845. They "complain that the buffalo are wantonly killed and scared off, which renders their only means of subsistence every year more precarious."[16]

LOSING THE WEST

The United States government was determined to protect its citizens—and to continue moving west. The United States hoped to create space for white settlers and to reduce conflict among settlers and tribes: In 1851 with the Treaty of Fort Laramie, Indians from all the major tribes on the northern Plains came together in a huge council and heard American proposals that Indians recognize and respect tribal boundaries. The United States hoped to restrict the tribes to designated areas in an effort to reduce intertribal conflict and prevent confrontations with Americans, but fighting broke out only a few years later. In 1854, a young army officer overreacted when a Brulé Sioux Indian killed an immigrant's cow. Lieutenant John Grattan led his command to the Indian village, demanded the killer be delivered up, and opened fire: when the smoke cleared, Grattan and his men lay dead. General William Harney retaliated by destroying an Indian village at Ash Hollow in Nebraska the following year and the stage was set for more than twenty years of open warfare between the Sioux and the United States army.

The American Civil War (1861–65) — in which some 20,000 Indians enlisted, fighting on both sides[17] — temporarily slowed migration westward and called most troops away from the frontiers, but conflicts with Indians continued with little respite.

Indian Wars and Treaties, 1851–68

In Minnesota, the Dakota Sioux, eastern relatives of the Lakotas, went to war in 1862. Their chief Little Crow for years pursued a policy of accommodation in dealing with the United States and took the lead in signing treaties selling Dakota lands. But the Americans failed to deliver the annuities, and the Indian agent told the hungry Dakotas to eat grass. In 1862, with his people on the verge of starvation, Little Crow agreed to lead his angry warriors in a desperate war. The war tore apart kinship and other relationships that had evolved over years as Dakota people intermarried and coexisted with white traders and neighbors. Families of mixed heritage faced divided loyalties. Dakota warriors killed more than one thousand settlers. But, as Little Crow had warned his angry young men when they demanded he lead them to war, the Americans were as thick as locusts in flight: "Count your fingers all day long and white men with guns will come faster than you can count."[18] American troops quelled the "Great Sioux Uprising." About 1,700 Sioux were marched to Fort Snelling and confined in a wooden stockade. Four hundred Indians were put on trial for murder, and 38 were eventually executed at Mankato in the largest public hanging in American history. Some Dakota refugees fled west to join their Lakota relatives on the Plains.

In 1864 occurred one of the worst massacres of the wars for the West. In 1858, gold was discovered in Colorado. Thousands of settlers poured into the area, transforming the front range of the Rockies and the Plains, destroying the Cheyenne Indians' way of life. Tensions escalated, heightened by settlers' fears that during the Civil War, the withdrawal of American troops east for war duty would precipitate an Indian uprising. Black Kettle's band of Cheyennes and some Southern Arapahos were camped at Sand Creek near Fort Lyon, Colorado, on land set aside by, and supposedly under the protection of, the U.S. government. There they were attacked by Colonel J. M. Chivington and the Third Colorado Cavalry. Black Kettle raised an American flag and a white flag, but the soldiers butchered some 270 Indians, mostly women and children. According to testimony gathered for a congressional investigation, the victims "were mutilated in the most horrible manner."[19]

In the Southwest, Colonel Edward Canby, General James Carleton, and Colonel Christopher (Kit) Carson, accompanied by Ute Indian allies, campaigned vigorously and mercilessly against the Navajos, destroying sheep herds and homes. Finally, many Navajos surrendered, and in 1864 thousands of Nava-

Little Crow

Artist Frank Blackwell Mayer sketched this portrait of the Mdwekanton chief Taoyateduta, or Little Crow (c. 1810–63), during negotiations of the Treaty of Traverse des Sioux in 1851, in which the Dakotas ceded much of their land to the United States. Mayer described Little Crow as an intelligent man in his forties, with a "very determined & ambitious nature, but withall exceedingly gentle and dignified in his deportment." His whole bearing, said Mayer, was "that of a gentleman." After attempting accommodation with the United States for a decade, Little Crow led his young men to war in 1862. The next year, he was shot dead by an American settler while picking raspberries with his son. His body was then scalped and dismembered by Americans. Newberry Library.

jos were removed to Bosque Redondo reservation at Fort Sumner, New Mexico, a four hundred-mile trek the Navajos called their "Long Walk." Carleton hoped that relocating the Navajos to Bosque Redondo would create a buffer zone protecting New Mexicans from Comanche raids. Confined to barren lands, the Navajos endured malnutrition and disease, bad water, drought, and grasshoppers. The government provided rations that were sometimes unfit for human consumption, and there were tensions with New Mexicans, and raids by Comanches. Meanwhile, the government tried to transform Navajos into farmers. After four years, the Navajos at Bosque Redondo met with the Indian Peace Commission. By the terms of the treaty signed June 1, 1868, they were allowed to return to their traditional homes with 15,000 head of sheep and goats as breeding stock to replenish their severely depleted herds and to begin rebuilding their communities. In return, they promised to stay on their reservation, to stop raiding, and to become farmers and ranchers. Like the Trail of Tears for the Cherokees, the "Long Walk" remained a traumatic and defining event in Navajo history.

"Winning the West" was a national goal that many believed could help restore unity and heal the wounds from the Civil War. Settlers moved west in increasing numbers into and across Indian homelands: "The whites are as numerous as the years," said one Sioux chief in 1867.[20] In the immediate aftermath of the Civil War, the Lakotas fought to protect their lands against the building of the Bozeman Trail, which was to run from Fort Laramie to gold fields in Montana. The Oglala Sioux chief Red Cloud fought the United States army to a standstill in 1866–67, and his warriors annihilated Captain William Fetterman's entire command in December 1866. In the Treaty of Fort Laramie in 1868 (see "Treaty with the Sioux and Arapaho, 1868," pages 305–12), the United States agreed to abandon the Bozeman Trail. Having won, Red Cloud kept his word and kept the peace. But American pressures on the Sioux only intensified: "We are melting like snow on the hillside, while you're grown like spring grass," Red Cloud told the secretary of the interior during a visit to Washington, D.C., in 1870. "When the white man comes in my country he leaves a trail of blood behind him."[21] Leadership of the Sioux warriors passed to younger men like Crazy Horse, Gall, and Sitting Bull.

After 1867, the government determined to confine the nomadic tribes of the Plains on small reservations where the Indians could be segregated, supervised, and educated in "civilized" ways. United States peace commissioners met with delegates of the Kiowas, Comanches, Plains Apaches, Southern Cheyennes, and Southern Arapahos at Medicine Lodge in Kansas in 1867, as well as with the Sioux at Fort Laramie, and induced the tribes to accept reservation lands. The army launched a series of campaigns to punish Indian raids and "bring in" tribes who refused to accept confinement. In 1868, George Armstrong Custer attacked Black Kettle's Southern Cheyenne village on the Washita River in the dead of winter. Black Kettle had survived Sand Creek, but he died at the Washita, along with his wife and more than one hundred of his people. In addition, Custer's command shot hundreds of Indian ponies: an Indian on foot was immobilized and easily defeated. The government failed to keep buffalo

Buffalo Skulls To Be Sold as Fertilizer, c. 1880
The slaughter of the buffalo herds in the late nineteenth century struck at the core of Plains Indian life and reduced once-independent peoples to dependence on government rations. Courtesy of the Burton Historical Collection, Detroit Public Library.

hunters out of the lands guaranteed to the Indians by the Medicine Lodge treaty, and tensions on the southern Plains erupted in the Red River War of 1874. In September 1874, at the Battle of Palo Duro Canyon in Texas, Colonel Ranald Mackenzie attacked an encampment of Comanches, Kiowas, and Southern Cheyennes, burning four hundred lodges and slaughtering 1,400 ponies. That winter starving Indians drifted into the reservations from the snow-covered Plains.

Other forces, more powerful than army bullets, were at work bringing an end to the Plains Indians' world. The first transcontinental railroad was completed in 1869; other lines proliferated in the years that followed, bringing more emigrants west and facilitating the movement of troops and supplies. At the same time the buffalo herds—the staple diet of the Plains Indians and the basis of their culture—were systematically slaughtered between 1867 and 1883. Some estimates based on the reports of travelers across the Plains in the early nineteenth century put buffalo numbers as high as 40 million or more. The influx of Indian peoples onto the Plains and the development of more efficient hunting techniques from horseback placed the herds under substantial pressure. Hunting for the American hide market, together with a drought in the 1840s and the possible impact of bovine diseases, further reduced buffalo populations, and there were reports of Indians starving even before 1850.[22] But American buffalo hunters, with the support and encouragement of the U.S. army, almost exterminated the buffalo so that fewer than a thousand survived in 1895.[23] "We believed for a long time that the buffalo would again come to us," recalled a Crow woman, Pretty Shield, "but they did not." Crow hunters rode far and wide looking for buffalo but came back empty-handed. " 'Nothing; we found nothing,' they told us; and then, hungry, they stared at the empty plains, as though dreaming."[24] With their food supply gone, Indians faced a choice between starvation and the reservation.

Battles for the Black Hills

For almost a century, the United States made treaties with Indian nations. But there was growing sentiment that the United States should treat Indians as wards of the government, not as independent nations. The House of Representatives, which was left out of the treaty-making process—the Senate ratified treaties—also wanted change, and in 1871 Congress declared an end to making treaties. In the years that followed, treaties that had already been made also came under attack. But the United States still needed mechanisms by which to deal with Indian tribes and create Indian reservations, and they did so by agreements, statutes, and presidential executive orders.[25] Indian people continued to resist the assault on their lands and, in many cases, fought rather than succumbed to the reservation system.

In 1872–73, the United States defeated the Modocs of southern Oregon and northern California in a brutal little war. Indian people felt the outside world rushing in on them. Red Dog, a Sioux chief who had visited Washington, told U.S. commissioners that when he was there he did not pull a twig from a tree

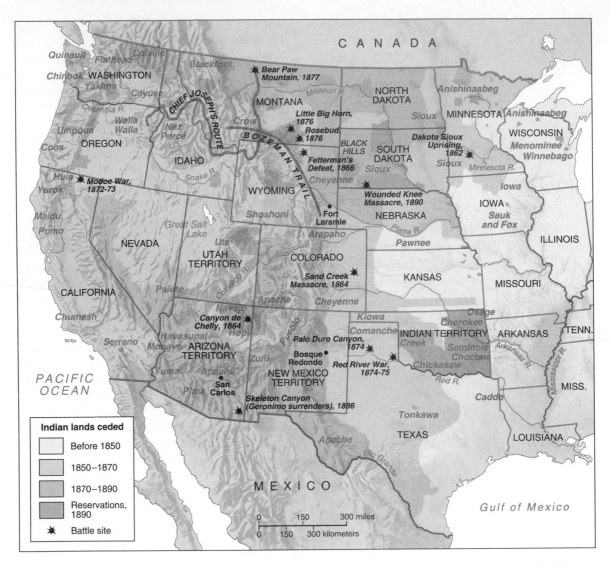

MAP 5.3 Conflicts with the United States and Indian Land Cessions, 1850–90
The rapid expansion of the United States in the second half of the nineteenth century demanded the defeat and dispossession of the Indian peoples living there. By 1890, Indian military resistance was broken and Indian homelands were reduced to a fraction of their original size.

or disturb anything, but Americans entering Indian land did not treat it with the same respect. "This is our country," he said, "and when white men come into it, it makes our hearts beat fast."[26] Red Dog had good reason to be anxious. In 1874, George Custer led an expedition into the Black Hills of South Dakota that verified reports of gold in the region. The Black Hills were sacred to the Sioux and had been guaranteed to them in the Treaty of Fort Laramie. Prospectors who trespassed there were killed. The government offered to purchase the Black Hills but the Sioux dismissed their offers. Sitting Bull said that the Black Hills were simply not for sale.

The United States resolved to take them anyway. The army sent an ultimatum ordering all Lakota and Northern Cheyenne bands onto the reservations by January 31, 1876, and then launched a three-pronged "pacification campaign" against the "hostiles" who refused to come in. Crazy Horse turned back one prong, led by General George Crook, at the Battle of the Rosebud. Custer and the Seventh Cavalry, approaching from the east, came upon a huge Indian village in the valley of the Little Big Horn and rashly attacked it. Sitting Bull had had a vision of soldiers without ears falling into the Indians' camp. The Lakotas and Cheyennes wiped out Custer's command in a battle that was refought and commemorated in countless movies and paintings (see Picture Essay "The Battle of the Little Big Horn in Myth and History," pages 327–33).

This most famous Indian victory occurred when Indians were nearing the end of fighting for their freedom. The bands which had congregated at the Little Big Horn split up and were tracked down and rounded up in the next year or two. Sitting Bull fled to Canada; Crazy Horse "came in" in 1877 and was bayoneted to death while "trying to escape." The Lakotas were confined to reservations, and Congress passed a law taking the Black Hills and extinguishing all Lakota rights outside the Great Sioux Reservation. After American troops destroyed the Northern Cheyenne village of Dull Knife and Little Wolf on the Powder River in Wyoming in November 1876, the Cheyennes were shipped to Indian Territory. In September 1878, about three hundred Cheyennes began a desperate 1,500-mile dash back north. Most were captured and many were killed, but some eventually were allowed to return home to a reservation in southern Montana.[27] In 1877, Chief Joseph and the Nez Percés of Oregon also made a 1,500-mile bid for freedom, trying to reach Canada rather than go to a reservation. They defeated and eluded various American armies sent in pursuit, but were caught just short of the border and exiled to Indian Territory (see "Chief Joseph's Plea for Freedom," pages 314–25).

Different Strategies for Survival

Not all Indians resisted American expansion westward; some participated in it and played an active role in bringing change to the West. One Delaware, Black Beaver, lived through the era of American exploration, conquest, and settlement of the West and participated in almost every phase of it. Born in Illinois in the year that Lewis and Clark returned from their western travels, Sekettu Maquah, or Black Beaver, became a trapper and trader, a guide, an army scout, and an interpreter. As a young man, he traveled west. Along with many other Delaware and Iroquois Indians, he worked as a trapper in the Rocky Mountain fur trade. He never learned to read or write but mastered the sign language of the Plains Indians and could speak several Indian languages as well as English, French, and Spanish. In 1834, he served as interpreter for an expedition to the Red River

Black Beaver

The ubiquitous Delaware, Black Beaver (1806–80), worked as trapper and trader, army scout and emigrant guide, interpreter and preacher, participating in key historic events in the nineteenth-century West. National Archives.

country of the Comanches, Kiowas, and Wichitas, led by Colonel Richard Dodge. A dozen years later, he was a scout for the U.S. army during the war with Mexico and commanded a company of thirty-five Delawares and Shawnees. He guided Captain Randolph Marcy and a company of dragoons° in establishing a route to Santa Fe and accompanying a wagon train of five hundred emigrants across the Southwest. Marcy said Black Beaver "had visited nearly every point of interest within the limits of our unsettled territory. . . . His life is that of a veritable cosmopolite, filled with scenes of intense and startling interest, bold and reckless adventure." In the 1850s, Black Beaver worked as a farmer, trader, and guide. By the Civil War, he had a ranch on the Wichita Agency in Indian Territory (Oklahoma). Along with many other Delawares, he served the Union; as a result, Confederates seized his cattle and horses and destroyed his ranch. In 1867, he acted as an interpreter at the Treaty of Medicine Lodge negotiations with the tribes of the southern Plains. In 1872, he was a member of an Indian delegation from the Wichita Agency to Washington, D.C. Toward the end of his life he became a Baptist minister. When he died in 1880, he had outlived most of the people he had known and whose roles in westward expansion were far more renowned.[28]

Like Black Beaver, some leaders opted for accommodation and attempted to control the pace of change. Washakie of the Shoshonis, Plenty Coups of the Crows, Red Cloud of the Oglalas after his successful war of resistance in the 1860s, and many others realized that the survival of their people depended upon dealing with the reality of American power and presence. They attempted to cooperate with government agents in the hope of securing better food, clothing, and shelter for their people, but continued the fight to be Indian. Some men who found themselves deprived of their traditional roles in society as warriors and hunters joined the Indian police as a means of attaining status and a way of helping their people make the transition through hard times.

For other Indian peoples, American expansion and wars against the Sioux offered an opportunity to secure powerful allies in their own struggles. Crows, Arikaras, Pawnees, and Shoshonis all, at one time or another, fought alongside the U.S. army in its battles against the Lakota Sioux and their allies. The westward expansion of the Lakotas in the late eighteenth and early nineteenth cen-

°Heavily armed troops on horseback.

MAP 5.4 Indian Reservations in the West, 1890

When Lewis and Clark journeyed across the West in the first decade of the nineteenth century, they entered an Indian world where they traveled at their risk and by Indian tolerance and guidance. By the end of the century, that world was transformed and Indian peoples were confined on patches of the lands they once occupied, or removed to Indian Territory. (See Map 5.6, page 299, for the Lakota Sioux reservations.) Based on maps by Harry Scott taken from The Indian Frontier of the American West, 1846–1890, *by Robert Utley. Copyright © 1984 University of New Mexico Press.*

tury had placed all these tribes on the defensive, and many of them had lost lands and relatives to the Lakotas. The Crows' rich hunting territories had come under virtual siege from neighboring tribes as buffalo herds in these tribes' lands diminished: "Look at our country, and look at our enemies," Crow chiefs declared in 1870, "they are all around it; the Sioux, Blackfeet, Cheyennes, Arapahos, and Flatheads, all want our country, and kill us when they can." It made sense for the Crows to align themselves with the Lakotas' new enemies, the Americans. In June 1876, Crows and Shoshonis fought with General Crook against Crazy Horse at the Battle of the Rosebud in South Dakota, where a Crow woman named Other Magpie fought to avenge her brother's death at the hands of the Lakotas. Crow and Arikara scouts guided Custer to the Little Big Horn. Before the so-called "Sioux War" of 1876–77 was over, Crows, Shoshonis, Arikaras, Utes, Bannocks, Pawnees, and even some Arapahos, Cheyennes, and Sioux had all served with the U.S. army.

A Crow Delegation to Washington, D.C., Spring 1880
The chiefs (from left to right) are Old Crow, Medicine Crow, Two Belly, Long Elk, Plenty Coups, and Pretty Eagle. Indian delegations to Washington were a regular feature of United States–Indian relations in the second half of the nineteenth century, as the government conducted negotiations with key chiefs and tried to impress them with American power. For the delegates, visiting the nation's capital offered an opportunity to represent their people's interests to the president, Congress, and senior officials. American Heritage Center, University of Wyoming.

The Crows and Shoshonis each managed to secure and retain a reservation in their traditional homelands in the late nineteenth century, when many Indian peoples were being uprooted and shipped off to Indian Territory. In later life, the Crow chief Plenty Coups explained that his people allied with the United States "not because we loved the whiteman [sic] who was already crowding other tribes into our country, or because we hated the Sioux, Cheyenne, and Arapaho, but because we plainly saw that this course was the only one which might save our beautiful country for us. When I think back my heart sings because we acted as we did. It was the only way open to us." Tribal historian Joe Medicine Crow agreed: "We were looking for survival and I think we played it smart." Like the Shoshonis, they used the United States as allies and it brought short-term gains.[29] The Crows survived their long military struggle against the Lakotas with the help of American allies, but they would soon face greater threats to their country and culture from their former allies.

Sharp Nose, Northern Arapaho
Sharp Nose (d. 1901), photographed here wearing his army uniform, served as a scout for General Crook in 1876 and fought in the campaign against the Cheyennes in the winter of 1876–77. He impressed army officers as a formidable warrior; one described him as an "inspiration" on the battlefield: "He handled men with rare judgment and coolness, and was as modest as he was brave." The Northern Arapahos settled on the Wind River reservation in Wyoming in 1878, and Sharp Nose became head council chief in 1893. National Archives.

The End of Apache Resistance

In Arizona and New Mexico, Apaches continued to raid into Mexico as they had for generations and steadfastly resisted American invasion of their homeland after 1848. Apache warriors fought with ferocity and Americans responded with equal ferocity. They killed the Mimbreño Apache chief, Mangas Coloradas, while he was shackled and under guard. They botched an attempt to capture the Chiricahua chief, Cochise, under a flag of truce, and, as the Mexicans had done for generations, they offered bounties on Apache scalps. "When I was young I walked all over this country, east and west, and saw no other people than the Apaches," said Cochise in 1866. "After many summers I walked again and found another race of people had come to take it. How is it? Why is it that the Apaches wait to die — that they carry their lives on their finger nails?"[30]

Eventually, the various Apache bands were confined on a reservation at San Carlos, Arizona Territory. Daklugie, an Apache who lived there as a child, told researcher Eve Ball in the 1940s that San Carlos was "the worst place in all the great territory stolen from the Apaches." The only vegetation was cacti. "Where there is no grass there is no game. . . . The heat was terrible. The insects were terrible. The water was terrible." Rattlesnakes and mosquitoes thrived there, but Apaches died of "the shaking sickness," malaria. San Carlos, said Daklugie, "Was considered a good place for the Apaches — a good place for them to die." Daklugie was the son of an Apache chief named Juh and retained an implacable hatred for white Americans. Even though he had spent a dozen years at Carlisle boarding school and worked as an interpreter, he pretended he could not speak English. "It took four years to get him to talk," said Ball.[31]

Not surprisingly, many Apaches rebelled against reservation confinement, preferring death in battle to a slow death at San Carlos. Victorio led his Warm Springs people off the reservation in 1877. "I will not go to San Carlos," he said. "I will not take my people there. We prefer to die in our own land under the tall cool pines. We will leave our bones with those of our people. It is bet-

Apache Leaders before Surrender
Geronimo, Naiche (wearing hat), and Naiche's son (standing next to Naiche), with an unidentified Apache and child in a photograph taken by C. S. Fly of Tombstone, Arizona, shortly before the Apaches first surrendered to General Crook in March, 1886. Courtesy of the Arizona Historical Society/Tucson. AHS #78162.

ter to die fighting than to starve."[32] For three years he outwitted, outmaneuvered, and outfought the troops sent against him. In 1880, driven across the Mexican border by pursuing American troops, Victorio's band clashed with a force of Mexicans and Tarahumara Indians in a two-day battle in Chihuahua. When the smoke cleared, Victorio lay dead. The United States also spent years chasing down a small band of Chiricahuas led by Geronimo and Naiche. General Crook employed Chiricahua scouts and always maintained that they "did most excellent service, and were of more value in hunting down and compelling the surrender of the renegades, than all other troops engaged in operations against them combined." Two Chiricahua scouts, Martine and Kayitah, risked their lives to get Geronimo to surrender to General Nelson Miles in 1886. Miles had five thousand soldiers, one-fourth of the Regular Army, under his command. Geronimo's band consisted of only eighteen warriors and some women and children. Even so, Geronimo and other Apaches agreed that Miles had to lie to them to get their surrender. Jasper Kanseah, Geronimo's nephew who was about fifteen at the time of the surrender and had been fighting with Geronimo for three years, said "Nobody ever captured Geronimo. I know. I was with him. Anyway," he added," who can capture the wind?"[33]

After Geronimo and his band of Chiricahua Apache holdouts surrendered in September 1886, they were sent to Fort Pickens, Florida. The rest of the Chiricahuas, most of whom had not supported Geronimo's war and some of whom had served the United States army as scouts against him, were also loaded on to trains to Fort Marion, a military prison in Florida. Martine and Kayitah, who had risked their lives to bring peace, were thrown on the train still wearing their army uniforms. Crowded into the rundown old fortress at Fort Marion, the Chiricahuas endured unfamiliar climate and malaria. "We were accustomed to dry heat," said James Kaywaykla, "but in Florida the dampness and the mosquitoes took toll of us until it seemed that none would be left. Perhaps we were taken to Florida for that purpose. . . ."[34] Army officers who had fought alongside the Apache scouts and the Indian Rights Association took up the Chiricahuas' cause, but succeeded only in having them removed to Alabama. In 1894, the surviving Chiricahuas were relocated to the Kiowa and Comanche reservation in Indian Territory. There Geronimo died of pneumonia in 1909. Not until 1913 were the Chiricahuas allowed to return to the Southwest, many of them joining the Mescalero Apaches in New Mexico. With the Apaches' defeat, American military conquest of the West was complete.

Return of the Prophets

For most Indians, the hard times following defeat and dispossession proved traumatic. They suffered defeat in war, saw their subsistence base destroyed, and lost most of their lands. Once prosperous and powerful, the Plains tribes were reduced to poverty, forced to rely on government handouts and the assistance of the agents. Once free and mobile, they were confined to arid, nonproductive reservations, which they could not leave without permission. Poor health and diet, a high mortality rate, and a low life expectancy became the norm on many Indian reservations. Even the environment was transformed as Americans pushed relentlessly to master the West and exploit its resources. The United States demanded that the defeat of the western tribes involve the destruction of their way of life as well as their military subjugation.

Some Indians sought escape from the harsh reality of their situation and succumbed to alcoholism. Others looked inward and tried to restore harmony and meaning to their world through religion and ritual. As had Handsome Lake and the Shawnee Prophet at the beginning of the century, new prophets were believed to have died, traveled to heaven, and returned with divine messages that promised deliverance from suffering and oppression and a new era for Indian people. They initiated religious movements that combined old beliefs and new teachings and offered an outlet for frustration and a source of solace for people in crisis. In the 1850s, Smohalla, a Wanapum Indian from the Columbia River region, began prophesying a restoration of the Indian world and the destruction of whites. He taught his followers to abstain from alcohol, to revive the old ways, and to purify themselves of white influences. His religion became known as the Dreamer religion, with believers spending long periods in meditation. Smohalla opposed the government's program of converting his people into farmers—"You ask me to plow the ground. Shall I take a knife and tear my mother's bosom?"—and rejected the Protestant work ethic promoted by Christian missionaries and Indian agents: "My young men shall never

Ghost Dancers of Big Foot's Miniconjou Band
Photographed with United States soldiers in the fall of 1890. The army kept a close watch on the Ghost Dance as fears increased that it would spark an uprising. Many of the Indians pictured here were killed at Wounded Knee in December. Library of Congress.

work. Men who work can not dream, and wisdom comes to us in dreams." Smohalla was persecuted and jailed, but the Dreamer religion he founded spread across the Pacific Northwest and survives today.[35]

Another Northwest Coast prophet, Squsachtun or John Slocum, founded the Indian Shaker religion in the Puget Sound region in 1881. Squsachtun, a Nisqually Indian, experienced trances in which he received divine messages on how Indian people could survive the trauma of reservation life. He taught his followers to believe in God and Christ, heaven and hell, but to rely on his prophecies for sacred guidance. His followers, who shook their bodies while ritually brushing away their sins, became known as Shakers. Like Smohalla, Squsachtun was harassed and imprisoned but, like the Dreamer religion, the Shaker sect survived. The religion spread through the Northwest and northern California and the Shaker Church was incorporated in 1910.

Prophetic movements on the northern Plains produced different, tragic results. A young Crow medicine man named Sword Bearer gained a following of frustrated young Crows who could no longer exist by war or hunting. He was reputed to have great power and preached an apocalyptic vision that alarmed the government and the citizens of Montana. The army was sent in, Sword Bearer was killed, and the potential movement crushed. A possible bloodbath was averted. Three years later the Lakotas were not so fortunate.

The Ghost Dance religion that swept the Plains at the end of the 1880s originated in the Nevada region. A Paiute Indian named Wovoka preached a religion that promised a return of the old ways that would reunite its practitioners with departed ancestors if they abstained from alcohol, lived in peace, and followed a prescribed ritual, including a dance in a circle called the Ghost Dance. It also promised that the white man would disappear. The religion spread rapidly on the Plains. The Lakotas sent messengers who traveled by train to receive the new religion.

As it reached the Lakotas and their neighbors, non-Indians became alarmed by reports of warriors performing a strange new dance that was supposed to result in the disappearance of whites and the return of the buffalo. Tensions intensified between the soldiers and the Lakotas. Sitting Bull—always regarded as a potential "troublemaker" by the authorities—was killed by Indian police as they tried to arrest him at his cabin on the Standing Rock reservation in mid-December 1890. Two weeks later, perhaps still smarting from their defeat at the Little Big Horn fourteen years before, the Seventh Cavalry massacred more than two hundred men, women, and children of Big Foot's band of Miniconjou Sioux at Wounded Knee in South Dakota. Many wounded Indians died as they were left to lie on the site of the massacre in subzero temperatures.

The Oglala holy man Black Elk, a young man at the time of the massacre, reacted with fury. Years later he reflected on how much more had ended at Wounded Knee. His words, as recorded by poet John G. Neihardt, have often been cited as elegiac testimony to the end of a way of life.

> When I look back now from this high hill of my old age, I can still see the butchered women and children lying heaped and scattered all along the crooked gulch as plain as when I saw them with eyes still young. And I can see that something else died there in the bloody mud, and was buried in the blizzard. A people's dream died there.

The "nation's hoop," concluded Black Elk, was "broken and scattered."[36] Wounded Knee put a grisly end to armed conflict on the northern plains, but Indian people around the country were already engaged in another desperate struggle. In time, the hoop of the Lakota nation would be mended.

References

1. Loretta Fowler, "The Great Plains from the Arrival of the Horse to 1885," in Bruce G. Trigger and Wilcomb E. Washburn, eds., *The Cambridge History of the Native Peoples of the Americas,* 2 vols. (Cambridge: Cambridge University Press, 1996), 2:8.
2. John Stands In Timber and Margot Liberty, *Cheyenne Memories* (Lincoln: University of Nebraska Press, 1972), 40, 117.
3. Frank B. Linderman, *Pretty-shield, Medicine Woman of the Crows* (Lincoln: University of Nebraska Press, 1972), 83.
4. Andrew C. Isenberg, *The Destruction of the Bison* (Cambridge: Cambridge University Press, 2000).

5. Elliott West, *The Way to the West: Essays on the Central Plains* (Albuquerque: University of New Mexico Press, 1995), 15; West, "Called Out People: The Cheyennes and the Central Plains," *Montana, The Magazine of Western History* 48 (Summer 1998), 2–15.

6. Richard White, "The Winning of the West: The Expansion of the Western Sioux in the Eighteenth and Nineteenth Centuries," *Journal of American History* 65 (1978), 319–43.

7. David La Vere, *Contrary Neighbors: Southern Plains and Removed Indians in Indian Territory* (Norman: University of Oklahoma Press, 2000).

8. Elizabeth Fenn, *Pox Americana: The Great Smallpox Epidemic of 1775–1782* (New York: Hill and Wang, 2001).

9. Russell Thornton, *American Indian Holocaust and Survival: A Population History since 1492* (Norman: University of Oklahoma Press, 1987), 94–99; Clyde D. Dollar, "The High Plains Smallpox Epidemic of 1837–38," *Western Historical Quarterly* 8 (1977), 15–38.

10. George Bird Grinnell, *The Cheyenne Indians: Their History and Ways of Life*, 2 vols. (Lincoln: University of Nebraska Press, 1972), 2:165.

11. John C. Cremony, *Life among the Apaches* (San Francisco: A. Roman & Co., 1868), chaps. 3–7.

12. Peter Nabokov, ed., *Native American Testimony* (New York: Harper and Row, 1979), 125–32.

13. Malcolm Margolin, ed., *The Way We Lived: California Indian Stories, Songs and Reminiscences* (Berkeley: Heyday Books and the California Historical Society, 1993), 173–74.

14. Robert F. Heizer, ed., *The Destruction of the California Indians: A Collection of Documents from the Period 1847 to 1865* (Santa Barbara and Salt Lake City: Peregrine Smith, Inc., 1974), 201.

15. Quoted in Albert L. Hurtado, *Indian Survival on the California Frontier* (New Haven, Conn.: Yale University Press, 1988), 193.

16. John D. Unruh, Jr., *The Plains Across: The Overland Emigrants and the Trans-Mississippi West, 1840–60* (Urbana: University of Illinois Press, 1979), quote at 128; figures at 144.

17. Laurence M. Hauptman, *Between Two Fires: American Indians in the Civil War* (New York: Free Press, 1995).

18. Gary Clayton Anderson and Alan R. Woolworth, eds., *Through Dakota Eyes: Narrative Accounts of the Minnesota Indian War of 1862* (St. Paul: Minnesota Historical Society Press, 1988), quote at 40.

19. Elliott West, *The Contested Plains: Indians, Goldseekers, and the Rush to Colorado* (Lawrence: University Press of Kansas, 1998); Stan Hoig, *The Sand Creek Massacre* (Norman: University of Oklahoma Press, 1961), 180.

20. Henry M. Stanley, *My Early Travels and Adventures in America and Asia*, 2 vols. (London: Sampson, Low, Marston and Co., 1895), 1:206.

21. *First Annual Report of the Board of Indian Commissioners for 1870* (Washington, D.C.: U.S. Government Printing Office, 1871), 41.

22. Dan Flores, "Bison Ecology and Bison Diplomacy: The Southern Plains from 1800 to 1850," *Journal of American History* 78 (1991), 465–85.

23. Thornton, *American Indian Holocaust and Survival*, 52. See also Isenberg, *Destruction of the Bison*.

24. Linderman, *Pretty-shield*, 250–51.

25. Francis Paul Prucha, *American Indian Treaties: The History of a Political Anomaly* (Berkeley: University of California Press, 1944) chs. 12–13.

26. *Annual Report of the Commissioner of Indian Affairs for 1873* (Washington, D.C.: U.S. Government Printing Office, 1874), 166.

27. Alan Boye, *Holding Stone Hands: On the Trail of the Cheyenne Exodus* (Lincoln: University of Nebraska Press, 1999).

28. Dee Brown, "Black Beaver," *American History Illustrated* 2 (1967), 32–40; Carolyn Thomas Foreman, "Black Beaver," *Chronicles of Oklahoma* 24 (1946), 269–92.

29. Colin G. Calloway, "Army Allies or Tribal Survival? The 'Other Indians' in the 1876 Campaign," in Charles E. Rankin, ed., *Legacy: New Perspectives on the Battle of the Little Bighorn* (Helena: Montana Historical Society Press, 1996), 62–81; quotes at 71 and 75–76. See also David D. Smits, "Fighting Fire with Fire: The Frontier Army's Use of Indian Scouts and Allies in the Trans-Mississippi Campaigns, 1860–1890," *American Indian Culture and Research Journal* 22 (1998), 73–116, and Thomas W. Dunlay, *Wolves for the Blue Soldiers: Indian Scouts and Auxiliaries with the United States Army, 1860–1890* (Lincoln: University of Nebraska Press, 1982).

30. W. C. Wanderworth, comp., *Indian Oratory: Famous Speeches by Noted Indian Chieftains* (Norman: University of Oklahoma Press, 1971), 125.

31. Eve Ball, *Indeh: An Apache Odyssey* (Provo: Brigham Young University Press, 1980), xv, 37.

32. Eve Ball, *In the Days of Victorio: Recollections of a Warm Springs Apache* (Tucson: University of Arizona Press, 1970; London: Corgi Books, 1973), 69.

33. General Crook is quoted in Dan L. Thrapp, *The Conquest of Apacheria* (Norman: University of Oklahoma Press, 1967), 364. S. M. Barrett, *Geronimo: His Own Life Story* (New York: Penguin, 1996), 132–38; Ball, *Indeh: An Apache Odyssey,* 106–12, quote at 110.

34. Ball, *In the Days of Victorio,* 210.

35. Clifford E. Trafzer and Margery Ann Beach, "Smohalla, the Washani, and Religion as a Factor in Northwestern Indian History," in Trafzer, ed., "American Indian Prophets: Religious Leaders and Revitalization Movements," *American Indian Quarterly* 9 (Special Issue, Summer 1995), 309–24; quotes at 316, 320.

36. John G. Neihardt, *Black Elk Speaks: Being the Life Story of a Holy Man of the Oglala Sioux* (Lincoln: University of Nebraska Press, 1988), 270.

Suggested Readings

Anderson, Gary. *Little Crow: Spokesman for the Sioux* (St. Paul: Minnesota Historical Society Press, 1986).

Ball, Eve. *Indeh: An Apache Odyssey* (Norman: University of Oklahoma Press, 1980).

Barrett, S. M. *Geronimo: His Own Story* (New York: Penguin, 1996).

Calloway, Colin G., ed. *Our Hearts Fell to the Ground: Plains Indian Views of How the West Was Lost* (Boston: Bedford Books, 1996).

Greene, Jerome A., ed. *Lakota and Cheyenne Indian Views of the Great Sioux War, 1876–1877* (Norman: University of Oklahoma Press, 1994).

Hoxie, Frederick E. *Parading through History: The Making of the Crow Nation in America, 1805–1935* (Cambridge: Cambridge University Press, 1995).

Isenberg, Andrew C. *The Destruction of the Bison* (Cambridge: Cambridge University Press, 2000).

Mooney, James. "The Ghost Dance Religion and the Sioux Outbreak of 1890," *14th Annual Report of the Bureau of American Ethnology,* 1892–93, part 2 (Washington, D.C.: U.S. Government Printing Office, 1896).

Moore, John H. *The Cheyenne* (Cambridge, Mass.: Blackwell, 1996).

Nabokov, Peter. *Two Leggings: The Making of a Crow Warrior* (Lincoln: University of Nebraska Press, 1982).

Robinson, Charles M. III. *A Good Year to Die: The Story of the Great Sioux War* (New York: Random House, 1995).

Stands In Timber, John, and Margot Liberty. *Cheyenne Memories* (Lincoln: University of Nebraska Press, 1972).

Utley, Robert. *The Indian Frontier of the American West, 1846–1890* (Albuquerque: University of New Mexico Press, 1984).

Utley, Robert. *The Lance and the Shield: The Life and Times of Sitting Bull* (New York: Henry Holt, 1993).

West, Elliott. *The Contested Plains: Indians, Goldseekers, and the Rush to Colorado* (Lawrence: University Press of Kansas, 1998).

D   O   C   U   M   E   N   T   S

Sixty Years of Kiowa History

⇒—•—⇐

All peoples devise ways of recording their history and preserving for posterity the events that give meaning to their collective lives. In oral cultures like those of the Plains Indians, the memories of the elders served as repositories of tribal histories. Recurrent retellings of significant events fastened them into the communal memory, just as songs, stories, dances, and other public performances fastened traditions in the lives of successive generations. Tribal historians on the Plains also compiled calendars of events—often called winter counts—significant to the community as a whole.

Usually painted on a buffalo robe in a spiral denoting successive years, these calendars chronicle the people's history with each year marked by a pictographic device symbolizing a memorable event. The symbols functioned as mnemonic devices, allowing the keeper of the chronicle at some future date to draw on his fund of memory and knowledge, recalling more details and other events. Sometimes a single individual would compile a winter count, recording the years of his own life; other calendars would be made over two or three generations, or compiled by one person in consultation with elders who remembered the events or who had received knowledge of them from people long since dead. The keepers of the chronicles would bring them out to be displayed and discussed around the campfires during winter evenings.

Winter counts are of great value to modern ethnohistorians when used in conjunction with documentary evidence. Most calendars record outbreaks of smallpox and other epidemics, and most note "the winter when the stars fell," the meteor shower visible throughout the western United States in November 1833. But sometimes these tribal records make no reference to things outsiders might assume would be significant: they contain many references to horse raids, the Sun Dance, battles with enemy tribes, deaths of prominent chiefs, and domestic squabbles that resulted in violence—things that were noteworthy in the community and also served to jog the memory about other events—but might ignore major battles and treaties with the United States.[1]

Like other historical sources, winter counts have limitations: their chronology usually cannot be established without cross-referencing to other sources. Interpretation of the mnemonic devices can vary considerably, and when winter counts were explained to outsiders it was not always clear how much of the interpretation came from the keeper of the calendar, how much from the translator, and how much from the ethnologist or other scholar who then transferred

Sam Kills Two

Sam Kills Two, Lakota, adds the symbol of another year to a winter count documenting 130 years of tribal history. The chronicles created and preserved by tribal recordkeepers such as Sam Kills Two supplemented oral histories handed down from generation to generation. Nebraska State Historical Society.

what he had been told into a written chronology of events. Nevertheless, they provide scholars with a unique research tool and, properly analyzed, allow integration of Indian and non-Indian records to create a richer story of the past.[2]

Moreover, winter counts are by no means the only source of history for Plains Indian societies who created and kept them. Lakota author Mary Crow Dog, recounting her life in the twentieth century, commented on some of the ways in which history survived among a people who did not record it in writing: "The Sioux used to keep winter counts, picture writings on buffalo skin, which told our people's story from year to year," she said. "Well, the whole country is one vast winter count. You can't walk a mile without coming to some family's sacred vision hill, to an ancient Sun Dance circle, an old battleground, a place where something worth remembering happened."[3]

The chronicle reproduced here records Kiowa history during sixty years of calamitous change. Kiowa traditions tell that the people entered the world through a hollow log "in the bleak northern mountains" in western Montana. Life there was hard, and in the late seventeenth century they began to migrate southward. "The great adventure of the Kiowas was a going forth into the heart of the continent," wrote Kiowa author N. Scott Momaday. They began a long migration from the headwaters of the Yellowstone River, east to the Black Hills, where they befriended the Crows. They acquired horses "and their ancient nomadic spirit was suddenly free of the ground." They acquired Tai-me, the sacred Sun Dance doll, and with it "the religion of the Plains." And they acquired "a love and possession of the open land." Pushed out of the Black Hills by the Sioux and Cheyennes, they moved south through Wyoming along the front range of the Rockies and toward the Ouachita Mountains in Oklahoma. By the time they reached the southern Plains, they had been transformed. "In the course of that long migration they had come of age as a people," said Moma-

Devil's Tower

Kiowa legend links the tribe to Devil's Tower in Wyoming. According to the legend, eight children—seven sisters and their brother—were playing when suddenly the boy was transformed into a bear and began to chase the girls. The terrified girls ran to the stump of a huge tree and scrambled up. As they did, the tree began to rise into the air. The bear lunged at them, but they were always just beyond its reach, and its claws scored long grooves into the bark of the great stump. The seven sisters were carried into the sky and became the stars of the Big Dipper. At the end of the twentieth century, Devil's Tower, by then a national monument as well as a sacred site to several Indian nations, was at the center of a legal battle when the National Parks Service attempted to restrict rock climbers from using Devil's Tower during the month of June when Indians conducted ceremonies at the site.

Wyoming State Archives, Department of State Parks and Cultural Resources.

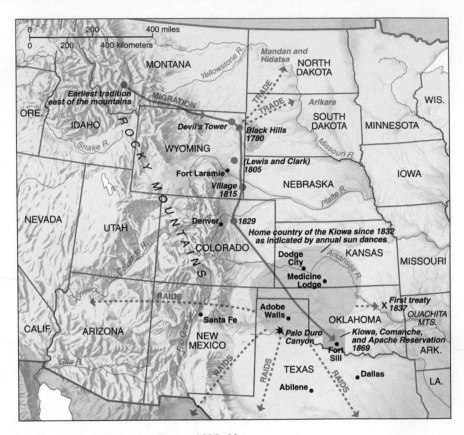

MAP 5.5 Kiowa Migration Route, 1832–69
Migration south across the Great Plains brought the Kiowas to new homes and a new way of life. But as they journeyed, the Kiowas encountered Americans, whose growing presence would soon change forever the way of life the Kiowas created on the Plains, and would eventually confine them on a reservation. James Mooney, Calendar History of the Kiowa Indians *(Washington, D.C.: U.S. Government Printing Office, 1898).*

day. "They had conceived a good idea of themselves; they had dared to imagine and determine who they were."[4]

By the early nineteenth century, the Kiowas were ranging across western Oklahoma, northern Texas, northeastern New Mexico, southeastern Colorado, and southwestern Kansas. They became allied with the Comanches sometime around 1790, and together they dominated the southern Plains. Kiowas traded with Pueblo peoples in New Mexico, but as the calendar indicates, they were also far-ranging raiders, striking deep into Mexico as well as against other Indian tribes. They lived in small, independent bands. But each summer the people came together for the Sun Dance, the central ceremony of the tribe, where they reaffirmed their unity, renewed relationships, and hunted buffalo, the foundation of Kiowa economy and culture. That way of life collapsed under the onslaught of American expansion in the years documented by the calendar.

▶ Questions for Consideration

1. What does the Dohasan Calendar (page 291) suggest about different ways of understanding and remembering history?

2. What things seem to have been important to the Kiowas? Are they the same kind of things that non-Indians might have recalled and recorded during these years?

3. What does the calendar tell us about Kiowa relations with other Indian tribes and about how the Kiowas witnessed their world changing before their eyes?

The Dohasan Calendar (1832–92)

This calendar was begun by a Kiowa chief named Dohasan, whom the artist George Catlin met and painted in 1834 and described as "a very gentlemanly and high minded man."[5] When Dohasan died in 1866, the calendar was continued to 1892 by his nephew, also called Dohasan. It contains two pictorial devices for each year — one representing the winter and one the summer. The chronicle was originally painted on hides which were renewed from time to time as they became worn out from age and handling, but Dohasan drew a copy with colored pencils on manila paper which he gave to Captain Hugh L. Scott of the Seventh Cavalry at Fort Sill in 1892. Four years later anthropologist James Mooney compiled an explanation of the events associated with each picture, primarily from information supplied to Scott by Dohasan before his death in 1893, and supplemented with information from other Kiowa chronicles.

The pictographs are arranged in a continuous spiral. The calendar on page 291 begins in the winter of 1832–33 at the lower left hand corner (1), when a man (indicated by his breech cloth) named Black Wolf (identified by the symbol above his head) was killed in an encounter with a party of Americans.[6] The next symbol (2) refers to an Osage attack on a Kiowa camp that summer, when the Osages cut off the heads of their victims.[7] Then, three stars (3) indicate the meteor shower in the winter of 1833, which, according to Momaday, "has a special place in the memory of the Kiowa people," and "marks the beginning as it were of the historical period in the tribal mind."[8] Black bars, representing dead vegetation, mark the winters; summers are usually indicated by a Sun Dance lodge with a door. (In years when the Sun Dance was not held, the season is marked by a tree in leaf or simply by the symbol for that summer's event between the two winter bars.) The major event of the season is indicated by a pictograph above or beside the winter mark or the Sun Dance lodge.[9]

The story recorded here is a familiar one in the histories of other peoples on the Plains. New diseases scythed the Kiowa population as American immigrants encroached on their territory. (The calendar records epidemics among the Kiowas in the winters of 1839–40 (4) and 1861–62 (6), and cholera in the summer of 1849 — the figure over the central Sun Dance lodge is doubled over with the pangs of cholera (5).[10]) Escalating tensions exploded in outbursts of sporadic violence and occasional pitched conflicts. The superior numbers, resources, and firepower of the United States compelled the Kiowas and their

Source: *A Chronicle of the Kiowa Indians, 1832–1892* (1968). Courtesy of the C. P. Apperson Hearst Museum of Anthropology and the Regents of the University of California.

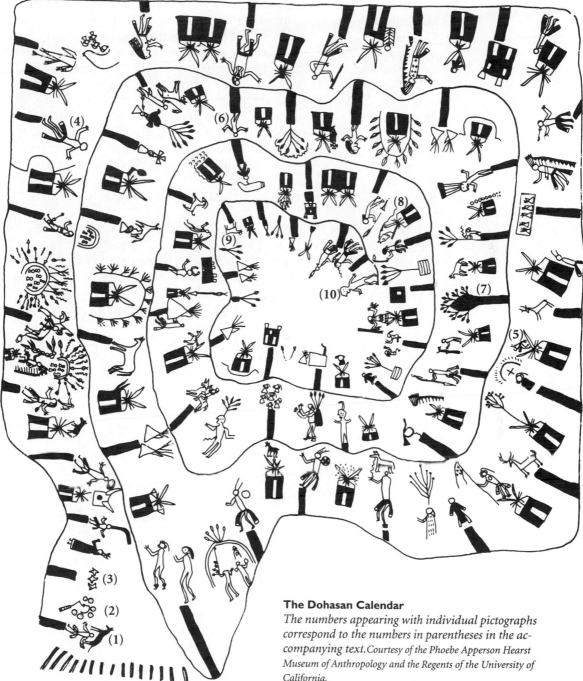

The Dohasan Calendar
The numbers appearing with individual pictographs correspond to the numbers in parentheses in the accompanying text. Courtesy of the Phoebe Apperson Hearst Museum of Anthropology and the Regents of the University of California.

neighbors to contemplate an unknown kind of life: in the Treaty of Medicine Lodge in 1867 ("Timber Hill winter" indicated by the large black tree (7)[11]), Kiowas, Comanches, Southern Cheyennes, Southern Arapahos, and Plains Apaches agreed to move on to a reservation in what is now Oklahoma. Meanwhile, the slaughter of the southern herds continued without respite, and in 1874, Kiowa and other southern Plains warriors went to war rather than die of hunger. The United States army responded with overwhelming force and destroyed the Kiowas' lodges and horse herds at the Battle of Palo Duro Canyon. The Kiowas surrendered to the army at Fort Sill, Oklahoma, and seventy-two "ringleaders" of the southern Plains Indians were shipped to Florida as prisoners of war. (The calendar records clashes with Texans and U.S. soldiers, and the arrests of chiefs.) "The young Plains culture of the Kiowas," wrote Momaday, "withered and died like grass that is burned in the prairie wind."[12]

The summer of 1879, marked by a horse head above a Sun Dance lodge (8) was remembered as the "Horse-Eating Sun Dance." The buffalo were so scarce that the Kiowas had to kill and eat their horses to keep from starving. "This may be recorded as the date of the disappearance of the buffalo from the Kiowa country," wrote Mooney. "Thenceforth the appearance of even a single animal was a rare event."[13] In subsequent years, as indicated by trees in leaf rather than Sun Dance lodges, the Sun Dance sometimes could not be held, because of the lack of buffalo. The last Kiowa Sun Dance in the nineteenth century was held in 1887. The buffalo and the Sun Dance were the anchors of Kiowa culture and experience. "Those were the two things that were always there. Things changed around them, but the buffalo and the Sun Dance stayed the same. Now they were both gone, together."[14] With buffalo gone, Kiowas began to lease grasslands to cattlemen, as indicated by the drawing of a cow (9).

The calendar ends with a measles epidemic in 1892 (10). The epidemic broke out at the reservation school and spread rapidly when the school superintendent sent the sick children home. When James Mooney visited the Kiowas in early summer the disease had spent its force, but deaths were still occurring every day or two and its impact was evident everywhere: "nearly every woman in the tribe had her hair cut off close to her head and her face and arms gashed by knives, in token of mourning, while some had even chopped off a finger as a sign of grief at the loss of a favorite child. The men also had their hair cut off at the shoulders and had discarded their usual ornaments and finery." Bereaved relatives wailed, burned blankets, tepees, and other property, and shot horses and dogs over the graves of their owners, "to accompany them to the world of shades." The scenes of mourning continued for months.[15]

The calendar provides a tribal record of the years when "the West was lost," when peoples like the Kiowas went from a life of mobility and independence to one of confinement and dependence. Those Kiowas who survived the wars and diseases of the nineteenth century had to learn new ways to survive in the world that had been imposed on them.

References

1. See, for example, Garrick Mallery, *Picture Writing of the American Indians, Tenth Annual Report of the Bureau of American Ethnology, 1888–89* (Washington, D.C.: U.S. Government Printing Office, 1893), 266–328; James Mooney, *Calendar History of the Kiowa Indians, Seventeenth Annual Report of the Bureau of American Ethnology, 1895–96,* pt. 1 (Washington, D.C.: U.S. Government Printing Office, 1898), 129–445.
2. Melburn D. Thurman, "Plains Indian Winter Counts and the New Ethnohistory," *Plains Anthropologist* 27 (1982), 173–75.
3. Mary Crow Dog, with Richard Erdoes, *Lakota Woman* (New York: HarperPerennial, 1991), 11.
4. Mooney, *Calendar History of the Kiowa Indians,* 152–64; quotations from N. Scott Momaday, *The Way to Rainy Mountain* (Albuquerque: University of New Mexico Press, 1969), 4, 6–7.
5. George Catlin, *Letters and Notes on the Manners, Customs, and Conditions of North American Indians,* 2 vols. (London, 1844; reprinted, New York: Dover, 1973), 2:74 and plate 178.
6. Mooney, *Calendar History of the Kiowa Indians,* 254–55.
7. Mooney, *Calendar History of the Kiowa Indians,* 257–60.
8. Momaday, *Way to Rainy Mountain,* 85.
9. Mooney, *Calendar History of the Kiowa Indians,* 143–44.
10. Mooney, *Calendar History of the Kiowa Indians,* 289.
11. Mooney, *Calendar History of the Kiowa Indians,* 320.
12. Momaday, *Way to Rainy Mountain,* 1.
13. Mooney, *Calendar History of the Kiowa Indians,* 344.
14. Alice Marriott, *The Ten Grandmothers* (Norman: University of Oklahoma Press, 1945), 144.
15. Mooney, *Calendar History of the Kiowa Indians,* 362–63.

Suggested Readings

Mallery, Garrick. *Picture Writing of the American Indians, Tenth Annual Report of the Bureau of American Ethnology, 1888–89,* reprinted (Washington, D.C.: U.S. Government Printing Office, 1893; New York: Dover, 1972).

Marriott, Alice. *The Ten Grandmothers* (Norman: University of Oklahoma Press, 1945).

Mayhall, Mildred P. *The Kiowas,* 2d ed. (Norman: University of Oklahoma Press, 1971).

Momaday, N. Scott. *The Way to Rainy Mountain* (Albuquerque: University of New Mexico Press, 1969).

Mooney, James. *Calendar History of the Kiowa Indians, Seventeenth Annual Report of the Bureau of American Ethnology, 1895–96,* pt. 1 (Washington, D.C.: U.S. Government Printing Office, 1898), 129–445 (reprinted, Washington, D.C.: Smithsonian Institution Press, 1979).

The Treaty of Fort Laramie and the Struggle for the Black Hills

Lakota people maintain that they emerged into this world from the Black Hills in western South Dakota. French sources and most historians locate the Sioux on the headwaters of the Mississippi in Minnesota at the time of first contact with Europeans, and the Crows, Kiowas, and other tribes have historical connections to the Black Hills. But whenever and however they arrived there, the Lakotas came to regard the Black Hills, Paha Sapa, as sacred ground, the center of their universe, "the heart of everything that is." The Sioux struggle to keep and to recover the Black Hills has been and remains at the heart of their relations with the United States.

In the first Treaty of Fort Laramie in 1851, the United States recognized the territory of the Lakotas or Teton Sioux as covering most of the present-day states of North and South Dakota and parts of Nebraska, Montana, and Wyoming, an enormous expense of territory comprising approximately five percent of the continental United States. The Black Hills lay within that territory.

When the United States attempted to establish the Bozeman Trail through Sioux territory to gold mines in Montana, the Lakotas and their Northern Cheyenne and Arapaho allies fought the army to a standstill in the so-called Red Cloud War. They laid siege to the posts the army built along the trail at Fort Reno, Fort Phil Kearny, and Fort C. F. Smith, and in December 1866 they annihilated the entire command of Captain William Fetterman who had boasted that with eighty men he could ride through the Sioux Nation. Faced with embarrassing defeats, the United States now looked for peace. The result was the second Treaty of Fort Laramie in 1868, one of the most significant and controversial treaties in the history of Indian–U.S. relations. It ended the war, planted the seeds for another war, and provided the legal foundation for Sioux claims to the Black Hills for more than a hundred years.

The United States Peace Commission consisted of military men — Generals William Tecumseh Sherman, William S. Harney, Alfred H. Terry, Christopher C. Augur, John B. Sanborn — and politicians and reformers — Commissioner of Indian Affairs Nathaniel G. Taylor, Senator John B. Henderson, and Indian agent Samuel F. Tappan. Its goals were to end warfare on the Plains and to consolidate the Indians on reservations.

In the spring of 1868, the commissioners dispatched messengers to the Indian encampments in the Powder River country, inviting Red Cloud, Man

Afraid of His Horses, and their followers to meet them at Fort Laramie. The more compliant bands who lived close to the fort—nicknamed the "Laramie loafers"—were happy to sign the treaty and receive gifts. Spotted Tail's Brulés met the commissioners in April. "I have helped you to make peace and I will help you again," Spotted Tail told them. Another Brulé, Baptiste, made clear that the United States had caused the war by placing soldiers and forts in Sioux country. Remove them, he said. "I do not want them to stay another night. . . . As long as they remain here it will look as if this road is a warpath."[1] Red Cloud and the more militant Oglalas remained aloof: "We are on the mountains looking down on the soldiers and the forts," he said. "When we see the soldiers moving away and the forts abandoned, then I will come down and talk."[2]

Over a six-month period, 159 chiefs from ten Sioux bands "touched the pen" to the treaty. The commissioners left in May without meeting Red Cloud. Only after the forts were abandoned and burned did Red Cloud ride into Fort Laramie and sign the treaty with the post commander in November. Having signed the treaty, Red Cloud kept it. The United States did not.

By the terms of the treaty, both sides agreed to end the war and live in peace. But the treaty also contained the seeds of future conflicts and included contradictory provisions. The government undertook to punish persons under U.S. jurisdiction who committed offenses against the Indians, but secured agreement that any Indians committing offenses against American citizens should be delivered to the United States for punishment. The Americans agreed to close the Bozeman Trail but, having just fought and won a war to close one road, the Lakotas now agreed to allow other roads and railroads to be built through their hunting grounds! The government set aside South Dakota west of the Missouri River as the "Great Sioux Reservation" and confirmed the country north of the North Platte River and east of the Big Horn Mountains as unceded hunting territory. But Article 11 of the treaty stipulated that, at some future date, the Indians "will relinquish all right to occupy permanently the territory outside their reservation." The treaty guaranteed the Indians the right to hunt north of the North Platte "so long as the buffalo may range thereon in sufficient numbers to justify the chase"; but the campaign to exterminate the buffalo herds was already under way on the southern Plains and it would soon spread north. The treaty contained provisions for transforming the Indians into farmers who would "compel" their children to attend schools where they would be educated out of Lakota ways and into American ways. The treaty supposedly guaranteed the northern Plains to the Lakotas, but Congress created Wyoming Territory the same year. The treaty also stipulated that no further cessions of reservation lands would be valid unless agreed to by three-quarters of the adult male population.

Military historian John Gray viewed a treaty as "so exclusively a white man's device . . . that it served primarily as an instrument of chicanery and a weapon of aggression." He had no doubt that the contradictions contained in

Sioux Chiefs at Fort Laramie in 1868
Some of the signatories of the treaty in this photograph by Alexander Gardner are (left to right): Spotted Tail, Roman Nose, Old Man Afraid of His Horses, Lone (One) Horn, Whistling Elk, Pipe, and Slow Bull. National Anthropological Archives, Smithsonian Institution.

the Fort Laramie treaty were inserted deliberately, to obtain from the Indians in peace what the army had been unable to seize in war:

> Here is a solemn treaty that cedes territory admittedly unceded; that confines the Indian to a reservation while allowing him to roam elsewhere; and that guarantees against trespass, unless a trespasser appears! The Indian was given to understand that he retained his full right to live in the old way in a vast unceded territory without trespass or molestation from whites. The treaty does indeed say precisely this. The fact that it also denies it, was no fault of the Indian. It was the Commission that wrote in the contradictions. There can be only one explanation—they designed one set of provisions to beguile and another to enforce.

Proof of Gray's contention came the following year. In June 1869, General Philip Sheridan issued a general order: All Indians on reservations were under the control and jurisdiction of their agents; outside the limits of their reservations they were under military jurisdiction "and as a rule will be considered hostile." The "unceded territory" had become "white territory."[3]

As had been the case in treaty councils between eastern Indians and European colonists, the Treaty of Fort Laramie represented a diplomatic forum

which the participants approached with different expectations and understandings. For the Indians, who lived in an oral culture, the council, the spoken
words, and the accompanying rituals of smoking together in peace were the important things. For the Americans, these parleys were just the prelude to the
"real thing": a written document on which the Indian delegates recorded their
agreement by "touching the pen" or making an X after their names.[4] As in the
forest diplomacy of the eighteenth century, so in the Plains diplomacy of the
nineteenth century, Indians affixed their names to documents that sometimes
differed greatly from what they had said in council. Sometimes Indian delegates
changed their minds or succumbed to persuasion or coercion. Sometimes errors in translation created genuine misunderstandings. Sometimes Indians
were deceived into signing documents that contained statements they were not
aware of, and to which they would never have agreed. "In 1868, men came out
and brought papers. We could not read them and they did not tell us truly
what was in them," said Red Cloud in a speech to the Cooper Union in New
York in 1870. "We thought the treaty was to remove the forts and for us to
cease from fighting." Another Sioux delegate, Bear in the Grass, said "these
words of the treaty were never explained. It was merely said that the treaty was
for peace and friendship among the whites. When we took hold of the pen
they said they would take the troops away so we could raise our children."[5]
From that day to this, Sioux people have been convinced that the treaty was altered after the delegates signed it. At a gathering of Northern Plains Native Nations at Fort Laramie in 1996, tribal elder Homer Whirl Wind Horse accused
white men of always speaking with duplicity. "With one of their tongues they
tell us good things, and the other tongue is a pencil," he said. "We understood
the words of the treaty, but when they wrote it down, the pencil changed it."[6]

Whatever contradictions and "gray areas" the Treaty of Fort Laramie contained, it soon became quite clear that the United States would have to break it.
In 1873, Pierre Jean De Smet, a Jesuit missionary, reported that there was gold
in the Black Hills. The next year, George Armstrong Custer led a military expedition into the hills and confirmed the news. The United States was in the grip
of a severe depression; the Lakotas would not be left in undisturbed possession
of the gold-rich Black Hills, no matter what the Fort Laramie Treaty said.

As miners began to risk their lives and trespass on Lakota hunting grounds,
the government tried to buy the Black Hills. A commission traveled to Lakota
country but met stiff opposition. Some chiefs refused to discuss selling the
hills; Little Big Man threatened to kill the first Indian who even spoke of doing
so. Others asked for far more than the United States was prepared to offer: Red
Cloud demanded enough money to feed his people for seven generations. The
commission returned to Washington and the army took over.

The Northwest Ordinance of 1787 had declared that the United States
would not disturb Indians in the rightful possession of their lands, except in
"just and lawful wars authorized by Congress." The army withdrew the troops
which, under the terms of the Fort Laramie treaty, were supposed to prevent

miners from entering the Black Hills. An ultimatum ordered all Lakota and Cheyenne bands to report to the agencies by January 31, 1876, and then declared that those who failed to come in were "hostile." The war against them *would* be just and lawful.

The army launched a three-pronged invasion to trap and crush Lakota resistance, but things did not go according to plan. Crazy Horse and his warriors turned back General George Crook's army at the Battle of the Rosebud in mid-June. Eight days later, on June 25, the Lakotas and Cheyennes routed an attack on their village in the Little Big Horn valley and annihilated Custer's immediate command. The army won its war, but it did so in a series of mopping-up operations, chasing scattered Indian bands over the northern Plains, attacking winter encampments, and killing women, children, and ponies in the snow. Crazy Horse surrendered and was killed. Sitting Bull fled to Canada.

With Lakota resistance broken, another commission, this one led by George Manypenny, arrived on the reservations to obtain consent to the transfer to the United States of the "unceded territory" that included the Black Hills. Congress cut rations to the agencies until the Lakotas agreed to cede the land. Lakota people recalled having to negotiate under the guns of American soldiers. The Lakotas protested but the reservation chiefs signed. The commissioners managed to secure the agreement of only about 10 percent of the adult males—about 65 percent short of what the Treaty of Fort Laramie required—but, in the wake of the "Custer Massacre," the government was in no mood to worry about such niceties. In February 1877, Congress passed a law taking the Black Hills and extinguishing all Sioux rights outside the Great Sioux Reservation.

The "Great Sioux Nation" had shrunk in less than twenty years from about 134 million acres as recognized in the 1851 Treaty of Fort Laramie to less than 15 million acres. It continued to shrink. The Sioux Act of 1888 applied the Dawes Allotment Act (see pages 339–42) to the Great Sioux Reservation, opening "surplus lands" to settlement and dividing the Lakotas into six separate reservations (see Map 5.6, "The Lakota Reservations, 1890," page 299).

Congress passed another Sioux Act in 1889 and dispatched another commission. This one included General George Crook, a veteran of Indian wars. Crook told the Indians there was a flood coming and they must save what they could or see it all swept away. He applied divide and conquer tactics. The commission found that "it was impossible to deal with the Indians as a body in general councils." The Lakotas in their own councils had already decided against agreement with the U.S. government and they presented the commissioners with a united front. The commissioners then "endeavored to convince individuals that substantial advantages to the Indians as a whole would result from an acceptance of the bill." For a time, they said in their report, "the task seemed almost hopeless, but persistence prevailed and interest was awakened. As soon as the question became debatable the situation changed and success was assured."[7] Congress cut the amount of rations the commission promised, and another nine million acres was stripped away from the reservation. Angry and divided, Lakota

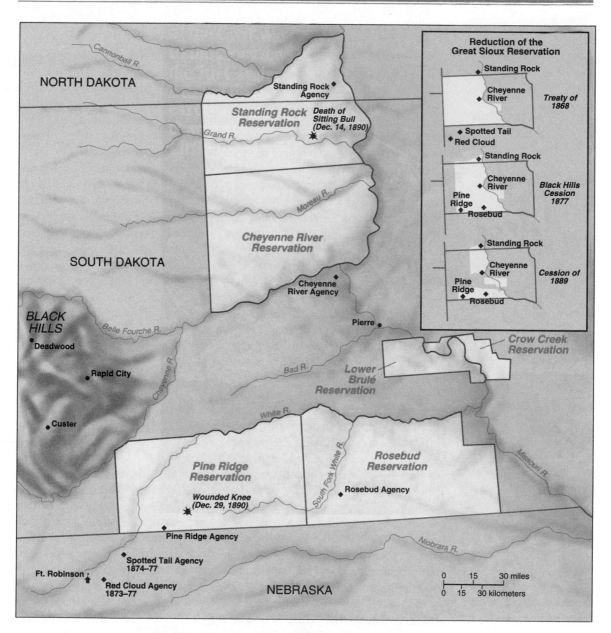

MAP 5.6 The Lakota Reservations, 1890

The Treaty of Fort Laramie in 1868 recognized the territory west of the Missouri River in South Dakota as the Great Sioux Reservation. Following the discovery of gold in the Black Hills and the defeat of the Sioux after the Little Big Horn, the United States systematically reduced Sioux territory, depriving the Lakotas of the sacred Black Hills and dividing them into half a dozen separate reservations. Based on maps by Harry Scott taken from The Indian Frontier of the American West, 1846–1890, *by Robert Utley. Copyright © 1984 University of New Mexico Press.*

people watched as settlers moved onto lands that less than twenty-five years earlier had been set apart for their "absolute and undisturbed use and occupation."

The Sioux never accepted the loss of the Black Hills.[8] In 1923 they filed suit with the United States Court of Claims demanding compensation. The Court of Claims dragged its feet until 1942 and then dismissed the claim. The United States Supreme Court refused to review the Court of Claims' decision. With the creation of the Indian Claims Commission in 1946, the Sioux tried again, but in 1954 the commission dismissed the case on the grounds that it had already been denied. In 1956, the Sioux fired their lawyer and had their claim reinstated on the basis that they had been represented by "inadequate counsel." Despite the Justice Department's attempt to secure a ruling granting "extraordinary relief" from continued litigation, in 1974 the Indian Claims Commission decided that the government had taken the land in violation of the Fifth Amendment because it had not paid just compensation. The commission awarded the Sioux $17.5 million plus interest. The government appealed and the Court of Claims reversed the decision on the basis of *res judicata,* that the claim had already been litigated and decided back in 1942. But the court declared that "a more ripe and rank case of dishonorable dealings will never, in all probability, be found in our history," and opened the door for the Sioux to seek compensation on the grounds of dishonorable dealings.[9] In 1978, Congress passed an act enabling the Court of Claims to rehear the case. The Court of Claims found that the United States had taken the Black Hills unconstitutionally and reinstated the $17.5 million award, plus interest of 5 percent, a total of $122.5 million. The Justice Department appealed the decision and, finally, in 1980, fifty-seven years after the Sioux first brought suit, the United States Supreme Court heard the Black Hills case. It found that the annexation act of 1877 constituted "a taking of tribal property which had been set aside by the treaty of Fort Laramie for the Sioux's exclusive occupation," and upheld the award.

The Sioux, having won their long-sought victory, turned down the money. T-shirts and bumper stickers echoed their position that "The Black Hills Are Not For Sale." Instead, Sioux people demanded that the United States return the Black Hills to them and pay the money as compensation for the billions of dollars of wealth that had been extracted and the damages done while whites illegally occupied the hills. In 1981, Russell Means and other activists established Yellow Thunder Camp in the Black Hills and announced it was the first step in reoccupying the land. Senator Bill Bradley of New Jersey and others proposed compromises, but most Sioux remained adamant that the Black Hills must be returned. The award remains uncollected and, with accumulated interest, stands at more than $400 million. The conflict between the Sioux and the United States remains unresolved.

▶ **Questions for Consideration**

By reprinting excerpts from the following treaty councils, as well as the final treaty itself, the following selections provide a sense of the concerns the Indians voiced—that the Bozeman Trail and forts be closed, that they receive trade and presents, and that they be able to continue living as Sioux—as well as the written articles by which they signified their agreement to live within reservation boundaries and embark on the "white man's road."

1. Which parts of the treaty are the ones the Lakota delegates are most likely not to have agreed to or understood?

2. What issues did Indians and treaty commissioners view differently?

3. What do the conversations and the text of the treaty suggest about the mechanics of treaty-making and the problems and pitfalls of translation?

Council with the Brulé Sioux, April 28, 1868

GENERAL SANBORN

We . . . offer you peace to save your nations from destruction. We speak the truth. But the truth is often unwelcome and grates harshly upon the ear. You will not believe me when I tell you that you can not protect yourselves from the white people. You will not believe me when I tell you that this military officer now here, a commissioner to meet you, had to use his authority to keep a great body of whites out of your country last year. You will not believe me when I tell you that the white soldiers whom you were killing and trying to kill last year were driving back the whites from your country and trying to save the country for you and to prevent your destruction. But all this is true, and you must have the protection of the President of the United States and his white soldiers or disappear from the earth.

We want you to see this yourselves, and not be compelled to believe it because we say so. That you may see how the case stands we request you to send some of your chiefs and braves to Washington now. Any of your friends among the whites that you desire may go along with you. You will then see and know what we know, and can determine what course it is best for your nations to take. You do not see the white soldiers when they are fighting the whites and keeping them out of your country, but only when they resist your attacks made upon them when marching along the road. The questions between you and the whites must soon be finally and forever settled.

Source: Vine Deloria, Jr. and Raymond DeMallie, intro., *Proceedings of the Great Peace Commission of 1867–1868* (Washington, D.C.: The Institute for the Development of Indian Law, 1975), 106–9, 117–20; Charles J. Kappler, ed., *Indian Affairs, Laws and Treaties,* 2 vols. (Washington: U.S. Government Printing Office, 1904), 2:998–1007.

If you continue to fight the whites you can not expect the President nor your friends among them to protect you in your country from those who are waiting to go there in large numbers. If you continue at war your country will soon be all overrun by white people. Military posts will be located on all the rivers. Your game and yourselves will be destroyed. This is the last effort of the President to make peace with you and save for you a country and home.

We therefore propose that you now make a treaty by which you can and will abide. By this treaty we will agree to protect you from the inroads of our people and keep them out of a portion of your present country described in the treaty. We shall agree to furnish you supplies in clothing and other useful articles while you continue to roam and hunt. We shall agree to furnish cattle, horses, cows, and implements to work the ground to each of your people as may at any time settle down and build a home and wish to live like the whites. Under this treaty you can roam and hunt while you remain at peace and game lasts; and when the game is gone you will have a home and means of supporting yourselves and your children. But you must understand that if peace is not now made all efforts on our part to make it are at an end.

We ask you now to consider this matter with the understanding of men and not with the malice of children; and when you reply speak your whole thoughts and feelings. If there are any here who do not design to remain at peace, we do not want them to sign any treaty. If there are any here who design to disturb the railroads or any of the ranches or white people south of the Platte River, we do not want them to sign any treaty, for such acts repeated will force the President to send soldiers into your country and to make war. But all who now conclude to make peace and abide by it, who intend to meet the whites in a friendly manner, and receive aid and protection from the President, we now request to sign the treaty tomorrow morning at 10 o'clock. This is all that we have been told to say to you.

GENERAL HARNEY

I am afraid you do not understand why we want to make peace. Perhaps you think we are afraid. You can not be such fools as that, I hope. We do not want to go to war with you because you are a small nation, a handful compared with us, and we want you to live. If we go to war we shall send out to meet you a large army. Suppose you kill the whole army, we have another to send in its place. A great many of you will be killed and you have nobody to take their places. We are kind to you here. You have true hearts and we want you to live. We have not been making war with you. You are at war with us. We have not commenced yet. I hope you will not drive us to war.

IRON SHELL (BRULÉ)

I am getting to be an old man. The talk you have just made is what I have always gone by since I was a young man. When I was about 30 years old I joined the sensible men and have been with them ever since. When I was a young man I looked for nothing good, but everything that was bad. I was out hunting buffalo, and I heard that there were some good men here waiting to see me and I came in. I heard that General Harney had left the warpath and was ready for peace, so I came in.

My father and grandfather used to be with the whites, and I have been with them, too. We used to treat them well, I do not recollect that there was any war while we were with the whites. We used to take pity on one another and did nothing bad to each other while we were together. I know that the whites are like the grass on the prairie. Anybody that takes anything from the whites must pay for it. You have come into my country without my consent and spread your soldiers all over it. I have looked around for the cause of the trouble and I can not see that my young men were the cause of it. All the bad things that have been done, you have made the road for it. That is the truth. I love the whites. You whites went all over my country, killing my young men, and disturbing everything in my country. My heart is not made out of rock, but of flesh, but I have a strong heart. All the bad deeds that have been done I have had no hand in, neither have any of our young men. I want to hear you give us good advice. I came here for that purpose. We helped you to stop this war between us and the whites. You have put us in misery; also these old traders whom the war has stopped. We want you to set us all right and put us back the same as in old times.

We want you to take away the forts from the country. That will leave big room for the Indians to live in. If you succeed about the forests all the game will come back and we will have plenty to eat. If you want the Indian to live do that and we will have a chance to live. One above us has created all of us, the whites the same as the Indians, and he will take pity on us. Our God has put us on earth to live in the way we do, to live on game. Our great father we depend on at Washington. We do not deliberate for ourselves, and we want him to take pity on us. Do you think that our God is for us the same as for the whites? I have prayed to God and asked him to make me succeed, and He has allowed it to me. I succeeded often. Your commissioners want to make peace and take pity on the Indians. Take away all these things if you intend to make peace, and we will live happy and be at peace. All we have is the land and the sky above. This war has set an example to our young men to make war on the whites. If it had not been for that we should have been at peace all the time.

You generally pick on bad white men to give them office which is the cause of our being put in trouble. From this our young men have learned all these bad things and we are in misery and have a hard time. Me and some others of the sensible men have been put in trouble by you. I have listened to your advice, General Sanborn, and I told the others to listen to you. You sent messengers to us last winter and we have come in to you. A few of us are inclined to do well out of way that are for

war, and we have pushed for you to make peace with you. The Single Horn [a chief, probably Lone Horn or One Horn] went to the Missouri. I brought a chief of the Sans Arcs to you, and I want you to send word by him to the Sans Arcs when he goes away.

You are passing over the foolish acts of our young men, and we are pleased at that. Try to get all the Indians in and give them good advice and it will be all right. Push, push as hard as you can, and in that way you will take great pity on me. I want to live. It goes slow, and there are a great many Indians who are pushing for peace. Go slow yourselves and you will succeed. Get through with the Brulés at once. I want to go home. You will have plenty of Indians in and will have enough to do. You will hear pretty much the same from the different tribes of Indians as you have heard from me. Three moons is too long in which to move the forts. I would like them to be moved before. Winter will come before that time.

GENERAL SANBORN

The forts will be removed as soon as possible.

IRON SHELL

Those forts are all that is in the way — wagons coming backward and forward. You have taken Spotted Tail away from me and have him to go around with you. That is good. I expect you will listen to him when he talks with you. You are right in bringing him here. There are a very few who are out yet. Often when you are persecuting me and the Indians with papers we do not get well thought of. I have one recommendation which I take good care of. I always talk to the whites in a good way and they generally listen to me. Today you tell us you will take pity on us. I have listened to it all. I will recollect all you have to say.

Our country is filling up with whites. Our great father has no sense; he lets our country be filled up. That is the way I think sometimes. Our great father is shutting up on us and making us a very small country. That is bad. For all that I have a strong heart. I have patience and pass over it, although you come over here and get all our gold, minerals, and skins. I pass over it all and do not get mad. I have always given the whites more than they have given me.

Yesterday you tell us we would have a council and last night I did not sleep; I was so glad. Now, I would like you to pick some good sensible young men, from one to four, and send them out, men who can be depended upon. I name Blue Horse, myself, and I want him to pick the others. We have been speaking very well together, and I am glad we get along so smoothly. The last thing I have to ask you about are the forts. This is sufficient and all right. We have got through talking. Give us our share of the goods and send them over to our village. We want to get back immediately as our children are crying for food. What you are doing with the Brulés will be a good example to the others. It will encourage them. We do not want to stay here and loaf upon you.

GENERAL HARNEY

We know very well that you have been treated very badly for years past. You have been cheated by everybody, and everybody has told lies to you, but now we want to commence anew. You have killed our people and have taken enough of our property and you ought to be satisfied. It is not the fault of your great father in Washington. He sends people out here that he thinks are honest, but they are people who cheat you and treat you badly. We will take care that you shall not be treated so any more. We will begin to move the forts as soon as possible. They will be removed as soon as the treaty is made with all the Indians. . . .

IRON SHELL

I will always sign any treaty you ask me to do, but you have always made away with them, broke them. The whites always break them, and that is the way that war has come up.

(The treaty was here signed by the chiefs and head soldiers of the Brulés.)

Council with the Oglala Sioux,
May 24–25, 1868

HIGH WOLF

I would like to know if the commissioners are in earnest in truth. I would like to know if the words are strong and binding and faithful. It is true that the posts will be removed? You are telling us that you are going to take pity on us. What are the posts that are going to be removed? You have been telling us that you are going to give us back our country. Why, then, do you interfere with our trading at this post?

AMERICAN HORSE

I would like to have my friends here to sign the treaty. I will sign, and if there is anything wrong afterwards I will watch the commissioners, and they will be the first one that I will whip.

KILLS THE BEAR

I will sign the treaty provided that the commissioners promise that they will remove the posts and give us a big present. I am a rascal, and if the whites don't fulfill this treaty I will show myself one.

FOUR BEARS

Look at me, commissioners, I am nobody. I sprang from Minnesota. I am binding myself to do what the chiefs are doing who are setting there.

I am the last to speak. All that you have said I have understood. I have watched you well. If you tell an untruth in saying that you will remove the posts, I will be even with you. The people at the posts make money and then go away. My wish is for the post to be abandoned. You say that you will protect us for thirty years, but I do not believe it.

Council with the Miniconjous,
May 27, 1868

ONE HORN

You and ourselves all wish for peace. I am the last to have a talk with you. I have not much to say to you. This Indian country we all (the Sioux Nation) claim as ours. I have never lost the place from my view. It is our home to come back to. I like to be able to trade here, although I will not give away my land. I don't ever remember ceding any of my land to anyone. If the whites had listened to me in times back, we should never have had any of this war. But they would not. Instead they established forts and drove away the game. I am 53 years old and do not remember ever having treated the whites wrongly. . . . The whites kept coming more and more through our country. I see that the whites blame the Indians, but it is you that acted wrong in the beginning. The Indians never went to your country and did wrong. This is our land, and yet you blame us for fighting for it. I remember your word that you told me. You told me whenever any wrong was done to tell you and you would make it right. I have told you that I did not like the military posts in my country, and that is what brought me over here. I would like the soldiers to leave as soon as possible that we may have plenty of game again.

You have come here in earnest to make peace, I believe. . . . There have been great lies told before you came, and it is often the fault of the interpreters. When you do send us interpreters, send good, honest men. . . .

Treaty with the Sioux — Brulé, Oglala,
Miniconjou, Yanktonai, Hunkpapa, Blackfeet, Cuthead,
Two Kettle, Sans Arcs, and Santee —
and Arapaho, 1868

Apr. 29, 1868.
15 Stats., 635.
  Ratified,
Feb. 16, 1869.
  Proclaimed,
Feb. 24, 1869.

Articles of a treaty made and concluded by and between Lieutenant-General William T. Sherman, General William S. Harney, General Alfred H. Terry, General C. C.

Augur, J. B. Henderson, Nathaniel G. Taylor, John B. Sanborn, and Samuel F. Tappan, duly appointed commissioners on the part of the United States, and the different bands of the Sioux Nation of Indians, by their chiefs and head-men, whose names are hereto subscribed, they being duly authorized to act in the premises.

ARTICLE 1. From this day forward all war between the parties to this agreement shall forever cease. The Government of the United States desires peace, and its honor is hereby pledged to keep it. The Indians desire peace, and they now pledge their honor to maintain it.

If bad men among the whites, or among other people subject to the authority of the United States, shall commit any wrong upon the person or property of the Indians, the United States will, upon proof made to the agent and forwarded to the Commissioner of Indian Affairs at Washington City, proceed at once to cause the offender to be arrested and punished according to the laws of the United States, and also re-imburse the injured person for the loss sustained.

If bad men among the Indians shall commit a wrong or depredation upon the person or property of any one, white, black, or Indian, subject to the authority of the United States, and at peace therewith, the Indians herein named solemnly agree that they will, upon proof made to their agent and notice by him, deliver up the wrongdoer to the United States, to be tried and punished according to its laws; and in case they wilfully refuse so to do, the person injured shall be re-imbursed for his loss from the annuities or other moneys due or to become due to them under this or other treaties made with the United States. And the President, on advising with the Commissioner of Indian Affairs, shall prescribe such rules and regulations for ascertaining damages under the provisions of this article as in his judgment may be proper. But no one sustaining loss while violating the provisions of this treaty or the laws of the United States shall be re-imbursed therefor.

ARTICLE 2. The United States agrees that the following district of country, to wit, viz: commencing on the east bank of the Missouri River where the forty-sixth parallel of north latitude crosses the same, thence along low-water mark down said east bank to a point opposite where the northern line of the State of Nebraska strikes the river, thence west across said river, and along the northern line of Nebraska to the one hundred and fourth degree of longitude west from Greenwich, thence north on said meridian to a point where the forty-sixth parallel of north latitude intercepts the same, thence due east along said parallel to the place of beginning; and in addition thereto, all existing reservations on the east bank of said river shall be, and the same is, set apart for the absolute and undisturbed use and occupation of the Indians herein named, and for such other friendly tribes or individual Indians as from time to time they may be willing, with the consent of the United States, to admit amongst them; and the United States now solemnly

Margin notes:
War to cease and peace to be kept.

Offenders against the Indians to be arrested, etc.

Wrongdoers against the whites to be punished.

Damages.

Reservation boundaries.

Certain persons not to enter or reside thereon.

agrees that no persons except those herein designated and authorized so to do, and except such officers, agents and employés of the Government as may be authorized to enter upon Indian reservations in discharge of duties enjoined by law, shall ever be permitted to pass over, settle upon, or reside in the territory described in this article, or in such territory as may be added to this reservation for the use of said Indians, and henceforth they will and do hereby relinquish all claims or right in and to any portion of the United States or Territories, except such as is embraced within the limits aforesaid, and except as hereinafter provided.

Additional arable land to be added, if, etc.

ARTICLE 3. If it should appear from actual survey or other satisfactory examination of said tract of land that it contains less than one hundred and sixty acres of tillable land for each person who, at the time, may be authorized to reside on it under the provisions of this treaty, and a very considerable number of such persons shall be disposed to commence cultivating the soil as farmers, the United States agrees to set apart, for the use of said Indians, as herein provided, such additional quantity of arable land, adjoining to said reservation, or as near to the same as it can be obtained, as may be required to provide the necessary amount.

Buildings on reservation.

ARTICLE 4. The United States agrees, at its own proper expense, to construct at some place on the Missouri River, near the center of said reservation, where timber and water may be convenient, the following buildings, to wit: a warehouse, a store-room for the use of the agent in storing goods belonging to the Indians, to cost not less than twenty-five hundred dollars; an agency-building for the residence of the agent, to cost not exceeding three thousand dollars; a residence for the physician, to cost not more than three thousand dollars; and five other buildings, for a carpenter, farmer, blacksmith, miller, and engineer, each to cost not exceeding two thousand dollars; also a school-house or mission-building, so soon as a sufficient number of children can be induced by the agent to attend school, which shall not cost exceeding five thousand dollars.

The United States agrees further to cause to be erected on said reservation, near the other buildings herein authorized, a good steam circular-saw mill, with a grist-mill and shingle-machine attached to the same, to cost not exceeding eight thousand dollars.

Agent's residence, office, and duties.

ARTICLE 5. The United States agrees that the agent for said Indians shall in the future make his home at the agency-building; that he shall reside among them, and keep an office open at all times for the purpose of prompt and diligent inquiry into such matters of complaint by and against the Indians as may be presented for investigation under the provisions of their treaty stipulations, as also for the faithful discharge of other duties enjoined on him by law. In all cases of depredation on person or property he shall cause the evidence to be taken in writing and forwarded, together with his findings, to the Commissioner of Indian Affairs, whose decision, subject to the revision of the Secretary of the Interior, shall be binding on the parties to this treaty.

Heads of families may select lands for farming.

ARTICLE 6. If any individual belonging to said tribes of Indians, or legally incorporated with them, being the head of a family, shall desire to commence farming, he shall have the privilege to select, in the presence and with the assistance of the agent then in charge, a tract of land within said reservation, not exceeding three hundred and twenty acres in extent, which tract, when so selected, certified, and recorded in the "land-book," as herein directed, shall cease to be held in common, but the same may be occupied and held in the exclusive possession of the person selecting it, and of his family, so long as he or they may continue to cultivate it.

Others may select land for cultivation.

Any person over eighteen years of age, not being the head of a family, may in like manner select and cause to be certified to him or her, for purposes of cultivation, a quantity of land not exceeding eighty acres in extent, and thereupon be entitled to the exclusive possession of the same as above directed.

Certificates.

For each tract of land so selected a certificate, containing a description thereof and the name of the person selecting it, with a certificate endorsed thereon that the same has been recorded, shall be delivered to the party entitled to it, by the agent, after the same shall have been recorded by him in a book to be kept in his office, subject to inspection, which said book shall be known as the "Sioux Land-Book."

Surveys.

The President may, at any time, order a survey of the reservation, and, when so surveyed, Congress shall provide for protecting the rights of said settlers in their improvements, and may fix the character of the title held by each. The United States may pass such laws on the subject of alienation and descent of property between the Indians and their descendants as may be thought proper. And it is further stipulated that any male Indians, over eighteen years of age, of any band or tribe that is or shall hereafter become a party to this treaty, who now is or who shall hereafter become a resident or occupant of any reservation or Territory not included in the tract of country designated and described in this treaty for the permanent home of the Indians, which is not mineral land, nor reserved by the United States for special purposes other than Indian occupation, and who shall have made improvements thereon of the value of two hundred dollars or more, and continuously occupied the same as a homestead for the term of three years, shall be entitled to receive from the United States a patent for one hundred and sixty acres of land including his said improvements, the same to be in the form of the legal subdivisions of the surveys of the public lands. Upon ap-

Alienation and descent of property.

Certain Indians may receive patents for 160 acres of land.

plication in writing, substained [sic] by the proof of two disinterested witnesses, made to the register of the local land-office when the land sought to be entered is within a land district, and when the tract sought to be entered is not in any land district, then upon said application and proof being made to the Commissioner of the General Land-Office, and the right of such Indian or Indians to enter such tract or tracts of land shall accrue and be perfect from the date of his first improvements thereon, and shall continue as long as he continues his residence and improvements, and no longer. And any Indian or Indians receiving a patent for land under the foregoing provisions, shall thereby and from thenceforth become and be a citizen of the United States, and be entitled to all the privileges and immunities of such citizens, and shall, at the same time, retain all his rights to benefits accruing to Indians under this treaty.

Such Indians receiving patents to become citizens of the United States.

Education.

ARTICLE 7. In order to insure the civilization of the Indians entering into this treaty, the necessity of education is admitted, especially of such of them as are or may be settled on said agricultural reservations, and they therefore pledge themselves to compel their children, male and female, between the ages of six and sixteen years, to attend school; and it is hereby made the duty of the agent for said Indians to see that this stipulation is strictly complied with; and the United States agrees that for every thirty children between said ages

Children to attend school.

Schoolhouses and teachers.

who can be induced or compelled to attend school, a house shall be provided and a teacher competent to teach the elementary branches of an English education shall be furnished, who will reside among said Indians and faithfully discharge his or her duties as a teacher. The provisions of this article to continue for not less than twenty years.

Seeds and agricultural implements.

ARTICLE 8. When the head of a family or lodge shall have selected lands and received his certificate as above directed, and the agent shall be satisfied that he intends in good faith to commence cultivating the soil for a living, he shall be entitled to receive seeds and agricultural implements for the first year, not exceeding in value one hundred dollars, and for each succeeding year he shall continue to farm, for a period of three years more, he shall be entitled to receive seeds and implements as aforesaid, not exceeding in value twenty-five dollars.

Instructions in farming.

And it is further stipulated that such persons as commence farming shall receive instruction from the farmer herein provided for, and whenever more than one hundred persons shall enter upon the cultivation of the soil, a second blacksmith shall be provided, with such iron, steel, and other material as may be needed.

Second blacksmith.

Physician, farmer, etc., may be withdrawn.

ARTICLE 9. At any time after ten years from the making of this treaty, the United States shall have the privilege of withdrawing the physician, farmer, blacksmith, carpenter, engineer, and miller herein provided for, but in case of such

Additional appropriation in such cases.

withdrawal, an additional sum thereafter of ten thousand dollars per annum shall be devoted to the education of said Indians, and the Commissioner of Indian Affairs shall, upon careful inquiry into their condition, make such rules and regulations for the expenditure of said sum as will best promote the educational and moral improvement of said tribes.

Delivery of goods in lieu of money or other annuities.

ARTICLE 10. In lieu of all sums of money or other annuities provided to be paid to the Indians herein named, under any treaty or treaties heretofore made, the United States agrees to deliver at the agency-house on the reservation herein named, on or before the first day of August of each year, for thirty years, the following articles, to wit:

Clothing.

For each male person over fourteen years of age, a suit of good substantial woolen clothing, consisting of coat, pantaloons, flannel shirt, hat, and a pair of home-made socks.

For each female over twelve years of age, a flannel skirt, or the goods necessary to make it, a pair of woolen hose, twelve yards of calico, and twelve yards of cotton domestics.

For the boys and girls under the ages named, such flannel and cotton goods as may be needed to make each a suit as aforesaid, together with a pair of woolen hose for each.

Census.

And in order that the Commissioner of Indian Affairs may be able to estimate properly for the articles herein named, it shall be the duty of the agent each year to forward to him a full and exact census of the Indians, on which the estimate from year to year can be based.

Other necessary articles.

And in addition to the clothing herein named, the sum of ten dollars for each person entitled to the beneficial effects of this treaty shall be annually appropriated for a period of thirty years, while such persons roam and hunt, and twenty dollars for each person who engages in farming, to be used by the Secretary of the Interior in the purchase of such articles as from time to time the condition and necessities of the Indians may indicate to be proper. And if within the

Appropriation to continue for thirty years.

thirty years, at any time, it shall appear that the amount of money needed for clothing under this article can be appropriated to better uses for the Indians named herein, Congress may, by law, change the appropriation to other purposes; but in no event shall the amount of this appropriation be withdrawn or discontinued for the period named. And the President shall annually detail an officer of the Army

Army officer to attend the delivery.

to be present and attest the delivery of all the goods herein named to the Indians, and he shall inspect and report on the quantity and quality of the goods and the manner of their delivery. And it is hereby expressly stipulated that each Indian over the age of four years, who shall have removed to and settled permanently upon said reservation and complied with the stipulations of this treaty, shall be entitled to receive from the United

States, for the period of four years after he shall have settled upon said reservation, one pound of meat and one pound of flour per day, provided the Indians cannot furnish their own subsistence at an earlier date. And it is further stipulated that the United States will furnish and deliver to each lodge of Indians or family of persons legally incorporated with them, who shall remove to the reservation herein described and commence farming, one good American cow, and one good well-broken pair of American oxen within sixty days after such lodge or family shall have so settled upon said reservation.

ARTICLE 11. In consideration of the advantages and benefits conferred by this treaty, and the many pledges of friendship by the United States, the tribes who are parties to this agreement hereby stipulate that they will relinquish all right to occupy permanently the territory outside their reservation as herein defined, but yet reserve the right to hunt on any lands north of North Platte, and on the Republican Fork of the Smoky Hill River, so long as the buffalo may range thereon in such numbers as to justify the chase. And they, the said Indians, further expressly agree:

1st. That they will withdraw all opposition to the construction of the railroads now being built on the plains.

2d. That they will permit the peaceful construction of any railroad not passing over their reservation as herein defined.

3d. That they will not attack any persons at home, or travelling, nor molest or disturb any wagon-trains, coaches, mules, or cattle belonging to the people of the United States, or to persons friendly therewith.

4th. They will never capture, or carry off from the settlements, white women or children.

5th. They will never kill or scalp white men, nor attempt to do them harm.

6th. They withdraw all pretence of opposition to the construction of the railroad now being built along the Platte River and westward to the Pacific Ocean, and they will not in future object to the construction of railroads, wagon-roads, mail-stations, or other works of utility or necessity, which may be ordered or permitted by the laws of the United States. But should such roads or other works be constructed on the lands of their reservation, the Government will pay the tribe whatever amount of damage may be assessed by three disinterested commissioners to be appointed by the President for that purpose, one of said commissioners to be a chief or headman of the tribe.

7th. They agree to withdraw all opposition to the military posts or roads now established south of the North Platte River, or that may be established, not in violation of treaties heretofore made or hereafter to be made with any of the Indian tribes.

ARTICLE 12. No treaty for the cession of any portion or part of

Margin notes:

Meat and flour.

Cows and oxen.

Right to occupy territory outside of the reservation surrendered.

Right to hunt reserved.

Agreements as to railroads.

Emigrants, etc.

Women and children.

White men.

Pacific Railroad, wagon roads, etc.

Damages for crossing their reservation.

Military posts and roads.

No treaty for cession of reservation to be valid unless, etc.

the reservation herein described which may be held in common shall be of any validity or force as against the said Indians, unless executed and signed by at least three-fourths of all the adult male Indians, occupying or interested in the same; and no cession by the tribe shall be understood or construed in such manner as to deprive, without his consent, any individual member of the tribe of his rights to any tract of land selected by him, as provided in Article 6 of this treaty.

United States to furnish physician, teachers, etc. **ARTICLE 13.** The United States hereby agrees to furnish annually to the Indians the physician, teachers, carpenter, miller, engineer, farmer, and blacksmiths as herein contemplated, and that such appropriations shall be made from time to time, on the estimates of the Secretary of the Interior, as will be sufficient to employ such persons.

Presents for crops. **ARTICLE 14.** It is agreed that the sum of five hundred dollars annually, for three years from date, shall be expended in presents to the ten persons of said tribe who in the judgment of the agent may grow the most valuable crops for the respective year.

Reservation to be permanent home of tribes. **ARTICLE 15.** The Indians herein named agree that when the agency house or other buildings shall be constructed on the reservation named they will regard said reservation their permanent home, and they will make no permanent settlement elsewhere; but they shall have the right, subject to the con-

ditions and modifications of this treaty, to hunt, as stipulated in Article 11 hereof.

Unceded Indian territory. **ARTICLE 16.** The United States hereby agrees and stipulates that the country north of the North Platte River and east of the summit of the Big Horn Mountains shall be held and considered to be unceded Indian territory, and also stipulates Not to be occupied by whites, etc. and agrees that no white person or persons shall be permitted to settle upon or occupy any portion of the same; or without the consent of the Indians first had and obtained, to pass through the same; and it is further agreed by the United States that within ninety days after the conclusion of peace with all the bands of the Sioux Nation, the military posts now established in the territory in this article named shall be abandoned, and that the road leading to them and by them to the settlements in the Territory of Montana shall be closed.

Effect of this treaty upon former treaties. **ARTICLE 17.** It is hereby expressly understood and agreed by and between the respective parties to this treaty that the execution of this treaty and its ratification by the United States Senate shall have the effect, and shall be construed as abrogating and annulling all treaties and agreements heretofore entered into between the respective parties hereto, so far as such treaties and agreements obligate the United States to furnish and provide money, clothing, or other articles of property to such Indians and bands of Indians as become parties to this treaty, but no further.

References

1. Vine Deloria, Jr. and Raymond DeMallie, intro., *Proceedings of the Great Peace Commission of 1867–1868* (Washington, D.C.: The Institute for the Development of Indian Law, 1975), 103.
2. James C. Olson, *Red Cloud and the Sioux Problem* (Lincoln: University of Nebraska Press, 1965), 74–75.
3. John S. Gray, *Centennial Campaign: The Sioux War of 1876* (Norman: University of Oklahoma Press, 1988), 11, 15.
4. For an excellent discussion of Indian treaties, and of the 1851 Treaty of Fort Laramie in particular, see Raymond J. DeMallie, "Touching the Pen: Plains Indian Treaty Councils in Ethnohistorical Perspective," in Frederick C. Luebke, ed., *Ethnicity on the Great Plains* (Lincoln: University of Nebraska Press, 1980), 38–51.
5. Quoted in Edward Lazarus, *Black Hills/White Justice: The Sioux Nation Versus the United States, 1775 to the Present* (New York: HarperCollins, 1991), 61–62. A full version of Red Cloud's Cooper Union speech as reported in the *New York Times* is in Wayne Moquin and Charles Van Doren, eds., *Great Documents in American Indian History* (New York: Praeger Publishers, 1973), 211–13.
6. *Indian Country Today,* vol. 16, issue 15 (Oct. 7–14, 1996), A2 (incorrectly identified as George Whirl Wind Horse).
7. Quoted in Robert M. Utley, *The Last Days of the Sioux Nation* (New Haven: Yale University Press, 1963), 53.
8. For a thorough account of the history of the Black Hills land claim, see Lazarus, *Black Hills/White Justice,* on which this survey relies.
9. Quoted in Lazarus, *Black Hills/White Justice,* 344.

Suggested Readings

Deloria, Vine, Jr., and Raymond DeMallie, intro. *Proceedings of the Great Peace Commission of 1867–1868* (Washington, D.C.: The Institute for the Development of Indian Law, 1975).

Getches, David H., and Charles F. Wilkinson, and Robert A. Williams, Jr. *Cases and Materials on Federal Indian Law,* 4th ed. (St. Paul, Minn.: West Group, 1998).

Lazarus, Edward. *Black Hills/White Justice: The Sioux Nation Versus the United States, 1775 to the Present* (New York: HarperCollins, 1991).

Olson, James C. *Red Cloud and the Sioux Problem* (Lincoln: University of Nebraska Press, 1965).

Ortiz, Roxanne Dunbar. *The Great Sioux Nation: Sitting in Judgment on America: An Oral History of the Sioux Nation and Its Struggle for Sovereignty* (New York: Random House, 1977).

Price, Catherine. *The Oglala People, 1841–1879: A Political History* (Lincoln: University of Nebraska Press, 1996).

Chief Joseph's Plea for Freedom

W hen Lewis and Clark stumbled down from the Lolo Trail across the Bitterroot Mountains on their way west to the Columbia River in the fall of 1805, they met the Nee-me-poo Indians, whom the French called Nez Percés or pierced noses. The Nez Percés had heard of Americans but few if any had seen them. They could have killed the hungry and exhausted explorers, but instead they welcomed them, fed them, and helped them on their way. Lewis and Clark developed respect and admiration for them. In part, the Nez Percés were extending traditional hospitality to strangers; in part, they were eager to receive the trade, and especially the guns, that Lewis and Clark promised to bring them in return. Like their Shoshoni neighbors, the Nez Percés were hard pressed by well-armed Blackfeet who ranged to their north and kept British guns out of their reach.

The Nez Percés lived where the present states of Washington, Idaho, and Oregon meet. After they acquired horses early in the eighteenth century, they built up huge herds and gained a reputation as skilled riders and breeders. From their first meeting with Americans in 1805, they pursued policies of peaceful coexistence with the newcomers. They traded with American fur traders and attended trappers' rendezvous in the 1820s. In 1831, they sent a delegation to St. Louis searching for the "book of heaven." Presbyterian missionaries Reverend Henry Spalding and his wife answered their call and went to live and work among the Nez Percés; other missionaries followed.

In 1855, the Nez Percés signed a treaty with Governor Isaac Stevens of Washington Territory, which set aside a large reservation for the tribe. But immigrants pressed in evergrowing numbers and miners encroached on the reservation after gold was discovered in 1860. In 1863, the Americans negotiated a new treaty with a chief named Lawyer, assigning the Nez Percés to a new, drastically smaller reservation at Lapwai on the Clearwater River in Idaho. Like most of the Nez Percé chiefs, Tu-ke-kas, whom the whites called Old Joseph, refused to sign the treaty; his band continued to live in the Wallowa valley in northeastern Oregon. Just before he died in 1871, Old Joseph made his son promise never to sell his homeland.

Young Joseph came under almost immediate pressure to break his promise. Settlers encroached on the Wallowa valley and the United States dispatched commissioners, first to investigate the situation and then to persuade Joseph to sell and join the "treaty party" on the Lapwai reservation. The commissioners, led by Oliver Otis Howard, a one-armed Civil War general and founder of

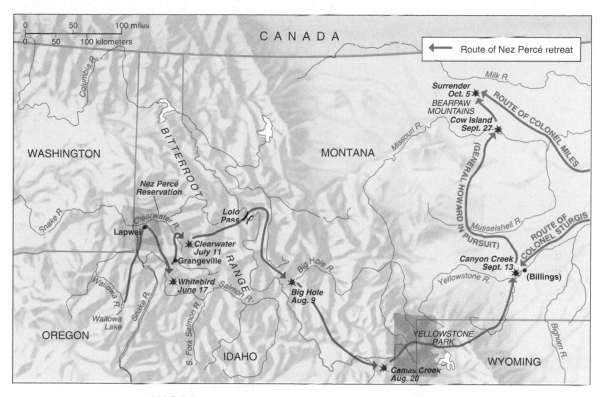

MAP 5.7 The Nez Percé Odyssey, 1877
Nez Percé men, women, and children trekked 1,500 miles and fought off pursuing American armies in a desperate but ultimately unsuccessful bid to reach freedom in Canada.

Howard University for African American students, declared that the Nez Percés who had not signed the 1863 treaty must come into the reservation or be moved there by force. The Indians pleaded to be allowed to remain on their homelands but Howard lost patience and had one old chief, Toohoolhoolzote, arrested and thrown into the guardhouse. The Nez Percés were given until April 1, 1877, to complete the move. According to Nez Percé warrior Yellow Chief, "That was what brought war, the arrest of this chief and showing us the rifle."[1]

Despite his promise to his father, Joseph persuaded his angry people to move rather than go to war. "None of the chiefs wanted war," said Yellow Wolf.[2] But events were moving beyond their control. Three young warriors killed some men along the Salmon River in revenge for the murder of a chief called Tipyahlanah Siskon, or Eagle Robe. The U.S. army was quick to respond and attacked the Nez Percés at White Bird Canyon. The Nez Percés routed the soldiers.

It was the first of a series of embarrassing defeats for the United States, and the beginning of a fifteen-hundred mile odyssey for the Nez Percés. Ably led by Joseph, his younger brother Ollokot, and the war chief Looking Glass, some eight hundred Nez Percés fled east. Fighting off Howard's troops, they crossed the Bitterroot Mountains into Montana where they hoped to find refuge with the Crows. They rested at the Big Hole River but Colonel John Gibbon struck them in a surprise dawn attack, killing men, women, and children. The warriors rallied and fought off Gibbon's troops until their families could escape. With American troops at their backs and news that Crow scouts were riding for the army, the Nez Percés decided to head for Canada. Passing through the newly created park, they frightened tourists in Yellowstone. They defeated General Samuel Sturgis's cavalry at Canyon Creek. Time and again they fended off pursuing troops. Reaching the Bear Paw Mountains, about thirty miles from the Canadian border, they halted in exhaustion, confident they had shaken off their pursuers.

But General Nelson Miles and six hundred men were rushing to head them off. Miles's Cheyenne scouts found the Nez Percés's tepees and Miles attacked immediately. Caught off guard, the Nez Percés were split into groups, and lost most of their horses. Ollokot and Toohoolhoolzote died in the fighting. The survivors dug rifle pits and settled down for a siege. It began to snow. "Most of our few warriors left from the Big Hole had been swept as leaves before the storm," recalled Yellow Wolf. He looked around: "Children crying with cold. No fire. There could be no light. Everywhere the crying, the death wail. . . . I felt the coming end."[3] Looking Glass was killed. White Bird and about three hundred people slipped past the army and made it to Canada. After five days of fighting and a botched attempt to take him prisoner, Joseph finally accepted Miles's entreaties to surrender. His surrender speech, as reported by Lieutenant Charles Erskin Wood, has become famous.

> "I am tired of fighting," he said as he handed Miles his rifle. "Our chiefs are killed. Looking Glass is dead. Toohoolhoolzote is dead. The old men are all dead. It is the young men who say yes or no. He who led the young men [Ollokot] is dead. It is cold and we have no blankets. The little children are freezing to death. . . . I want to have time to look for my children, and see how many of them I can find. Maybe I shall find them among the dead. Hear me my chiefs! I am tired. My heart is sick and sad. From where the sun now stands, I will fight no more forever."[4]

The Nez Percés's epic trek and Joseph's dignified conduct and tragic speech all captured public attention. Newspapers across the country carried reports of the war and of the Nez Percés's military exploits. Even their adversaries expressed admiration. General William Tecumseh Sherman admitted that they "displayed a courage and skill that elicited universal praise; they abstained from scalping, let captive women go free, did not commit indiscriminate murder of

Chief Joseph
Joseph (c. 1840–1904) is seen here shortly after his surrender to General Miles in 1877. Handsome and dignified in defeat, Joseph came to symbolize the heroic resistance of the Nez Percés. National Anthropological Archives, Smithsonian Institution.

peaceful families which is usual, and fought with almost scientific skill, using advance and rear guards, skirmish-lines and field-fortifications."[5] Ollokot and Looking Glass had been the masterminds behind the military retreat, but they were dead. Joseph, handsome and dignified in defeat, became a celebrity.

Nevertheless, the Nez Percés were betrayed again. Contrary to Miles's assurances that they would be allowed to return home if they surrendered, they were loaded on trains and sent first to Fort Leavenworth, then to Indian Territory (Oklahoma). Miles's role in the betrayal is uncertain (he argued consistently that the Nez Percés be allowed to return home, but the promises made and broken when Joseph surrendered to him are strikingly similar to the promises made and broken when Geronimo surrendered to him seven years later). Secretary of the Interior Carl Schurz and Commissioner of Indian Affairs Ezra Hayt concurred with General Sherman and General Philip Sheridan that the Nez Percés should not be allowed to return home.

Four hundred eighteen Nez Percés arrived at Fort Leavenworth in late November and were put in a winter camp close to the Missouri River. Commissioner Hayt described it as "the worst possible place that could have been selected"; another observer compared what he saw to the horrors of Andersonville, the Confederate prison camp during the Civil War. "We were not badly treated in captivity," said Yellow Wolf. "Only the climate killed many of us. All the newborn babies died, and many of the old people too. It was the climate. Everything so different from our old homes. No mountains, no springs, no clear running rivers. We called where we were Eeikish Pah [Hot Place]."[6] In the summer of 1878, the Nez Percés were moved to the northeastern corner of present-day Oklahoma. Huddled in refugee camps, they endured hunger, misery, and malaria. By the end of the year, reported Hayt, they had "lost by death more than one-quarter of their entire number."[7]

Joseph tried to secure relief for his people. In January 1879, he and another chief, Yellow Bull, were permitted to travel to Washington to plead that the Nez Percés be sent home. Arthur Chapman accompanied them as interpreter. Chapman was a rancher who had fought against the Nez Percés during the war but he had an Indian wife, spoke Nez Percé fluently, and was Joseph's friend. They met President Hayes and Secretary Schurz and received a sympathetic hearing in the East. Joseph made a two-hour speech to a gathering of cabinet members, congressmen and others in Lincoln Hall and received a standing ovation. In March he met with Commissioner Hayt. A month later his speech was published in the *North American Review*. Some critics have suggested that Chapman, or even the periodical's editor, embellished Joseph's words, but the views are clearly Nez Percé. Joseph's speech focused public attention on the injustices suffered by the Nez Percés, but Western politicians effectively resisted any efforts to let them go home.

In 1885, the Nez Percés were finally allowed to return to the Northwest. One group of about 188 people who agreed to become Christians went to the Lapwai agency. The others, about 150 people including Joseph, were sent to the Colville Reservation in Washington Territory, where they joined San Poils, Okanogans, Colvilles, Palouses, Wenatchees, and other Indians. Joseph continued the fight to be allowed to return home to the land where his father had died, the land he had promised never to sell. In 1897, he traveled to Washington again to plead his case with President McKinley. In 1903, he was back and met with President Theodore Roosevelt. In 1904, he had his photograph taken with his old enemy, General Howard. But Joseph did not get to return home. He died that fall, at sixty-four, probably of a heart attack. The agency doctor said he died of a broken heart. Joseph was buried on the Colville Reservation.

▶ Questions for Consideration

What do the extracts from Chief Joseph's speech tell about the war's causes and the conduct of United States Indian policy? "One side of war story is that told by the white man," said Yellow Chief. In his old age he told "the Indian side" of "the war we did not want," exposing the falsehoods reported by General Miles and others. That was in the 1930s, more than fifty years after the war, and Yellow Wolf gave his story for "the young generation behind me." Joseph gave his version of the war less than eighteen months after its end, to the generation that fought against him.

1. What does it reveal about the options and strategies, and the role and authority of an Indian leader in a time of crisis?

2. To what extent does Joseph seem to be speaking in a context and terms defined by whites?

3. How effectively does Joseph convey "the Indian side . . . of the war we did not want"?

CHIEF JOSEPH
"An Indian's View of Indian Affairs" (1879)

The United States claimed they had bought all the Nez Percés country outside the Lapwai Reservation, from Lawyer and other chiefs, but we continued to live on this land in peace until eight years ago, when white men began to come inside the bounds my father had set. We warned them against this great wrong, but they would not leave our land, and some bad blood was raised. The white men represented that we were going upon the warpath. They reported many things that were false.

The United States Government again asked for a treaty council. My father had become blind and feeble. He could no longer speak for his people. It was then that I took my father's place as chief. In this council I made my first speech to white men. I said to the agent who held the council:

"I did not want to come to this council, but I came hoping that we could save blood. The white man has no right to come here and take our country. We have never accepted any presents from the Government. Neither Lawyer nor any other chief had authority to sell this land. It has always belonged to my people. It came unclouded to them from our fathers, and we will defend this land as long as a drop of Indian blood warms the hearts of our men."

The agent said he had orders, from the Great White Chief at Washington, for us to go upon the Lapwai Reservation, and that if we obeyed he would help us in many ways. "You must move to the agency," he said. I answered him: "I will not. I do not need your help; we have plenty, and we are contented and happy if the white man will let us alone. The reservation is too small for so many people with all their stock. You can keep your presents; we can go to your towns and pay for all we need; we have plenty of horses and cattle to sell, and we won't have any help from you; we are free now; we can go where we please. Our fathers were born here. Here they lived, here they died, here are their graves. We will never leave them." The agent went away, and we had peace for a little while.

Soon after this my father sent for me. I saw he was dying. I took his hand in mine. He said: "My son, my body is returning to my mother earth, and my spirit is going very soon to see the Great Spirit Chief. When I am gone, think of your country. You are the chief of these people. They look to you to guide them. Always remember that your father never sold this country. You must stop your ears whenever you are asked to sign a treaty selling your home. A few years more, and white men will be all around you. They have their eyes on this land. My son, never forget my dying words. This country holds your father's body. Never sell the bones of your father and your mother." I pressed my father's hand and told him I would protect his grave with my life. My father smiled and passed away to the spirit land.

I buried him in that beautiful valley of winding waters. I love that land more than all the rest of the world. A man who would not love his father's grave is worse than a wild animal.

For a short time we lived quietly. But this could not last. White men had found gold in the mountains around the land of winding water. They stole many horses from us, and we could not get them back because we were Indians. The white men told lies for each other. They drove off a great many of our cattle. Some white men branded our young cattle so they could claim them. We had no friend who would plead our cause before the law councils. It seemed to me that some of the white

Source: "An Indian's View of Indian Affairs," *North American Review*, April 1879.

men in Wallowa were doing these things on purpose to get up a war. They knew that we were not strong enough to fight them. I labored hard to avoid trouble and bloodshed. We gave up some of our country to the white men, thinking that then we could have peace. We were mistaken. The white man would not let us alone. We could have avenged our wrongs many times, but we did not. Whenever the Government has asked us to help them against other Indians, we have never refused. When the white men were few and we were strong we could have killed them all off, but the Nez Percés wished to live at peace.

If we have not done so, we have not been to blame. I believe that the old treaty has never been correctly reported. If we ever owned the land we own it still, for we never sold it. In the treaty councils the commissioners have claimed that our country had been sold to the Government. Suppose a white man should come to me and say, "Joseph, I like your horses, and I want to buy them." I say to him, "No, my horses suit me, I will not sell them." Then he goes to my neighbor, and says to him: "Joseph has some good horses. I want to buy them, but he refuses to sell." My neighbor answers, "Pay me the money, and I will sell you Joseph's horses." The white man returns to me, and says, "Joseph, I have bought your horses, and you must let me have them." If we sold our lands to the Government, this is the way they were bought.

On account of the treaty made by the other bands of the Nez Percés, the white men claimed my lands. We were troubled greatly by white men crowding over the line. Some of these were good men, and we lived on peaceful terms with them, but they were not all good.

Nearly every year the agent came over from Lapwai and ordered us on to the reservation. We always replied that we were satisfied to live in Wallowa. We were careful to refuse presents or annuities which he offered.

Through all the years since the white men came to Wallowa we have been threatened and taunted by them and the treaty Nez Percés. They

have given us no rest. We have had a few good friends among white men, and they have always advised my people to bear these taunts without fighting. Our young men were quick-tempered, and I have had great trouble in keeping them from doing rash things. I have carried a heavy load on my back ever since I was a boy. I learned then that we were but few, while the white men were many, and that we could not hold our own with them. We were like deer. They were like grizzly bears. We had a small country. Their country was large. We were contented to let things remain as the Great Spirit Chief made them. They were not; and would change the rivers and mountains if they did not suit them.

Year after year we have been threatened, but no war was made upon my people until General Howard came to our country two years ago and told us he was the white war-chief of all that country. He said: "I have a great many soldiers at my back. I am going to bring them up here, and then I will talk to you again. I will not let white men laugh at me the next time I come. The country belongs to the Government, and I intend to make you go upon the reservation." . . .

I knew I had never sold my country, and that I had no land in Lapwai; but I did not want bloodshed. I did not want my people killed. I did not want anybody killed. Some of my people had been murdered by white men, and the white murderers were never punished for it. I told General Howard about this, and again said I wanted no war. I wanted the people who lived upon the lands I was to occupy at Lapwai to have time to gather their harvest.

I said in my heart that, rather than have war, I would give up my country. I would give up my father's grave. I would give up everything rather than have the blood of white men upon the hands of my people.

General Howard refused to allow me more than thirty days to move my people and their stock. I am sure that he began to prepare for war at once.

When I returned to Wallowa I found my people very much excited upon discovering that the soldiers were already in the Wallowa Valley. We held a council and decided to move immediately, to avoid bloodshed.

Too-hool-hool-suit, who felt outraged by his imprisonment, talked for war, and made many of my young men willing to fight rather than be driven like dogs from the land where they were born. He declared that blood alone would wash out the disgrace General Howard had put upon him. It required a strong heart to stand up against such talk, but I urged my people to be quiet, and not to begin a war.

We gathered all the stock we could find, and made an attempt to move. We left many of our horses and cattle in Wallowa, and we lost several hundred in crossing the river. All of my people succeeded in getting across in safety. Many of the Nez Percés came together in Rocky Cañon to hold a grand council. I went with all my people. This council lasted ten days. There was a great deal of war talk, and a great deal of excitement. There was one young brave present whose father had been killed by a white man five years before. This man's blood was bad against white men, and he left the council calling for revenge.

Again I counseled peace, and I thought the danger was past. We had not complied with General Howard's order because we could not, but we intended to do so as soon as possible. I was leaving the council to kill beef for my family, when news came that the young man whose father has been killed had gone out with several other hot-blooded young braves and killed four white men. He rode up to the council and shouted: "Why do you sit here like women? The war has begun already." I was deeply grieved. All the lodges were moved except my brother's and my own. I saw clearly that the war was upon us when I learned that my young men had been secretly buying ammunition. I heard then that Too-hool-hool-suit, who had been imprisoned by General Howard, had succeeded in organizing a war party. I knew

that their acts would involve all my people. I saw that the war could not be prevented. The time had passed. I counseled peace from the beginning. I knew that we were too weak to fight the United States. We had many grievances, but I knew that war would bring more. We had good white friends, who advised us against taking the war path. My friend and brother, Mr. Chapman, who has been with us since the surrender, told us just how the war would end. Mr. Chapman took sides against us, and helped General Howard. I do not blame him for doing so. He tried hard to prevent bloodshed. We hoped the white settlers would not join the soldiers. Before the war commenced we had discussed this matter all over, and many of my people were in favor of warning them that if they took no part against us they should not be molested in the event of war being begun by General Howard. This plan was voted down in the war council.

There were bad men among my people who had quarreled with white men, and they talked of their wrongs until they roused all the bad hearts in the council. Still I could not believe that they would begin the war. I know that my young men did a great wrong, but I ask, Who was first to blame? They had been insulted a thousand times; their fathers and brothers had been killed; their mothers and wives had been disgraced; they had been driven to madness by whisky sold to them by white men; they had been told by General Howard that all their horses and cattle which they had been unable to drive out of Wallowa were to fall into the hands of white men; and, added to all this, they were homeless and desperate.

I would have given my own life if I could have undone the killing of white men by my people. I blame my young men and I blame the white men. I blame General Howard for not giving my people time to get their stock away from Wallowa. I do not acknowledge that he had the right to order me to leave Wallowa at any time. I deny that either my father or myself ever sold that land. It is still our land. It may never again be our home, but my father sleeps there, and I love it as I love my mother. I left there, hoping to avoid bloodshed.

If General Howard had given me plenty of time to gather up my stock, and treated Too-hool-hool-suit as a man should be treated, there would have been no war.

My friends among white men have blamed me for the war. I am not to blame. When my young men began the killing, my heart was hurt. Although I did not justify them, I remembered all the insults I had endured, and my blood was on fire. Still I would have taken my people to the buffalo country without fighting, if possible.

I could see no other way to avoid a war. We moved over to White Bird Creek, sixteen miles away, and there encamped, intending to collect our stock before leaving; but the soldiers attacked us, and the first battle was fought. We numbered in that battle sixty men, and the soldiers a hundred. The fight lasted but a few minutes, when the soldiers retreated before us for twelve miles. They lost thirty-three killed, and had seven wounded. When an Indian fights, he only shoots to kill; but soldiers shoot at random. None of the soldiers were scalped. We do not believe in scalping, nor in killing wounded men. Soldiers do not kill many Indians unless they are wounded and left upon the battle field. Then they kill Indians.

Seven days after the first battle, General Howard arrived in the Nez Percés country, bringing seven hundred more soldiers. It was now war in earnest. . . .

We heard nothing of General Howard, or Gibbon, or Sturgis. We had repulsed each in turn, and began to feel secure, when another army, under General Miles, struck us. This was the fourth army, each of which outnumbered our fighting force, that we had encountered within sixty days.

We had no knowledge of General Miles' army until a short time before he made a charge upon us, cutting our camp in two, and capturing nearly all of our horses. About seventy men, myself among them, were cut off. My little daughter, twelve years old, was with me. I gave her a rope, and told her to catch a horse and join the others who were cut off from the camp. I have not seen her since, but I have learned that she is alive and well.

I thought of my wife and children, who were now surrounded by soldiers, and I resolved to go to them or die. With a prayer in my mouth to the Great Spirit Chief who rules above, I dashed unarmed through the line of soldiers. It seemed to me that there were guns on every side, before and behind me. My clothes were cut to pieces and my horse was wounded, but I was unhurt. As I reached the door of my lodge, my wife handed me my rifle, saying: "Here's your gun. Fight!"

The soldiers kept up a continuous fire. Six of my men were killed in one spot near me. Ten or twelve soldiers charged into our camp and got possession of two lodges, killing three Nez Percés and losing three of their men, who fell inside our lines. I called my men to drive them back. We fought at close range, not more than twenty steps apart, and drove the soldiers back upon their main line, leaving their dead in our hands. We secured their arms and ammunition. We lost, the first day and night, eighteen men and three women. General Miles lost twenty-six killed and forty wounded. The following day General Miles sent a messenger into my camp under protection of a white flag. I sent my friend Yellow Bull to meet him.

Yellow Bull understood the messenger to say that General Miles wished me to consider the situation; that he did not want to kill my people unnecessarily. Yellow Bull understood this to be a demand for me to surrender and save blood. Upon reporting this message to me, Yellow Bull said he wondered whether General Miles was in earnest. I sent him back with my answer, that I had made up my mind, but would think about it and send word soon. A little later he sent some Cheyenne scouts with another message. I went out to meet them. They said they believed that

General Miles was sincere and really wanted peace. I walked on to General Miles' tent. He met me and we shook hands. He said, "Come, let us sit down by the fire and talk this matter over." I remained with him all night; next morning Yellow Bull came over to see if I was alive, and why I did not return.

General Miles would not let me leave the tent to see my friend alone.

Yellow Bull said to me: "They have got you in their power, and I am afraid they will never let you go again. I have an officer in our camp, and I will hold him until they let you go free."

I said: "I do not know what they mean to do with me, but if they kill me you must not kill the officer. It will do no good to avenge my death by killing him."

Yellow Bull returned to my camp. I did not make any agreement that day with General Miles. The battle was renewed while I was with him. I was very anxious about my people. I knew that we were near Sitting Bull's camp in King George's land, and I thought maybe the Nez Percés who had escaped would return with assistance. No great damage was done to either party during the night.

On the following morning I returned to my camp by agreement, meeting the officer who had been held a prisoner in my camp at the flag of truce. My people were divided about surrendering. We could have escaped from Bear Paw Mountain if we had left our wounded, old women, and children behind. We were unwilling to do this. We had never heard of a wounded Indian recovering while in the hands of white men.

On the evening of the fourth day General Howard came in with a small escort, together with my friend Chapman. We could now talk understandingly. General Miles said to me in plain words, "If you will come out and give up your arms, I will spare your lives and send you to your reservation." I do not know what passed between General Miles and General Howard.

I could not bear to see my wounded men and women suffer any longer; we had lost enough already. General Miles had promised that we might return to our own country with what stock we had left. I thought we could start again. I believed General Miles, or I never would have surrendered. I have heard that he has been censured for making the promise to return us to Lapwai. He could not have made any other terms with me at that time. I would have held him in check until my friends came to my assistance, and then neither of the generals nor their soldiers would have ever left Bear Paw Mountain alive.

On the fifth day I went to General Miles and gave up my gun, and said, "From where the sun now stands I will fight no more." My people needed rest — we wanted peace.

I was told we could go with General Miles to Tongue River and stay there until spring, when we would be sent back to our country. Finally it was decided that we were to be taken to Tongue River. We had nothing to say about it. After our arrival at Tongue River, General Miles received orders to take us to Bismarck. The reason given was, that subsistence would be cheaper there.

General Miles was opposed to this order. He said: "You must not blame me. I have endeavored to keep my word, but the chief who is over me has given the order, and I must obey it or resign. That would do you no good. Some other officer would carry out the order."

I believe General Miles would have kept his word if he could have done so. I do not blame him for what we have suffered since the surrender. I do not know who is to blame. We gave up all our horses — over eleven hundred — and all our saddles — over one hundred — and we have not heard from them since. Somebody has got our horses.

General Miles turned my people over to another soldier, and we were taken to Bismarck. Captain Johnson, who now had charge of us, received an order to take us to Fort Leavenworth. At Leavenworth we were placed on a low river bottom, with no water except river water to drink and cook with. We had always lived in a healthy country, where the mountains were high and the water was cold and clear. Many of my people sickened and died, and we buried them in this strange land. I can not tell how much my heart suffered for my people while at Leavenworth. The Great Spirit Chief who rules above seemed to be looking some other way, and did not see what was being done to my people.

During the hot days (July, 1878) we received notice that we were to be moved farther away from our own country. We were not asked if we were willing to go. We were ordered to get into railroad cars. Three of my people died on the way to Baxter Springs. It was worse to die there than to die fighting in the mountains.

We were moved from Baxter Springs (Kansas) to the Indian Territory, and set down without our lodges. We had but little medicine, and we were nearly all sick. Seventy of my people have died since we moved there.

We have had a great many visitors who have talked many ways. . . .

At last I was granted permission to come to Washington and bring my friend Yellow Bull and our interpreter with me. I am glad we came. I have shaken hands with a great many friends, but there are some things I want to know which no one seems able to explain. I can not understand how the Government sends a man out to fight us, as it did General Miles, and then breaks his word. Such a government has something wrong about it. I can not understand why so many chiefs are allowed to talk so many different ways, and promise so many different things. I have seen the Great Father Chief (the President), the next Great Chief (Secretary of the Interior), the Commissioner Chief (Hayt), the Law Chief (General Butler), and many other law chiefs (Congressmen), and they all say they are my friends, and that I shall have justice, but while their mouths all talk right I do not understand why nothing is done for my people. I have heard talk and talk, but nothing is done. Good words

do not last long unless they amount to something. Words do not pay for my dead people. They do not pay for my country, now overrun by white men. They do not protect my father's grave. They do not pay for all my horses and cattle. Good words will not give me back my children. Good words will not make good the promise of your War Chief General Miles. Good words will not give my people good health and stop them from dying. Good words will not get my people a home where they can live in peace and take care of themselves. I am tired of talk that comes to nothing. It makes my heart sick when I remember all the good words and all the broken promises. There has been too much talking by men who had no right to talk. Too many misrepresentations have been made, too many misunderstandings have come up between the white men about the Indians. If the white man wants to live in peace with the Indian he can live in peace. There need be no trouble. Treat all men alike. Give them the same law. Give them all an even chance to live and grow. All men were made by the same Great Spirit Chief. They are all brothers. The earth is the mother of all people, and all people should have equal rights upon it. You might as well expect the rivers to run backward as that any man who was born a free man should be contented when penned up and denied liberty to go where he pleases. If you tie a horse to a stake, do you expect he will grow fat? If you pen an Indian up on a small spot of earth, and compel him to stay there, he will not be contented, nor will he grow and prosper. I have asked some of the great white chiefs where they get their authority to say to the Indian that he shall stay in one place, while he sees white men going where they please. They can not tell me.

I only ask of the Government to be treated as all other men are treated. If I can not go to my own home, let me have a home in some country where my people will not die so fast. I would like to go to Bitter Root Valley. There my people would be healthy; where they are now they are dying.

Three have died since I left my camp to come to Washington.

When I think of our condition my heart is heavy. I see men of my race treated as outlaws and driven from country to country, or shot down like animals.

I know that my race must change. We can not hold our own with the white men as we are. We only ask an even chance to live as other men live. We ask to be recognized as men. We ask that the same law shall work alike on all men. If the Indian breaks the law, punish him by the law. If the white man breaks the law, punish him also.

Let me be a free man—free to travel, free to stop, free to work, free to trade where I choose, free to choose my own teachers, free to follow the religion of my fathers, free to think and talk and act for myself—and I will obey every law, or submit to the penalty.

Whenever the white man treats an Indian as they treat each other, then we will have no more wars. We shall all be alike—brothers of one father and one mother, with one sky above us and one country around us, and one government for all. Then the Great Spirit Chief who rules above will smile upon this land, and send rain to wash out the bloody spots made by brothers' hands from the face of the earth. For this time the Indian race are waiting and praying. I hope that no more groans of wounded men and women will ever go to the ear of the Great Spirit Chief above, and that all people may be one people.

In-mut-too-yah-lat-lat has spoken for his people.

References

1. L. V. McWhorter, *Yellow Wolf: His Own Story* (Caldwell, Idaho: Caxton Printers, 1940, 1995), 41.
2. McWhorter, *Yellow Wolf,* 42.
3. McWhorter, *Yellow Wolf,* 211–12.
4. Quoted in Alvin M. Josephy, Jr., *The Nez Percé Indians and the Opening of the Northwest* (New Haven: Yale University Press, 1965), 630.
5. Quoted in Bruce Hampton, *Children of Grace: The Nez Percé War of 1877* (New York: Henry Holt, 1994), 311.
6. *Annual Report of the Commissioner of Indian Affairs,* 1878, 464, quoted in Hampton, *Children of Grace,* 321–22. See also McWhorter, *Yellow Wolf,* 289.
7. *Annual Report of the Commissioner of Indian Affairs,* 1878, 464; quoted in Hampton, *Children of Grace,* 323.
8. McWhorter, *Yellow Wolf,* 18, 226.

Suggested Readings

Beal, Merrill D. *I Will Fight No More Forever: Chief Joseph and the Nez Percé War* (Seattle: University of Washington Press, 1963).

Haines, Francis. *The Nez Percés* (Norman: University of Oklahoma Press, 1955).

Hampton, Bruce. *Children of Grace: The Nez Percé War of 1877* (New York: Henry Holt, 1994).

Josephy, Alvin M., Jr. *The Nez Percé Indians and the Opening of the Northwest* (New Haven: Yale University Press, 1965).

McBeth, Kate. *The Nez Percés Since Lewis and Clark* (Moscow: University of Idaho Press, 1993 reprint).

McWhorter, L. V. *Yellow Wolf: His Own Story* (Caldwell, Idaho: Caxton Printers, 1940, 1995).

Slickpoo, Allen P., Sr., and Deward E. Walker, Jr. *Noon Nee-Me-Poo (We, The Nez Percés): Culture and History of the Nez Percés* (Nez Percé Tribe of Idaho, 1973).

The Battle of the Little Big Horn in Myth and History

The Battle of the Little Big Horn is the exception to the rule that the winners write history. In this case the losers transformed a defeat into a mythic symbol of nation-building. Almost immediately after the death of George Custer and his men on June 25, 1876, Americans began to construct an image of the battle that became part of a national mythology. Even among people who know little or nothing of the battle or its historical circumstances, the very words "Custer's Last Stand" conjure up images of the blond-haired officer and his gallant band of soldiers surrounded by hordes of Indian warriors.

FIGURE 5.1 William Carey, *The Death Struggle of General Custer* (1876)
Library of Congress.

FIGURE 5.2 *Custer's Last Fight* (c. 1896)
Buffalo Bill Historical Center, Cody, Wyoming. Gift of Edgar William and Bernice Chrysler Garbisch; 10.68.

For many Americans then and since, the battle was the epic struggle of Western history, a final clash between two ways of life, between the old and the new, between "savagery" and "civilization." It is the soldiers, not the Indians whose land is invaded and whose villages are attacked, who are fighting for their lives. Surrounded and doomed, they become martyrs to the cause of westward expansion and their deaths justify the eventual victory. After Gettysburg, the Little Big Horn is probably America's most famous battlefield, and it continues to generate heated emotions 120 years after the event. Recent events—appointing the first Indian (a woman) as National Parks superintendent of the site, renaming the battlefield the Little Big Horn instead of the Custer Battlefield, and erecting a monument to the Indians alongside the monument to the Seventh Cavalry—have raised controversy. These actions have also helped to heal wounds for some people. The battle means different things to different people, but it remains a defining event in American history. Even as society's values have changed and Custer in some circles has tumbled from gallant hero, to bumbling incompetent, to genocidal maniac, the central image of the battle—beleaguered soldiers on the hilltop—has endured.[1]

FIGURE 5.3 *Custer's Last Stand (1904)*
Buffalo Bill Historical Center, Cody, Wyoming; 19.69.

Yet this enduring image of the battle was created by people who were not there. The only survivors and eyewitnesses were Indians, most of whom remained tight-lipped about the battle and their role in it, fearing retribution even into the twentieth century. Stories and memories of what really happened survived among the Lakotas and Cheyennes, but most Americans imagined or preferred a different story, one perpetuated in countless books, paintings, and movies.

Less than a month after the battle, William Carey sketched the first image of the fight, subtitled *The Death Struggle of General Custer* (Figure 5.1). It set the standard for subsequent portrayals. Twenty years later, the Anheuser-Busch Brewing Association began distribution of Otto Becker's 1896 lithograph, *"Custer's Last Fight"* (Figure 5.2). It was reprinted repeatedly; generations of Americans sat in barrooms drinking in Becker's interpretation of the battle. In his Wild West shows around the turn of the century, Buffalo Bill Cody got in on the act by staging reenactments that both perpetuated and popularized the heroic image of the battle (Figure 5.3). Twentieth-century movie audiences

FIGURE 5.4 *They Died with Their Boots On* (1941)
Photofest.

saw numerous renditions of the battle in films like *They Died with Their Boots On* (1941, Figure 5.4), where Errol Flynn's Custer was the last man standing at the Last Stand, and *Custer of the West* (1968, Figure 5.5), where actor Robert Shaw's Custer was a more complex character but, again, died alone, surrounded by his Indian enemies. By the time of *Little Big Man* (1970), Custer's reputation was at a low ebb. Few Americans who anguished about their country's actions in Vietnam could admire the Indian-killing Custer. The film portrayed him, like his country, as bloodthirsty, arrogant, and ultimately mad (Figure 5.6). The hero turned villain still died alone on the hill.[2]

From the fury and chaos
of the Civil War
to the glory days of
the 7th Cavalry
...to the final
earth-shaking
charge at
Little Big Horn!

CINERAMA RELEASING CORP
presents
ROBERT SHAW
as
CUSTER
OF THE
WEST

FIGURE 5.5 *Custer of the West (1968)*
Photofest.

But other images of the battle existed. Lakota and Cheyenne participants, in keeping with the traditional practice of recording and recounting warriors' heroic deeds, produced pictographic accounts of the fight. These pictures, like the oral traditions of the battle passed down within the tribes, usually depict it as a rout rather than a heroic last stand (Figure 5.7). Increasingly sophisticated battlefield archaeology that employs metal detectors and forensic techniques, together with the very placement of the grave markers where the bodies of dead soldiers were found, suggest an interpretation of the battle that more closely resembles that offered by the Indians than that presented by

FIGURE 5.6 *Little Big Man* (1970)
Photofest.

Anheuser-Busch or Hollywood: a breakdown of command occurred, discipline disintegrated, and the men of the Seventh Cavalry died in a series of desperate, piecemeal actions—plenty of tragedy (Figure 5.8), but little heroism.

Yet the old images endure and will continue to do so, and they are historically significant. They may distort understanding of what really happened at the Battle of the Little Big Horn but they have become historical documents in their own right, showing how people view the past and exerting powerful influences even to this day.

FIGURE 5.7 Lakotas Fighting Custer's Command
National Anthropological Archives, Smithsonian Institution.

▶ **Questions for Consideration**

1. What do the images in this picture essay suggest about the power of art—and more recently the movies—in shaping history?

2. Can a comparison be drawn between the competing and changing views of this battle, and the opposing views of King Philip's War offered in the documents on pages 121–30? If King Philip's War was also a "war of words," can the Little Big Horn be described as a "battle of images"?

3. What do the changing images indicate about how, even when one side controls the interpretations, those interpretations change over time?

FIGURE 5.8 Custer's Dead Cavalry
National Anthropological Archives, Smithsonian Institution.

References

1. For further discussion of the issues surrounding the battle, see the essays in Charles E. Rankin, ed., *Legacy: New Perspectives on the Battle of the Little Bighorn* (Helena: Montana Historical Society, 1996).
2. On Custer imagery in art and film, see the essays by Brian W. Dippie and Paul Andrew Hutton in Rankin, ed., *Legacy,* 206–70, and Dippie, *Custer's Last Stand: The Anatomy of an American Myth* (1976; reprinted Lincoln: University of Nebraska Press, 1994).

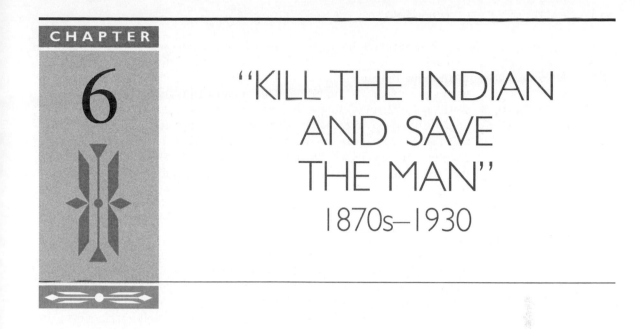

"KILL THE INDIAN AND SAVE THE MAN"
1870s–1930

AMERICANIZING THE AMERICAN INDIAN

Relating his life story in old age, Two Leggings, a Crow warrior, concentrated on his search for a vision and his aspirations and achievements as a warrior. He ended his story at the point when his people were confined to the reservation. Nothing in his warrior tradition and training prepared him for reservation life. "Nothing happened after that," he said. "We just lived. There were no more war parties, no capturing of horses from the Piegans and the Sioux, no buffalo to hunt. There is nothing more to tell."[1] But Two Leggings lived for another forty years after the end of the old days. There was plenty more to tell.

As the wars for the West came to an end, Indian people found themselves subjected to attacks of a different kind. Various organizations mobilized in the late 1870s and 1880s for a reform of Indian policies. President Grant had established precedent by using churchmen as officials and agents as part of his "peace policy," and some of his appointees had brought an element of humanitarianism to Indian affairs. In later years, groups which saw themselves as the "friends of the Indian" attempted to take things further. Tragic events such as the pursuit and relocation of the Nez Percés in 1877, the uprooting of the Ponca tribe to make room for new Sioux reservations the same year, and the desperate flight in 1878 of some three hundred Northern Cheyennes from a reservation in Indian Territory—all described in moving terms by reformer Helen Hunt Jackson in her 1881 book, *A Century of Dishonor*—left an ugly taste in the mouths of those who believed the United States should be extending the blessings of civilization to Indian people, not shooting them down in the snow.

The need for a thorough reform of Indian affairs was clear. The Board of Indian Commissioners, established by Congress in 1869 to curb mismanagement in the Bureau of Indian Affairs, investigated conditions on reservations where corruption was notorious. The Indian Rights Association, founded in 1882, pledged to protect the rights and interests of the Indians; its reformers attended annual conferences at Lake Mohonk resort in upstate New York where they discussed what was best for "the Indian." The Indian Rights Association did champion Indian causes and on occasion backed Indian cases in the courts, but they shared the commitment of other reform groups to "save" the Indians by assimilating them.

Policies of Detribalization

Influential groups in American society combined with the federal government in a sustained campaign to remake Indians in the image of white American citizens. Like earlier generations of Euro-Americans, they wanted to "civilize" Indians and have them lead sedentary lives on fixed plots of land, be self-supporting, and practice Christianity. As the first step in this transformation, American reformers believed it was necessary to eradicate all vestiges of tribal life and culture—to "destroy the Indian and save the man." Powerful forces acted to suppress Indian culture, undermine tribal ways, and destroy the economic base of tribal life. The American government and reformers sought to apply a single model of transformation to all tribes, regardless of their differences. Like the European immigrants who were streaming into eastern cities, the first peoples in America were to be made into "Americans." The result was tremendous suffering and hardship for Indian peoples who saw their land domains diminish, their heritage distorted, and their certainties questioned. But tribal culture and society proved more resilient than the reformers imagined.

With the defeat of the resistive groups, many of the Indian "ringleaders" were rounded up and sent away as prisoners of war, while their people were herded onto reservations. Seventy-two southern Plains war leaders were incarcerated in Fort Marion, a military prison in Florida. There Captain Richard Henry Pratt subjected them to an experimental program of "civilization by immersion." Pratt took off their shackles, cut their hair, gave them army uniforms, and attempted to impose rapid and complete assimilation.

At the same time, the government in the late nineteenth century refined its policies for dealing with the Indians on the reservations. The new Indian policies employed a hierarchy of command that ran from the Department of the Interior, down through the Bureau of Indian Affairs to the regional superintendents, and to the Indian agents on the reservations. The reservation was the context in which the process of detribalization was to occur. But in the long-term policy of assimilating Indians, reservations were regarded as temporary, a stage on the road to incorporating Indians into mainstream American society. The agents were the key figures in the administration and enforcement of the government's Americanization policies on the reservations. They relied for assistance on the clerks, doctors, field matrons, farmers, teachers, and black-

Ration Day on the Pine Ridge Reservation, 1891
With the buffalo herds gone, Plains Indians were reduced to unaccustomed poverty and dependence on government rations. Here, Oglala people wait in line to receive their supplies. Denver Public Library, Western History Collection.

smiths who worked on the agencies; they also relied on the reservation police and the Courts of Indian Offenses, both of which were staffed by Indians and assigned with the suppression of tribal culture and traditional activities. In this way, resentment against government policies at the community level often became channeled against Indians charged with implementing those policies rather than against the federal government or its agents. If the system failed and resentment erupted in open resistance, the army could be called in to restore order and enforce compliance.

Some agents were dedicated and honest men who worked hard to ease the Indians' transition to a new way of life and who displayed genuine sympathy for their charges. Many were not. Often, agents were political appointees in a system that encouraged graft and corruption, and they made matters worse for the people they were supposed to administer. Sarah Winnemucca saw her Paiute people decline into poverty after they were confined to a reservation in Nevada in 1860 and then relocated to Oregon in 1879. Indians will "never be civilized," she wrote for a white audience in 1883, "if you keep on sending us such agents as have been sent to us year after year, who do nothing but fill their pockets, and the pockets of their wives and sisters, who are always put in as teachers, . . . and yet they do not teach." Indians complained regularly to the government about corrupt agents, "Yet it goes on, just the same, as if they did not know."[2] Sarah Winnemucca went on the lecture circuit, dressed as a Paiute "princess," to de-

Sarah Winnemucca as "Princess" in the Dress of a Paiute
Sarah Winnemucca gave more than four hundred speeches in the United States and in Europe in an effort to improve conditions for her people. Nevada Historical Society.

nounce the government's policies and call attention to her people's plight, but died in 1891 without seeing the Paiutes receive justice.

Resistance Takes New Forms

As Indian peoples confronted a painful readjustment to new constraints, they found ways to shield their own ways and values from the prying eyes of Indian agents and maintained ties of family, clan, and community. Indian officials sometimes evaded or diluted the impact of the laws they were supposed to enforce: Wooden Leg, a Northern Cheyenne who fought at the Little Big Horn and later served as a tribal judge, sent away one of his two wives in compliance with the government's ban on polygyny, but when he heard that some of the older men refused to obey the order he "just listened, said nothing, and did nothing." The government originally conceived of Indian judges as men who would simply enforce the rules, but many judges had other ideas. In time, notes historian Frederick E. Hoxie, Crow judges evolved into "government-sanctioned elders who worked to reconcile their oaths of office with individual behavior and the standards of their communities."[3]

For generations Indians were forced to practice their religious ceremonies illegally and covertly. For example, in American eyes, conversion to Christianity required that rituals such as the Sun Dance be suppressed as "heathenish practices." But efforts at suppression did not match Indian insistence on preservation: Kiowas, for instance, transferred elements from the Sun Dance, which was banned, into the new Gourd Dance, which was not, and Indians repeatedly found ways to evade government regulations and opportunities to hold dances.[4] As the practice of native ceremonies on reservations today indicates, the government's attempts at "cultural genocide" and religious oppression were partially successful at best.

Reformers realized that, despite the massive assaults on Indian life and cultures, the reservations were failing in one of their primary purposes: Indians were not abandoning the old ways; they refused to stop being Indians. Reservations were supposed to be crucibles of change where tribalism would perish and "civilization" flourish, but Indians made them into homelands where

The Twilight of the Indian (1897)
Indians who accepted allotment were expected to give up the tepee, bow, and hunting shirt in favor of a cabin, plow, and farming clothes. As Frederic Remington's painting and title indicate, most Americans believed that once Indians lived on and farmed their own plots of land, they embarked on the path to a new life: they would not only cease being hunters, they would also eventually cease being Indian. Courtesy of The R. W. Norton Art Gallery, Shreveport, Louisiana.

tribal ways refused to die. In the eyes of reformers determined to save Indians from themselves, the reservations came to be "obstacles to progress."

The Dawes Allotment Act (1887)

"Friends of the Indian" now advocated that reservations be dismantled as the best way to push Indians into the modern world. In some cases, concentrating Indians on reservations stimulated tribal organization and identity—the far-ranging Comanche bands, for example, came together as a nation after they

MAP 6.1 Confining the Comanches, 1865–1901
The Comanche experience dramatically illustrates the impact of the assault on tribal lands that culminated in the Allotment Act. For much of the nineteenth century, the Comanches ranged across a huge region from north of the Arkansas River to south of the Rio Grande. The Treaty of the Little Arkansas in 1865 began to compress the tribal domain, and the end of the Civil War initiated new pressures on Indian lands. In the Treaty of Medicine Lodge in 1867, the Comanches ceded most of their lands to the United States and agreed to live on a 3-million-acre reservation. After the Allotment Act was applied around the turn of the century, the reservation shrank to a patchwork of individual holdings. In the view of the U.S. government, swift and massive territorial reductions, such as those the Comanches experienced, were necessary to transform Indian land into American real estate and to speed the transition of Indians from nomadic hunters to settled farmers. For Indian people, land loss meant a shift from mobility, prosperity, and independence to confinement, poverty, and dependence, and also separation from familiar sites linked to individual, family, and tribal memories. Adapted from The American Indian: Prehistory to the Present, *first edition, by Arrell M. Gibson. Copyright © 1980 by D.C. Heath and Company. Used by permission of Houghton Mifflin Company.*

were confined to a reservation in the 1870s. But reformers wanted to dismantle the *tribes* themselves. "The organization of the Indian tribes is, and has been, one of the most serious hindrances to the advancement of the Indian toward civilization," the 1884 Lake Mohonk Conference proclaimed: "every effort should be made to secure the disintegration of all tribal organizations."[5] The reformers wanted to grant Indians citizenship and to educate them in Christian and American ways. They rejected the notion that Indians were different; they should dissolve tribal ties and assimilate into American society like everyone else. Reformers and federal officials shifted their support from a policy based on reservations to a policy based on *breaking up* reservations.

In 1887, Congress passed the Dawes or General Allotment Act to abolish reservations and allot lands to individual Indians as private property. Reformers saw these provisions as the way to radically change federal Indian policy and initiate a new era for American Indians. Like the Indian removal policy of the 1830s, allotment was a program on which both pro- and anti-Indian groups could agree as a "solution" to the "Indian problem." The new policy would terminate communal ownership, push Indians into mainstream society, and offer for sale "surplus" land not used by Indians. The law was an attempt to impose a revolution on Indian societies. Allotment, its advocates believed, would liberate Indians from the stifling hold of community and instill individual ambition, American ideas of property rights, habits of thrift and industry. It would also break up extended families and undermine leaders who worked for the collective good. Indians could progress no further as long as they held land in common, said Senator Henry Dawes of Massachusetts, the main proponent of the Allotment Act. "There is no selfishness,

An Anishinaabe Family, c. 1905
Dressed in their best and displaying beautiful beadwork and embroidery, this family posed about the time the assault on White Earth reservation lands began. Note the drawn pistol. Minnesota Historical Society.

which is at the bottom of civilization."[6] Thus the acquisition of private property was vital if an Indian was to become a fully participating and competing member of American society. "The wish for a home of his own awakens him to new efforts," declared Merrill Gates, a member of the Board of Indian Commissioners. "Discontent with the tepee and the starving rations of the Indian camp in winter is needed to get the Indian out of the blanket and into trousers, — and trousers with a pocket in them, and with a *pocket that aches to be filled with dollars!*"[7] Theodore Roosevelt put it more bluntly: allotment, he said, was "a vast pulverizing engine to break up the tribal mass."[8]

The Dawes Allotment Act passed through Congress and was implemented with speed. It contained the following provisions:

1.   The president was authorized to assign allotments of 160 acres to heads of families, with lesser amounts to younger persons and orphans.

2.   Indians were to select their own lands, but if they failed to do so, the agent would make the selection for them. Reservations were to be surveyed and rolls of tribal members prepared prior to allotment.

3.   The government was to hold title to the land in trust for twenty-five years, preventing its sale until allottees could learn to treat it as real estate.

4.   All allottees and all Indians who abandoned their tribal ways and became "civilized" were to be granted citizenship.

5.   "Surplus" reservation lands could be sold.

The law remained in force from 1887 to 1934. Its main effect was to strip Indian people of millions of acres of land. The protections provided to Indian allottees were steadily whittled away. In 1902, Congress allowed Indian heirs to sell inherited land without approval from the Secretary of the Interior. In 1906, the Burke Act declared that Indians whom the Secretary of the Interior deemed "competent" to manage their own affairs could be granted patents in fee simple, which meant they no longer had to wait twenty-five years before they could sell their allotments.

On the White Earth reservation in northern Minnesota, American businessmen and speculators steadily eroded the land base of the Anishinaabe residents. The U.S. government established White Earth in 1867 as a reservation for all Anishinaabe people, and the various bands who lived there made a promising start. But the rich timber lands in the eastern part of the reservation and fertile farm lands to the west attracted the attention of outsiders. In 1899, the Nelson Act mandated that all the land be allotted under the terms of the Dawes Act. In 1906, Minnesota Senator Moses A. Clapp, a former lumber baron, attached a rider to the annual Indian appropriations bill stating that "mixed-blood" adults on White Earth were "competent" to dispose of their land parcels immediately. One Anishinaabeg, a school superintendent from 1903 to 1911, said that the Clapp rider "brought grief and happiness to many people." Speculators approached Indian people who knew nothing about the legislation and got witnesses to "subscribe to affidavits that the Indian in question had white blood in his veins and in many cases the white blood ran through the branches of the family for many generations to some remote Canadian Frenchman."[9] Powerful lumber interests bought up timber-rich allotments for a fraction of their value and proceeded to clear the northern forests that had sustained Anishinaabe people for centuries.

As reservation lands and resources dwindled, social and political conflicts within Anishinaabe society increased. Before the 1906 Clapp rider, the people of White Earth had been adapting relatively well to life on the reservation and to the demands and opportunities of a market economy; an investigation in 1909 found them with "no lands, no money." By 1920, "most of the reservation land base had been transferred to Euroamerican hands," and by 1994, "only 7 percent of White Earth's land base remained under Indian control."[10]

Even as allotment was implemented, however, Indians found ways to evade its assimilationist intent. Some Indians—Jicarilla Apaches and the bands on the Grand Ronde reservation in western Oregon, for example—actually requested allotment and used it to secure control of land and to build new agricultural communities defined as much by their own choices and standards as by government policies. Others—the Nez Percés for instance—selected their allotments of land "with agendas other than assimilation in mind." They used space in Indian rather than Euroamerican ways, occupied land as families and communities rather than as individual property owners, and perpetuated rather than terminated traditional environmental practices.[11]

Indian Territory Becomes Oklahoma

The "Five Civilized Tribes" in Indian Territory were originally excluded from the provisions of the Allotment Act. The Cherokees, Creeks, Choctaws, Chickasaws, and Seminoles had rebuilt their economic, educational, and political structures after removal, had weathered the divisive effects of the Civil War, and functioned as autonomous societies. In 1889, Congress provided for allotment of the lands of all Indians in the area except for the five tribes. But in 1890, In-

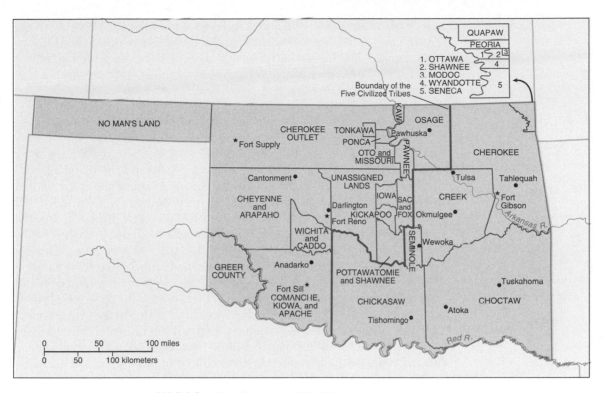

MAP 6.2 Indian Territory, 1866–89

Following the Indian Removal Act of 1830, thousands of Indian people from the East were relocated to Indian Territory. Other peoples from other regions were moved there in later years. They rebuilt their societies in what was originally supposed to be "permanent" Indian territory, but allotment produced huge losses of land in what became the state of Oklahoma. Francis Paul Prucha, Atlas of American Indian Affairs *(Lincoln: University of Nebraska Press, 1990).*

dian Territory was divided into Oklahoma Territory and Indian Territory, and in 1893 Congress appointed a commission to negotiate allotment agreements with the five tribes. Many tribal leaders opposed allotment, but the Curtis Act of 1898 terminated the Indian governments and allotment proceeded in the remainder of Indian Territory. In 1907, Congress combined Indian Territory and Oklahoma Territory to create the new state of Oklahoma. Although the Muskogee (Creek) National Council agreed to allotment, some Creeks followed the lead of Chitto Harjo, or Crazy Snake, in resisting allotment. After violence erupted with whites, the Oklahoma National Guard was called out in 1909 to quell the "uprising." In the meantime, fraud and chicanery characterized the allotment process in Oklahoma. Non-Indians married Indians to get on the tribal rolls and thereby become eligible for allotments, cheated them out of their allotments with words or whiskey, and, in the view of one Oklahoma historian, "lurked about the Indian nations, a predacious wolf pack lusting for the last parcels of Indian land."[12] When the Osages were forced to accept the allotment of their lands in 1907, they wisely insisted that the tribe continue to own the subsurface materials—oil had been discovered beneath the Osage reservation ten years before. The Osages benefitted from an oil bonanza, but non-Indians resorted to swindling, bribery, and even a spate of murders in the 1920s. "The Osage Reign of Terror" attracted national attention and FBI investigations.[13]

In the United States as a whole between 1887 and 1934, the entire tribal estate was reduced from some 138 million acres to about 48 million acres. The allotment of 160 acres was often insufficient for Indians to make a living by farming or herding, especially as the lands were usually arid and marginally fertile. By the late nineteenth century many white American farmers were finding it hard to make ends meet, even on good lands. Moreover, the original 160 acres often were broken up into smaller parcels as they were divided among the heirs of the original allottee. Many Indians were persuaded to lease their lands. As non-Indian settlers bought up surplus lands, many reservations assumed a "checkerboard" pattern of Indian and non-Indian property (see "Dismantling Tribes and Their Homelands," pages 367–73). The Navajo population and reservation increased in the late nineteenth century as the tribe rebuilt their economy around stockraising, but they were an exception to the general rule.[14] With their already reduced tribal domain further diminished and disrupted (see Map 6.1, "Confining the Comanches, 1865–1901," page 340, for example), most Indians living on allotted reservations endured increasing poverty, despondency, and discrimination.

THE EDUCATIONAL ASSAULT ON INDIAN CHILDREN

While allotment tried to break up the reservations as obstacles to progress, education was seen as the key to making progress and saving the Indian. In the eyes of reformers like Merrill Gates, allotment and education went hand in hand (see "Dismantling Tribes and Their Homelands," pages 367–73). If necessary, both would be forced upon Indians. Like the children of European immigrants, Indian children were expected to jettison their old ways and language and become English-speaking "Americans." The Board of Indian Commissioners in 1880 outlined its view of the Indian:

> As a savage we cannot tolerate him any more than as a half-civilized parasite, wanderer or vagabond. The only alternative left is to fit him by education for civilized life. The Indian, though a simple child of nature with mental facilities dwarfed and shriveled, while groping his way for generations in the darkness of barbarism, already sees the importance of education. . . .[15]

Deprived of their lands and reduced to poverty, Indians had to learn to support themselves as wage laborers.

Removing Children from the Tribe

Reformers aimed to educate Indian adults. Captain Richard Henry Pratt imposed his program of civilization on the Plains Indian prisoners of war in Fort Marion, attempting to immerse them in white culture. But Indian children became the main targets of American education efforts. Congress in 1877 appropriated $20,000 for the express purpose of Indian education. Funding rose and reached almost $3 million by 1900. The numbers of students enrolling in school also increased: 3,598 in 1877; 21,568 in 1900.[16] Some children attended day schools on the reservations, but reformers preferred off-reservation boarding schools where children could be isolated from the "contaminating" influences of parents, friends, and family. "Our purpose," said the superintendent of Rainy Mountain Boarding School in Oklahoma, which hundreds of young Kiowas attended between 1893–1920, "is to change them forever."[17]

MAP 6.3 U.S. Government Boarding Schools, 1889

Twenty years after Richard Henry Pratt opened his school at Carlisle, Pennsylvania, Indian country was dotted by two dozen off-reservation boarding schools and many more reservation boarding schools, such as Keams Canyon on the Hopi reservation, which Helen Sekaquaptewa attended (see page 347). Francis Paul Prucha, Atlas of American Indian Affairs *(Lincoln: University of Nebraska Press, 1990).*

A Crow Indian Girl Wearing an Elks'-tooth Dress and Riding a Richly Bedecked Horse, c. 1905–10

When this photograph was taken, government policy aimed to separate children from their families and to educate them out of their Indian ways. Richard Throssel (1882–1933), who took this photograph, was of Cree heritage and an adopted Crow. He worked on the Crow reservation in Montana for the U.S. Indian Service from 1902 to 1911 and took more than a thousand photographs, compiling an invaluable visual record of the Crows during an era of tremendous change. American Heritage Center, University of Wyoming.

Hampton Institute, established in 1868 as a school for former slaves, admitted Indian students ten years later. In 1879, Pratt opened Carlisle Indian School in Pennsylvania. These schools became famous, or infamous, and served as models for other Indian educational facilities in their curriculum, discipline, regimen, and goals. Two dozen more boarding schools were opened in the next twenty-three years.

Attendance was mandatory. In 1891, Congress authorized the Commissioner of Indian Affairs "to make and enforce by proper means" rules and regulations to ensure that Indian children of suitable age attended the schools established for them. Two years later, Congress went further and authorized the Indian office to withhold rations and annuities from parents who refused to send their children to school. Many children were hauled off to school by soldiers or Indian police enforcing the agents' instructions. In 1886, the agent at the Mescalero Apache agency reported:

> Everything in the way of persuasion and arguments having failed, it became necessary to visit the camps unexpectedly with a detachment of police, and seize such children as were proper and take them away to school, willing or unwilling. Some hurried their children off to the mountains or hid them away in camp, and the police had to chase and capture them like so many wild rabbits. This unusual proceeding created quite an outcry. The men were sullen and muttering, the women loud in their lamentations, and the children almost out of their wits with fright.[18]

When the government built a boarding school at Keams Canyon, Arizona, in 1887, the Hopis at first refused to send their children there. In 1890, the government established a quota system for the attendance of Hopi children in schools and the next year sent African American troops to round up children. Don Talayesva, a Hopi, remembered hearing about it as a child: "The people said it was a terrible sight to see Negro soldiers come and take our children away from their parents." Using African American troops to round up Native American children may have been a deliberate policy to pit one oppressed group against another, but Hopis recognized who was responsible. Talayevsa "grew up believing that Whites are wicked, deceitful people."[19] Helen Sekaquaptewa, a Hopi woman, recalled in 1969 the bewilderment she and other children felt in 1906 when they were lined up, loaded into wagons, and taken from their families under military escort:

> It was after dark when we reached the Keams Canyon boarding school and were unloaded and taken into the big dormitory, lighted with electricity. I had never seen so much light at night. . . . Evenings we would gather in a corner and cry softly so the matron would not hear and scold or spank us. . . . I can still hear the plaintive little voices saying, "I want to go home. I want my mother." We didn't understand a word of English and didn't know what to say or do. . . . We were a group of homesick, lonesome, little girls. . . .[20]

Life in the Schools

Schools such as that at Carlisle, Pennsylvania, were designed not only to educate the Indian students who attended but also to completely transform them. They tried to provide students with the kind of skills that America deemed appropriate and even necessary for their survival and to remake them as individual citizens, not tribal members. To this end, boarding schools imposed strict discipline and regimented the students' activities, from morning until prayers before bedtime. When Indian children arrived at the boarding schools, they were given new Anglo-American names. The boys had their hair cut, and all students had to wear stiff uniforms in place of their native clothing. Writing in

Chiricahua Apache Children on Arrival at Carlisle School.
National Anthropological Archives, Smithsonian Institution.

the 1930s Luther Standing Bear, a Lakota and one of the first students to attend Carlisle, remembered the discomfort of high collars, stiff shirts, and leather boots; then the students were issued red flannel underwear for the winter and "discomfort grew into actual torture."[21] They ate a monotonous diet, endured harsh discipline, and followed daily routines to acquire systematic habits. Educational policy at the boarding schools discouraged—and often prohibited—students from returning home during vacations or at times of sickness and death among family members, to the distress of parents and students alike.[22] Most students suffered from homesickness. Basil Johnston, a Canadian Anishinaabeg who attended a Jesuit school in Ontario, remembered the emotional toll on the youngest children. These "babies" clung to one of the Jesuit priests or huddled in the corner; they "seldom laughed or smiled and often cried and whimpered during the day and at night." Some of the older students carved toys for them but the children did not play with them; "they just held on to them, hugged them and took them to bed at night, for that was all they had

Chiricahua Apache Children after Four Months at Carlisle
National Anthropological Archives, Smithsonian Institution.

in the world when the lights went out, and they dared not let it go."[23;°] Many students suffered from trachoma, a contagious viral disease of the eye. Many died of tuberculosis, coughing up blood as the disease attacked their lungs. Between 1885 and 1913, one hundred Indians students, from thirty-seven tribes, were buried in the cemetery at Haskell Indian School in Kansas. Most were teenagers, but some were only six or seven years old. Some committed suicide. "The change in clothing, housing, food, and confinement combined with lonesomeness was too much," recalled Standing Bear. "In the graveyard at Carlisle most of the graves are those of little ones."[24]

°In 1998 the Canadian government issued a formal apology to the victims of sexual and physical abuse in the residential school system and committed $350 million to support the development of community-based healing to help deal with the legacy of that abuse.

Navajo Tom Torlino as He Came to Carlisle (left) and after Three Years at Carlisle
National Anthropological Archives, Smithsonian Institution.

The ravages of disease were not confined to boarding schools far from home, of course. Don Talayesva attended school at New Oraibi on the Hopi reservation and recalled hearing just before Christmas, 1899, that smallpox was spreading west across Hopi country. "Within a few weeks news came to us that on Second Mesa the people were dying so fast that the Hopi did not have time to bury them, but just pitched their bodies over the cliff." The government employees and some of the teachers fled Oraibi. Another Hopi, Edmund Nequatewa, was at the Keams Canyon boarding school when the epidemic struck: "the whole reservation was condemned," he remembered. "They had to draw the line between the school and the Hopi village. There were guards going back and forth day and night. No one could come in to the school from the Hopi villages." For several months, students at the school were cut off from news of their relatives in the disease-ridden villages. When Nequatewa was allowed home in the spring, he found his parents alive but two aunts dead. "Some of those people that had had smallpox were very hard to recognize," he recalled. "Their faces were all speckled and they looked awful."[25]

In the classroom, teachers taught reading and writing by rote, pushed "American" values on the children, and taught patriotism and a version of American history that distorted or ignored the Indians' role. Teachers punished those caught speaking their native language. Many parents who had attended missionary or government boarding schools refused to teach their children their native tongue in order to save them from having the language beaten out of them in school. Eleven-year-old Elsie Allen, a Pomo girl, was beaten with a strap for speaking her language at the Covelo boarding school in California. "[E]very night I cried and then I'd lay awake and think and think and think. I'd think to myself, 'If I ever get married and have children I'll *never* teach my children the language or all the Indian things that I know. I'll *never* teach them that, I don't want my children to be treated like they treated me.' That's the way I raised my children."[26]

Boys acquired vocational and manual skills; girls were taught the domestic skills thought appropriate for a Victorian mother and homemaker, or trained for work as maids in middle-class families. In fact, many students found themselves in a twilight world: they were not equipped or allowed to enter American society as equals, yet they had been subjected to sufficient change as to make returning to the reservations difficult and sometimes traumatic.

Surviving the Schools, Using the Education

After the turn of the century, the Bureau of Indian Affairs relaxed its policy of sending Indians away to boarding schools, and more students attended schools on the reservations. The boarding school experience and the educational philosophy of the government left a legacy of bitterness, confusion, and heartbreak that continues to affect Indian people, as they struggle to revive languages that were almost destroyed and restore pride in a heritage that was denied any worth for so long.

But the boarding schools were also places where young Indian people found ways of resisting the educational crusade intended to transform them. They often engaged in acts of subversion and rebellion against petty authority, built bonds of loyalty and friendship with other students, and found humor and humanity in the midst of loneliness, hardship, and regimentation. Interviews with alumni from the Chilocco Indian School in northeastern Oklahoma convinced Tsianina Lomawaima, an anthropologist and daughter of a former Chilocco student, that Indians at boarding schools "actively created an ongoing educational and social process." They built their own world within the confines of boarding-school life, and in the process, they turned an institution founded and controlled by the federal government into an Indian school. Some students even had pride in their school, and most found ways to enjoy themselves. Indian people, she concludes, "made Chilocco their own."[27]

Many Indian students took the knowledge, experience, and literacy acquired during their school years and applied it in their work, their lives, and their understanding of the world. Like Luther Standing Bear (see the document by Standing Bear on pages 380–84), they saw Western education and traditional education as two systems of knowledge. They tried to combine the best of both systems in adapting to the demands of a rapidly changing world. Many boarding school alumni returned to reservations as teachers themselves — in 1899, 45 percent of the United States Indian School Service employees were Indians.[28] For Wolf Chief, a Hidatsa who went to school for the first time when he was thirty years old, education was a source of power. He learned arithmetic so he could check traders' weights and later operate his own store on the Fort Berthold reservation in North Dakota. He also employed his literary skills to bombard the Office of Indian Affairs with complaints and concerns: "He has contracted the letter writing habit and cannot be suppressed," said one exasperated agent in 1886. He wrote to newspapers and magazines and even wrote to the president, and his letters got results.[29] Anna Moore Shaw, a Pima who attended school with Helen Sekaquaptewa and became the first Indian woman high-school graduate in Arizona, wrote that her generation was "the first to be educated in two cultures, the Pima and the white. Sometimes the values were in conflict, but we were learning to put them together to make a way of life different from anything the early Pimas ever dreamed of."[30]

Two Omaha sisters, Susan and Suzette LaFlesche, used their education in the non-Indian world to champion Indian rights, lecturing and lobbying Congress, while their brother, Francis, became one of the first Indian anthropologists. Suzette studied at reservation mission schools, private schools in the East, and the University of Nebraska. She worked as a volunteer nurse among the Poncas. After Standing Bear led his people back to their Nebraska homeland in 1879, she and her brother accompanied him on a tour of eastern cities. On the lecture circuit in both America and Great Britain, using the name Bright Eyes and dressed in ceremonial Omaha clothing, she spoke out about the unjust treatment of Indians and the need for Indians to become citizens to gain full protection under the Constitution. Her sister Susan graduated from the Hampton Institute in 1886 and the Women's Medical College in Philadelphia in 1889 to become the first female Indian physician. She returned west, serving as the government reservation doctor for the Omahas and also went on the lecture circuit with her sister. She lobbied for the eradication of tuberculosis and the prohibition of alcohol on reservations. She campaigned against government corruption, incompetence, and unjust laws that kept Indians dependent. She also supported individual ownership of land, allowing Omahas to sell and lease their property free from government supervision.

The Two Worlds of Ohiyesa and Charles Eastman

Perhaps no individual better personified the changing times in which Indians lived than did Charles Alexander Eastman. Eastman was born in Minnesota in 1858, the youngest of five children. His father, Many Lightnings, was a Wahpeton Dakota Sioux; his mother, who died soon after his birth, was Mary Eastman, daughter of soldier-turned-artist Seth Eastman. Named Hakadah, "the pitiful last," at birth, the boy earned the name Ohiyesa, "the winner," in a lacrosse game. Raised in traditional Dakota ways by his paternal grandmother, as an adult Ohiyesa lived in two worlds and earned distinction in American society as Dr. Charles Eastman, physician, writer, and reformer. After the Minnesota Sioux uprising of 1862, Many Lightnings was imprisoned and the family fled to Ontario, Canada, where Ohiyesa lived until the age of fifteen. Ohiyesa believed his father had been hanged in the mass execution of Santee Sioux war-

Charles Eastman
Charles Eastman (Ohiyesa, 1858–1939) was photographed while he was a student at Dartmouth College. Dartmouth College Library.

riors at Mankato, but in 1873, Many Lightnings returned. He had escaped the gallows by President Lincoln's pardon and instead had served three years in jail in Davenport, Iowa. He then converted to Christianity and took the surname of his deceased wife's father, calling himself Jacob Eastman. He named his son Charles Eastman and urged him to learn white Americans' ways. "We have now entered upon this life, and there is no going back," he told his son. "Besides, one would be like a hobbled pony without learning to live like those among whom we must live."[31]

Jacob Eastman sent his son to school. "It is the same as if I sent you on your first warpath," he told him. "I shall expect you to conquer."[32] Charles first attended Santee Normal Training School in Nebraska. "I hardly think I was ever tired in my life until those first days of boarding school," he wrote later. "All day things seemed to come and pass with a wearisome regularity, like walking railway ties — the step was too short for me. At times I felt something of the fascination of the new life, and again there would arise in me a dogged resistance, and a voice seemed to be saying, 'It is cowardly to depart from the old things.'"[33] In September 1876, just months after the Battle of the Little Big Horn, Eastman entered Beloit College in Wisconsin. "I was now a stranger in a strange country," he recalled, "and deep in a strange life from which I could not retreat."[34] After stints at Knox College in Illinois and Kimball Union in New Hampshire, he graduated from Dartmouth College, and then earned his M.D. degree at Boston University.

Committed to using his education and skills for the benefit of his people, Eastman became the agency physician at the Pine Ridge reservation in 1890, just as the tensions revolving around the Ghost Dance (see pages 280–81) were reaching a breaking point. There he met Elaine Goodale, a young New England woman who was teaching on the reservation and who spoke Sioux. They married in 1891 and had six children. But their courtship had been overshadowed by the tragedy at Wounded Knee. Eastman treated wounded and mutilated Indians and went over the field searching for survivors. He found a woman's body three miles from the scene of the massacre "and from this point on we found them scattered along as they had been relentlessly hunted down and slaughtered while fleeing for their lives." He stood, stunned, amid the fragments of burned tepees and the frozen bodies of old men, women, and children. It was, he wrote, "a severe ordeal for one who had so lately put all his faith in the Christian love and lofty ideals of the white man."[35]

Nevertheless, Eastman remained a staunch advocate of educating the Sioux in American ways. Many of his later writings reflected the ideas of the Social Darwinism of the time that asserted that unchanging Indians were a vanishing race. "The North American Indian was the highest type of pagan and uncivilized man," he wrote in 1902. "But the Indian no longer exists as a natural and free man. Those remnants which now dwell upon the reservations present only a sort of tableau—a fictitious copy of the past."[36] He became prominent as a "Red Progressive," supported the Dawes Allotment Act, and worked for the Bureau of Indian Affairs. In the age of the self-made man, reformers held him up as a model for what Indians could achieve if they would only abandon their Indian ways and learn to live like other Americans.

But Charles Eastman never entirely stopped being Ohiyesa. Although he worked to bring about assimilation of Indians into mainstream society, he had been raised in the traditional ways and remained strongly attached to Sioux values. He wrote extensively—often in collaboration with his wife—for a non-Indian audience that contained many influential people. To some extent, he told them what they wanted to hear, but he also supported Indian rights and was a founding member of the Society of American Indians. He criticized American injustice and hypocrisy, and insisted that Americans had much to learn from Indian society about morality and spirituality. He attacked corrupt Indian agents and took on the Indian Service. Before his death in 1939, he returned to Ontario. There he lived and died in a forest cabin, thereby completing the circle by returning from "civilization" to "the deep woods."[37] In the rapidly changing world of American Indians, Eastman demonstrated that one could adapt without totally assimilating. One biographer wrote that he "could wear both a war bonnet and a high starched collar with equal aplomb."[38] He insisted that he could be both an Indian and an American. "I am an Indian," he wrote at the end of his autobiography, "and while I have learned much from civilization, for which I am grateful, I have never lost my Indian sense of right and justice. I am for development and progress along social and spiritual lines, rather than those of commerce, nationalism, or material efficiency. Nevertheless, so long as I live, I am an American."[39]

A CHANGING WORLD

In 1900, the United States census estimated there were a mere 250,000 Indians in the country. Their count was low—the census takers decided who was or was not Indian, and recorded many Indians as black, mulatto, or colored, while Indians who could pass as white often found that safer to do than attracting racist attention by proclaiming their Indian identity. Nevertheless the figures reflected four hundred years of demographic decline. In the eyes of most Americans, Indians were doomed to extinction, "a vanishing race."

At the same time, Indians found themselves with declining legal protection and subjected to increasing state and federal legislation. After the Supreme Court decision in *Ex Parte Crow Dog* in 1883 assured tribes some autonomy in settlement of criminal cases, Congress in 1885 passed the Major Crimes Act making it a federal crime for Indians to commit rape, murder, manslaughter, assault with intent to kill, arson, or larceny against another Indian on a reservation. (In later years, the list of crimes was expanded to fourteen, adding kidnapping, incest, assault with a dangerous weapon, assault resulting in serious bodily injury, burglary, robbery, and sexual relations with a female under sixteen years of age.) In *United States v. Kagama* (1886), a case involving the murder of an Indian by another Indian on the Hoopa Valley reservation in California, the Supreme Court affirmed the constitutionality of the Major Crimes Act. In 1903, with the support of the Indian Rights Association, the Kiowas sued the Secretary of the Interior to stop the transfer of their lands by a fraudulent agreement that blatantly contravened the Treaty of Medicine Lodge. In *Lone Wolf v. Hitchcock* (1903), the Supreme Court declared that Congress had complete constitutional authority over Indian affairs and could abrogate its own treaties. The Supreme Court in *Winters v. United States* (1908) recognized Indians as having federally reserved water rights,[40] but on the whole, Congress had the power to dispose of Indian lands as it saw fit.

"I Still Live": Indians in American Society

In spite of past population losses and legal constraints, the twentieth century was to be a time of endurance and survival, not decline and disappearance, in Indian country and in Indian communities. Surviving the dark years of the late nineteenth and early twentieth century built resources for later resurgence in a different social and political climate.

With their traditional economies in ruins, many Indian peoples found that they had to find new ways of making a living. Mohawk men from Kahnawake near Montreal began working as steelworkers on high-rise projects at the end of the nineteenth century. Many traveled south to New York during the city's building boom in the 1920s, working on the Empire State Building, the Chrysler Building, and the George Washington Bridge. Railroads brought a flood of immigrants to the Puget Sound region of western Washington after the Civil War. Some Indians were pushed out of their homelands, but others found new opportunities for employment and barter — selling fish, logging and working in lumber mills, cultivating hops — that brought them into daily contact with their new neighbors.[41] In Alaska, Tlingit people continued the subsistence economies of old but also joined the labor market. Tlingit men fished for the canneries and worked in mining and lumbering operations; women sold baskets and handicrafts to tourists on the streets of Sitka or processed fish alongside Chinese immigrant workers.[42] Although exploitation of Indian land, labor, and resources devastated environments, disrupted communities, and generated dependence, some Indian people participated in the market economy in ways that helped fend off white domination.

A Meeting of the Indian Council of New England, Providence, Rhode Island, 1924
By donning Plains Indian-style headdresses and buckskins, the council members made a public proclamation of Indian identity and presence in an area of the country where most Americans believed Indians had long since disappeared. Haffenreffer Museum of Anthropology, Brown University, Providence.

Menominees in Wisconsin who worked as loggers and mill laborers and Metlakatlan Tsimshians who harvested timber and salmon in British Columbia achieved a measure of prosperity but used the proceeds to strengthen their communities and preserve their cultural independence.[43]

In New England, Indian women continued to make baskets, but now they sold them door-to-door or to tourists. Many young Indian women found employment in textile mills in Lowell, Massachusetts, or Manchester, New Hampshire. Native American men continued, as they had since the eighteenth century, to go to sea, while others found work closer to home as trappers, as guides (Henry David Thoreau had hired Penobscot guides for his excursions through

Maine), or in the logging industry. Some migrated to the cities. Micmac Indians from northern Maine and the Maritime Provinces of Canada worked as seasonal laborers, picking potatoes and blueberries. Some traveled west to work on building the Canadian Pacific Railroad. Others moved south to work in Boston. Native people in New England maintained important ties of kinship and community and began to develop regional networks and pan-Indian organizations. In 1923, when most white Americans assumed Indians had long since disappeared from the area, the New England Indian Council formed, adopting as its motto "I still live."

On the Plains, many women earned cash by selling bead work and other crafts to off-reservation markets. Plains Indian men, whose economy and role had rested so heavily on hunting buffalo, faced a particularly bleak future now that the buffalo herds were destroyed. Many adjusted to the new conditions and the post-allotment world by hunting smaller game, herding, gardening, and working for wages. But the government's exhortations to settle down and take up farming on 160 acres of land had little appeal for many young men. Instead, a few found employment in a venture that took them far from the hard times on the reservations and required them to dress and act like Indians "of old."

For a generation after the end of the wars for the Great Plains, entrepreneurs like William F. (Buffalo Bill) Cody hired Indians to travel the East and Europe as members of Wild West shows. They donned headdresses, rode bareback, attacked wagon trains, and danced for audiences in the eastern United States, England, France, Belgium, Germany, Austria, Poland, Russia, and even Australia. Even Sitting Bull participated in Buffalo Bill's show for a time. "Show Indians" earned money and got to see the world; they became tourists as well as entertainers. Some met presidents, queens, and kings; some attended theater and opera; some, like the Oglala Red Shirt, became celebrities on the tour circuit. Black Elk, another Oglala who later became a spiritual leader, joined the show as a young man "for adventure." Some of the performers died in cities far from home. Indian commissioners, members of Congress, humanitarian reformers, and some members of the Society of American Indians opposed the shows for exploiting Indians and perpetuating an image of Indian "barbarism." Some scholars have seen the Indians who participated as victims of commercial capitalism that marginalized Native people. Certainly the Wild West shows and the people who "played Indian" in them helped to create a popular stereotype of all Indians as feather-bonneted, horseriding warriors. But the Indians who participated in the shows do not seem to have seen themselves as victims or pawns. They got paid for displaying a part of their history and culture that the government was intent on destroying and many seem to have enjoyed themselves doing it. As one scholar of the Wild West show concludes, it was "the only place to be Indian—and defiantly so—and still remain relatively free from the interference of missionaries, teachers, agents, humanitarians, and politicians."[44]

At home, some individuals forged new roles for themselves and found new ways to represent their people. Quanah Parker, a Comanche warrior and son of captive Cynthia Ann Parker, fought against the Americans in the Red River War of 1874–75 but then rose to prominence as the principal Comanche chief

Quanah Parker
Quanah Parker (c. 1852–1911) with To-pay and Cho-ny, two of his seven wives, c. 1892. The government worried about what it called Quanah's "much married condition" and pressured him to give wives up in accordance with its regulations. Quanah swore "to give up and relinquish all claims to To-pay as my wife." But To-pay stayed with him and bore him two children. Quanah Parker had two wives when he died in 1911. Western History Collections, University of Oklahoma Library.

and a savvy politician after his people were confined to the reservation. He made himself useful to the U.S. government as a chief who would comply with the new policies being implemented on the reservation. He leased grazing rights on Comanche lands to local cattlemen. He achieved wealth and position, owning a large herd of cattle and living in an impressive house. He sent his children away to receive an American education. But he also used his position to represent his people; he refused to cut his hair or to comply with the government's rules forbidding polygyny, and he became a leader in the peyote religion.[45]

Peyote buttons had been used in Mexico and in religious rituals along the Rio Grande for centuries. Now, in the late nineteenth and early twentieth centuries, a new religion based on the use of peyote entered Indian territory in the United States and then spread north across the Plains. It grew to become the Native American Church of the twentieth century. Though some of the rituals differed among regions and tribes, the religion had widespread appeal because it combined Christian elements with ancient tribal roots and provided "a bridge between traditional faiths and the realities of contemporary life."[46] Whereas many older ceremonies, such as the Sun Dance, took place in the open during the day, peyote ceremonies were performed quietly at night and could more easily escape the prying eyes of Indian agents intent on suppressing tribal religions. The religion was opposed by many non-Indians—and by some Indians. But in 1918 the Native American Church was formally organized in Oklahoma. Its declared purpose was to promote Christian religious belief using "the practices of the peyote sacrament" and to teach Christian morality and self-respect. The church prohibited alcohol and advocated monogamy, family responsibility, and hard work as means of combating the social problems that plagued many Indian communities. The use of peyote in ceremonies continued to draw opposition: fourteen states outlawed the drug by 1923; the Navajo tribal council banned it from the reservation in 1940; it was the subject

Sherman Coolidge and Black Coal
*Arapaho Episcopalian Minister Sherman Coolidge (1862–1932)
stands with his left hand on the shoulder of Northern Arapaho
chief, Black Coal (1843–93), who was called Tag-ge-tha-the
(Shot-off Fingers) because of his three missing fingers. Like
Coolidge, Black Coal became an advocate of new ways. He was
one of the first Arapahos to convert to Catholicism, sent his son to
boarding school, and earned praise as the "hidden hero of the
Rockies" from the white minister, Rev. John Roberts, whom he
helped to establish a government school. American Heritage Center,
University of Wyoming.*

of a Supreme Court case and new federal
legislation in the 1990s. Nevertheless, the
Native American Church of the United
States was organized in 1944 and functions as an important element in the lives
of thousands of Indian people today.

A New Generation of Leaders

In the first decades of the twentieth century, some Indians began to "talk back" to
the United States. They subjected American society to searching scrutiny and challenged the supposed superiority of "civilization" by pointing to enduring qualities
in Indian life and culture.[47]

A new generation of Indians,
schooled in American ways, united for the
first time by a common language, English,
and aware of the challenges confronting
their people, founded the Society of
American Indians in 1911. The members
included some of the more influential Indians of the day: Charles Eastman; the
Rev. Sherman Coolidge, an Arapaho Episcopalian minister who had been captured
at the age of seven by American troops,
raised by an army captain, and lived many
years in New York City; Carlos Montezuma, a Yavapai Apache who had been
captured by Pima Indians as a boy, sold to
an itinerant Italian photographer who
changed his name to Carlos Montezuma,
later earned a medical degree and became
a respected physician in Chicago; Henry
Roe Cloud, a Winnebago who obtained
bachelor's and master's degrees from Yale
and became a Presbyterian minister;
Arthur S. Parker, a Seneca anthropologist;
the Sioux writer Gertrude Bonnin (also
known as Zitkala-Sa) (see "Two Sioux
School Experiences," pages 384–89). These
people became known as the "Red Pro-
gressives." According to Sherman Coolidge,
the establishment of the Society of American Indians, an organization "managed solely for and by the Indians," meant that "the hour has struck when the

Jim Thorpe (1887–1953), Playing Football at Carlisle
National Archives.

best educated and most cultured of the race should come together to voice the common demands, to interpret correctly the Indians' heart, and to contribute in a more united way their influence and exertion with the rest of the citizens of the United States in all lines of progress and reform, for the welfare of the Indian race in particular, and all humanity in general."[48] The Society favored assimilation but also lobbied for citizenship, improved health care on reservations, a special court of claims for Indians, and other reform issues. Disputes over the Bureau of Indian Affairs and the Native American Church caused it to decline by the 1920s, but it represented a first step toward the kind of pan-Indian unity that would play a vital role in the protection of Indian rights and the preservation of Indian culture in later years. Far to the north, Tlingit and other Alaskan communities formed the Alaskan Native Brotherhood in 1912, and lobbied to protect Native resources and rights, and to end discrimination.

For a few Indians, sports provided access to temporary fame and fortune. Louis Francis Sockalexis, a Penobscot from Maine, played baseball at Holy Cross College and Notre Dame. In 1897, he broke into the major leagues, playing for Cleveland. In his first season, he played the outfield, batted .338, and stole sixteen bases, but alcoholism cut short his career and he died at the age of forty-two in 1913.[49] A more famous Indian athlete, Jim Thorpe, was born on the Sauk and Fox reservation in Oklahoma in 1887, the year the Allotment Act was passed. In 1898, his father sent him to the Haskell Institute in Lawrence, Kansas, where the eleven-year-old learned to play football. But Jim was an indifferent student at best, and in 1904 his father sent him to Carlisle, partly because it was too far for the youth to run away to home. At Carlisle, he found his niche in athletics and earned varsity letters in eleven sports: football, track, baseball, boxing, wrestling, lacrosse, gymnastics, swimming, hockey, handball, and basketball. In 1912, he competed for the United States in the Olympic Games in Stockholm, winning gold medals in both the pentathlon and the decathlon, an achievement unequaled in Olympic history. A year later, however, the U.S. Amateur Athletic Union stripped him of his medals and erased his name from the record books after discovering that he had once played baseball for a minor league team in North Carolina for $25 a week and was therefore a professional. Thorpe went on to play baseball for the New York Giants and other teams and then played professional football. In 1920, he became the first president of the American Professional Football Association (now the National Football League). Press polls judged Thorpe the greatest athlete of the first half of the twentieth century, but after he quit football in 1928 his life was marked by failed marriage, struggles with alcohol, and odd jobs, including bit roles in "cowboy and Indian" movies. Thirty years after his death in 1953, a court ruled that he had been unjustly stripped of his medals and duplicate medals were restored to his children.

Soldiers and Citizens

In 1917, the United States entered the First World War, which had been raging in Europe since 1914. About sixteen thousand Indians served in the armed forces, and many more contributed to the cause on the home front. American society, and the press in particular, interpreted the Indians' participation as evidence of their assimilation: "it may seem strange to see an Apache in a sailor's blue uniform," said one paper, "but it merely shows that he has become an American and has passed the tribal stage." That Indians were now fighting for the United States and defending Western values and democracy constituted, in the words of one scholar, "the ultimate vindication of U.S. expansionism, since it proved that the vanquished were better off for having been conquered." Indians pointed to their patriotism and sacrifice as evidence of their readiness for full citizenship: "Challenged, the Indian has responded and shown himself a citizen of the world," said Seneca Arthur C. Parker, president of the Society for American Indians.[50]

Although many Indians volunteered, some resisted the draft on the basis that they were not citizens and could not vote or because they saw it as an infringement of their tribal sovereignty and treaty rights. Carlos Montezuma criticized the drafting of Indians as "another wrong perpetuated on the Indian without FIRST bestowing his just title—THE FIRST AMERICAN CITIZEN."[51] The Iroquois Confederacy made a separate declaration of war against Germany, emphasizing that they were independent nations and fighting the war as allies, not as subjects, of the United States.° In 1924, Congress passed the Indian Citizenship Act, extending citizenship and suffrage to all American Indians. Roughly two-thirds of Indian people, including those who had taken allotments or served in World War I, had already been accorded citizenship, but passage of the act affirmed the belief that America's first peoples had become sufficiently assimilated to take up their role as participating American citizens. But things were not that simple. Some states continued to place obstacles in the way of Indian voting, and not all Indians eagerly embraced their new status. "The law of 1924 cannot . . . apply to Indians," declared one Mohawk, "since they are independent nations. Congress may as well pass a law making Mexicans citizens."[52] As events throughout the twentieth century would demonstrate, the place of American Indians in American society and the relations of Indian nations with the United States were far from resolved.

Indian Affairs on the Eve of the Great Depression

The 1920s were a time of unprecedented affluence for many Americans. Indians became United States citizens, but, unlike the Osages (see page 344), few shared in the prosperity that many Americans enjoyed during the "roaring twenties." In 1926, the Department of the Interior commissioned a team of scholars, headed by anthropologist Lewis Meriam, to conduct a survey of Indian affairs. Henry Roe Cloud, the Winnebago graduate of Yale University and Auburn Theological Seminary and one of the founding members of the Society of American Indians, was one of the principal investigators. The commission's report, published two years later as *The Problem of Indian Administration* and popularly known as the Meriam Report, detailed the problems confronting American Indians and drew attention to the poverty, ill health, and despair that beset Indian communities. Indians could not, said the report, live in "a glass case" and the clock could not be turned back; the traditional economic foundations of Indian culture could not be restored. Nevertheless, the report recommended reforms in the Bureau of Indian Affairs (BIA) to increase its efficiency and promote the social and economic advancement of Indians "so that they may be absorbed into the prevailing civilization or be fitted to live in the presence of that civilization at least in accordance with a minimum standard of health and decency."[53] These minimum goals had rarely been attained since

---

°The Six Nations of Canada sent a delegation to London in 1921 and to the League of Nations in Geneva in 1923 to argue their case that as a sovereign nation they were exempt from Canada's laws.

the Allotment Act had weakened the communal and family basis of Indian life. The report called for an end to allotment and advocated phasing out Indian boarding schools, where "provisions for the care of the Indian children . . . are grossly inadequate." The Indian Service, said the report, "has not appreciated the fundamental importance of a family life and community activities in the social and economic development of a people."[54]

In 1929, the stock market crashed and the United States entered the worst depression in its history. Millions of Americans found themselves unemployed, and stark pictures of breadlines and starving children replaced images of national prosperity. In 1932, Democrat Franklin Delano Roosevelt was swept into the Oval Office with a mandate for reform. Roosevelt committed the federal government to unprecedented levels of economic planning and social responsibility. He promised a new deal for "the forgotten man" — and no one was more forgotten than American Indians.

References

1. Peter Nabokov, *Two Leggings: The Making of a Crow Warrior* (Lincoln: University of Nebraska Press, 1982), 197.
2. Sarah Winnemucca Hopkins, *Life among the Piutes* (Reno: University of Nevada Press, 1994), 89–90.
3. Wooden Leg quoted in Colin G. Calloway, ed., *Our Hearts Fell to the Ground: Plains Indian Views of How the West Was Lost* (Boston: Bedford Books, 1996), 159; Frederick E. Hoxie, *Parading through History: The Making of the Crow Nation in America, 1805–1935* (Cambridge: Cambridge University Press, 1995), 309.
4. Clyde Ellis, "'There Is No Doubt . . . the Dances Should Be Curtailed': Indian Dances and Federal Policy on the Southern Plains, 1880–1930," *Pacific Historical Review* 70 (2001), 543–69.
5. *Second Annual Address to the Public of the Lake Mohonk Conference* (Philadelphia: Indian Rights Association, 1884), 6–7.
6. D. S. Otis, ed., *The Dawes Act and the Allotment of Indian Lands* (Norman: University of Oklahoma Press, 1973), 10.
7. Quoted in David Wallace Adams, *Education for Extinction: American Indians and the Boarding School Experience, 1875–1928* (Lawrence: University Press of Kansas, 1995), 23.
8. Virgil Vogel, ed., *This Country Was Ours: A Documentary History of the American Indian* (New York: Harper and Row, 1972), 193.
9. Now-ah-quay-gi-shig (N. B. Hurr) quoted in Ignatia Broker, *Night Flying Woman: An Ojibway Narrative* (St. Paul: Minnesota Historical Society Press, 1983), xi–xii.
10. Melissa L. Meyer, *The White Earth Tragedy: Ethnicity and Dispossession at a Minnesota Anishinaabe Reservation, 1889–1920* (Lincoln: University of Nebraska Press, 1994), quotes at 161, 171, 229.
11. The people of Grand Ronde Reservation made the transition from a hunting and gathering subsistence economy to an agricultural community and accepted allotment before the Dawes Act was passed. Tracy Neal Leavelle, "'We Will Make It Our Own Place': Agriculture and Adoptation at the Grand Ronde Reservation, 1856–1887," *American Indian Quarterly* 22 (1998), 433–56; Emily Greenwald, *Re-*

configuring the Reservation: The Nez Percés, Jicarilla Apaches, and the Dawes Act (Lincoln: University of Nebraska Press, 2002).

12. Arrell M. Gibson, *The American Indian: Prehistory to the Present* (Lexington, Mass.: D. C. Heath, 1980), 502.

13. Terry P. Wilson, *The Underground Reservation: Osage Oil* (Lincoln: University of Nebraska Press, 1985), chap. 6; "FBI File on Osage Indian Murders," 3 rolls of microfilm (Wilmington, Del.: Scholarly Resources, Inc., 1986). Charles H. Red Corn's novel, *A Pipe for February* (Norman: University of Oklahoma Press, 2002), deals with the experiences of Osage people amid the wealth and murders of the 1920s.

14. Richard White, *The Roots of Dependency: Subsistence, Environment, and Social Change among Choctaws, Pawnees, and Navajos* (Lincoln: University of Nebraska Press, 1983), 212.

15. Francis Paul Prucha, ed., *Americanizing the American Indians: Writings by the "Friends of the Indian," 1880–1920* (Lincoln: University of Nebraska Press, 1978), 194.

16. Adams, *Education for Extinction,* 26–27.

17. Clyde Ellis, *To Change Them Forever: Indian Education at the Rainy Mountain Boarding School, 1893–1920* (Norman: University of Oklahoma Press, 1996).

18. Adams, *Education for Extinction,* 63, 211.

19. Helen Sekaquaptewa, *Me and Mine: The Life Story of Helen Sekaquaptewa as Told to Louis Udall* (Tucson: University of Arizona Press, 1969), 8; Leo W. Simmons, ed., *Sun Chief: The Autobiography of a Hopi Indian, by Don C. Talayesva* (New Haven: Yale University Press, 1942), 88–89.

20. Sekaquaptewa, *Me and Mine,* 92–93, 96.

21. Luther Standing Bear, *Land of the Spotted Eagle* (Lincoln: University of Nebraska Press, 1978), 232–33.

22. Brenda J. Child, *Boarding School Seasons: American Indian Families, 1900–1940* (Lincoln: University of Nebraska Press, 1998).

23. Basil H. Johnston, *Indian School Days* (Norman: University of Oklahoma Press, 1988), 60.

24. Luther Standing Bear, *Land of the Spotted Eagle,* 234 Bette; Child, *Boarding School Seasons,* 66–67, 112–15.

25. Simmons, ed., *Sun Chief: The Autobiography of a Hopi Indian,* 90–91; P. David Seaman, ed., *Born a Chief: The Nineteenth Century Hopi Boyhood of Edmund Nequatewa* (Tucson: University of Arizona Press, 1993), 107–9.

26. Malcolm Margolin, ed., *The Way We Lived: California Indian Stories, Songs and Reminiscences* (Berkeley: Heyday Books and the California Historical Society, 1993), 182.

27. K. Tsianina Lomawaima, *They Called It Prairie Light: The Story of Chilocco Indian School* (Lincoln: University of Nebraska Press, 1994), 167.

28. Wilbert H. Ahern, "An Experiment Aborted: Returned Indian Students in the Indian School Service, 1881–1908," *Ethnohistory* 44 (1997), 263–304.

29. Carolyn Gilman and Mary Jane Schneider, *The Way to Independence: Memories of a Hidatsa Indian Family, 1840–1920* (St. Paul: Minnesota Historical Society Press, 1987), 153–54, 226.

30. Quoted in Gretchen M. Bataille and Kathleen Mullen Sands, *American Indian Women: Telling Their Lives* (Lincoln: University of Nebraska Press, 1984), 84.

31. Charles A. Eastman, *From the Deep Woods to Civilization: Chapters in the Autobiography of an Indian* (1916; reprinted Lincoln: University of Nebraska Press, 1977), 25.

32. Eastman, *From the Deep Woods to Civilization,* 31–32.

33. Eastman, *From the Deep Woods to Civilization,* 47.

34. Eastman, *From the Deep Woods to Civilization,* 54.

35. Eastman, *From the Deep Woods to Civilization*, 111–14.
36. Charles A. Eastman, *Indian Boyhood* (New York: McClure, Phillips and Co., 1902), v.
37. Hertha Dawn Wong, *Sending My Heart Back Across the Years: Tradition and Innovation in Native American Autobiography* (New York: Oxford University Press, 1992), 140.
38. Raymond Wilson, *Ohiyesa: Charles Eastman, Santee Sioux* (Urbana: University of Illinois Press, 1983), 191.
39. Eastman, *From the Deep Woods to Civilization*, 195.
40. John Shurts, *Indian Reserved Water Rights: The Winters Doctrine in Its Social and Legal Context, 1830s–1930s* (Norman: University of Oklahoma Press, 2000).
41. Alexandra Harmon, *Indians in the Making: Ethnic Relations with Indian Identities around Puget Sound* (Berkeley: University of California Press, 1998), chap. 4.
42. Sergei Kan, *Memory Eternal: Tlingit Culture and Russian Orthodox Christianity, 1794–1994* (Seattle: University of Washington Press, 1999), chap. 7.
43. Brian C. Hosmer, *American Indians in the Marketplace: Persistence and Innovation among the Menominees and Metlakatlans, 1870–1920* (Lawrence: University Press of Kansas, 1999).
44. L. G. Moses, *Wild West Shows and the Images of American Indians, 1883–1933* (Albuquerque: University of New Mexico Press, 1996), 278. James Welch, *The Heartsong of Charging Elk* (New York: Random House, 2000), provides a fictional account of a "show Indian" who gets stranded in France.
45. William T. Hagan, *Quanah Parker, Comanche Chief* (Norman: University of Oklahoma Press, 1993).
46. Carol Hampton, "Native American Church," in Frederick E. Hoxie, ed., *Encyclopedia of North American Indians* (Boston: Houghton Mifflin, 1996), 418.
47. Frederick E. Hoxie, ed., *Talking Back to Civilization: Indian Voices from the Progressive Era* (Boston: Bedford/St. Martin's, 2001).
48. Sherman Coolidge, "The Function of the Society of American Indians," in Bernd Peyer, ed., *The Elders Wrote: An Anthology of Early Prose by North American Indians 1768–1931* (Berlin: Dietrich Reimer, 1982), 161.
49. Colin G. Calloway, *The Abenaki* (New York: Chelsea House, 1989), 81.
50. Russel Lawrence Barsh, "American Indians in the Great War," *Ethnohistory* 38 (1991), 276–303; quotes at 276, 287, 288.
51. Hoxie, *Talking Back to Civilization*, 126.
52. Quoted in Laurence M. Hauptman, *The Iroquois and the New Deal* (Syracuse: Syracuse University Press, 1981), 6.
53. Francis Paul Prucha, ed., *Documents of United States Indian Policy* (Lincoln: University of Nebraska Press, 1975), 219–21.
54. Margaret Connell Szasz, *Education and the American Indian: The Road to Self-Determination since 1928*, 3d ed. (Albuquerque: University of New Mexico Press, 1999), chap. 3.

Suggested Readings

Adams, David Wallace. *Education for Extinction: American Indians and the Boarding School Experience, 1875–1928* (Lawrence: University Press of Kansas, 1995).

Archuleta, Margaret L., Brenda J. Child, and K. Tsianina Lomawaima, eds. *Away from Home: American Indian Boarding School Experiences, 1879–2000* (Phoenix: The Heard Museum, 2000).

Child, Brenda J. *Boarding School Seasons: American Indian Families, 1900–1940* (Lincoln: University of Nebraska Press, 1998).

Eastman, Charles A. *From the Deep Woods to Civilization: Chapters in the Autobiography of an Indian* (Lincoln: University of Nebraska Press, 1977).

Harring, Sidney L. *Crow Dog's Case: American Indian Sovereignty, Tribal Law, and United States Law in the Nineteenth Century* (Cambridge: Cambridge University Press, 1994).

Hoxie, Frederick E. *The Final Promise: The Campaign to Assimilate the Indians, 1888–1920* (Lincoln: University of Nebraska Press, 1984).

Hoxie, Frederick E. *Parading through History: The Making of the Crow Nation in America, 1805–1935* (Cambridge: Cambridge University Press, 1995).

Hoxie, Frederick E., ed. *Talking Back to Civilization: Indian Voices from the Progressive Era* (Boston: Bedford/St. Martin's, 2001).

Iverson, Peter. *Carlos Montezuma and the Changing World of American Indians* (Albuquerque: University of New Mexico Press, 1982).

Lomawaima, K. Tsianina. *They Called It Prairie Light: The Story of Chilocco Indian School* (Lincoln: University of Nebraska Press, 1994).

McDonnell, Janet A. *The Dispossession of the American Indian, 1887–1934* (Bloomington: Indiana University Press, 1991).

Meyer, Melissa L. *The White Earth Tragedy: Ethnicity and Dispossession at a Minnesota Anishinaabe Reservation, 1889–1920* (Lincoln: University of Nebraska Press, 1994).

Moses, L. G. *Wild West Shows and the Images of American Indians, 1883–1933* (Albuquerque: University of New Mexico Press, 1996).

Moses, L. G., and Raymond Wilson, eds. *Indian Lives: Essays on Nineteenth- and Twentieth-Century Native American Leaders* (Albuquerque: University of New Mexico Press, 1985).

Pratt, Richard Henry. *Battlefield and Classroom: Four Decades with the American Indian, 1867–1904,* edited by Robert M. Utley (New Haven: Yale University Press, 1964).

Prucha, Francis Paul. *The Great Father: The United States Government and the American Indians.* 2 vols. (Lincoln: University of Nebraska Press, 1984).

Smith, Sherry L. *Reimagining Indians: Native Americans through Anglo Eyes, 1880–1940* (New York: Oxford University Press, 2000).

Standing Bear, Luther. *My People the Sioux* (Boston: Houghton Mifflin, 1928).

D O C U M E N T S

Dismantling Tribes and Their Homelands

Looking at the devastating effects on Indian life and lives of the policies of the late nineteenth century, it is easy to forget that many of those advocating and implementing these policies believed they were working in the Indians' best interests. The assault on tribalism that culminated in the Allotment Act of 1887 stemmed in part from concern that the government was mishandling Indian affairs, mistreating Indian people, and missing the opportunity to transform American Indians into American citizens. Leaders in the movement to reform Indian affairs were "a group of earnest men and women who unabashedly called themselves 'the friends of the Indian,'" wrote historian Father Francis P. Prucha. They "set about to solve the 'Indian problem' in terms of religious sentiment and patriotic outlook that were peculiarly American. They had great confidence in the righteousness of their cause, and they knew that God approved."[1]

Convinced of the superiority of Anglo-Saxon Protestant civilization, they saw little or nothing of value in Indian civilization. The "Indian problem" would disappear, they believed, when individual Indian people were swallowed up by American society and Indian tribes ceased to exist. They had no compunction about dictating to Indians what was best for them; after all, they were saving them from themselves and from extinction. They championed Indian rights in some important cases, but their main goals were to revolutionize Indian policy and thoroughly assimilate Indians. Private property, citizenship, and education were the keys to "Americanizing" American Indians.

The reformers were organized and vocal, and they exerted tremendous influence in Congress on the direction of Indian policy. To understand the changes in Indian policy and the intensity of the assault on Indian life, we must try to understand the people who spearheaded the movement. We need to consider how they saw things at the end of the nineteenth century. "They were an articulate lot," said Prucha. They "employed rhetoric as a weapon in their crusade" and "hammered incessantly on the public conscience" in speeches, pamphlets, press releases, articles, editorials, and letters to congressmen and government officials. Only by reading their words "can one begin to appreciate the strength of their convictions and the lengths to which they were willing to go in their program of Americanizing the Indians."[2]

Merrill Gates was one of the most prominent Indian reformers of the time. He had been president of Rutgers University and of Amherst College and was appointed to the Board of Indian Commissioners by President Chester Arthur in 1884. He served as president of the board and was an active participant at the Lake Mohonk conferences. In 1885, Gates prepared a long paper on Indian policy, which was printed in the *Annual Report of the Board of Indian Commissioners.* It is, says Prucha, "a remarkable example of the reformers' mentality."[3] It also shows what Indian peoples faced in their struggle to preserve their cultures and communities in late nineteenth-century America.

▶ **Questions for Consideration**

1. What criticisms does Gates level against the U.S. government's Indian policies, and what recommendations does he make for changing them?

2. What does he identify as the defining characteristics of tribal life that "hold Indians back," and what are the characteristics of Anglo-Saxon Protestant life with which he seeks to replace them?

3. What does Gates's paper reveal about how reformers, and eventually the federal government, were able to shift from a policy based on reservations to a policy based on dismantling reservations and yet remain consistent in their ultimate goal of "civilizing" Indians?

4. His crusade ultimately failed; are seeds of its failure evident in the arguments and assumption of the paper?

MERRILL E. GATES

From the *Seventeenth Annual Report of the Board of Indian Commissioners* (1885)

. . . For what ought we to hope as the future of the Indian? What should the Indian become?

Source: *Seventeenth Annual Report of the Board of Indian Commissioners* (1885), 17–19, 26–35; reprinted in Francis Paul Prucha, ed., *Americanizing the American Indians: Writings by the "Friends of the Indian," 1880–1900* (Lincoln: University of Nebraska Press, 1978), 45–54.

To this there is one answer—and but one. He should become an intelligent citizen of the United States. There is no other "manifest destiny" for any man or any body of men on our domain. To this we stand committed by all the logic of two thousand years of Teutonic and Anglo-Saxon history, since Arminius with his sturdy followers made a stand for liberty against the legions of

Rome. Foremost champions of that peculiarly Anglo-Saxon idea, that supports a strong central government, moves as a whole, yet protects carefully the local and individual freedom of all the parts, we are, as a matter of course, to seek to fit the Indians among us as we do all other men for the responsibilities of citizenship. And by the stupendous precedent of eight millions of freedmen made citizens in a day, we have committed ourselves to the theory that the way to fit men for citizenship is to make them citizens. The dangers that would beset Indian voters solicited by the demagogue would not be greater than those which now attend him unprotected by law, the prey of sharpers, and too often the pauperized, ration-fed pensioner of our Government, which, when it has paid at all the sums it has promised to pay to Indians, has paid them in such a way as to undermine what manhood and self-respect the Indian had. For one, I would willingly see the Indians run the risk of being flattered a little by candidates for Congress. None of their tribes are destitute of shrewd men who would watch the interests of the race.

Has our Government in its dealings with the Indians hitherto adopted a course of legislation and administration, well adapted to build up their manhood and make them intelligent, self-supporting citizens?

They are the wards of the Government. Is not a guardian's first duty so to educate and care for his wards as to make them able to care for themselves? It looks like intended fraud if a guardian persists in such management of his wards and such use of their funds intrusted to him as in the light of experience clearly unfits them and will always keep them unfit for the management of their own affairs and their own property. When a guardian has in his hands funds which belong to his wards, funds which have been expressly set apart for the education of those wards, funds which from time to time he has publicly professed himself to be about to use for that particular end, yet still retains the money from year to year while his wards suffer sadly in the utter lack of proper educational facilities, we call his conduct disgraceful—an outrage and a crying iniquity. Yet our Commissioner of Indian Affairs again and again calls attention to the fact that the Government has funds, now amounting to more than $4,000,000, which are by treaty due to Indians for educational purposes alone. Who can doubt that a comprehensive plan looking to the industrial and the general education of all Indians should be undertaken at once? . . .

But it is not merely in neglecting to provide direct means for their education that we have been remiss in our duty to the Indians. The money and care which our Government has given to the Indians in most cases has not been wisely directed to strengthening their manhood, elevating their morals, and fitting them for intelligent citizenship. We have massed them upon reservations, fenced off from all intercourse with the better whites. We have given them no law to protect them against crimes from within the tribe—almost none to protect them against aggression from without. And above all else we have utterly neglected to teach them the value of honest labor. Nay, by rations dealt out whether needed or not, we have interfered to suspend the efficient teaching by which God leads men to love and honor labor. We have taken from them the compelling inspiration that grows out of His law, "if a man will not work, neither shall he eat!" Why, if a race inured to toil were cut off from all intercourse with the outside world, and left to roam at large over a vast territory, regularly fed by Government supplies, how many generations would pass before that race would revert to barbarism?

We have held them at arm's length, cut them off from the teaching power of good example, and given them rations and food to hold them in habits of abject laziness. A civilization like ours would soon win upon the Indians and bring them rapidly into greater harmony with all its ideas if as a nation in our dealings with them we had shown a true spirit of humanity, civilization, and Christianity.

But such a spirit cannot be discerned in the history of our legislation for the Indians or our treaties with them. We have never recognized the obligation that rests upon us as a dominant, civilized people, the strong Government, to legislate carefully, honorably, disinterestedly, for these people. We boast of the brilliant adaptations of science to practical ends and everyday uses as the distinctive mark of American progress. Where are the triumphs of social science discernible in the treatment Americans have given to this distinctively American question? We have not shown in this matter anything approaching that patient study of social conditions which England has shown for the uncivilized natives in her domain. The great mass of our legislation regarding Indians has had to do with getting land we had promised them into our possession by the promise of a price as low as we could fix and yet keep them from making border warfare upon us in sheer despair. The time of would-be reformers has been occupied too constantly in devising precautions to keep what had been appropriated from being stolen before it reached the Indians. And when it has reached them it has too often been in the form of annuities and rations that keep them physically and morally in the attitude of lazy, healthy paupers. We have not seemed to concern ourselves with the question, How can we organize, enforce, and sustain institutions and habits among the Indians which shall civilize and Christianize them? The fine old legend, *noblesse oblige*, we have forgotten in our broken treaties and our shamefully deficient legislation. . . .

Two peculiarities which mark the Indian life, if retained, will render his progress slow, uncertain and difficult. These are:

(1) The tribal organization.

(2) The Indian reservation.

I am satisfied that no man can carefully study the Indian question without the deepening conviction that these institutions must go if we would save the Indian from himself.

And first, the tribe. Politically it is an anomaly—an *imperium in imperio*. Early in our history, when whites were few and Indians were relatively numerous and were grouped in tribes with something approaching to a rude form of government, it was natural, it was inevitable, that we should treat with them as tribes. It would have been hopeless for us to attempt to modify their tribal relations. But now the case is entirely different. There is hardly one tribe outside the five civilized tribes of the Indian Territory which can merit the name of an organized society or which discharges the simplest functions of government. Disintegration has long been the rule. Individualism, the key-note of our socio-political ideas in this century, makes itself felt by sympathetic vibrations even in the rude society of the Indian tribes. There is little of the old loyalty to a personal chief as representing a governing authority from the Great Spirit. Perhaps there never was so much of this as some have fancied among the Indians. Certainly there are few signs of it now. A passive acquiescence in the mild leadership of the promising son of a former leader, among the peaceable tribes of the southwest, or a stormy hailing by the young braves of a new and reckless leader, bloodthirsty for a raid upon the whites—these are the chief indications of the survival of the old spirit.

Indian chiefs are never law-makers, seldom even in the rudest sense law-enforcers. The councils where the chief is chosen are too often blast-furnaces of anarchy, liquefying whatever forms of order may have established themselves under a predecessor. The Indians feel the animus of the century. As personal allegiance to a chieftain and the sense of tribal unity wanes, what is taking its place? Literally, nothing. In some cases educated but immoral and selfish leaders take advantage of the old traditions to acquire influence which they abuse. On the whole, however, a rude, savage individuality is developing itself, but not under the guidance of law, moral, civil, or religious.

Surely the intelligence of our nation should devise and enforce a remedy for this state of affairs. . . .

The highest right of man is the right to be a man, with all that this involves. The tendency of the tribal organization is constantly to interfere with and frustrate the attainment of his highest manhood. The question whether parents have a right to educate their children to regard the tribal organization as supreme, brings us at once to the consideration of the family.

And here I find the key to the Indian problem. More than any other idea, this consideration of the family and its proper sphere in the civilizing of races and in the development of the individual, serves to unlock the difficulties which surround legislation for the Indian.

The family is God's unit of society. On the integrity of the family depends that of the State. There is no civilization deserving of the name where the family is not the unit of civil government. Even the extreme advocates of individualism must admit that the highest and most perfect personality is developed through those relations which the family renders possible and fosters. . . .

The tribal organization, with its tenure of land in common, with its constant divisions of goods and rations per capita without regard to service rendered, cuts the nerve of all that manful effort which political economy teaches us proceeds from the desire for wealth. True ideas of property with all the civilizing influences that such ideas excite are formed only as the tribal relation is outgrown. . . .

But the tribal system paralyzes at once the desire for property and the family life that ennobles that desire. Where the annuities and rations that support a tribe are distributed to the industrious and the lazy alike, while almost all property is held in common, there cannot be any true stimulus to industry. And where the property which a deceased father has called his own is at the funeral feast distributed to his adult relatives, or squandered in prolonged feasting, while no provision whatever is made for the widow or the children, how can the family be perpetuated, or the ideal of the permanence and the preciousness of this relation become clear and powerful. Yet this is the custom in by far the greater number of the Indian tribes. . . .

As the allegiance to tribe and chieftain is weakened, its place should be taken by the sanctities of family life and an allegiance to the laws which grow naturally out of the family! Lessons in law for the Indian should begin with the developing and the preservation, by law, of those relations of property and of social intercourse which spring out of and protect the family. First of all, he must have land in severalty.°

Land in severalty, on which to make a home for his family. This land the Government should, where necessary, for a few years hold in trust for him or his heirs, inalienable and unchargeable. But it shall be his. It shall be patented to him as an individual. He shall hold it by what the Indians who have been hunted from reservation to reservation pathetically call, in their requests for justice, "a paper-talk from Washington, which tells the Indian what land is his so that a white man cannot get it away from him." "There is no way of reaching the Indian so good as to show him that he is working for a home. Experience shows that there is no incentive so strong as the confidence that by long, untiring labor, a man may secure a home for himself and his family." The Indians are no exception to this rule. There is in this consciousness of a family-hearth, of land and a home in prospect as permanently their own, an educating force which at once begins to lift these savages out of barbarism and sends them up the steep toward civilization, as rapidly as easy divorce laws are sending some sections of our country down the slope toward barbaric heathenism. . . .

Thus the family and a homestead prove the salvation of those whom the tribal organization and the reservation were debasing. It was a step in advance when Agent Miles began to issue rations to families instead of to the headmen of the tribe. Every measure which strengthens the family tie and makes clearer the idea of family life, in which selfish interests and inclinations are sacrificed for

---

°Individual ownership of a tract of land.

the advantage of the whole family, is a powerful influence toward civilization.

In this way, too, family affection and care for the education and the virtue of the young are promoted. Thus such law as is necessary to protect virtue, to punish offenses against purity, and to abolish polygamy, will be welcomed by the Indians. These laws enforced will help still further to develop true family feeling. Family feeling growing stronger and stronger as all the members of the family work on their own homestead for the welfare of the home, will itself incline all toward welcoming the reign of law, and will increase the desire of all for systematic education. The steadying, educating effect of property will take hold upon these improvident children of the West, who have for too long lived as if the injunction, "Take no thought for the morrow," in its literal sense, were their only law.

We must as rapidly as possible break up the tribal organization and give them law, with the family and land in severalty as its central idea. We must not only give them law, we must force law upon them. We must not only offer them education, we must force education upon them. Education will come to them by complying with the forms and the requirements of the law. . . .

While we profess to desire their civilization, we adopt in the Indian reservation the plan which of all possible plans seems most carefully designed to preserve the degrading customs and the low moral standards of heathen barbarism. Take a barbaric tribe, place them upon a vast tract of land from which you carefully exclude all civilized men, separate them by hundreds of miles from organized civil society and the example of reputable white settlers, and having thus insulated them in empty space, doubly insulate them from Christian civilization by surrounding them with sticky layers of the vilest, most designingly wicked men our century knows, the whiskey-selling whites and the debased half-breeds who infest the fringes of our reservations, men who have the vices of the barbarian plus the worst vices of the reckless fron-

tiersman and the city criminal, and then endeavor to incite the electrifying, life-giving currents of civilized life to flow through this doubly insulated mass. If an Indian now and then gets glimpses of something better and seeks to leave this seething mass of in-and-in breeding degradation, to live in a civilized community, give him no protection by law and no hope of citizenship. If he has won his way as many have done through the highest institutions of learning, with honor, tell him that he may see many of our largest cities ruled by rings of men, many of whom are foreigners by birth, ignorant, worthless, yet naturalized citizens, but that he must not hope to vote or to hold office.

If he says "I will be content to accumulate property, then," tell him "you may do so; but any one who chooses may withhold your wages, refuse to pay you money he has borrowed, plunder you as he will, and our law gives you no redress." Thus we drive the honest and ambitious Indian, as we do the criminals, back to the tribe and the reservation; and cutting them off from all hopes of bettering themselves while we feed their laziness on Government rations, we complain that they are not more ambitious and industrious.

Christian missionaries plunge into these reservations, struggle with the mass of evil there, and feeling that bright children can be best educated in the atmosphere of civilization, they send to Eastern institutions these Indian children plucked like fire-stained brands from the reservations. They are brought to our industrial training schools. The lesson taught by the comparison of their photographs when they come and when they go is wonderful. (See pages 348–50.)

The years of contact with ideas and with civilized men and Christian women so transform them that their faces shine with a wholly new light, for they have indeed "communed with God." They came children; they return young men and young women; yet they look younger in the face than when they came to us. The prematurely aged look of hopeless heathenism has given way to that dew of eternal youth which marks the difference between the savage and the man who lives in the thoughts of an eternal future. . . .

Break up the reservation. Its usefulness is past. Treat it as we treat the fever-infected hospital when life has so often yielded to disease within its walls that we see clearly the place is in league with the powers of death, and the fiat goes forth, "though this was planned as a blessing it has proved to be a curse; away with it! burn it!"

Guard the rights of the Indian, but for his own good break up his reservations. Let in the light of civilization. Plant in alternate sections or townships white farmers, who will teach him by example. Reserve all the lands he needs for the Indian. Give land by trust-deed in severalty to each family.

Among the parts of the reservation to be so assigned to Indians in severalty retain alternate ranges or townships for white settlers. Let only men of such character as a suitable commission would approve be allowed to file on these lands. Let especial advantages in price of land, and in some cases let a small salary be offered, to induce worthy farmers thus to settle among the Indians as object-teachers of civilization. Let the parts of the reservations not needed be sold by the Government for the benefit of the Indians, and the money thus realized be used to secure this wise intermingling of the right kind of civilized men with the Indians. Over all, extend the law of the States and Territories, and let Indian and white man stand alike before the law. . . .

References

1. Francis Paul Prucha, ed., *Americanizing the American Indians: Writings by the "Friends of the Indian," 1880–1900* (Lincoln: University of Nebraska Press, 1978), 1.
2. Prucha, ed., *Americanizing the American Indians,* 8–9.
3. Prucha, ed., *Americanizing the American Indians,* 46.

Suggested Readings

Hagan, William T. *The Indian Rights Association* (Tucson: University of Arizona Press, 1985).

Hoxie, Frederick E. *The Final Promise: The Campaign to Assimilate the Indians, 1880–1920* (Lincoln: University of Nebraska Press, 1984).

Keller, Robert H., Jr. *American Protestantism and United States Indian Policy 1869–1882* (Lincoln: University of Nebraska Press, 1983).

Mathes, Valerie Sherer. *Helen Hunt Jackson and Her Indian Reform Legacy* (Austin: University of Texas Press, 1990).

Priest, Loring Benson. *Uncle Sam's Stepchildren: The Reformation of United States Indian Policy, 1865–1887* (Lincoln: University of Nebraska Press reprint edition, 1969).

Prucha, Francis P. *American Indian Policy in Crisis: Christian Reformers and the Indians, 1865–1900* (Norman: University of Oklahoma Press, 1976).

Prucha, Francis Paul, ed. *Americanizing the American Indians: Writings by the "Friends of the Indian," 1880–1900* (Lincoln: University of Nebraska Press, 1978).

An Indian View of the Indian Bureau

◆—●—◆

Carlos Montezuma (c. 1866–1923) was born in central Arizona at a time when the influx of settlers and prospectors was disrupting the world of his Yavapai people. Named Wassaja by his parents, the young boy was captured by Pima Indians in 1871 and sold to an Italian photographer, Carlos Gentile, for thirty dollars. Gentile gave him a new name and an education. Montezuma attended the University of Illinois and graduated from Chicago Medical College in 1889. He took an appointment in the Indian Service and worked at the Fort Stevenson Indian School in North Dakota, the Western Shoshone Agency in Nevada, and the Colville Reservation in Washington. He served as medical officer at Richard Henry Pratt's school in Carlisle from 1894–96, and then opened a private practice in Chicago.

Montezuma believed in the values of hard work and individualism espoused by people like Merrill Gates, and he believed Indian people had what it took to achieve great things if given the chance. But he complained bitterly about the government's Indian policies and believed that the Indian Bureau stood in the way of the very "progress" that the government claimed to be promoting among Indians. He came into conflict with bureau personnel, gave lectures in which he criticized the bureau and the reservation system it supported, and advocated citizenship for Indian people. He supported assimilation but also argued for taking pride in Indian ways. He was one of the founding members of the Society of American Indians and the following excerpt comes from an essay he published in the society's *Quarterly Journal* in 1914. But not everyone in the society agreed with his outspoken views, and he later left the society. In 1916 he founded the magazine *Wassaja* (his Yavapai name) as a forum for his ideas.

Montezuma rebuilt his ties with the Yavapai community at Fort McDowell in Arizona. He visited when he could and he assisted the community in their fights to preserve their land and water. After he was diagnosed with tuberculosis, he returned to the Southwest and died at Fort McDowell in January 1923 — a year before Congress granted Indians citizenship.

▶ **Questions for Consideration**

1. Compare Montezuma's view of Indian society and Indian policy with that expressed by Merrill Gates. In what essential ways do they differ?

2. What does Montezuma advocate for Indian people? Do these goals seem attainable as he outlines them?

3. Compare Montezuma's view with some of the views expressed by later Indian activists in Chapter 7.

CARLOS MONTEZUMA
"What Indians Must Do" (1914)

We must free ourselves. Our peoples' heritage is freedom. Freedom reigned in their whole make-up. They harmonized with nature and lived accordingly. Preaching freedom to our people on reservations does not make them free any more than you can, by preaching, free those prisoners who are in the penitentiary. Reservations are prisons where our people are kept to live and die, where equal possibilities, equal education and equal responsibilities are unknown. . . .

We must do away with the Indian Bureau. The reservation system has debarred us as a race from acquiring that knowledge to appreciate our property. The government after teaching us how to live without work has come to the conclusion "that the Indians are not commercialists" and, therefore, "we (his guardian) will remove them as we think best and use them as long as our administration lasts and make friends."° The Indian Department has drifted into commercialism at the expense of our poor benighted people. So they go on and say, "Let us not allot those Indians on that sweet flowing water because there are others who will profit by damming it up and selling it out to the newcomers; that the Indians do not use or develop their lands; five acres of irrigated land is all that one Indian can manage, but in order to be generous, we will give him ten acres and close up the books and call it square; that their vast forest does them no good, before the Indian can open his eyes let us transfer it to the Forestry Reserve Department. Never mind, let the Indian scratch for his wood to cook with and to warm himself in the years to come; that the Indians have no use for rivers, therefore, we will go into damming business and build them on their lands without their consent. Pay? No! Why should we?" They give us "C" class water instead of "A" class. They have got us! Why? Because we do not know the difference.

"In this valley the Indians have too much land. We will move them from where they have lived for centuries (by Executive order in behalf of the coming settlers). Even if he had cultivated and claims more than that, we will allot that Indian only ten acres. If he rebels and makes trouble, we will put him in jail until he is ready to behave himself." This poor Indian may try to get an Indian friend to help him out of his predicament. But right there the Indian helper is balked by the Indian Department and is told he is not wanted on the reservation. When an Indian collects money from among his tribe to defray expenses to Washington and back in order to carry their complaints, and to be heard and considered in their rights, the superintendent with the aid of the Indian policeman takes this Indian, takes the money away from him and gives back the money to those who contributed, put[s] him in jail and brands him s a grafter. . . .

The sooner the Government abolishes the Indian Bureau, the better it will be for we Indians in every way. The system that has kept alive the Indian Bureau has been instrumental in dominating over our race for fifty years. In that time the Indian's welfare has grown to the secondary and the Indian Bureau the whole thing, and therefore a necessary political appendage of the government. It sends out exaggerated and wonderful reports to the public in order to suck the blood of our race, so that it may have perpetual life to sap your

Source: Carlos Montezuma, "What Indians Must Do," *Quarterly Journal* 2 (1914), 294–99; reprinted in Frederick E. Hoxie, ed., *Talking Back to Civilization: Indian Voices from the Progressive Era* (Boston: Bedford/St. Martin's, 2001), 92–95.

°Apparently these quotations are fictitious. Montezuma used them as rhetorical devices to make his point that the Indian Office cared little for its charges' welfare. Hoxie, ed. *Talking Back to Civilization, 93.*

life, my life and our children's future prospects. There are many good things to say about the Indian Department. It started out right with our people. It fed them, clothed them and protected them from going outside of the reservations. It was truly a place of refuge. Then they were dominated by agents; now they are called superintendents. On the reservation our people did not act without the consent of the Superintendent; they did not express themselves without the approval of the Superintendent, and *they did not dare to think,* for that would be to rival, to the Superintendent. Yesterday, today, our people are in the same benighted condition. As Indians they are considered nonentities. They are not anything to themselves and not anything to the world. . . .

We must be independent. When with my people for a vacation in Arizona I must live outdoors; I must sleep on the ground; I must cook in the fire on the ground; I must sit on the ground, I must eat nature's food and I must be satisfied with inconveniences that I do not enjoy at my Chicago home. Yet those blood relations of mine are independent, happy, because they were born and brought up in that environment, while as a greenhorn I find myself dependent and helpless in such simple life. In order for we Indians to be independent in the whirl of this other life, we must get into it and used to it and live up to its requirements and take our chances with the rest of our fellow creatures. Being caged up and not permitted to develop our facilities has made us a dependent race. We are looked upon as hopeless to save and hopeless to do anything for ourselves. The only Christian way, then, is to leave us alone and let us die in that condition. The conclusion is true that we will die that way if we do not hurry and get out of it and hustle for our salvation. Did you ever notice how other races hustle and bustle in order to achieve independence? Reservation Indians must do the same as the rest of the wide world.

As a full-blooded Apache Indian° I have nothing more to say. Figure out your responsibility and the responsibility of every Indian that hears my voice.

°Yavapais are sometimes referred to as Yavapai Apaches.

Suggested Readings

Hoxie, Frederick E., ed. *Talking Back to Civilization: Indian Voices from the Progressive Era* (Boston: Bedford/St. Martin's, 2001).

Iverson, Peter. *Carlos Montezuma and the Changing World of American Indians* (Albuquerque: University of New Mexico Press, 1982).

Sioux School Experiences

Individuals who underwent the cultural transformation programs at the boarding schools had mixed experiences. For many Indian students, the experience was heartbreaking and humiliating; they left these schools with bitter memories, little education, and few prospects. But some of those who endured the painful process and found fault with the system also learned from it and employed the knowledge and skills they acquired in their subsequent careers. The government viewed a boarding school education as a powerful weapon of assimilation, and many Indian students rejected it for that same reason. But two Sioux writers, Luther Standing Bear and Gertrude Bonnin or Zitkala-Ša, illustrate the ambivalent relationships which some alumni had with the boarding school system and their ability to use the education they received for their own purposes.

Stripped of much of their traditional culture yet regarded by American society as capable only of the most menial employment, many students came out of the schools as confused and bewildered as when they went in. The story of Plenty Horses graphically illustrates the plight of many Carlisle graduates. In 1890, during the Ghost Dance troubles on Pine Ridge reservation, the twenty-two-year-old Lakota shot and killed an army officer. He was tried for murder. When asked why he killed the officer, Plenty Horses responded: "I am an Indian. Five years I attended Carlisle and was educated in the ways of the white man. . . . I was lonely. I shot the lieutenant so I might make a place for myself among my people. Now I am one of them. I shall be hung and the Indians will bury me as a warrior." The federal court, however, confronted a dilemma: if Plenty Horses was guilty of murdering the army officer, were not the officers and men of the Seventh Cavalry guilty of murdering Lakota men, women, and children at Wounded Knee? The court decided that Plenty Horses had acted as a belligerent during a state of war and acquitted him. The case made legal history but it did not help Plenty Horses, who lived out his life in poverty and despondency.[1]

Born around the time of the Treaty of Fort Laramie in 1868, Plenty Kill was raised in traditional ways during traumatic years for his Lakota Sioux people. He participated in a buffalo hunt as a boy and was trained to become a Lakota warrior, but such male roles were soon precluded as the Lakotas became confined to reservations. In 1879, his father, Standing Bear, enrolled him in the first class at the new boarding school established in Carlisle, Pennsylvania. There his name was changed from Plenty Kill to Luther Standing Bear; he was subjected to the school's assimilationist curriculum, and he endured a sustained assault

Plenty Horses *Smithsonian Institution.*

on his Lakota heritage and identity. But Standing Bear weathered the assault and did well at school.

When he graduated in 1884, he returned to the Rosebud reservation. At Carlisle he had been trained as a tinsmith, but found no use for his skills on the reservation. He became an assistant at the government school on the reservation and in 1891 was appointed superintendent of one of the day schools on the Pine Ridge reservation. He did a stint with Buffalo Bill's Wild West show and spent almost a year in England with the troupe. After a variety of jobs, he moved to California in 1912 and began a career as a film actor, playing Indian characters in silent movies and B westerns. He became president of the Indian Actors Association.

Standing Bear died in 1939. On the surface, his life and career might point to the success of Carlisle in separating him from his Lakota community and paving the way for assimilation into modern society. He left the reservation and "made it" in modern America. But Standing Bear's writings — *My People the Sioux* (1928), *Indian Boyhood* (1931), *Land of the Spotted Eagle* (1933), and *Stories of the Sioux* (1934) — champion the values of Indian cultures and implicitly reject the assimilationist policies and philosophies that drove Carlisle. He also became a severe critic of the government's reservation policies and of the repressive hand of Indian agents on Indian lives.

Zitkala-Ša (Red Bird), a Yankton Sioux, went to Carlisle not as a student, but as a teacher. Born Gertrude Simmons (to a Yankton mother and a white father) in 1876, she left her home in South Dakota for Indiana at eight years old, lured by the promise of "red apples" at a Quaker-sponsored school, White's Indian Manual Labor Institute. Despite poor health, she continued her education at Earlham College in Indiana, where she became a skillful orator and musician. She also studied at the New England Conservatory of Music. In 1898, Richard Henry Pratt hired her to teach at Carlisle. Increasingly, however, she found that her education and career were pulling her away from her mother and her people. About this time she published a series of autobiographical essays under her self-given Yankton name Zitkala-Ša. The essays were later published as *American Indian Stories* (1921), and in the words of one scholar "serve as emblems of the experience of many Indians living in transition between two worlds—the remembered past and the alien present, tradition and change."[2] The passages reprinted here recount her experiences as a student and a teacher. In 1902, she left Carlisle and returned to Yankton. She broke her engagement to Carlos Montezuma, who lived in Chicago and was unwilling to relocate, and married a Yankton man, Raymond Bonnin.

Raymond Bonnin worked for the Indian Service and the family was assigned to the Uintah Ouray Ute reservation in Utah, where they lived for fourteen years. Gertrude Bonnin taught, did public speaking, and became active in the Society of American Indians formed in 1911. When she was elected president of the society in 1916, the family moved to Washington, D.C. She edited the society's magazine, lobbied for reform of Indian policies, campaigned for Indian citizenship and, like Pratt, strongly opposed peyote. She worked with the Indian Rights Association and the American Indian Defense Association, and in 1926 she and her husband formed the National Council of American Indians. She also served as president of the association until she died in 1938, just a year before Standing Bear.[3]

▶ Questions for Consideration

Plenty Horses, Standing Bear, and Bonnin each experience a personal journey from traditional life to the modern world via the boarding school. Standing Bear and Bonnin used their literary and oratorical talents to defy, not promote, the assimilationist education policies of the time. Zitkala-Ša writes about "testing the chains which tightly bound my individuality."

1. In what ways do these authors test those chains and manage to preserve both individual and tribal identity despite the "iron routine" of the "civilizing machine"?

2. What do their writings reveal about the tensions they experienced in walking between two ways of life? In what ways do they take issue with the educational system and the assimilationist policies of the time?

3. What is their audience and in what ways might they also be described as interpreters and culture brokers?

4. What conflicts and contradictions are suggested in the photograph of Plenty Horses, a Carlisle graduate, wearing braids, blanket, and moccasins, standing next to an army gun shortly after the Wounded Knee massacre?

LUTHER STANDING BEAR
"What a School Could Have Been Established" (1933)

I grew up leading the traditional life of my people, learning the crafts of hunter, scout, and warrior from father, kindness to the old and feeble from mother, respect for wisdom and council from our wise men, and was trained by grandfather and older boys in the devotional rites to the Great Mystery. This was the scheme of existence as followed by my forefathers for many centuries, and more centuries might have come and gone in much the same way had it not been for a strange people who came from a far land to change and reshape our world.

At the age of eleven years, ancestral life for me and my people was most abruptly ended without regard for our wishes, comforts, or rights in the matter. At once I was thrust into an alien world, into an environment as different from the one into which I had been born as it is possible to imagine, to remake myself, if I could, into the likeness of the invader.

By 1879, my people were no longer free, but were subjects confined on reservations under the rule of agents. One day there came to the agency a party of white people from the East. Their presence aroused considerable excitement when it became known that these people were school teachers who wanted some Indian boys and girls to take away with them to train as were white boys and girls.

Now, father was a 'blanket Indian,'° but he was wise. He listened to the white strangers, their offers and promises that if they took his son they would care well for him, teach him how to read and write, and how to wear white man's clothes. But to father all this was just 'sweet talk,' and I know that it was with great misgivings that he left the decision to me and asked if I cared to go with these people. I, of course, shared with the rest of my tribe a distrust of the white people, so I know that for all my dear father's anxiety he was proud to hear me say 'Yes.' That meant that I was brave.

I could think of no reason why white people wanted Indian boys and girls except to kill them, and not having the remotest idea of what a school was, I thought we were going East to die. But so well had courage and bravery been trained into us that it became a part of our unconscious thinking and acting, and personal life was nothing when it came time to do something for the tribe. Even in our play and games we voluntarily put ourselves to various tests in the effort to grow brave and fearless, for it was most discrediting to be called *can'l wanka,* or a coward. Accordingly there were few cowards, most Lakota men preferring to die in the performance of some act of bravery than to

---

Source: Luther Standing Bear, *Land of the Spotted Eagle.* (Lincoln: University of Nebraska Press, 1978), 229–37. Copyright 1933 and renewed © 1960 by May Jones. Reprinted with the permission of the University of Nebraska Press.

°The term "blanket Indian" was often used to describe a person who adhered to the old ways. In the parlance of white reformers, it carried pejorative connotations, and Indian students who "returned to the blanket"—i.e., went home to live as Indians on the reservation rather than making new lives for themselves in American society—were regarded with particular disdain by people like Richard Pratt.

Luther Standing Bear (c. 1868–1939)
Library of Congress.

die of old age. Thus, in giving myself up to go East I was proving to my father that he was honored with a brave son. In my decision to go, I gave up many things dear to the heart of a little Indian boy, and one of the things over which my child mind grieved was the thought of saying good-bye to my pony. I rode him as far as I could on the journey, which was to the Missouri River, where we took the boat. There we parted from our parents, and it was a heart-breaking scene, women and children weeping. Some of the children changed their minds and were unable to go on the boat, but for many who did go it was a final parting.

On our way to school we saw many white people, more than we ever dreamed existed, and the manner in which they acted when they saw us quite indicated their opinion of us. It was only about three years after the Custer battle, and the general opinion was that the Plains people merely infested the earth as nuisances, and our being there simply evidenced misjudgment on the part of Wakan Tanka [the Great Mystery]. Whenever our train stopped at the railway stations, it was met by great numbers of white people who came to gaze upon the little Indian 'savages.' The shy little ones sat quietly at the car windows looking at the people who swarmed on the platform. Some of the children wrapped themselves in their blankets, covering all but their eyes. At one place we were taken off the train and marched a distance down the street to a restaurant. We walked down the street between two rows of uniformed men whom we called soldiers, though I suppose they were policemen. This must have been done to protect us, for it was surely known that we boys and girls could do no harm. Back of the rows of uniformed men stood the white people craning their necks, talking, laughing, and making a great noise. They yelled and tried to mimic us by giving what they thought were war-whoops. We did not like this, and some of the children were naturally very much frightened. I remember how I tried to crowd into the protecting midst of the jostling boys and girls. But we were all trying to be brave, yet going to what we thought would end in death at the hands of the white people whom we knew had no love for us. Back on the train the older boys sang brave songs in an effort to keep up their spirits and ours too. In my mind I often recall that scene — eighty-odd blanketed boys and girls marching down the street surrounded by a jeering, unsympathetic people whose only emotions were those of hate and fear; the conquerors looking upon the conquered. And no more understanding us than if we had suddenly been dropped from the moon.

At last at Carlisle the transforming, the 'civilizing' process began. It began with clothes. Never, no matter what our philosophy or spiritual quality, could we be civilized while wearing the moccasin and blanket. The task before us was not only that of accepting new ideas and adopting new manners, but actual physical changes and discomfort has to be borne uncomplainingly until the body adjusted itself to new tastes and habits. Our accustomed dress was taken and replaced with clothing that felt cumbersome and awkward. Against trousers and handkerchiefs we had a distinct feeling — they were unsanitary and the trousers kept us from breathing well. High collars, stiff-bosomed shirts, and suspenders fully three inches in width were uncomfortable, while leather boots caused actual suffering. We longed to go barefoot, but were told that the dew on the grass would give us colds. That was a new warning for us, for our mothers had never told us to beware of colds, and I remember as a child coming into the tipi with moccasins full of snow. Unconcernedly I would take them off my feet, pour out the snow, and put them on my feet again without any thought of sickness, for in that time colds, catarrh, bronchitis, and *la grippe* were unknown. But we were soon to know them. Then, red flannel undergarments were given us for winter wear, and for me, at least, discomfort grew into actual torture. I used to endure it as long as possible, then run upstairs and quickly take off the flannel garments and hide them. When inspection time came, I ran and put them on again, for I knew that if I were found disobeying the orders of the school I should be punished. My niece once asked me what it was that I disliked the most during those first bewildering days, and I said, 'red flannel.' Not knowing what I meant, she laughed, but I still remember those horrid, sticky garments which we had to wear next to the skin, and I still squirm and itch when I think of them. Of course, our hair was cut, and then there was much disapproval. But that was part of the transformation process and in some mysterious way long hair stood in the path of our development. For all the grumbling among the bigger boys, we soon had our heads shaven. How strange I felt! Involuntar-

ily, time and time again, my hands went to my head, and that night it was a long time before I went to sleep. If we did not learn much at first, it will not be wondered at, I think. Everything was queer, and it took a few months to get adjusted to the new surroundings.

Almost immediately our names were changed to those in common use in the English language. Instead of translating our names into English and calling Zinkcaziwin, Yellow Bird, and Wanbli K'leska, Spotted Eagle, which in itself would have been educational, we were just John, Henry, or Maggie, as the case might be. I was told to take a pointer and select a name for myself from the list written on the blackboard. I did, and since one was just as good as another, and as I could not distinguish any difference in them, I placed the pointer on the name Luther. I then learned to call myself by that name and got used to hearing others call me by it, too. By that time we had been forbidden to speak our mother tongue, which is the rule in all boarding-schools. This rule is uncalled for, and today is not only robbing the Indian, but America of a rich heritage. The language of a people is part of their history. Today we should be perpetuating history instead of destroying it, and this can only be effectively done by allowing and encouraging the young to keep it alive. A language, unused, embalmed, and reposing only in a book, is a dead language. Only the people themselves, and never the scholars, can nourish it into life.

Of all the changes we were forced to make, that of diet was doubtless the most injurious, for it was immediate and drastic. White bread we had for the first meal and thereafter, as well as coffee and sugar. Had we been allowed our own simple diet of meat, either boiled with soup or dried, and fruit, with perhaps a few vegetables, we should have thrived. But the change in clothing, housing, food, and confinement combined with lonesomeness was too much, and in three years nearly one half of the children from the Plains were dead and through with all earthly schools. In the graveyard at Carlisle most of the graves are those of little ones.

I am now going to confess that I had been at Carlisle a full year before I decided to learn all I could of the white man's ways, and then the inspiration was furnished by my father, the man who has been the greatest influence in all my life. When I had been in school a year, father made his first trip to see me. After I had received permission to speak to him, he told me that on his journey he had seen that the land was full of 'Long Knives.' 'They greatly outnumber us and are here to stay,' he said, and advised me, 'Son, learn all you can of the white man's ways and try to be like him.' From that day on I tried. Those few words of my father I remember as if we talked but yesterday, and in the maturity of my mind I have thought of what he said. He did not say that he thought the white man's ways better than our own; neither did he say that I could be like a white man. He said, 'Son, try to be like a white man.' So, in two more years I had been 'made over.' I was Luther Standing Bear wearing the blue uniform of the school, shorn of my hair, and trying hard to walk naturally and easily in stiff-soled cowhide boots. I was now 'civilized' enough to go to work in John Wanamaker's fine store in Philadelphia.

I returned from the East at about the age of sixteen, after five years' contact with the white people, to resume life upon the reservation. But I returned, to spend some thirty years before again leaving, just as I had gone — a Lakota.

Outwardly I lived the life of the white man, yet all the while I kept in direct contact with tribal life. While I had learned all that I could of the white man's culture, I never forgot that of my people. I kept the language, tribal manners and usages, sang the songs and danced the dances. I still listened to and respected the advice of the older people of the tribe. I did not come home so 'progressive' that I could not speak the language of my father and mother. I did not learn the vices of chewing tobacco, smoking, drinking, and swear-

ing, and for all this I am grateful. I have never, in fact, 'progressed' that far.

But I soon began to see the sad sight, so common today, of returned students who could not speak their native tongue, or, worse yet, some who pretended they could no longer converse in the mother tongue. They had become ashamed and this led them into deception and trickery. The boys came home wearing stiff paper collars, tight patent-leather boots, and derby hats on heads that were meant to be clothed in the long hair of the Lakota brave. The girls came home wearing muslin dresses and long ribbon sashes in bright hues which were very pretty. But they were trying to squeeze their feet into heeled shoes of factory make and their waists into binding apparatuses that were not garments — at least they served no purpose of a garment, but bordered on some mechanical device. However, the wearing of them was part of the 'civilization' received from those who were doing the same thing. So we went to school to copy, to imitate; not to exchange languages and ideas, and not to develop the best traits that had come out of uncountable experiences of hundreds and thousands of years living upon this continent. Our annals, all happenings of human import, were stored in our song and dance rituals, our history differing in that it was not stored in books, but in the living memory. So, while the white people had much to teach us, we had much to teach them, and what a school could have been established upon that idea! However, this was not the attitude of the day, though the teachers were sympathetic and kind, and some came to be my lifelong friends. But in the main, Indian qualities were undivined and Indian virtues not conceded. And I can well remember when Indians in those days were stoned upon the streets as were the dogs that roamed them. We were 'savages,' and all who had not come under the influence of the missionary were 'heathen,' and Wakan Tanka, who had since the beginning watched over the Lakota and his land, was denied by these men of God. Should we not have been justified in thinking them heathen? And so the 'civilizing' process went on, killing us as it went.

When I came back to the reservation to resume life there, it was too late to go on the warpath to prove, as I had always hoped to prove to my people, that I was a real brave. However, there came the battle of my life—the battle with agents to retain my individuality and my life as a Lakota. I wanted to take part in the tribal dances, sing the songs I had heard since I was born, and repeat and cherish the tales that had been the delight of my boyhood. It was in these things and through these things that my people lived and could continue to live, so it was up to me to keep them alive in my mind.

Now and then the Lakotas were holding their tribal dances in the old way, and I attended. Though my hair had been cut and I wore civilian clothes, I never forsook the blanket. For convenience, no coat I have ever worn can take the place of the blanket robe; and the same with the moccasins, which are sensible, comfortable, and beautiful. Besides, they were devised by people who danced—not for pastime, excitement, or fashion—but because it was an innate urge. Even when studying under the missionary, I went to the dances of my tribe.

ZITKALA-ŠA

"The Melancholy of Those Black Days" (1921)

THE SCHOOL DAYS OF AN INDIAN GIRL

The Land of Red Apples

There were eight in our party of bronzed children who were going East with the missionaries. Among us were three young braves, two tall girls, and we three little ones, Judéwin, Thowin, and I.

We had been very impatient to start on our journey to the Red Apple Country, which, we were told, lay a little beyond the great circular horizon of the Western prairie. Under a sky of rosy apples we dreamt of roaming as freely and happily as we had chased the cloud shadows on the Dakota plains. We had anticipated much pleasure from a ride on the iron horse, but the throngs of staring palefaces disturbed and troubled us.

On the train, fair women, with tottering babies on each arm, stopped their haste and scrutinized the children of absent mothers. Large men, with heavy bundles in their hands, halted near by, and riveted their glassy blue eyes upon us.

I sank deep into the corner of my seat, for I resented being watched. Directly in front of me, children who were no larger than I hung themselves upon the backs of their seats, with their bold white faces toward me. Sometimes they took their forefingers out of their mouths and pointed at my moccasined feet. Their mothers, instead of

Source: Zitkala-Ša (Gertrude Bonnin), *American Indian Stories* (Washington: Hayworth Publishing House, 1921; reprinted Lincoln: University of Nebraska Press, 1985), 47–51, 65–68, 81–84, 95–99.

Gertrude Simmons Bonnin, Zitkala-Ša (1878–1938)
Courtesy of South Dakota Historical Society—State Archives.

stopped, on my way down the road, to hold my ear against the pole, and, hearing its low moaning, I used to wonder what the paleface had done to hurt it. Now I sat watching for each pole that glided by to be the last one.

In this way I had forgotten my uncomfortable surroundings, when I heard one of my comrades call out my name. I saw the missionary standing very near, tossing candies and gums into our midst. This amused us all, and we tried to see who could catch the most of the sweetmeats.

Though we rode several days inside of the iron horse, I do not recall a single thing about our luncheons.

It was night when we reached the school grounds. The lights from the windows of the large buildings fell upon some of the icicled trees that stood beneath them. We were led toward an open door, where the brightness of the lights within flooded out over the heads of the excited palefaces who blocked our way. My body trembled more from fear than from the snow I trod upon.

Entering the house, I stood close against the wall. The strong glaring light in the large white-washed room dazzled my eyes. The noisy hurrying of hard shoes upon a bare wooden floor increased the whirring in my ears. My only safety seemed to be in keeping next to the wall. As I was wondering in which direction to escape from all this confusion, two warm hands grasped me firmly, and in the same moment I was tossed high in midair. A rosy-cheeked paleface woman caught me in her arms. I was both frightened and insulted by such trifling. I stared into her eyes, wishing her to let me stand on my own feet, but she jumped me up and down with increasing enthusiasm. My mother had never made a plaything of her wee daughter. Remembering this I began to cry aloud.

They misunderstood the cause of my tears, and placed me at a white table loaded with food. There our party were united again. As I did not hush my crying, one of the older ones whispered to me, "Wait until you are alone in the night."

reproving such rude curiosity, looked closely at me, and attracted their children's further notice to my blanket. This embarrassed me, and kept me constantly on the verge of tears.

I sat perfectly still, with my eyes downcast, daring only now and then to shoot long glances around me. Chancing to turn to the window at my side, I was quite breathless upon seeing one familiar object. It was the telegraph pole which strode by at short paces. Very near my mother's dwelling, along the edge of a road thickly bordered with wild sunflowers, some poles like these had been planted by white men. Often I had

It was very little I could swallow besides my sobs, that evening.

"Oh, I want my mother and my brother Dawée! I want to go to my aunt!" I pleaded; but the ears of the palefaces could not hear me.

From the table we were taken along an upward incline of wooden boxes, which I learned afterward to call a stairway. At the top was a quiet hall, dimly lighted. Many narrow beds were in one straight line down the entire length of the wall. In them lay sleeping brown faces, which peeped just out of the coverings. I was tucked into bed with one of the tall girls, because she talked to me in my mother tongue and seemed to soothe me.

I had arrived in the wonderful land of rosy skies, but I was not happy, as I had thought I should be. My long travel and the bewildering sights had exhausted me. I fell asleep, heaving deep, tired sobs. My tears were left to dry themselves in streaks, because neither my aunt nor my mother was near to wipe them away. . . .

Iron Routine

A loud-clamoring bell awakened us at half-past six in the cold winter mornings. From happy dreams of Western rolling lands and unlassoed freedom we tumbled out upon chilly bare floors back again into a paleface day. We had short time to jump into our shoes and clothes, and wet our eyes with icy water, before a small hand bell was vigorously rung for roll call.

There were too many drowsy children and too numerous orders for the day to waste a moment in any apology to nature for giving her children such a shock in the early morning. We rushed downstairs, bounding over two high steps at a time, to land in the assembly room.

A paleface woman, with a yellow-covered roll book open on her arm and a gnawed pencil in her hand, appeared at the door. Her small, tired face was coldly lighted with a pair of large gray eyes.

She stood still in a halo of authority, while over the rim of her spectacles her eyes pried nervously about the room. Having glanced at her long list of names and called out the first one, she tossed up her chin and peered through the crystals of her spectacles to make sure of the answer "Here."

Relentlessly her pencil black-marked our daily records if we were not present to respond to our names, and no chum of ours had done it successfully for us. No matter if a dull headache or the painful cough of slow consumption had delayed the absentee, there was only time enough to mark the tardiness. It was next to impossible to leave the iron routine after the civilizing machine had once begun its day's buzzing; and as it was inbred in me to suffer in silence rather than to appeal to the ears of one whose open eyes could not see my pain, I have many times trudged in the day's harness heavy-footed, like a dumb sick brute.

Once I lost a dear classmate. I remember well how she used to mope along at my side, until one morning she could not raise her head from her pillow. At her deathbed I stood weeping, as the paleface woman sat near her moistening the dry lips. Among the folds of the bedclothes I saw the open pages of the white man's Bible. The dying Indian girl talked disconnectedly of Jesus the Christ and the paleface who was cooling her swollen hands and feet.

I grew bitter, and censured the woman for cruel neglect of our physical ills. I despised the pencils that moved automatically, and the one teaspoon which dealt out, from a large bottle, healing to a row of variously ailing Indian children. I blamed the hard-working, well-meaning, ignorant woman who was inculcating in our hearts her superstitious ideas. Though I was sullen in all my little troubles, as soon as I felt better I was ready again to smile upon the cruel woman. Within a week I was again actively testing the chains which tightly bound my individuality like a mummy for burial.

The melancholy of those black days has left so long a shadow that it darkens the path of years that have since gone by. These sad memories rise above those of smoothly grinding school days. Perhaps my Indian nature is the moaning wind which stirs them now for their present record. But, however tempestuous this is within me, it comes out as the low voice of a curiously colored seashell, which is only for those ears that are bent with compassion to hear it.

AN INDIAN TEACHER AMONG INDIANS

My First Day

Though an illness left me unable to continue my college course, my pride kept me from returning to my mother. Had she known of my worn condition, she would have said the white man's papers were not worth the freedom and health I had lost by them. Such a rebuke from my mother would have been unbearable, and as I felt then it would be far too true to be comfortable.

Since the winter when I had my first dreams about red apples I had been traveling slowly toward the morning horizon. There had been no doubt about the direction in which I wished to go to spend my energies in a work for the Indian race. Thus I had written my mother briefly, saying my plan for the year was to teach in an Eastern Indian school. Sending this message to her in the West, I started at once eastward.

Thus I found myself, tired and hot, in a black veiling of car smoke, as I stood wearily on a street corner of an old-fashioned town, waiting for a car. In a few moments more I should be on the school grounds, where a new work was ready for my inexperienced hands.

Upon entering the school campus, I was surprised at the thickly clustered buildings which made it a quaint little village, much more interesting than the town itself. The large trees among the houses gave the place a cool, refreshing shade, and the grass a deeper green. Within this large court of grass and trees stood a low green pump.

The queer boxlike case had a revolving handle on its side, which clanked and creaked constantly.

I made myself known, and was shown to my room, — a small, carpeted room, with ghastly walls and ceiling. The two windows, both on the same side, were curtained with heavy muslin yellowed with age. A clean white bed was in one corner of the room, and opposite it was a square pine table covered with a black woolen blanket.

Without removing my hat from my head, I seated myself in one of the two stiff-backed chairs that were placed beside the table. For several heart throbs I sat still looking from ceiling to floor, from wall to wall, trying hard to imagine years of contentment there. Even while I was wondering if my exhausted strength would sustain me through this undertaking, I heard a heavy tread stop at my door. Opening it, I met the imposing figure of a stately gray-haired man. With a light straw hat in one hand, and the right hand extended for greeting, he smiled kindly upon me. For some reason I was awed by his wondrous height and his strong square shoulders, which I felt were a finger's length above my head.

I was always slight, and my serious illness in the early spring had made me look rather frail and languid. His quick eye measured my height and breadth. Then he looked into my face. I imagined that a visible shadow flitted across his countenance as he let my hand fall. I knew he was no other than my employer.

"Ah ha! so you are the little Indian girl who created the excitement among the college orators!" he said, more to himself than to me. I thought I heard a subtle note of disappointment in his voice. Looking in from where he stood, with one sweeping glance, he asked if I lacked anything for my room.

After he turned to go, I listened to his step until it grew faint and was lost in the distance. I was aware that my car-smoked appearance had not concealed the lines of pain on my face.

For a short moment my spirit laughed at my ill fortune, and I entertained the idea of exerting myself to make an improvement. But as I tossed my hat off a leaden weakness came over me, and I felt as if years of weariness lay like water-soaked logs upon me. I threw myself upon the bed, and, closing my eyes, forgot my good intention. . . .

Retrospection

. . . As months passed over me, I slowly comprehended that the large army of white teachers in Indian schools had a larger missionary creed than I had suspected.

It was one which included self-preservation quite as much as Indian education. When I saw an opium-eater holding a position as teacher of Indians, I did not understand what good was expected, until a Christian in power replied that this pumpkin-colored creature had a feeble mother to support. An inebriate paleface sat stupid in a doctor's chair, while Indian patients carried their ailments to untimely graves, because his fair wife was dependent upon him for her daily food.

I find it hard to count that white man a teacher who tortured an ambitious Indian youth by frequently reminding the brave changeling that he was nothing but a "government pauper."

Though I burned with indignation upon discovering on every side instances no less shameful than those I have mentioned, there was no present help. Even the few rare ones who have worked nobly for my race were powerless to choose workmen like themselves. To be sure, a man was sent from the Great Father to inspect Indian schools, but what he saw was usually the students' sample work *made* for exhibition. I was nettled by this sly cunning of the workmen who hookwinked [sic] the Indian's pale Father at Washington.

My illness, which prevented the conclusion of my college course, together with my mother's stories of the encroaching frontier settlers, left me in no mood to strain my eyes in searching for latent good in my white co-workers.

At this stage of my own evolution, I was ready to curse men of small capacity for being the dwarfs their God had made them. In the process of my education I had lost all consciousness of the nature world about me. Thus, when a hidden rage took me to the small white-walled prison which I then called my room, I unknowingly turned away from my one salvation.

Alone in my room, I sat like the petrified Indian woman of whom my mother used to tell me. I wished my heart's burdens would turn me to unfeeling stone. But alive, in my tomb, I was destitute!

For the white man's papers I had given up my faith in the Great Spirit. For these same papers I had forgotten the healing in trees and brooks. On account of my mother's simple view of life, and my lack of any, I gave her up, also. I made no friends among the race of people I loathed. Like a slender tree, I had been uprooted from my mother, nature, and God. I was shorn of my branches, which had waved in sympathy and love for home and friends. The natural coat of bark which had protected my oversensitive nature was scraped off to the very quick.

Now a cold bare pole I seemed to be, planted in a strange earth. Still, I seemed to hope a day would come when my mute aching head, reared upward to the sky, would flash a zig-zag lightning across the heavens. With this dream of vent for a long-pent consciousness, I walked again amid the crowds.

At last, one weary day in the schoolroom, a new idea presented itself to me. It was a new way of solving the problem of my inner self. I liked it. Thus I resigned my position as teacher; and now I am in an Eastern city, following the long course of study I have set for myself. Now, as I look back upon the recent past, I see it from a distance, as a whole. I remember how, from morning till evening, many specimens of civilized peoples visited the Indian school. The city folks with canes and eyeglasses, the countrymen with sunburnt cheeks and clumsy feet, forgot their relative social ranks in an ignorant curiosity. Both sorts of these Christian palefaces were alike astounded at seeing the children of savage warriors so docile and industrious.

As answers to their shallow inquiries they received the students' sample work to look upon. Examining the neatly figured pages, and gazing upon the Indian girls and boys bending over their books, the white visitors walked out of the schoolhouse well satisfied: they were educating the children of the red man! They were paying a liberal fee to the government employees in whose able hands lay the small forest of Indian timber.

In this fashion many have passed idly through the Indian schools during the last decade, afterward to boast of their charity to the North American Indian. But few there are who have paused to question whether real life or long-lasting death lies beneath this semblance of civilization.

References

1. Robert M. Utley, *The Indian Frontier of the American West, 1846–1890* (Albuquerque: University of New Mexico Press, 1984), 227–28, 245.
2. Dexter Fisher, "Foreword," to Zitkala-Ša, *American Indian Stories* (Lincoln: University of Nebraska Press, 1985), vi.
3. P. Jane Hafen, "Zitkala-Ša" in Frederick E. Hoxie, ed., *Encyclopedia of North American Indians* (Boston: Houghton Mifflin, 1996), 708–10.

Suggested Readings

Adams, David Wallace. *Education for Extinction: American Indians and the Boarding School Experience, 1875–1928* (Lawrence: University Press of Kansas, 1995).

Hafen, P. Jane, ed. *Dreams and Thunder: Stories, Poems, and the Sun Dance Opera,* by Zitkala-Ša (Lincoln: University of Nebraska Press, 2001).

Pratt, Richard Henry. *Battlefield and Classroom: Four Decades with the American Indian, 1867–1906,* edited by Robert M. Utley (New Haven: Yale University Press, 1964).

Standing Bear, Luther. *Land of the Spotted Eagle* (Lincoln: University of Nebraska Press, 1978).

Standing Bear, Luther. *My People the Sioux* (Lincoln: University of Nebraska Press, 1975).

Zitkala-Ša, *American Indian Stories* (Lincoln: University of Nebraska Press, 1985).

The Fort Marion Artists

When history books include examples of Indian art or pictographic records, they tend to place them at the beginning, as examples of unchanging Native traditions that would be replaced. But Indian art was constantly evolving. Like Indian cultures generally, it altered as a result of contact with new influences, but it did not disappear or lose touch with its traditional roots. Plains Indian warriors depicted their heroic deeds on tepee covers and buffalo robes; when white men arrived with paints, pencils, and paper, Indian artists readily employed the new materials. The Mandan chief Four Bears not

FIGURE 6.1 Howling Wolf, Cheyenne Warrior Striking an Enemy
Allen Memorial Art Museum, Oberlin College, Ohio. Gift of Mrs. Jacob D. Cox, 1904.

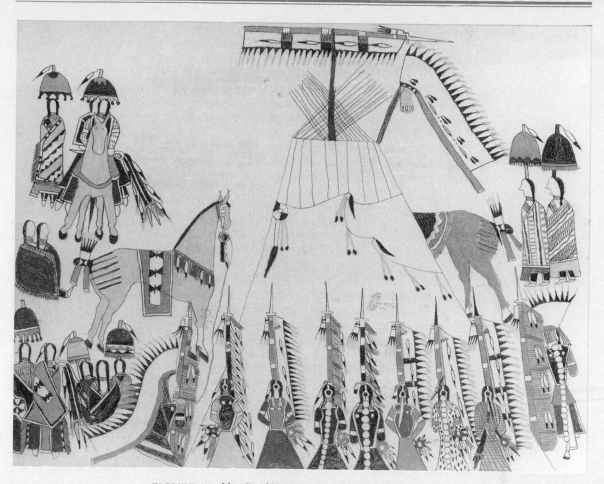

FIGURE 6.2 Howling Wolf, Gathering for a Dance
Yale Collection of Western Americana, Beinecke Rare Book and Manuscript Library.

only posed for George Catlin and Karl Bodmer, he also watched them at work and adopted some of their techniques in his own representational art.

In the late nineteenth century, a new type of Indian art emerged out of circumstances that seemed more likely to stifle than to stimulate artistic creativity: "under the strains and stresses of their disintegrating world, talented Indian artists transformed painting into an expressive and vital art form."[1] Plains Indians acquired new materials with which to work and new subjects to portray. Since many of the sketches they produced were done on pages torn from account books, the new art form became known as ledger art.

Warrior artists produced a rich visual record of coup-counting and combat on the Plains,[2] but some of the most famous and significant Plains Indian ledger art was produced thousands of miles from the Plains. In 1875, seventy-

FIGURE 6.3 Courtship Scene
National Anthropological Archives, Smithsonian Institution.

two Southern Cheyenne, Arapaho, Kiowa, and Comanche warriors whom the government identified as "ringleaders" in the Red River War of 1874 were manacled, chained, and loaded on a train bound for exile and imprisonment at Fort Marion, in St. Augustine, Florida. Their jailor, Captain Richard H. Pratt regarded their incarceration as an opportunity to test his program for assimilating Indians into American society. As he would do later as superintendent of the boarding school at Carlisle, Pennsylvania, Pratt stripped the Indians of their clothes and gave them army uniforms; he cut their long hair short, and he made them follow a regimented routine of working, schooling, eating, and sleeping that he felt would instill the values and industrious habits they needed to become "civilized." He also encouraged them to draw and gave them the materials to do so.

With time on their hands, the Fort Marion prisoners produced hundreds of drawings. Some sold books of their work to tourists. Far from their homes and loved ones, and with no idea of what the future held for them, they were poised on the edge of old and new ways of life. Their drawings reflected that dualism in form and content. Some of the artists painted nostalgic scenes from the old ways—hunting buffalo, raiding for horses, counting coup—and employed

On the parapet of Ft Marion next day after arrival

FIGURE 6.4 **Paul Caryl Zotom, *On the Parapet of Ft. Marion Next Day after Arrival***
National Cowboy and Western Heritage Museum, Oklahoma City, [96.17.0203A].

traditional conventions. These included: right to left flow of action; pictographic shorthand, such as hoof prints to indicate previous movements; symbols above the head to identify an individual, such as the warrior named Sitting Bull (not the famous Hunkpapa) in Figure 6.1.

But the heroic events that warrior-artists had traditionally recorded were things of the past. The artists experimented with new subjects and new forms of composition and introduced new elements of personal expression and individual style. They painted scenes of pageantry from Plains Indian life, as in the Southern Cheyenne artist Howling Wolf's picture of men and women, bedecked in blankets and finery, gathering for a dance. The women carry bright umbrellas and the warriors hold feathered lances and rattles[3] (Figure 6.2).

FIGURE 6.5 Distribution of Goods

Yale Collection of Western Americana, Beinecke Rare Book and Manuscript Library.

Warriors who had once been concerned only with depicting heroic deeds now drew scenes of courtship (Figure 6.3). They turned their attention and skills to aspects of the strange world into which they had been thrust, as when the Kiowa Zotom drew the newly arrived prisoners standing on the parapet at Fort Marion, getting their first look at the Atlantic Ocean (Figure 6.4), as well as scenes of the new way of life that was being imposed back home on the reservations, such as the distribution of annuities or treaty goods (Figure 6.5).

Some of the Fort Marion artists continued to draw and paint long after they had been released and returned home in 1878. Their work constitutes a unique collection of historical documents, a record of a people experiencing

WOHAW

FIGURE 6.6 Wohaw, Self-Portrait
Missouri Historical Society, St. Louis.

revolutionary change. As the self-portrait of the Kiowa Wohaw, with a foot in each world but wearing long hair and traditional breech cloth, graphically illustrates (Figure 6.6), many were unsure about their place in the future.

▶ Questions for Consideration

1. What do the compositions of these pictures suggest about the artists' purposes?

2. What elements of these pictures suggest that the artists had new materials and time on their hands, as well as new subjects to paint?

3. What value do pictures such as these have in depicting scenes that could be effectively portrayed by American artists and photographers of the time?

References

1. Arthur Silberman "The Art of Fort Marion," in *Making Medicine: Ledger Drawing Art from Fort Marion* (Oklahoma City: Center of the American Indian, 1984), n.p. For additional studies of Plains Indian Ledger Art, see Berlo, Janet Catherine, ed. *Plains Indian Drawings, 1865–1935: Pages from a Visual History* (New York: Harry N. Abrams, 1996); Maurer, Evan M., et al. *Visions of the People: A Pictorial History of Plains Indian Life* (Minneapolis Institute of Arts, 1992); Peterson, Karen Daniels. *Plains Indian Art from Fort Marion* (Norman: University of Oklahoma Press, 1971); Szabo, Joyce M. *Howling Wolf and the History of Ledger Art* (Albuquerque: University of New Mexico Press, 1994); Viola, Herman J. *Warrior Artists: Historic Cheyenne and Kiowa Indian Ledger Art Drawing by Making Medicine and Zotom* (Washington, D.C.: National Geographic Society, 1998).
2. Jean Afton, David Fridtjof Halaas, and Andrew E. Masich, *Cheyenne Dog Soldiers: A Ledgerbook History of Coups and Combat* (Niwot, Colo.: University of Colorado Press and the Colorado Historical Society, 1997).
3. Szabo, *Howling Wolf and the History of Ledger Art*, 105.

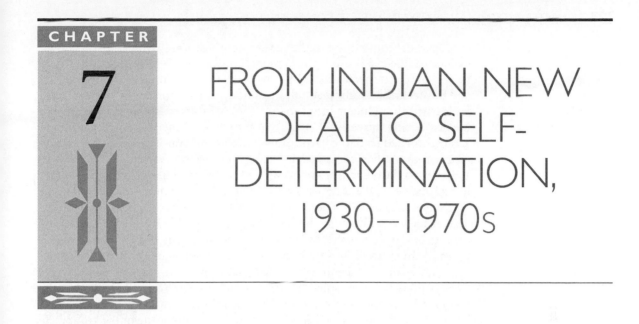

7

FROM INDIAN NEW DEAL TO SELF-DETERMINATION, 1930–1970s

SHIFTING POLICIES AND INDIAN ACTIVISM

The Great Depression changed the way the U.S. government conceived of its role and responsibilities toward American society and the economy. It also brought changes in United States policies towards American Indians. The New Deal brought the first of several shifts in government Indian policy during the twentieth century. Yet, while policies changed, underlying problems often remained the same, as did the underlying goals of assimilating Indian people and gaining access to Indian resources. Indian communities responded to the policy shifts emanating from Washington, D.C., but they also worked both within and against the system to effect change. They took increasing responsibility for implementing programs in their own communities, and eventually for formulating policies. By 1980, the U.S. government was formally committed to a policy of self-determination, but what that actually meant was often, and sometimes bitterly, contested.

John Collier and the Indian New Deal

Franklin Delano Roosevelt's presidency reversed some of the disastrous policies of the previous fifty years. FDR appointed as his Commissioner of Indian Affairs John Collier, who served from 1933 to 1945. Collier envisioned and implemented far-reaching changes in the relationship between the U.S. government and the Indian tribes within its borders. He attempted to restore an emphasis on community in the government's dealings with Indian peoples. Collier had been a social worker among immigrants in New York City, where he became concerned with what he saw as the fragmentation of community life and the decline of traditional cultures among immigrants to the United States. He learned about Indian life primarily from his visits to Pueblo peoples in New Mexico during the early 1920s. At that time many American intellectuals and idealists turned from the havoc of the First World War in Europe to seek harmony in the Indian communities of the Southwest. A visit to Taos Pueblo in 1920 changed Collier's life and convinced him that Indian cultures had something fundamental to offer American society. "He saw modernity as a disaster that was defeating man's perfectibility," Collier's son recalled. "He saw the Indian as the last remnant of natural perfection, a model that must be preserved for human rejuvenation."[1] Modern American life seemed shallow, materialistic, individualistic; Indian life, as evidenced by the Pueblos, seemed deeply spiritual and communal. Despite "repeated and immense historical shocks," wrote Collier in his autobiography, Pueblo communities "were going right on in the production of states of mind, attitudes of mind, earth-loyalties and human loyalties, amid a context of beauty which suffused all the life of the group." He thought that Indians might be the only people in the western hemisphere who still possessed "the fundamental secret of human life—the secret of building great personality through the instrumentality of social institutions." But he feared that Indian life might not survive.[2] Like many other idealists before and since, Collier saw in Indian society the chance for the salvation of his own society.

Collier helped to establish the All-Pueblo Council, which lobbied successfully against the Bursum bill of 1922 that threatened to deprive the Pueblos of land and water rights by placing jurisdiction over those rights in the state courts and legitimizing the claims of many non-Indians on Pueblo lands. He became executive secretary of the American Indian Defense Association in 1923. As Commissioner of Indian Affairs, Collier introduced his own beliefs in the formulation of Indian policy. For a century and a half, the federal government had tried to break up and sell off tribal land holdings, dismantle tribal governments, stamp out native languages, and eradicate tribal cultures. Now the government tried to reverse the assault on Indian lands, rejuvenate tribal governments, preserve native languages, and revive tribal cultures. The late anthropologist D'Arcy McNickle, a metis° and enrolled member of the Flathead tribe who worked on Collier's staff, said that the Roosevelt administration, with Collier's prompting, "accepted the radical concept that the Indian race was not headed for early extinction."[3] Instead, it was committed to promoting revitalization of Indian life. The "Indian New Deal," masterminded by Collier, charted a new direction in United States Indian policy which, despite efforts to reverse it after 1945, had a lasting impact throughout Indian America. (See "Two Views of the Indian Reorganization Act," pages 426–37.)

°Metis generally means "mixed blood" but in Canada indicates an Indian-French ethnic group.

In some ways the Indian New Deal was not new, but rather another attempt by non-Indians to do what they regarded as the right thing for Indians. It was another paternalistic promise to bring a "new era" in Indian affairs, one of many twentieth-century shifts in Indian policy that left Indian people distrustful of anything coming out of Washington. It was another blueprint for reform, mandating one policy for all Indians and making little allowance for the tremendous diversity of Indian America.

Collier was devoted to championing Indian rights as he understood them, and he did so with a zeal that both attracted and alienated others. In the assessment of historian Alvin M. Josephy, Jr., Collier possessed "the zeal of a crusader who knew better than the Indians what was good for them."[4] Collier's long-term goals included the eventual absorption of Indian people into mainstream American society, but he opposed his predecessors' concept of rapid assimilation and tried to develop a program that would preserve much more of the tribal heritage. The aims of his Indian New Deal included ending allotment and consolidating tribal lands, allowing Indians to play a more active role in running their own affairs, organizing tribal governments, supporting Indian cultures, ending government suppression of tribal rituals, and allowing Indian children to attend day schools on their home reservations. He was only partially successful in achieving these goals.

To some extent, Indians benefited from general New Deal legislation that provided jobs and relief, built schools and hospitals. Collier succeeded in channeling funds from other agencies and programs to benefit Indians. But Collier also managed to get specific programs passed by Congress. Long-overdue improvements were made in the field of Indian education, with more focus on community, new curriculum more suited to the needs of Indian students, and more and better trained teachers. The emphasis shifted from off-reservation boarding schools, the core of the government's educational crusade for the past fifty years, to day schools on reservations; between 1933 and 1941 almost one hundred day schools were built, almost half of them on the Navajo reservation.

Under the Johnson-O'Malley Act of 1934, the Secretary of the Interior was authorized to negotiate contracts with any state for financial relief in areas of Indian education, medical aid, agricultural assistance, and welfare. The federal government funded school districts to provide services for the Indian children attending public schools. The idea was that state and federal government would work together to improve the quality of Indian education. Only Arizona, California, Minnesota, and Washington made contracts in the 1930s. In some areas, the system worked well, but Indian children in public schools still encountered racism and prejudice and some school districts drew Johnson-O'Malley money without making any provision for the needs of their Indian students. Nevertheless, the Indian New Deal took bold steps departing from past educational policy and promoting bilingual and bicultural education that bore fruit in the late 1960s and '70s.[5] In another federal initiative, in 1935 the Indian Arts and Crafts Board was established within the Department of the Interior to promote and preserve traditional crafts and arts by helping Indian people form craft cooperatives, authenticate items of Indian manufacture, and establish marketing networks.

The Indian Reorganization Act

The centerpiece of Indian New Deal legislation was the Indian Reorganization Act (IRA). "The repair work authorized by Congress under the terms of the act," Collier said in his report as commissioner in 1934, "aims at both the economic and the spiritual rehabilitation of the Indian race."[6] Passed in 1934, the IRA aimed to protect Indians in their religion and lifestyle and represented an open admission that the Dawes Act was a mistake. The original bill stated:

1. Indians living on reservations were allowed to establish local self-government and tribal corporations to develop reservation resources. The Secretary of the Interior would issue a charter of home rule, granting an Indian community greater responsibility over its own affairs, and the Indians would vote to accept it in tribal elections.

2. The federal government was to train Indians in such issues as land management, public health, and law enforcement and prepare them for employment in the Bureau of Indian Affairs (BIA), as well as provide scholarship money for Indian students.

3. The Dawes Act was terminated. Further allotments of Indian lands were prohibited. The bill provided for consolidation of allotted lands into units for com-

John Collier
Newly appointed Commissioner of Indian Affairs John Collier (1884–1968) shakes hands with Oglala chiefs in 1933. Buechel Memorial Lakota Museum.

munity use and provided $2 million each year to purchase lands for the tribes. Any "surplus" land remaining from allotment would be restored to the reservations.

4. A special court of Indian Affairs was to be established.

The bill that finally passed Congress was substantially modified,[7] including the deletion of the special court provision.

Tribes were required to accept or reject the IRA by referendum; the establishment of tribal self-government was to be decided the same way. When a majority of adult tribal members approved the IRA, they could then write a constitution, which had to be approved by another majority vote and by the Secretary of the Interior. Tribes who accepted the IRA could elect a tribal council. The IRA applied only to those tribes that accepted it, and Oklahoma and Alaska were left out of its provisions. (Congress passed laws in 1936 to encourage the establishment of tribal and village governments in those areas.) Collier spent much time and energy selling his program to Indian communities and he held ten regional conferences in the spring of 1934 to explain the philosophy, operation, and importance of the IRA. For the first time, a Commissioner of Indian Affairs traveled around the country to explain legislation to Indian people.

Opposing and Disputing the IRA

Despite his enthusiasm, Collier encountered opposition which slowed the progress of his reform program. Many Indians and non-Indians feared that after generations of painful adjustment the reversal of policies would mean a "return to the blanket." Some Indian traditionalists disliked the proposed changes in tribal government. The Indian Rights Association argued that the new legislation perpetuated segregation, and some members of Congress opposed it for protecting communal ownership.

Some tribes were divided over the New Deal. Collier underestimated the diversity of Indian life and wanted Indians to function as unified tribes. In fact, the IRA proposed to impose rigid and alien political and economic systems on Indian communities. Majority rule went against traditional practices in those societies that reached decisions by consensus, and it seemed to ride roughshod over the views of the minority. In Indian country, not voting was often viewed as a negative vote; in western-style democracy, however, those who do not vote have no voice. From the viewpoint of many Indians, the referenda on the IRA were rigged to produce an affirmative vote. On the Santa Ysabel reservation in California, for instance, forty-three people voted against the IRA and only nine voted in favor. But the sixty-two eligible voters who did not vote were counted as being in favor and IRA was applied.[8]

Eventually, some 174 tribes accepted the IRA and 135 communities drafted tribal constitutions. The Blackfeet of Montana voted for it, seeing it as the best vehicle for change available at the time. They used it to improve their political and economic situation and to try "to reorganize relations with the federal government on their own terms and to construct an American community of their own design."[9] But 78 tribes rejected it. The Seneca activist Alice Lee Jemison was a vocal critic of both Collier and the Indian New Deal and helped found the American Indian Federation, a group that campaigned against Collier's program. The Senecas regarded the Indian New Deal as a threat to their treaty rights and to the elective self-government they had established in 1848. With the other Iroquois tribes of New York, they voted heavily against the IRA (although the Wisconsin Oneidas accepted it). The Crows, unlike most Plains groups, rejected it, despite the influential support of Robert Yellowtail, the Crow Indian Superintendent. The Navajos rejected it.

After their return from confinement at Bosque Redondo in 1868, the Navajos rebuilt their communities around sheep and herding. While Plains Indians experienced population collapse and loss of subsistence base with the slaughter of buffalo herds, Navajo numbers and Navajo herds grew steadily. The government even enlarged the Navajo reservation to accommodate the increase of human and animal population. By 1933, the Navajos numbered more than 40,000 and were self-sufficient sheepherders. Issued 14,000 sheep (less than 2 per capita) with which to rebuild their herds in 1868, the Navajos had increased their stock to about 800,000 sheep and goats (21 per capita) by the eve of the Great Depression.[10] But, combined with natural erosion cycles in the area, and the intrusions of Anglo-American cattlemen who restricted Navajo grazing areas, the increase in livestock took a toll on the Navajo environment. A period of severe drought aggravated the problem. The government feared that overgrazing and trampling hooves broke down soils and that accumulations of silt from the reservation threatened the functioning of the huge Boulder Dam (later renamed Hoover Dam). Built on the Colorado River in northwestern Arizona and completed in 1936, the dam provided water, flood control, and electricity to the southwestern United States and Los Angeles. The government advocated a program of livestock reduction to relieve the stress on the land.[11]

In an effort to limit production and raise prices, the government imposed livestock reductions on American farmers during the New Deal era, but Collier underestimated the importance of sheep, goats, and horses in Navajo life. He persuaded the Navajo tribal council to accept a program of stock reduction and promised to secure additional lands for the reservation. The tribal council had been formed under government auspices in the 1920s to facilitate access to oil deposits on the reservation; it hardly spoke for the majority of Navajos scattered across a reservation the size of West Virginia. The council agreed to a 10 percent reduction in stock, but this was only the first stage in a program that continued for more than a decade and cut Navajo herds by half. Most Navajos saw the causes of erosion as drought and insufficient access to acreage for grazing — too little land, not too many sheep. The program was brutal and devastating for Navajo families who watched the slaughter of their animals with outrage and heartbreak. "It haunts me now, more than a half century later," wrote an anthropologist who worked on the Navajo reservation at the time of the stock reductions, "and it still haunts the Navajos even more profoundly."[12]

Many Navajos held Collier personally responsible for their most bitter experience since the Long Walk to Bosque Redondo. They felt betrayed when he failed to deliver on promises he had made to expand the reservation eastwards.

When Collier visited the reservation in 1934 to promote the IRA, he encountered fierce opposition from Navajos led by J. C. Morgan. When the referendum was held, 98 percent of the eligible voters cast ballots. The voting was close but in the end the largest tribe in the country rejected the IRA and Collier's vision of a new era in Indian affairs. Collier offered his own interpretation of what had happened. (See "Two Views of the Indian Reorganization Act," pages 430–31.)

The IRA failed to achieve many of its goals. Nevertheless, the Indian New Deal produced some dramatic changes in government policy. Indian tribes regained several million acres of lands that had been lost under the allotment program and moved forward in the areas of education, cultural preservation, and control of their own affairs. As Commissioner of Indian Affairs, Collier displayed sympathy for Indian heritage and recognized the importance of allowing Indian tribes a measure of self-determination. However, in 1941, the United States entered the Second World War, which had broken out in Europe two years before. Concern for righting wrongs at home diminished as the nation focused its energies on winning the war for democracy abroad.

Indians and World War II

About twenty-five thousand Indians served in the armed forces during World War II. Some were drafted, others volunteered. The Iroquois challenged the right of the federal government to compel Indian men to fight, and a group of Iroquois issued a formal declaration of war against the Axis powers in 1942, indicating that they were participating in the war as sovereign nations, not as subordinates of the United States. Some Indian soldiers won lasting fame—Navajo code talkers in the Pacific theater baffled the Japanese with a code based on Navajo words, and Ira Hayes, a Pima Indian, participated in the famous flag-raising by American marines on Iwo Jima. More than five hundred Indians were killed in the war. Another forty thousand Indian men and women worked in war-related industries. The war took Indians away from home, often for the first time, brought them into contact with new people and new ideas, and gave them new pride in having helped win the great fight for democracy.

But not all Native people could feel such pride. After the Japanese landed troops on two islands in the Aleutian Chain off the Alaska Peninsula, the U.S. government forced Aleutian and Alaska Natives to evacuate their homes on the islands to make way for military defense preparation. More than 850 Aleuts were forcefully evacuated. They lost their homes and belongings and suffered hardship, disease, and misery in hastily constructed camps in southeastern Alaska and Washington state. When they returned home after the war, they found their homes had been used to billet troops and much of their property had been destroyed.[13]

Many Indians returning from the war expected to find improved living conditions and better relations with their white neighbors. Many Indian veterans took advantage of the GI Bill to pursue education and vocational training. But Indian people in general faced more hard times and a renewed assault on their tribalism.

Banning the Swastika
A Navajo woman signs a multitribal resolution outlawing the use of the swastika. South-western Indians had formerly employed the motif in blanket weaving, basketmaking, and sand painting, but Nazi Germany's adoption of the symbol gave it new and sinister con-notations. "A symbol of friendship among our forefathers for many centuries has been desecrated," stated the resolution. Bettmann/CORBIS.

TERMINATION

In the late 1940s and the 1950s, the pendulum of public opinion and govern-ment support swung away from the reform impetus of the New Deal to con-servatism and conformity, marked by commitment to "Americanism," fear of communism, and resentment of those who did not seem to fit in with main-stream society. Many Americans saw Indian participation in the war as evidence of their readiness for final assimilation into American society. The government decided to hasten the process of assimilation by ending, or "terminating," its re-lationship with Indian tribes.

After the war, the government implemented a three-part program of com-pensation, termination, and relocation. Acknowledging that injustices had been committed in the past, Congress aimed to "wipe the slate clean" by settling once and for all the claims that Indian tribes had against the government for loss of lands; it wanted to eliminate special tribal status and turn jurisdiction over the Indians to state and local authorities; and it imagined that Indians

Living in Two Worlds: Molly Spotted Elk

*Some Indian people already led lives that were very much en-
twined in the outside world, and for one Indian woman, the war
brought wrenching personal experiences. Born on the Penobscot
reservation at Indian Island in Maine, Molly Spotted Elk
(1903–77) became a dancer, and starred in a Hollywood movie,*
The Silent Enemy, *in 1930, about the time this photograph was
made. She made her way to Paris where she married a French
journalist. The German occupation of France forced her to flee
with her young daughter, crossing the Pyrenees Mountains into
Spain on foot. She returned safely to the United States, but never
saw her husband again. Throughout her career, Molly had
wrestled with her need to make a living and her desire for a dancing career on the one hand, and her revulsion at having to do so
by donning headdresses and skimpy buckskin costumes to act out
stereotypes on the other. Back home in rural Maine after travels
in New York, California, and Paris, she struggled to readjust. Her
childhood home, in the words of her biographer, "was like an old
pair of moccasins that one dreamed of during years of high-heeled
city life—only to find, upon slipping into them, that they felt less
comfortable than remembered because the shape of one's feet had
changed." She was not the first Indian to experience the tensions
of moving from reservation to city and back again: Molly Spotted
Elk completed her life's circle on Indian Island, where she died in
1977.* Molly Spotted Elk: A Penobscot in Paris *by Bunny McBride, published by the University of Oklahoma Press (1995), quote at 223. Photo courtesy of Jean A. Moore, daughter of Molly Spotted Elk.*

would more easily enter the mainstream
of American life if they moved from their
reservations to cities.

Indian Claims Commission

From 1778 (the first United States treaty
with the Delawares) to 1871 (when Congress ended the treaty-making process in
favor of executive agreements), the United
States negotiated nearly four hundred
treaties with Indian tribes. However, many
of the provisions of these treaties were
never implemented, and many tribes
never received payment stipulated in
treaties for lands they had ceded. In 1946,
Congress established the Indian Claims
Commission to review tribal grievances
over treaty enforcement and management
of resources and to resolve lingering disputes between Indian tribes and the U.S.
government. Tribes were allowed five years
in which to file grievances; they had to
prove aboriginal title to the lands in question and then bring suit for settlement.
The commission would then review their
case and assess the amount, if any, to be
paid in compensation. The whole process
was expected to be completed in ten years.

The work of the Claims Commission
was beset with problems. The Justice Department often discouraged or hindered
tribes that wanted to file claims. Some Indian groups had conflicting claims to aboriginal occupancy of the same lands. In addition, some Indians rejected the idea that
cash payment could settle land issues.
Land, not money, was the basis of their
culture. For example, the Taos Indians rejected an offer of $10 million for Blue Lake
in northwestern New Mexico because it
was sacred to them and not "for sale." The
Pit River Indians in northern California
rejected the offer of a measly 47 cents per
acre for the lands they had lost.

When compensation was paid, other
problems arose. People often disagreed

over whether the payments should be made per capita to individual tribal members or whether they should be invested by tribal officials in the reservation economy. Tribal members who lived off the reservations often differed with their relatives who had stayed behind. In the case of per capita payments, tribal rolls had to be drawn up and verified, producing further disputes over who qualified as a member.

By the time the Indian Claims Commission ended its operations in 1978 it had settled 285 cases, and paid out more than $800 million in settlements. The Crows received a $10 million payment and allocated 50 percent for per capita payments and invested the rest in health, housing, education, scholarships, land purchases, and social services. Some Indians squandered their payments; others were cheated out of them by unscrupulous local businessmen.

Removing the Government's Trust Responsibilities

The period also saw a growing call to end federal services to Indian tribes and remove the government's trust relationship established by treaties and the Constitution. Influential western congressmen such as Senator Arthur Watkins of Utah and Representative E. Y. Berry of South Dakota were among the most vocal advocates of this termination policy. In 1950, Dillon S. Myer, the former head of the War Relocation Authority which had taken thousands of Japanese Americans from the West Coast and put them in internment camps, became Commissioner of Indian Affairs. The new commissioner was hostile to many of the reforms implemented by John Collier in the 1930s. In Myer's view, the BIA should "not do anything which others can do as well or better and as cheaply. The Bureau should do nothing for Indians which Indians can do for themselves and we should lean over backward to help them learn to do more things on their own."[14] He began to implement a government policy of termination and relocation of Indian tribes. His successor, Glenn Emmons, who took over as commissioner in 1953, carried on his work.

Tribes deemed to have made most "progress" were identified as eligible for termination. The government's list included the Six Nations of New York, the Prairie Potawatomis of Kansas, the Menominees of Wisconsin, the Flatheads of Montana, the Klamaths of Oregon, the Hoopas of northern California, and various southern California bands. In 1953, House Concurrent Resolution 108 proposed ending federal relations with a number of these eligible tribes. The goal of termination expressed in House Concurrent Resolution 108 was "as rapidly as possible, to make the Indians within the territorial limits of the United States subject to the same laws and entitled to the same privileges and responsibilities as are applicable to other citizens of the United States, to end their status as wards of the United States, and to grant them all the rights and prerogatives pertaining to American citizenship."[15] The resolution passed both houses of Congress unanimously. Two weeks later, Congress passed Public Law 280, transferring jurisdiction over tribal lands to state and local governments in California, Oregon, Nebraska, Minnesota, and Wisconsin. PL 280 represented a major step toward extending state control over Indian reservations.

Other states could unilaterally adopt it if they chose (until 1968, after which the consent of the reservation was required). In 1954, responsibility for Indian health was transferred from the BIA to the Public Health Service. In the next decade Congress terminated federal services to more than sixty Indian groups.

In 1960, John F. Kennedy was elected president and spoke of a "new frontier," but his words brought little comfort to Indian people "who had bad memories of the old frontier." Kennedy had little real interest in Indians, and termination remained the official policy throughout his administration.[16]

Termination's Impact: Menominees and Klamaths

As had the proponents of allotment in the 1880s, advocates of termination justified their new policy as one that would liberate Indian people from the stifling atmosphere of reservation life and dependence on government support. In fact, the withdrawal of special federal services to Indian tribes was often disastrous. The Menominees and the Klamaths were especially hard hit. The Menominees were fairly self-sufficient in 1950, with their tribal lumbering operation and sawmill providing employment and paying for most of their community services. Termination struck at their prosperity and society. In 1953, the Menominees were seeking distribution of an earlier settlement on a per capita basis. Payment required congressional approval; it passed in the House, but encountered stiff opposition before the Senate Committee on Interior Affairs. Utah Senator Arthur Watkins, a termination advocate, supported an amendment calling for the termination of federal assistance to the Menominees and then informed the Menominees that agreeing to termination was a precondition to obtain the payments in question.[17] With little understanding of the exact termination provisions, most of those Menominees who voted for termination were probably only voting to receive their per capita payments. In June 1954, President Eisenhower signed the Menominee Termination Act. The law gave the tribe four years in which to establish their own municipal, educational, health, and other services previously provided by the federal government. The Menominees won a deadline extension to 1961. They reorganized the tribe as a corporation, Menominee Enterprises Incorporated, to manage the lands and lumber mill formerly owned and operated by the tribe, and the reservation became a county. Nevertheless, the impact of termination was devastating. The once-thriving tribal lumber industry was deprived of federal contracts at a time of a nationwide slump in housebuilding. Menominees had to sell land to pay taxes. Hospitals closed and health problems increased. A plan to save the federal government money cost more than ever in the form of welfare payments.

The law terminating the Klamaths was passed in 1954 and went into effect in 1961. Like the Menominees, the Klamaths impressed government officials as a model tribe for termination because of their rich timber resources and relative prosperity, with a gross annual income of $2 million from sale of tribal timber.[18] But the Klamaths relied heavily on federal services and contracts, and, as in the case of the Menominees, termination brought economic disaster. Cutting off health and education services previously provided by the federal government

Ada Deer
Social worker Ada Deer (b. 1935) lobbied in Washington against the Menominee Termination Act. In 1972, President Nixon signed the Menominee Restoration Act, redesignating the Menominees as a federally recognized tribe. Deer served as chairperson of the Menominee Restoration Committee from 1973 to 1976 and became the first Native American woman to head the BIA. Milwaukee Journal Sentinel, *January 31, 1974.* © 2002, *Journal Sentinel, Inc. Reproduced with permission.*

caused additional suffering. Some communities had little choice but to sell lands which the government had previously held in trust. Many Indians regarded termination as another land grab, with lumber interests influencing policy and lumber companies emerging as the actual beneficiaries of a policy that was supposed to "liberate" Indian people.[19]

The National Congress of American Indians (NCAI) led the fight against termination, under its chairman Joseph Garry, a Coeur d'Alene veteran of World War II and an Idaho state legislator. "Reservations do not imprison us," declared the NCAI, "they are our ancestral homelands, retained by us for our perpetual use and enjoyment. We feel we must assert our right to maintain ownership in our own way, and terminate it only by our consent."[20] Both the Menominees and the Klamaths fought for restoration of tribal status. A young Menominee social worker named Ada Deer led the movement to reverse Menominee termination, lobbying in Washington until Congress passed the Menominee Restoration Act, which President Nixon signed in 1973. The Klamaths secured restoration of tribal status in 1986. But the experience of both tribes stood as a warning to others: economic success could bring termination.

Relocation

The government also introduced a program of urban relocation. Since colonial times, some Indians had moved to cities in the wake of dispossession and the disruption of their traditional economies. After the Allotment Act placed them on small plots of land, more Indians began to leave the reservations and look for work elsewhere. During World War II, large numbers of Indians moved to the cities to work in war-related industries. The Indian population of Minneapolis, for example, rose from less than 1,000 in the 1920s to more than 6,000 by the end of World War II.[21] After the war, endemic unemployment on the reservations and new social and economic opportunities in the cities prolonged the trend. Kahnawake Mohawks continued to travel to New York City for jobs in steel construction. Los Angeles was "an industrial boom

"Come to Denver"
BIA leaflets such as this promoted the advantages of city life among reservation communities. National Archives.

town" after the war, offering blue-collar jobs in the petroleum, construction, aircraft, and other manufacturing industries. The government seized on this trend and initiated its relocation program as the means of ending reservation poverty and accelerating the pace of assimilation. Many Indians had already relocated from rural reservations to urban areas on their own initiative and successfully adjusted to urban life, and the BIA encouraged other young families to make the move. In 1948, the BIA experimented with a relocation program to move Navajos to Denver, Salt Lake City, and Los Angeles. Between 1952 and 1960, the BIA provided incentive and means to move more than 30,000 Indians from their reservations to the cities; by 1973, more than 100,000 Indians had gone on relocation. Relocation became a nationwide policy, and Indian people continued to move to the cities, with and without government assistance. There were no more than 5,000 Indians in Los Angeles County before World War II; by 1980, 50,000 lived there.[22] In 1950, only 13.4 percent of Indians counted by the U.S. Census lived in urban areas; by 1970, the proportion had risen to 44 percent; by 1980 half of American Indians lived in cities.[23] (See the Census figures in Chapter 8, page 490.)

Thousands of Indians were given one-way bus tickets to cities where they were expected to live and work like other Americans. Usually, the BIA moved relocatees long distances—Anishinaabe and Sioux people from Minnesota and South Dakota to California, Alaskan Natives and Navajos to Chicago, for instance—to discourage them from returning to their reservation homes. The BIA established relocation centers in key cities, gave help with moving and finding accommodations, offered job training, provided free medical care for one year, and paid a month's subsistence until the relocatees became settled. Relocation officials made arrangements for the move, greeted the relocatees on their arrival in the city, and attempted to prepare them for adjustment to city life. But, like other immigrants from rural areas, many of the newcomers faced new problems. Accustomed to close-knit extended families and small communities, Indian migrants had to adjust to the anonymity of life in a city of millions. Accustomed to a philosophy of communal responsibility and sharing,

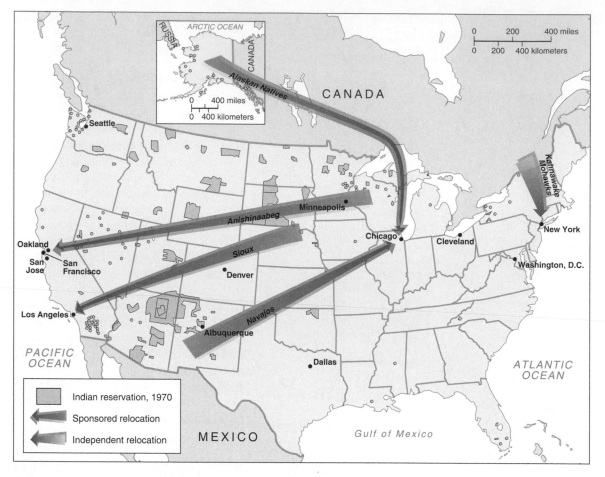

MAP 7.1 Selected Indian Relocations, 1950–70

The government's policy of relocation intensified ongoing Indian movement to the cities. This map shows sample migrations, but members of a single tribe might move to a variety of cities, and any city was likely to become home to people from many different tribes and regions.

Adapted from The Settling of North America: The Atlas of the Great Migrations into North America from the Ice Age to Ellis Island and Beyond *by Helen Hornbeck Tanner, Janice Reiff, and John H. Long, editors. Copyright © 1995 by Swanston Publishing Ltd.*

they had to survive in a world of individual capitalist competition. Accustomed to a slower pace of life on rural reservations where family demands and ceremonial calendars took precedence, many struggled to keep up with the hectic routine and daily time-keeping required by urban employers. Unaccustomed to demanding their rights and not motivated by the financial and property ideals of middle-class America, urban Indians often saw themselves left behind in a race dominated by white Americans. For many Indians, urban life meant poverty, poor housing, and unemployment. "They never told us it would be like this," they said.[24] As many as a third of the relocatees returned to the reservations.

Drowning Homelands

Back on the reservations, some Indian peoples faced new assaults on their homelands as well as on their tribal status. Some found their homes targeted for flooding. After a series of floods in the lower Missouri basin states in the spring of 1943, the Army Corps of Engineers built Garrison Dam on the Fort Berthold reservation in North Dakota as part of a massive six-dam project to harness the power of the Missouri River. When the dam was completed in 1953, the floodwaters covered one quarter of the total reservation land base, split the reservation in half, and drowned 90 percent of the best agricultural land. The Mandan, Hidatsa, and Arikara people who lived on the reservation had opposed the

Losing a Homeland
Members of the Fort Berthold Tribal Business Council watch — some in tears — as the Secretary of the Interior signs a contract selling reservation lands to the government for construction of the Garrison Dam in 1950. AP/Wide World Photos.

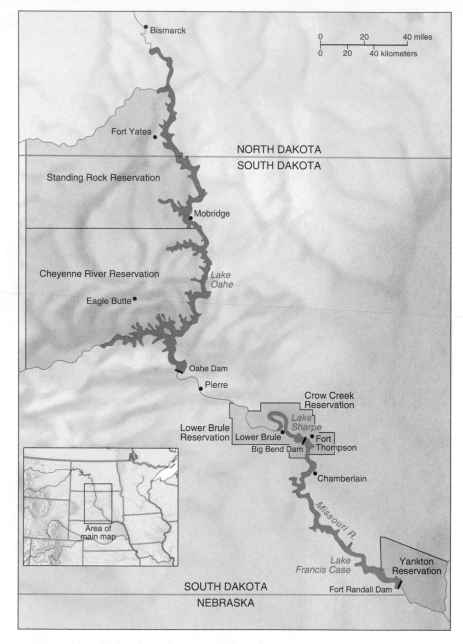

MAP 7.2 Sioux Lands Inundated by the Pick-Sloan Projects

*Between 1944 and 1980, the Pick-Sloan Plan flood control and water development pro-
gram in the Missouri River basin affected Indian peoples along the length of the river.
The dams at Oahe, Big Bend, and Fort Randall flooded more than 200,000 acres of
Sioux land on the Standing Rock, Cheyenne River, Lower Brulé, Crow Creek, and Yankton reservations.* Adapted from Michael Lawson, Dammed Indians: The Pick-Sloan Plan and the
Missouri River Sioux *(Norman: University of Oklahoma Press). Copyright © 1982, 1994. Reprinted by
permission.*

Seneca Elders at Kinzua Dam
Seneca leaders George D. Herron (left) and Sidney Carney take a last walk over tribal lands about to be flooded by the Kinzua Dam. AP/Wide World Photos.

dam and now most were forced to relocate. Many became scattered and many went from supporting their families as farmers to becoming wage laborers or welfare recipients. (Today, the Mni Sose Intertribal Water Rights Coalition, an alliance of twenty-six of the twenty-eight tribes along the Missouri River basin, is lobbying for an allocation of hydropower to reduce its electric utility rates, which remain among the highest in the nation despite the promise of low-cost hydroelectric power from the dams that flooded their homelands.)

In Iroquois country, Mohawk communities at Kahnawake near Montreal and at Akwesasne on the U.S.–Canadian border lost land when the St. Lawrence Seaway was built in the 1950s. The industrialization that followed devastated Akwesasne's dairy industry and left the community with heavily polluted fishing waters. The Senecas fought for years to prevent the Army Corps of Engineers from building the Kinzua Dam on the Allegheny River in northwestern Pennsylvania. But, in contravention of the Treaty of Canandaigua in 1794 which assured the Senecas that the United States would never claim or disturb their reservation lands, the dam was completed in 1965, drowning ten thousand acres. An attempt to halt the dam went all the way to the United States Supreme Court, but to no avail. Justice Hugo Black, in a strongly worded dissent, reminded his colleagues that "great nations, like great men, should keep their word." Seneca families were relocated and the remains of chief Cornplanter, who had led the tribe during and after the Revolution, were removed as the floodwaters covered his grave.

In the Northwest, the Bonneville, Grand Coulee, and Dalles dams destroyed ancient fishing sites and reduced the Columbia River to a shadow of its former power. In the Southeast, Cherokees and environmentalists fought to stop construction of the Tellico Dam on the Little Tennessee River and invoked the American Indian Religious Freedom Act to protect their sacred sites, but the project was pushed through Congress in 1979 and the dam was built. Chota, the site of the old Cherokee capital, and numerous other archaeological sites were flooded. In northern Quebec, Cree Indians in the 1970s saw dams built and lands flooded—and then embarked on a long battle to prevent further destruction of their homelands.

A YOUNGER GENERATION RESPONDS

Twentieth-century pan-Indian political action started with the work of Charles Eastman, Carlos Montezuma, and the Society of American Indians, and the National Congress of American Indians (NCAI), founded in 1944 to fight termination. In the 1950s and 1960s, Seneca people protested against the Kinzua Dam, and Wallace Mad Bear Anderson, a Tuscarora, helped the Mohawks of St. Regis resist New York State's attempt to impose state income taxes on the reservation and led nonviolent resistance to prevent seizures of Tuscarora land by the New York Power Authority.[25]

The government's termination and relocation policies largely backfired, generating increased resistance and organization among many American Indian groups. As happened when Indians were sent to boarding schools, a new generation of Indians emerged with a new, unifying experience. Mass migrations of Indians fostered a growing pan-Indian identity and a determination to preserve Indian community and heritage (exactly the opposite of what the government relocation program intended to achieve; see "Indians in the Cities," pages 438–46). Some lobbied effectively in Congress for change; others took to the streets and seized property to confront American society with its shameful record and continuing injustices. Indian activism reached new levels in the 1960s and 1970s, as increasing numbers of Indian people insisted on self-determination, and the right to run their own affairs free from the stifling control of the BIA, while holding the government to promises it had made in past treaties.

Urban Indians

Indians who stayed in the cities built a new life in an alien setting. Newcomers sought out Indian people who had already established themselves in the cities, and Indians tended to concentrate in certain areas, such as Uptown, Chicago and Bell Gardens and Cudahy, Los Angeles. They built support networks with people who lived in the same neighborhoods, worked at the same jobs, attended the same churches, and frequented the same bars. In many cities they es-

Defying the State
*Tuscarora Wallace Mad Bear Anderson burns an injunc-
tion issued by the state of New York prohibiting demonstrations against road construction on the Onondaga
reservation. Anderson wears a* gustoweh, *the traditional
headdress of Iroquois men. The beaded headband represents the Hiawatha Belt, the wampum belt that recorded
the formation of the Iroquois League of Nations.*
Bettmann/CORBIS.

tablished American Indian centers which provided social services and functioned as a cultural
focus. Urban Indians also developed new ways
of sustaining ties with their reservation communities. For example, before World War II, almost
all Comanches lived in southwestern Oklahoma;
since the war, about half of the enrolled tribal
members have left home and taken jobs elsewhere. Many Comanches, and other Indian
groups, find that returning home to take part in
pow wows and social and ceremonial gatherings
allows them to celebrate their culture, express
shared tribal values, and reinforce their identity.[26]

Like African American civil rights activists
and militants who were winning long-denied
rights, many young urban Indians came to believe it was futile to wait patiently for conditions
to improve: American society would respond
only to political confrontation and the threat of
militancy. Growing Indian activism in the cities
generated a revival of nationalism on many
reservations, and many young urban Indians returned to the reservations to relearn traditional
ways. By the 1960s, young Indians, more vocal
and militant than their parents, were demanding
a better deal for Indian people. They insisted
that the government cease its assault on Indian
tribes and fulfill its treaty obligations; they demanded that Indian people be more involved in
formulating policy and in running their own affairs; and they demanded respect for Indian
rights and culture. Many young urban Indians
actively promoted the Indian identity and culture that the termination and relocation programs were designed to eradicate.

After debate and controversy, relocation
programs were reduced in the 1970s. But jobs
and social opportunities attracted young Indians long after the government's
program of relocation faded. By 1980, more Indians lived in urban areas than
on reservations. Los Angeles, Seattle, Albuquerque, Phoenix, Denver, Minneapolis, and Chicago contained large composite Indian communities. Urbanization was not the death knell of Indian society: it was another phase in an
ongoing history of Indian change and adaptation to contact with non-Indian
society. Much of Indian America was now urban and parts of urban America
were now Indian. By the end of the century, more than two-thirds of American
Indians lived in urban areas, many of them third-generation citydwellers.[27]

Rise of Indian Militancy

The turmoil in American society in the 1960s helped to create a mood for reform in Congress and the courts, but things were not moving quickly enough for many young Indians, who were angry and frustrated by years of dealing with the federal bureaucracy. In 1961, over four hundred delegates from sixty-five tribes attended the American Indian Chicago Conference and composed a Declaration of Indian Purpose which they sent to President John F. Kennedy. Later in the year, younger participants from the Chicago conference voiced their discontent and impatience in trying to work with the U.S. government and formed the National Indian Youth Council (NIYC) in Gallup, New Mexico. The NIYC demanded a new role for Native Americans in determining the policies that affected their lives.

President Lyndon Johnson's War on Poverty and attempts to create a Great Society increased federal assistance programs and prompted greater Indian participation in those programs. In 1964, Congress created the Office of Economic Opportunity, with a special "Indian desk." A year later the Department of Housing and Urban Development was created, which assisted many reservation communities in building new housing. Vine Deloria, Jr., director of the NCAI at the time, said the government's poverty program meant that "for the first time tribes

Fish-In
In the 1960s, Indian people in the Northwest openly asserted their rights to fish despite harassment from state authorities and non-Indian neighbors. Here, Indian fishermen stage a "fish-in" on the Nisqually River in Olympia, Washington. Note the TV cameras.
Bettmann/CORBIS.

can plan and run their own programs for their people without someone in the BIA dictating to them."[28] "We are not free," declared NIYC president Clyde Warrior in 1967. Instead of relying on the government to run their affairs, Indians sought freedom to make their own decisions, make their own futures, make their own mistakes.[29] (See "Documents of Indian Militancy," pages 450–52.)

Some of the first causes to generate support for the NIYC and attract public attention occurred on the northwest Pacific coast and Columbia River. Indian peoples there depended on rich and regular harvests of salmon. Salmon were as important in the life and culture of the coastal tribes as buffalo were to the peoples of the Plains or corn was to the Iroquois. In the 1850s, Governor Isaac Stevens of Washington Territory had secured a series of treaties that deprived the tribes of most of their lands but that recognized the Indians' right to continue fishing in their "usual and accustomed places." The Americans were interested in farming and lumbering, not in fishing, and they gave little thought to the issue of guaranteeing the Indian fishing rights. In the next century, however, the population of the Northwest increased dramatically. Pollution, dams, and increasing sport and commercial fishing took a heavy toll on salmon runs. Indians struggled to harvest enough fish to live on and found themselves arrested for fishing out of season and without licenses. Denied justice in state courts, they began in the 1960s to stage "fish-ins" to draw attention to their grievances and publicize their treaty rights. Many Indians went to jail.

American Indian Movement

The growing pan-Indian activism was particularly strong among young city Indians. About ten thousand Indians lived in Minneapolis and St. Paul, drawn mainly from the Anishinaabe and Sioux populations of Minnesota and the Dakotas. The Indian community complained frequently of harassment by the police, and Minneapolis Anishinaabeg formed an "Indian patrol" to monitor the activities of police in Indian neighborhoods (much like the Black Panthers in the ghettoes of Oakland, California). Three patrol leaders, Clyde Bellecourt, Dennis Banks, and George Mitchell, went further and organized the American Indian Movement (AIM) in the summer of 1968.

Other Indian groups also took direct action to achieve their goals or publicize their grievances. That same year, Mohawk Indians blockaded the International Bridge between Canada and New York, forcefully protesting the infringement of rights of free passage guaranteed them by the Jay Treaty of 1794. In 1969, a group of young Indians seized Alcatraz Island in San Francisco harbor. Under the name "Indians of All Tribes," they issued a "Proclamation to the Great White Father," ironically employing the rhetoric of old treaties to demonstrate their grievances. (See "Proclamation to the Great White Father and *All His People*," page 453.) The seizure of Alcatraz increased awareness of Indian grievances and galvanized many Indian people into activism. Young urban Indians often returned to their reservations in search of support and spiritual guidance from the traditional people at home, forging new alliances in the struggle for Indian rights.

The "Native American Embassy"

Members of the American Indian Movement stand ready to defend their occupation of the BIA building—here renamed the Native American Embassy—in November 1972. Bettmann/ CORBIS.

AIM protesters staged demonstrations in 1970 at Plymouth Rock and Mayflower II at Thanksgiving (which Russell Means declared a national day of mourning) and in 1971 on Mount Rushmore (where the sculpted heads of "enemy" presidents look out over Lakota land). AIM leaders were active in efforts to secure and protect fishing rights in the Great Lakes region in 1972–73. AIM demonstrators protested against the beatings, unlawful imprisonment, and deaths of Indians such as when Raymond Yellow Thunder, an Oglala from Pine Ridge, was beaten to death in Gordon, Nebraska, a reservation border town in February 1972, and when Leroy Shenandoah, an Onondaga Green Beret veteran and a member of the honor guard at President Kennedy's funeral, was beaten and shot to death by Philadelphia police, who called the killing "justifiable homicide." The new sense of political aggressiveness culminated in the "Trail of Broken Treaties" in 1972. A caravan of Indians traveled across the United States, via Minneapolis to Washington, arriving there in November with more than five hundred protesters. The protesters brought a twenty-point document (see "A Summary of the Twenty Points," pages 454–55.) proposing that the federal government reestablish a treaty-making relationship with Indians. The protest almost resulted in violence when Indian militants occupied the BIA building for six days, but with a national election looming, the government did not want open conflict with the first Americans in the streets of the nation's capital. They agreed to review the protesters' twenty demands and provide funds for their transportation home.

Siege at Wounded Knee

The new strategies of direct confrontation on the part of the militant pan-Indian leaders also produced strains and divisions within Indian society. Young AIM radicals questioned the legitimacy of tribal governments set up under the

IRA and criticized many tribal leaders as self-serving BIA pawns. On the other hand, many tribal chairmen had worked hard within the system to obtain services for their communities. They, and other older, more conservative Indians, sometimes disliked AIM; they regarded the new tactics and political aggression as inappropriate and not in their people's best interests, fearing the militants would create a backlash. When young militants returned to the Wind River reservation in Wyoming and called on the Arapahos to embrace the new activism, their ignorance of tribal protocol and their own language alienated Arapaho elders.[30]

The differences between the militants and the tribal chairman on the Pine Ridge reservation came to a head in South Dakota in 1973. In January, a young Lakota named Wesley Bad Heart Bull was stabbed to death, and his accused white killer was charged with only second-degree manslaughter. Angry Lakotas demanded the charge be changed to one of murder, and AIM protesters clashed with police in Custer, South Dakota. Wesley Bad Heart Bull's mother was arrested, charged with assaulting a police officer, and sentenced to three to five years in jail. The tribal chair, Richard Wilson, condemned AIM and banned it from Pine Ridge. As tensions and violence mounted, the BIA requested federal marshals at Pine Ridge. Confronted with this display of federal force, AIM leaders Dennis Banks, Russell Means, and about two hundred activists, with the support of Oglala traditional leaders, took over the village of Wounded Knee in February 1973. They announced the creation of the Oglala Sioux Nation, declared independence from the United States, and defined their national boundaries as those established by the Treaty of Fort Laramie in 1868. Federal marshals, FBI agents, troops, and armored vehicles surrounded the village and the world's media flocked to Wounded Knee. Wounded Knee was the site of the massacre of Big Foot's band in 1890 and was well known to the American public from the title of Dee Brown's best-selling indictment of the Indian wars, *Bury My Heart at Wounded Knee,* published in 1971. Banks and Means chose the place as a symbolic location to dramatize their opposition to the BIA and their demands for self-determination and a return of tribal sovereignty.

The Wounded Knee siege lasted seventy-one days against a background of violence, murder, and suspicion. Two Indians were killed and several others wounded as the military fired more than half a million rounds of ammunition into the AIM compound. At one point, the government considered launching an open assault on the village, but after protracted negotiations between AIM and the FBI, the Indians finally agreed to end their occupation on condition that the government hold a full investigation into their grievances and demands. "Once again, we Indians had accepted the white man's promises — just as our ancestors had," reflected Russell Means. "Once again, the government of the United States had lied."[31] Means then ran for tribal chairman, but the election was accompanied by arson, violence, intimidation, and murder attributed to tribal chair Richard Wilson's men. Wilson won by a narrow margin, but conditions on Pine Ridge remained tense. In 1975, two FBI agents were murdered, a crime for which AIM activist Leonard Peltier was arrested, tried, convicted, and sentenced to double life imprisonment on what many regarded as the shakiest of evidence. The election of Al Trimble as tribal chairman in 1976

Wounded Knee Settlement
Russell Means (foreground) and Assistant U.S. Attorney General Kent Frizzell sign an agreement. Frizzell smoked a sacred pipe with AIM leaders, but the peace settlement failed. Means said "the government broke it before the ink was dry." (Quoted in Robert Burnett and John Koster, The Road to Wounded Knee. *[New York: Bantam Books, 1974], 245.)*
AP/Wide World Photos.

restored a measure of calm to the reservation. But Peltier remains in jail and his case remains a source of heated controversy and, for many, a symbol of America's continuing oppression of its Native peoples.[32]

Legacies of Wounded Knee: Toward Self-Determination

Media coverage of the events at Wounded Knee tended to present a "war correspondents" approach, focusing on exchanges of gunfire and resurrecting western movie images of "hostile Indians" rather than examining the root issues of the conflict.[33] Those roots stretched back to the Treaty of Fort Laramie in 1868 (see "The Treaty of Fort Laramie and the Struggle for the Black Hills," pages 294–312), the annexation of the Black Hills, and the establishment of a new style of tribal government under the IRA in 1934, which imposed minority government on Pine Ridge. In June 1973, after the siege ended, Senator James Abourezk of South Dakota, the chairman of the United States Senate Subcommittee on Indian Affairs, held hearings at Pine Ridge to investigate the causes of the confrontation. Ramon Roubidoux, Russell Means's Sioux attorney, pinned much of the blame on the IRA, which was supposed to restore self-government. "But as you know," Roubidoux told the committee, "self-government by permission is not self-government at all. . . . I think this committee should realize that we have got a very serious situation throughout the country."[34] The confrontation at Wounded Knee, then, was more than a media event or even an attempt to overthrow a corrupt tribal government. Its goal was to free Pine Ridge from the shackles imposed by the federal government and to inspire other tribes to follow suit. By restoring responsible governments of their own, Indian peoples would regain their sovereignty, take care of their own affairs, and be able to determine their own futures. But in the opinion of Lakota writer and activist Vine Deloria, Jr., Wounded Knee gave AIM only temporary visibility in the media and failed to resolve deeper problems between Indians and the United States. AIM became "stalled in its own rhetoric" and the movement lost momentum. "Wounded Knee," concluded Paul Chaat Smith and Robert Allen Warrior, "proved to be the final performance of AIM's daring brand of political theater."[35]

Other less dramatic demonstrations and developments followed. In 1974, the International Indian Treaty Council was organized, with the goal of bringing the struggles of indigenous peoples around the globe to the attention of the world community. In 1978, Clyde Bellecourt led the "Longest Walk" of Indian protesters from Alcatraz to Washington, D.C. Gradually though, legal assault and FBI persecution drove many AIM leaders into hiding.[36]

Some observers, Native and non-Native, criticized the AIM leaders as publicity hounds — "the media's chiefs" — while the real work of reforming Indian policy went on outside the spotlight. Northern Cheyenne elder and tribal leader Ted Rising Sun said AIM "excited people for the moment" but produced no lasting positive results: "AIM was a big disturbance, but no real substance." Anishinaabe writer Gerald Vizenor disparaged the AIM leaders as "mouth warriors."[37] Some Indian women believed that AIM did not adequately represent their concerns and in the mid-1970s they established the activist group WARN (Women of All Red Nations). WARN tackled issues such as domestic violence and involuntary sterilization of Native women by the Indian Health Service, and tried to reassert Native rights and protect Native cultures.

Others, Native and non-Native, see AIM and the broader Red Power movement as a galvanizing and transformative force that generated an Indian demographic and cultural renaissance; increased numbers of Indian organizations, newspapers, tribal colleges and American Indian Studies Programs; dramatically raised the level of awareness and political action; and served as a catalyst for an American Indian ethnic renewal whose impact is seen in census figures in the late twentieth century.[38] (See the census figures in Chapter 8, page 490.) Russell Means said AIM lit a fire that brought renewed hope and pride across Indian country and struck a huge blow for Native sovereignty.[39] The AIM activists had effectively focused public concern on the plight and protests of Native Americans. AIM also gave many young Indian people a cause and a new direction in life. Mary Crow Dog remembered, "my early life, . . . before I went to Wounded Knee, was just one endless, vicious cycle of drinking and fighting, drinking and fighting."[40] Commitment to AIM's work ended the self-destructive spiral for Mary Crow Dog. AIM today continues to work for Indian rights and Indian communities, but with less militant confrontation and much less media visibility.

Whatever else it achieved, AIM demonstrated dramatically that the "Indian wars" did not end in 1890, that Indian people had not disappeared, and that Indian–U.S. relations would continue to be marked by conflict as long as American society encroached on Indian resources and denied Indian rights. Mounting Indian activism and growing public awareness of the continuing injustices in the government's dealings with the first Americans prompted yet another change in policy. In 1968, President Johnson called for a new Indian policy "expressed in programs of self-help, self-development, self-determination." In the years to come, the federal government acknowledged the Indians' unique political and legal status and, using that relationship as a foundation, set U.S.-Indian relations on the course of self-determination, but the struggle for self-determination was far from over.

References

1. John Collier, Jr., "Foreword" to Lawrence C. Kelly, *The Assault on Assimilation: John Collier and the Origins of Indian Policy Reform* (Albuquerque: University of New Mexico Press, 1983), xiii.
2. John Collier, *From Every Zenith* (Denver: Sage Books, 1963), 126.
3. D'Arcy McNickle, *Native American Tribalism: Indian Survivals and Renewals* (New York: Oxford University Press, 1973), 93.
4. Alvin M. Josephy, Jr., *Now That the Buffalo's Gone: A Study of Today's American Indians* (Norman: University of Oklahoma Press, 1984), 218.
5. Margaret Connell Szasz, *Education and the American Indian: The Road to Self-Determination since 1928*, 3d ed. (Albuquerque: University of New Mexico Press, 1999), chaps. 4–8.
6. Reprinted in Wilcomb E. Washburn, comp., *The American Indian and the United States: A Documentary History*, 4 vols. (Westport, Conn.: Greenwood Press, 1973), 2:910.
7. Elmer R. Rusco, *A Fateful Time: The Background and Legislative History of the Indian Reorganization Act* (Reno: University of Nevada Press, 2000).
8. David E. Wilkins, *American Indian Politics and the American Political System* (Lanham, Md.: Rowman and Littlefield, 2002), 134.
9. Paul C. Rosier, *Rebirth of the Blackfeet Nation, 1912–1954* (Lincoln: University of Nebraska Press, 2001), quote at 3–4.
10. Klara B. Kelley and Peter M. Whiteley, *Navajoland: Family Settlement and Land Use* (Tsaile, Ariz.: Navajo Community College Press, 1989), 11.
11. Richard White, *The Roots of Dependency: Subsistence, Environment, and Social Change among the Choctaws, Pawnees, and Navajos* (Lincoln: University of Nebraska Press, 1983), chap. 10 discusses the environmental factors.
12. Edward T. Hall, *West of the Thirties: Discoveries among the Navajo and Hopi* (New York: Doubleday, 1994), 136. For fuller treatment of these issues, see Peter Iverson, *Diné: A History of the Navajos* (Albuquerque: University of New Mexico Press,

2002) and Peter Iverson, ed., *"For Our Navajo People": Diné Letters, Speeches, and Petitions, 1900–1960* (Albuquerque: University of New Mexico Press, 2002).

13. Dean Kohlhoff, *When the Wind Was a River: Aleut Evacuation in World War II* (Seattle: University of Washington Press, 1995).

14. Quoted in Robert M. Kvasnicka, *The Commissioners of Indian Affairs, 1824–1977* (Lincoln: University of Nebraska Press, 1979), 294–95.

15. Francis Paul Prucha, ed., *Documents of United States Indian Policy* (Lincoln: University of Nebraska Press, 1975), 233.

16. George P. Castile, *To Show Heart: Native American Self-Determination and Federal Indian Policy, 1960-1975* (Tucson: University of Arizona Press, 1998), quote at 13.

17. Deborah Shames, ed., *Freedom with Reservation: The Menominee Struggle to Save Their Land and People* (Madison: University of Wisconsin Press, 1972), 7–8.

18. Donald Fixico, *Termination and Relocation: Federal Indian Policy, 1945–1960* (Albuquerque: University of New Mexico Press, 1986), 116–17.

19. Fixico, *Termination and Relocation,* 185.

20. Quoted in Wilcomb E. Washburn, ed., *Handbook of North American Indians,* vol. 4, *History of Indian-White Relations* (Washington, D.C.: Smithsonian Institution Press, 1988), 315.

21. Nancy Shoemaker, "Urban Indians and Ethnic Choices: American Indian Organizations in Minneapolis, 1920–1950," *Western Historical Quarterly* 19 (1988), 434.

22. Joan Weibel-Orlando, *Indian Country, L.A.: Maintaining Ethnic Community in Complex Society* (Urbana: University of Illinois Press, 1991), 1, 22.

23. J. Matthew Shumway and Richard H. Jackson, "Native American Population Patterns," *The Geographical Review* 85 (Spring 1995), 185–201 figures at 187, 193; Donald L. Fixico, *The Urban Indian Experience in America* (Albuquerque: University of New Mexico, 2000); Matthew C. Snipp, *American Indians: The First of This Land* (New York: Russell Sage Foundation, 1989), 83.

24. Fixico, *Urban Indian Experience in America.*

25. Laurence M. Hauptman, *The Iroquois Struggle for Survival: World War II to Red Power* (Syracuse: Syracuse University Press, 1985).

26. Morris W. Foster, *Being Comanche: A Social History of an American Indian Community* (Tucson: University of Arizona Press, 1991), 131.

27. Fixico, *The Urban Indian Experience in America.*

28. Quoted in George Pierre Castile, *To Show Heart: Native American Self-Determination and Federal Indian Policy, 1960–1975* (Tucson: University of Arizona Press, 1998), 41.

29. Alvin M. Josephy, Jr., ed., *Red Power: The American Indians' Fight for Freedom* (New York: McGraw-Hill, 1972), 71–77.

30. Loretta Fowler, *Arapahoe Politics, 1851–1978* (Lincoln: University of Nebraska Press, 1982), 282–84.

31. Russell Means with Marvin J. Wolf, *Where White Men Fear to Tread: The Autobiography of Russell Means* (New York: St. Martin's Press, 1995), 293.

32. Harvey Arden, ed., *Leonard Peltier, Prison Writings: My Life Is My Sun Dance* (New York: St. Martin's Press, 1999).

33. Mary Ann Weston, *Native Americans in the News: Images of Indians in the Twentieth Century Press* (Westport, Conn.: Greenwood Press, 1996), 142–45.

34. Quoted in Alvin M. Josephy, Jr., *Now That the Buffalo's Gone,* 217–18.

35. Robert Allen Warrior, "'Temporary Visibility': Deloria on Sovereignty and AIM," in Alan R. Velie, ed., *Native American Perspectives on Literature and History* (Norman: University of Oklahoma Press, 1994), 51–61, quote at 58; Paul Chaat Smith

and Robert Allen Warrior, *Like a Hurricane: The Indian Movement from Alcatraz to Wounded Knee* (New York: The New Press, 1996), 269.

36. Rex Weyler, *Blood of the Land* (New York: Everett House, 1982); Ward Churchill and James Vander Wall, *Agents of Repression: The FBI's Secret Wars against the Black Panther Party and the American Indian Movement* (Boston: South End Press, 1988); Ward Churchill, "The Bloody Wake of Alcatraz: Political Repression of the American Indian Movement during the 1970s," *American Indian Culture and Research Journal* 18 (1994), 253–300.

37. Ted Rising Sun quoted in Joanne Nagel, *American Indian Ethnic Renewal: Red Power and the Resurgence of Identity and Culture* (New York: Oxford University Press, 1996), 136, 169; Gerald Vizenor, "Dennis of Wounded Knee," *American Indian Quarterly* 7 (1983), 51–65, quote at 64; Castile, *To Show Heart*, chap. 5.

38. Nagel, *American Indian Ethnic Renewal*.

39. Means, *Where White Men Fear to Tread*.

40. Mary Crow Dog and Richard Erdoes, *Lakota Woman* (New York: HarperCollins, 1990), 54.

Suggested Readings

American Indian Culture and Research Journal 18 (1994), no. 4. Special Issue: "Alcatraz Revisited."

Baringer, Sandra K. "Indian Activism and the American Indian Movement: A Bibliographical Essay." *American Indian Culture and Research Journal* 21 (1997), 217–50.

Bernstein, Alison. *American Indians and World War II: Toward a New Era in Indian Affairs* (Norman: University of Oklahoma Press, 1990).

Castile, George Pierre. *To Show Heart: Native American Self-Determination and Federal Indian Policy, 1960–1975* (Tucson: University of Arizona Press, 1998).

Cohen, Fay G. *Treaties on Trial: The Continuing Controversy over Northwest Indian Fishing Rights* (Seattle: University of Washington Press, 1986).

Cornell, Stephen. *The Return of the Native: American Indian Political Resurgence* (New York: Oxford University Press, 1988).

Crow Dog, Mary, and Richard Erdoes. *Lakota Woman* (New York: HarperCollins, 1990).

Deloria, Vine, Jr. *Custer Died for Your Sins: An Indian Manifesto* (New York: Macmillan, 1969).

Deloria, Vine, Jr., and Clifford Lytle. *The Nations Within: The Past and Future of American Indian Sovereignty* (New York: Pantheon, 1984).

Fixico, Donald L. *The Invasion of Indian Country in the Twentieth Century : American Capitalism and Tribal Natural Resources* (Niwot: University Press of Colorado, 1998).

Fixico, Donald L. *Termination and Relocation: Federal Indian Policy, 1945–1960* (Albuquerque: University of New Mexico Press, 1986).

Fixico, Donald L. *The Urban Indian Experience in America* (Albuquerque: University of New Mexico Press, 2000).

Iverson, Peter, *Diné: A History of the Navajos* (Albuquerque: University of New Mexico Press, 2002).

Iverson, Peter. *"We Are Still Here": American Indians in the Twentieth Century* (Wheeling, Ill.: Harlan Davidson, 1998).

Iverson, Peter, ed. *"For Our Navajo People": Diné Letters, Speeches, and Petitions, 1900–1960* (Albuqueque: University of New Mexico Press, 2002).

Jaimes, M. Annette, ed. *The State of Native America: Genocide, Colonization, and Resistance* (Boston: South End Press, 1992).

Josephy, Alvin M., Jr. *Now That the Buffalo's Gone: A Study of Today's American Indians* (Norman: University of Oklahoma Press, 1984).

Means, Russell, with Marvin J. Wolf. *Where White Men Fear to Tread: The Autobiography of Russell Means* (New York: St. Martin's Press, 1995).

Nagel, Joanne. *American Indian Ethnic Renewal: Red Power and the Resurgence of Identity and Culture* (New York: Oxford University Press, 1996).

Olson, James S., and Raymond Wilson. *Native Americans in the Twentieth Century* (Urbana: University of Illinois Press, 1984).

Parman, Donald L. *Indians and the American West in the Twentieth Century* (Bloomington: Indiana University Press, 1994).

Philp, Kenneth R., ed. *Indian Self-Rule: First-Hand Accounts of Indian-White Relations from Roosevelt to Reagan* (Salt Lake City: Howe Brothers, 1986).

Rawls, James J. *Chief Red Fox Is Dead: A History of Native Americans since 1945* (Fort Worth: Harcourt Brace, 1996).

Smith, Paul Chaat, and Robert Allen Warrior. *Like a Hurricane: The Indian Movement from Alcatraz to Wounded Knee* (New York: The New Press, 1996).

Townshend, Kenneth William. *World War II and the American Indian* (Albuquerque: University of New Mexico Press, 2000).

D O C U M E N T S

Two Views of the Indian Reorganization Act

Drafted by John Collier and a team of lawyers, the bill that became the Indian Reorganization Act (IRA) contained forty-eight pages. It was introduced in Congress in February 1934 by Senators Burton K. Wheeler of Montana and Edgar Howard of Nebraska and endured a stormy passage that stripped it of some key provisions—notably, Collier's plans to consolidate Indian landholdings and establish a separate federal court of Indian affairs. President Roosevelt signed the amended bill into law in June. The act ended the policy of allotment and alienation of Indian land; it promoted economic development in Indian communities by establishing a revolving credit fund; and it encouraged tribes to take back responsibility for running their own affairs.

But it was a limited measure of self-government and it often produced unrepresentative minority tribal administrations. The forms of government that the tribes were invited and encouraged to establish and vote on were not their own traditional governments guided by clan or spiritual leaders; they were American-style representative governments and bureaucracies, created and operated under the supervision of the Bureau of Indian Affairs (BIA) and the Secretary of the Interior. In that sense, the IRA represented a shift in strategy rather than a fundamental change in policy, with assimilation still the ultimate goal. "The IRA and the Indian New Deal set out to grant to Indians a limited but enlarged degree of control over their affairs and destinies," writes sociologist Stephen Cornell, "but did so in the service of ends preselected by the dominant society and through methods given by that society, after its own models." Instead of trying to break up tribal communities and assimilate individuals, the IRA sought to make communities the vehicles of assimilation. Indian tribes as political constructs would survive, but as they "voluntarily formed constitutional governments, undertook the development of their own resources, and joined with the federal government in the assault on poverty and ignorance, assimilation would necessarily follow. American economic and political institutions would be reproduced within Indian societies, as a result of Indian efforts."[1]

The IRA revealed and fueled divisions in some Indian communities. Among the Lakotas, some people who became known as "new dealers" enthusiastically embraced Collier's vision of Indian self-government. But others "had their own ideas about what Indian self-government should look like" and wanted nothing to do with a system imposed from Washington.[2] On the Pine Ridge reservation in South Dakota, only 13 percent of the eligible Oglala voters accepted the IRA in the tribal referendum; 12 percent voted against it. The other 75 percent failed to vote, which from their perspective probably meant voting in the negative by having nothing to do with the process. "But," explains Alvin Josephy, "a majority of those who voted had said 'Yes,' and a minority of 13 percent was thus used to foist upon the other 87 percent a form of self-government that White men had chosen for them."[3] The elected BIA-style tribal governments often represented a minority who supported assimilation and acted as rubber stamps for federal policies; many more traditional people continued to look to spiritual leaders and did not participate in, or identify with, the new government. This situation led to open conflict in the early 1970s when traditional Oglalas and American Indian Movement (AIM) militants joined forces to try and oust the corrupt political machine of tribal chair Richard Wilson.

Combative and controversial in his own day, Collier and his legacy as architect of the Indian New Deal remain controversial today. Some people revere Collier for having pulled tribal governments from the brink of extinction; others see him as just another Washington politician who imposed his own ideas on Indian communities with little regard for their needs. Clarence Wesley, a San Carlos Apache leader, said Collier's policy "was the best thing that ever happened to Indian tribes." Rupert Costo, a Cahuilla Indian and president of the American Indian Historical Society, denounced Collier as "vindictive and overbearing," "a rank opportunist" who "betrayed us." For Costo, Collier's Indian New Deal was the "Indian Raw Deal."[4]

Collier had no ambivalence about the IRA. In his view it was the key to the survival of Indian tribes in modern America, and he worked tirelessly for its acceptance and implementation. The original draft of the Wheeler-Howard bill declared "that those functions of government now exercised by the Federal Government through the Department of the Interior and the office of Indian Affairs shall be gradually relinquished and transferred to the Indians." According to Collier as he left office in 1945, "We tried to extend to the tribes a self-governing self-determination without any limits beyond the need to advance by stages to the goal." As Collier envisioned the IRA, and as he explained it to the tribes, the tribal governments established under the IRA would be allowed to govern in fact, not just in legislation.[5]

Ben Reifel, a Brulé Sioux born in 1906 on the Rosebud reservation, worked for the government to explain the provisions of the Wheeler-Howard bill in meetings with the various tribes in South Dakota in the early 1930s; he "was impressed with the opportunities" it outlined. Reifel, who had a long career in the BIA before winning a seat in Congress in 1960, believed much of the opposition to the IRA among Lakota people stemmed from the nature of the relationship between the government and the Indian tribes. The government held Indian lands in trust and made "every honest effort . . . to protect the Indians in the use of their property," but the same rules and regulations that were established to protect or exercise that trust meant that the Secretary of the Interior retained ultimate control and created the feeling "that the tribal council did not get enough authority to really do the things they wanted to do on behalf of the people they represented." Looking back after fifty years, Reifel insisted "there is nothing in the Indian Reorganization Act that harms any Indian tribe or any Indian individual who has property." The IRA created the tribal constitutions; it was "up to the people to amend those constitutions and make them useful."[6]

But Robert Burnette, a Brulé of another generation, writing in the wake of the violent confrontation at Wounded Knee in 1973, offers a very different view of the IRA. Burnette was born in Rosebud, South Dakota, in 1926. He served in the Marines during World War II and returned home to face continued racism and the threat of termination. He blamed much of the poverty and the loss of land he saw in Lakota country on collusion between corrupt tribal officials and the BIA. In 1952, he was elected to the Rosebud Tribal Council; two years later he was elected tribal president. From the 1950s until his death in 1984, he was known as a combative champion of Indian civil rights, tribal self-determination, and sovereignty. He became executive director of the National Congress of American Indians in 1961 and served as a mediator and advocate of nonviolent resistance during AIM's takeover of the BIA building in Washington in 1972 and at the siege of Wounded Knee in 1973. His book *The Tortured Americans* was published in 1971, and in 1974 he coauthored *The Road to Wounded Knee,* which traced the root causes of the siege back to the kind of tribal governments established under the Indian New Deal. One of his earliest memories was of campaigning in school against his tribe's acceptance of the IRA. He was eight years old at the time. "I remember John Collier coming to the Rosebud Indian Boarding School and exactly what he said there," Burnette said half a century later. "I felt like we were being fooled."[7]

▶ **Questions for Consideration**

1. What does Collier's discussion of the Indian Reorganization Act in his annual report of 1935 illustrate about his vision of the IRA and his hopes for its impact on Indian America? What does the extract also reveal about his attitudes toward Indian people and toward those who did not share his vision? To what extent was he justified in talking about an "Indian renaissance"?

2. To what extent do Burnette's statements about the workings of the IRA refute Collier's claims that the act marked a decisive shift in the direction of Indian policy and initiated a new era in relations between Indians and the U.S. government?

3. Despite its shortcomings, its paternalism, and its continuing colonialism, did the Indian New Deal break with past government policies? What was new about the Indian New Deal after all?

JOHN COLLIER

An "Indian Renaissance," from the *Annual Report* of the Commissioner of Indian Affairs (1935)

This annual report is burdened with overcondensed statements of things done and more things yet to do; with urgencies, programs, and life-and-death necessities, all under the compulsion of speed.

It is all true. But the foundations of Indian life rest in a quiet earth. Indian life is not tense, is not haunted with urgencies, and does not fully accept the view that programs must be achieved, lest otherwise ruin shall swiftly befall.

Indian life is happy. Even the most poverty-stricken and seemingly futureless Indians still are happy. Indians have known how to be happy amid hardships and dangers through many thousand years. They do not expect much, often they expect nothing at all; yet they are able to be happy. Possibly this is the most interesting and important fact about Indians.

THE ACCELERATED TASK

The Indians and the Indian Service have had a difficult and challenging year, due to drought and depression; on the other hand, many Indians, and Indian property, have benefited from the generous relief appropriations. The effort to spend these relief funds wisely has meant extra work for the Service staff, which already had assumed the additional burden of launching the Indian reorganization program without benefit of new funds or personnel.

REORGANIZING INDIAN LIFE

The Indian Reorganization (modified Wheeler-Howard) Act was approved June 18, 1934. Its passage made mandatory a complete change in the traditional Federal Indian policy of individual allotment of land—which resulted in the break-up of Indian reservations—and of destroying Indian organization, institutions, and racial heritage to the end that the Indian as an Indian might disappear from the American scene with the utmost speed.

The next result of this policy has been the loss of two-thirds of the 139,000,000 acres owned by Indian tribes in 1887, the year when the General Allotment Act was adopted; and the individualization policy has broken up the land remaining on allotted reservations, has disrupted tribal bonds, has destroyed old incentives to action, and has created a race of petty landlords who in the generous Indian manner have shared their constantly shrinking income with the ever-increasing number of their landless relatives and friends.

The Indian Reorganization Act prohibits future allotments, and the sale of Indian lands except to the tribes; it restores to the tribes the unentered remnants of the so-called surplus lands of the allotted reservations thrown open to white settlement; it authorizes annual appropriations for the purchase of land for landless Indians, provides for the consolidation of Indian lands, and sets up a process which enables Indians voluntarily to return their individual landholdings to the

Source: John Collier, *Annual Report of the Commissioner of Indian Affairs for 1935*, reprinted in Wilcomb E. Washburn, comp., *The American Indian and the United States: A Documentary History*, 4 vols. (Westport, Conn.: Greenwood Press, 1973), 2:921–26.

protection of tribal status, thus reversing the dis-integration policy.

The act also authorizes a ten-million-dollar revolving loan fund, the use of which is restricted to those tribes which organize and incorporate so as to create community responsibility. It is expected that the organization of Indians in well-knit, functional groups and communities will help materially in the creation of new incentives for individual and collective action. The Indian is not a "rugged individualist"; he functions best as an integrated member of a group, clan, or tribe. Identification of his individuality with clan or tribe is with him a spiritual necessity. If the satisfaction of this compelling sentiment is denied him—as it was for half a century or more—the Indian does not, it has been clearly shown, merge into white group life. Through a modernized form of Indian organization, adapted to the needs of the various tribes (a form of organization now authorized by law), it is possible to make use of this powerful latent civic force.

The Indian Reorganization Act was passed a few days before the end of the Seventy-third Congress. None of the authorized appropriations, however, became available until May 1935. For land purchases the authorized appropriation was reduced to one-half, or $1,000,000; the revolving credit fund was limited to a quarter of the authorization, or $2,500,000; for organizing expenses the amount was reduced from $250,000 to $175,000.

THE INDIANS HOLD THEIR FIRST ELECTIONS

Congress had ordained in section 18 that each tribe must be given the unusual privilege of deciding at a special election whether it wanted to accept these benefits or reject them. Beginning with August 1934 and ending June 17, 1935, a series of 263 elections resulted in the decision by 73 tribes, with a population of 63,467 persons, to ex-clude themselves from the benefits and protection of the act, and by 172 tribes, with the population of 132,426 persons, to accept the act.

The participation of the Indians in these referendum elections was astonishingly heavy. In national elections, when a President is chosen and the interest of the voters is aroused through a long, intensive campaign, the average number of ballots cast does not exceed 52 percent of the total number of eligible voters; in referendum elections deciding on such matters as constitutional ratifications, bond issues, etc., when no personalities are injected into the campaign, less than 35 percent of the eligible voters participate. The referendum election on the Indian Reorganization Act did not concern itself with candidates and personalities, yet 62 percent of all adult Indians came to the polls and cast their ballots. . . .

The rejection of the Reorganization Act on 73 reservations, most of them very small (but including the largest reservation, that of the Navajos), was due in the main to energetic campaigns of misrepresentation carried on by special interests which feared that they would lose positions of advantage through the applications of the act. Joining hands in this campaign of misrepresentation were stockmen who feared that the Indians would run their own stock on land hitherto leased to white interests; traders who were afraid of losing their business through the competition of Indian consumers' cooperatives; merchants and politicians in white communities on the edge of reservations; a few missionaries who resented the extension of the constitutional guarantee of religious liberty and freedom of conscience to Indians (not an element in the Reorganization Act, but enforced as a policy by the present administration); lumber interests which did not want to see Indian tribes exploit their own forest resources. These interests, working frequently by the historic method of defrauding Indian tribes with the connivance of certain of their own leaders, spread extreme and bizarre falsehoods concerning the effects of the act.

Among the myths spread by adverse interests on various reservations were such as these: Acceptance of the act would cause Indian owners of allotments to lose their land, which would then be distributed among those Indians who had disposed of their allotments; all farm crops would be impounded in warehouses and thereafter would be equally distributed among the population; the Indians would be segregated behind wire fences charged with electricity; all the livestock would be taken from certain tribes; unalloted reservations would be thrown open to white entry; Indian dances and other religious ceremonies would be suppressed; Indians would not be allowed to go to Christian churches; certain Southwestern reservations would be turned over to Mexico, etc.

THE NAVAJO VOTE

On the Navajo Reservation, certain interests disseminated the most fantastic fictions in their effort to induce the 43,500 Navajos to reject the help the Federal Government was offering them. With the aid of these fictions, and by falsely connecting the referendum on the Reorganization Act with the unpopular but necessary stock reduction program, the propagandists succeeded in bringing about the exclusion of the Navajo Reservation by a very narrow margin of votes: 7,608 for acceptance; 7,992 against acceptance. Immediately after the result became known, Navajo leaders started a movement to reverse it through a renewed referendum which will be possible only through a new enabling act of Congress.

THE INDIAN RENAISSANCE

Considering the long history of broken treaties, pledges, and promises, the fact that 172 tribes with an Indian population of 132,000 accepted the word of the Government that the fundamental reorganization of their lives would not harm them is evidence of a new, more satisfactory relationship between the Indians and the Indian Service. The referendum elections served a most valuable purpose. They were palpable proof to the Indians that the Government really was ready to give them a voice in the management of their own affairs, and that the period of arbitrary autocratic rule over the tribes by the Indian Service had come to an end.

This evidence of good faith was reinforced by the request that the tribes begin immediately to formulate the constitutions and charters authorized by the act. Reservation committees and groups set to work at the unaccustomed task of drafting constitutions and of making plans and programs for the economic rehabilitation of the tribes. Charters and constitutions under the Reorganization Act, when once adopted, cannot be revoked or changed by administrative action. Personal government of the tribes by the Secretary of the Interior and the Indian Commissioner is brought to an end.

INDIAN EMERGENCY WORK

In the revivifying of the Indian spirit, the wide-opened benefits of Indian emergency conservation and of other relief work played an important part. It must be remembered that on many reservations the kind of depression which struck the Nation in 1929 had been a chronic condition for a long time, becoming acute when land sales dropped off and the revenue from farm and grazing lands leased to whites dropped almost to the vanishing point. Opportunities for wage work had been all but nonexistent on most reservations, and the psychology of the chronically unemployed had prevailed for so long that it was feared that most of the Indians had become unemployable.

This fear proved to be groundless. Indians young and old not merely accepted emergency relief work, but almost fought for the chance to labor. And they labored effectively. Through their effort the physical plant, the land, the water, the forests, have had many millions of dollars added to their use value in the last 2 years. Incalculable benefits have been derived from the improvement of 20 million acres of range, through the development of springs and wells and the construction of thousands of stock-water dams, through roads and truck trails, through the construction of thousands of miles of fences and telephone lines. There is not one reservation which, as a result of the emergency and relief work, is not a better place to live on, an easier place in which to gain a living from the soil.

A clear gain to the Indians—and to many white communities in the Indian country—accrued out of the grants from Public Works funds for new Indian community-school buildings, hospitals, and sanatoria, many of them built entirely by Indian labor. Yet the pressing need for structures of this kind has not been half filled. Nor is the Indian irrigation program, financed from emergency grants, more than one-third completed.

AFTER THE DEPRESSION—WHAT?

The benefit derived by the Indians from the emergency and relief work has many aspects. Thousands of the Indian workers have, for perhaps the first time in their lives, learned what it means to have sufficient nourishment of the right kind regularly. Other thousands have been able to acquire minimal household goods, clothing, livestock, and farm implements. Thousands of savings accounts have been started at the various agencies out of earnings of $2.10 per day for 20 days in the month during part of the year.

There have been entries on the debit side also. The number of bootleggers on the fringe of many reservations has multiplied; law enforcement has become more and more difficult. Automobile dealers with second-hand wrecks for sale have encouraged the younger Indians to obligate their potential earnings for years ahead; some traders have encouraged credit buying on far too lavish a scale.

But more important than these shortcomings due to the innate generosity of a race unfamiliar with wise consumption habits is the problem that arises from the introduction of a wage economy on reservations which will supply almost no permanent opportunity for wage work. After the depression is over and the emergency grants cease, what will happen to the now-working Indians?

REHABILITATION EMPHASIZED

To prepare for this inevitable crisis additional funds must be obtained for rehabilitation projects, such as land purchase, housing, the construction of barns and root cellars, the development of domestic water and sanitary facilities, the subjugation of land, the financing of purchases of seeds, implements, and livestock, the stimulation and development of Indian arts and crafts, and the organization and financing of sawmills, fisheries, and other industrial enterprises. This amended program would mean a playing down of the wage motive, a playing up of production for use.

If the necessary grants for this program be made, the Indians on many reservations should be able to pass gradually from relief work to subsistence farming, craft, and other supplemental industrial work of their own.

ROBERT BURNETTE AND JOHN KOSTER
"A Blueprint for Elected Tyranny" (1974)

Under the IRA, the once all-powerful agent was pushed from his dictatorial position in favor, usually, of a chairman-council form of elective government. For the first time in fifty years the Indians were allowed to pick their own leaders. This was a radical change from the traditional tribal government which had total democracy in council, advised by a smaller council of wise elders who had to agree unanimously on every decision and even then could not force their decisions on any adult male. Built into the BIA's chairman-council system were all the weaknesses, but none of the strengths, of local government in middle America. The white agent was retained in the form of the *superintendent,* a white BIA appointee who holds veto power over tribal finances. Through the superintendent, the BIA could still tell the Indian people how many cows they could buy or sell, how much timber they could cut, and what their school curricula should be. There was no system of checks and balances, no procedure through which inequities could be righted. It was a blueprint for elected tyranny. . . .

Before the IRA, there were almost as many tribal governing bodies as there were tribes. Owing to restrictive federal policies, some tribes were actually without a government. The actual power on the reservations, as far as the government was concerned, was the Indian agent, acting on behalf of the secretary of the interior. The tribes themselves sometimes managed to maintain a link with their past in the form of traditional governing bodies. The form differed tribe by tribe. The Red Lake

Chippewas of Minnesota maintained their traditional chief system, in which chieftainship was hereditary. The Sioux across South Dakota were operating under the three-quarters-majority council system that stemmed from the Sioux Treaty of 1868. This required that three-fourths of all adult males sign any legislation affecting the tribe. The Pueblo tribes of the Southwest operated their traditional Kiva system, which was strongly linked to their religion. The Crow tribe of Montana kept their general council system, a forum of one hundred people empowered to represent the rest of the tribe.

On their own, the Indian peoples had developed the checks and balances that were needed to keep a brake on ambition. Most plains tribes originally had at least two governing bodies that kept the power decentralized. Among the Cheyenne, for example, four old man chiefs served as advisers and executives, and a council of forty chiefs made up the legislative body. The police duties were assumed by three or more warrior societies, which were rotated to prevent any group from gaining power. Each warrior society was headed by a big war chief, assisted by nine little war chiefs. The various council chiefs expressed the will of the people, and the government had no right to compel anyone to take any action unless to do otherwise would threaten the whole tribe. . . .

The New Deal's Indian Reorganization Act of 1934 carried the promise of constitutional guarantees of liberty; finances for economic growth; an end to the steady loss of Indian lands; legal counsel needed by the tribes in order to cope with modern society; and lastly, the right to self-government to those who chose to adopt it.

Despite the golden promises, many traditional leaders were wary of anything that would

Source: From Robert Burnette and John Koster, *The Road to Wounded Knee* (New York: Bantam Books, 1974), 15–16, 180–87. Copyright © 1974 by Robert Burnette. Used by permission of Bantam Books, a division of Random House, Inc.

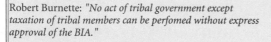

Robert Burnette: *"No act of tribal government except taxation of tribal members can be perfomed without express approval of the BIA."*

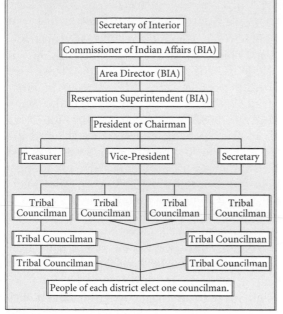

CHART 7.1 IRA-Style Tribal Government, According to Robert Burnette

Robert Burnette and John Koster, The Road to Wounded Knee *(New York: Bantam Books, 1974), 295.*

disrupt the forms of government the Indians had created for themselves. The bitterly fought battle of the traditionals against the Indian Reorganization Act raged from 1934 until 1940. In the end, the Indian opposition was the victim of a provision of the act that allowed it to be adopted by 30 percent of the voting-age population of the reservation. This was a deviation both from Indian tradition and American democracy, since it allowed less than a majority to rule. The same provision that sets 30 percent as a quorum supposedly allows the Indians to petition for a referendum to recall the tribal constitution by securing at least 30 percent of the voting-age population's signatures. Yet the secretary of the interior has in-

variably ignored this and has categorically refused to hold referendums to repeal the tribal government system set up by the IRA. Thus the government has twisted its own rules for its own convenience.

In actual practice, a tribal council is a strange vintage of constitutional government: the federal government is divided into the executive, legislative, and judicial branches; the tribal constitutions created by the federal government provide for one single governing body, which tends to operate under constant conflicts of interest.

Under the IRA, the tribal president, chairman, or chief is generally empowered only to carry out the resolutions, ordinances, or directives of the tribal council. Thus, Indians have an executive who can only function whenever the tribal council orders him to act. Likewise, the vice-president, vice-chairman, or vice-chief can only act in the absence of the president, chairman, or chief.

The tribal secretary, although he may be a constitutional officer, is the keeper of the tribal records and as such is subject to the powers of the tribal council. The tribal treasurer is the custodian of all tribal funds and can disburse such funds only by orders of the tribal council.

The size of the tribal council depends on the size of the tribe. Many have as few as six members; the Navajo tribe has seventy-two. The average number is around sixteen.

These councilmen are elected by various methods. On the Sioux reservations of Rosebud and Pine Ridge, among others, the tribe has an open nonpartisan primary, in which anyone with the required number of signatures on his nominating petition can get on the ballot. The primary narrows the field down to two candidates for each office. These two vie for office in the final election, usually about two months after the primary.

On other reservations, like the Crow reservation of Montana, there is no primary. The general election is open, with as many as a dozen candidates running as spoilers to take votes away from their friend's political opponents. Anyone who thinks that Indian people lack political sophistication would find some of the elections held by the north plains tribes, the Sioux in particular, to be very instructive. Not the least compelling reason for seeking office is that tribal chairmen receive a five-figure income—not easy to come by on a reservation—and can control a great deal of patronage, such as jobs for relatives.

Tribal constitutions specifically grant tribal councils the power to act for and in behalf of the entire tribe, without consulting the wishes of the people.

The tribal council has the power to negotiate with the federal, state, and local governments; to legislate the economic, social, educational, and domestic affairs of the tribe; to establish a tribal court, maintain a law-and-order code; to control domestic relations; to charter subordinate tribal enterprises; and to regulate the appointment of guardians for minors and mental incompetents.

In the area of land, the tribal council was empowered with restricting undesirable persons from the reservation; making assignments of tribal land to members; employing legal counsel for the advancement and protection of the tribe; purchasing lands through condemnation in courts of competent jurisdiction; governing the inheritance of real and personal property; and executing leases on tribal land. In addition, the council had the power to veto any action that would destroy tribal property.

The council also had the power to expend tribal funds; to levy taxes on tribal members or require the performance of labor in lieu of taxes; to regulate tribal elections; to advise the secretary of the interior on budget estimates prior to submission to Congress or the Bureau of the Budget; and to regulate their own procedure.

Despite this impressive list of powers, tribal self-government was a charade. The tribal constitution provides that the secretary of the interior approve the tribal council's actions, which means that the conflict of interest inherent in Interior's control over the Indian tribes is written right into their constitutions.

To add to the confusion, the Department of the Interior holds that the charters issued to the tribes are separate and distinct documents with no application or control over the tribal constitutions. This is an extremely contradictory position for the Department of the Interior to take, since the tribal constitutions, *Powers of the Tribal Council,* say bluntly:

"To manage economic affairs and enterprises of the tribe in accordance with the terms of the charter which may be issued to the tribe by the Secretary of the Interior . . ."

Thus the government set up for the Indians by Congress violates the Congress's own form of government. Indians hate this second-class form of government because their original, traditional tribal governments were invariably far superior.

Time and again, the Department of the Interior has interfered in tribal affairs against the Indians' best interests. For instance, a tribe may have a tremendous reserve of oil and gas on their reservation and have no desire to have some oil company exploit their wealth. They would prefer to form a tribally owned oil company employing their own people and profiting the tribe. But government officials will be bribed and the BIA will begin applying pressure to force the tribal council members to enact a resolution to advertise the oil and gas leases in their reservation for public bids. . . . The BIA has habitually meddled in tribal business, usually to the tribe's detriment.

After the BIA had established blocks of land known as range units, they began making loans to the tribes to establish Indian credit corporations, under the tribal council's authority to charter subordinate organizations. The tribal credit corporation was totally controlled by the BIA's required secretarial-approval clause. This credit corporation was intended to advance money for Indians who desired to enter business. The funds were supposed to provide capital for opening filling stations and grocery stores, or buying livestock or farm machinery to be used in working the Indians' land. In actual practice, the BIA would only approve loans that led to Indian indebtedness.

Nearly every loan client was limited to a loan of five thousand dollars or less, when twelve thousand dollars would have ensured success. But despite the fact that the loans were failure-bound, the Indian Loan System had a national loss rate of less than 1 percent. The Indian—unlike the government—paid his debts.

This Indians' relations with the federal government began and usually ended with the BIA superintendent, and it was the superintendent, not the tribal council, who held the real power on most reservations. Except in rare cases, the balance of power has not changed since the days of the 1880s when the Indian agent ran his reservation like an army camp. Tribal government, as provided for by the Indian Reorganization Act and administered by the BIA, is now and always has been such a mess that those few tribes who escaped from the IRA government, like the Onondagas of upstate New York, feel that they are much better off under their traditional form of government.

In battles between the all-powerful superintendents and the Indian people, all too many elected officials washed their hands of the whole affair and let their constituents do their own fighting. Those elected officials who chose to try to defend their people were drawn into constant battles with the superintendents, but because of the pervasive apathy of reservation living and because of their lack of knowledge of how to appeal a decision, most individual Indians seemed to think that attempts to protect their people were hopeless. One could hardly expect the Indians to be informed on Indian law when 99.44 percent of the nation's lawyers know nothing of the matter either.

Another very special fact is that Indians or anyone else affected have the right to an administrative appeals system. This is a tiresome and almost endless process because the government on any level is not subject to time limitations. Most Indian appeals taken in this manner die a natural death for lack of persistence on the part of those who seek such adjudication.

Unlike the Indians, who felt strangled and frustrated by this morass of white tape, BIA officials seemed to thrive on it. But they took pains to stifle any challenge to their powers.

References

1. Stephen Cornell, *The Return of the Native: American Indian Political Resurgence* (New York: Oxford University Press, 1988), 94–95.
2. Thomas Biolsi, *Organizing the Lakota: The Political Economy of the New Deal on the Pine Ridge and Rosebud Reservations* (Tucson: University of Arizona Press, 1992), xx.
3. Alvin M. Josephy, Jr., *Now That the Buffalo's Gone: A Study of Today's American Indians* (Norman: University of Oklahoma Press, 1984), 219.
4. Kenneth R. Philp, ed., *Indian Self-Rule: First-Hand Accounts of Indian-White Relations from Roosevelt to Reagan* (Salt Lake City: Howe Brothers, 1986), 28–29, 47–48, 101.
5. Quotes from Biolsi, *Organizing the Lakota,* 126–27.
6. Reifel's views are expressed in Joseph H. Cash and Herbert T. Hoover, eds., *To Be an Indian: An Oral History* (St. Paul: Minnesota Historical Society Press, 1995), 124–25, and Philp, ed., *Indian Self-Rule,* 76–78.

7. Alvin M. Josephy, Jr., "Burnette, Bob," in Frederick E. Hoxie, ed., *Encyclopedia of North American Indians* (Boston: Houghton Mifflin, 1996), 88–90; Burnette quote in Philp, ed., *Indian Self-Rule*, 104.

Suggested Readings

Biolsi, Thomas. *Organizing the Lakota: The Political Economy of the New Deal on the Pine Ridge and Rosebud Reservations* (Tucson: University of Arizona Press, 1992).

Burnette, Robert, and John Koster. *The Road to Wounded Knee* (New York: Bantam Books, 1974).

Kelly, Lawrence C. *The Assault on Assimilation: John Collier and the Origins of Indian Policy Reform* (Albuquerque: University of New Mexico Press, 1983).

Philp, Kenneth R. *John Collier's Crusade for Indian Reform, 1920–1945* (Tucson: University of Arizona Press, 1977).

Philp, Kenneth R., ed. *Indian Self-Rule: First-Hand Accounts of Indian-White Relations from Roosevelt to Reagan* (Salt Lake City: Howe Brothers, 1986).

Rosier, Paul C. *Rebirth of the Blackfeet Nation, 1912–1954* (Lincoln: University of Nebraska Press, 2001).

Taylor, Graham D. *The New Deal and American Indian Tribalism: The Administration of the Indian Reorganization Act, 1934–45* (Lincoln: University of Nebraska Press, 1980).

Indians in the Cities

W hen Glenn Emmons, a banker from New Mexico, became Commissioner of Indian Affairs under President Eisenhower in 1953, he devoted considerable energy toward improving the relocation program established by his predecessor, Dillon S. Myer. Emmons moved the Bureau of Relocation headquarters from Washington, D.C., to Denver to bring it closer to Indian populations and opened new field offices, secured additional funding, and stepped up publicity for the program. He placed great faith in relocation's ability to weaken tribalism and promote assimilation. In his annual report for 1954 he described the program in optimistic terms.

Indian individuals and families looked for jobs and new lives in urban America long before the BIA program provided additional incentives; they continued to do so long after the program was phased out. Those who made the move often saw things quite differently from Emmons. "The decision to leave their homelands," writes historian Kenneth Philp, "was more than a response to the prodding of federal bureaucrats who favored termination. It was a stride toward freedom from Indian Bureau paternalism, economic insecurity, racial injustice, segregation, and second-class citizenship."[1] The accounts reprinted here by anonymous Indian people living in Chicago and by Ignatia Broker, an Ojibway or Anishinaabe elder and storyteller who moved from the White Earth reservation to Minneapolis during World War II, reveal a variety of motivations, experiences, and achievements.

▶ Questions for Consideration

1. What reasons do migrants in the following selections give for making the move to the cities?

2. In which cases, and in what ways, was urban migration and adjustment to city life the result of Indian, not government, efforts?

3. What evidence do the accounts provide to support the view that the relocation was a "stride toward freedom"?

4. What causes of difficulty and despair do the accounts reveal? What do they tell us about how people managed to adjust to their new urban environment, rebuild communities, and maintain their identities?

5. What new relationships and perspectives emerged out of their urban experiences?

GLENN L. EMMONS
From the *Annual Report of the Commissioner of Indian Affairs* (1954)

... During the 1954 fiscal year, 2,163 Indians were directly assisted to relocate under the Bureau's relocation program. This included 1,649 persons in over 400 family groups, and 514 unattached men and women. In addition, over 300 Indians left reservations without assistance to join relatives and friends who had been assisted to relocate. At their destination, Bureau Relocation Offices assisted this group also to adjust to the new community. The total number of relocations represented a substantial increase over relocations during the previous fiscal year.

Of the 2,163 Indians assisted to relocate, financial assistance, to cover all or part of the costs of transportation to the place of relocation and short-term temporary subsistence, were provided to 1,637 Indians, in addition to relocation services. This number included 1,329 persons in over 300 family groups, and 308 unattached men and women. An additional 526 Indians, including 320 in approximately 100 family groups and 206 unattached men and women, were assisted to relocate without financial assistance, but were provided relocation services only. These services included counseling and guidance prior to relocation, and assistance in establishing residence and securing permanent employment in the new community.

In addition to the above-mentioned persons who were assisted to relocate, Bureau Relocation Offices assisted a number of Indian workers to se-

cure employment which did not involve relocation, and cooperated with public employment offices and the Railroad Retirement Board in recruitment of Indians for temporary and seasonal work. However, in order to concentrate on providing relocation services, placement activities which do not involve relocation have been progressively decreased and responsibility for such placement activities has been largely left to established employment agencies. In recognition of this emphasis, and following the recommendation of the survey team for the Bureau of Indian Affairs, the name of the former Branch of Placement and Relocation was changed during the year to the Branch of Relocation.

Approximately 54 percent of the Indians assisted to relocate came from 3 northern areas (Aberdeen, Billings, and Minneapolis), and 46 percent came from 4 southern areas (Anadarko, Gallup, Muskogee, and Phoenix). They went to 20 different States. The Los Angeles and Chicago metropolitan areas continued to be the chief centers of relocation.

On the reservations there was continued interest in relocation throughout the year. Relocation assistance funds were used up in almost every area, and at the end of the year there was a backlog of applications for relocation. Letters from relocated Indians to friends and relatives back on the reservation, describing their experiences and new standards of living, served to stimulate interest as did a decrease in employment opportunities in the vicinity of some of the reservations and a marked decrease in railroad employment.

There was a slight tightening of the labor market during part of the year. However, through

Source: Glenn L. Emmons, *Annual Report of the Commissioner of Indian Affairs for 1954,* reprinted in Francis Paul Prucha, ed., *Documents of United States Indian Policy* (Lincoln: University of Nebraska Press, 1975), 237–38.

intensive efforts on the part of field relocation offices, it was still possible to assure permanent types of employment to almost all qualified workers who requested assistance in settling away from reservations. Field relocation offices followed a policy of securing employment for Indians in diversified industries and with a large number of employers. This policy proved of great benefit when industrial disputes developed in certain industries on the west coast. . . .

The Chicago Field Relocation Office, in recognition of the needs of the growing number of relocatees in that city and in accordance with the Bureau policy of encouraging the development of non-Bureau facilities for Indians, assisted in the establishment of an All-Tribes American Indian Center in Chicago. This center raised its own funds, and under the directorship of a board composed almost entirely of Indians, began providing opportunities for Indian relocatees to meet, engage in social and recreational programs, exchange experiences, and assist each other. Its operations were completely independent of the Bureau. . . .

ANONYMOUS

Life in the City: Chicago (c. 1970)

I more or less knew what to expect. I had relatives who had moved to the city, and they came home and talked about it. I needed work, and the relocation program seemed like a good idea to me. Sometimes I got mad at the BIA. Seems like they tried to confuse me sometimes. But I finished the training and got a job, and then I changed jobs on my own, and I still have that job—four years almost—and I think it is a good idea to help people make it to the places where there are jobs. We could have used more money, though, while I was in training.

—*Male, age 37*

I didn't come because the BIA or anyone else helped me. We heard in Wisconsin that there were jobs in Chicago. I knew something about welding, so I came, and I've been here ever since—except I go back to visit and I travel around some. I

like it here. I raised my kids here. Sometimes they got in with the wrong crowd and there was some trouble, but they're all grown now, and everything worked out OK. My children are real city kids. They like to visit in Wisconsin, but Chicago is their home. One boy even went to junior college—Wilson. All of them married whites. I don't care and my wife doesn't care either. That's their business. We have seven grandchildren, and I don't think they consider themselves Indians at all. Oh, they know where their grandparents came from, but they're all just part of the city. There's a lot of dirt and noise, and when the children were little, I used to worry about the traffic, but I think they got a better education here than they would back home, and I like the things to do in a city, lots of people, and much better jobs. It may cost more to live in the city, but with a job you can afford it. What is there back home? When I go back I see no jobs, nothing to do, everyone just drinks.

—*Male, age 53*

Source: Merwyn S. Garbarino, "Life in the City: Chicago," in Jack O. Waddell and O. Michael Watson, eds. *The American Indian in Urban Society* (Boston: Little, Brown, 1971), 171, 179–82.

I heard about relocation on the reservation. It's a good idea. Sometimes it doesn't work too well. When I first came, I had some training, and then things got bad and I lost my job. The BIA helped me get another one, but it didn't pay too good, and we had a hard time making out. We had to get some welfare at times. That sort of embarrassed me at first, but then in those days lots of people were out of work. At first it was just my wife and me. That wasn't so bad. She did some day jobs, you know, just line up each morning and see if there's a job for the day. That helped get some money. She didn't like it much. Some people say that it is easier to be alone, but I'm glad I had her along. Then we had a baby, a boy, and that could have been bad, but the jobs began to get better. I heard of a better job from a friend and I changed. No, I didn't think about going back to the reservation. Jobs were even worse there. There are things in the city that I like — the museums, movies, things like that. There are things to do, and the jobs did get better. We have quite a family now. Three girls and two boys, and I can take care of them all. Some people say that it is easier if you are alone, but I am glad that I have my family. I take the children to the zoo, and things. My wife never has to work any more. I think I'd like some other cities too. I like Chicago, but I have visited some smaller cities like Green Bay, and I think I might like to live there. But I can say I like a city.

— Male, age 49

Well, I think an Indian ought to go back to his reservation and help the people there. It's not that I don't like Chicago, but I think if everyone young and educated leaves the reservation, who is going to run things? You know tribal politics can be damn dirty, and someone who knows something ought to go back and watch those guys. I am going back someday, but first I am going to finish my education and get some experience.

I came under the relocation program. I applied through the agency back on the reservation, and I came to Chicago to go to school. I went to a business school in a suburb, and I liked it out there. It was really beautiful, the trees and that.

All the kids coming in for training lived at the Y. We don't any more.

I took secretarial training, and some of the teachers were good and some weren't. I used to think . . . I still think that sometimes they just passed us with good grades because they knew the BIA would go on paying. So maybe we really didn't get a very good education always. But I must have learned all right because I applied for a job as a secretary, and I got it OK, and I am still doing it. I think the relocation program is a good thing, but the BIA just never seems to do anything right. They really don't seem to take an interest in the students, and they ran us through like cattle, but the idea is still good. And some of the advisors are real nice and helpful. Well, anyhow, I have a job now that pays enough and I can save some money. It is my hope to go to college someday.

I think that people who really make it in the city and on relocation are people who are quite independent. If you are too dependent on the BIA or anyone else, you'll probably drop out and go back home. You have to have some idea or goal in mind. I want an education. I have traveled about a lot. I guess someone who had never been off a reservation might have a hard time, but I didn't. I don't know if I'll stay here, but I can't say that I don't like cities. There is so much going on, like if you want to go to these art places and if you want to go see one of the latest movies that's out and what not and things like the Buckingham Fountain, and things like that you never see anywhere. Also all the things you can learn from other people because they're all from different backgrounds, like on the job, you know, the boss finds out you're Indian, so he talks about his German history or something like this, and you kind of learn a lot from them too. That's what I like about the city. I don't like what is so dirty, and it's expensive. I think city people are sort of unfriendly. I mean you could fall over in front of somebody and I don't think they'd pick you up.

— Female, age 24

I wish we had never left home. This will never be a home to me. It's dirty and noisy, and people all around, crowded. The apartment is too small, and it seems like I never see the sky or trees. Seems like nothing goes right anymore. First my husband got sick and lost his job. He still isn't working. I have a job, but it never seems like we have enough money. Everything costs so much, shoes, clothes, books, and stuff like that the kids need for school. I have to get help from welfare and have to ask for things. But what can I do? I wish my husband would go back to work. Things would be different then. He says the doctors tell him he can't work yet. I guess they know, but he seems to be able to do the things he wants to do. I wish he'd take more interest in the children. They're always in trouble somehow. After I leave for work, I don't know what's going on. The girl has been picked up on truancy a couple of times, and the boys have gotten into trouble too. They've been up in juvenile court, but they got put on probation. The probation officer is a real nice man, and he tries to help me, but the boys don't listen to me. Next time they'll probably get sent to IYC [the Illinois Youth Commission], and that means reformatory, I guess. My husband ought to do something about them. He just doesn't know how to control them . . . he doesn't even try. I can't be there, and they don't listen to me anyhow. They did something bad. They stole because they wanted some money to spend. I can't give them any money. And once or twice, maybe more, they've gotten an older man to buy them beer and stuff because they're too young to buy it themselves. Well, back on the reservation maybe they'd get beer too, but then I don't think they'd get into so much trouble. They wouldn't get picked up by the police. Maybe the schools are better here, but half the time my kids just don't go to school. They start out, but they never get there—or else I guess they leave before school is out. I just don't know what to do with them. The counselor always wants me to come and talk, but how can I when I have to go to work. When the boys were in juve-

nile court, I had to take off from work because the mother or father is supposed to go too. I just don't know why my husband can't do more—just sits around and drinks beer with friends. I don't like living here, but we have no other choice.

—*Female, age 48*

I don't like living in Chicago. I'm here on the relocation training program, and I'm glad to learn a trade, but I sure don't like the city. The BIA doesn't give us enough money to live in Chicago. It's awfully expensive here. But it's not just that. People are different here—even the Indians. They don't talk to you. Bus drivers are bastards, and I got lost on the "el"° and no one would help me. City people are in such a hurry. As soon as I finish school, I'm going away—maybe back to the reservation, but to a small town anyhow. I'd rather be in a small town and not have such a good job as stay in the city.

—*Male, age 25*

Most of my life I've been coming back and forth to the city. I'm thirty now. I used to stay with my mother's sister. When I was a teenager, I thought the city was wonderful. My aunt was married and had a family. Sometimes I had to babysit for her. But I liked to come to visit. Then I got into trouble. That's how I got these tattoos. In Bridewell [prison], for strong-arm robbery. So, like I say, I'd stay here for a few years then go back for a few years. I just couldn't get along either place really. I got a lot of relatives both places, and pretty soon we'd start fighting and I'd move on. Maybe I shouldn't feel that way, but I don't belong any place. Do you ever get that feeling that you don't belong? Well, I do, and then I start to drink. And I got married, but I didn't like her. I just don't fit in anywhere . . . relatives, marriage. And I'm always getting into fights, especially with Puerto Ricans. The Indians here ain't like they used to be

---

°The local name for Chicago's elevated train system.

when I was young. So I go back, but there's nothing to do there. It's prettier than the city—but somehow even there the people seem different and I come back to the city. Maybe I ought to get my GED [General Education Diploma]—finish my education, but I don't seem to be able to do anything.

—Male, age 30

IGNATIA BROKER
"Brought to a Brotherhood" (1983)

I got off the city bus and walked the short one-and-a-half blocks home as I have been doing for years around five o'clock each evening. Because this evening was warm, I walked slower than usual, enjoying the look and feel of the early spring. The earth that had been white was now brown, left uncovered by the melting snow. This brown was turning to green and the air was fragrant with the opening of spring.

Daylight still lingered and as I walked I looked at my neighborhood and thought about it. When I first moved here in the mid-1950s this was a mixed neighborhood of Spanish-speaking people and Catholic whites, and there were many children. Now the Spanish-speaking people are all gone. They left when the parochial school closed its doors, although the church is still here. Now the neighborhood is only four blocks long and two blocks wide, whittled down by urban renewal and the freeways which reach their tentacles all around us.

I reached my doorstep and sat enjoying the good day and remembering the past. It was funny, really, when I think about it. That day thirty years ago when we moved here, me and my children, we were the aliens looking for a place to fit in, looking for a chance of a new life, moving in among these people, some of whose "forefathers" had displaced my ancestors for the same reason: looking for a new life. Their fathers were the aliens then, and now they, the children, are in possession of this land.

For a long time I was that Indian person with the two children. But it is good that children have a natural gift of accepting people, and so my children became a part of the neighborhood.

Thirty years in this neighborhood. My children went to school from here, they went to church from here, they were married from here and even though they are in faraway places they seem to have their roots here, for they had lived no other place while growing up.

I talked to my children, even when they were very small, about the ways of the Ojibway people. They were good children and they listened, but I had a feeling that they listened the same as when I read a story about the Bobbsey twins or Marco Polo. I was speaking of another people, removed from them by rock and roll, juvenile singers, and the bobbing movement of the new American dance.

My two, born and raised in Minneapolis, are of that generation of Ojibway who do not know what the reservation means, or the Bureau of Indian Affairs, or the tangled treaties and federal—so called—Indian laws which have spun their webs for a full century around the Native People, the First People of this land.

Source: Reprinted from Ignatia Broker, *Night Flying Woman: An Ojibway Narrative* (St. Paul: Minnesota Historical Society Press, 1983), 1–7. Copyright 1983 by the Minnesota Historical Society.

Now my children are urging me to recall all the stories and bits of information that I ever heard my grandparents or any of the older Ojibway tell. It is important, they say, because now their children are asking them. Others are saying the same thing. It is well that they are asking, for the Ojibway young must learn their cycle.

I have been abroad in this society, the dominating society, for two-thirds of my life, and yet I am a link in a chain to the past. Because of this, I shall do as they ask. I can close my eyes and I am back in the past.

I came to the Twin Cities from the reservation in 1941, the year Pearl Harbor was attacked. I went to work in a defense plant and took night classes in order to catch up on the schooling I had missed. I was twenty-two years old and aching for a permanent, settling-down kind of life, but the war years were unstable years for everyone, and more so for the Indian people.

Although employment was good because of the labor demand of the huge defense plants, Indian people faced discrimination in restaurants, night clubs, retail and department stores, in service organizations, public offices, and worst of all, in housing. I can remember hearing, "This room has been rented already, but I got a basement that has a room. I'll show you." I looked at the room. It had the usual rectangular window, and pipes ran overhead. The walls and floors were brown cement, but the man with a gift-giving tone in his voice said, "I'll put linoleum on the floor for you and you'll have a toilet all to yourself. You could wash at the laundry tubs."

There was of course, nothing listed with the War Price and Rationing Board, but the man said it would cost seven dollars a week. I know that he would have made the illegal offer only to an Indian because he knew of the desperate housing conditions we, the first Americans, faced.

I remember living in a room with six others. It was a housekeeping room, nine by twelve feet in size, and meant for one person. It was listed with the price agency at five dollars a week, but the good landlady collected five dollars from each of us each week. However, she did put in a bunk bed and a rollaway which I suppose was all right because we were on different shifts and slept different times anyway. It was cramped and crowded but we had a mutual respect. We sometimes shared our one room with others who had no place, so that there might be nine or ten of us. We could not let friends be out on the street without bed or board. As long as our landlady did not mind, we helped and gave a place of rest to other Ojibway people.

Our paydays were on different days and so whoever had money lent carfare and bought meat and vegetables. Stew was our daily fare because we had only a hot plate and one large kettle.

I mention this practice because I know other Indian people did the same thing, and sometimes whole families evolved from it. This was how we got a toehold in the urban areas—by helping each other. Perhaps this is the way nonmaterialistic people do. We were a sharing people and our tribal traits are still within us.

I think now that maybe it was a good thing, the migration of our people to the urban areas during the war years, because there, amongst the millions of people, we were brought to a brotherhood. We Indian people who worked in the war plants started a social group not only for the Ojibway but for the Dakota, the Arikara, the Menominee, the Gros Ventres, the Cree, the Oneida, and all those from other tribes and other states who had made the trek to something new. And because we, all, were isolated in this dominant society, we became an island from which a revival of spirit began.

It was not easy for any of us during the war years and it became more difficult after the war had ceased. Many Native People returned to the reservations after our soldiers came home from the foreign lands, but others like me stayed and took the buffeting and the difficulties shown us by an alien society.

The war plants closed and people were without jobs. The labor market tightened up and we, the Native People—even skilled workers—faced bias, prejudice, and active discrimination in employment. I know because when I was released from my defense job I answered many advertisements and always I was met with the words, "I'm sorry but we don't hire Indians because they only last the two weeks till payday. Then they quit."

It was around this time that I met and married a veteran who was passing through to the reservation. He got a job with the railroad. To be close to that job and because of the bias in housing, we moved to the capitol side of the river, to an area of St. Paul called the river flats. It was a poor area. Many of the houses had outdoor toilets; many were but tar-paper shacks. Surprising, but it was so in this very large city. It was here our two children were born and I, like a lot of other Indian women, went out and did day work—cleaning and scrubbing the homes of the middle-income people.

Many Indian families lived on the river flats, which became vibrant with their sharing. People gave to each other because times were bad. No Indian family dared approach the relief and welfare agencies of the Twin Cities. They knew that they would only be given a bus ticket and be told to go back to the reservation where the government would take care of them as usual. This was the policy of the public service agencies, and we put up with it by not asking for the help to which we had a legal right. We also suffered in other ways of their making. My husband was recalled to service and died in Korea. After this I moved from the river flats. I took the clerical training and got my first job at a health clinic.

Because my husband died fighting for a nation designed for freedom for all, I felt that I must help extend that freedom to our people. I joined a group of Indians who had banded together to form an Indian help agency. We built a welfare case to challenge the policy of sending our people back to the reservation, and we were successful. After that, the tide of Indians moving to Minnesota's urban areas increased, and today there are ten thousand of us. As the number grew, new-fangled types of Indian people came into being: those demanding what is in our treaties, those demanding service to our people, those working to provide these services—and all reaching back for identity.

When I see my people every day and know how they are doing, I do not feel so lost in the modern times. The children of our people who come to our agency have a questioning look, a dubious but seeking-to-learn look, and I truly believe that they are reaching back to learn those things of which they can be proud. Many of these children were born and raised in the urban areas and they do not make any distinctions as to their tribes. They do not say, "I am Ojibway," or "I am Dakota," or "I am Arapaho," but they say, "I am an Indian." Now they, too, are looking to their tribal identity.

References

1. Kenneth R. Philp, "Stride Toward Freedom: The Relocation of Indians to Cities, 1952–1960," *Western Historical Quarterly* 16 (1985), 175–90, quote at 176–77.

Suggested Readings

Fixico, Donald. *The Urban Indian Experience in America* (Albuquerque: University of New Mexico Press, 2000).

Lobo, Susan, and Kurt Peters, eds. *American Indians and the Urban Experience* (Walnut Creek, Calif.: Altamira Press, 2001).

Philp, Kenneth R. "Stride Toward Freedom: The Relocation of Indians to Cities, 1952–1960," *Western Historical Quarterly* 16 (1985), 175–90.

Shoemaker, Nancy. "Urban Indians and Ethnic Choices: American Indian Organizations in Minneapolis, 1920–1950," *Western Historical Quarterly* 19 (1988), 431–47.

Thornton, Russell, Gary D. Sandefur, and Harold G. Grasmick. *The Urbanization of American Indians: A Critical Bibliography* (Bloomington: Indiana University Press for the Newberry Library, 1982).

Waddell, Jack O., and O. Michael Watson, eds. *The American Indian in Urban Society* (Boston: Little, Brown, 1971).

Weibel-Orlando, Joan. *Indian Country, L. A.: Maintaining Ethnic Community in Complex Society* (Urbana: University of Illinois Press, 1991).

Documents of Indian Militancy

The dramatic takeover in 1969 of Alcatraz Island by Indian students often serves as a starting point for discussing the Red Power movement. With the Trail of Broken Treaties in 1972, the takeover of the BIA building in Washington, the siege at Wounded Knee in 1973, and other confrontations around the country, American Indian Movement (AIM) leaders such as Dennis Banks and Russell Means increasingly attracted the media spotlight. But the dramatic events and charismatic personalities that capture public attention usually emerge from, and often obscure, deeper movements, longer lasting developments, and the contributions of other individuals. The militant spirit that flared into open confrontation after 1969 had been gathering momentum throughout the decade. The arguments for Indian self-determination, the fundamental goals of AIM, had been articulated by young Indians even before AIM was founded in 1968. One was Clyde Warrior, a young Ponca activist from eastern Oklahoma, whose story "qualifies as the top story the press missed in the years leading up to Alcatraz."[1]

American society was in turmoil in the late 1960s. The country was divided over the war in Vietnam. People of different generations, genders, ethnicities, and classes clashed over issues of morality, power, and privilege, and argued about the kind of society America was, or could be. College campuses erupted in protest and violence; race riots devastated many American cities; families split around old and new values. Like African Americans, college students, and antiwar protesters, young Indians, many of them college-educated, declared that it was up to them to bring about change, to save America from itself. The National Indian Youth Council (NIYC) began to carry out acts of protest and civil disobedience. Young Indian speakers began to appear on college campuses, at meetings of national organizations, and at hearings of government agencies which affected Indian life, but which usually operated without input from Indian people. They distrusted non-Indian politicians and denounced some older tribal leaders as "Uncle Tomahawks" who held on to their positions by cozying up to those non-Indian politicians. They raised the level of debate on Indian affairs to new levels and introduced it in areas where it had never been discussed before. Historian Alvin Josephy, who served as a consultant on Indian affairs to Secretary of the Interior Stewart Udall, knew many of the young Indian activists. "They were a new generation," he wrote, "proud of their Indian heritage, unwilling to share their fathers' acceptance of white paternalism, and contemptuous of the society of the white man, which everywhere around them seemed to be falling into disarray."[2]

Clyde Warrior was "with little doubt the most compelling and important leader of this emerging youth movement."[3] Born near Ponca City, Oklahoma, in 1939, he was raised by his grandparents and as a teenager traveled Indian country as a pow wow dancer. He became increasingly vocal about the need for Indians to reject white images of them, to take pride in their Indian heritage, and to hold on to traditional values in modern times. He became a founding member and president of the NIYC and advocated taking direct action to effect change. Indians, said Warrior, were "getting fed up" and it was only a question of time before they did something about it.[4] Like Malcolm X in the Black Power movement, Warrior was eloquent and militant in his prophecies and prescription for revolution, and like Malcolm X he alarmed white America and discomfited many of his own people. But he became "almost a legendary hero to young Indians throughout the country."[5]

In speeches and in writings, Warrior repeatedly articulated the demands and desires of Indian people for freedom. President Lyndon Johnson's administration was pledged to a War on Poverty, with programs like Head Start and other initiatives administered through the Office of Economic Opportunity (OEO). But Warrior insisted that Indians would never escape poverty so long as white men continued to run their affairs and make decisions for them. He delivered the speech reprinted here at a hearing of the President's National Advisory Commission on Rural Poverty in Memphis, Tennessee, in 1967.

Even as he worked to free Indian people from dependency on white America and its government, Warrior succumbed to dependency of another sort. Known as a hard drinker, he battled alcoholism. In the summer of 1968, as events began to spin out of control in southeast Asia and the United States, his liver failed and he died within a few days. He was twenty-eight. In the next five years, Indian activists seized Alcatraz, marched on the nation's capital, and battled U.S. armed forces on the plains of South Dakota. The world's media was there to record it all, but "the prophet of Red Power wasn't around to see what would become of his prophecies."[6]

In November 1969, eighty-nine young Indians seized Alcatraz Island, "the Rock," in San Francisco Bay, which had been abandoned as a maximum-security federal penitentiary six years earlier. Mostly urban Indians and college students from the Bay area, the occupiers identified themselves as "Indians of All Tribes," and proclaimed the island Indian land. They also called for an American Indian university, museum, and cultural center to be established there. The government cut off water and electricity supplies in the spring of 1970 and eventually the seizure of Alcatraz fizzled out. Media attention became diverted elsewhere. In June 1971, nineteenth months after the takeover began, federal marshals quietly removed the fifteen remaining protesters. But Alcatraz made a lasting impact that carried over into the escalating activism of the 1970s. The protests there brought Indians and their grievances to the attention of the world. Alcatraz served as a warning for the United States that Indian rights could no longer be ignored and became a symbol of hope for Indian people who realized that they need no longer suffer in silence. Wilma Mankiller (see "Two Indian Leaders," pages 530–32) who visited the island many times during the takeover, recalled: "I'd never heard anyone actually tell the world that we needed someone to pay attention to our treaty rights, that people had given up an entire continent, and many lives, in return for basic services like health care and education, but nobody was honoring those agreements. For the first time, people were saying things I felt but hadn't known how to articulate. It was very liberating."[7]

Hank Adams, a former member of the NIYC who had been shot in the stomach in 1971 during the fish-in protests on the Northwest coast, played a leading role in the Trail of Broken Treaties in 1972. After the marchers voiced their grievances and proposed solutions en route, recalled Russell Means, "Hank shut himself in a motel room for forty-eight hours and produced a twenty-point document summarizing our key issues."[8] The protesters intended to present the document to the government in Washington and demand a commitment to, and a timetable for, implementing each of the points. As part of the agreement for ending the takeover of the BIA building, the protesters were told that the White House would consider the Twenty Points, but the points did not make their way into the policies of the Nixon administration.

▶ Questions for Consideration

1. To what extent do Clyde Warrior's views of the system parallel those of Robert Burnette (see "Two Views of the Indian Reorganization Act," pages 433–36)?

2. Non-Indians, bewildered by the new wave of militancy, would sometimes ask, "What do Indians want?" What answers do Warrior's speech, the declaration from Alcatraz, and the Twenty Points provide?

3. How do these documents seem to define self-determination for Indian peoples?

4. Do the goals they describe seem achievable in modern America?

CLYDE WARRIOR

"We Are Not Free":
From Testimony before the President's National Advisory Commission on Rural Poverty (1967)

Most members of the National Indian Youth Council can remember when we were children and spent many hours at the feet of our grandfathers listening to stories of the time when the Indians were a great people, when we were free, when we were rich, when we lived the good life. At the same time we heard stories of droughts, famines and pestilence. It was only recently that we realized that there was surely great material deprivation in those days, but that our old people felt rich because they were free. They were rich in things of the spirit, but if there is one thing that characterizes Indian life today it is poverty of the spirit. We still have human passions and depth of feeling (which may be something rare in these days), but we are poor in spirit because we are not free—free in the most basic sense of the word. We are not allowed to make those basic human choices and decisions about our personal life and about the destiny of our communities which is the mark of free mature people. We sit on our front porches or in our yards, and the world and our lives in it pass us by without our desires or aspirations having any effect.

We are not free. We do not make choices. Our choices are made for us; we are the poor. For those of us who live on reservations these choices and decisions are made by federal administrators, bureaucrats, and their "yes men," euphemistically called tribal governments. Those of us who live in non-reservation areas have our lives controlled by local white power elites. We have many rulers. They are called social workers, "cops," school teachers, churches, etc., and now OEO employees. They call us into meetings to tell us what is good for us and how they've programmed us, or they come into our homes to instruct us and their manners are not always what one would call polite by Indian standards or perhaps by any standards. We are rarely accorded respect as fellow human beings. Our children come home from school to us with shame in their hearts and a sneer on their lips for their home and parents. We are the "poverty problem" and that is true; and perhaps it is also true that our lack of reasonable choices, our lack of freedoms, our poverty of spirit is not unconnected with our material poverty.

The National Indian Youth Council realizes there is a great struggle going on in America now between those who want more "local" control of programs and those who would keep the power and the purse strings in the hands of the federal government. We are unconcerned with that struggle because we know that no one is arguing that the dispossessed, the poor, be given any control over their own destiny. The local white power elites who protest the loudest against federal control are the very ones who would keep us poor in spirit and worldly goods in order to enhance their own personal and economic station in the world.

Source: Testimony of Clyde Warrior before the President's National Advisory Commission on Rural Poverty, February 2, 1967, reprinted in Alvin M. Josephy, Jr., ed., *Red Power: The American Indians' Fight for Freedom* (New York: McGraw-Hill, 1971), 72–77.

Nor have those of us on reservations fared any better under the paternalistic control of federal administrations. In fact, we shudder at the specter of what seems to be the forming alliances in Indian areas between federal administrators and local elites. Some of us fear that this is the shape of things to come in the War on Poverty effort. Certainly, it is in those areas where such an alliance is taking place that the poverty program seems to be "working well." That is to say, it is in those areas of the country where the federal government is getting the least "static" and where federal money is being used to bolster the local power structure and local institutions. By "everybody being satisfied," I mean the people who count and the Indian or poor does not count. . . .

Fifty years ago the federal government came into our communities and by force carried most of our children away to distant boarding schools. My father and many of my generation lived their childhoods in an almost prison-like atmosphere. Many returned unable even to speak their own language. Some returned to become drunks. Most of them had become white haters or that most pathetic of all modern Indians—Indian haters. Very few ever became more than very confused, ambivalent and immobilized individuals—never able to reconcile the tensions and contradictions built inside themselves by outside institutions. As you can imagine, we have little faith in such kinds of federal programs devised for our betterment nor do we see education as a panacea for all ills. In recent days, however, some of us have been thinking that perhaps the damage done to our communities by forced assimilation and directed acculturative programs was minor compared to the situation in which our children now find themselves. There is a whole generation of Indian children who are growing up in the American school system. They still look to their relatives, my generation, and my father's to see if they are worthy people. But their judgment and definition of what is worthy is now the judgment most Americans make. They judge worthiness as competence and

competence as worthiness. And I am afraid me and my fathers do not fare well in the light of this situation and judgment. Our children are learning that their people are not worthy and thus that they individually are not worthy. Even if by some stroke of good fortune, prosperity was handed to us "on a platter" that still would not soften the negative judgment our youngsters have of their people and themselves. As you know, people who feel themselves to be unworthy and feel they cannot escape this unworthiness turn to drink and crime and self-destructive acts. Unless there is some way that we as Indian individuals and communities can prove ourselves competent and worthy in the eyes of our youngsters there will be a generation of Indians grow to adulthood whose reaction to their situation will make previous social ills seem like a Sunday School picnic.

For the sake of our children, for the sake of the spiritual and material well-being of our total community we must be able to demonstrate competence to ourselves. For the sake of our psychic stability as well as our physical well-being we must be free men and exercise free choices. We must make decisions about our own destinies. We must be able to learn and profit by our own mistakes. Only then can we become competent and prosperous communities. We must be free in the most literal sense of the word—not sold or coerced into accepting programs for our own good, not of our own making or choice. Too much of what passes for "grassroots democracy" on the American scene is really a slick job of salesmanship. It is not hard for sophisticated administrators to sell tinsel and glitter programs to simple people—programs which are not theirs, which they do not understand and which cannot but ultimately fail and contribute to already strong feelings of inadequacy. Community development must be just what the word implies, Community Development. It cannot be packaged programs wheeled into Indian communities by outsiders which Indians can "buy" or once again brand themselves as unprogressive if they do not "cooperate." Even the best of outside programs suffer from one very large defect—if the program falters helpful outsiders too often step in to smooth over the rough spots. At that point any program ceases to belong to the people involved and ceases to be a learning experience for them. Programs must be Indian creations, Indian choices, Indian experiences. Even the failures must be Indian experiences because only then will Indians understand why a program failed and not blame themselves for some personal inadequacy. A better program built upon the failure of an old program is the path of progress. But to achieve this experience, competence, worthiness, sense of achievement and the resultant material prosperity Indians must have the responsibility in the ultimate sense of the word. Indians must be free in the sense that other more prosperous Americans are free. Freedom and prosperity are different sides of the same coin and there can be no freedom without complete responsibility. And I do not mean the fictional responsibility and democracy of passive consumers of programs; programs which emanate from and whose responsibility for success rests in the hands of outsiders—be they federal administrators or local white elitist groups.

Many of our young people are captivated by the lure of the American city with its excitement and promise of unlimited opportunity. But even if educated they come from powerless and inexperienced communities and many times carry with them a strong sense of unworthiness. For many of them the promise of opportunity ends in the gutter on the skid rows of Los Angeles and Chicago. They should and must be given a better chance to take advantage of the opportunities they have. They must grow up in a decent community with a strong sense of personal adequacy and competence.

America cannot afford to have whole areas and communities of people in such dire social and economic circumstances. Not only for her economic well-being but for her moral well-being as well. America has given a great social and moral message to the world and demonstrated (perhaps not forcefully enough) that freedom and responsibility as an ethic is inseparable from and, in fact, the "cause" of the fabulous American standard of living. America has not however been diligent enough in promulgating this philosophy within her own borders. American Indians need to be given this freedom and responsibility which most Americans assume as their birth right. Only then will poverty and powerlessness cease to hang like the sword of Damocles over our heads stifling us. Only then can we enjoy the fruits of the American system and become participating citizens— Indian Americans rather than American Indians.

Perhaps, the National Indian Youth Council's real criticism is against a structure created by bureaucratic administrators who are caught in this American myth that all people assimilate into American society, that economics dictates assimilation and integration. From the experience of the National Indian Youth Council, and in reality, we cannot emphasize and recommend strongly enough the fact that no one integrates and disappears into American society. What ethnic groups do is not integrate into American society and economy individually, but enter into the mainstream of American society as a people, and in particular as communities of people. The solution to Indian poverty is not "government programs" but in the competence of the person and his people. The real solution to poverty is encouraging the competence of the community as a whole.

[The] National Indian Youth Council recommends for "openers" that to really give these people "the poor, the dispossessed, the Indians," complete freedom and responsibility is to let it become a reality not a much-heard-about dream and let the poor decide for once, what is best for themselves. . . .

Proclamation to the Great White Father
and to All *His* People (1969)

We, the native Americans, re-claim the land known as Alcatraz Island in the name of all American Indians by right of discovery.

We wish to be fair and honorable in our dealings with the Caucasian inhabitants of this land, and hereby offer the following treaty:

We will purchase said Alcatraz Island for twenty-four dollars (24) in glass beads and red cloth, a precedent set by the white man's purchase of a similar island about 300 years ago. We know that $24 in trade goods for these 16 acres is more than was paid when Manhattan Island was sold, but we know that land values have risen over the years. Our offer of $1.24 per acre is greater than the 47¢ per acre the white men are now paying the California Indians for their land.°

We will give to the inhabitants of this island a portion of the land for their own to be held in trust by the American Indian Affairs and by the bureau of Caucasian Affairs to hold in perpetuity—for as long as the sun shall rise and the rivers go down to the sea. We will further guide the inhabitants in the proper way of living. We will offer them our religion, our education, our life-ways, in order to help them achieve our level of civilization and thus raise them and all their white brothers up from their savage and unhappy state. We offer this treaty in good faith and wish to be fair and honorable in our dealings with all white men.

We feel that this so-called Alcatraz Island is more than suitable for an Indian Reservation, as determined by the white man's own standards. By this we mean that this place resembles most Indian reservations in that:

1. It is isolated from modern facilities, and without adequate means of transportation.
2. It has no fresh running water.
3. It has inadequate sanitation facilities.
4. There are no oil or mineral rights.
5. There is no industry and so unemployment is very great.
6. There are no health care facilities.
7. The soil is rocky and non-productive; and the land does not support game.
8. There are no educational facilities.
9. The population has always exceeded the land base.
10. The population has always been held as prisoners and kept dependent upon others.

Further, it would be fitting and symbolic that ships from all over the world, entering the Golden Gate, would first see Indian land, and thus be reminded of the true history of this nation. This tiny island would be a symbol of the great lands once ruled by free and noble Indians.

American Indian Center

Source: Reprinted in Virgil J. Vogel, ed., *This Country Was Ours: A Documentary History of the American Indian* (New York: Harper and Row, 1972), 228–29.

°A reference to the money offered to the Pit River Indians of northern California by the Indian Claims Commission as compensation for the loss of their lands.

A Summary of the Twenty Points (1972)

1. Restoration of Constitutional Treaty-Making Authority: This would force federal recognition of each Indian nation's sovereignty.

2. Establishment of a Treaty Commission to Make New Treaties: Reestablishes all exising treaties, affirms a national commitment to the future of Indian people, and ensures that all Indians are governed by treaty relations without exception.

3. An Address to the American People and Joint Sessions of Congress: This would allow us to state our political and cultural cases to the whole nation on television.

4. Commission to Review Treaty Commitments and Violations: Treaty-based lawsuits had cost Indian people more than $40 million in the last decade alone, yet Indian people remain virtual prisoners in the nation's courtrooms, being forced constantly to define our rights. There is less need for more attorney assistance than for an institution of protections that reduce violations and minimize the possibilities for attacks on Indian rights.

5. Resubmission of Unratified Treaties to the Senate: Many nations, especially those in California, have made treaties that were never ratified. Treaty status should be formalized for every nation.

6. All Indians To Be Governed by Treaty Relations: Covers any exceptions to points 1, 2, and 5.

7. Mandatory Relief against Treaty Violations: Federal courts to automatically issue injunctions against non-Indians who violate treaties, eliminating costly legal delays.

8. Judicial Recognition of Indian Right to Interpret Treaties: A new law requiring the U.S. Supreme Court to hear Indian appeals arising from treaty violations.

9. Creation of Congressional Joint Committee on Reconstruction of Indian Relations: Reconfigurement of all committees dealing with Indian affairs into a single entity.

10. Land Reform and Restoration of a 110-million-acre Native Land Base: Termination of all Indian land leases, reversion of all non-Indian titles to land on reservations, consolidation of all reservation natural resources under local Indian control.

11. Restoration of Rights to Indians Terminated by Enrollment and Revocation of Prohibition Against "Dual Benefits": An end to minimum standards of "tribal blood" for citizenship in any Indian nation, which serves to keep people with mixed Indian ancestors from claiming either heritage.

12. Repeal of State Laws Enacted under Public Law 280: Eliminates all state powers over Indians, thereby ending disputes over jurisdiction and sovereignty.

13. Resume Federal Protective Jurisdiction over Offenses against Indians: Since state and local courts have rarely been able to convict non-Indians of crimes against Indians, Indian grand juries should have the power to indict violators, who will then be tried in federal courts.

14. Abolition of the Bureau of Indian Affairs: The BIA is so much a prisoner of its past that it can never be expected to meet the needs of Indians. Better to start over with an organization designed to meet requirements of new treaties.

15. Creation of an Office of Federal Indian Relations and Community Reconstruction: With one thousand employees or fewer, this agency would report directly to the president and preserve equality between Indian nations and the federal government.

16. Priorities and Purpose of the Proposed New Office: The previous agency would address the breakdown in the constitutionally prescribed

Source: Reprinted in Russell Means with Marvin J. Wolf, *Where White Men Fear to Tread: The Autobiography of Russell Means* (New York: St. Martin's Press, 1995), 228–30.

relationship between the United States and the Indian nations.

17. Indian Commerce and Tax Immunities: Eliminate constant struggles between Indian nations and the states over taxation by removing states' authority for taxation on reservations.

18. Protection of Indian Religious Freedom and Cultural Integrity: Legal protection must be extended to Indian religious expression, and existing statutes do not do this.

19. National Referendums, Local Options, and Forms of Indian Organization: An appeal to restrict the number of Indian organizations and to consolidate leadership at every level.

20. Health, Housing, Employment, Economic Development, and Education: Increased funding, better management, and local control.

References

1. Paul Chaat Smith and Robert Allen Warrior, *Like a Hurricane: The Indian Movement from Alcatraz to Wounded Knee* (New York: The New Press, 1996), 38.
2. Alvin M. Josephy, Jr., ed., *Red Power: The American Indians' Fight for Freedom* (New York: McGraw-Hill, 1971), 71.
3. Smith and Warrior, *Like a Hurricane*, 38.
4. Quoted in Smith and Warrior, *Like a Hurricane*, 37.
5. Josephy, *Red Power*, 71.
6. Smith and Warrior, *Like a Hurricane*, 58.
7. Quoted in Troy R. Johnson, *The Occupation of Alcatraz Island: Indian Self-Determination and the Rise of Indian Activism* (Urbana: University of Illinois Press, 1996), 128.
8. Russell Means with Marvin J. Wolf, *Where White Men Fear to Tread: The Autobiography of Russell Means* (New York: St. Martins Press, 1995), 228.

Suggested Readings

Deloria, Vine, Jr. *Custer Died for Your Sins: An Indian Manifesto* (New York: Macmillan, 1969).

Johnson, Troy R. *The Occupation of Alcatraz Island: Indian Self-Determination and the Rise of Indian Activism* (Chicago: University of Illinois Press, 1996).

Johnson, Troy, Joanne Nagel, and Duane Champagne, eds. *American Indian Activism: Alcatraz to the Longest Walk* (Urbana: University of Illinois Press, 1997).

Josephy, Alvin M., Jr., ed. *Red Power: The American Indians' Fight for Freedom* (New York: McGraw-Hill, 1971).

Nagel, Joanne, *American Indian Ethnic Renewal: Red Power and the Resurgence of Identity and Culture* (New York: Oxford University Press, 1996).

Smith, Paul Chaat, and Robert Allen Warrior. *Like a Hurricane: The Indian Movement from Alcatraz to Wounded Knee* (New York: The New Press, 1996).

Steiner, Stan. *The New Indians* (New York: Dell, 1968).

Twentieth-Century Indian Artists
Depict Indian Life

Although non-Indians have dominated the representation of Indian history and life in literature, art, and film, they have not monopolized it. Indian people interpret their history in their own ways in spoken and written word, and in still and moving pictures. In the twentieth-century Indian artists looking at the past offered non-Indian audiences a fresh, and sometimes troubling,

FIGURE 7.1 Fred Beaver, *Florida Seminole Women—Daily Life* (1962)
Watercolor on board, museum purchase, The Philbrook Museum of Art, Tulsa, Oklahoma, 1962.7.

FIGURE 7.2 Patrick DesJarlait, *Making Wild Rice* (1946)
Watercolor on paper, museum purchase, The Philbrook Museum of Art, Tulsa, Oklahoma, 1947.22.

perspective on a familiar story; they also provided commentary on Indian experiences and change in the twentieth century, and depicted aspects of Indian
life that non-Indian artists had often missed or ignored. They helped to dismantle old notions among some non-Indians that "Indian art" constituted
only baskets, blankets, and pottery, and they employed new forms of expression
while responding to traditional inspirations and values.[1]

Creek artist Fred Beaver said the purpose of his art was "to change the
non-Indians' image of my people, and . . . to help my own people understand
themselves, especially the young."[2] Beaver's village scene (Figure 7.1) shows
Seminoles who had resisted removal and remained in their Florida homelands
practicing aspects of traditional life. The painting focuses squarely on the world
of Seminole women. It has a very modern "feel" about it, but the log fire, the

FIGURE 7.3 Timothy Begay, *Navajo Girls and Lambs* (c.1950)

Watercolor on woven paper, gift of the Phillips Petroleum Company, The Philbrook Musuem of Art, Tulsa, Oklahoma, 1946, 45.4.

FIGURE 7.4 Quincy Tahoma, *First Furlough* (1943)

Courtesy National Museum of the American Indian Smithsonian Institution (23.6014). Photo by David Heald.

FIGURE 7.5 Woody Crumbo, *Land of Enchantment* (c. 1946)
Watercolor on board, gift of Clark Field, The Philbrook Museum of Art, Tulsa, Oklahoma, 1946. 45.4.

huts, and the clothing suggests that little has changed in Seminole daily life or in the roles Seminole women play.

Anishinaabe Patrick DesJarlait "felt compelled to tell the story of my people through paintings"[3] and developed a unique style, as exemplified in *Making Wild Rice* (Figure 7.2) DesJarlait records in one picture the process of preparing wild rice after it had been harvested in late summer: winnowing, hulling by treading on the grain to remove the outer husks, and boiling. Again, the artist brings his own particular style to depicting a very old process that was central to the Indian cultures of the Great Lakes.

Three paintings depict continuity and change in Navajo country. Navajo Timothy Begay's picture (Figure 7.3) of two girls, their lambs, and a kitten captures an ordinary human moment and also conveys something of the attachment of Navajo families to their sheep that made the livestock reduction pro-

FIGURE 7.6 **Arnold Jacobs, _Reflections: Tribute to Our Iron Skywalkers_ (1983)**
Courtesy of the artist, Arnold Jacobs, from the collection of the Woodland Cultural Center, Brantford, Ontario, Canada.

gram of the 1930s so devastating. Quincy Tahoma painted _First Furlough_ (Figure 7.4) in the midst of World War II. Although Navajos are best known for their services as code talkers in that conflict, Tahoma reminds us that the war also affected the Navajo home front. Depicted so often in stereotypical and negative terms themselves, Indian artists have often turned the tables and poked fun at white society. Weaving for the tourist trade offered Navajo women new economic opportunities in the early twentieth century although, as Potawatomi/Creek artist Woodrow W. Crumbo's _Land of Enchantment_ (Figure 7.5) makes clear, it also brought new intrusions in Navajo life.

Urban migration provided new subjects and new contexts. Embracing new economic opportunities and developing new skills while guided and protected by traditional values, an Iroquois steelworker looks out over the skyscrapers of New York City in Onondaga Arnold Jacobs's 1983 painting _Reflections: Tribute to Our Iron Skywalkers_ (Figure 7. 6). Harry Fonseca, an artist of Maidu/Por-

FIGURE 7.7 Harry Fonseca, *When Coyote Leaves the Reservation (A Portrait of the Artist as a Young Coyote*, (1980)
Heard Museum, Phoenix, Arizona.

tuguese/Hawaiian descent, has painted a series of pictures featuring the trick-ster figure Coyote. "I believe my Coyote paintings to be the most contemporary statements I have painted in regard to traditional beliefs and contemporary reality," said Fonseca. "I have taken a universal Indian image, Coyote, and have placed him in a contemporary setting."[4] Figure 7.7 is entitled *When Coyote Leaves the Reservation (A Portrait of the Artist as a Young Coyote).*

FIGURE 7.8 **T. C. Cannon, *Osage with Van Gogh or Collector #5***
(c. 1975)
Fine Arts Collection, Heard Museum, Phoenix, Arizona.

In *Osage with Van Gogh* or *Collector #5* (Figure 7.8), Caddo/Kiowa artist
T. C. Cannon took a humorous look at notions of what constitutes Indian art,
at the same time positioning it in a larger international artistic tradition. Wearing traditional dress and surrounded by the art he has collected (including Van
Gogh's painting *Wheatfield* and a Navajo rug), the Osage art collector frowns
at his audience.[5]

Most of these paintings combine traditional and new elements in their
subject matter, composition, and style. Some have been painted with a non-
Indian audience in mind. They offer insights into Indian life and reflect ways
in which Indian people in the twentieth century adjusted to the modern world
while remembering the values and traditions of the past.

These pictures all represent identifiable "Indian" subjects, but they display
diversity of style, content, and technique. Other Indian artists, many more recent than those represented here, have developed other styles, breaking the bar-
riers of what was long regarded as "Indian art."

► Questions for Consideration

1. What is the effect of the composition in Figure 7.3? What can one read from the painting about the place of these animals in the Navajo world? Of Navajos in the animals' world?

2. What does Figure 7.4 tell us about Native American participation in World War II? What might the way it is constructed suggest about Native American expectations at the end of the war?

3. Figure 7.5 was painted the year after the war ended and depicts a situation that was becoming increasingly common on the Navajo reservation. How are the Indians and tourists depicted, and how does what we see of them, and how much we see, help deliver the artist's message?

4. Figure 7.6 shows us a modern Indian in a modern urban environment and is rendered in a modern style. How does the artist nevertheless imply a sense of tradition and history here? What is the effect of partially obscuring the eagle by the figure of the steelworker?

5. In what ways does Figure 7.7 make similar and different suggestions about Indians in the city?

6. What commentary does the content and composition of Figure 7.8 offer on notions of Indians' space, their role in the art world, and the nature of their art?

7. Do the works shown here offer only illustrations from Indian life, or do they provide evidence of evolving art forms?

8. Apart from the subject matter, what things might distinguish these paintings from works by non-Indian artists?

References

1. See, for example, the fine art of the Santa Fe Indian School directed by Dorothy Dunn beginning in 1932. Bruce Bernstein and W. Jackson Rushing, *Modern by Tradition: American Indian Painting in the Studio Style* (Santa Fe: Museum of New Mexico Press, 1995).
2. Quoted in Lydia L. Wyckoff, ed., *Visions and Voices: Native American Painting from the Philbrook Museum of Art* (Tulsa, Okla.: Philbrook Museum of Art, 1996), 72.
3. Quoted in Wyckoff, ed., *Visions and Voices,* 116.
4. Quoted in Margaret Archuleta and Rennard Strickland, *Shared Visions: Native American Painters and Sculptors in the Twentieth Century,* 2nd ed. (New York: The Free Press, 1993), 95.
5. Archuleta and Strickland, *Shared Visions,* 18.

NATIONS WITHIN A NATION: INDIAN COUNTRY TODAY

MOVING BEYOND FAILED POLICIES

In 1970, President Richard Nixon delivered a "Special Message on Indian Affairs" to Congress. Denouncing past policies of federal termination and federal paternalism, Nixon called instead for a new era of self-determination for Indian people in which the federal government and Indian communities played complementary roles.[1] (see "President Nixon and the Supreme Court Address Self-Determination," pages 511–14). Nixon selected a Mohawk, Louis R. Bruce, to head the Bureau of Indian Affairs (BIA), but Bruce himself saw that a new generation of Indians was pushing for self-determination as they, not Washington, understood it. "Not in this century has there been such a volume of creative turbulence in Indian country," he said. "The will for self-determination has become a vital component of the thinking of Indian leadership. . . . It is an irreversible trend, a tide in the destiny of American Indians that will eventually compel all of America once and for all to recognize the dignity and human rights of Indian people."[2] Elected Navajo tribal chairman in 1970, Peter MacDonald outlined the goals of his administration in his inaugural address in January 1971:

> First, what is rightfully ours, we must protect; what is rightfully due us we must claim. Second, what we depend on from others, we must replace with the labor of our own hands, and the skills of our own people. Third, what we do not have, we must bring into being. We must create for ourselves.[3]

Indian leaders in modern America strive to prepare their nations for the twenty-first century without sacrificing the values of the past that made them

Indian Country in 2000

- ○ Federal Indian reservations
- △ State Indian reservations

MAP 8.1 State and Federally Recognized Indian Reservations in the United States, 2000

Indian Country today comprises about 550 different Indian tribes, bands, and Alaskan village corporations. The majority of Indian people today live in urban areas, and there are also many non-recognized groups and groups without reservation land. This map shows the reservations recognized by the federal government and the individual states.

into who they are. To survive, Indian nations must protect their lands, manage their own resources, preserve their traditions, build their economies, and educate their young people. Achieving these goals involves defending their unique status as nations within a nation and reasserting their inherent sovereign rights which, they stress, existed before conquest and can be eroded but not erased.

European nations and the United States recognized these rights when they made treaties with Indians, the United States Constitution recognizes them, and the Supreme Court reaffirmed them in *Worcester v. Georgia* (1832). But Indian nations in modern America struggle constantly to preserve their sovereignty. Indians reside within the United States and within the borders of individual states, both of which have impinged on their sovereign powers. The situation produces complexity and ambiguity in daily lives as well as in American law. Tribes have the right to exercise self-determination, but states try to interfere and the federal government sometimes exercises its trust responsibility to Indian tribes in ways that undermine self-determination.

The tribal sovereignty that many people regard as crucial to the survival of Indian nations in the twenty-first century is repeatedly challenged and threatened, sometimes negotiated and compromised, and often simply not understood.[4]

Working out relations between the United States and more than 550 tribes on a multitude of issues remains a formidable task. Tribal members are in fact "triple citizens" — of their tribe, of the states in which they reside, and of the United States.[5] At the same time, many non-Indian people live on reservations and therefore fall under the jurisdiction of tribal governments in some respects, even though they are citizens of the United States and individual states but not of the tribe. Indians not on reservations are generally subject to federal, state, and local laws. Only federal and tribal laws apply on reservations, however, unless Congress has provided otherwise. Consequently, when Indians step off the reservation they become subject to local or state jurisdiction; a non-Indian who enters a reservation is subject to tribal jurisdiction in civil matters. In states where Public Law 280 applies, the state has some form of jurisdiction over the reservations. The relationship of federal/state/Indian law is a tangle of overlapping and sometimes conflicting jurisdictions. What, for instance, are the rights of non-Indian residents of Indian reservations who are subject to tribal laws, courts, and taxes but have no say in tribal government?

From Paternalism to Partnership

In line with Nixon's recommendations, Congress in the 1970s passed a series of laws ranging from land claims and political status to education, social services, and religious freedom, which promised to protect Indian rights and increase Indian participation in running their own affairs. In 1970, Nixon signed a bill returning Blue Lake to Taos Pueblo, ending a sixty-four-year fight by the people of Taos to regain the lands that President Theodore Roosevelt had proclaimed part of what is now Carson National Forest. Other lands were returned to the

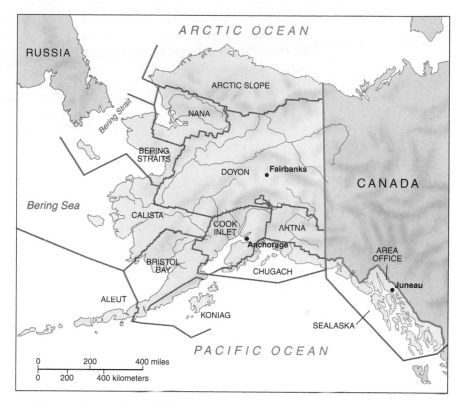

MAP 8.2 Alaska's Native Regional Corporations
The ANCSA in 1971 created a dozen regional corporations and more than two hundred villages' corporations.

Yakama Nation in Washington State and to Warm Springs in Oregon.

In 1965, Alaska Natives had created the Alaska Federation of Natives, a statewide organization designed to pursue the land claims of Alaska's Native peoples. Oil discoveries on Alaska's North Slope in the 1950s and 1960s brought Native land issues to national attention. The Alaska Native Claims Settlement Act (ANCSA) of 1971 was intended to resolve those land claims. The act also aimed to open the area to pipeline construction by transferring 44 million acres to more than 200 village corporations and a dozen regional for-profit corporations, allocating almost $1 billion in funds for Alaskan natives. Native discontent with some of ANCSA's provisions led not only to modification of the legislation but also to a lack of trust in the government's self-determination policies.

In 1973, responding to tireless lobbying by Ada Deer and other Menominee leaders, Congress passed the Menominee Restoration Act, returning the Menominees' tribal status and restoring their access to federal programs. The Indian Education Act of 1972 provided funding for Indian children who attended public schools. The Indian Finance Act in 1974 authorized federal grants and loans to federally recognized tribes to promote economic development and led to the creation of the Indian Business Development Program. The Indian Self-Determination and Educational Assistance Act of 1975 gave tribes instead of government officials the right to administer federal assistance programs. Tribal governments could now contract to provide services previously carried out by the Departments of Interior, Health, and Human Services.

In 1978, the Indian Child Welfare Act renounced the practice of transferring care of Indian children to non-Indians and placed responsibility for the welfare of Indian children squarely with the tribe. That same year, in the American Indian Religious Freedom Act, Congress declared its intention "to protect and preserve for American Indians their inherent right of freedom to believe, express, and exercise" their traditional religions, "including but not limited to access to sites, use and possession of sacred objects, and the freedom to worship through ceremonials and traditional rights."[6]

Sovereignty Goes to Court

In the past, Indian warriors fought battles to defend their lands and their way of life and they lost. In the late twentieth century, Indians took their fights to the courtroom—and frequently they won. Indians and their attorneys, often with the support of the Native American Rights Fund, founded in 1970, reached back into history and uncovered laws and treaties that were supposed to guarantee and protect their rights, but that were often ignored in days when Indians had no voice in the courts. In the new social and political climate of reform created by the upheavals of the 1960s and 1970s, judicial opinion was more sympathetic to the notion that the nation should live up to its treaty commitments. The courtroom replaced the battlefield as the arena where Indians could best promote and protect their people's interests.

Examples of these courtroom conflicts occurred all across the country. In Nevada, Northern Paiutes watched for decades as a dam across the Truckee River lowered water levels at Pyramid Lake, nearly destroying the rare cui cui, the Lahontan trout on which they had subsisted from time immemorial, and threatening to destroy the lake itself. In 1970, the Paiutes filed suit to have the water level restored and won their case. In Maine, the Penobscot and Passamaquoddy Indians brought suit for the return of about two-thirds of the state's land to the tribes. The Indian Trade and Intercourse Act of 1790 declared that no transfers of Indian land were valid unless they had the approval of Congress, but none of the land sales that occurred in Maine after that date had been submitted for approval. If the United States was to respect its own laws, the Indians believed they had a watertight case. In 1980, President Carter signed the Maine Indian Settlement Act, paying the Indians $81.5 million in compensation for lands taken in contravention of the 1790 law. Also in 1980, the Supreme Court found in favor of the Sioux in the Black Hills case (see "The Treaty of Fort Laramie and the Struggle for the Black Hills," pages 294–312). In both cases, however, Anglo-American justice was limited by its own remedies:

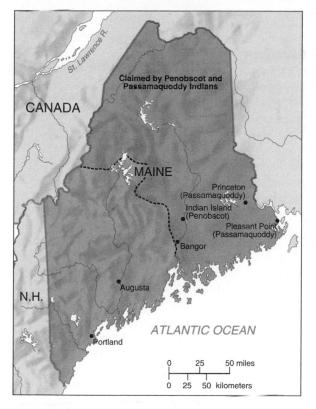

MAP 8.3 Indian Land Claims in Maine

The Penobscot and Passamaquoddy tribes claimed that about two-thirds of the state (roughly the area north and east of the line) had been taken from them illegally. In 1980, the tribes were paid $81.5 million in compensation.

Indian people who insisted that the land be returned saw the settlements as "selling out" ancestral lands.

Indians went to court not only to bring land claims but also to defend treaty rights, to assert their sovereign rights to manage their reservation resources and protect their environments, and to clarify their right to define tribal membership. While some people feared the Indian Civil Rights Act of 1968 would erode the autonomy of tribal governments, in *Santa Clara v. Martinez* (1978), the Supreme Court declared that the Indian Civil Rights Act was enforceable in tribal courts; only persons detained by tribal law could seek relief in federal court. Santa Clara Pueblo was traditionally a matrilineal society but had adopted European patrilineal patterns of descent. In 1939, the tribal council passed an ordinance denying membership to the children of women who married outside the tribe, but granting it to the children of Santa Clara men who married outside. Julia Martinez, a Santa Clara woman, married a Navajo. Her children were denied membership in the Santa Clara Pueblo. Martinez sued the tribe. The tribal council argued that the tribe had the right to establish its own membership criteria. The Supreme Court agreed, noting that Indian tribes were "distinct, independent political communities retaining their original natural rights in matters of local self-government" and that tribal governments "have the power to make their own substantive law in internal matters."[7] A tribe's right to determine its own membership is a crucial attribute of sovereignty.

The struggle for fishing rights that began with "fish-ins" in the 1960s produced some significant legal victories in the 1970s and 1980s. In 1973, the United States, representing fourteen tribes, sued the state of Washington over the issue of fishing rights. The next year, U.S. District Court Judge George Boldt ruled that Indians were entitled to catch up to 50 percent of the fish returning to "the usual and accustomed places" designated by the treaties of the 1850s. Non-Indian fishermen reacted in anger and disbelief—Judge Boldt was burned in effigy and there were outbreaks of violence. A federal task force was appointed to try to avert a "fishing war" in Washington, but the struggle over fishing rights continued, even as most people came to realize that environmental destruction reduced the stakes. What good was the right to 50 percent of the harvest if there were no salmon to harvest, or if the fish that were caught were unfit to eat?

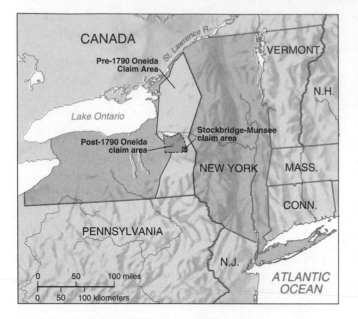

MAP 8.4 Oneida Land Claims, c. 1985
Most Oneidas sided with the Americans during the Revolution, but they nonetheless lost millions of acres in the years following American independence from Britain. The Oneida land claims involved areas lost by the tribe before 1790 and approximately one-quarter of a million acres lost since. The Oneidas claimed that New York State violated postrevolutionary treaties and the Indian Trade and Non-Intercourse Act of 1790, which required congressional approval of all Indian land sales. Adapted from Christopher Vecsey and William A. Starna, eds., Iroquois Land Claims *(Syracuse: Syracuse University Press, 1988).*

To many Americans, it seemed that Indians, who should be treated "just like everyone else," were claiming and receiving special rights and privileges. In 1983, for instance, a U.S. Court of Appeals upheld the Wisconsin Anishinaabe claims that the treaties they had signed guaranteed their right to continue hunting, fishing, and gathering in the areas ceded by those treaties. The *Voigt* decision, as it became known, generated a backlash among local fishermen, and there was racial violence every spring spearfishing season during the 1980s as Indians attempted to exercise their rights. And after the Penobscot and Passamaquoddy won a land settlement in 1980, several Iroquois tribes brought successful land claims cases in upstate New York. In 1985, the Oneida Nation won a significant victory when the courts declared that claims brought under the Trade and Intercourse Act were not barred by the passage of time, leaving the way open for the Oneidas to file suit.

Land claims often put a cloud over property titles and generated a backlash among non-Indian property owners, most of whom bought their lands in good faith long after the Indians lost them, and felt they were being punished for the sins of past generations. A common response was "the Indians sold the land, didn't they?"[8]

The backlash against Indian attempts to assert their rights was not limited to New York State. In 1997, Senator Slade Gorton (of Washington State) introduced legislation that would have required tribes to waive their sovereign immunity as a precondition to receiving federal funds.[9]

Tired of complaints that Indians enjoyed unfair privileges, Anishinaabe leader Marge Anderson responded:

When Indian incomes are level with yours, when our schools are as good as yours, our houses as warm, our kids as safe and our woods and streams as clean as yours, when our babies first open their eyes to a future as bright as yours, then we'll talk about level playing fields. Whether out of greed or out of racism or out of ignorance, there are always some who will go after Indian self-determination and economic development in ways as old as Columbus, as bold as Custer and as devious as any federal land grabber.[10]

Unfortunately for Indian people, one of the key figures "going after" Indian self-determination seems to have been the Chief Justice of the United States Supreme Court.

Chipping Away at Tribal Sovereignty

Reaching back to *Worcester v. Georgia* in 1832, the Supreme Court often "served as the conscience of federal Indian law, protecting tribal powers and rights against state action, unless and until Congress clearly states a contrary intention." But since the mid-1980s the Court has tended to favor state sovereignty over tribal sovereignty. Under Chief Justice Burger (1969–85), the Supreme Court ruled in favor of Indians in 58 percent of the cases that came before it; under Chief Justice Rehnquist, from 1986 to 2001, the Court ruled *against* Indians in 77 percent of cases.[11]

In *Oliphant v. Suquamish*, (1978), with Judge Rehnquist writing for the majority, the Supreme Court struck down tribal jurisdiction over crimes committed by non-Indians on their reservations (see "President Nixon and the Supreme Court Address Self-Determination," pages 514–18). Subsequently, in *Duro v. Reina* (1990), the Rehnquist Court further limited the scope of tribal criminal jurisdiction, holding that a tribe's right to govern its own affairs does not include criminal jurisdiction over an Indian who is not a tribal member. Congress overrode the *Duro* decision in 1991 by passing legislation that affirmed the authority of tribes to exercise criminal jurisdiction over all Indians within their reservation. In 1981, in *Montana v. United States*, the Supreme Court reversed a lower court ruling and declared that the Crow Tribe did not have authority to regulate hunting and fishing by non-Indians on non-Indian-owned land within their reservation.

Congress passes laws, but the effect of those laws often depends on how the Supreme Court interprets them. The American Indian Religious Freedom Act of 1978 contained no enforcement provisions, and the declaration of policy did not translate into immediate and actual protection of Indian religious freedoms. Indians had to fight in court for the rights to take eagle parts (federal law protects eagles as an endangered species) for religious ceremonies, to wear long hair or hold sweat lodges when in prison, and to protect sacred sites. In 1988, in *Lyng v. Northwest Indian Cemetery Protective Association*, the Supreme Court overturned a lower court injunction on the building of a logging road in the Six Rivers National Forest in California which the Yurok Indians argued would cause irreparable damage to sacred sites. In April 1990, in the case of two members of the Native American Church who had been dismissed from their jobs by the Oregon Department of Education for using peyote, the United States Supreme Court ruled that state governments could prosecute people who used controlled substances as part of a religious ritual without violating their constitutional rights of religious freedom. Many Americans, Indian and non-Indian, saw the court's decision as a major threat to Native American religion and to religious freedom in general. Responding to overwhelming public sentiment, Congress passed the Native American Free Exercise of Religion Act in

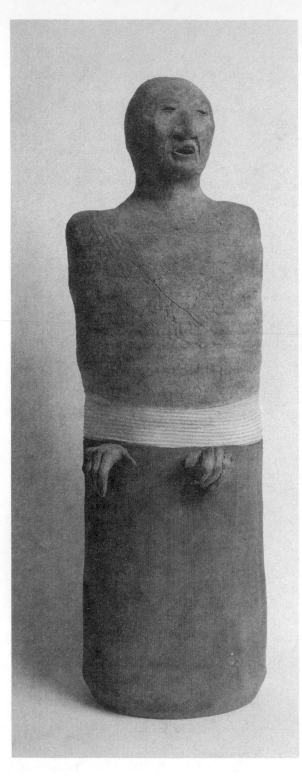

Sovereign Indian

Indian tribes enjoy unique political status as sovereign nations within the United States. But, as this sculpture by Onondaga Peter Jones suggests, their efforts to control their own lives and lands are often severely curtailed. The legacies of conquest and colonialism continue to limit Indian opportunities. Loss of lands, depletion of resources, lack of economic bases, limited educational opportunities, erosion of languages and traditions, pressing health and social problems, all hamper Indian political aspirations, even as they motivate them. Racist attitudes and stereotypes, intrusions by the federal and state governments, as well as the sometimes stifling hand of the BIA also present obstacles to self-government. Tribal sovereignty exists by inherent right: the Supreme Court in 1832 said Indian tribes "had always been considered distinct, independent political communities, retaining their original natural rights," and found that states could not execute their laws within Indian nations protected by treaties and the United States Constitution (pages 246–47). But issues affecting key attributes of tribal sovereignty—the right to levy taxes, to determine tribal membership, to exercise criminal and civil jurisdiction within reservation boundaries—are often tested in the courts. How might one interpret the bound arms on Peter Jones' sculpture in the light of Supreme Court rulings over the last twenty-five years?

Courtesy of Iroquois Indian Museum, Howes Cave, New York.

1994, which protected Native American rights to use peyote in traditional religious ceremonies and strengthened the American Indian Religious Freedom Act.[12]

By the turn of the century, many Indian people and scholars of Indian law were convinced that the United States Supreme Court had abandoned its historic role, and the foundations on which it had traditionally based its decisions, in favor of an assault on the sovereignty of Indian tribes.[13] The Alaska Native Claims Settlement Act granted lands to Native villages in fee simple,° but in 1998, in *Alaska v. Native Village of Venetie Tribal Government*, the Supreme Court ruled that Venetie's 1.8 million acres of fee simple land was not "Indian country" and consequently the tribal government lacked authority to tax a non-Native contractor who was building a school in the village. In 2001, the Supreme Court ruled in *Nevada v. Hicks* that tribes do not have civil jurisdiction over the conduct of state officials operating on the reservation, and, in *Atkinson Trading Company v. Shirley*, that the Navajo Nation had no right to tax non-Indian businesses operating on fee land within the reservation. The Rehnquist Court has taken such a consistently "anti-Indian" stance that some legal scholars fear it may be pursuing a policy of "judicial termination."[14]

More than half a century ago, legal scholar Felix S. Cohen wrote that "like the miner's canary, the Indian marks the shift from fresh air to poison gas in our political atmosphere, and our treatment of Indians, even more than our treatment of other minorities, reflects the rise and fall in our democratic faith."[15] Frank Pommersheim, a law professor and appellate justice on the Rosebud Sioux and Cheyenne River Sioux reservations, reports that "the present ratio of fresh air to gas is not necessarily encouraging." Worse, there seems to be "no national moral commitment to ensure that the fresh air will not dissipate further."[16]

Changes at the BIA

In an effort to eradicate "excessive bureaucracy" and streamline the process by which tribes administered BIA and Indian Health Service funds, Congress passed the Indian Self-Determination Act Amendments of 1994, specifying the terms of contracts entered into by the federal government and tribal organizations. That same year, President Bill Clinton pledged to honor tribal sovereignty based on the government's "unique legal relationship with Native American tribal governments." The BIA role was becoming increasingly advisory, as Indian tribes assumed greater responsibility over their own affairs, developed their own businesses, and planned for their futures; the bureau itself experienced dramatic downsizing in the 1990s. "The role of the federal government should be to support and to implement tribally inspired solutions to tribally de-

---

°Full ownership.

The BIA on Trial
*Interior Secretary Gale Norton and Assistant Secretary for Indian Affairs Neal McCaleb
(Chickasaw) were required to answer charges of contempt of court during the Indian
Trust Fund scandal. As the presence of the man in a headdress behind them suggests, In-
dian people watched to see if the BIA would act in good faith toward those it is supposed
to serve. In September 2002 the U.S. District Court for the District of Columbia held
Norton and McCaleb in contempt of court and cited four instances in which they had
committed fraud on the court. © Scripps Howard News Service.*

fined problems," said Ada Deer, whom Clinton appointed as the first woman assistant secretary of Indian affairs. "The days of federal paternalism are over."[17]

In 2000, then Assistant Secretary for Indian Affairs Kevin Gover, a Pawnee,
issued a public apology on behalf of the BIA to the Indian people of the United
States. In it he acknowledged that the bureau had sometimes harmed the communities it was meant to serve, and he promised stronger commitment to
"serve the cause of renewed hope and prosperity for Indian Country."[18] But the
slate was not wiped clean. In 1996, another Pawnee, John Echohawk, executive
director of the Native American Rights Fund, had filed a class action suit against
Secretary of the Interior Bruce Babbit on behalf of half a million beneficiaries
for misuse of billions of dollars held in trust by the BIA. The Indian Trust Fund
was established in the late nineteenth century, and the disbursement of oil and
gas royalties and other income from resources on Indian trust lands was assigned to the BIA. But the United States had no accurate accounting for hundreds of thousands of Indian beneficiaries nor of billions of dollars owed them.
The United States District Court of the District of Columbia ruled in the Indians' favor. The judge said the government was guilty of "fiscal and govern-

mental irresponsibility in its purest form" and gave the Departments of the Interior and the Treasury five years to correct the situation.[19] The Department of the Interior's failure to address the problems in a timely fashion, and charges of contempt of court leveled against Interior Secretary Gale Norton and Neal McCaleb, President George W. Bush's appointee as Assistant Secretary for Indian Affairs, left many people feeling that it was "business as usual" at the BIA. Senator Ben Nighthorse Campbell, a Cheyenne from Colorado, commented: "There seems to be an institutional rot that does not seem to go away."[20]

THE STRUGGLE FOR NATURAL RESOURCES AND NATIVE RIGHTS

In the nineteenth century, the United States wanted Indian land; in the twentieth century, it wanted Indian resources. Coal, gas, oil, uranium, timber, and water were vital to the nation's economy and, some said, to national security. For Indian communities whose reservation lands contained such resources, they offered the potential for economic development. But since World War II, access to natural and energy resources on Native American lands has increasingly been debated as an issue of sovereign rights. As Native Americans embrace self-determination and realize goals of education, they also struggle to protect rights regarding resources as vital to their traditional and spiritual way of life.

Fighting for and against Water

In the arid American West, water is a scarce and precious resource. Population growth, irrigation, power plants, and desert cities like Phoenix and Las Vegas place enormous demands on the West's limited water supply. At the same time, Indian tribes in the West need water to sustain and develop their reservations, and even to survive. "Water is the life blood, the key to the whole thing," declared Madonna Thunderhawk, a Lakota water rights activist on the Standing Rock reservation in North Dakota, in 1985.[21] The struggle for water has brought Indians into competition and conflict with non-Indian ranchers and state governments and into court. To the chagrin of many of their neighbors, Indians have prevailed some in these cases. But, in keeping with other rulings since 1970, the Supreme Court has ruled against tribes in 90 percent of the water-related cases it has ruled on.[22]

The basis for water rights cases was laid in the first decade of the twentieth century when the Supreme Court decided the case of *Winters v. United States*. The suit was brought to prevent a white settler from damming the Milk River and diverting water from the Fort Belknap reservation in Montana. Although the court at that time was generally unsympathetic to Indians, it found in favor of the tribe. The *Winters* Doctrine, as the court's decision became known, declared that when Congress established reservations it did so with the implicit intention that the Indians should have sufficient water to live. In-

MAP 8.5 James Bay

Cree Indian people have lived around James Bay for thousands of years. Subsisting by hunting, fishing, and trapping, they developed reciprocal and spiritual relationships with the animals who shared their world. When Europeans arrived about three hundred years ago, they introduced changes, but the Crees were able to adapt to the demands of the European fur trade without undermining their traditional way of life. They lived far to the north of major population centers, and their land seemed remote and inhospitable to Canadians to the south.

dian reservations, said the court, had "reserved water rights" that the federal government was bound to protect. For much of the century, the *Winters* Doctrine remained a paper victory, and non-Indians continued to divert water from Indian lands. Nevertheless, the courts have upheld *Winters,* and the doctrine is the foundation on which western tribes have won important water rights cases. The *Winters* Doctrine has been a source of tension, as non-Indian ranchers during droughts had their water supply terminated while flows to neighboring Indian reservations continued uninterrupted. American society has had a hard time adjusting to the realization that, in the words of one legal scholar of water rights, "the debt has come due" and one way or another "it must be paid."[23] Competition for water in the West continues with numerous lawsuits over how much water tribes are entitled to, how they can use it, whether they can lease it, and so on. The tribes, the states, and the federal government continue to wrestle with finding equitable ways to allocate an ever-diminishing resource in an area of the country where control of water means power and prosperity.

The assault on Native resources and communities has not been restricted to the United States, nor have Indian peoples within U.S. borders been the only ones to feel the impact of American energy consumption. The struggle of Cree Indians in northern Quebec attracted attention in both the United States and Canada in the late twentieth century as a test case of modern society's exploitation and disregard of Native peoples and the environment—and in this case, the Indians are fighting *against* water.

In 1970, the premier of Quebec announced plans for Hydro-Quebec, the largest hydroelectric project in the world, to dam major rivers that drained into James Bay, which is at the southern end of Hudson Bay and is the largest bay and estuary system on the continent. The project subsequently expanded to include dams on the La Grande River, the third largest river in Quebec. Construction began two years later. Five major rivers were dammed or diverted and more than four thousand square miles of forest were flooded to generate electric power for eastern Canada and the northeastern United States. "One day, after we had lived in our land for thousands of years," said Grand Chief Matthew Coon-Come, "a decision was made to block our rivers, cut down our forests, and flood our lands. No one came to talk to us. We were not told of these plans. All of this just happened."[24]

By 1985, Phase I of the Hydro-Quebec project had been completed at a cost of $20 billion, but the costs to the Crees were also considerable. People were relocated to make way for dams that flooded ancient hunting territories and sacred places. Migrating birds found nowhere to land. A sudden release of water from one reservoir drowned ten thousand migrating caribou in 1984. As Anishinaabe activist Winona LaDuke explains: "There are many things Cree people have taken for granted over countless generations: that the rivers will always flow, the sun and moon will alternate, and there will be six seasons of the year. . . . That is how the time is counted here in the North, in seasons based on the migrations of caribou, geese, sturgeons, and other relations and on the ebb and flow of ice and water." But, since Hydro-Quebec went into effect, "the rivers do not always flow, the animals are not always there, and strange as it may seem, there are no longer six seasons in some parts of this land."[25]

Having failed to stop Phase I in the courts, the Crees widened their campaign against Phase II. They lobbied for non-Native support in Canada and the United States, pointing out to audiences in New York and New England that *they* bore a share of responsibility for the devastation of the Cree homeland and that what was going on to the north was environmental racism and just as threatening as the destruction of the Amazonian rain forests. "This is what I want you to understand," said Coon-Come. "It is not a dam. It is a terrible and vast reduction of our entire world. It is the assignment of vast territories to a permanent and final flood."[26]

As the environmental impact of such projects becomes apparent, Indian people struggling to protect their homelands have found increasing numbers of allies among concerned non-Indians. LaDuke, who ran as vice-presidential candidate of the Green Party in the 1996 and 2000 elections, articulated a growing awareness that "at some point, there will be no more 'frontiers' to conquer. There will be no more resources to mine, rivers to dam, trees to fell, or capital to invest."[27] Contracts for selling the power in the United States began to be delayed and canceled. In 1994, the new premier of Quebec shelved Phase II of the James Bay project. Coon-Come was awarded the Goldman Environmental Prize for his fifteen-year fight against the project, but Hydro-Quebec continued to propose plans for diverting and damming the Great Whale and Rupert Rivers which run through the heart of Cree territory. In 2002, in a move that surprised and alarmed many environmentalists, the James Bay Cree High Council endorsed a new agreement with Hydro-Quebec: in return for a share of the profits from a huge new hydroelectric plant, the Crees agreed to support a project to divert much of the Rupert River to the plant.

Exploitation's Impact: Black Mesa and Laguna Pueblo

When the United States assigned Indians to reservations in the nineteenth century, it generally placed them on barren lands other Americans did not want. Ironically, many western reservations lay on one of the world's richest mineral belts. It is estimated that reservations contain one-third of all western low-sulphur coal, one-fifth of the country's reserves of oil and natural gas, and over half

Boy and Four Corners Power Plant
Power plants were built in Indian country to service distant cities, not the local communities. Navajos continued to herd sheep in the shadow of the Four Corners Power Plant, but they and their flocks suffered from the pollution and environmental degradation the plants produced. Courtesy Rock Point Community School, Arizona.

the nation's uranium deposits. With the onset of the Cold War after 1945 and the escalating energy demands of modern America, Indian tribes came under intense pressure from the U.S. government and from energy companies to develop and market these resources. With few economic alternatives, tribal leaders found themselves negotiating—or, at that time, found the BIA negotiating for them—with outsiders eager to get at their resources, just as their ancestors had. In some cases, Indian reservations became transformed into energy colonies, exporting their valuable resources to the outside world and getting little in return.[28]

The Navajo reservation became the scene of extensive exploitation of energy resources and enduring conflict. The program of livestock reduction in the 1930s and 1940s eroded the traditional Navajo economy and generated widespread poverty. World War II offset some of the worst effects by providing jobs in war-related industries and service in the armed forces. But Navajos who returned home after the war faced an economic crisis. With their traditional economy disrupted, they needed other sources of income. They found the

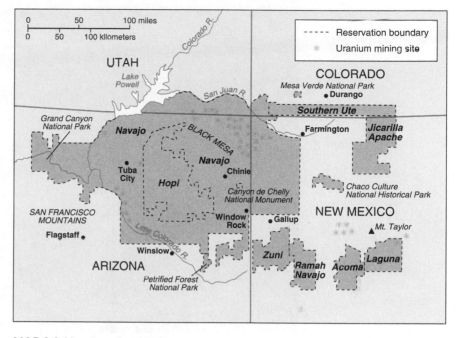

MAP 8.6 Uranium Ore Mining Areas

The four corners area of the United States, regarded by many people as a special and sacred place, became pockmarked with uranium mining sites in the twentieth century.
Adapted from a map by Deborah W. Reade for Peter Eichstaedt, If You Poison Us: Uranium and Native Americans, published by Red Crane Books, 1994.

promise of prosperity in what seemed at the time to be attractive offers to develop the coal, oil, gas, and uranium resources of the Navajo reservation.

Royalties from these operations injected much-needed income into the Navajo economy, provided funds for Navajo Community College, and scholarships for Navajo students. Some Navajos, notably tribal chairman Peter Mac-Donald who worked closely with energy companies in the 1970s and 1980s, grew rich. But most Navajos benefited little from the power they were producing for other people. Like the people of a third world country, most Navajos remained poor as the benefits and profits from exploitation of their rich resources left the reservation. Navajo energy resources provided electricity for Albuquerque, Phoenix, Los Angeles, and other cities, but many Navajo homes lacked running water or electricity. Smoke from the huge power plant at Four Corners blackened the sky. Navajo lambs were stunted, spat blood, and died. In July 1979, the nation's worst release of radioactivity occurred when United Nuclear Corporation's uranium tailings dam failed at Church Rock, just outside the Navajo reservation: 100 million gallons of radioactive water flooded into the Rio Puerco and ten thousand sheep died.

Peabody Coal Company signed leases with the Hopis and Navajos in 1966 to begin coal strip mining operations on Black Mesa. But many Navajos bitterly

Navajo Miner

At a time when jobs were scarce and Navajos were still feeling the impact of the government's stock reduction program, many men earned what seemed like good wages working in coal and uranium mines. This young man was photographed drilling in a uranium mine on the reservation in the 1950s. The dangers of exposure to excessive radiation levels were not so well understood then, and companies sometimes cut corners on what safety regulations did exist. Many Navajos like this young man contracted lung cancer and other ailments in later life as a consequence of working in the mines. Courtesy of the Arizona Historical Society/Tucson PC196f.485/13.

opposed the ensuing despoiling of the area. Navajo men working in uranium mines were exposed to excessive radiation levels, and many contracted lung cancer and other respiratory ailments. In 1990, the United States issued a formal apology and promised to compensate the families of Navajo men injured or killed by radiation in the government mines, but for victims' families such compensation was too little too late.

At Laguna Pueblo in New Mexico, Anaconda Corporation operated the world's largest uranium strip mine from 1952 to 1981. At its peak of operations, the mine employed 650 workers. The Laguna tribe became relatively wealthy, but the local economy changed completely from agriculture to wage-based mining. When the extractable ore played out, Anaconda pulled out, and the Lagunas were left with a huge crater and piles of radioactive slag. (Anaconda later agreed to pay the tribe $34.6 million for cleanup and reclamation projects.) Lagunas who had become accustomed to earning regular wages were now unemployed. In addition, many people suffered from mining related ailments; many of the new homes built with the mine profits were found to be radioactive, and local water sources were all contaminated.

Black Mesa and Laguna served as warnings to other tribes of the long-term damage that could be incurred in return for short-term gain. By the 1970s, Indian tribes with valuable mineral resources were becoming more organized and less vulnerable to exploitation by energy companies. In 1975, leaders from more than twenty tribes formed CERT, the Council of Energy Resource Tribes, whose goal was to secure better terms from corporations and to exert political influence through collective action. The Jicarilla Apaches of New Mexico and the Assiniboines and Sioux of Fort Peck in Montana drilled their own oil wells.

Choosing Homelands over Wastelands

The days are over when the BIA and energy companies could decide between them how to exploit reservation resources. Now Indian tribes themselves call the shots. But they still come under intense pressure, face formidable political and economic realities in making choices, and sometimes find that achieving economic prosperity may not be compatible with traditional values. In 1982, Congress passed the Indian Mineral Development Act to encourage tribes to mine their lands as a way to become economically self-sufficient. But, after seeing the impact of America's energy demands, many tribes took a cautious approach. The Northern Cheyennes in Montana sit on between 5 and 10 million tons of strippable coal, but in the 1970s they took the unprecedented step of canceling their coal mining leases and designating the air above their reservation Class I quality. They continue to fend off proposals to turn their Montana homeland into the largest coal strip mine in the United States. "I feel like I have lived a lifetime fighting coal strip mining," says Gail Small of Native Action, a grassroots organization committed to fight coal development and ensure the survival of the Northern Cheyenne community.[29]

Navajo people continue to deal with pressures to exploit the energy resources in their homelands. The government's attempt to settle conflicts between Navajos and Hopis who inhabited a "joint use area" by removing Navajo families has been seen by many people as an effort to open the region's rich coal resources to exploitation. Navajos who regarded the area as sacred land refused to move.[30] The Navajo Nation established its own Environmental Protection Agency, and in 1987 the Navajos and Hopis renegotiated their leases with Peabody Coal. In 1996, approximately 75 percent of the Navajo Nation's operating budget depended on royalties from coal sales.[31]

Some tribes ceased being energy colonies and became energy developers. Many argue that unless the tribes can make economic progress they stand to lose their traditional culture in the face of poverty and dependence. Others maintain that the land is sacred and should not be scarred by mining operations. They question the wisdom of pursuing quick wealth by extracting mineral resources from their reservations, or from storing radioactive waste in and on their land. "Where will we all be 20 or 25 years from now when the coal is

MAP 8.7 Nuclear Waste in Indian Country

The construction of nuclear waste storage facilities on some reservations may offer short-term economic opportunities to the tribes, but many Indians and non-Indians regard the dumping of nuclear waste as a prime example of "environmental racism" that poses long-term threats to neighboring communities. Adapted from Winona LaDuke, All Our Relations (Cambridge, Mass.: South End Press, 1999).

all consumed and the companies operating these gasification plants have cleaned up all the resources and moved away?" one Navajo asked. "There will be nothing; they will be working elsewhere and we will be sitting on top of a bunch of ashes with nothing to live on."[32]

The pressure to generate economic development on the reservations has led tribal governments to consider housing more toxic wastes. The United States Department of Energy (DOE) offered $100,000 study grants to encourage tribes and rural communities to explore storing nuclear waste in monitored retrievable storage (MRS) facilities until a permanent DOE site at Yucca Mountain, Nevada, can be licensed. The Skull Valley Goshute, Mescalero Apache, Northern Arapaho, Fort McDermitt Paiute-Shoshone, Lower Brulé Sioux, Chickasaw, Sac and Fax, Alabama-Coushatta, Ponca, Eastern Shawnee, Caddo, Yakima, and other Native groups applied for the study grants. Some of these tribes have since reconsidered, but others continue to explore the projects, and several have accepted MRS facilities on their reservations.[33]

The economic incentives offered are attractive in communities where unemployment and poverty are commonplace, but critics of MRS facilities point out that the long-term environmental problems outweigh any short-term economic benefits. They denounce the dumping of nuclear waste on Indian reservations as "environmental racism": American society wants the benefits of nuclear power but no one wants the waste in their backyard, so they send it to Indian country.

In February 1994, the Mescalero Apache Tribal Council signed an agreement with Minnesota's Northern States Power Company, representing thirty-three nuclear energy companies, to establish a private site for forty thousand metric tons of spent nuclear fuel from commercial power plants. Tribal chair Wendell Chino explained the move as a step toward achieving tribal economic independence and self-sufficiency by providing jobs and income for the tribe. Other Mescaleros opposed the decision as violating sacred land and jeopardizing their children's futures. The Skull Valley Goshutes in Nevada also leased land for an MRS facility. Although tribes are subject to federal environmental laws, they are exempt from state acts that often are stricter, and tribal opponents of MRS sometimes dismiss state opposition by invoking their sovereignty. Other Indian peoples are demanding federal enforcement of environmental laws and are creating their own regulations to protect their people and resources.

The threat of contamination from leakage of nuclear waste is perhaps most acute at Prairie Island, Minnesota, where the Mdwekanton community lives literally next door to a nuclear power plant and a nuclear waste storage plant. When Northern States Power Company planned to store waste from its Prairie Island reactors outside, on a historic site and burial ground in the Mississippi floodplain, an alliance of Indians, environmental groups, and other concerned citizens formed the Prairie Island Coalition to oppose the plan. In 1994, the Minnesota state legislature passed a law limiting the number of storage casks at the site to seventeen and requiring the power company to find a new site. The Mdwekanton Dakota and their allies refuse to accept official assurances that the plant and storage facility are safe and continue to lobby for removal of the nuclear waste.

The Department of Energy plans to open an underground repository at Yucca Mountain by 2010, but the Western Shoshones are fighting the project, arguing that the site is on land guaranteed to them by treaty in 1863. Many more Americans worry about the dangers involved in transporting nuclear waste to the new site.

Pollution of the air, land, and water, destruction of animal and plant life, and relentless exploitation of natural resources all run counter to traditional Native ideals of living with the earth. The Arctic tundra is being used as a dumping ground for nuclear waste, and PCBs have been found in Eskimo mothers' milk. At the Mohawk community of Akwesasne, in upstate New York on the banks of the St. Lawrence River, where the people used to hunt, farm and fish, so many chemicals were dumped into the water by nearby industrial plants that it became unsafe to eat fish or game, cultivate the soil, or raise cattle. Scientists have caught snapping turtles with so many PCBs in their bodies that they constitute toxic waste, an event with ominous significance for a people whose creation stories tell that the world was formed on the back of a huge sea turtle. The pollution that threatens Navajos in Arizona and Mohawks at Akwesasne threatens everyone. "The earth hurts," said the late Navajo elder Roberta Blackgoat, a long-time opponent of the desecration of Navajo land. "The planet is in danger. . . . It is everybody's future."[34]

Many Indian people regard a return to traditional ways as the only chance for humanity to survive in the twenty-first century. More than a quarter century ago, Iroquois delegates to the Non-Governmental Organizations of the United Nations in Geneva, Switzerland, issued a "call to consciousness" to the western world. "The way of life known as Western Civilization is on a death path on which their own culture has no viable answers," they warned. "When faced with the reality of their own destructiveness, they can only go forward into areas of more efficient destruction." The delegates saw the air becoming foul, water being poisoned, trees dying, and animals disappearing. Even the weather seemed to be changing. It was time to break away from Western concepts of exploiting and subjugating the natural world, and embrace Native ways of living with the natural world. "The traditional Native peoples hold the key to the reversal of the processes in Western Civilization which hold the promise of unimaginable future suffering and destruction."[35] Today, Anishinaabe environmental activist Winona LaDuke warns that America "must move from a society based on conquest to one steeped in the practice of survival."[36]

BUILDING PROSPERITY IN INDIAN COUNTRY: GAMING, A DEVIL'S BARGAIN?

In the past, the laws and policies of the federal government were seen as the key factors in economic development on Indian reservations. But by the end of the twentieth century, many Indian tribes had taken charge of their own economic affairs and were demonstrating that Indian sovereignty rather than federal policy seems to be the crucial factor in determining prosperity in Indian country today. When the tribes, rather than the BIA or other outsiders, take the responsibility for their own economic futures—deciding, implementing, and being accountable for their own economic strategies—and pursue projects compatible with their cultures and values, they can achieve sustainable economic development and rebuild their nations.[37] From this perspective, tribal sovereignty becomes a valuable economic resource—and assaults on tribal sovereignty pose an even greater threat to tribal survival.

The Mississippi Band of Choctaws provides a clear example of economic success, achieved by a tribe on its own terms. In 1979, unemployment on the Choctaw reservation was about 80 percent. Today, under the leadership of Chief Philip Martin, the tribe runs several manufacturing plants as well as gaming and tourism, and uses the income generated on the reservation to supplement federal contracts in providing educational, health, and other services to Choctaw people. The Mississippi Band of Choctaw Indians is one of the ten largest employers in Mississippi, providing more than eight thousand jobs for tribal members and others (more than 65 percent of its workforce is non-Indian). Tribal revenues have helped the Choctaw to reinvest more than $210 million in economic development projects in Mississippi.[38]

While the Choctaws are a success story, tribes with few resources and limited economic opportunities have turned in the late twentieth century to gaming as a way of generating income and employment. In this they are not alone. As one scholar of Indian gaming notes, state and local governments have also turned to games of chance to fund services in an age of federal cutbacks: "Government-sponsored gambling has become the revenue-raising activity of choice among governments in the United States."[39] The unique status of Indian tribes and their lands—generally, income generated on reservation land is exempt from federal and state taxes—makes gambling extremely lucrative in Indian country. Some tribes have staged "economic miracles." But gaming is a contentious issue in many parts of the country.

The Seminole Indians in Florida opened a bingo hall in 1979 and offered prizes of $10,000, ignoring a state law that prohibited jackpots of more than $100. The state of Florida tried to close down the bingo hall, but the Seminoles sued in federal court and the United States Supreme Court upheld the right of the Seminoles and other tribes to operate bingo games free from state regulation. In 1987, the Supreme Court ruled in *California v. Cabazon* that, despite Public Law 280, a state which permitted any form of gambling could not prohibit Indians from operating gambling facilities.

The next year, Congress passed the Indian Gaming Regulatory Act (IGRA). Under the act, a tribe that wants to operate Class III or "casino-type" gambling must request the state in which its lands are located to enter into negotiations for a "compact," in which the tribe submits to state jurisdiction while the state permits gaming on the reservation. If a state fails to negotiate "in good faith," the tribe may sue in federal court. States complain that the IGRA violates their

**The Foxwoods Casino and the Mashantucket Pequot Museum
and Research Center**

*The Foxwoods casino, owned and operated by the 530-member Mashantucket Pequot
tribe of southern Connecticut, brings in millions of dollars every year. Attracting about
50,000 vistors a day, it also offers entertainment by world-famous stars, elegant dining,
and specialty shopping. Some critics claim the Pequots and other tribes who go into the
gaming business are "selling out," capitalizing on their Indian heritage but sacrificing traditional values for easy money. Others respond that the criticism stems from the fact that
the Pequots are shattering stereotypes of Indian poverty, and that the new wealth serves to
preserve and revive the culture, not to undermine it. The income for Foxwoods*

sovereign immunity under the Eleventh Amendment° to the Constitution and
violates the Interstate Commerce Clause of the Constitution, which states that
only the federal government can deal with Indian tribes (a position the United
States Supreme Court supported in 1996). Some tribes complain that the compacts violate their sovereignty.

In 1998, Indian gaming was a $500 million business; in 2002, 290 Indian
casinos reported a combined revenue of $12.7 billion.⁴⁰ The development of
gaming operations on Indian reservations has opened unprecedented oppor-

---

°The Eleventh Amendment protects states against suit "by Citizens of another state, or by Citizens or Subjects of any Foreign State."

provided funds for one example of cultural preservation. In August 1998, after five years of construction, the Mashantucket Pequots opened the $193-million Mashantucket Pequot Museum and Research Center, featuring exhibits of Pequot history and culture and housing an extensive library to serve as a research center for other tribes, scholars, schools, and the general public. "We want to show that Native peoples are not a static part of history, but are still evolving, vital contributors to modern society," said spokesman David Holahan. "We will show that Native peoples may not be what the public often expects or envisions them to be. That's part of the learning process." Mashantucket Pequot Tribal Nation.

tunities for economic growth for some tribes. For 130 years after they hid in the Everglades to avoid forced removal to Oklahoma, the Florida Seminoles lived in poverty. They now enjoy millions of dollars in annual revenues from gaming operations on their South Florida reservations. In addition to monthly payments to tribal members, the Florida Seminoles and the Cabazon band are able to fund community services and scholarships for their members.[41]

Perhaps more than any other tribe, the Mashantucket Pequots have demonstrated the transformative power of gaming. The Pequots of Connecticut were a major economic and political power in southern New England at the beginning of the seventeenth century. After the English destroyed their main village in 1637 and declared the tribe extinct, for almost 350 years the Pequots seemed to be on the verge of disappearing. But the Pequots held on to their tiny land base and their identity. In 1983, the Mashantucket Pequots won federal recognition as an Indian tribe. After experimenting with a number of ventures for economic development, they turned first to bingo and then to high-stakes gambling. Within easy driving distance of several major cities, the Mashantucket Pequots' Foxwoods Casino is widely believed to be the most profitable casino in the world and does a billion dollars of business every year. Profits provide the tribe housing, health care, education, care for the elderly, and cultural programs. The Mashantuckets have built a huge museum that displays Pequot artifacts of history and culture and are involved in archaeological research to recover material evidence of their history. The casino employs ten thousand workers, a boost to the once-flagging economy of southern Connecticut. Today the Pequots are once again a major economic and political power in the region. In an ironic twist of history, some local residents see the Pequot tribe as an expanding business entity threatening to engulf their small towns in a flood of tourists and traffic.

Many tribes hope to emulate the Pequots' success, or at least win a measure of economic independence by going into bingo and gaming. The Pequots' neighbors in Connecticut, the Mohegans, opened their casino in the fall of 1996. In its first six months, the casino earned a pretax profit of $55.3 million, of which the tribe gets 60 percent. The Mohegans have used the money for college scholarships, a new home for the elderly, and a campaign to retrieve tribal artifacts.[42]

Some states and individuals who stand to lose money to Indian gaming have been vocal in protesting against it. Donald Trump even brought a lawsuit against the federal government, claiming that Indian gaming operations had an "unfair advantage" over his own Atlantic City casinos because they did not have to comply with state regulations as he did. But with an economic downturn at the beginning of the new century, many states showed a new willingness to cooperate with Indian gaming to secure a piece of the pie, notably in New York State where the economic effects of September 11 were most severe.[43]

Contrary to some popular notions that all Indians eagerly pursue the get-rich-quick opportunities it offers, gaming has generated tensions and differences of opinion within Indian country and Indian communities. In some Iroquois communities, disputes between pro- and antigaming factions escalated to intimidation, violence, and arson. In 1994 and again in 1997, Navajos in a tribal referendum voted against gaming on their reservation, but they later voted to allow slot-machine gaming. Many leaders question the wisdom of entering into compacts with state governments, as required under the Indian Gaming Regulatory Act, to operate high-stakes gaming: does not such action compromise a tribe's sovereignty in pursuit of quick money?

The National Indian Gaming Association, a non-profit organization established in 1985, says: "Today, gaming has replaced the buffalo as the mechanism used by American Indian people for survival. . . . [It is] the first—and only—economic development tool that has ever worked on reservations."[44] But not all Indian people hunted buffalo, and not all Indian people agree on the benefits of gaming. Supporters of gaming point out that the income generated goes back into the community, providing jobs, social service programs, utility services, clinics, housing, schools, scholarships, and hope for the future. "Every cent of Indian gaming revenue goes right back into services for tribal people," said Marge Anderson, former Chief Executive of the Mille Lacs Band of Ojibwe in Minnesota, in 1993. "Two years ago, unemployment for my 2,400 member tribe in Minnesota was 45 percent and is now zero."[45]

With prosperity comes self sufficiency, opportunities for economic diversification, and the ability to exercise true self-determination. Gaming tribes can afford the costly legal battles necessary to protect tribal rights and resources and can exert political influence in the form of lobbying and campaign contributions which, it could be argued, effect improvements for all Indian people. Others denounce it as a social vice and an affront to their tribal values. They worry about the impact of gaming and the sudden influx of money and people into communities unaccustomed to dealing with either in large quantities. They fear it will undermine tribal community, culture, and values, and caution that a new stereotype of Indians as wealthy casino operators distorts reality and may prove harmful to all Indians. Casino revenues disproportionately benefit a relatively small number of tribes, and in some cases non-Indian financial backers seem to take the lion's share of the profits. Some fear that Congress may respond to growing fears about Indian gaming by returning to termination tactics, arguing that the government need no longer maintain its trust relationship with tribes who are independently wealthy. The success of tribes like the Mohegans and Mashantuckets has generated a backlash among some non-Indians, renewed concern in some circles about the powers and the unique status of Indian nations within the United States, and brought heightened attention to questions of Indian identity.[46]

NUMBERS, IDENTITIES, AND IMAGES

In 1900, the United States Census reported an Indian population of only 237,196. In those days, census enumerators classified race on the basis of observation — in other words, you were counted as an Indian if you "looked" like one. By 2000, with the Census Bureau using self-identification as its criterion and allowing respondents to check more than one box, Indian population had risen to 2.5 million, with an additional 1.6 million people identifying themselves as part Indian. But the question of who is an Indian is a contentious one that goes beyond mere numbers to the issue and nature of tribal and cultural survival in the twenty-first century. Although improved health conditions, higher birth rates, and lower death rates accounted for some of the increases, the huge rise in American Indian population in the second half of the twentieth century was due to changing patterns in ethnic identity rather than natural increase: more Indians were being born and living longer, but far more people were calling themselves Indians.[47]

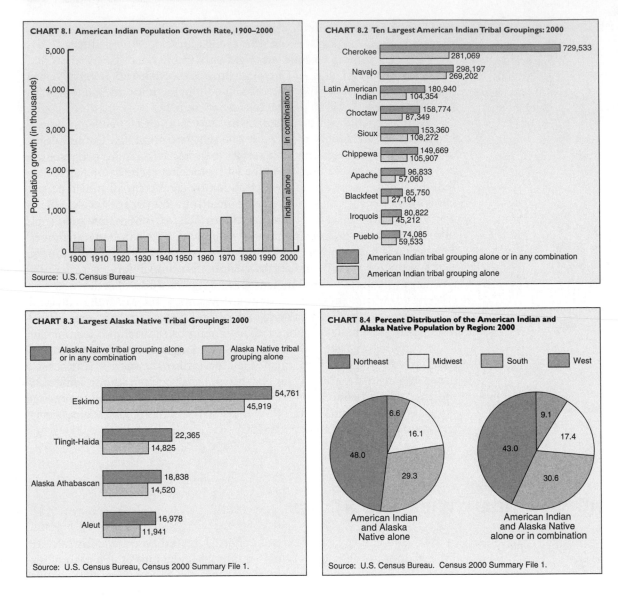

CHART 8.1 American Indian Population Growth Rate, 1900–2000

Source: U.S. Census Bureau

CHART 8.2 Ten Largest American Indian Tribal Groupings: 2000

Cherokee 729,533 / 281,069
Navajo 298,197 / 269,202
Latin American Indian 180,940 / 104,354
Choctaw 158,774 / 87,349
Sioux 153,360 / 108,272
Chippewa 149,669 / 105,907
Apache 96,833 / 57,060
Blackfeet 85,750 / 27,104
Iroquois 80,822 / 45,212
Pueblo 74,085 / 59,533

American Indian tribal grouping alone or in any combination
American Indian tribal grouping alone

CHART 8.3 Largest Alaska Native Tribal Groupings: 2000

Alaska Naitve tribal grouping alone or in any combination
Alaska Native tribal grouping alone

Eskimo 54,761 / 45,919
Tlingit-Haida 22,365 / 14,825
Alaska Athabascan 18,838 / 14,520
Aleut 16,978 / 11,941

Source: U.S. Census Bureau, Census 2000 Summary File 1.

CHART 8.4 Percent Distribution of the American Indian and Alaska Native Population by Region: 2000

Northeast   Midwest   South   West

American Indian and Alaska Native alone: 48.0, 6.6, 16.1, 29.3

American Indian and Alaska Native alone or in combination: 43.0, 9.1, 17.4, 30.6

Source: U.S. Census Bureau. Census 2000 Summary File 1.

Census 2000: A Profile of Indian America

American Indians were first counted as a separate group in the United States Census in 1860, but that census did not include Indian people living on reservations and in Indian territory. Not until 1890 were Indians counted throughout the country. In 1900, the Indian population of the United States was recorded at less than a quarter million, clear evidence, many people believed, that Indians were on the brink of extinction. But the 1900 census was off the mark: census counters failed to identify many Indian people, and many Indians chose not to be identified. Instead of continued decline and disappearance in the twentieth century, Indian population rebounded, at first slowly and then

Census Director Kenneth Prewitt in Alaska
The annual census requires huge — and sometimes extraordinary — efforts to achieve an accurate population count: In this photograph, Census Bureau Director Kenneth Prewitt heads for an Alaskan Native village by dogsled. Nevertheless, some people complain that, as in the past, Native American populations in 2000, were significantly undercounted. Photographed by David A. Predeger for the U.S. Census Bureau, © David A. Predeger.

dramatically (see Chart 8.1). In a changing social climate marked by increased Indian activism, increased interest in Indian cultures, and increased prestige and opportunities associated with Indian heritage, many people who have not done so before are literally standing up to be counted as Indians.[48]

In 2000, for the first time, the census allowed respondents to identify themselves as belonging to more than one racial category. Respondents could identify themselves as "part Indian" — American Indian and white, American Indian and black, and so on — and were listed in the "American Indian in combination" category, rather than in the "American Indian alone" category. The figures for American Indians in 2000 included Native people who had migrated to the United States from Canada and Mexico. The 2000 census also calculated tribal populations, again including an "in combination" category. Cherokee and Navajos were reported as the largest tribes (see Chart 8.2). Alaska Natives have been counted since 1880 but were generally reported in the "American Indian" category until 1940, when they began to be enumerated separately as Eskimo and Aleut. In 2000, the census used a combined "American Indian or Alaska Native" response category to gather data on both population groups (see Chart 8.3). The state with the highest proportion of Native population is Alaska, where 19 percent of the population identifies itself as full or part American Indian or Native Alaskan (see Map 8.8, "Indian Populations, 2000", page 494).

In addition to huge increases in the numbers of people reporting as Indians, the 2000 census confirmed patterns of population distribution that earlier censuses had already identified: most American Indians are located in the West and Midwest, with more than 50 percent living in just ten states (see Chart 8.4). One in four Indian people reside in either Oklahoma or California, and more than half of America's Indian population lives in urban areas.

Who Is an Indian?

There is no simple answer. Neither Indian tribes nor the federal government apply a single criterion for identifying who is an Indian. Different Indian nations have different rules for membership. Urban Indians may have different criteria for identifying as Indians than do reservation Indians.[49] The BIA defines Indians as people who are members of federally recognized tribes, or who have (depending on the purpose) one-half or one-quarter ancestry. Some Indian people do not belong to recognized tribes. Degree of ancestry, or "blood," in itself might not be sufficient for membership in one tribe, but may not be required at all for membership in another. Residence, status in the community, and many other factors can play into whether one is regarded as Indian. The same person might be regarded as Indian by some people and not Indian by others. Individuals may think of themselves as ethnically, culturally, or politically Indian. As ethnic identities become increasingly complex and flexible, the same person might consider him or herself Indian for some purposes and in some situations, and not in others.

Indian nations historically determined membership with little or no regard to "blood." Members of other tribes and even Europeans could become tribal members through marriage, adoption, or even choice. In many areas of the country, intermarriage between Indians and non-Indians was more common than armed conflict. Around Puget Sound, for example, Native people and their offspring had extensive and intimate relations with immigrants and their offspring, with the result that the descendants of the Indians who were there when Europeans first arrived are now "inextricably tangled in the cultural, economic, and racial threads of a social fabric designed by non-Indians."[50] In many areas, Indian people and African Americans have had long histories of intermarriage, with the result that some people identify themselves as black Indians. Ethnic groups change as human relations change, and many Indian peoples define themselves on their own terms, perhaps distinguishing themselves from outsiders on the basis of clan and kinship or involvement in community and ceremony, rather than a measured tribal and ethnic identity.[51] "Blood" has little to do with it.

But the U.S. government attempted to institutionalize definitions of Indianness. The terms Indian and tribe, introduced by non-Indians, became crucial terms for classifying a huge array of people. Federal bureaucrats tried to reduce many ways of being Indian to simple and static categories. Government criteria for identifying Indians in the wake of extensive intermarriage with non-Indians introduced concepts of blood quotas, which remain to this day, though they are often inconsistently applied and with damaging results. Generally the federal government applies a 25 percent "blood quantum" (that is, one must be at least one-quarter Indian to qualify). As Indian people continue to marry non-Indians, this level of "Indian blood" will inevitably become less common, or "diluted," with the result that Indians will eventually "disappear" or be defined out of existence if they continue to be identified according to this measure. As activist and writer Ward Churchill sees it: "North America's Native peoples have been bound ever more tightly into the carefully crafted mechanisms of oppression and eventual negation."[52]

Today, even though census figures show a growing number of Native Americans, and a willingness to let Natives define themselves (at least statistically), identity is still a crucial issue. More than 50 percent of all Indians are married to non-Indians. If current trends continue, it has been projected that only about 8 percent of Indian people will have one-half or more Indian ancestry by the

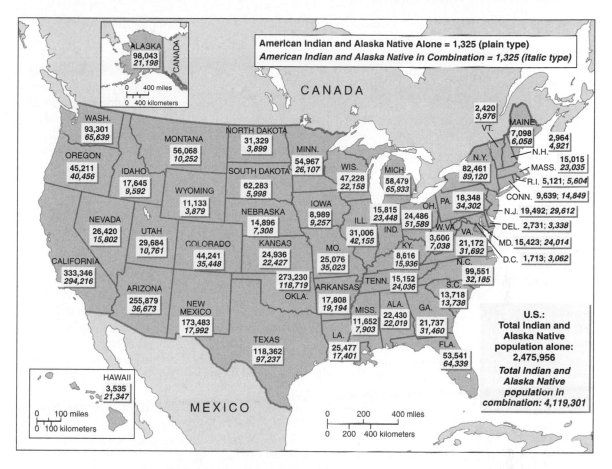

MAP 8.8 Indian Populations, 2000

At the end of the twentieth century, Indian populations were growing steadily in every state, rebounding dramatically after the massive declines of previous centuries. The 2000 census was the first time the census allowed people to identify themselves as belonging to more than one ethnic category.

year 2080. As Cherokee demographer Russell Thornton predicts, "a point will be reached—perhaps not too far in the future—when it will no longer make sense to define American Indians in genetic terms, only as tribal members or as people of Indian ancestry or ethnicity."[53] Journalist Fergus Bordewich asks: "How much blending can occur before Indians finally cease to be Indians?"[54]

Census figures based on self-identification are not always good enough for skeptics, Native and non-Native, who point out that an Indian identity might provide access to land claim settlements, casino wealth, scholarships, health benefits, mineral and resource royalties, or other privileges. Are some of the "new Indians" instead "wannabees"? Are people who self-identify as Indian but who lack tribal affiliation really Indian? Should urban Indians who have never lived on the reservation qualify as tribal members, especially when membership means access to tribal services or per capita payments from oil and gas leases?

Should blood quota have any role to play in measuring "Indianness"? If not, what criteria should be applied? Should the federal government or other outside agencies have any say regarding how Indian communities determine their own membership?

Some Indian communities today are attempting to tighten up the tribal rolls and exclude people who marry non-Indians or the children of people who have married outsiders, but it is uncertain what the long-term effects of such policies will be. Other communities reject the idea of measuring "Indian blood": on Pine Ridge reservation in South Dakota, the Oglalas abandoned blood quantum as a criterion of tribal enrollment, basing membership instead on factors such as residency and commitment to the Oglala people.[55] The Cherokee Nation of Oklahoma determines membership by tracing descent from a person on the 1906 tribal roll rather than on the degree of blood. What it means to be Indian continues to be a complex and sometimes divisive issue.[56]

"Recognized" and "Nonrecognized" Tribes

The question "Who is really an Indian?" is posed to tribes as well as to individuals.[57] The BIA acts not only as trustee for Indian resources, it also decides which groups are formally recognized as Indian tribes. Tribes with whom the United States made treaties or otherwise established a governmental relationship are recognized. There are more than 550 federally recognized tribes, including more than 220 Native Alaskan villages.[58] Many Indian groups are not formally recognized as Indian "tribes" by the U.S. government; some are recognized by the state in which they live but not by the federal government. Many unrecognized groups are quite small, but the Lumbees of Robeson County, North Carolina, with more than forty thousand members, are the largest Indian tribe east of the Mississippi and are not yet recognized by the federal government. The Lumbees have a long history of intermarrying with people of European and African origin, and in the biracial South of the nineteenth century they were classified as "nonwhite." Nevertheless, Lumbees have steadfastly maintained their community and asserted their Indian identity. They maintained their own school system, drove the Ku Klux Klan out of Robeson County in 1958, and secured state recognition as an Indian tribe. The federal government, however, has not found them eligible for recognition. Indian groups who lack federal recognition do not qualify for federal assistance programs for Indians; nor do they benefit from the status of being identified as Indians. For example, they are not recognized as Indians for the purposes of the Indian Arts and Crafts Act of 1990, which requires Indian artists to be certified to guarantee the authenticity of their "Indian art."[59]

In 1901, in *Montoya v. United States*, the United States Supreme Court adopted a working definition of tribe as "a body of Indians of the same or similar race, united in community under one leadership or government, and inhabiting a particular though sometimes ill-defined territory." But how groups "fit" what is essentially a non-Indian category has always been and remains a problem. In 1978, Congress created the Federal Acknowledgment Project and the Branch of Acknowledgment and Research in the BIA to evaluate the claims of nonrecognized tribes. The government expects petitioning groups to provide a paper trail documenting such things as common Indian ancestry, continuous community and political leadership, and historical association with a particular territory. The BIA modified its acknowledgment procedures in the 1990s, but the process remained expensive, time-consuming, often demeaning, and potentially divisive. Petitioning groups expend a tremendous amount of money and energy in compiling the necessary documentation, with no guarantee that their claim will be successful. Tribes who have secured recognition include the Grand Traverse Band of Ottawa and Chippewa (1980), the Narragansetts (1983), the Gay Head Wampanoags (1987), the San Juan Southern Paiutes (1990), and the Mohegans (1994). Congress has also acknowledged some other tribes, including the Pascua Yaqui near Tucson (1978), the Mashantucket Pequots (1983), the Aroostook Micmacs of Maine (1991), and the Match-E-Be-Nash-She-Wish Band of Potawatomis in Michigan (1999). Members of President Clinton's administration extended eleventh-hour recognition to several tribes (including the Nipmucs in Massachusetts and the Duwamish outside Seattle), only to have the citations revoked by appointees of President George W. Bush. Many nonrecognized groups are small, heavily intermarried with non-Indian neighbors, and do not easily fit in with standard notions of "Indianness." They often resent the fact that they have to comply with criteria laid down by someone else to be recognized for who they say and know they are.

Stereotypes Old and New

Indian people today are found in virtually all walks of life and, as they always have, display tremendous diversity in culture, behavior, and opinion. One thing they have in common is that they can expect to deal with non-Indian stereotypes, whether in the form of media images, innocent questions from new friends at college, insensitive behavior by sports fans, or openly racist hostility from anti-Indian groups.

From first contacts with a few Native peoples, Europeans tended to generalize about all Indians. Many modern Americans likewise expect all Indians to look, dress, speak, and live like horseback-riding, buffalo-hunting Indians they have seen depicted on TV or in the movies; Indian people who do not fit these images are often regarded as somehow "less Indian." The public, the media, and even the courts subscribe to the notion that Indians who change with the times "lose" their culture. All cultures change, indeed they must if they are to survive, and change is constant in American culture. But some people feel that Indians cannot be Indians if they drive pickup trucks instead of ride horses, live in condominiums in town instead of tepees on reservations, wear business suits instead of buckskins, or communicate by e-mail instead of smoke signals. Such ideas freeze Indian people in an unchanging past that, for many Indians, was never part of their culture in the first place.

A glance at the names of automobiles, such as Jeep Cherokee, or the logos on products on the shelves of grocery stores, such as Land O' Lakes butter,

HAVE YOU EVER SEEN A REAL INDIAN?

AMERICAN INDIAN
COLLEGE FUND
EDUCATION IS STRENGTH

Have You Ever Seen a Real Indian?
In 2001 the American Indian Tribal College Fund began an advertising campaign to combat persisting stereotypes about Native Americans. This ad features Rick West, Southern Cheyenne, founding director of the National Museum of the American Indian. West is an attorney; he is also a traditional pow wow dancer. Other ads in the campaign feature Dr. Lori Arviso Alvord, surgeon and associate dean at Dartmouth Medical School; director and screenwriter Dean Bear Claw; and college students. American Indian College Fund.

shows that using stereotypical Indian images is common in American popular culture. Professional and high school sports teams use Indian logos or "mascots," a practice that has become increasingly controversial as more people take offense at distorted images and cultural appropriations (see "Mascots and Playing Indian," pages 536–37). Indians themselves sometimes employ the same clichés that other people find offensive: a visitor to the Mashantucket Pequot casino, for instance, will see Plains Indian style statues and décor; generic "Indian" symbols such as tomahawks, arrows, feathers and buffalos; and cocktail waitresses in headbands and short, fringed dresses.

Many negative stereotypes stem from generations of contact and colonialism: loss of land and hope, and economic and social disruption have produced alcoholism, poverty, and unemployment in many communities; but these stereotypes are often regarded as characteristic of all Indians. As more people question the values of modern American society and worry about the environmentally destructive path we are on, new, more positive stereotypes have emerged: Indians are spiritual people who live in harmony with nature and possess virtues our own society seems to have lost. Stressing the positive aspects of Indian society as an implicit criticism of non-Indian society is not new—Jean Jacques Rousseau and other eighteenth-century writers did it with their depictions of "the noble savage." Any stereotyping, whether negative or positive, holds people to different standards and tends to dehumanize them.

TAKING BACK EDUCATION

Important new initiatives in Indian education stemmed from the growing movement toward self-determination in the 1960s and 1970s. Traditionally, Native American parents and elders taught their children in a community setting. But well into the twentieth century, government-sponsored schools made every effort to separate Indian students from their communities and rid them of their tribal heritage, language, and understandings, so that they could act, speak, and think like non-Indian Americans, not Native Americans. The schools and colleges that Indian students attended operated to meet the goals of American society. They failed to meet many of the needs of their Indian students and, not surprisingly, Indian students frequently failed at those institutions (see Chapter 6.) Indian people established their own schools early on—the Cherokee Nation established its own educational system in the nineteenth century and the nondenominational Cherokee Female Seminary in eastern Oklahoma in 1851[60]—but not until the 1960s and 1970s were Indian people and communities able to have a significant voice in planning and running some of their institutions of higher education.

In 1969, a Senate subcommittee published a report on Indian education called "A National Tragedy—A National Challenge." The committee declared, "We are shocked at what we discovered."[61] The report marked an end to the government's educational assault on Indian cultures and languages, but the legacy of that assault left Indian peoples and communities with a formidable task as they began to repair what had been broken in the past, to prepare for future challenges, and to educate Indian children to succeed in modern American society while at the same time cultivating traditional values and ways of knowledge.

In 1966, the Navajos established the Rough Rock Demonstration School near Chinle, Arizona. Two years later, they founded the first tribal college on the Navajo reservation: Navajo Community College—now Diné College—in Tsaile, Arizona. Students who previously had to leave the reservation for higher education in an alien environment now had the option of attending college closer to home in an institution that tried to incorporate Navajo values in its administration and classes. In the words of a former dean of instruction, the college's mission has always been "to perpetuate Navajo-ness"; to find ways to synthesize Navajo and Western knowledge "and instill this knowledge into young Navajo men and women so they will survive in the dominant society while maintaining their heritage."[62] Fifteen more two-year institutions were founded by Indian tribes in the next decade. Tribal colleges, created and administered by Indian people and generally located on or near Indian reservations in the West, grew out of a widespread conviction that most institutions of higher education had failed abysmally to provide a learning environment for Indian people of traditional background. In 1972, tribes formed the American Indian Higher Education Consortium to help Indian students gain access to higher education. The consortium's lobbying in Congress resulted in passage of the Tribally Controlled Community Colleges Act in 1978, which provided funding for the colleges.

Severe budget cuts during the Reagan presidency threatened to eradicate many of the gains made. A task force commissioned to evaluate education among American Indians and Alaska Native people issued its report in 1991, entitled "Indian Nations at Risk." Indian educators lobbied hard to hold the government to its treaty commitments and trust responsibility to provide an education for Indian children. In 1992, President Clinton held a White House Conference on Indian Education. In 1995, a "National American Indian/Alaska Native Education Summit" was held in Washington, D.C. From that summit,

Pow Wow Dancers
*Indian dancers compete at a Northern Plains pow wow at the Buffalo Bill
Historical Center in Cody, Wyoming, 1995. Kevin R. Morris/©Corbis.*

*The word "pow wow" derives from an Algonquian term for medicine men, and early European colonists often applied
it to any gatherings in which medicine men participated. Today the term refers to Indian social events that revolve
around dancing, drumming, and singing. Always a crucial part of Native American religious and communal life,
dancing persisted even while missionaries and government agents tried to suppress what they regarded as "heathenish
practices." Some dances even spread from tribe to tribe during the reservation era. In the late twentieth century, pow
wows flourished as Indian people across the United States and Canada sought ways to come together to celebrate their
heritage, preserve traditional dances, and demonstrate new forms of cultural expression.*

*Pow wows are usually annual events of several days. After an opening grand entry, flag-raising ceremony, and
prayer, participants wearing different styles of regalia perform different dances to the rhythm and singing of drum
groups. Some dances are traditional; others, like the swirling fancy dance with bustles and feathers, have developed in
modern times. There are dances for men, and dances, like the shawl and jingle dances, exclusively for women. There
are dance contests for children. There are dances in which only certain people participate, and dances, like the round
dance, in which all participants and visitors, Indian and non-Indian, are welcome.*

*As many as two thousand pow wows are held each year in North America. Some are huge events, like the ones
held each summer at Gallup, New Mexico, and at Crow Fair in Montana, or in cities like Denver and Chicago. Others*

MAP 8.9 Selected Pow Wow Sites, 1995

Adapted from The Settling of North America: The Atlas of the Great Migrations into North America from the Ice Age to Ellis Island and Beyond *by Helen Hornbeck Tanner, Janice Reiff, and John H. Long, eds., page 193. Copyright © 1995 by Swanston Publishing, Ltd.*

Indian educators produced a draft that was circulated among Indian educational organizations, and after revisions, was eventually submitted to the White House. In 1998, President Clinton signed an "Executive Order on American In-

are smaller local affairs, hosted by a particular reservation community. Some state universities now host pow wows, as do private colleges like Stanford and Dartmouth. Some people spend much of the summer traveling the pow wow circuit, competing for prizes or simply enjoying the opportunities to socialize with friends and relatives. Some urban Indians return to their reservations during pow wow time to maintain connections with their community and culture. For many Indian people in modern America, pow wows are an important way to reaffirm their identity and participate in their culture in a dramatic and public way.

dian and Alaskan Native Education," which affirmed "the unique political and legal relationship" between the federal and tribal governments and recognized "the unique educationally and culturally related academic needs" of Native students. Many Indian educators regarded it as a landmark event, even as they recognized how much work remained to be done and knew too well that the Indian education budget was vulnerable to political mood swings and economy-minded lawmakers.[63]

Meanwhile, tribal colleges continued to wage their own struggle to provide Indian people with an Indian education in their own communities. (See "Tribal Colleges: Indian Education for Indian People," pages 520–26.) At the same time, increasing numbers of Native people insisted on greater intellectual and cultural sovereignty. History is contested ground. Who tells it, who "owns the past," matters. Until recently, the writing of Indian history has been monopolized by non-Indians. Colonial writers often dehumanized Indian people, early historians regularly dismissed them, and modern scholars rarely incorporate Native American knowledge and voices in their work. Filmmakers have been equally insensitive and uninformed, offering negative and stereotypical portrayals of Indian people and the Indian past. Now many Indians argued that knowledge from Indian communities should stay in the communities and that Indian people should tell their own stories, write their own history using Native sources of knowledge, speak their own languages, and make their own films and videos.[64] All Native peoples confront the challenge of preserving traditional culture and tribal heritage in the modern world. Just as the U.S. government in the late nineteenth century saw destruction of Indian languages as an effective means of erasing tribal culture and identity, so Indian people today see language revival as a means of restoring it. In 1990, Congress passed the Native American Languages Act. The law recognized that "the traditional languages of Native Americans are an integral part of their cultures and identities and form the basic medium for the transmission, and thus survival, of Native American cultures, literature, histories, religions, political institutions, and values."[65] Additional legislation provided grants for recording oral histories and teaching languages in classrooms, but Indian people realize that language preservation and revitalization lie in their own hands: if they don't use it, they will lose it.[66]

BUILDING WELL NATIONS°

Although standards of health have improved, Indian communities confront major challenges in AIDS and HIV, diabetes, teen suicides, and other problems common to modern American society. At the end of the twentieth century,

---

°The concept of Well Nations is taken from *Well Nations Magazine*, a new publication designed to provide Indian and other people with helpful information regarding physical, emotional, mental, and spiritual health.

tuberculosis rates among Indian people were more than seven times the national average; alcohol-related deaths were ten times higher; fetal alcohol syndrome thirty-three times more common; and suicide rates were four times greater among Indian teenagers than among non-Indians. Type 2 diabetes (also known as adult-onset diabetes) affects more than 12 percent of Indian adults, compared to 4% for the rest of the population; it is approaching epidemic proportions in some Indian communities.[67] Restoring the physical health of Indian communities involves restoring the spiritual health of Indian America after centuries of invasion, colonialism, dispossession, cultural genocide, and racism. In some areas, it involves restoring the health of land that has been scarred by extraction of uranium, coal, and other energy resources and contaminated by cancer-causing pollutants. It also involves greater control by Indian people of their governments, health services, education, and cultural property.

Confronting Alcoholism

In 1987, the tribal council of the Cheyenne River Sioux declared war on alcoholism with the goal of eliminating it from the reservation by the year 2000.[68] Injected into Indian country from colonial times onward as a means of stimulating trade and undermining Indian independence, alcohol continues to disrupt Indian communities, break up Indian families, shatter Indian lives, and threaten Indian futures. Many tribal leaders regard alcoholism as their primary enemy. In 1977, the American Indian Policy Review Commission declared alcohol abuse "the most severe and widespread health problem among Indians," and things are little better today. Estimates of alcoholism on some Indian reservations range from 50 percent to 80 percent. Growing up on a reservation in South Dakota, Mary Crow Dog recalled, "I started drinking because it was the natural way of life. My father drank, my stepfather drank, my mother drank. . . . I think I grew up with the idea that everybody was doing it." She said, "The men had nothing to live for so they got drunk and drove off at ninety miles an hour in a car without lights, without brakes, and without destination, to die a warrior's death."[69] Seventy percent of all treatment services provided by the Indian Health Service in the early 1990s were alcohol-related. So many Indian babies are affected by fetal alcohol syndrome that some Indian people insist that if they do not halt it, "we will cease to exist as Indians."[70]

Myths and stereotypes about Indian drinking are common and damaging.[71] In fact, Indian people have resisted and protested against the use of alcohol since colonial times.[72] Today, many Indian people fight alcoholism by returning to Indian ways and values. "I haven't touched a drop of liquor for years," writes Mary Crow Dog, "ever since I felt there was purpose to my life, learned to accept myself for what I was. I have to thank the Indian movement for that, and Grandfather Peyote, and the pipe."[73]

Balancing Ways of Healing

Some Indian communities supplement the western-style medicine provided by the Indian Health Service (HIS) with more holistic, community-based, and culturally connected forms of healing. The Navajos have moved "closer to true self-determination in medical care" not only by playing a greater role in the delivery of IHS services and producing their own physicians but also by preserving traditional herbal, ceremonial, and cultural ways of healing. At the same time, many non-Indian physicians have begun to take more note of Native healing practices. They increasingly recognize that both traditions have a role to play, an approach that Dr. Lori Arviso Alvord, the first Navajo woman to become a surgeon, has consistently advocated. The benefits of combining Native and western approaches and healing practices was demonstrated in 1993 when a "mystery illness" struck the Southwest. Navajo healers helped the Center for Disease Control to identify the cause of the disease—the hantavirus carried by deer mice and other rodents—and western medical practitioners were able to bring it under control.[74] Combining western and traditional knowledge in holistic and culturally centered approaches to healing has been shown to work—even to be necessary—in restoring the health of communities. Whether it can work to restore the health of the planet remains to be seen.

Repatriation

Many Indian communities are involved in an ongoing campaign to have skeletal remains and sacred objects returned to them. The struggle concerns cultural patrimony, human respect, and access to knowledge. It is also, for many Indian people, a question of health. Human remains and sacred objects that have been wrenched from their proper place may jeopardize the spiritual well-being and the physical health of a community, even of a universe.

In the 1970s, Indian activists began to challenge the right of non-Indian museums to hold religious and other artifacts and skeletal remains of Indian people. For generations, soldiers, tourists, scientists, and collectors had looted Indian country of material culture and human remains. Museums had put Indian artifacts and even Indian bones on display without regard to Indian peoples' feelings about the significance of the objects or the offensiveness of the display. The 1906 Antiquities Act and the 1979 Archaeological Resources Protection Act declared Indian bones and objects found on federal land the property of the United States, and between 600,000 and 2 million skeletal remains were housed in museums, laboratories, historical societies, and universities across the county. The Smithsonian Institution alone held the remains of about 18,500 people. Archaeologists and anthropologists studied Indian bones to learn about diet, mortuary customs, levels of health, and causes of death, but most Indian people regarded this as continuing exploitation and a denial of their status as human beings. In the 1980s, the Pawnees waged a bitter fight to recover ancestral remains from the Nebraska State Historical Society and other repositories. Pawnee people believed that many of their social problems stemmed from the disturbance of graves and demanded ceremonial reburial of the bones to free the spirits of their ancestors by returning them to the earth. Some scholars argued that this would be a terrible loss to science, but public opinion favored the Indians' position that it was a question of basic human decency—their grandparents should be left to rest in peace—and the state returned the bones for reburial.

The Zunis of New Mexico demanded the return of carved wooden war gods from museums and private collections. They pointed out that since the war gods are communally owned and cannot be sold or given away, any war gods that have been removed from their proper shrines must be stolen property. "They are the spiritual guardians of the Zuni People. When they are removed from their shrines Zuni religious leaders cannot pray to them, and their vast powers cause fires, earthquakes, wars, storms, and wanton destruction in our world."[75] Once recovered, the gods could be placed in the desert and continue the cycle of decay back to the earth. The Iroquois demanded the return of twelve wampum belts from the New York State Museum, arguing that these were the tribal archives and belonged in Onondaga (where the records of the Iroquois Confederacy were kept), not on display in Albany. The twelve belts were restored to Onondaga chiefs in a ceremony in Albany in 1989.

In 1989, Congress passed a law requiring the Smithsonian Institution to return most of its skeletal remains and grave goods to Indian communities. In 1990, President George H. W. Bush signed into law the Native American Grave Protection and Repatriation Act, requiring all institutions receiving federal funds to inventory their collections of Indian artifacts and human remains, share the lists with Indian tribes, and return, when appropriate, the items the tribes requested. The act initiated a new era of unprecedented cooperation between museums and Indian communities as they worked together to determine what should be returned, where, and how. Some individuals and institutions complied reluctantly with the legislation. Contentious issues remain, as illustrated by the continuing controversy over the disposition of the skeletal remains of Kennewick Man (see pages 15–16). But in general public opinion and national law came to agree that human remains and religious objects should be returned to their original communities and not be pored over by anthropologists or displayed for tourists. For many Indian people, recovering their ancestors' bones or important sacred objects was an emotional and healing experience that began to restore to the world some of the harmony that had been lost.

Indian America in the Twenty-First Century

Indian America continues to defy easy and narrow descriptions. The legacies of conquest, colonization, cultural assault, and failed government policies continue to shape the world that Indian peoples inhabit and the choices they make. Some Indian reservations remain notorious for poverty, alcoholism, and unemployment. But prosperity, tribal sovereignty, political influence, and cul-

Change and Continuity in Indian America
Today, as they have for centuries, Havasupai Indians continue to live on the floor of the Grand Canyon. Their community is accessible by foot, by horse and mule, and by helicopter. In this photograph, satellite dishes are being delivered. Will embracing such modern technology undermine tribal ways of life and erode traditional values? Or will Indian people, as they have so often in the past, manage to balance the old and the new, and build stronger communities in the twenty-first century? StarBand Communications.

tural revitalization are also creating new conditions, new rules, and new relations with American society.

Many Indian people look to the seventh generation as a guide for living, with concern for how their actions will affect those yet unborn. In the rapidly changing and tumultuous modern era, the responsibility of handing on a good world across seven generations is truly formidable. Tribal communities are working hard to ensure that lands and resources, languages, traditions, values, education, community health, and tribal sovereignty are handed down intact.

References

1. Francis Paul Prucha, ed., *Documents of United States Indian Policy* (Lincoln: University of Nebraska Press, 1975), 256–58.
2. Quoted in Mark N. Trahant, "The 1970s: New Leaders for Indian Country," in Frederick E. Hoxie and Peter Iverson, eds., *Indians in American History,* 2d ed. (Wheeling, Ill.: Harlan Davidson, 1998), 238.

3. Quoted in Peter Iverson, *The Navojo Nation* (Albuquerque: University of New Mexico Press, 1981), 130–31.

4. David E. Wilkins, *American Indian Politics and the American Political System* (Lanham, Md.: Rowman and Littlefield, 2002), 56.

5. Wilkins, *American Indian Politics and the American Political System*.

6. Francis Paul Prucha, ed., *Documents of United States Indian Policy*, 2d ed. (Lincoln: University of Nebraska Press, 1990), 288–89.

7. David H. Getches, Charles F. Wilkinson, and Robert A. Williams, Jr., *Cases and Materials on Federal Indian Law*. 4th ed. (St. Paul: West Group, 1998), 509–20; John R. Wunder, *"Retained by the People": A History of American Indians and the Bill of Rights* (New York: Oxford University Press, 1994), 153–56.

8. Christopher Vecsey and William A. Starna, eds., *Iroquois Land Claims* (Syracuse: Syracuse University Press, 1988).

9. Getches, Wilkinson, and Williams, *Cases and Materials on Federal Indian Law*, 251–52, 438–39.

10. Quoted in Wilkins, *American Indian Politics and the American Political System*, 157.

11. Ben Welch, "A Slippery Slope," in *American Indian Report* 17 (October 2001), 12–17.

12. Getches, Wilkinson, and Williams, *Cases and Materials on Federal Indian Law*, chap. 10; Carolyn N. Long, *Religious Freedom and Indian Rights: The Case of* Oregon v. Smith (Lawrence: University Press of Kansas, 2000).

13. See, for example, "Indians in Court: A Look at the Rise and Decline of Indian Law," *American Indian Report*, Special Issue, 17 (October 2001).

14. For detailed discussions, see Getches, Wilkinson, and Williams, *Cases and Materials on Federal Indian Law*, 253–55; Bruce Duthu, "Implicit Divestiture of Tribal Powers: Locating Legitimate Sources of Authority in Indian Country," *American Indian Law Review* 19 (1994), 353–402; David H. Getches, "Conquering the Cultural Frontier: The New Subjectivism of the Supreme Court in Indian Law," *California Law Review* 84 (December 1996), 1573–1655; David E. Wilkins, *American Indian Sovereignty and the U.S. Supreme Court: The Masking of Justice* (Austin: University of Texas Press, 1997), chaps. 5–6; Philip P. Frickey, "A Common Law for Our Age of Colonialism: The Judicial Divestiture of Indian Tribal Authority over Nonmembers," *Yale Law Review* 109 (October 1999), 1–85.

15. Quoted in Getches and Wikinson, *Cases and Material on Federal Indian Law*, 2d ed. (St. Paul: West Publishing Co., 1986), xxx.

16. Frank Pommersheim, *Braid of Feathers: American Indian Law and Contemporary Tribal Life* (Berkeley: University of California Press, 1995), 51.

17. Quoted in Fergus M. Bordewich, *Killing the White Man's Indian: Reinventing Native Americans at the End of the Twentieth Century* (New York: Doubleday, 1996), 313.

18. "Gover Issues Historic Apology," *American Indian Report* 16 (October 2000), 10.

19. Wilkins, *American Indian Politics and the American Political System*, 3–5.

20. Quoted in *American Indian Report* 15 (April 1999), 3.

21. Quoted in Marianna Guerrero, "American Indian Water Rights: The Blood of Life in Native North America," in M. Annette Jaimes, ed., *The State of Native America: Genocide, Colonization, and Resistance* (Boston: South End Press, 1992), 207–08.

22. Wilkins, *American Indian Politics and the American Political System*, 76.

23. Lloyd Burton, *American Indian Water Rights and the Limits of the Law* (Lawrence: University Press of Kansas, 1991), 140–41; Getches, Wilkinson, and Williams, *Cases and Materials on Federal Indian Law*, chap. 11.

24. Matthew Coon-Come, "A Reduction of Our World," in Kurt Russo, ed., *Our People . . . Our Land: Reflections on Common Ground—500 Years* (Bellingham, Wash.: Florence Kluckhohn Center, 1992), 82.

25. Winona LaDuke, "Foreword" to Boyce Richardson, *Strangers Devour the Land* (1976; reprinted, Post Mills, Vt.: Chelsea Green Publishing Co., 1991), ix.

26. Coon-Come, "A Reduction of Our World," 82.

27. LaDuke, "Foreword" to Richardson, *Strangers Devour the Land,* xiv.

28. Donald L. Fixico, *The Invasion of Indian Country in the Twentieth Century: American Capitalism and Tribal Natural Resources* (Niwot: University Press of Colorado, 1998).

29. Quoted in Winona LaDuke, *All Our Relations: Native Struggles for Land and Life* (Cambridge, Mass.: South End Press, 1999), 85.

30. Emily Benedek, *The Wind Won't Know Me: A History of the Navajo-Hopi Land Dispute* (Norman: University of Oklahoma Press, 1999).

31. *News from Indian Country* 10, no. 17 (mid-September 1996), 8A.

32. Quoted in Donald A. Grinde and Bruce E. Johansen, *Ecocide of Native America: Environmental Destruction of Indian Lands and Peoples* (Santa Fe: Clear Light Publishers, 1995), 138.

33. On the controversies surrounding MRS facilities; see David R. Lewis, "Native Americans and the Environment: A Survey of Twentieth Century Issues." *American Indian Quarterly* 19 (1995), 423–50; and LaDuke, *All Our Relations,* chap. 5.

34. Grinde and Johansen, *Ecocide of Native America,* cover.

35. Akwesasne Notes, ed., *Basic Call to Consciousness* (1st ed., 1978; rev. ed., Summertown, Tenn.: Book Publishing Co., 1991), 71–79.

36. LaDuke, *All Our Relations,* 197.

37. Stephen Cornell and Joseph P. Kalt, *What Can Tribes Do? Strategies and Institutions in American Economic Development* (Los Angeles: UCLA American Indian Studies Center, 1992).

38. See http://www.choctaw.org. See also Robert H. White, *Tribal Assets: The Rebirth of Native America* (New York: Henry Holt, 1990), chap. 2.

39. W. Dale Mason, *Indian Gaming: Tribal Sovereignty and American Politics* (Norman: University of Oklahoma Press, 2000), 43.

40. Donald L. Bartlett and James B. Steele, "Special Report: Indian Casinos, Wheel of Misfortune," *Time,* vol. 160. no. 25, Dec. 16, 2002, 44–56; see also Montie R. Deer, "National Indian Gaming Commission," testimony before the Senate Committee on Indian Affairs, U.S. Senate, July 19, 2000, cited in Nicholas C. Peroff, "Indian Gaming, Tribal Sovereignty, and American Indian Tribes as Complex Adaptive Systems," *American Indian Culture and Research Journal* 25, no. 3 (2001), 144.

41. "Gaming: Seminoles Ace in the Hole," *Fort Lauderdale Sun-Sentinel,* 1 April 1996, 1A; James J. Rawls, *Chief Red Fox Is Dead: A History of Native Americans since 1945* (Fort Worth-Harcourt Brace, 1996), 156.

42. *New York Times,* 4 June 1997, A27.

43. Jeff Hinkle, "Deal: State Lawmakers Willing to Play for a Piece of the Gaming Pie," *American Indian Report* 18 (January 2002), 12–15.

44. Quoted in Peroff, "Indian Gaming, Tribal Sovereignty, and American Indian Tribes," 144.

45. *Indian Country Today,* 25 August 1993.

46. Bartlett and Steele, "Indian Casinos: Wheel of Misfortune"; Jeff Benedict, *Without Reservation* (New York: HarperCollins, 2001); Kim Isaac Eisler, *Revenge of the Pequots* (New York: Simon and Schuster, 2001).

47. Joanne Nagel, *American Indian Ethnic Renewal: Red Power and the Resurgence of Identity and Culture* (New York: Oxford University Press, 1996), chap. 4; Nancy Shoemaker, *American Indian Population Recovery in the Twentieth Century* (Albuquerque: University of New Mexico, 1999).

48. Nagel, *American Indian Ethnic Renewal,* chap. 4; Shoemaker, *American Indian Population Recovery in the Twentieth Century.*

49. Susan Lobo, "Is Urban a Person or a Place? Characteristics of Urban Indian Country," in Susan Lobo and Steve Talbot, eds., *Native American Voices: A Reader, 2d ed.* (Upper Saddle River, N.J.: Prentice Hall, 2001), 56–66.

50. Alexandra Harmon, *Indians in the Making: Ethnic Relations and Indian Identities around Puget Sound* (Berkeley: University of California Press, 1998), 2.

51. See, for example, Harmon, *Indians in the Making*; Morris W. Foster, *Being Comanche: A Social History of an American Indian Community* (Tucson: University of Arizona Press, 1991).

52. Ward Churchill, "The Crucible of American Indian Identity: Native Tradition versus Colonial Imposition in Postconquest North America," in Duane Champagne, ed., *Contemporary Native American Cultural Issues* (Walnut Creek, Calif.: Altamira Press, 1999), 40.

53. Russell Thornton, *American Indian Holocaust and Survival: A Population History since 1492* (Norman: University of Oklahoma Press, 1987), 236–37.

54. Bordewich, *Killing the White Man's Indian*, 300, 333.

55. M. Annette Jaimes, "Federal Indian Identification Policy: A Usurpation of Indigenous Sovereignty in North America," in Jaimes, ed., *The State of Native America*, 134.

56. Nagel, *American Indian Ethnic Renewal*, chap. 9.

57. Nagel, *American Indian Ethnic Renewal*, 237.

58. See http://www.doi.gov/bia/tribes/telist for the list. [At the time of publication, this Web site is unavailable due to the Cobell Litigation. Please call 202-208-3710 for general BIA information.]

59. Gail K. Sheffield, *The Arbitrary Indian: The Indian Arts and Crafts Act of 1990* (Norman: University of Oklahoma Press, 1997).

60. Devon A. Mihesuah, *Cultivating the Rosebuds: The Education of Women at the Cherokee Female Seminary, 1851–1909* (Urbana: University of Illinois Press, 1993).

61. "Indian Education: A National Tragedy and Challenge," in Alvin M. Josephy, Jr., ed., *Red Power: The American Indians' Fight for Freedom* (New York: McGraw-Hill, 1971), 155–62.

62. Paul Willeto, "Diné College Struggles to Synthesize Navajo and Western Knowledge," *Tribal College Journal* 9 (Fall 1997), 11.

63. Margaret Connell Szasz, *Education and the American Indian: The Road to Self-Determination since 1928,* 3d ed. (Albuquerque: University of New Mexico Press, 1999), chap. 8. Clinton's 1998 Executive Order is reprinted as Appendix 3.

64. For discussion of such issues, see Devon A. Mihesuah, *Natives and Academics: Researching and Writing about American Indians* (Lincoln: University of Nebraska Press, 1998); Beverley R. Singer, *Wiping the War Paint off the Lens: Native American Film and Video* (Minneapolis: University of Minnesota Press, 2001).

65. "Native American Languages Act," *United States Code Annotated* (St. Paul: West Publishing Co., 1995), chap. 31 in Title 25.

66. *Tribal College: The Journal of American Indian Higher Education* 11 (Spring 2000) is dedicated to Native languages and contains a resource guide.

67. Shelley Swift, "Diabetes: Native America Wrestles with a Dangerous Epidemic," *American Indian Report* 16 (November 2000), 12–15.

68. Statistics on alcoholism are from Bordewich, *Killing the White Man's Indian,* 247–49. Peter C. Mancall, *Deadly Medicine: Indians and Alcohol in Early America* (Ithaca: Cornell University Press, 1995), examines the introduction and impact of alcohol on Indians in colonial times.

69. Mary Crow Dog and Richard Erdoes, *Lakota Woman* (New York: HarperCollins, 1990), 15, 45.

70. Roberta Ferron, a Rosebud Sioux, quoted in Rawls, *Chief Red Fox Is Dead,* 86.

71. Philip A. May, "The Epidemiology of Alcohol Abuse among American Indians: The Mythical and Real Properties," in Champagne, ed., *Contemporary Native American Cultural Issues,* 227–44.

72. See, for example, the speech of the Catawba chief, Hagler, in 1754, in Colin G. Calloway, ed., *The World Turned Upside: Indian Voices from Early America* (Boston: Bedford Books, 1994), 108.

73. Crow Dog and Erdoes, *Lakota Woman,* 45.

74. Wade Davies, *Healing Ways: Navajo Health Care in the Twentieth Century* (Norman: University of Oklahoma Press, 2001); Maureen Trudelle Schwarz, *Navajo Lifeways: Contemporary Issues, Ancient Knowledge* (Norman: University of Oklahoma Press, 2001); Lori Arviso Alvord and Elizabeth Cohen Van Pet, *The Scalpel and the Silver Bear* (New York: Bantam Books, 1999).

75. Roger Anyon, "Zuni Repatriation of War Gods," reprinted in Lobo and Talbot, eds., *Native American Voices,* 329.

Suggested Readings

Ambler, Marjane. *Breaking the Iron Bonds: Indian Control of Energy Development* (Lawrence: University Press of Kansas, 1990).

American Indian Report: Indian Country's News Magazine, Fairfax, Va.

Bordewich, Fergus M. *Killing the White Man's Indian: Reinventing Native Americans at the End of the Twentieth Century* (New York: Doubleday, 1996).

Chamberlain, Kathleen P. *Under Sacred Ground: A History of Navajo Oil, 1922–1982* (Albuquerque: University of New Mexico Press, 2000).

Davis, Mary B., ed. *Native America in the Twentieth Century: An Encyclopedia* (New York: Garland, 1994).

Deloria, Vine, Jr., and Clifford Lytle. *The Nations Within: The Past and Future of American Indian Sovereignty* (New York: Pantheon, 1984).

Edmunds, R. David, ed. *The New Warriors: Native American Leaders since 1900* (Lincoln: University of Nebraska Press, 2001).

Eichstaedt, Peter H. *If You Poison Us: Uranium and Native Americans* (Santa Fe: Red Crane Books, 1994).

Fixico, Donald L. *The Invasion of Indian Country in the Twentieth Century: American Capitalism and Tribal Natural Resources* (Niwot: University Press of Colorado, 1998).

Grinde, Donald A., and Bruce E. Johansen. *Ecocide of Native America: Environmental Destruction of Indian Lands and Peoples* (Santa Fe: Clear Light Publishers, 1995).

Indian Country Today (newspaper), Rapid City, S.D., 1981–.

Iverson, Peter, *Diné: A History of the Navajos* (Albuquerque: University of New Mexico Press, 2002).

Iverson, Peter. *"We Are Still Here": American Indians in the Twentieth Century* (Wheeling, Ill.: Harlan Davidson, 1998).

Jaimes, M. Annette, ed. *The State of Native America: Genocide, Colonization, and Resistance* (Boston: South End Press, 1992).

King, C. Richard, and Charles Fruehling Springwood, eds., *Team Spirits: The Native American Mascot Controversy* (Lincoln: University of Nebraska Press, 2001).

LaDuke, Winona, *All Our Relations: Native Struggles for Land and Life* (Cambridge, Mass.: South End Press, 1999).

Lobo, Susan, and Steve Talbot, eds. *Native American Voices: A Reader.* 2d ed. (Upper Saddle River, N.J: Prentice Hall, 2001).

Mason, W. Dale. *Indian Gaming: Tribal Sovereignty and American Politics* (Norman: University of Oklahoma Press, 2000).

Morrison, Dane, ed. *American Indian Studies: An Interdisciplinary Approach to Contemporary Issues* (New York: Peter Lang, 1997).

Parman, Donald L. *Indians and the American West in the Twentieth Century* (Bloomington: Indiana University Press, 1994).

Rawls, James J. *Chief Red Fox Is Dead: A History of Native Americans since 1945* (Fort Worth: Harcourt Brace, 1996).

Tiller, Veronica E. Velarde, ed. and comp. *Tiller's Guide to Indian Country: Economic Profiles of American Indian Reservations* (Albuquerque: BowArrow Publishing Co., 1996).

Utter, Jack. *American Indians: Answers to Today's Questions*, 2d ed. (Norman: University of Oklahoma Press, 2001).

Wilkins, David E. *American Indian Politics and the American Political System* (Lanham, Md.: Rowman and Littlefield, 2002).

Wilkins, David E. *American Indian Sovereignty and the U.S. Supreme Court: The Masking of Justice* (Austin: University of Texas Press, 1997).

Wilkins, David E., and K. Tsianina Lomawaima. *Uneven Ground: American Indian Sovereignty and Federal Law* (Norman: University of Oklahoma Press, 2001).

President Nixon and the Supreme Court Address Self-Determination

President Nixon's Message to Congress in 1970 seemed to mark a new era of optimism for Indian peoples. Nixon clearly rejected past federal policies of paternalism and termination and espoused a policy of self-determination as beneficial to Indian peoples and to the nation as a whole. In the years between Nixon's address and the Supreme Court decision in *Oliphant v. Suquamish* in 1978, some of the promise contained in Nixon's message was realized. Important new legislation passed through Congress, and Indian communities took significant steps in managing programs, running their own schools, and exerting political influence, both within Congress and through the media. They even won some landmark victories in American courts.

But tribal sovereignty—the rights of Indian nations to govern themselves—remained vulnerable. A nation's self-government includes the right to make and impose one's own laws, both on one's own citizens and on outsiders who enter the nation. In Indian country, this became a complicated and contentious issue as more and more non-Indians took up residence within reservation boundaries. On many reservations, allotment had created a checkerboard pattern of land holding, with non-Indians living alongside Indians. Further sales and leases, migrations of Indians to the cities, and intermarriage brought more non-Indians on to reservations, with the result that by the late twentieth century some reservations contained more non-Indian than Indian residents. What was their legal status? Were they subject to tribal law, even though they were not tribal citizens? Did someone fall under tribal law the moment they stepped on to the reservation? If not, how could tribes regulate and police their own communities? More and more cases challenging Indian sovereignty in this respect reached the Supreme Court.

Mark Oliphant, a non-Indian, was arrested by tribal authorities on the Port Madison reservation of the Suquamish Tribe near Seattle. The reservation was small, and non-Indian residents heavily outnumbered Indian residents. Oliphant challenged the tribe's authority to prosecute him, arguing in federal court that, as a non-Indian, he was immune from tribal law and subject only to state or federal law. The Marshall cases in the 1830s seemed to have made clear that Indian tribes are "distinct political communities, having territorial boundaries, within which their authority is exclusive," but the Supreme Court now found new limits on tribal sovereignty. Overturning the rulings of lower courts, the Supreme

Court decided that tribal courts do *not* have criminal jurisdiction over non-Indians. The ruling applied not only to small reservations such as Suquamish, where Indians residents were in a minority, but to all Indian country.

The *Oliphant* decision has been strongly criticized by both Native and non-Native legal scholars as a calculated assault on Indian tribes' inherent powers of self-government. Many see it as "result-oriented"; that is, that the Court intended from the outset to limit tribal sovereignty and used shaky evidence and faulty legal reasoning to do so. Peter Maxfield, a non-Indian law professor at the University of Wyoming, not accustomed to making extreme statements, concluded: "The justification that the Court used to reach its result can only be characterized as reprehensible."[1]

► Questions for Consideration

1. What effects does the *Oliphant* ruling (page 514) have on tribal sovereignty? Does the ruling contradict the assertion in President Nixon's message to Congress that "we must assure the Indian that he can assume control of his own life"?

2. What arguments and evidence does the Court present to support its decision?

3. What is the relevance of the demographic information provided in the Court's Note 1 (page 514) to the outcome of the case?

4. What does the dissenting opinion identify as the only basis for removing an aspect of tribal sovereignty?

5. Apache Chief Wendell Chino once described tribal sovereignty as "a bundle of rights." What does this decision do to that bundle?

6. What does tribal sovereignty amount to when it is subject to the plenary power of Congress (as it is) and to limitations imposed by the courts?

PRESIDENT RICHARD NIXON
Special Message to Congress on Indian Affairs (1970)

To the Congress of the United States:

The first Americans—the Indians—are the most deprived and most isolated minority group in our nation. On virtually every scale of measurement—employment, income, education, health—the condition of the Indian people ranks at the bottom.

This condition is the heritage of centuries of injustice. From the time of their first contact with European settlers, the American Indians have

Source: H.R. Doc. No. 91-363, 91st Cong., 2d session (July 8, 1970).

been oppressed and brutalized, deprived of their ancestral lands and denied the opportunity to control their own destiny. Even the Federal programs which are intended to meet their needs have frequently proven to be ineffective and demeaning.

But the story of the Indian in America is something more than the record of the white man's frequent aggression, broken agreements, intermittent remorse and prolonged failure. It is a record also of endurance, of survival, of adaptation and creativity in the face of overwhelming obstacles. It is a record of enormous contributions to this country—to its art and culture, to its strength and spirit, to its sense of history and its sense of purpose.

It is long past time that the Indian policies of the Federal government began to recognize and build upon the capacities and insights of the Indian people. Both as a matter of justice and as a matter of enlightened social policy, we must begin to act on the basis of what the Indians themselves have long been telling us. The time has come to break decisively with the past and to create the conditions for a new era in which the Indian future is determined by Indian acts and Indian decisions.

SELF-DETERMINATION WITHOUT TERMINATION

The first and most basic question that must be answered with respect to Indian policy concerns the historic and legal relationship between the Federal government and Indian communities. In the past, this relationship has oscillated between two equally harsh and unacceptable extremes.

On the one hand, it has—at various times during previous Administrations—been the stated policy objective of both the Executive and Legislative branches of the Federal government eventually to terminate the trusteeship relationship between the Federal government and the In-

dian people. As recently as August of 1953, in House Concurrent Resolution 108, the Congress declared that termination was the long-range goal of its Indian policies. This would mean that Indian tribes would eventually lose any special standing they had under Federal law: the tax exempt status of their lands would be discontinued; Federal responsibility for their economic and social well-being would be repudiated; and the tribes themselves would be effectively dismantled. Tribal property would be divided among individual members who would then be assimilated into the society at large.

This policy of forced termination is wrong, in my judgment, for a number of reasons. First, the premises on which it rests are wrong. Termination implies that the Federal government has taken on a trusteeship responsibility for Indian communities as an act of generosity toward a disadvantaged people and that it can therefore discontinue this responsibility on a unilateral basis whenever is sees fit. But the unique status of Indian tribes does not rest on any premise such as this. The special relationship between Indians and the Federal government is the result instead of solemn obligations which have been entered into by the United States Government. Down through the years, through written treaties and through formal and informal agreements, our government has made specific commitments to the Indian people. For their part, the Indians have often surrendered claims to vast tracts of land and have accepted life on government reservations. In exchange, the government has agreed to provide community services such as health, education and public safety, services which would presumably allow Indian communities to enjoy a standard of living comparable to that of other Americans.

This goal, of course, has never been achieved. But the special relationship between the Indian tribes and the Federal government which arises from these agreements continues to carry immense moral and legal force. To terminate this relationship would be no more appropriate than to terminate the citizenship rights of any other American.

The second reason for rejecting forced termination is that the practical results have been clearly harmful in the few instances in which termination actually has been tried. The removal of Federal trusteeship responsibility has produced considerable disorientation among the affected Indians and has left them unable to relate to a myriad of Federal, State and local assistance efforts. Their economic and social condition has often been worse after termination than it was before.

The third argument I would make against forced termination concerns the effect it has had upon the overwhelming majority of tribes which still enjoy a special relationship with the Federal government. The very threat that this relationship may someday be ended has created a great deal of apprehension among Indian groups and this apprehension, in turn, has had a blighting effect on tribal progress. Any step that might result in greater social, economic or political autonomy is regarded with suspicion by many Indians who fear that it will only bring them closer to the day when the Federal government will disavow its responsibility and cut them adrift.

In short, the fear of one extreme policy, forced termination, had often worked to produce the opposite extreme: excessive dependence on the Federal government. In many cases this dependence is so great that the Indian community is almost entirely run by outsiders who are responsible and responsive to Federal officials in Washington, D.C., rather than to the communities they are supposed to be serving. This is the second of the two harsh approaches which have long plagued our Indian policies. Of the Department of the Interior's programs directly serving Indians, for example, only 1.5 percent are presently under Indian control. Only 2.4 percent of HEW's° Indian health programs are run by Indians. The result is a burgeoning Federal bureaucracy, programs which are far less effective than they ought to be, and an erosion of Indian initiative and morale.

I believe that both of these policy extremes are wrong. Federal termination errs in one direction, Federal paternalism errs in the other. Only by clearly rejecting both of these extremes can we achieve a policy which truly serves the best interests of the Indian people. Self-determination among the Indian people can and must be encouraged without the threat of eventual termination. In my view, in fact, that is the only way that self-determination can effectively be fostered.

This, then, must be the goal of any new national policy toward the Indian people: to strengthen the Indian's sense of autonomy without threatening his sense of community. We must assure the Indian that he can assume control of his own life without being separated involuntarily for the tribal group. And we must make it clear that Indians can become independent of Federal control without being cut off from Federal concern and Federal support. My specific recommendations to the Congress are designed to carry out this policy. . . .

The recommendations of this Administration represent an historic step forward in Indian policy. We are proposing to break sharply with past approaches to Indian problems. In place of a long series of piecemeal reforms, we suggest a new and coherent strategy. In place of policies which simply call for more spending, we suggest policies which call for wiser spending. In place of policies which oscillate between the deadly extremes of forced termination and constant paternalism, we suggest a policy in which the Federal government and Indian community play complementary roles.

But most importantly, we have turned from the question of *whether* the Federal government has a responsibility to Indians to the question of *how* that responsibility can best be fulfilled. We have concluded that the Indians will get better

---

°The Department of Health, Education, and Welfare.

programs and that public monies will be more effectively expended if the people who are most affected by these programs are responsible for operating them.

The Indians of America need Federal assistance—this much has long been clear. What has not always been clear, however, is that the Federal government needs Indian energies and Indian leadership if its assistance is to be effective in improving the conditions of Indian life. It is a new and balanced relationship between the United States government and the first Americans that is at the heart of our approach to Indian problems. And that is why we now approach these problems with new confidence that they will successfully be overcome.

SUPREME COURT OF THE UNITED STATES
Oliphant v. Suquamish Indian Tribe (1978)

MR. JUSTICE REHNQUIST delivered the opinion of the Court.

. . . Located on Puget Sound across from the city of Seattle, the Port Madison Reservation [of the Suquamish Tribe] is a checkerboard of tribal community land, allotted Indian lands, property held in fee-simple by non-Indians, and various roads and public highwayss maintained by Kitsap County.[1]

Source: 435 U.S. 191 S. Ct. 1011, 55 L. Ed. 2d. 209; reprinted in David H. Getches, Charles F. Wilkinson, and Robert A. Williams, Jr., *Cases and Materials on Federal Indian Law,* 4th ed. (St. Paul: West Group, 1998), 532–39.

1. According to the District Court's findings of fact, "[T]he Port Madison Indian Reservation consists of approximately 7276 acres of which approximately 63% thereof is owned in fee-simple absolute by non-Indians and the remainder 37% is Indian owned lands subject to the trust status of the United States, consisting mostly of unimproved acreage upon which no persons reside. Residing on the reservation is an estimated population of approximately 2,928 non-Indians living in 976 dwelling units. There lives on the reservation approximately 50 members of the Suquamish Indian Tribe. Within the reservation are numerous public highways of the State of Washington, public schools, public utilities and other facilities in which neither the Suquamish Indian Tribe nor the United States has any ownership or interest." . . .

The Suquamish Indians are governed by a tribal government which in 1973 adopted a Law and Order Code. The Code, which covers a variety of offenses from theft to rape, purports to extend the Tribe's criminal jurisdiction over both Indians and non-Indians. Proceedings are held in the Suquamish Indian Provisional Court. Pursuant to the Indian Civil Rights Act of 1968, 25 U.S.C. § 1302, defendants are entitled to many of the due process protections accorded to defendants in federal or state criminal proceedings. However, the guarantees are not identical. Non-Indians, for example, are excluded from Suquamish tribal court juries.

Both petitioners are non-Indian residents of the Port Madison Reservation. Petitioner Mark David Oliphant was arrested by tribal authorities during the Suquamish's annual Chief Seattle Days celebration and charged with assaulting a tribal officer and resisting arrest. After arraignment before the tribal court, Oliphant was released on his own recognizance. Petitioner Daniel B. Belgarde was arrested by tribal authorities after an alleged high-speed race along the reservation highways that only ended when Belegarde collided with a tribal police vehicle. Belegarde posted bail and was released. Six days later he was arraigned and charged under the tribal code with "recklessly endangering another person" and injuring tribal property. Tribal court proceedings against both petitioners have been stayed pending a decision in this case. . . .

I

Respondents do not contend that their exercise of criminal jurisdiction over non-Indians stems from affirmative congressional authorization or treaty provision. Instead, respondents urge that such jurisdiction flows automatically from the "Tribe's retained inherent powers of government over the Port Madison Indian Reservation." . . .

The Suquamish Indian Tribe does not stand alone today in its assumption of criminal jurisdiction over non-Indians. Of the 127 reservation court systems that currently exercise criminal jurisdiction in the United States, 33 purport to extend that jurisdiction to non-Indians. . . .

The effort by Indian tribal courts to exercise criminal jurisdiction over non-Indians, however, is a relatively new phenomenon. And where the effort has been made in the past, it has been held that the jurisdiction did not exist. Until the middle of this century, few Indian tribes maintained any semblance of a formal court system. Offenses by one Indian against another were usually handled by social and religious pressure and not by formal judicial processes; emphasis was on restitution rather than on punishment. In 1834 the Commissioner of Indian Affairs described the then status of Indian criminal systems: "With the exception of two or three tribes, who have within a few years past attempted to establish some few laws and regulations amongst themselves, the Indian tribes are without laws, and the chiefs without much authority to exercise any restraint." H.R.Rep. No. 474, 23d Cong., 1st Sess., at 91 (1834).

It is therefore not surprising to find no specific discussion of the problem before us in the volumes of United States Reports. But the problem did not lie entirely dormant for two centuries. A few tribes during the 19th century did have formal criminal systems. From the earliest treaties with these tribes, it was apparently assumed that the tribes did not have criminal jurisdiction over non-Indians absent a congressional statute or treaty provision to that effect. For example, the 1830 Treaty with the Choctaw Indian Tribe, which had one of the most sophisticated of tribal structures, guaranteed to the Tribe "the jurisdiction and government of all the persons and property that may be within their limits." Despite the broad terms of this governmental guarantee, however, the Choctaws at the conclusion of this treaty provision "express a *wish* that Congress *may grant* to the Choctaws the right of punishing by their own laws any white man who shall come into their nation, and infringe any of their national regulations." Such a request for affirmative congressional authority is inconsistent with respondents' belief that criminal jurisdiction over non-Indians is inherent in tribal sovereignty. Faced by attempts of the Choctaw Tribe to try non-Indian offenders in the early-1800's the United States Attorneys General also concluded that the Choctaws did not have criminal jurisdiction over non-Indians absent congressional authority. See 2 Opinions of the Attorney General 693 (1834); 7 Opinions of the Attorney General 174 (1855). . . .

At least one court has previously considered the power of Indian courts to try non-Indians and it also held against jurisdiction. . . . *Ex parte Kenyon,* 14 Fed. Cases 353 (WD Ark. 1878). . . . The conclusion of Judge Parker was reaffirmed only recently in a 1970 Opinion of the Solicitor of the Department of the Interior. See 77 I.D. 113 (1970).

While Congress was concerned almost from its beginning with the special problems of law enforcement on the Indian reservations, it did not initially address itself to the problem of tribal jurisdiction over non-Indians. For the reasons previously stated, there was little reason to be concerned with assertions of tribal court jurisdiction over non-Indians because of the absence of formal tribal judicial systems. . . .

It was in 1834 that Congress was first directly faced with the prospect of Indians trying non-Indians. In the Western Territory Bill, Congress proposed to create an Indian territory beyond the western-directed destination of the settlers; the territory was to be governed by a confederation of Indian tribes and was expected ultimately to become a State of the Union. While the bill would have created a political territory with broad governing powers, Congress was careful not to give the tribes of the territory criminal jurisdiction over United States officials and citizens traveling through the area. The reasons were quite practical:

> Officers, and persons in the service of the United States, and persons required to reside in the Indian country by treaty stipulation, must necessarily be placed under the protection, and subject to the laws of the United States. To persons merely travelling in the Indian country the same protection is extended. The want of fixed laws, of competent tribunals of justice, which must for some time continue in the Indian country, absolutely requires for the peace of both sides that this protection be extended.

H.R.Rep. No. 474, 23d Cong., 1st Sess., at 18 (1834). Congress' concern over criminal jurisdiction in this proposed Indian Territory contrasts markedly with its total failure to address criminal jurisdiction over non-Indians on other reservations, which frequently bordered non-Indian settlements. The contrast suggests that Congress shared the view of the Executive Branch and lower federal courts that Indian tribal courts were without jurisdiction to try non-Indians.

This unspoken assumption was also evident in other congressional actions during the 19th century. [The opinion discusses amendments to the Nonintercourse Act in 1854 and the Major Crimes Act of 1885.]

. . . While Congress never expressly forbade Indian tribes to impose criminal penalties on non-Indians, we now make express our implicit conclusion of nearly a century ago that Congress consistently believed this to be the necessary result of its repeated legislative actions.

In a 1960 Senate Report, that body expressly confirmed its assumption that Indian tribal courts are without inherent jurisdiction to try non-Indians, and must depend on the Federal Government for protection from intruders. In considering a statute that would prohibit unauthorized entry upon Indian land for the purpose of hunting or fishing, the Senate Report noted:

> . . . One who comes on such lands without permission may be prosecuted under State law but a non-Indian trespasser on an Indian reservation enjoys immunity. *This is by reason of the fact that Indian tribal law is enforcible against Indians only; not against non-Indians.*
>
> *Non-Indians are not subject to the jurisdiction of Indian courts and cannot be tried in Indian courts on trespass charges.* Further, there are no Federal laws which can be invoked against trespassers. . . .

S.Rep. No. 1686, 86th Cong., 2d Sess., 2–3 (1960) (emphasis added).

II

While not conclusive on the issue before us, the commonly shared presumption of Congress, the Executive Branch, and lower federal courts that tribal courts do not have the power to try non-Indians carries considerable weight. "Indian law" draws principally upon the treaties drawn and executed by the Executive Branch and legislation passed by Congress. These instruments, which beyond their actual text form the backdrop for the intricate web of judicially made Indian law, cannot be interpreted in isolation but must be read in light of the common notions of the day and the assumptions of those who drafted them.

While in isolation the Treaty of Point Elliott, 12 Stat. 927 (1855), would appear to be silent as to tribal criminal jurisdiction over non-Indians, the addition of historical perspective casts substantial doubt upon the existence of such jurisdiction. In the Ninth Article, for example, the Suquamish "acknowledge their dependence on the Government of the United States." As Chief Justice Marshall explained in *Worcester v. Georgia*, 6 Pet. 515, 551–552, 554 (1832), such an acknowledgement is not a mere abstract recognition of the United States' sovereignty. "The Indian nations were, from their situation, necessarily dependent on [the United States] for their protection from lawless and injurious intrusions into their country." *Id.*, at 555. By acknowledging their dependence on the United States, in the Treaty of Point Elliott, the Suquamish were in all probability recognizing that the United States would arrest and try non-Indian intruders who came within their Reservation. Other provisions of the Treaty also point to the absence of tribal jurisdiction. Thus the Tribe "agree[s] not to shelter or conceal offenders against the laws of the United States, but to deliver them up to the authorities for trial." Read in conjunction with 18 U.S.C. § 1152, which extends federal enclave law to non-Indian offenses on Indian reservations, this provision implies that the Suquamish are to promptly deliver up any non-Indian offender, rather than try and punish him themselves.

By themselves, these treaty provisions would probably not be sufficient to remove criminal jurisdiction over non-Indians if the Tribe otherwise retained such jurisdiction. But an examination of our earlier precedents satisfies us that, even ignoring treaty provisions and congressional policy, Indians do not have criminal jurisdiction over non-Indians absent affirmative delegation of such power by Congress. Indian tribes do retain elements of "quasi-sovereign" authority after ceding their lands to the United States and announcing their dependence on the Federal Government. See *Cherokee Nation v. Georgia*, 5 Peters 1, 15 (1831). But the tribes' retained powers are not such that they are limited only by specific restrictions in treaties or congressional enactments. As the Court of Appeals recognized, Indian tribes are proscribed from exercising both those powers of autonomous states that are expressly terminated by Congress *and* those powers *"inconsistent with their status."*

Indian reservations are "a part of the territory of the United States." *United States v. Rogers,* 4 How. 567, 571 (1846). Indian tribes "hold and occupy [the reservations] with the assent of the United States, and under their authority." *Id.*, at 572. Upon incorporation into the territory of the United States, the Indian tribes thereby come under the territorial sovereignty of the United States and their exercise of separate power is constrained so as not to conflict with the interests of this overriding sovereignty. "[T]heir rights to complete sovereignty, as independent nations [are] necessarily diminished." *Johnson v. McIntosh,* 8 Wheat. 543, 574 (1823).

We have already described some of the inherent limitations on tribal powers that stem from their incorporation into the United States. In *Johnson v. McIntosh,* supra, we noted that the Indian tribes' "power to dispose of the soil at their own will, to whomsoever they pleased," was inherently lost to the overriding sovereignty of the United States. And in *Cherokee Nation v. Georgia,* supra, the Chief Justice observed that since Indian tribes are "completely under the sovereignty and dominion of the United States, . . . any attempt [by foreign nations] to acquire their lands, or to form a political connexion with them, would be considered by all as an invasion of our territory, and an act of hostility."

. . . Protection of territory within its external political boundaries is, of course, as central to the sovereign interest of the United States as it is to any other sovereign nation. But from the formation of the Union and the adoption of the Bill of Rights, the United States has manifested an equally great solicitude that its citizens be protected by the United States from unwarranted intrusions on their personal liberty. The power of the United States to try and criminally punish is an important manifestation of the power to restrict personal liberty. By submitting to the overriding sovereignty of the United States, Indian tribes therefore necessarily give up their power to try non-Indian citizens of the United States except in a manner acceptable to Congress. This principle would have been obvious a century ago when most Indian tribes were characterized by a "want of fixed laws [and] of competent tribunals of justice." H.R.Rep. No. 474, 23d Cong., 1st Sess., at 18 (1834). It should be no less obvious today, even though present-day Indian tribal courts embody dramatic advances over their historical antecedents.

In *Ex parte Crow Dog,* 109 U.S. 556 (1883), the Court was faced with almost the inverse of the issue before us here — whether, prior to the passage of the Major Crimes Act, federal courts had jurisdiction to try Indians who had offended against fellow Indians on reservation land. In concluding that criminal jurisdiction was exclusively in the tribe, it found particular guidance in the "nature and circumstances of the case." The United States was seeking to extend United States

> law, by argument and inference only, . . . over aliens and strangers; over the members of a community separated by race [and] tradition, . . . from the authority and power which seeks to impose upon them the restraints of an external and unknown code . . . ; which judges them by a standard made by others and not for them. . . . It tries them, not by their peers, nor by the customs of their people, nor the law of their land, but by . . . a different race, according to the law of a social state of which they have an imperfect conception. . . . *Id.* at 571.

These considerations, applied here to the non-Indian rather than Indian offender, speak

equally strongly against the validity of respondents' contention that Indian tribes, although fully subordinated to the sovereignty of the United States, retain the power to try non-Indians according to their own customs and procedure. . . .

. . . We recognize that some Indian tribal court systems have become increasingly sophisticated and resemble in many respects their state counterparts. We also acknowledge that with the passage of the Indian Civil Rights Act of 1968, which extends certain basic procedural rights to *anyone* tried in Indian tribal court, many of the dangers that might have accompanied the exercise by tribal courts of criminal jurisdiction over non-Indians only a few decades ago have disappeared. Finally, we are not unaware of the prevalence of non-Indian crime on today's reservations which the tribes forcefully argue requires the ability to try non-Indians. But these are considerations for Congress to weigh in deciding whether Indian tribes should finally be authorized to try non-Indians. They have little relevance to the principles which lead us to conclude that Indian tribes do not have inherent jurisdiction to try and punish non-Indians. The judgments below are therefore

Reversed.

MR. JUSTICE BRENNAN took no part in the consideration or decision of this case.

MR. JUSTICE MARSHALL, with whom The Chief Justice joins, dissenting.

I agree with the court below that the "power to preserve order on the reservation . . . is a sine qua non of the sovereignty that the Suquamish originally possessed." In the absence of affirmative withdrawal by treaty or statute, I am of the view that Indian tribes enjoy as a necessary aspect of their retained sovereignty the right to try and punish all persons who commit offenses against tribal law within the reservation. Accordingly, I dissent.

References

1. Peter C. Maxfield, "*Oliphant v. Suquamish Tribe:* The Whole Is Greater Than the Sum of the Parts," *Journal of Contemporary Law* 19 (1993), 391, quoted in David H. Getches, Charles F. Wilkinson, and Robert A. Williams, Jr., *Cases and Materials on Federal Indian Law*, 4th ed. (St. Paul: West Group, 1998), 542. See also N. Bruce Duthu, "Implicit Divestiture of Tribal Powers: Locating Legitimate Sources of Authority in Indian Country," *American Indian Law Review* 19 (1994), 353–402.

Suggested Readings

Castile, George Pierre. *To Show Heart: Native American Self-Determination and Federal Indian Policy, 1960–1975* (Tucson: University of Arizona Press, 1998).

Deloria, Vine, Jr., and Clifford M. Lytle. *American Indians, American Justice* (Austin: University of Texas Press, 1983).

Deloria, Vine, Jr., and Clifford M. Lytle. *The Nations Within: The Past and Future of American Indian Sovereignty* (New York: Pantheon, 1984).

Getches, David H., Charles F. Wilkinson, and Robert A. Williams, Jr. *Cases and Materials on Federal Indian Law,* 4th ed. (St. Paul: West Group, 1998), 532–43.

Pommershcim, Frank. *Braid of Feathers: American Indian Law and Contemporary Tribal Life* (Berkeley: University of California Press, 1995).

Wilkins, David E. *American Indian Sovereignty and the U.S. Supreme Court: The Masking of Justice* (Austin: University of Texas Press, 1997).

Tribal Colleges: Indian Education for Indian People

In a characteristically scathing indictment of Western education, the Lakota scholar Vine Deloria, Jr., criticizes American colleges for training professionals but not producing people. "Education," he writes, "is more than the process of imparting and receiving information, . . . it is the very purpose of human society and . . . human societies cannot really flower until they understand the parameters of possibilities that the human personality contains."[1] Many non-Indian educators share Deloria's sentiments, but the sense that Western education does not address the whole person has permeated Indian responses to non-Indian teachers and schools from colonial times to the present. Tribal colleges offer a more holistic approach to learning and the kind of education that young Indian people can rarely find in mainstream American colleges.

There are thirty-two tribally controlled community colleges in the United States, with about 30,000 students. They integrate Native American traditions into their curriculum, providing classes in tribal language, art, philosophy, and history at the same time they offer students access to the skills needed in the modern world. Most colleges have relatively small enrollments and minuscule budgets. Inadequate facilities and low salaries are typical, and college administrators sometimes struggle just to keep the doors open. But the colleges have impressive rates of success where federal education policies and mainstream colleges have failed. In the words of one study, more has been accomplished in the years "since the founding of the first tribal college to meet the higher education needs of the tribes and their members than in the two hundred years since the first Indian graduated from Harvard University."[2] One reporter called tribal colleges "underfunded miracles."[3] In Deloria's opinion, "tribal colleges may be the most important movement we have in Indian country today."[4]

The colleges are community institutions. They provide support services for students, many of whom are older and must overcome financial obstacles and competing family commitments to attend school and complete their degrees. They train people for work on and off the reservation, and also prepare students for transfer to four-year colleges, where their rate of success is far higher than that of Indian students who go directly from reservation communities. "While we want to give our graduates the ability to go anywhere they want," said Janine Pease-Pretty on Top, former president of Little Big Horn College on the Crow reservation, "we need them all desperately here on the reservation. Our first goal is to train young people to serve their own community: we need engineers, data processors, dental technicians, specialists in animal husbandry, premed, everything." Students study the Crow language and "come out of here knowing what it is to be Crow," she said, but they "must also pass college algebra."[5]

According to Paul Boyer, former editor of the journal *Tribal College* and author of a report on tribal colleges prepared after a two-year study for the Carnegie Foundation for the Advancement of Teaching, the colleges "are, deliberately, institutions that bridge two worlds. They are built on a foundation of tribal culture and values, but teach the knowledge of both Indian and non-Indian communities. In this way, they are cultural translators, sitting on the fulcrum between two very distinct societies."[6] In certain fundamental ways, says Deloria, "they are the only transitional institution standing between the reservation population and the larger society that can bring services and information to Indian people."[7]

In 2002, President George W. Bush vowed a new commitment to tribal colleges. Calling them "integral and essential" to their communities, the president signed an executive order creating the White House Initiative on Tribal Colleges and Universities and a President's Board of Advisers on Tribal Colleges and Universities.

▶ Questions for Consideration

1. Why and in what ways have tribal colleges succeeded where other institutions of higher education have failed?

2. What does the Carnegie report suggest about the abilities of communities to achieve important goals despite inadequate funding?

3. How do the colleges attempt to blend education and tradition?

4. Do tribal colleges appear to be realizing Luther Standing Bear's dream of a school built on the exchange of knowledge between Indian America and Anglo-America (see "Two Sioux School Experiences," page 383)?

5. What roles do colleges have to play in building communities and promoting tribal sovereignty?

THE CARNEGIE FOUNDATION
From *Tribal Colleges: Shaping the Future of Native America* (1989)

TRIBAL COLLEGES: A NEW ERA

The story of the Native American experience has been described, almost always, in the language of despair. Indian life is filled with images of poverty, and the government policy has consistently been called a failure. We often speak of "the plight of the Indians" and conclude with resignation that little can be done.

But there is in fact a lot that can be done. We report here on some of the great beginnings that have been accomplished for the Indians themselves, and offer recommendations for support that should be offered to help assure their continued support.

At the heart of the spirit of renewal among the Indian is a network of Native American colleges providing education and community service in a climate of self-determination. . . .

The challenges these institutions confront cannot be overstated. A typical tribal college necessarily charges low tuition but lacks a tax base to support the full education costs. Meanwhile, the limited federal support these colleges receive—the backbone of their funding—fails to keep pace with their enrollment growth. Classes at tribal colleges frequently are held in shabby buildings, even in trailers, and students often use books and laboratory equipment that are embarrassingly obsolete. At the same time, the colleges are educating many first-generation students who usually have important but competing obligations to their families and local communities.

Tribal colleges also offer vital community services—family counseling, alcohol abuse programs and job training—with little financial or administrative support. Successful programs frequently end abruptly because of budget cuts. Considering the enormously difficult conditions tribal colleges endure, with resources most collegiate institutions would find unacceptably restrictive, their impact is remarkable. It became unmistakably clear during our visits that, even as they struggle to fulfill their urgent mandates, tribal colleges are crucial to the future of Native Americans, and of our nation.

First, tribal colleges establish a learning environment that encourages participation by and builds self-confidence in students who have come to view failure as the norm. The attrition rate among Indian students, at both the school and college levels, greatly exceeds the rate for white students. Isolated by distance and culture, many have come to accept that they cannot complete school. College seems to many Native Americans an impossible dream. Tribal colleges offer hope in this climate of despair.

Second, tribal colleges celebrate and help sustain the rich Native American traditions. For many Americans, Indian culture is little more than images of tepees, peace pipes, and brightly colored rugs. But in many reservation communities, traditional cultural values remain a vital part of the social fabric. Tribal languages are still spoken, and traditional arts and crafts and spiritual beliefs are respected.

While non-Indian schools and colleges have long ignored Indian culture, tribal colleges view it as their curricular center. They argue that it is through a reconnection to these longstanding cultural skills and beliefs that Indians can build a strong self-image and participate, with confidence, in the dominant society. Each of the tribal colleges offers courses, sometimes taught by tribal elders, in native language, story-telling, history, and arts.

Third, tribal colleges provide essential services that enrich the communities surrounding them. These colleges are, in the truest sense, community institutions. Located on reservations, nearly all colleges offer social and economic programs for tribal advancement. Some offer adult education, including literacy tutoring, high school equivalency programs, and vocational training. Others work cooperatively with local businesses and industries to build a stronger economic base.

Fourth, the colleges are often centers for research and scholarship. Several have established cooperative programs with state universities to conduct scientific research, while others sponsor seminars and studies about economic development needs. . . .

These institutions have taken on a breathtaking array of responsibilities. As they move beyond their infancy, successes are now clearly visible; their value is well documented. But recognition and acceptance happen despite the federal government's benign neglect and a lack of national awareness of their merits. . . .

A PLACE FOR TRADITIONAL CULTURE

Tribal colleges, in sharp contrast to past federal policies, argue that there is still a central need for traditional culture.

Indeed, they view traditional culture as their social and intellectual frame of reference. These institutions have demonstrated eloquently that the traditional Indian cultures, rather than being disruptive or irrelevant, are supportive and nurturing influences on Indian students.

Individuals firmly rooted in their own heritage can participate with more confidence in the complex world around them. In this way, tribal colleges are "cultural translators," according to a counselor at one Indian college. "Many students need to learn how to fit into the twentieth century and still be a Chippewa," he said.

While American education policy towards Indians has matured considerably since the first students were enrolled, it was not until Indians themselves became participants in determining their future that true advancement and productive interaction began. Tribal colleges are a major part of this trend and their success in the future will, in a very real way, assure the continued emergence of a dynamic and self-sustaining Indian population.

EDUCATIONAL PHILOSOPHY AND CURRICULUM

All Indian-controlled colleges share a common goal of cultural understanding and tribal development, but there is diversity in educational philosophy from college to college and each curriculum reflects the priorities of that tribe. Each focuses on the needs of its own community and provides opportunity for students who choose to remain on the reservation.

A native studies program is a significant feature of all tribal colleges. Some students concentrate on native culture; others take courses in tribal languages, art, history, society, and politics, for personal understanding. Many colleges infuse a Native American perspective throughout the college and the curriculum. Navajo Community College, for example, has structured its campus and programs to reflect the traditional emphasis on the four compass points and values attached to each. Turtle Mountain Community College seeks to insert an Indian perspective in all of its courses.

In addition, most colleges offer a broad curriculum that provides a firm and rigorous general education. Not merely centers of vocational education, they provide a full range of academic courses that challenges what one tribal college president called the "good with their hands syndrome." . . .

THE TRIBAL COLLEGES IN CONTEXT

Tribal colleges play an important role in their local communities. But for the potential of these institutions to be fully understood, we must place them in the context of the larger Indian movement now building. There is a movement among Native Americans even more sweeping in its significance than the New Deal reforms. It's a movement that is resilient because it is self-directed. For the first time since becoming wards of the state 150 years ago, American Indians are building institutions and developing skills to control their own lives, a strategy that can, they believe, outlast Washington's shifting political winds.

Today's era of Indian self-determination reveals that constructive change in Indian society can occur when it is self-directed. Freed from aggressive abuse and misdirected intervention and ready to assert their cultural uniqueness in their own ways, American Indians are feeling a new spirit of opportunity and hope in many of their reservation communities. Tribal leaders are defining priorities of their own, and American Indian communities are combining, by their own choice, the values of two worlds — Indian and Anglo. While acknowledging that Indian society cannot retreat from the non-Indian culture, Native Americans have also reaffirmed those traditions and values that have sustained Indians for generations.

The emerging consensus is that you can be a lawyer and dance a pow-wow. "Cultural adaptation and change can take place if it is not forced and if there is a free interplay of ideas between cultures," according to researcher Jon Reyhner. In advocating self-determination in Indian educa-

tion, he declared: "Indian education must be a synthesis of the congruent strengths of the dominant and tribal cultures rather than a process of erasure of the Indian culture and the transference of American culture."

The impact of the current Indian movement is not just philosophical or legal, illustrated by the highly publicized claim of a legal right included in several treaties between the United States and these sovereign Indian nations. The influence of the movement is also inward, touching the quality of life on the reservation, providing tangible impact on the lives of Indian people. And the reinforcement of native culture has become a crucial part of this new movement.

NATIVE CULTURE: A FORCE FOR CHANGE

Anglo leaders of the past saw Indian culture as an annoying barrier to change. Today most leaders, both within and outside Indian society, recognize just that the opposite is true. Rather than being a hindrance, traditional culture is an important force for constructive change. But for much of white society, Indian culture still means little more than stereotypic childhood images of feathered Indians on the warpath. Native Americans are often seen as people of the past, identified by the artifacts they left behind. And in Indian Country today — the vast empty expanses of America's West where many reservations are found — these images are exploited for the tourist trade.

But beneath the surface, there are still the bonds of shared values and heritage that sustain Indian communities. Increasingly Native Americans are learning this lesson of self-identity, in a true renaissance of traditional culture. Albert White Hat, an instructor at the Rosebud Sioux Community College, stated: "We're trying to bring a positive image back. We're telling the young people that they can be proud of who they are and what they are. They don't necessarily have to wear a feather to be an Indian, but what is inside — how they look at themselves — is what's important. You know, traditions can be carried on whether you wear blue jeans or traditional costumes." . . .

COLLEGES THAT BUILD COMMUNITIES

Native Americans are constructing new and more supportive communities, and tribes are working to preserve the traditional values of their cultures. The Indians, having experienced the loss of so much of what bonds a society, feel an urgency to rediscover and rebuild. Strengthening their communities depends on retrieving and preserving traditions which have come close to extinction. The need for social bonding is deep-rooted and is one shared by all societies. Tribal colleges are working, not to return to the past, but to see the past as the foundation for a better present and a sounder future. In this way, reconciliation with the Native American heritage is as essential to Indian culture as an understanding of Jeffersonian thought is to Anglo-American culture.

In Indian society, as well as in the non-Indian world, education plays a central role in this search for interaction. According to Native American historian Jack Forbes, Indian-controlled colleges can fulfill the same cultural and social role in their communities that white-controlled colleges have traditionally provided in theirs. Tribally controlled colleges, in fact, are among the most successful examples of institutions that are rebuilding shared traditions. Like their community college counterparts across the United States, tribal colleges are expected to serve the needs of both individuals and communities. What we found remarkable is that while most of these institutions have existed for only a decade or less, they already provide their tribal societies with unity and human understanding that much of American society is still seeking.

Tribally controlled colleges are, at first glance, a study in diversity. Curricula, teaching styles, and campus architecture mirror the surrounding tribal cultures, each college possessing a unique character. Some focus on general education, others emphasize vocational training. A few have campuses that would be the envy of any small rural college, while others offer classes in mismatched trailers. Beyond the differences, all tribal colleges share common goals. They seek to strengthen respect for their cultural heritage, create greater social and economic opportunities for the tribe and its members, and create links to the larger American society. The watchword at Indian colleges is not simply education, but empowerment.

All tribal colleges seek first to rebuild, among students, an understanding of their heritage, and in some settings this has been a particularly challenging task. On many reservations, native beliefs, language, and traditional arts were not strong. Values once shared through a rich tradition of storytelling were not being preserved — traditional culture existed to a large degree only in textbooks, while Anglo values remained alien and unaccepted.

Tribal colleges are in the vanguard of a cultural renaissance in all of their communities. Courses in Native American culture are centerpieces. . . . They are the bridge to tribal unity and individual pride. . . a bridge to the past — and to the future, too. . . .

. . . In the larger American society the impact of a few hundred college graduates is difficult to see. But on the reservations with populations that range from three to eight thousand, the impact of new-found knowledge and expertise is pervasive. But the benefits of tribal colleges go far beyond job placement, as important as this is. In small communities, graduates can advance all of tribal society, and their value as role models is substantial. Graduates who remain on the reservations after graduation offer the seeds of social stability, economic growth, and future leadership. These tribal colleges offer more than a degree; they are the key to a healthy culture.

It must also be noted that the contribution of the colleges and their students goes far beyond the boundaries of their reservations. By offering services—ranging from day care and GED testing to alcohol counseling and literacy tutoring—tribal colleges have become a powerful, often the most powerful, social force in their communities. Indeed, on some reservations, the college is the only institution—government or tribal—that is examining all community needs, and working to provide real solutions. Graduates with knowledge and skills enrich all of American society. The country as a whole could learn from the tribal college's ability to connect to its society.

As the United States looks to rebuild a commitment to service and renewal, it could do no better than to examine the most dynamic and successful tribal colleges. Through the emphasis on traditional culture, social responsibility and economic development, these institutions have become the single most important force in their nations. In the end, college officials insist, all of American society benefits.

References

1. Vine Deloria, Jr., *Indian Education in America* (Boulder, Colo.: AISES, 1991), 20–21.
2. Norman T. Oppelt, *The Tribally Controlled Indian College: The Beginnings of Self-Determination in American Indian Education* (Tsaile, Ariz.: Navajo Community College Press, 1990), x.
3. "Tribal Colleges: Gains for 'Underfunded Miracles,'" *Christian Science Monitor,* 21 May 1997, 12.
4. Quoted in Margaret Connell Szasz, *Education and the American Indian: The Road to Self-Determination since 1928,* 3d ed. (Albuquerque: University of New Mexico Press, 1999), 239.
5. Quoted in Fergus M. Bordewich, *Killing the White Man's Indian: Reinventing Native Americans at the End of the Twentieth Century* (New York: Doubleday, 1996), 275–78. (At the time of the interview, her name was Pease-Windy Boy.)
6. Paul Boyer, "Tribal College of the Future," *Tribal College* 7, no. 1 (Summer 1995), 15.
7. Deloria quoted in Szasz, *Education and the American Indian,* 239.

Suggested Readings

Deloria, Vine, Jr. *Indian Education in America* (Boulder, Colo: AISES, 1991).

Oppelt, Norman T. *The Tribally Controlled Indian College: The Beginnings of Self-Determination in American Indian Education* (Tsaile, Ariz.: Navajo Community College Press, 1990).

Szasz, Margaret Connell. *Education and the American Indian: The Road to Self-Determination since 1928,* 3rd ed. (Albuquerque: University of New Mexico, 1999).

Tribal College: Journal of American Indian Higher Education.

Two Indian Leaders

$\Longrightarrow\!\bullet\!\Longleftarrow$

Throughout their history, Indian people and communities have struggled to adapt to new conditions. Some tribes, like the Navajos and Cherokees, have done so successfully time and time again in the face of recurrent setbacks and severe adversity. Successful adjustment has usually entailed balancing old and new, holding on to the past as well as embracing the future. As historian Frederick Hoxie noted from his study of Crow leadership during the difficult era around the beginning of the century, "political cultures respond to new environments and new pressures with a 'modern' version of their traditional culture."[1] Many tribal leaders still try to cope with a changing world in a manner consistent with tribal values and practices. The following autobiographical passages show the importance two prominent Indian leaders—Cherokee Wilma Mankiller, who served as Principal Chief of the Cherokee Nation of Oklahoma from 1985 to 1995, and Onondaga Oren Lyons—attach to traditional values and tribal history as guides to personal and political behavior in the modern world. Mankiller interspersed passages of Cherokee history in her autobiography; Lyons refers to the traditional beliefs of the Haudenosaunee or Iroquois and to the role expected of a leader by the laws of the Great League (see "The Iroquois Great League of Peace," pages 44–54).

Traditionally, the name *Mankiller* was a title conferred on Cherokee war leaders. Cherokee women who distinguished themselves, sometimes in battle, earned the title of *Ghigau* or "Beloved Woman." Perhaps the most famous Mankiller of the eighteenth century, Outacite, visited London as part of a Cherokee delegation to the king, but he has been surpassed in history by a namesake and beloved woman of the twentieth century. Wilma Mankiller is the first woman ever elected to the office of principal chief of the Cherokee Nation.

Wilma Mankiller was born in 1945 to a Cherokee father and a Dutch-Irish mother. One of eleven children, she grew up in rural poverty in Adair County, Oklahoma, in a house with no electricity or running water. The house was located on Mankiller Flats, a 160-acre allotment granted to her grandfather in 1907 when the federal government dismantled the Cherokee government, divided up the land, and created the state of Oklahoma. In 1956, the family moved to San Francisco under the BIA relocation program. Like many other young Indians of her generation, Mankiller found that mixing with other Indians in a new urban environment generated increased political consciousness and commitment to her Indian heritage, exactly the opposite of what the government hoped to achieve by its relocation program. She became active in the Indian rights movement in San Francisco, visiting Alcatraz during its occupation by Indian students.

Wilma Mankiller
Wilma Mankiller (b. 1945), the first woman to be elected chief of a major Indian tribe, and the Principal Chief of the Cherokee Nation for ten years. Photo © by James Schnepf.

In 1977, after divorcing her husband of eleven years, she returned to Oklahoma. She had two daughters, Felicia and Gina, no job, and no car. She began working for the Cherokee Nation as a volunteer, started new programs, and obtained grants to run them. In 1981, she became director of the Cherokee Nation Community Development Department and, in 1983, was elected deputy chief. Two years later, when President Reagan appointed Cherokee Chief Ross Swimmer head of the BIA, she stepped into the office he vacated. Critics gave her little chance of being elected in her own right, and she fought gender prejudice. The next year she married Charlie Soap, a Cherokee traditionalist and community worker, without whom she says her life "would have taken a very different path."[2]

Reelected to a four-year term in 1987, and reelected with more than 80 percent of the vote in 1991, Mankiller served as principal chief of the Cherokee Nation for ten years. During her tenure, she initiated a revitalization in Cherokee country. Tribal membership increased from 55,000 to 156,000; the number of tribal employees almost doubled to 1,271, and the tribal budget doubled to $86 million. The tribe built three health centers and added nine children's programs. Mankiller testified before Congress on issues ranging from health care to Indian sovereignty, and met with three presidents.[3] She compared her job as Cherokee chief to that of a chief executive officer running a small country.[4] "We are more of a republic than a reservation and exist in a complex set of laws in relationship to the U.S. government," she explained. "We view it as a dual citizenship."[5] Mankiller brought to politics a strong belief in the importance of maintaining traditional values and applying them to the solution of contemporary problems. She also brought a belief in a leadership role for women in politics. "Women can help turn the world right side up," she told an audience in Denver in 1994. "We bring a more collaborative approach to government. And if we do not participate, then decisions will be made for us."[6] *Ms.* magazine named her Woman of the Year in 1987 and she was inducted into the

National Women's Hall of Fame in 1993. In 1998, President Clinton awarded her the Medal of Freedom — the highest civilian award given by the U.S. government — in recognition of her extraordinary efforts on behalf of Indian-peoples.

In her book, *Mankiller,* written with journalist Michael Wallis, she relates her personal odyssey from childhood in rural Oklahoma, to life as an unhappy housewife in the San Francisco area, through the civil rights struggles of the 1960s, back to the Cherokee Nation in the late 1970s, and into national and international prominence in the 1980s and 1990s. She weaves her own story with the history of the Cherokee people. It was, she said, inconceivable to do it any other way.[7] Her own life story of struggle, courage, and triumph in the face of adversity parallel a larger struggle by Indian peoples to overcome the legacies of the past. "We will," says Mankiller, "enter the 21st century more on our own terms than we have entered any other century."[8] Chad Smith, elected chief in 1999, led the Cherokees into the new century committed to building a Cherokee future on Cherokee terms and using Cherokee talent.[9]

In 1979, Wilma Mankiller was involved in a freak head-on collision with a car driven by her best friend, Sherry Morris. Morris died; Mankiller almost died. Surgeons operated seventeen times and at one point considered amputating her right leg. A year after the accident, she was diagnosed with myasthenia gravis, a debilitating disease of the nervous system. In 1989, she was hospitalized with a severe kidney infection and the next year underwent a kidney transplant. In the winter of 1996, while a fellow at Dartmouth College, she was diagnosed with lymphoma, a form of cancer, but has since battled her health problems successfully.

The extracts from her autobiography reprinted here focus on her term as deputy chief and her election as principal chief in her own right. In the words of historian Theda Perdue, Mankiller's courage in the face of adversity and her service to her community embodied the values of past generations of Cherokee women, values that had survived recurrent assault. Mankiller herself believes she could not have achieved what she did had it not been for the ordeals she suffered and survived: "After that, I realized I could survive anything," she said. "I had faced adversity and turned it into a positive experience — a better path. I had found the way to be of good mind."[10]

Oren Lyons was born in 1930. After a career as a commercial artist in New York City, he returned to Onondaga to take up the duties of Faithkeeper of the Turtle Clan, one of whose mandates is to keep alive the traditions and stories of his people. He sits in the Grand Council of Chiefs of the Six Nations. He holds a B.A. from Syracuse University and an honorary law degree from City University of New York. A writer and teacher, he also serves as director of Native American Studies at the State University of New York at Buffalo. He has spoken before congressional and United Nations committees in defense of Iroquois rights and indigenous sovereignty, and has long argued for the need to adopt a Native perspective in confronting environmental issues. "Exploitation of the earth without regard to the seventh generation to come" has produced "a very bleak future," says Lyons. "What about that seventh generation?" he asked years ago. "Where are you taking them? What will they have?"[11] His questions remain unanswered.

▶ Questions for Consideration

1. What do Mankiller and Lyons regard as the major challenges confronting Indian people?

2. In what ways do they find indigenous solutions to modern-day problems?

3. To what extent do the duties and character of a chief as described by Lyons reflect the ideals of chieftainship as outlined in "The Iroquois Great League of Peace," pages 44–54?

4. Mankiller and Lyons both stress the power and the necessity of being "of good mind." What does this phrase mean? How can something that seems so simple serve as a guide in the fast-paced and complex modern world?

WILMA MANKILLER
"Returning the Balance" (1993)

"I, Wilma P. Mankiller, do solemnly swear, or affirm, that I will faithfully execute the duties of Principal Chief of the Cherokee Nation. And will, to the best of my abilities, preserve, protect, and defend the Constitutions of the Cherokee Nation and the United States of America. I swear, or affirm, further that I will do everything within my power to promote the culture, heritage, and tradition of the Cherokee Nation.". . .

Source: Wilma Mankiller and Michael Wallis, *Mankiller: A Chief and Her People* (New York: St. Martin's Press, 1993), 242–51. Copyright © 1993 by Wilma Pearl Mankiller and Michael Wallis. Reprinted with the permission of St. Martin's Press, Inc.

By the time I took the oath of office, my eldest daughter, Felicia, had married, and I had my first grandchild, Aaron Swake. I was a forty-year-old grandmother, as well as the first woman to serve as chief of a major tribe. I told the reporters, who seemed to materialize from out of nowhere, that the only people who were really worried about my serving as chief were members of my family. That was because all of them knew very well how much time I tended to devote to my job. My daughters were, of course, concerned about my health. But my little grandson thought it was great that his grandma was the chief. . . .

One thing that I never tried to become as chief was "one of the boys," nor am I a "good ol' girl." I never will be. That goes against my grain. I do know how to be political and to get the job done, but I do not believe that one must sacrifice one's principles. Gradually, I noticed changes within the tribe and especially within the council.

Rural development was, and still remains, a high priority on my list of goals. For me, the rewards came from attempting to break the circle of poverty. My feeling is that the Cherokee people, by and large, are incredibly tenacious. We have survived so many major political and social upheavals, yet we have kept the Cherokee government alive. I feel confident that we will march into the twenty-first century on our own terms.

We are staffed with professionals — educators, physicians, attorneys, business leaders. Already, in the 1800s, we fought many of our wars with lawsuits, and it was in the courts where many of our battles were won. Today, we are helping to erase the stereotypes created by media and by western films of the drunken Indian on a horse, chasing wagon trains across the prairie. I suppose some people still think that all native people live in tepees and wear tribal garb every day. They do not realize that many of us wear business suits and drive station wagons. The beauty of society today is that young Cherokee men and women can pursue any professional fields they want and remain true to traditional values. It all comes back to our heritage and our roots. It is so vital that we retain that sense of culture, history, and tribal identity.

We also are returning the balance to the role of women in our tribe. Prior to my becoming chief, young Cherokee girls never thought they might be able to grow up and become chief themselves. That has definitely changed. From the start of my administration, the impact on the younger women of the Cherokee Nation was noticeable. I feel certain that more women will assume leadership roles in tribal communities. . . .

In 1987, after I had fulfilled the balance of Ross Swimmer's term as chief, I made the decision to run on my own and to win a four-year term of office. It was not an easy decision. I knew the campaign would be most difficult. I talked to my family and to my people. I spent long hours discussing the issues with Charlie Soap, whom I had married in 1986. Charlie had contracted with private foundations to continue development work with low-income native community projects. His counsel to me was excellent. He encouraged me to run. So did many other people.

But there were others who were opposed to my continuing as chief. Even some of my friends and advisers told me they believed the Cherokee people would accept me only as deputy, not as an elected principal chief. Some of those people came to our home at Mankiller Flats. I would look out the window and see them coming down the dirt road to tell me that I should give up any idea of running for chief. Finally, I told Charlie that if one more family came down that road and told me not to run, I was going to run for sure. That is just what happened.

I made my official announcement in early 1987, calling for a "positive, forward-thinking campaign." I chose John A. Ketcher, a member of the tribal council since 1983, as my running mate for the June 20 election. In 1985, John had been elected by the council to succeed me as deputy chief when I became principal chief. An eleven-sixteenths bilingual Cherokee, John was born in southern Mayes County in 1922. A veteran of World War II and a graduate of Northeastern State University in Tahlequah, Ketcher, as I do, considered unity and economic development to be the two priorities for the Cherokee Nation. . . .

I drew three opponents in the race for principal chief. I had to face Dave Whitekiller, a postal assistant from the small community of Cookson and a former councilman; William McKee, deputy administrator at W.W. Hastings Indian Hospital, in Tahlequah; and Perry Wheeler, a former deputy chief and a funeral home director from Sallisaw, in Sequoyah County.

From the beginning, the best description of the campaign came from someone on the council, who said there was an "undercurrent of viciousness." I ignored things that were going on around me. I did the same thing I had always done — went out to the communities and talked to as many of the Cherokee people as possible about the issues. I tried to answer all their questions. My critics claimed that I had failed to properly manage and direct the Cherokee Nation, which was obviously false. Our revenue for 1986 was up $6 million, higher than it had ever been to that point. I was not about to lose focus by warring with my opponents.

The election eliminated all the candidates except for Perry Wheeler and me. None of us had received more than 50 percent of the votes. I had polled 45 percent to Wheeler's 29 percent. We had to face each other in a July runoff. My supporters worked very hard during those last few weeks. Charlie was one of my main champions. On my behalf, Charlie visited many rural homes where English is a second language to remind the people that prior to the intrusion of white men, women had played key roles in our government. He asked our people to not turn their backs on their past or their future.

Charlie's help was especially important because I was stricken with my old nemesis, kidney problems, during the final weeks of the campaign. Finally, just before the election, I had to be hospitalized in Tulsa, but the physicians never determined the exact location of the infection and could not bring it under control. The lengthy infection and hospitalization would nearly cost me not only the election but also my life, since it brought on extensive and irreversible kidney damage. From that point forward, I was repeatedly hospitalized for kidney and urinary-tract infections, until I underwent surgery and had a kidney transplant in 1990.

Wheeler, an unsuccessful candidate for the chief's job against Ross Swimmer in 1983, tried to make my hospitalization a major issue. He waged a vigorous and negative runoff campaign. He publicly stated that I had never been truthful about my health. It all reminded me of the way Swimmer had been attacked when he was battling cancer. Wheeler, whom I can best describe as an old-style politician, also made claims that I had not hired enough Cherokee people for what he called the higher-paying tribal posts. . . .

When all the ballots from thirty-four precincts plus the absentee votes were tallied, the woman who supposedly knew nothing about politics was declared the winner. The night of the runoff election, we went to the Tulsa Powwow, where my daughter Gina was being honored. In a photograph taken that evening, Charlie, Gina, Felicia, and I look very tired and worn, as if we had just been through a battle. Later that night, we returned to Tahlequah to check on the election results. When the votes of the local precincts were counted, it appeared that I had won easily. Everyone around me was celebrating, but I was concerned about the absentee votes. Once that vote was included, I allowed myself to celebrate.

At last, the Cherokee Nation had elected its first woman as principal chief — the first woman chief of a major Native American tribe. I had outpolled Wheeler, and John Ketcher had retained his post as deputy chief. Wheeler conceded victory to me shortly before midnight.

At long last, I had the mandate I had wanted. I had been chosen as principal chief of the Cherokee Nation by my own people. It was a sweet victory. Finally, I felt the question of gender had been put to rest. Today, if anyone asks members of our tribe if it really matters if the chief is male or female, the majority will reply that gender has no bearing on leadership. . . .

If I am to be remembered, I want it to be because I am fortunate enough to have become my tribe's first female chief. But I also want to be remembered for emphasizing the fact that we have indigenous solutions to our problems. Cherokee values, especially those of helping one another and of our interconnections with the land, can be used to address contemporary issues.

OREN LYONS
"It Is in Our Hands" (1997)

My name is Jo-Ag-Quis-Ho, which is an old name. It comes from the Wolf Clan. My clan is the Wolf, but as I sit in council as a chief of the Onondaga Nation, I sit on behalf of the Turtle Clan. I'm what they called a "borrowed chief." The Turtles have borrowed me for twenty-four years. When I die, that name will be up for use again.

I was brought up in the Onondaga Nation territory my whole life, and I still live there. My grandmother lived there, my mother lives there, all my relations are there. I remember the Onondaga Indian school as a sort of an outpost of white people on Indian land. We all looked upon it as a battlefield of wills. I remember some of the principals attempted to change our direction forcibly, but we've always been independent and managed to survive.

We had one extraordinary woman who taught my father and our children after. But I also remember the hostility from other non-Indian teachers. Eventually I just dropped out of school. They didn't like me and I didn't like them. I'd rather hunt and fish. That was my school for the next seven years.

I grew up as a hunter, in the woods. They've been my best teacher throughout all of life. My father was a good hunter and I learned from him. He left the family when I was quite young, but he was a good influence on my life. I learned from myself, too, just being in the woods.

I grew up having to help feed a family. I had six brothers, one sister, and my mother. My

Source: Lois Crozier-Hogle and Darryl Babe Wilson, eds., *Surviving in Two Worlds: Contemporary Native American Voices* (Austin: University of Texas Press, 1997), 12–18. Copyright © 1997 by Lois Crozier-Hogle, Darryl Babe Wilson, and Jay Liebold. Reprinted with the permission of University of Texas Press.

mother was very, very strong. She held the family together. The entire family owes her everything.

I was the oldest. I spent many days and years in the woods with my shotgun. I learned to respect everything, how bountiful it is, a place where you can have true peace. It's a shame we're losing that. Some of our children may not have the privilege of knowing a real woods, a real forest, at the rate we're going.

I grew up in hardwood country. There's a lot of maple, oak, hickory, ironwood, poplar. I grew up in that area where you have real strong falls and real strong springs. Clear seasons. Cold winters and hot summers. Central New York is a beautiful place. It's the place we chose to stay and live from the beginning, and by good luck and good fortune we're still there. The hills still furnish us with what we need.

My mother was a Christian. My father was a longhouse chief. He was the Faithkeeper. They never had any problems. There were never any arguments. I remember him saying to my mother, "All I ask of you is that when we have the ceremonies, you are there with the children to make sure they behave." I learned to respect everyone's beliefs.

I always looked up to the chiefs. I remember as a young boy of six or seven, walking up to Chief George Thomas's house. He was the head of the Six Nation Confederacy. I remember knocking on his door. He was a big man and his wife was very kind. He looked at me and I said, "I want you to tell me about the nation. How does it work?"

He took me inside and gave me something to drink and we spent a little time. I don't remember much of the conversation. He said, "Keep coming to the longhouse. You'll learn."

I knew when there was smoke coming out of the longhouse, the chiefs were meeting. That always made me feel good. I wondered what they did there. The door was always open, so I'd peek in and see them sitting there. It was kind of scary so I usually wouldn't go in.

It seems like all of our people have very strong identity and strong vision. I don't think anybody trains us to it. Maybe the fact that we have the longhouse and our traditions and ceremonies helps.

I got my high school equivalency in the army, and I went to the University of Syracuse on an art and athletic scholarship. I was a bit rebellious as a child, but my art was pretty good. It seems to run in the family. If I had my preference, I'd be an artist. I never intended to be a teacher. I made the dean's list because I was a good artist, and I won several athletic awards, which surprised everybody, including myself.

When you become educated, it's important to be grounded in who you are. Once you are secure in your own identity, then you can learn anything anywhere in the world. But if you're not secure in your identity, when you go into a university you become whatever the university is. It is important to have pride in your own heritage. Know who you are first. Know your nation, your history, your clan and family. Even if you learn all you can in school, it's only half of what you already have.

When I came out of the army, Coach Roy Simmons at Syracuse University asked if I would consider playing lacrosse for them. He had a lot to do with my development outside of the territory. I learned patience from that man.

Patience is manifested in Indian life. I learned patience by hunting. I would sit still for hours. If you can sit still for hours, you learn something. But I learned patience from Coach Simmons, too. He had a lot of confidence in my abilities.

Lacrosse is a major tradition with the Iroquois. It's played around the world, but it originated with us. We call it "the Creator's game." There are two sides to it. We use it as a medicine game, and also for entertainment.

A whole community revolves around lacrosse. I love the game. It's one of the gifts we've given to the world. As a matter of fact, we made all the sticks, until plastics came in. All the universities came to the Six Nations. I still use a wood stick.

I played from 1945 to 1972. Last summer we took the Iroquois national team to Australia and competed as a nation against the United States, Canada, Australia, and England. It was the first time an indigenous nation participated. On the day of the games, our flag went up and everyone's hats went off to us. That was a great day for indigenous people.

When I was put up as a chief in 1967, it was a lifetime commitment. It says you will put the interests of your people ahead of your own interests. We must make our own living and do the work as well. The chiefs do not receive a salary. That makes for a quality leader.

I see spirituality simply as a service. Growing up, getting away from your own self and turning your concerns to other people. People who are out there doing service are about as spiritual as you can be.

The spiritual beliefs are in our ceremonies in the longhouse. I've been brought up with that all my life. When the people see the chief there, there's great attendance. That's how we carry on. We don't sit down and talk about spiritual beliefs. We just do what we're supposed to do. We sing the songs and carry on the ceremonies.

We are instructed to give thanks. We do our ceremonies and give thanks around the calendar. We have just completed our thanksgiving for the maple. The next thanksgiving will be for the first fruit, the strawberry, then the beans and squash, and then the green corn. After that will be the harvest, then the winter ceremony. The children see this and they gain the same respect. Eventually they understand it.

The earth is our mother. We believe that. I've met indigenous people from around the world and I've yet to find a difference of opinion on that.

It's much more than a saying, it's much more than a word, it's a real compassion and a longevity.

There's never a time when we're not in some kind of communication with the earth. The ceremonies are the best way to be in close communion. It's a reminder in the community from the smallest child to the oldest person. You pay your respects for what life is all about.

It's imperative that we carry on the ceremonies. As long as we do, life will continue. But we are coming to times now when some of our people are starting to lose that. The world is in flux, and there's a danger of losing touch entirely.

Indians have been losing touch by attrition. It's not that the Indians wanted to do it, it's not as if we were just benignly standing by and watching it happen. It's been a policy of the federal government. They took our language away, they forced our children out, they moved people about, taking them away from the earth—I mean, what do you expect? It's amazing that we do have any connection at all at this point.

These past few years we've had some serious disruptions. Some of our young people took this idea of independence and coupled it with economics. They picked up the idea of becoming powerful through commerce. They got into the idea of high-stakes gambling, casinos, smuggling. Mohawks have been fighting among themselves because of that influence. They've been victims of this commerce and it's very disruptive.

We're getting hooked in, just like the white man. They have gotten to our young people. We see them carrying automatic weapons and firing at their own people through the influence of organized crime. Are you going to blame Indian people for that when there's such outside pressure?

It's not so easy just to come back. It's not a simple thing. You have to deal with the communities. You have to stand there with your arms folded and say to them, "Whatever possessed you?"

The Indians are losing the high moral ground they used to hold. Some still hold that ground.

The elders do, the traditional Circle of Elders. But we're losing those values. I know from my experience that I don't have near the knowledge of the elders. Although I'm getting older, I'm lacking in fundamental knowledge. If I don't have it, how will it go on to the next generation? If things don't turn around now, there won't be any teachers left.

The only power that's left to maintain the planet is the spiritual power. Spiritual power will outlast and outgrow the manifestations of economics, although it may be at severe penalty of human life. There isn't going to be a winner. You can't think in those terms.

The instruction for the Haudenosaunee chief is that we must make all of our decisions on behalf of the seventh generation that is coming. They must be able to enjoy life to the same degree that we have it here. We should not think only in terms of ourselves or our families or even our nation. We're talking about life itself on this earth. We're talking about animal life, the water, life as we see it in the world around us.

We don't question spiritual instructions. Someone might ask, "Why is it the seventh generation?" They will never get an answer. I don't know why the seventh. We just take it on faith.

We have an instruction and it's very clear. You'll find that in all the Indian territories. Everywhere I go, we are welcomed into ceremonies by the Lakota, Hopi, or any Indian nation. We don't have to have an explanation of how they live or what their principles are. That's a unity that we'd like to extend to the rest of the world.

Our prophecies say it's a very hard future we're looking at. We've been told that it's inevitable that man is going to destroy himself. It's similar to the vision Black Elk° had. There were

---

°The Oglala holy man whose teaching's were recorded in the 1930s and 1940s by the writer and poet, John G. Neihardt. John G. Neihardt, *Black Elk Speaks: Being the Life Story of a Holy Man of the Oglala Sioux* (Lincoln: University of Nebraska Press, 1988).

only the stumps of trees. The grass was no longer green and the color was brown. There were no leaves, no animals; there was devastation. One of our leaders, a man named Ganiodaio, "Handsome Lake," was shown these visions. He said the same thing: "This will happen, inevitably. Just don't let it be your generation."

That means that as long as each generation strives, works, and does what it is supposed to do, there will be continuity. It puts it squarely in the hands of each generation. The generation that lets this happen will suffer beyond description. That's all there is to it.

There will never be peace until we stop making war on Mother Earth. We are bound to her from birth until death. When we lose the rhythm of the seasons and the moon, we are in trouble. It is up to the people to bring things back into balance. The next generation will make a difference as to whether life will continue on the earth.

If we can get the leaders of this nation to look seven generations ahead, we can have a change of direction. But the world is at dire risk at this moment. There has to be a new paradigm of life. As I sit here, I think of my people back home who still carry water in buckets. There is a great disparity in this land. Somewhere there has to be a sharing. We have to change this idea of supremacy of human beings as the ultimate authority. The human being is given a great deal of responsibility and he's not carrying that out at all.

I'm a champion of the continuation of the indigenous voice of sovereign Native nations. They have a lot to offer. The first basic principle of Native nations is peace. The second is equality and justice for the people. The third principle is discussion—the power of good minds. We hope to impart that.

We're publishing a book called *Exiled in the Land of the Free.*° We decided to do this book when the United States was taking these big bows for the two-hundredth anniversary of the Constitution. We said, "Wait a minute, we'd better step in here and explain where democracy came from."

It certainly didn't come over on the boats of the Europeans, because they were fleeing kings and queens who were burning people at the stake. So where was the land of the free? Well, everybody here was free. Freedom was rampant here in the whole of North America. We didn't know anything else. We had true democracy and we had respect, personal respect and honor. We didn't write anything down because the spoken word would be honored. A spoken commitment was enough. More than enough.

So that process of having power with the people is an old one with us. The leaders do not really have any power. We don't have a police force, we don't have an army, so there's no way for us to enforce anything. We can only present and persuade the people, and a chief is servant of the people.

It's a lifelong work of serving the people. No, it's hard work. Nobody wants to be chief.

°Oren Lyons, et al., *Exiled in the Land of the Free: Democracy, Indian Nations, and the U.S. Constitution* (Santa Fe: Clear Light Publishers, 1992).

References

1. Frederick E. Hoxie, "Building a Future on the Past: Crow Indian Leadership in an Era of Division and Reunion," in Walter Williams, ed., *Indian Leadership* (Manhattan, Kan.: Sunflower University Press, 1984), quote at 84.
2. Wilma Mankiller and Michael Wallis, *Mankiller: A Chief and Her People* (New York: St. Martin's Press, 1993), ix.

3. *New York Times,* 6 April 1994.

4. *The Dartmouth,* 19 April 1994.

5. *Los Angeles Times,* 1 November 1993.

6. Mankiller and Wallis, *Mankiller,* 242.

7. Comments at Native American Studies Colloquium, Dartmouth College, Winter 1996.

8. *The Dartmouth,* 24 January 1996.

9. Chad Smith, "Rebuilding a Nation," public talk at Dartmouth College, November 1999.

10. Theda Perdue, *Cherokee Women: Gender and Culture Change, 1700–1835* (Lincoln: University of Nebraska Press, 1998), 195; Mankiller and Wallis, *Mankiller,* 229.

11. Oren Lyons, "An Iroquois Perspective," in Christopher Vecsey and Robert W. Venables, eds., *American Indian Environments: Ecological Issues in Native American History* (Syracuse, N.Y.: Syracuse University Press, 1980), 171–74.

Suggested Readings

Edmunds, R. David. *The New Warriors: Native American Leaders since 1900* (Lincoln: University of Nebraska Press, 2001).

Lyons, Oren, et al. *Exiled in the Land of the Free: Democracy, Indian Nations, and the U.S. Constitution* (Santa Fe: Clear Light Publishers, 1992).

Mankiller, Wilma and Michael Wallis. *Mankiller: A Chief and Her People* (New York: St. Martin's Press, 1993).

Mascots and Playing Indian

Non-Indians have "played Indian" at least since colonists donned Indian attire and dumped British tea in Boston harbor. In modern days, troubled by environmental degradation, postindustrial society, and a host of other ills in the world, many people continue to "turn" to Indians. Emulating what they believe to be Indian ways, they hope they will somehow acquire greater wisdom, live at one with the earth, reconnect with their better inner selves, find freedom, or give themselves a new identity. Some Indians cater to this desire to "play Indian" by staging ceremonies, conducting sweatbaths, and bestowing Native wisdom for a price. Many more are bemused by it, while others are enraged by what they regard as continuing colonial exploitation and cultural appropriation. Whatever the motivations and meanings of "playing Indian," it generates images and ideas about "Indianness" that can be damaging and troubling for Indian people themselves.[1]

In April 1999, the federal Trademark Trial and Appeal Board voided the trademark rights of the Washington Redskins on the basis that the team's name and logo were disparaging to Native Americans and therefore violated the law. The case, initiated seven years earlier by a group of Native Americans that included Vine Deloria, Jr., and Susan Shown Harjo, was probably the most publicized of an ongoing series of attempts by Indian people to get professional, college, and high school sports teams, and other groups and organizations, to stop using Indian names, mascots, and logos to help rally support or market their products. Dartmouth College, the University of Oklahoma, and Stanford University retired their Indian mascots in the 1970s (although, at least at Dartmouth, pockets of resistance to the change remain and individual displays of the old Indian symbol are a recurrent problem). But the University of Illinois, Florida State University, and many other universities and colleges continue to use Indian names, symbols, and logos, while fans wear "war paint," perform "war dances" and chants, and, literally, "drum up" support. In face of protests and complaints from Indian people, many high schools have changed the names of their sports

Chief Wahoo
Many sports teams continue to use Indian symbols and mascots, despite protests that such images are offensive and dehumanizing. Supporters sometimes argue that the use of Indian symbols is meant to "honor" Indian people. "Chief Wahoo," above, is the logo of the Cleveland Indians baseball team. Cleveland Indians.

Mascot Protester at Super Bowl
A 12-year-old Anishinaabe boy joins protesters at the 1992 Superbowl in Minneapolis, where the Washington Redskins played the Buffalo Bills. © Eric Haase/Contact Press Images.

teams from "Chiefs," "Warriors," and "Braves" and have dropped the use of Indian symbols; others refuse to change. And despite the April 1999 finding, sports fans and the general public regularly see derogatory depictions of Indian people and culture whenever the Washington Redskins, Kansas City Chiefs, Chicago Blackhawks, Cleveland Indians, and Atlanta Braves play.

Many non-Indians find it difficult to understand why Indian people get so upset about these representations. With so many problems to confront, they say, don't Indians have anything better to do? Other people tell Indians, and themselves, that the caricatures and grotesque performances they use are intended to "honor" the country's first peoples.

Some Indian people are not bothered by these images, and some Indian teams use Indian logos themselves. Most, however, find them offensive and demeaning, believing that their use points to deep issues of power and racism that still pervade American society and popular culture. Stereotypical images dehumanize Indian people by reducing them to props and invoking them for their association with "wildness," violence, or supposed physical attributes. For many non-Indians, who never meet a real Indian person, these clichés come to represent all that it means to be Indian. Like the racist stereotypes that have been served up to the general public by movies and television, they adversely affect daily human relationships and individual self-esteem, and feed into "more tangible" problems such as alcohol abuse, college and high school dropout rates, unemployment, poverty, and, some would argue, the treatment of Native people by state and local government and of Native issues by the courts.[2]

Using Indian mascots and dressing up in paint and feathers for a sports event constitutes the most contested example of "playing Indian," which in its many forms ranges from role playing by children through cultural appropriation to outright racism.

Tim Giago, editor of the *Lakota Times* (which became *Indian Country Today*) is just one of many Indian people who have written and spoken out against the continued use of Indian symbols and mascots. Like many others, he understood that, while there were die-hard opponents, many Americans needed to be "educated" to see the issue in different ways.

▶ **Questions for Consideration**

1. What arguments and tactics does Giago employ in this article written shortly before the Columbus Quincentennial? How effective are his arguments?

2. Are there counterarguments that stand in the face of his criticisms?

3. Why do these issues appear to have such staying power in American society?

TIM GIAGO
Mascots, Spirituality, and Insensitivity (1991)

Indians as mascots has been a point of contention for many years among Native Americans.

Most of our ranting and raving has fallen on deaf ears lo these many years.

Suddenly, as the Atlanta Braves fought their way to the World Series, other voices picked up our indignant shouts and the issue has taken on national stature.

As a columnist and newspaper editor, these are things we have struggled to get on the front pages of the national media for years and we are pleased to see it become a national issue.

As an American Indian writer who has spent much of his life "covering the coverage," it does my heart good to get this kind of support, support vitally needed by the Indian people if we are to see change.

The media has centered its attention on whether the sham rituals and painted faces in the stands at Braves' baseball games border on racism. In our minds (Indians) it does, but there is another side of this coin I have written about that needs to be expanded at this time.

Source: Time Giago, *Lakota Times,* 23 October 1991.

The sham rituals, such as wearing of feathers, smoking of so-called peace pipes, beating of tom-toms, fake dances, horrendous attempts at singing Indian songs, the so-called war whoops, and the painted faces, address more than the issue of racism. They are direct attacks upon the spirituality (religion) of the Indian people.

Suppose a team like the New Orleans Saints decided to include religious rituals in their half-time shows in keeping with their name. Would different religious groups feel insulted to see these rituals on national television?

For instance: suppose Saints' fans decided to emulate Catholicism as part of their routine. What if they carried crosses, had a mascot dressed up like the Pope, spread ashes on their forehead, and displayed enlarged replicas of the sacramental bread of Holy Communion while drinking from chalices filled with wine?

Would Catholics consider these routines anti-Catholic?

Eagle feathers play an important role in the spirituality of Native Americans. Faces are painted in a sacred way.

The Pipes that became known to the white man as "peace pipes" are known to most Indians who use them as part of their spirituality as Sacred Pipes. . . . To most tribes of the Great Plains, the Pipe was, and is, their Bible.

Because the treaties signed between the sovereign Indian nations and the U.S. government were so sacred and so important to the Indian nations, the signing was usually attended by the smoking of a Sacred Pipe.

This spiritual gesture was intended to show the white man that the document just signed was a sacred one and would be treated as such by Indian people.

Since most of the treaties were intended to bring about peace between white man and Indian, the *wasicu* (white man) called the Sacred Pipe a peace pipe.

The point I hope to make here is that there is a national insensitivity when it comes to the religious beliefs, traditional values and the culture of the American Indian.

It is bad enough that American [sic] sees nothing wrong in naming football teams after the color of a people's skin. Jack Kent Cooke (owner of the Redskins) considers the name Washington Redskins complimentary to the Indian people.

Would he consider a team called the Minnesota White-skins complimentary to the white race?

The Christian Bible says, "Do unto others as you would have them do unto you." Would God-fearing Christians use sports mascots that would insult the Jewish people, Muslims, Buddhists, Shintoists, Hindus or any other minority religious group?

If not, then why in the world would they do this to the indigenous people of the Western Hemisphere, the American Indian?

As we approach the Quincentennial of Columbus, it is important that America take a long, hard look at itself and its dealing with Native Americans over the past 500 years.

Most foreigners, particularly those from countries that have been colonized by others (African nations), look upon America as a nation with two faces.

One face shows it to the world as a land of democracy and freedom, the other it shows to its indigenous peoples as uncaring, greedy, dictatorial and often times racist.

By the time December 31, 1992, rolls around, most of us will be sick of Christopher Columbus, revisionists, and politically correct thinkers, but that doesn't mean there is not a whole lot of truth in the things that Native Americans are complaining about.

Stop insulting the spirituality and the traditional beliefs of the Indian people by making us mascots for athletic teams. Is that asking so much of America?

References

1. Philip J. Deloria, *Playing Indian* (New Haven: Yale University Press, 1998); Colin G. Calloway, Gerd Gemünden, and Susanne Zantop, eds., *Germans and Indians: Encounters, Fantasies, and Projections* (Lincoln: University of Nebraska Press, 2002).
2. Carol Spindel, *Dancing at Halftime: Sports and the Controversy over American Indian Mascots* (New York: New York University Press, 2000); C. Richard King and Charles Fruehling Springwood, eds., *Team Spirits: The Native American Mascot Controversy* (Lincoln: University of Nebraska Press, 2001).

Suggested Readings

Berkhofer, Robert F., Jr. *The White Man's Indian: Images of the American Indian from Columbus to the Present* (New York: Knopf, 1978).

Deloria, Philip J. *Playing Indian* (New Haven: Yale University Press, 1998).

King, C. Richard, and Charles Fruehling Springwood, eds. *Team Spirits: The Native American Mascot Controversy* (Lincoln: University of Nebraska Press, 2001).

Spindel, Carol. *Dancing at Halftime: Sports and the Controversy over American Indian Mascots* (New York: New York University Press, 2000).

American Indians and the American Flag

The American flag features frequently in American Indian art and craftwork, at pow wows and ceremonies, and in Native American political activism. For Indian people to display the symbol of the power that has dispossessed and oppressed them seems ironic and contradictory. In fact, the long and varied association between Native Americans and the Stars and Stripes illustrates the sometimes ambiguous position of Indians in American society and the often ambivalent relations between Indian tribes and the United States.°

FIGURE 8.1   A Lakota Baby Bonnet, c. 1875–1900

Thaw Collection, Fenimore House Museum, Cooperstown, New York; photo by John Bigelow Taylor.

°Toby Herbst and Joel Kopp, *The Flag in American Indian Art* (New York State Historical Association and the University of Washington Press, 1993).

FIGURE 8.2 Dancing beneath the Flag
Western History Collections, University of Oklahoma Library.

Lewis and Clark distributed flags on their trip up the Missouri River in 1804, although the Indians who received them probably thought they were accepting gifts, perhaps even tribute, not placing themselves under American sovereignty and protection. The Southern Cheyenne chief Black Kettle displayed an American flag in his village at Sand Creek in 1864 as a sign of government protection but it did him little good. During the reservation era, national holidays were some of the few occasions when agents permitted traditional dances; consequently, Indians took the opportunity presented by the Fourth of July, Lincoln's birthday, and other holidays to celebrate their tribal culture and heritage, performing the old dances under the sanction of the Stars and Stripes. Indian riders in Buffalo Bill's Wild West shows carried flags and wore stars and stripes on their costumes. Indian soldiers served in the United States armed forces—from the Revolution to the Gulf War—under the country's flag; a Pima Indian marine, Ira Hayes, helped raise the flag in the famous World War II photograph of the Iwo Jima landing; and Indian veterans commonly lead pow wows and other gatherings by honoring the flag. Indian war-

FIGURE 8.3 Black Heart

Buffalo Bill Historical Center, Cody, Wyo. Vincent Mercaldo Collection. p. 71.609.

riors occasionally included American flags in their sacred war bundles which provided spiritual protection, signifying the special powers that their owners attributed to them.

The geometric design of stars and stripes also lent itself to incorporation into Indian artwork. Navajo women wove the flag design into rugs and blankets as early as the 1870s; Plains Indian women used it in their beadwork to decorate vests, leggings, moccasins, shirts, and caps; Plains men displayed it in

FIGURE 8.4 The Flag as Protest
Bettmann/CORBIS.

FIGURE 8.5 An Indian Stars and Stripes
Photographer: Arnoose, Great Lakes Indian Fish and Wildlife Commission. Chippewa Valley Museum, Eau Claire, Wis.

FIGURE 8.6 Fritz Scholder, *Indian, 1976*
Courtesy of artist and the Institute of American Indian Arts Museum.

their ledger art; and Plateau Indians incorporated the design in woven cornhusk bags and containers.

The display of the flag, therefore, meant different things in different circumstances: the U.S. government might take it to mean that the Indians were subject peoples or fully assimilated American citizens. For Indians, it could have many meanings: a symbol of protection; a symbol of patriotism and allegiance to the United States; a symbol of a warrior's record of service; a symbol of their status as real Americans; a symbol of deliberate irony or, inverted, a symbol of protest. In some cases, it was no doubt just an attractive design that increased craft sales to tourists.

The pictures reproduced here illustrate some of the diverse occasions and meanings of displaying the flag—on clothing, during dances, and in protest. The images reflect the ambiguous status of Indian tribes as nations within a nation. A baby's bonnet (Figure 8.1), beaded with love and attention to detail by a Lakota woman in the late nineteenth or early twentieth century, exemplifies the incorporation of stars and stripes designs into Plains Indian beadwork. A baby wearing a similar bonnet is reputed to have been found dead after the massacre at Wounded Knee in 1890.

Despite the assault on their lands, lives, and culture being waged by the U.S. government, a group of Lakota men perform the Omaha or War Dance on the Rosebud reservation in South Dakota in 1893 under the banners of the United States (Figure 8.2), while Black Heart (Figure 8.3), who performed in Paris with Buffalo Bill's Wild West Show in 1889, wears a shirt with stars and stripes on it as part of his show attire.

During the protest movements of the 1960s and 1970s, Indian activists often displayed the American flag upside down to reflect the broken treaties and record of injustices that characterized United States treatment of Indian people. The woman wrapped in the flag in Figure 8.4 took part in the occupation of the BIA building in Washington, D.C., in 1972. During protests over spear fishing in the Great Lakes in the 1970s and 1980s, Wisconsin Indians displayed American flags with the image of an Indian superimposed, as symbol that they, the Indians, were the law-abiding citizens, invoking their legal rights under past treaties in the face of non-Indian racism and violence (Figure 8.5).

In *Indian, 1976* (Figure 8.6), Luseño artist Fritz Scholder portrays a Native American wearing an American flag on the bicentennial of the country's birth.

▶ Questions for Consideration

The American flag means many things to many people and has great symbolic and emotive power.

1. What do these images suggest about the meaning of the American flag to Indian people in different times and places? What messages do these images send?

2. Are Indians accepting the flag or appropriating it for their own purposes?

3. What different interpretations could one attach to Figure 8.6 as a reflection of the place of American Indians in American society?

TIMELINE

—◀━●━▶—

c. 11,000 B.C.	Clovis spear point developed
c. 10,500 B.C.	Evidence of human presence at Monte Verde, Chile
c. 3400–3000 B.C.	Mound complex built at Watson Brake, Louisiana
c. 3500–1500 B.C.	Beginnings of agriculture in the Southwest
c. 1000 B.C.	Poverty Point Mounds built
c. 800–100 B.C.	Adena culture in Eastern Woodlands; Great Serpent Mound built c. 400 B.C.
c. 100–300 A.D.	Hopewellian culture in Eastern Woodlands
c. 100–1400	Hohokam culture in the Southwest
c. 700	Cahokia established
c. 700–1550	Mississippian chiefdoms flourish throughout the Southeast
c. 900–1300	Anasazi culture at its peak in the four-corners region of Utah, Colorado, Arizona, and New Mexico
c. 1000	Vikings voyage to North America; Norsemen settle in southern Greenland
c. 1100	Chaco Canyon in northwest New Mexico at height; Mesa Verde built in southern Colorado
c. 1200–1400	Ancestors of Navajos and Apaches separate from northern Athabascans and migrate to the Southwest
c. 1300	Droughts and enemy raids prompt abandonment of Anasazi towns in the Southwest
Pre-1400	Iroquois Great League of Peace formed
1492	Christopher Columbus voyages to America
1513	Juan Ponce de León opens Spanish contact with Indians in Florida
1519–21	Hernán Cortés conquers Aztec empire in Mexico
1520s	First epidemics of Old World diseases in North America
1523–24	Giovanni da Verrazzano sails Atlantic coast from Carolinas to Newfoundland
1528	Pánfilo de Narváez leads Spanish expedition to Gulf of Mexico; over the next six years, Álvar Núñez Cabeza de Vaca and other members travel into the Southwest
1533	Spanish conquer Inca empire in Peru
1534–41	Jacques Cartier travels up the St. Lawrence River
1539–43	Hernando de Soto invades the Southeast
1540–42	Francisco Vasquez de Coronado invades New Mexico

1565	Spanish found St. Augustine, Florida		Hudson Bay Company chartered
1585–86	English settle at Roanoke Island, North Carolina	1675–76	King Philip's War in New England
1598	Juan de Oñate establishes Spanish colony in New Mexico; takes Ácoma by assault in 1599	1680	Pueblo War of Independence drives Spaniards from New Mexico
1603–15	Samuel de Champlain voyages in the Northeast; clashes with Iroquois in 1609	1681–82	René-Robert Cavelier, Sieur de La Salle travels down the Mississippi and claims the Mississippi valley for Louis XIV (Louisiana)
1607	English settle at Jamestown, Virginia	c. 1680–1750	Plains Indians acquire horses
1608	French found Quebec	1689–97	King William's War
1610	Spanish found Santa Fe	1692–98	Diego de Vargas reconquers New Mexico
1614	Dutch establish trading post on Hudson River near Albany, New York	1700–01	Iroquois establish peace with France and Britain
1616–19	Major epidemic among New England Indians	1702–13	Queen Anne's War
1620	Pilgrims establish Plymouth Colony	1703–04	English and Indian allies destroy Spanish mission system in northern Florida
1622	Powhatan Indians go to war against English in Virginia	1704	French and Indians raid Deerfield, Massachusetts
1630s	"Great Migration" of 20,000 English Puritans to New England	1711–13	Tuscarora War
1633–34	Smallpox epidemic throughout the Northeast	1715	Yamassee War
		1720–35	French wars against the Fox Indians in the western Great Lakes
1632–50	Jesuit missionaries active in Huronia	1722	Tuscaroras migrate north from the Carolinas and join the Iroquois Confederacy; the "Five Nations" become the "Six Nations"
1636–37	Puritan war against the Pequots		
1640s	Mayhew family missionaries active on Martha's Vineyard	1738	Smallpox kills half the Cherokee population
1644	Second Powhatan war against the English	1741	Vitus Bering opens Russian trade with Native people of the Gulf of Alaska
1646–75	John Eliot's missionary work in New England	1744–48	King George's War
1649	Iroquois destroy Huron villages	1754	Albany Congress: English colonies meet to discuss unified colonial Indian policy
1670	Charlestown, South Carolina, founded		

1755	French and Indians defeat Edward Braddock
1756–63	Seven Years' War or "French and Indian War"
1759–61	War between the Cherokees and colonists
1763	Treaty of Paris ends French empire in North America
1763–64	Pontiac's War
1768	Treaty of Fort Stanwix: Iroquois cede lands south of Ohio River to Sir William Johnson
1769	First Franciscan mission established in California
1774	Lord Dunmore's War between the Shawnees and Virginia
1775	Treaty of Sycamore Shoals: Richard Henderson's purchase from the Cherokees
1776–78	Captain James Cook begins English trade with Northwest Coast peoples
1776–83	American Revolution
1778	Treaty between the Delawares and the U.S.; first treaty between U.S. and Indians
1779	General John Sullivan invades Iroquoia
1779–83	Massive smallpox epidemic from Mexico to Canada
1783	Peace of Paris: Britain recognizes the independence of its thirteen former colonies
1786	Governor Juan Bautista de Anza makes peace between New Mexico and the Comanches
	Treaty of Fort Finney between the Shawnees and the U.S.
1787	Northwest Ordinance pledges U.S. to conduct Indian affairs with "the utmost good faith"

1789	Congress assigns Indian affairs to the War Department
	U.S. Constitution gives Congress sole power to regulate commerce with Indian tribes
1790	Congress passes the first Indian Trade and Intercourse Act
	Northwestern tribes defeat General Josiah Harmar
1791	Northwestern tribes defeat General Arthur St. Clair
1791–93	George Vancouver trades with Indian peoples on Northwest Pacific coast
1794	Anthony Wayne defeats northwestern tribes at Fallen Timbers
	First U.S.–Indian treaty providing education for Indians (Oneidas, Tuscaroras, and Stockbridges)
1795	Treaty of Greenville: northwestern tribes cede most of Ohio to U.S.
1799	Handsome Lake's Longhouse Religion begins among the Senecas
1803	U.S. purchases Louisiana Territory from France
1804–06	Expedition of Meriwether Lewis and William Clark from St. Louis to the Pacific
1805–11	Tecumseh and Tenskwatawa attempt to unite tribes of the East
1809	Treaty of Fort Wayne: Indians cede three million acres along the Wabash River
1811	Battle of Tippecanoe
1812–15	War of 1812 between Britain and U.S.; death of Tecumseh in 1813
1813–14	Creek War; Battle of Horseshoe Bend, 1814
1817–18	First Seminole War in Florida

1820–23	Mexico wins independence from Spain
1821	Sequoyah completes Cherokee syllabary
1824	Secretary of War creates a Bureau of Indian Affairs within the War Department
1827	Cherokees adopt a constitution, modeled on the U.S. Constitution
1828–30	Georgia "abolishes" tribal government and expands authority over Cherokee country
1830	Indian Removal Act
1831	*Cherokee Nation v. Georgia:* U.S. Supreme Court describes Indian tribes as "domestic dependent nations"
1832	*Worcester v. Georgia:* U.S. Supreme Court declares state laws do not extend to Indian country
1832	Black Hawk War
1833–34	German Prince Maximilian and Swiss artist Karl Bodmer travel up Missouri River
1835	Treaty of New Echota: "Treaty Party" agrees to give up Cherokee lands in the Southeast in exchange for land in Indian Territory
1836	Creek removal
1835–42	Second Seminole War
1837	Smallpox epidemic on the northern plains
1838	Cherokee Trail of Tears
1845	Texas enters the Union
1846–48	War with Mexico; Mexico cedes most of present Southwest to U.S., 1848
1848	Gold discovered in California; produces massive decline in California Indian population

1849	Bureau of Indian Affairs transferred from War Department to new Department of the Interior
1849–50	Cholera epidemic on the Great Plains
1851	Cherokee Female Seminary opens as the first school for girls west of the Mississippi
	Treaty of Fort Laramie establishes tribal boundaries on the Plains
1853	Gadsden Purchase acquires additional Indian lands from Mexico
1855	Yakima and Rogue River wars in the Northwest
1861–65	American Civil War
1862	"Great Sioux Uprising" in Minnesota
1864	Sand Creek Massacre
	Navajo Long Walk to Bosque Redondo
1866–67	"Red Cloud's War" to close the Bozeman Trail
1867	Treaty of Medicine Lodge between the U.S. and southern Plains tribes
	U.S. purchases Alaska from Russia
1868	Navajo Indian Reservation created
	Second Treaty of Fort Laramie
1869	Act creating Board of Indian Commissioners
	Ely S. Parker becomes the first Indian to head the BIA
	Transcontinental railroad completed
1869–70	Smallpox epidemic on the northern Plains
1871	Congress terminates treaty-making with Indian tribes
1871–79	Slaughter of the buffalo herds
1872–73	Modoc War in California and Oregon
1874–75	Red River War on the southern Plains

1876–77	"The Great Sioux War"; Sioux and Cheyenne defeat 7th cavalry at Little Big Horn
1877	Nez Percé War and flight
1879	Carlisle Indian School established
1880	U.S. bans the sun dance
1881	Sitting Bull surrenders
1883	*Ex Parte Crow Dog*
1885	Major Crimes Act
	Last buffalo herd in the U.S. exterminated
1886	End of Apache military resistance
1887	Dawes Allotment Act
1889	Unassigned lands in Indian Territory opened by white settlers known as "boomers"
1890	Oklahoma Territory organized out of western half of Indian Territory
	Sitting Bull assassinated
	Wounded Knee massacre in South Dakota
	Indian population in U.S. reaches all-time low of less than 250,000
1893	Cherokee Outlet opened for white settlement
1898	Curtis Act aims to extend allotment to Oklahoma tribes
	U.S. annexes Hawaii
1903	Supreme Court in *Lone Wolf v. Hitchcock* rules Congress has power to abrogate treaties with Indian tribes
1906	Burke Act amending Dawes Act, allows "competent" Indians to sell allotments
	Alaska Allotment Act
1907	Oklahoma statehood combines Indian and Oklahoma territories; tribal governments dissolved

1908	*Winters v. United States* defines federally reserved water rights for Indian tribes
1911	Society of American Indians formed
1912	Jim Thorpe wins pentathlon and decathlon at Stockholm Olympic Games
	Alaskan Native Brotherhood established
1914–18	World War I (for U.S., 1917–18)
1918	Native American Church incorporated
1919	U.S. grants citizenship to Indian veterans of World War I
1922	All Pueblo Council formed to resist Bursum legislation
1923	American Indian Defense Association formed
	Navajo Tribal Council formed
1924	All Indians granted citizenship
	Indian Health Division established within the BIA
1928	Meriam Report published
1930s	Navajo livestock reduction program
1934	Indian Arts and Crafts Board established
	Johnson–O'Malley Act passed
	Indian Reorganization Act passed
1939–45	World War II (for U.S., 1941–45); Iroquois declare war on Germany, 1942
1944	National Congress of American Indians established
1946	Indian Claims Commission established
1953	House Concurrent Resolution 108 calling for termination of federal trusteeship over lands and affairs of Indian tribes
	Public Law 280

1956   Relocation Act passed to encourage relocation of Indian people to urban centers

1961   American Indian Chicago Conference

National Indian Youth Council founded

1968   Indian Civil Rights Act

American Indian Movement (AIM) founded

1969   Indian activists take over Alcatraz

Navajo Community College opens

1970   President Richard Nixon's message to Congress calls for a new era of Indian self-determination

Blue Lake returned to Taos Pueblo

1971   Alaska Native Claims Settlement Act

Native American Rights Fund (NARF) founded

1972   Trail of Broken Treaties march on Washington, D.C.

1973   Siege at Wounded Knee, South Dakota

Menominee reservation restored

1974   "Boldt decision" *(United States v. Washington)* finds in favor of Indian fishing rights in Pacific Northwest

Women of All Red Nations (WARN) founded

1975   Indian Self-Determination and Educational Assistance Act

Council of Energy Resource Tribes (CERT) formed

Leonard Peltier convicted of shooting two FBI agents on Pine Ridge

1977   American Indian Policy Review Commission Report

1978   Indian Child Welfare Act

American Indian Religious Freedom Act

Congress creates Federal Acknowledgment project

Longest Walk from Alcatraz to Washington, D.C.

Supreme Court decides *Oliphant v. Suquamish,* depriving tribes of criminal jurisdiction over non-Indians on the reservation

1980   Maine Indian Land Claims Settlement Act

Supreme Court decides for Sioux, upholding the $122 million judgment against the U.S. for illegal taking of the Black Hills

1981   President Ronald Reagan's administration initiates policy of severe cutbacks on funding for Indian social programs

1982   Indian Mineral Development Act

1985   Wilma Mankiller becomes principal chief of the Cherokee Nation

1988   Indian Gaming Regulatory Act

1989   Senate Select Committee on Indian Affairs report recommends a new era of voluntary agreements

1990   Native American Grave Protection and Repatriation Act

Native American Languages Act

1992   Mashantucket Pequots open Foxwoods Casino in Connecticut

1994   Representatives of all federally recognized tribes meet with President Clinton

1998   Mashantucket Pequot Museum and Research Center opens

2000   Assistant Secretary Kevin Gover apologizes to the Indian people of the U.S. for the BIA's past record

U.S. Census records American Indian and Alaskan Native population at almost 2.5 million, with an additional 1.6 million people identifying themselves as part Indian

APPENDIX II

GENERAL REFERENCE WORKS

Bonvillain, Nancy. *Native Nations: Cultures and Histories of Native North America.* Upper Saddle River, N.J.: Prentice/Hall, 2001.

Surveys the cultures, histories, and contemporary lives of the Native peoples of North America. Provides overviews of the major culture areas, supplemented by tribal case studies.

Champagne, Duane, ed. *Chronology of Native North America History: From Pre-Columbian Times to the Present.* Detroit: Gale Research, 1994.

Provides a convenient reference guide and time chart with chronologically arranged entries on important events, individuals, and developments in Indian history in both the United States and Canada.

Champagne, Duane, ed. *Native America: Portrait of the Peoples.* Detroit: Visible Ink Press, 1994.

An abridged version of *The Native North American Almanac* (see next entry).

Champagne, Duane, and Cynthia Rose, eds. *The Native North American Almanac.* 4 vols. Detroit: UXL, 1994.

Some sixty contributing authors profile Native experiences in the United States and Canada with chapters on chronology, demography, major culture areas, languages, law and policy, activism, environmental issues, urban populations, religion, arts, literature, media, health, education, economic issues, and biographies of prominent individuals.

Davis, Mary B., ed. *Native America in the Twentieth Century: An Encyclopedia.* New York: Garland, 1994.

Essays by contributors cover tribal groups and topics from "Anthropologists and Native Americans" to "Urbanization."

Deloria, Philip J., and Neal Salisbury, eds. *A Companion to American Indian History.* Malden, Mass.: Blackwell, 2002.

A collection of essays on key aspects of Native American history.

Dickason, Olivia Patricia. *Canada's First Nations: A History of Founding Peoples from Earliest Times.* Norman: University of Oklahoma Press, 1992.

A survey of Native history north of the U.S. border.

Edmunds, R. David, Frederick E. Hoxie, and Neal Salisbury. *The People: A History of Native America.* Boston: Houghton Mifflin, 2005.

A major new Native American textbook by authoritative authors.

Hoxie, Frederick E., ed. *Encyclopedia of North American Indians: Native American History, Culture, and Life from Paleo-Indians to the Present.* Boston: Houghton Mifflin, 1996.

Some 250 contributors provide essays on a wide range of subjects, from "Abenaki" to "Zuni."

Hoxie, Frederick E., Peter C. Mancall, and James H. Merrell, eds. *American Nations: Encounters in Indian Country, 1850 to the Present.* New York: Routledge, 2001.

A collection of essays focusing primarily on the varied responses of Indian peoples in dealing with the United States.

Hurtado, Albert L., and Peter Iverson, eds. *Major Problems in American Indian History.* Lexington, Mass.: D. C. Heath, 1994; 2d ed., Boston: Houghton Mifflin, 2001.

Introduces students to a range of primary sources and scholarly articles.

Indian Country Today. Rapid City, S.D.: Native American Publishing Co., 1981–.

http://www.indiancountry.com

A weekly newspaper covering events nationwide concerning Indians.

Josephy, Jr., Alvin M., et al. *The Native Americans: An Illustrated History.* Atlanta: Turner Publishing, 1992.

A lavishly illustrated "coffee table book," with chapters contributed by leading scholars in the field.

Klein, Barry T. *Reference Encyclopedia of the American Indian.* 7th ed. West Nyack, N.Y.: Todd Publications, 1995.

Annotated lists and addresses of tribal councils, reservations, government agencies, Indian schools, and health services; national, state and local associations; relevant museums and libraries; bibliographies and brief biographies of prominent individuals.

Lobo, Susan, and Steve Talbot. *Native American Voices: A Reader.* New York: Longman, 1998; 2d ed. 2001.

A collection of writings that serve as an introduction to the diverse and interdisciplinary field of Native American Studies.

Mancall, Peter C., and James H. Merrell, eds. *American Encounters: Natives and Newcomers from European Contact to Indian Removal, 1500–1850.* New York: Routledge, 2000.

A collection of essays representing some of the best writing on the ethnohistory of early America.

Maynard, Jill, ed. *Through Indian Eyes: The Untold Story of Native American Peoples.* Pleasantville, N.Y.: Reader's Digest Association, 1996.

Chapters by eleven scholars in a richly illustrated volume.

Nabokov, Peter, ed. *Native American Testimony: A Chronicle of Indian–White Relations from Prophecy to the Present, 1492–1992.* New York: Viking-Penguin, 1991.

A compilation of Indian statements and comments on their encounters with Euro-Americans.

Nichols, Roger L. *Indians in the United States and Canada: A Comparative History.* Lincoln: University of Nebraska Press, 1998.

An overview of the historical experiences of Indian peoples on both sides of the border, tracing their paths from independence through colonization and marginalization to twentieth-century political, economic, and cultural resurgence.

Oliver, Phil. *The American Indian.* CD-ROM. Carmel: Guild Press of Indiana, 1998.

A comprehensive encyclopedic CD-ROM resource on North American Indians. Over 350 treaties, guides to the National Archives, BIA statistics, and Native culture. Western Indian sign language and biographical information on best-known tribal chiefs are also included.

Perdue, Theda, ed. *Sifters: Native American Women's Lives.* New York: Oxford University Press, 2001.

A variety of authors present essays on the different aspects of Indian women's lives.

Pritzker, Barry M. *A Native American Encyclopedia: History, Culture and Peoples.* New York: Oxford University Press, 2000.

Arranged by geographic/culture area and tribe. Some odd captions accompany the photo section.

Prucha, Francis Paul. *Atlas of American Indian Affairs.* Lincoln: University of Nebraska Press, 1990.

Maps of land cessions, reservations, army posts and battles, agencies, schools and hospitals, and census information.

Prucha, Francis Paul. *The Great Father: The United States Government and the American Indians.* 2 vols. Lincoln: University of Nebraska, 1984.

A comprehensive study of U.S. Indian policy by a leading scholar of the subject.

Ray, Arthur J. *I Have Lived Here Since the World Began: An Illustrated History of Canada's Native People.* Toronto: Lester Publishing and Key Porter Books, 1996.

A survey of Canadian Indian history by a prominent scholar of the fur trade.

Shoemaker, Nancy, ed. *American Indians.* Malden, Mass.: Blackwell, 2001.

A classroom reader divided into seven chapters from precontact to the 1970s, with documents and essays by scholars.

Sturtevant, William C., ed. *Handbook of North American Indians.* Washington, D.C.: Smithsonian Institution Press, 1978–.

When completed, this series of twenty projected volumes will stand as a standard reference work for scholars and students of American Indian history. Some volumes cover particular culture areas; others focus on key topics. Volume 4 (1988), edited by the late Wilcomb E. Washburn, is a history of Indian–white relations.

Trafzer, Clifford E. *As Long as the Grass Shall Grow and Rivers Flow: A History of Native Americans.* Fort Worth: Harcourt Brace, 2000.

A textbook of Native American history that also includes chapters on contemporary Native American arts and literature.

Trigger, Bruce G., and Wilcomb E. Washburn, eds. *North America.* Vol. 1 of *The Cambridge History of the Native Peoples of the Americas.* Cambridge: Cambridge University Press, 1996.

The two-part set strives to be a comprehensive synthesis. It includes essays on Native views of history and on Native peoples in historiography and addresses developments in Canada as well as in the United States. The contributors are all scholars who have made their own mark on the field.

Waldman, Carl. *Atlas of the North American Indian.* New York: Facts on File, 1985; revised ed., New York: Checkmark, 2000.

The text provides information on standard aspects of Indian history and culture in the United States, Canada, and Middle America, and is supported by more than one hundred maps.

Weeks, Philip. *"They Made Us Many Promises": The American Indian Experience, 1524–Present.* 2d ed. Wheeling, Ill.: Harlan, 2002.

A collection of essays by a variety of scholars.

Wilson, James. *The Earth Shall Weep: A History of Native America.* New York: Grove Press, 1998.

Traces Indian people's five hundred-year struggle for survival, from first invasion to contemporary Indian activism.

Woodhead, Henry, ed. *The American Indians.* Alexandria, Va.: Time-Life Books, 1992–96.

A multivolume, richly illustrated series; each volume focuses on a particular region, period, or theme.

INTERNET RESOURCES

Links to the resources listed here and to additional relevant sites reside in the Bedford/St. Martin's Links Library at bedfordstmartins.com/historylinks, where students can access annotated links to topics covered in each chapter of *First Peoples*. Note that when this book went to press, the sites listed below were active and maintained except as noted. The author and the publisher do not endorse the information offered through these sites. This list is not comprehensive; the sources were chosen with an eye toward usefulness for students from among many available sites on American Indians.

Bureau of Indian Affairs

http://www.doi.gov/bureau-indian-affairs.html

This site, hosted by the U.S. Department of the Interior, is presently unavailable due to litigation. When available, it is a central location for statistical information on federally recognized tribes, with tables that organize data on population (alphabetically by state, then by tribe within states), labor statistics, links to the BIA mission statement, a list of tribal leaders and federally recognized tribes, a map of Indian lands, a way to "trace your Indian ancestry," and other government sites dealing with Native American legislation and issues. The homepage is still accessible at **http://www.doi.gov.**

Circumpolar and Aboriginal North America Resources

http://natsiq.nunanet.com/~nic/WWWVL-ANA.html

A component of The World Wide Web Virtual Library, and is maintained by the Nunavut Implementation Commission, its links cover not only circumpolar tribes (in Alaska, northern Canada, Greenland, and the Nordic countries), but also southern Canada, Hawaii, and the continental United States. Helpful annotations describe the contents of each link (text and photographs, news releases, art, and online catalogs). Not all links are annotated, however.

The Cradleboard Teaching Project

http://www.cradleboard.org/mainmenu.htm

The Cradleboard Teaching Project, founded by songwriter and educator Buffy Sainte-Marie to improve the teaching of Native American history and culture in schools, maintains a Web site with links to other Native American sources.

EnviroTech On-Line

http://www.envirotech.org/cgi-bin/freedb/uslaws.pl

> This catalog of environmental information includes a collection of legal documents. One section is devoted to Native American issues, and includes treaties, executive orders, memoranda, and proclamations from 1700 to the present, and TRIBLAW, a set of laws and rules written by tribal leaders. Access to Native American-related documents is free.

The Fourth World Documentation Project

http://www.halcyon.com/FWDP/fwdp.html

> Documents pertaining to Native Americans, including treaties, council meeting proceedings, coalition papers, and memoranda from the U.S. Commission on Civil Rights, can be found at this site. The Fourth World Documentation Project archives important documents by or about fourth-world nations, which are defined as "nations forcefully incorporated into states which maintain a different political culture, but are internationally unrecognized."

Index of Native American Resources on the Internet

http://hanksville.phast.umass.edu/misc/Naresources.html

> A vast index of Native American resources organized by category. Within the history category, links are organized under subcategories: Oral History, Written History, various geographical areas, Timelines, and Photographs.

Indian Country Today Online

http://www.indiancountry.com

> The largest Native American newspaper in the United States, published weekly with international circulation, *Indian Country Today* publishes an online version including the full text of all headline stories. There is no archive of past articles, so the site is good only for the most current events.

Indian Data Center

http://www.indiandata.com

> The stated mission of the Indian Data Center is to provide information about today's Indian tribes and reservations. Currently, the primary resource is a collection of maps showing reservations, gaming institutions, and geography, plus a list of addresses, phone, and fax numbers for all twelve BIA area offices.

Indian Health Service

http://www.tucson.ihs.gov

> Primarily a set of links to other sites (unannotated but organized into categories such as art, genealogy, language, and food), this site also includes statistical data on Indian health issues grouped into e .pdf files of text, tables, and charts. To view these files, users need the Adobe Acrobat Reader.

Native American Anthology: Internet Resources

http://www.wsu.edu:8080/~dee/NAINRES.HTM

> The anthology is organized into broad categories (history, art, texts, literature, nations, languages), as well as more specific ones, such as groups and tribes.

Native American Documents Project

http://coyote.csusm.edu/projects/nadp

> From California State University, San Marcos, this site continually adds documents that reveal the effects of federal policy on Native peoples. There are three sets of data: (1) published reports of the Commission of Indian Affairs and the Board of Indian Commissioners for 1871; (2) Allotment Data Collection (10 tables of annotated quantitative data); and (3) 111 indexed documents in the Rogue River War and Siletz Reservation Collection. A very straightforward site, NADP is text-only.

Native Americans and the Environment

http://conbio.rice.edu/nae

> This well-maintained site is "dedicated to promoting education and research on environmental issues facing Native American and First Nations communities." It includes articles on current Native American issues in the environment, a map of ecological and cultural regions, bibliographies, and a series of links to other environment-related sites. The site also includes links to primary documents, such as treaties that involve environmental issues.

Native American Resources on the Internet

http://www.tucson.ihs.gov/PublicInfo/AmerIndian/index.asp

> This clearly designed site lists dozens of links to other Native American sites arranged by category. Links useful to the history student are listed under genealogy, nations, maps, government, and the Bureau of Indian Affairs.

NativeWeb

http://www.nativeweb.org

One of the best-organized and most accessible sites available on Native American issues, NativeWeb combines an events calendar and message boards with history, statistics, a list of news sources, archives, a selection of new and related sites updated each week, and documents.

Smithsonian: Native American History and Culture

http://www.si.edu/resource/faq/nmai/start.htm

Most useful links on this site are extensive lists of suggested readings on varied topics, such as particular nations, Native American women, and Native American literature, cuisine, crafts, and architecture.

Web Pages and Other Resources for American Indian Schools and Students

http://indy4.fdl.cc.mn.us/~isk

This user-friendly site has many maps, including complex GIS (Geographical Information Systems) maps that organize data in relationship to location and geography, cover topics like North American precontact housing styles, environmental threats to Native lands, U.S. federally owned lands. A full U.S. map allows users to click on individual states to search for particular tribes and BIA area offices. This site also includes links to tribal homepages, divided between Canada and the U.S. This site has extensive resources on Canadian tribes.

VIDEO RESOURCES

━━●━━

There are literally hundreds of films about American Indians. Most of them have contributed to damaging stereotypes about Indian people and are not particularly useful for students of American Indian history. Even among the many documentaries produced in recent years, quality varies greatly. The following list offers titles of videos that are both well made and appropriate for teaching American Indian history.

Acts of Defiance. Produced and written by Mark Zannis. Directed by Alec G. MacLeod. 104 mins. National Film Board of Canada, 1992. Videocassette.

Traces the confrontation between Mohawks and Quebec at Oka in 1990, a stand-off that lasted seventy-eight days — longer than the siege at Wounded Knee.

Broken Treaty at Battle Mountain. Produced and directed by Joel L. Friedman. Narrated by Robert Redford. 16mm, 60 mins. Cinnamon Productions, 1975.

Portrays the Western Shoshones' struggle to stop the government from clearing thousands of acres of sacred pinion trees.

Contrary Warriors: A Story of the Crow Tribe. Produced by Connie Poten and Pamela Roberts. 16 mm, 58 mins. Rattlesnake Productions, 1985. Distributed by Direct Cinema.

Award-winning documentary focusing on the life of Robert Yellowtail as a leader exemplifying the tradition of the brave-hearted "contrary warrior."

The Dakota Conflict. Co-narrated by Floyd Red Crow Westerman and Garrison Keillor. 60 mins. KTCA/Twin Cities Public Television, 1990.

An account of the so-called Great Sioux War in Minnesota in 1862.

Geronimo and the Apache Resistance. Produced and directed by Neil Goodwin. 60 mins. Peace River Films for the PBS series *The American Experience,* 1988. Videocassette.

Relates the famous Chiricahua medicine man's struggle, with testimony from his descendants.

Homeland. Produced and directed by Jilann Spitzmiller and Hank Rogerson. 57 mins. Philomath Films, 1999. Videocassette.

Traces the lives of four Lakota families on the Pine Ridge Reservation in South Dakota.

Incident at Oglala: The Leonard Peltier Story. Produced by Arthur Chobanian. Directed by Michael Apted. 35 mm, 90 mins. Miramax Films, 1992.

Examines the murder of two FBI agents on the Pine Ridge Reservation in

1975 and the controversial trial and continued imprisonment of Leonard Peltier.

Indians, Outlaws, and Angie Debo. Produced by Barbara Abrash. Directed and written by Martha Sandlin. 60 mins. Institute for Research in History and WGBH-Boston for the PBS series *The American Experience,* 1988. Video- cassette.

Traces the life and career of historian Angie Debo who, at a time when neither women nor Indians received much attention in academic circles, exposed the underside of Oklahoma history and identified those who had benefited from the exploitation of the state's Indian residents.

In the Light of Reverence. Produced by Christopher McLeod and Malinda Maynor. Directed by Christopher McLeod. 72 mins. Sacred Land Film Project of Earth Island Institute, 2001. Videocassette and DVD.

Best Feature Documentary Award at the American Indian Film Festival, 2001. Documents the struggles of Native people to protect sacred landscapes: Devil's Tower in Wyoming, the Four Corners in the Southwest, and Mt. Shasta in California.

In the Spirit of Crazy Horse. Produced by Michael DuBois and Kevin McKiernan. 60 mins. PBS series *Frontline,* 1990. Videocassette.

Focuses on the confrontations of the 1960s and 1970s, the clashes over the Black Hills, and the violence on Pine Ridge at the time of Wounded Knee.

In the White Man's Image. Produced and written by Christine Lesiak. 60 mins. Native American Public Broadcasting Consortium for the PBS series *The American Experience,* 1992. Videocassette.

Traces the U.S. government assault on Indian culture through education, from the "experiment" on prisoners at Fort Marion to the boarding school system.

In Whose Honor?: American Indian Mascots in Sports. By Jay Rosenstein. 46 mins. New Day Films 1997. Videocassette

Tackles the controversial issue from the perspective of those who fight against, and suffer from, the use of mascots.

Kanehsatake: 270 Years of Resistance. Produced by Wolf Koenig and Alanis Obomsawin. Directed, written, and narrated by Alanis Obomsawin. 119 mins. National Film Board of Canada, 1993. Videocassette.

Abenaki filmmaker Alanis Obomsawin's documentary about a seventy-eight-day armed confrontation between armed Mohawks from the Kahnawake Reserve and the Canadian National Guard, filmed from within the Mohawk camp.

Lakota Woman: Siege at Wounded Knee. Produced by Fred Berner. Directed by Fred Pierson. 150 mins. Turner Network Television, 1994. Videocassette.

Based on the life story of Mary Crow Dog.

Lewis and Clark: The Journey of the Corps of Discovery. Produced by Dayton Duncan and Ken Burns. Directed by Ken Burns. Written by Dayton Duncan. 240 mins. PBS Home Video, 1997. 2 videocassettes.

Focuses on the two captains and their expedition through Indian country.

Power: The James Bay Cree versus Hydro-Quebec. 76 mins. Cineflex/National Film Board of Canada, 1996.

Covers the Cree's fight to continue their traditional way of life.

Thieves of Time. Produced by Don Hopfer for KAET-TV. Narrated by Tony Hillerman. 30 mins. PBS Video. 1998. Videocassette.

Examines the history of plundering Indian burial grounds and the changes that occurred as a result of the Native American Graves Protection and Repatriation Act.

To Protect Mother Earth: Broken Treaty II. Produced and directed by Joel L. Friedman. Narrated by Robert Redford. 16mm, 60 mins. Cinnamon Productions, 1989.

A sequel to *Broken Treaty at Battle Mountain,* the film portrays the Western Shoshone confrontation with the federal government at the Nevada nuclear test site.

Transitions: Destruction of a Mother Tongue. By Darrell Kipp and Joe Fisher. 30 mins. Native Voices Public Television Workshop, 1991. Videocassette.

This film by Blackfeet producers traces the decline of the Blackfeet language and the impact of language loss on Native communities, as well as efforts at revitalization.

Seasons of the Navajo. Produced by KAET-TV. 60 mins. PBS. Video, 1998. Videocassette.

Follows a year in the life of a Navajo family who tell, in their own words, what "living well" means for a traditional Navajo.

Views of a Vanishing Frontier. Directed by Craig B. Fisher. Written by Craig B. Fisher and Helen Ashton. 58 mins. Metropolitan Museum of Art, 1988. Videocassette.

Documents the journey of Prince Maximilian zu Wied and Swiss artist Karl Bodmer up the Missouri River in 1833–34, combining extracts from the prince's journals with examples of Bodmer's paintings.

Who Owns the Past? Produced and Directed by N. Jed Riff. 56 mins. PBS Video, 2002. Videocassette.

Traces the American Indian struggle for control of ancestral remains, the Native American Graves Protection and Repatriation Act, and the controversy over Kennewick Man.

Wiping the Tears of Seven Generations. Produced by Gary Rhine. Directed by Gary Rhine and Fidel Moreno. 57 mins. Kifaru Productions, 1991. Videocassette.

Relates the story of the Big Foot Memorial Ride, when three hundred Lakotas rode 250 miles in December 1990 to help bring their people out of one hundred years of mourning for the losses suffered at Wounded Knee in 1890.

INDEX

A note about the index:

Pages containing the main coverage or description of a topic or person are set in **boldface** for easy reference. Terms and the pages on which they are defined in the text also are set in **boldface.**

Letters in parentheses following pages refer to:
- (d) for documents
- (e) for picture essays
- (i) for illustrations
- (m) for maps
- (t) for tables